Interpersonal Communication

THIRD EDITION

Interpersonal Communication

SARAH TRENHOLM

Ithaca College

ARTHUR JENSEN

Syracuse University

Wadsworth Publishing Company

I T P® An International Thomson Publishing Company

Belmont • Albany • Bonn • Boston • Cincinnati • Detroit • London • Madrid • Melbourne • Mexico City •
New York • Paris • San Francisco • Singapore • Tokyo • Toronto • Washington

Communication Studies Editor: Todd R. Armstrong
Assistant Editor: Lewis DeSimone
Editorial Assistant: Michael Gillespie
Production Services Coordinator: Debby Kramer
Production: Tina Samaha
Designer: Janet Wood
Print Buyer: Barbara Britton

Permissions Editor: Robert Kauser
Copy Editor: Tina Samaha
Photo Researcher: Photosynthesis
Cover Designer: Janet Wood
Compositor: TBH/Typecast
Printer: R. R. Donnelley & Sons/Crawfordsville
Cover Printer: Color Dot Litho

Printed in the United States of America
2 3 4 5 6 7 8 9 10

For more information, contact Wadsworth Publishing Company:

Wadsworth Publishing Company
10 Davis Drive
Belmont, California 94002, USA

International Thomson Publishing Europe
Berkshire House 168-173
High Holborn
London, WC1V 7AA, England

Thomas Nelson Australia
102 Dodds Street
South Melbourne 3205
Victoria, Australia

Nelson Canada
1120 Birchmount Road
Scarborough, Ontario
Canada M1K 5G4

International Thomson Editores
Campos Eliseos 385, Piso 7
Col. Polanco
11560 México D.F. México

International Thomson Publishing GmbH
Königswinterer Strasse 418
53227 Bonn, Germany

International Thomson Publishing Asia
221 Henderson Road
#05-10 Henderson Building
Singapore 0315

International Thomson Publishing Japan
Hirakawacho Kyowa Building, 3F
2-2-1 Hirakawacho
Chiyoda-ku, Tokyo 102, Japan

Library of Congress Cataloging-in-Publication Data

Trenholm, Sarah
        Interpersonal communication / Sarah Trenholm, Arthur Jensen.—
  3rd ed.
            p.   cm.
        Includes bibliographical references and indexes.
        ISBN 0-534-26394-1
        1. Interpersonal communication.   I. Jensen, Arthur
  II. Title.
  BF637.C45T72   1995
  153.6—dc20   95-32039

Contents in Brief

Contents

Preface

TO THE INSTRUCTOR

Writing the third edition of *Interpersonal Communication* has been an extremely satisfying experience for us. We thank all who have used and responded favorably to the previous editions, particularly those who have served as reviewers for this edition. Such a stamp of approval has not only been gratifying, but has been accompanied by enthusiastic suggestions on how to make this edition even better.

Reviewer responses prompted several changes in the structure and content of the text, and other changes grew out of the spirit of their concerns as well. We have attempted to make the central and most enduring themes of the text even more explicit, while introducing and expanding other themes in new directions. At the heart of this edition remains the primary goal of *helping students achieve interpersonal competence in a social world that is at once deeply cultured and yet openly challenged by new modes of thought and action.* Understanding and managing interpersonal interaction and relationships in such a world is seldom easy, but new research and theory points out further complications. We now understand that contemporary American patterns of interpersonal communication are not only culturally, but historically situated. In previous editions of *Interpersonal Communication* we were content to allude to historical contexts with boxed material tangential to the primary text. In this edition, the importance of the cultural and historical

backdrops is woven into our model of communication competence, drawn out in several new boxes and in various discussions throughout the text, and summarized in the final chapter.

Among other changes in this edition, you will find a revised model of communication competence; a more pronounced emphasis on competence in each chapter, with summary sections on improving competence in each of the four relational context chapters (family, intimate, and professional relationships, and a new final chapter on cultural/historical perspectives). In addition, fifteen new boxes ranging from a history of dating to the politics of multicultural talk have replaced outdated or less intriguing material. We have also updated the research base in each chapter, trying to reflect the state of the art in as many areas as possible, given the limitations of space and the reader's attention span. Finally, for those who do want to read more, we have updated the Suggested Readings section at the end of each chapter.

In keeping with the emphasis on communicative competence, the structure of the text has been modified to emphasize that theme throughout the text. Part 1 introduces the reader to basic perspectives on interpersonal communication. A newly revised model of competence is introduced in Chapter 1. The model shows how five key elements (perceptual, role, self, goal, and message competence) are interrelated and shaped by cultural and historical influences. One of these elements, message competence, is further delineated in terms of verbal, nonverbal, and relational codes. In Chapter 2, we focus more specifically on interpersonal communication, explaining what it means to form interpersonal bonds.

Each element of the competence model becomes the focus of separate chapters in Part 2 and Part 3. Part 2 examines the ways in which we send and receive messages, beginning with nonverbal competence in Chapter 3 and addressing verbal competence in Chapter 4. New material on the role of language in promoting the interests of some groups in society and silencing the voices of others has been added to this chapter. The section concludes with a discussion of relational competence in Chapter 5. The rationale for dealing with message making prior to other elements of the model is twofold. First, it makes interaction the prominent site from which the other elements (perceptions, roles, relationships, and self-concepts) are derived or in which they are displayed. And second, it offers the instructor an opportunity to prompt discussion on such issues as the relationship between cognition and behavior. Under what conditions do we behave first and then reflect on what our behavior means? When is our communication behavior an intentional reflection of previously held attitudes?

Part 3 looks more closely at the other basic processes linked to message construction and interpretation. Chapter 6 examines the relationship between perception and successful communication. The discussion of cognitive schemata has been clarified to improve student understanding as to how cognition and communication are related. Chapters 7 and 8 focus on how social and personal identities are formed and how they affect interactions. A new emphasis on how gender and other cultural/historical narratives influence role behavior informs Chapter 7, while an historical perspective on how each historical era calls for decidedly different self-concepts is introduced in Chapter 8. Finally, Chapter 9 shows how we use the interpersonal influence process to achieve goals in a competent fashion.

In Part 4, we investigate how communication principles are applied in the context of different kinds of relationships. Chapter 10 discusses interpersonal communication in the family. As in many other chapters, we introduce an historical perspective to help us better understand current communication patterns. We have also provided a more thorough discussion of parent-child communication in this edition. Chapter 11, on how intimate relationships work, is once again the chapter with the most new research to report. This reflects researchers' interests as well as the importance our culture attaches to close relationships. In Chapter 12 we examine professional, role-oriented relations. Some reviewers have suggested that we cut this chapter, as it seemed to them out of place in a text primarily focused on the close, personal relationships of family and friends. We resist doing that, on the basis that our culture already trivializes role relations and other forms of public, impersonal interaction. We believe that democracy rests very heavily on the civil interaction of people who do not know one another personally and feel no compulsion to make every relationship a personal one (or to attach value only to the most personal of relationships). Finally, Chapter 13 draws together the thematic influences that culture and history exercise on interpersonal communication. This chapter is, for all practical purposes, a new one. It incorporates some material on cross-cultural communication from the previous edition, but the historical overview of interpersonal communication patterns is all new. Each of the chapters in Part 4 concludes with a new section examining how the material in that chapter relates to the recurring theme of developing and enhancing our communication competence.

Throughout the text you will find boxed materials. These contain interesting and unusual applications of communication principles. Fifteen of these boxes are completely new or have been substantially rewritten. Drawn from anthropology, ethnology, history, psychology, philosophy, education, linguistics, popular culture, and the like, they demonstrate that communication occurs in many different contexts. We've included them not only because we think they are interesting, but also because they provide sources for additional reading and study.

At the end of each chapter, you will still find a section devoted to enhancing a particular communication skill relevant to the thrust of the chapter. This section describes the principles, steps, or subskills necessary for improving the skill. In effect, it offers practical ways to put the content of the chapter to work. The other end-of-the chapter materials in the section entitled "Process to Performance" are designed to move students toward application as well. This section includes discussion questions, observational assignments, and classroom exercises that further aid in skill development.

We have also updated the *Instructor's Manual,* which now includes a student handout of review questions for each chapter, many more test items, additional classroom activities, and other handout material. We hope you will find this material helpful in your teaching efforts.

TO THE STUDENT

We hope that reading this book will open your eyes to a new world of interaction. While you've communicated all your life, you've probably never really *seen* communication. Most people don't take time to observe and analyze familiar everyday activities. When they do, often they are amazed at the richness and complexity they find. We believe that after reading this book, you will never again dismiss communication as uninteresting or commonplace. You'll have the tools to observe the context in which communication takes place and to increase your own communication competence.

ACKNOWLEDGMENTS

We are indebted to those who have reviewed this and previous editions of *Interpersonal Communication.* We believe (and readily admit our bias) that each edition has been improved in terms of both the comprehensive nature of its content, and in the arrangement of ideas and materials. Our reviewers are largely responsible for those improvements. We would like to thank Brant R. Burleson, Purdue University; Mindy Chang, University of Richmond; Kenneth Cissna, University of South Florida; Richard K. Curtis, Indiana University; Lawrence W. Hugenberg, Youngstown State University; Randall J. Koper, University of the Pacific; Sandra Metts, Illinois State University; Martha W. Moore, Murray State University; Sally K. Murphy, California State University at Hayward; Charles Petrie, SUNY-Buffalo; Sally Planalp, University of Colorado at Boulder; Marilyn Root, Boston University; Karyn Rybacki, Northern Michigan University; Gregory J. Shepherd, University of Kansas; Ralph Smith, Southwest Missouri State; Robbyn J. Turner-Matthews, Miami University (Ohio); Michael Waltman, University of North Carolina, Chapel Hill; Lynne Webb, University of Florida; Jerry L. Winsor, Central Missouri State University. We also owe a debt of gratitude to the following folks at Wadsworth: Todd Armstrong, our editor, for his persistence and ability to keep us on track, and his flair for arranging conference calls; Laura Murray, editorial assistant, for her gracious and timely assistance on matters too numerous to mention; and Tina Samaha, our production editor, for seeing to all the details. Finally, we are grateful to our colleagues and students at Ithaca College and Syracuse University for their encouragement and support.

Sarah Trenholm

Arthur Jensen

1

INTRODUCTORY PERSPECTIVES

In attempting to understand our world, we often look outward toward the remote and the exotic. Everyday processes, however, are equally fascinating and complex. We can discover worlds in our own behavior.

1

Introduction:
Communication and Competence

Now, I do not deny, nor do I doubt, that should communication be opened, the reaction among mankind would be very strong — not because of the content of the message but simply from the fact that a message could in fact be received. Such an experience would say to us human beings "We are not alone in the universe." And this, I think . . . might by itself quite justify any expenditures made in the search for extraterrestrial intelligence.[1]

W. H. McNeill

Only a few years ago the idea that humans might one day communicate with extraterrestrials seemed ridiculous. Those who believed it possible were considered to be, at best, misguided and, at worst, lunatics. Nowadays, however, some very high-powered astrophysicists are taking the idea seriously. They are convinced that communication with alien intelligence may one day be possible.[2]

Think about it for a minute. Try to put yourself in the place of these scientists. Imagine that you are trying to make contact with alien beings. Remember that the beings you are trying to reach — if they exist at all — have given you no address. All you know is that they live somewhere in the vast stretches of the universe, hundreds or thousands of light years away. And even if you succeed in making contact, you still have to design an intelligible message. Movies like *E.T.* and *Close Encounters of the Third Kind* notwithstanding, extraterrestrials are unlikely to respond (or even look) like any organism you have ever seen. The chances of their being able to understand human language, let alone English, are infinitesimally small. How can you be sure that aliens will recognize your communications? How will you be able to recognize theirs? What if you have already come in contact with their messages without realizing it?

In the face of all these problems, your only choice would be to do exactly what all of us do

3

when we communicate: rely on guesswork and faith. You would begin by assuming a desire for cooperative communication. You would then try to guess what extraterrestrials are like and how they see the world, searching for a point of similarity upon which to make connection. After that, you would simply wait and hope. Of course, the subject of this book is not interstellar communication but a much more mundane one: the way normal human beings communicate as they go about their everyday lives. We believe, though, that unusual examples help us see the commonplace in new ways.[3]

If you think about it, there are some interesting similarities between earthbound and intergalactic communication. First of all, in both cases we must resist "communicative chauvinism," the belief that everyone else thinks and acts as we do. Communication depends on sensitivity to differences and on a real desire to establish common ground. Second, people who wish to communicate must learn to "speak the same language"; they must take the time and trouble to adjust to one another. Cooperation and coordination are necessary for any kind of communication, whether it's with neighbors in the next street or with beings in the next galaxy.

We often take interpersonal communication for granted, overlooking what an amazing process it really is. The purpose of this book is to help you see interpersonal communication in a new light. While it may not be as exotic as interstellar communication, it is still a complex and fascinating process. We hope that by the time you finish this book, you will have a better understanding of how it works.

What Is Communication?

Although communication has been written about for over 25 centuries,[4] there is still disagreement about how to define it. In this section we'll look at a number of definitions of human communication, offer our own, and then explore its implications.

DEFINITIONS OF HUMAN COMMUNICATION

In 1973 Frank Dance and Carl Larson surveyed the field for definitions of communication. They found 126.[5] Even more have been formulated since then. Obviously, a process as complex as communication is hard to summarize or define. Each person who thinks seriously about it brings a different perspective to the task. There are many valid ways to view a process, each providing a different insight.

We will give you a number of definitions to consider, but before we do, stop and jot down your own ideas about communication. Then, compare your definition with those that follow. Ask yourself which comes closest to your understanding of what communication is. More importantly, ask yourself why.

Communication is the discriminatory response of an organism to a stimulus.[6]

Communication . . . is an "effort after meaning," a creative act initiated by man in which he seeks to discriminate and organize cues so as to orient himself in his environment and satisfy his changing needs.[7]

Speech communication is a human process through which we make sense out of the world and share that sense with others.[8]

Communication: the transmission of information, ideas, emotions, skills, etc. by the use of symbols . . .[9]

Communication is a process by which a source transmits a message to a receiver through some channel.

The purpose of a definition is to set boundaries and to focus attention. Definitions ask people to look at certain parts of a process while ignoring others. The question to ask in evaluating a definition is not, "Is it right or wrong?" Rather, the question should be, "Is it a useful guide for inquiry?" Each focuses on a different part of the phenomenon we call communication.

The first definition is very broad. According to this view any response by any living organism counts as communication. A plant seeking out the sun, prey sensing the presence of a predator, a human being reading a book — all would be examples of communication. Furthermore, this definition concentrates on the part the receiver plays in communication and gives almost no attention to the part played by the sender. In comparison, the next definition is narrower, focusing our attention on human communication and emphasizing the reasons we communicate. The third definition adds another concept, that of sharing. According to this definition communication is more than the processing of information; it is also the transmission of that information to others. The fourth definition also takes up the idea of transmission but adds a further limitation: Messages created by humans are made up of symbols. The final definition focuses on the means by which this transmission of messages takes place and introduces the idea of the sender as the initiator of communication.

Each definition tells us something about the process of communication, yet each leaves something out. Each asks us to examine a different aspect of the process. While you may prefer one definition over another, one is not necessarily right and the others wrong. Rather, each may be useful for a different purpose. Below we offer yet another definition, not because our definition is necessarily closer to what communication *really* is, but because it allows us to take a more social perspective on communication and because it emphasizes the

We live in a world of constructed realities. Consider this ferocious warrior guardian: To us the image may seem nothing but a curious artifact, but to the people of 13th-century Japan, its significance was quite different.

creativity of interaction. We believe that this definition will be particularly useful in helping us understand communication in the interpersonal context.

CHARACTERISTICS OF COMMUNICATION

For us, **communication** is *the process whereby humans collectively create and regulate social reality.* Let's try to understand what this definition has to say about communication by looking at each of its parts.

Communication as Process

Any object or activity can be viewed as either a thing or a process. Things are static, bound in time, and unchanging. **Processes** are moving, have no beginning and no end, and constantly change. Our first point, then, is that communication is a process, not a thing.

The communication process is like a river: active, continuous, and flowing, never the same from one minute to the next. If we try to understand a river by analyzing a bucket of water drawn from it, we are not studying the river as a whole. The same is true of communication. Individual sentences, words, or gestures make sense only when we see them as part of an ongoing stream of events. To understand communication, we have to look at how what we do and say is connected to what others do and say. We have to view communication as an ongoing process.

Communication as Uniquely Human

The term *communication* has been used to describe the behavior of many organisms. Geneticists, for example, describe the instructions for

development and growth in the DNA of cells as a kind of communication. Physiologists use the term to describe how the human body maintains and regulates itself. Biologists see all kinds of animal behaviors as communication, including the distress signals of birds, the courtship ritual of jumping spiders, the use of threat displays by Siamese fighting fish, and the play behavior of gorillas and baboons.[10]

The kind of communication we are interested in, however, is *human* communication. We believe that humans communicate in unique and powerful ways that differ markedly from those used by other animals. Although there have been several recent attempts to teach higher primates to use human communication codes, results of these studies are inconclusive. Box 1.1 summarizes some of the research on this subject.

Most everyone will agree that only people use language naturally and spontaneously, giving us a flexibility and creativity denied to all other creatures. Of course, as Aldous Huxley pointed out, this power is not always to our advantage:

For evil, then, as well as for good, words make us the human beings we actually are. Deprived of language, we should be as dogs or monkeys. Possessing language, we are men and women able to persevere in crime no less than in heroic virtue, capable of intellectual achievements beyond the scope of any animal, but at the same time capable of systematic silliness and stupidity such as no dumb beast could ever dream of.[11]

Communication as Collective Activity

All languages depend on social agreement for their meaning. This brings us to the next part of our definition: Communication is collective. The relationship between human society and human communication is circular; one could not exist without the other. On the one hand, what holds a society together is the ability of its members to act as a coordinated whole, which would be impossible without communication. On the other hand, communication presupposes social cooperation; interpersonal communication cannot occur unless at least two people mutually engage in creating meaning.

Joost Meerloo tells us that the word *communication* comes from *munia*, meaning service and connoting "mutual help, exchange, and interaction of those belonging to the same community."[12] In ancient times, members of the community who were exempt from public service were referred to as having *immunity*. If an individual committed an offense so terrible that he or she was no longer deemed fit to experience things in common with the rest of society, the offender was *excommunicated*. Meerloo explains, "Wherever the concept of communication comes into play, the emphasis is on the common sharing of material and ideological wealth, on social intercourse, mutual exchange, and the bestowing of feelings and thoughts onto each other."[13]

Communication as Creative Endeavor

A direct result of human communication is human *creativity*. When we agree with others that something can be talked about, we create that thing: We cause it to exist. While some things we agree to talk about (such as books or telephones) already exist in the physical world, others (like truth or justice) exist only in the shared symbolic world created by language. This doesn't mean, however, that symbolic things do not have powerful effects upon us.

Let's take the word *demon*. For most of us, this word has little reality. For many people in many parts of the world, however, demons have a real and objective existence. In Bali, for example, demons can cause human illness; they can make crops fail, pigs die, and volcanoes erupt. In order to survive, the Balinese must pacify and cajole them. On the Day of Silence, for example, everyone must sit "silent and immobile all day long in order to avoid contact with a sudden influx of demons chased momentarily out of hell."[14] The Balinese live in a symbolic world inhabited by — among other things — demons.

Are we superior to the Balinese? Is our world any less symbolic and more real than theirs? Think for a minute about how much of what you know and believe comes to you from direct experience and how much is a product of talk. You may be surprised to find that most of your reality is created and sustained through communication.

Communication as Regulatory

Communication allows us not only to create the world around us but to take possession of it as well. Through communication we can act on our world. In this sense communication is *regulatory*. If you have ever come down with a bad case of laryngitis, you know how helpless you feel when you can't speak. Such a loss illustrates the connection between communication and power.

This connection is as old as civilization. Even today words are associated with magic. By reciting incantations or writing an enemy's name on a piece of paper and then burning it, primitive people try to control others.[15] Even sophisticated moderns retain some superstitions about communication. One of the most common is reluctance to speak about good or bad fortune. If two friends are studying for an exam and the first asks, "What if we fail?" the other is likely to respond, "Don't even talk about something like that." We still retain vestiges of the belief that talking about something can either make it come true or jinx it.

BOX **1.1**

Bonzo Goes to College: Attempts to Teach Language to Primates

Part of what we are, part of how we communicate and behave, has been inherited from our animal ancestors. But how much? What is the difference between animal and human behavior and what difference does it make? Studies of animal behavior can help answer these questions.

A number of studies have focused on whether primates other than human beings can be taught to use "language." Since the 1950s, when an infant chimpanzee named Vicki was adopted by a human family and taught four human words, a number of chimps have been given language lessons. Four of the most famous of these "students" were Washoe and Nim Chimsky (who were instructed in the use of American sign language); Sarah (who was taught to manipulate magnetized plastic tokens); and Lana (a computer-trained chimp). The results of these experiments have led most people to revise their ideas about the

nature of the boundaries between human and animal thought.

All of the chimps learned to associate arbitrary signs with physical referents. They could recognize symbols for such objects as bananas, monkey chow, and cola. They could also use symbols to ask for rewards from their keepers. Washoe, for example, could ask her trainer to tickle her, and Lana could type on her console, "Start pour coke stop" to activate a soft-drink dispenser.

The chimps were also capable of more abstract tasks. Sarah, for example, learned to use the tokens symbolizing *same* and *different* in very sophisticated ways. She was able to solve simple visual analogies. For example, if asked whether an apple and a knife were the same as a piece of paper and a pair of scissors, she would indicate that they were. When the scissors was replaced with a bowl of water, she would indicate that the sets were now different. She also seemed able to recognize the class to which tokens belonged. Thus, when given the token "banana" and asked whether it was a name or a color, she would correctly identify it as a name. Similarly she would label the "yellow" token as a color.

Just what can we make of these achievements? The chimps were able to recognize the communicative function of symbols and make simple associations between these symbols and objects in much the same way young human chil-

Superstitions aside, communication is a powerful regulator of action. Through communication we can persuade, dissuade, anger, hurt, comfort, soothe, entertain, or bore one another. We can even use communication to control our own actions, talking ourselves into taking risks or comforting ourselves when we are afraid. Communication is a powerful way of regulating and controlling our world.

Summary and Implications

All definitions have implications. What are the implications of our definition of communication? Although we see at least four, perhaps you will be able to think of more.

1. Much of what we think of as real is actually the product of communication. This im-

Chimps also did not exhibit linguistic creativity, nor did they use language to direct their activities, as human children do when they guide themselves through a task by talking out loud. Finally, they never spontaneously developed a language of their own. As Stephen Walker points out, "In a state of nature, we expect humans to talk, and, by comparison, the most unrelenting efforts to induce our closest living relatives to reveal hidden linguistic potential have left the discontinuities [between human speech and animal communication] bloodied but unbowed."

SOURCE: Stephen Walker, *Animal Thought* (London: Routledge & Kegan Paul, 1983).

ADDITIONAL READINGS

Gardner, Beatrice T., and R. Allen Gardner. "Two-Way Communication with an Infant Chimpanzee." In *Behavior of Nonhuman Primates,* Vol. 4. Allan Martin Scheier and Fred Stollnitz, eds. New York: Academic Press, 1971, pp. 117–83. (Washoe.)

Hayes, Keith J., and Catharine Hayes. "The Intellectual Development of a Home-Raised Chimpanzee." *Proceedings of the American Philosophical Society 95* (1951): 105–9. (Vicki.)

Premack, David. *Intelligence in Ape and Man.* Hillsdale, N.J.: Lawrence Erlbaum, 1976. (Sarah.)

Rumbaugh, Duane M., ed. *Language Learning by a Chimpanzee*: The LANA Project. New York: Academic Press, 1977. (Lana.)

dren do when they begin to learn language. However, the chimps never learned to link symbols together into complex "sentences." Although they used language to gain immediate goals, they showed no interest in using it to comment on the world. The ability to make up stories, which develops very early in human children, was absent.

plies that there is no single reality. Instead, *through communication we each create our own reality.* People with different communication experiences will see the world in different ways. We can never be totally sure that others see the world as we do. If we stop from time to time to check our perceptions, if we try to view things from others' perspectives, we may be surprised to see how different the world looks.

2. The fact that reality is a product of communication also has another implication: *Too often we allow what we have created through communication to control us.* When the Balinese created demons as an explanation for natural events, they put themselves in the position of spending the rest of their lives placating a concept. We too create our own kinds of demons. The expectations we have for ourselves — about

Communication allows the formation of close personal ties and a coordination of activity.

(Paul Gauguin, *Breton Girls Dancing, Pont Aven,* 1888)

things like success, perfection, and reputation — are examples of concepts that can control our lives and relationships.

3. Of course, individuals are not totally free to create any reality they want. Most of us are strongly influenced by the cultures in which we live. *Communication always takes place in a cultural context.* To forget this fact is to become a prisoner of culture. Erving Goffman has analyzed the powerful but unstated social rules that govern interaction.[16] Although we will have more to say about Goffman throughout

this book, it might be useful to introduce one of his concepts now, the concept of face.

Goffman defines **face** as an approved social identity, what we present to others for their approval. He believes that we spend a great deal of our time trying to fit face both to situation and to self-image. Communication that is incongruent with face will be judged as socially unacceptable. For Goffman, although face may be an individual's most cherished possession, "it is only on loan to him from society; it will be withdrawn unless he conducts himself in a way that is worthy of it. Approved attributes and their relation to face make of each man his own jailer; this is a fundamental social constraint even though each man may like his cell."[17]

Clearly, many of our most personal behaviors are culturally derived. One tension we all experience is that between independence and conformity. To communicate successfully, we must conform to social rules; to act creatively we must often oppose them. This tension will be discussed in more detail in Chapter 2.

4. Finally, communication requires cooperation. We are influenced not only by our cultures but by every individual we communicate with. This means that *what is important in interpersonal communication is what people do when they are together, not what each does separately.* Throughout this text we will stress the idea that interpersonal communication is mutual. In order to understand relationships we must look at the relationship itself, not at each individual participant. Most of the time we don't do this. For example, when a relationship fails, most of us try to figure out who to blame. We may blame the other person, feeling he or she is insensitive or egocentric; or we may blame ourselves, wishing we had been more open or less selfish. The truth is that communication is never the product of only one person's efforts. In order for relationships to work, *both* parties have to strive to be competent communicators.

Through competent communication we create lasting bonds. Who we become is often a function of early communicative experience.

(Jean-François Millet, *The Knitting Lesson*, 1869)

The Nature of Communicative Competence

Communication doesn't always run smoothly. This may be one of the main reasons you've decided to study interpersonal communication. If you're like most people, at some time in your life you've run into communication problems. You've probably been in situations where you couldn't think of what to say next. Or you may

have been unable to express yourself clearly. Perhaps you insulted someone unintentionally or blurted out something thoughtlessly. If you've experienced any of these situations, you know how important it is to be able to communicate competently.

What, exactly, does it mean to communicate competently? **Communicative competence** is the *ability to communicate in a personally effective and socially appropriate manner.* Although this definition appears very simple, competence is a complex subject that has generated a lot of research and discussion. One reason is that competent communication involves two separate levels: (1) a surface level, consisting of the part of competence that can be seen — the actual performance of day-to-day behaviors — and (2) a deeper level, consisting of everything we have to know in order to perform. Although the surface level has many different names, we will call it **performative competence.** It is demonstrated every time someone actually produces effective and appropriate communication behaviors. The second, underlying level we will call **process competence.** It consists of all the cognitive activity and knowledge necessary to generate adequate performance.

For example, when you hear someone give a particularly gracious compliment, what you observe is only the surface level. What you cannot see is the mental activity that led up to it. Giving a compliment involves a lot of thought. It entails knowing when a compliment is appropriate and when it isn't; predicting whether the recipient will be pleased or embarrassed; choosing content that sounds sincere but not ingratiating; and knowing how to phrase the compliment in a graceful and pleasing style. All of this is part of process competence.

A MODEL OF COMMUNICATIVE COMPETENCE

There are many different models of communicative competence. Some focus on performative aspects,[18] some on process,[19] and some do a little of both.[20] The model presented in Figure 1.1 is primarily a process model. It is our way of answering the question *What does a person have to know or be able to do in order to communicate in a personally effective and socially appropriate manner?* Figure 1.1 is a representation of the processes we think are involved.

We believe that people who wish to be competent communicators must know how to do five things well: (1) assign meanings to the world around them; (2) set goals strategically; (3) take on social roles appropriately; (4) present a valued image of themselves to the world; and (5) generate intelligible messages. These abilities correspond to the types of process competence outlined in our model: interpretive

competence, goal competence, role competence, self competence, and message competence.

When we say that people who wish to be competent must "know" how to do the things listed previously, we are talking about implicit rather than explicit knowledge. Implicit knowledge is knowledge we don't stop to think about, that we use unconsciously to guide our behavior. Grammatical knowledge is a good example. From the time we are quite young we can say things in well-structured and meaningful ways. We can even recognize and correct errors when we make them. However, most children (and indeed most adults) would be hard-pressed to recite the rules of grammar. The formal grammatical rules we learn in English class are attempts to express explicitly the implicit rules we follow when speaking.

The first kind of **implicit knowledge** we need about the world is perceptual. In order to communicate, we must be able to assign meaning to the world; we must know how to "see" it. This kind of competence we call interpretive competence. We must also be able to set communicative goals, to foresee the results of communication and make adequate plans. This we refer to as goal competence. Next, we must adapt to the needs and expectations of others. We must know what behaviors are appropriate and expected and what are prohibited. Doing this involves us in role competence. At the same time we are learning to adapt to others, we must also learn to be true to self. We must develop our own individual styles based on our sense of self. This is called self competence. Finally, we must be able to use all of this knowledge in actual speech situations. To do this we need message competence, the competence that allows us to express verbal, nonverbal, and relational messages. If we lack any of these kinds of process competence, communication becomes impossible: messages are unclear and relationships flawed.

In the remainder of this chapter, we will give a brief overview of each of the elements in our

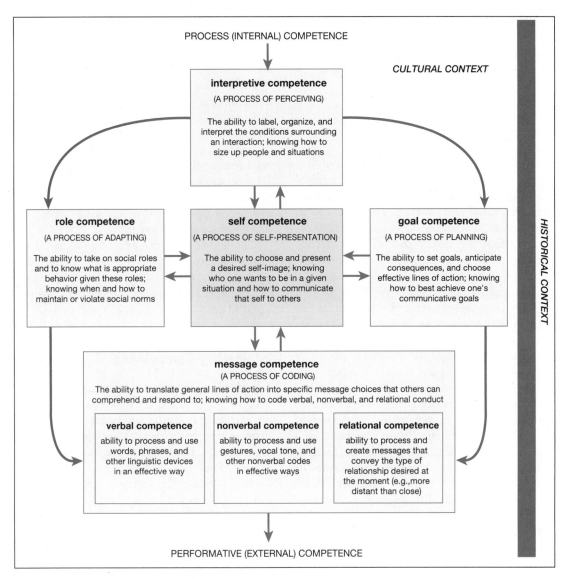

PROCESS (INTERNAL) COMPETENCE

CULTURAL CONTEXT

interpretive competence

(A PROCESS OF PERCEIVING)

The ability to label, organize, and interpret the conditions surrounding an interaction; knowing how to size up people and situations

role competence

(A PROCESS OF ADAPTING)

The ability to take on social roles and to know what is appropriate behavior given these roles; knowing when and how to maintain or violate social norms

self competence

(A PROCESS OF SELF-PRESENTATION)

The ability to choose and present a desired self-image; knowing who one wants to be in a given situation and how to communicate that self to others

goal competence

(A PROCESS OF PLANNING)

The ability to set goals, anticipate consequences, and choose effective lines of action; knowing how to best achieve one's communicative goals

message competence

(A PROCESS OF CODING)

The ability to translate general lines of action into specific message choices that others can comprehend and respond to; knowing how to code verbal, nonverbal, and relational conduct

verbal competence

ability to process and use words, phrases, and other linguistic devices in an effective way

nonverbal competence

ability to process and use gestures, vocal tone, and other nonverbal codes in effective ways

relational competence

ability to process and create messages that convey the type of relationship desired at the moment (e.g.,more distant than close)

PERFORMATIVE (EXTERNAL) COMPETENCE

HISTORICAL CONTEXT

F I G U R E **1.1**

A model of interpersonal communication competence

model. Later in this book, we will revisit each kind of competence in more detail. As you read the brief descriptions below, remember that all five types of competence are interconnected. Because interpretive competence is at the top of our model and message competence is at the bottom, it may appear that interpretation comes before message-making. This isn't necessarily the case. There are times when we make language choices based on prior perceptions, but there are also times when the way we talk about something affects the way we perceive it.

To emphasize the fact that the relationship between types of competence is complex and nonlinear, we will start our discussion with message competence and then move on to the other types of competence.

Message Competence

Probably the first kind of competence most people think of when they think of communication is **message competence,** *the ability to make message choices that others can comprehend as well as to respond to the message choices of others.* Without the ability to code and decode messages, communication would be impossible. Schizophrenics, for example, use language in a bizarre and individualistic way. Their lack of message competence means that they must live apart from others in an impenetrable private world. Luckily, this kind of disruption in basic competence is rare. Most of us have an innate ability to understand and create messages.

The most obvious part of message competence is **verbal competence,** *the ability to process and use linguistic devices to convey content in effective ways.* Language is the basic currency through which meanings are exchanged. Without the ability to understand the rules of language, we would be unable to communicate in a fully human way. But language isn't everything. To communicate effectively we also need **nonverbal competence,** *the ability to process and use nonverbal codes to convey content in effective ways.* Body movement, facial expression, use of time and space, physical appearance, and vocal characteristics all convey meaning. To communicate competently, we must understand verbal codes as well as the nonverbal codes that accompany and often modify their meaning.

Verbal and nonverbal codes combine to create two kinds of meaning, content and relational meaning. Content meaning conveys the explicit topic of a message; it consists of the ideas or feelings the speaker is trying to share. Relational meaning is more implicit and contextual; it defines our relationship with the speaker. Whereas content meaning is contained in *what* is said, relational meaning lies in *how* something is said. Communicators often concentrate only on content and disregard relational meaning. To emphasize how important this second kind of message is, we have added relational competence to our model. For us, **relational competence** consists of *the ability to process and create messages that convey the type of relationship assumed or desired by a communicator at a given moment.*

The ability to make effective linguistic and nonverbal choices lies at the heart of communication. But message competence does not exist in a vacuum. It is connected to each of the other kinds of competence shown in our model.

Interpretive Competence

In order to make effective message choices, we need to gather basic data about the context in which communication will occur. This involves **interpretive competence:** *the ability to label, organize, and interpret the conditions surrounding an interaction.* We live and communicate in a world full of diverse stimuli. Because we cannot pay attention to everything, we must learn to pick out information that is important and disregard information that is irrelevant.

If you have ever been in a completely unfamiliar situation, you know how difficult it can be to sort out sensory impressions. First-time campers lying alone in a tent in the dead of night hear all kinds of unfamiliar and inexplicable sounds, sounds that an experienced camper could easily dismiss as unimportant. Novices in any situation lack interpretive experience: they pay attention to meaningless details while overlooking important information and often don't know how to organize what they do see. If they have basic interpretive competence, however, they quickly learn what is important and what is not.

The need to interpret the world correctly is especially important in interpersonal interactions. In order to communicate effectively, we must understand the situations in which we find ourselves as well as the kind of people we are dealing with. We must also be able to identify our own feelings and needs. If we misinterpret our surroundings or misjudge our partners or overlook our own feelings, we may find ourselves in serious trouble. Without basic data about people and situations, we are likely to say the wrong thing at the wrong time. The kind of people who blurt out whatever they think, with no regard for where they are or who they are with, lack interpretive competence.

Interpretive competence helps us size up situations and people, name them, identify their outstanding characteristics, and, inevitably, decide upon an attitude toward them. If we succeed at this, we will make appropriate message choices; if not, we will do or say the wrong thing and will appear to be personally insensitive and impervious to our surroundings.

Role Competence

Communication is a cooperative activity, a transaction in which people adapt to one another. Because of this, effective message choices must be culturally approved and socially shared. This brings us to a kind of competence we call **role competence,** *the ability to take on social roles and to know what is appropriate behavior given these roles.*

In order to communicate effectively, we must know who we may safely be in any situation; we must recognize what behaviors are appropriate and what are off limits. When conflicting social demands arise, we must be able to choose between them. We must also be able to maintain our own social identities while protecting the identities of others. If we fail to recognize the subtle rules that govern interaction, our message choices will seem odd or out of place. This often happens when we leave the safety of our own cultures. While most of us manage to learn the norms of our own groups, we're often at a loss when we have to interact with people not brought up as we were. The individual who is snatched from his or her own environment and placed in a very different one often lacks role competence. Plays and movies are full of such characters. The working-class heroine who suddenly finds herself in high society (*My Fair Lady*) or the time traveler who somehow ends up in a different era (*Back to the Future*) are examples of characters who must somehow learn new ways of behaving. While their ineptness is a source of comedy in the movies, in real life the consequences of role-inappropriate behavior are more serious. Although a certain amount of individuality is charming, too much is socially costly. People who lack role competence often make message choices that lead others to perceive them as rude or willful or crazy.

Self Competence

Of course communicating competently is not just a matter of following social rules. People who follow every rule of etiquette precisely, who let society define them completely, are merely social robots. We label such people as phony or fake, for they lack an essential characteristic that most of us value highly: individuality. Because all of us are individuals with our own unique thoughts and feelings, we must express them in our own ways. Thus, another important part of communicative competence is **self competence,** *the ability to choose and present a desired self-image.* Individuals with self competence know who they are and who they want to be and can convey that self to others.

One of the most important aspects of growing up is developing a sense of individuality and a personal communication style. Central to this process is the development of a healthy **self-concept,** for who we think we are is closely tied to how we present ourselves to others. If our self-concept contains negative elements (if our **self-esteem** is low) we are likely to avoid certain communication situations and to communicate tentatively and self-consciously. If, on the other hand, our self-concept is positive and our self-esteem high, we will communicate with confidence in a variety of situations. People who lack role competence lack a consistent communication style. Because they are not sure of who they are, they have trouble expressing thoughts and feelings. Others may perceive them as inconsistent or cold.

Goal Competence

A final process necessary for communicative competence is planning. This process involves **goal competence,** *the ability to set goals, anticipate probable consequences, and choose effective lines of action.* Although not all communication is intentional, a great deal involves "strategic verbal choice-making." In order to make adequate message choices, a communicator must know what he or she is trying to achieve, determine the obstacles that lie in the path of goal attainment, and find a line of action that will overcome those obstacles.[21] This sequence is well known to salespeople who often carefully plan their approaches and use "canned" sales pitches to make sure their goals are achieved. Everyday planning takes a great deal more creativity and imagination. Seldom are our objectives completely clear and our lines of argument explicitly laid out; we must be able to think "on our feet."

Goal competence doesn't come easily. If we lack goal competence, we have few behavioral alternatives. We don't know how to approach others or what to do once we gain their attention. People without goal competence can't imagine the world as others see it, and their

range of behaviors is limited. They don't know how to frame an argument or make an effective appeal. They may realize that their way of communicating is not working, but they don't know what to do about it. People who lack this form of competence make poor strategic choices. People are impervious to their messages and may well perceive them as awkward or offensive.

The Effects of Culture and History

It is easy to forget that communication is culturally constrained. As we go about our daily lives, making friends and sharing experiences, our communication choices seem to be unique and individual. It is hard to imagine that the emotions we feel and the beliefs we hold are, as often as not, prescribed for us by others. The way we do things seems so natural that it is almost impossible to think of other ways of acting. Yet communication has a large cultural component as we have indicated in our model of communication competence. Everything we do is embedded within the constraints of culture and history.

Throughout this book we will try to make you more aware of the effects of culture on interpersonal arrangements. We will discuss ways other cultures define communication competence, and we will devote an entire chapter to cultural and historical influences. As an introduction, consider the description of communicative behavior given in Box 1.2. We think it will point up the fact that different cultures solve interpersonal problems in different ways and that what makes us competent in one culture may make us incompetent in another.

Cultures, of course, are in a constant state of evolution. Since Lee wrote his article, outside influences have encroached on the culture of the !Kung. To survive they have had to develop new ways of life. This happens in every culture. As time passes, social, economic, and technological changes occur, and these changes affect interpersonal patterns. What seems modern and new to one generation seems hopelessly outdated and old-fashioned to the next. To be competent, communicators must be willing to accept and adapt to change.

To indicate the influence of temporal change on communication patterns, we have added a historical dimension to our model. Throughout this text we have included historical case studies as well as discussions of the potential effects of technology on future communication patterns. To further illustrate the importance of time on concepts of competence, we have also included a discussion of the social history of interpersonal communication in the last chapter. By the time you finish this book, you should have a clearer understanding of how culture and time affect interpersonal communication.

THE LINK BETWEEN PROCESS AND PERFORMANCE

The five processes we have discussed are all necessary for good performance. Unfortunately, knowing how to communicate does not guarantee we will say or do the right thing.[22] A person can know perfectly well what is required in a given situation and still not perform adequately. A number of factors can cause communication to fail: individual physical states such as fatigue or anxiety; contradictory attitudes, beliefs, and values; poor motivation; and sheer stubbornness. Finally, lack of practice can cause a performance to come off as stilted and artificial.

In this book we'll provide you with some of the theoretical knowledge you'll need to understand and analyze communication. After defining interpersonal communication in the next chapter, we revisit the five kinds of competence outlined in our model. We begin with message competence, because the sending and receiving of messages is the heart of all interpersonal communication. In Chapter 3 we look at nonverbal communication codes and note the kinds of meanings they convey. In Chapter 4 we note

the importance of language on thought and action, while in Chapter 5 we explore ways both codes are used to send relational messages. Chapter 6 looks at interpretive competence, examining the relationship between communication and perception. Chapter 7 investigates role competence while Chapter 8 focuses on self competence and issues of identity formation. Chapter 9 centers on goal competence and strategic communication. Chapters 10 through 12 focus on competence in important communication contexts: these chapters discuss how we can improve our interactions with family, intimates, and colleagues. Finally, we end with a chapter dedicated to understanding how culture and history affect interpersonal patterns in all contexts.

While we believe that the first step to becoming a better communicator is understanding the basic processes of competence, we believe theory is not the whole picture. To be fully competent you must be able to translate theory into practice. To help you do that, at the end of each chapter we include a section on skill building. These sections offer guidelines to help you improve your interpersonal skills. Through classroom activities and by working through some of the assignments in the "Process to Performance" sections that follow each chapter, we hope you will find a way to take these general guidelines and make them work for you.

Skill Building: On Taking a Process Perspective

As we progress through the text, we will be looking at ways to improve specific skills like listening, giving and receiving feedback, becoming more assertive, and so on. For now, we want to say a few general words about how to build skills. An important step in improving

BOX **1.2**

Insulting the Meat: An Interpersonal Communication Ritual

Cultural understandings guide virtually every aspect of our lives. They show us how to dress and move and speak. They tell us how to make friends, how to make enemies, and how to make love. They indicate what objects to hoard, what people to value, and what gods to worship. But precisely because they tell us so much, we often fail to realize their influence. Studying the customs of different cultures can remind us that the way we do things is not the only natural and proper way.

One example of how another culture communicates is described by Richard Lee, who studied the Dobe !Kung, the so called Bushmen of the Kalahari. The !Kung are nomadic foragers who survive in a harsh environment by hunting and gathering. They have developed a number of

rituals that have helped them adapt to this way of life. One of the most interesting is known as "insulting the meat."

In !Kung society the wild game and edible plants gathered by members of the group are normally shared with the entire tribe. A lot of time and attention is devoted to the fair distribution of goods, particularly meat. One way of ensuring fair distribution is demonstrated by the following communication pattern.

Strict norms govern the way a hunter announces his results when he returns from a successful hunt. He must sit in silence until someone asks him how the hunt went. He must then say that he found nothing of any worth. On the following day, when his companions go out with him to collect the kill, they are expected to do so with a minimum of enthusiasm, complaining loudly about the distance and wretchedness of the game. Instead of being offended, the hunter agrees, apologizing for his lack of skill.

What can we make of this behavior? Wouldn't it be more "natural" for a hunter to boast of a good kill? Lee tells us that the "heavy joking and derision are directed toward one goal: the leveling of potentially arrogant behavior in a successful hunter." Lee believes that "insulting the meat" is a way of maintaining a sense of

your communication is learning to take what we call a **process perspective.** This means becoming aware of what's going on when you communicate; beginning to recognize how the underlying processes involved in communication manifest themselves in everyday performance. Too often people communicate in a mindless kind of way. They are so busy thinking about *what* they are saying or doing (the content of communication) that they fail to consider *how* they are going about it (the form of communication). Taking a process perspective means concentrating on form in addition to

content. It means sitting back and watching yourself as you communicate.

At first this is not an easy thing to do, for it involves a kind of "double consciousness." The competent communicator must be able to act naturally and spontaneously and at the same time observe and analyze communication patterns. This is somewhat like being a good actor. On the one hand, actors exist within the imaginary world of the play, reacting as their characters would. On the other hand, they remain aloof and in control, watching for the cues that signal exits and entrances, remembering their

he thinks of us as his servants or inferiors. We can't accept this. We refuse one who boasts, for someday his pride will make him kill somebody. So we always speak of his meat as worthless. In this way we cool his heart and make him gentle.

For most of us, this is a peculiar way of doing things. We believe that people should take pride in their accomplishments and show gratitude for generosity. But stop for a moment and think about the social results of concepts such as "gratitude" and "accomplishment" and "generosity." How do they affect our relationships with others? The answer to this question may make you see more clearly how seemingly innocent and trivial patterns of communication are tied to larger social issues.

equality. Because the !Kung depend on sharing for survival, generosity is something that should not be praised but simply expected. Praise might lead to pride and arrogance, potential threats to the !Kung way of life. As Tomazho, one of the !Kung, expressed it:

When a young man kills much meat, he comes to think of himself as a chief or a big man, and

SOURCE: Richard B. Lee, *The Dobe !Kung* (New York: Holt, Rinehart & Winston, 1984).

ADDITIONAL READINGS

Geertz, Clifford. *The Interpretation of Cultures.* New York: Basic Books, 1973.
Spradley, James P., and David W. McCurdy, eds. *Conformity and Conflict: Readings in Cultural Anthropology,* 5th ed. Boston: Little, Brown, 1984.

positions and lines, and adjusting to audience reaction. Beginning actors often have a hard time finding just the right mixture of involvement and distance.

The beginning speech communication student must also find the right balance point between performing and analyzing. At first students have problems removing themselves from the content level; they have not yet learned to see process. Later on, as they learn more about communication, they may become too analytical, annoying their friends by giving instant analyses of every interaction. But with

practice it is possible to learn when to act and when to analyze. The transitions become easy and automatic.

We cannot stress strongly enough how important it is to begin to start analyzing interactions. For one thing, it will make learning theory more interesting and enjoyable. You will begin to see connections between what you read about in this text and what you and those around you actually do. Even more important, developing the ability to observe behavior will allow you to diagnose and improve your own performance.

Process to Performance

REVIEW TERMS

The following is a list of major concepts introduced in this chapter. The page where the concept is first mentioned is listed in parentheses.

communication   (6)
process   (6)
face   (10)
communicative competence   (11)
performative competence   (12)
process competence   (12)
implicit knowledge   (12)
message competence   (14)
verbal competence   (14)
nonverbal competence   (14)
relational competence   (14)
interpretive competence   (14)
role competence   (15)
self competence   (15)
self-concept   (16)
self-esteem   (16)
goal competence   (16)
process perspective   (18)

SUGGESTED READINGS

Civikly, Jean M. *Contexts of Communication.* New York: Holt, Rinehart & Winston, 1981. Essays that give an overview of the field of speech communication by examining the forms communication takes in a variety of contexts. Easy reading, and useful if you want to get a feel for what is studied in speech communication.

Matson, Floyd W., and Ashley Montagu. *The Human Dialogue: Perspectives on Human Communication.* New York: Free Press, 1967. A compilation of essays from a variety of fields, including works by mathematicians, physicists, psychoanalysts, philosophers, theologians, sociologists, psychologists, novelists, and essayists. Hannah Arendt, Jacques Barzun, Martin Buber, Albert Camus, Erich Fromm, Oliver Wendell Holmes, and E. B. White are just a few of the contributors.

Savage-Rumbaugh, Sue, and Roger Lewin, *Kanzi: The Ape at the Brink of the Human Mind.* New York: John Wiley & Sons, 1994. A story of one of the remarkable apes who has learned to understand human language. Sue Savage-Rumbaugh describes her attempts to teach Kanzi language and invites us to share her discoveries.

Shweder, Richard A., *Thinking Through Cultures: Expeditions in Cultural Psychology.* Cambridge: Harvard University Press, 1991. An interesting and thoughtful discussion of some of the philosophic questions raised by social constructionism. Not as easy to read as some of the other sources, it is well worth the effort just for its insights into other cultures.

Sigman, Stuart J., *Introduction to Human Communication: Behavior, Codes, and Social Action.* Needham Heights, Mass.: Ginn, 1992. A collection of readings on such diverse topics as interpersonal deception, visual elements in television news, dance as communication, and the paintings of van Gogh.

Walker, Stephen. *Animal Thought.* London: Routledge & Kegan Paul, 1983. If you are at all intrigued by animal communication, you will find this book fascinating. It is clear and easy to read, but it also does a thorough job of evaluating the scientific literature.

TOPICS FOR DISCUSSION

1. In the introduction to this chapter, we tried to draw a parallel between extraterrestrial and interpersonal communication. Think of at least five additional ways that the process of communicating across cultures is like the process of communicating interpersonally. (We consider communication with extraterrestrials to be the ultimate in cross-cultural communication.)

2. Define communication. What kinds of behaviors are included in and excluded from your definition? According to your definition, would a person sitting alone in a room thinking about a friend be communicating? Would a blush of embarrassment be communication? If you became tongue-tied, so that the message you were trying to get across became distorted, would communication have taken place? For a behavior to qualify as communication, does it have to involve two people? Be intentional? Be successful?

3. In this chapter we suggested that the realities people create through communication often control them. We used the example of Balinese demon worship. Can you think of words or concepts that control the lives of people in our culture? Discuss.

4. Goffman argues that much of what we do, including our communication, we do because society says we must. To what extent do you believe you are controlled by social rules and roles? How much freedom do you have?

5. Perception is a complex process involving the ability to interpret what is going on in situations and episodes, what other people are like, and what we ourselves are thinking and feeling. Think of at least three examples of how problems in perception could lead to failures in communication.

6. Discuss the relationship between role competence and goal competence. Is it possible to have one without the other? What would a person who was role competent but had no goal competence be like? Is it possible to be goal competent without being role competent?

7. Assume that a visitor from another planet asked you to give it some advice on how to get along at your college or university. Pick a simple activity, say, attending a one-hour class, working at the gym, or going out for pizza. Perceptually, what would the alien have to be able to do to handle these situations? What social roles would it have to master? What kinds of plans and strategies would it need? What verbal and nonverbal rules would it have to follow to be communicatively competent?

8. Have you ever been in a situation where your inability to handle language effectively caused an interpersonal problem? Have you ever committed a nonverbal *faux pas*? If they aren't too personal, share these experiences. What do they tell you about message competence?

9. In this chapter we argued that mastering process doesn't always lead to perfect performance. What factors can intervene between process and performance? What can be done about them?

10. Discuss the ritual of insulting the meat (Box 1.2). Can you think of other rituals in our culture that have a social-control function?

OBSERVATION GUIDE

1. Analyze a recent conversation by applying the model of communication competence presented in this chapter. Identify the level of interpretive, goal, role, and message competence you and your partner achieved. For instance, how successful were you in sizing up the situation? Did you accurately perceive your partner's intentions? How many message strategies did you consider? Did you have a clear understanding of the social roles called for? Were there any verbal or nonverbal misunderstandings? Judge your performance. How well did you do what you wanted to?

2. Take a look at the other courses you're enrolled in this semester. How can these courses give you an understanding of communication? Make a list of at least 15 topics from other courses that are related to interpersonal communication. Take one and describe what it taught you about the communication process. For example, you may have read a short story in a literature class that described interpersonal relationships. You may have come across a theory in psychology that explains some aspect of communication. Describe in detail what you learned.

EXERCISES

1. Work in pairs. Begin by individually thinking of the best and worst communicators you ever knew. Describe them to your partner. Working together, come up with a list of at least ten attributes that differentiate your good and bad communicators. Now ask your partner to describe his or her best and worst communicators and repeat the process. How did your ideas differ? How do you stack up on both your own and your partner's list? What is your strongest point? What areas need more work? Discuss.

2. Taking a process perspective means becoming aware of how people communicate with one another. It means looking for cues that signal what's going on between people. Choose a partner and go to a public area on campus. Find a group of people who look interesting and observe them for 10 or 15 minutes. As you observe, make notes on what's going on in their interaction. Share your notes with your partner. From your combined observations, make a list of all of the things you were able to tell about interpersonal relationships just by observing. At the next class, share your list with others. Together come up with an observation guide — a list of things to look for in interaction. Use this observation guide to observe another group. You should begin to see more and more happening as you gain experience in observing others.

3. A model is a simplified explanation of a process. Models can help us understand the characteristics of a process, the factors that affect it, the way it operates, and so on. There are many ways of describing any process; consequently there are many models of it.

a. To get some practice in model making, think of a fairly complex process or object that you're familiar with (a football game, eating at a restaurant, graduating from high school, a first date). Working in groups, construct a model of that process. Pretend that you are preparing materials for people from a vastly different culture who will be visiting your college. Your model will help these people learn how things are done in your culture. You can create a verbal description, a flowchart, a diagram, a rule book. Share your model with the class.

b. Now try constructing your own model of communication.

Interpersonal communication always changes us. When it works, we touch each other's lives; when it fails, we are disconnected and alone.

(Dale Kennington, *Caffe Florian*.)

2

Interpersonal Communication:
Building Relationships

Communication takes many forms. It can be as simple and direct as a smile or as complex and eloquent as a novel. It can occur between two people or among thousands, with a small group of friends or in an impersonal bureaucracy. Because communication takes so many different forms, it is easy to forget that all are part of the same process: the act of creating and sharing meaning. No matter how technologically sophisticated the channels or how vast the audience, communicators must share meaning with one another. It is for this reason that communication is, at heart, an interpersonal process.

One of the authors of this text was once asked at a party what he taught. When he answered, "Interpersonal communication," he was asked, "But isn't all communication interpersonal? Doesn't it always occur between people? Doesn't it always occur between people?" The question is not a bad one. Although it is common to reserve the label interpersonal for intimate communication between two people in face-to-face interaction, clearly all communication is, in a sense, interpersonal.

In this chapter we explore the relationship between interpersonal and other forms of communication. We begin by looking at traditional approaches to interpersonal communication and by offering our own definition. We then describe what happens to people when they form interpersonal bonds, and we consider how interpersonal communication and intimacy are related. Finally, we look at the special kind of competence it takes to build relationships.

What Is Interpersonal Communication?

There are several ways to distinguish interpersonal from other forms of communication. In this section we will discuss and criticize two of the most popular approaches: the situational and the developmental.

25

THE SITUATIONAL APPROACH

The **situational approach** holds that the situation in which communication occurs determines what kind of communication is going on; different situations result in different forms of communication.[1]

When we're alone, for example, our communication is often quite different from our communication when we are with others. First of all, it is silent, taking place inside our heads. Most people believe that this kind of communication, called **intrapersonal communication,** is also more disconnected and repetitive and less logical than other forms of communication.[2] Whenever you daydream or fantasize, consider a difficult personal problem, or try to make sense of the world around you, you are engaging in intrapersonal communication. You are both sender and receiver of your own message.

According to the situational approach, intrapersonal communication can be distinguished from **interpersonal communication,** communication between two people, generally in face-to-face interaction. Another name for this form of communication is *dyadic.* Dyadic communication is generally spontaneous and informal; the participants receive maximum feedback from each other. Roles are relatively flexible, as partners alternately act as senders and receivers. When you sit down with a friend to recall old times, when you ask a professor what will be on the test, or when you have a serious discussion with someone you love, you are engaging in interpersonal communication.

As soon as a third person joins an interaction, it ceases to be interpersonal and becomes **small-group communication.** While the size of a small group may vary, it must be small enough that everyone can interact freely. In a dyad the participants are connected directly; if the link between them is severed, the relationship no longer exists. In a small group, communication is not destroyed when the link between two of the members is cut. Members can communicate with one another in a variety of ways.

Coordinating group interaction is relatively complex. For most of us, groups are psychologically more difficult to handle than dyads. One of the reasons formalized roles like that of leader emerge is to allow groups to handle the difficult problem of coordinating activity.[3] Students working on a class project together, cabinet members setting government policy, sports teams, and social clubs all engage in small-group communication.

The next situational level involves **organizational communication**. This form of communication occurs in complex organizations such as large businesses and industries and government institutions. Here communication takes place within a strongly defined hierarchy. Organizational members also experience, in addition to interpersonal and group relationships with coworkers, a relationship to the organization itself and to the bureaucracy that organizes and runs it. Roles tend to be more specialized and differentiated than at other levels, and rules for behavior more formalized. Successful communication requires knowledge of these roles and rules, often referred to as "organizational culture."[4]

When a single speaker addresses a large group of individuals simultaneously, he or she engages in **face-to-face public communication.** The speaker doesn't know audience members personally and must therefore compose the message for a hypothetical receiver. Because of the size of the audience, mutual interaction is also impossible. The speaker therefore acts as sender while the audience takes on a more passive receiver role. Clear organization, careful planning, and a fairly formal, nonconversational style are hallmarks of public communication. A political candidate on a whistle-stop tour, an evangelist exhorting a congregation, even a lecturer in a mass-enrollment course are examples of people communicating on the public level.

Finally, when speaker and audience become separated in both space and time, indirect ways of sending and receiving messages must be used. Messages must be stored until they can be received by their intended audience. When the

Interpersonal relationships are varied — some fleeting and public, others long-lasting and intimate. Each relationship will follow its own unique trajectory.

(Pierre-Auguste Renoir, *The Luncheon of the Boating Party*, 1881)

audience is large but the transmission is indirect, we call it **mediated public** (or **mass**) communication. Whenever "a medium replicates, duplicates, and disseminates identical content to a geographically widespread population," mass communication is taking place.[5] Radio and TV broadcasts, newspaper and magazine articles, and recorded music are examples.

According to the situational view, as we move from intrapersonal to mass communication, the following elements change: (1) the number of interactants, (2) their physical proximity, (3) their ability to deliver and receive feedback immediately, (4) the level of formality

of communication roles, (5) the ability of interactants to adapt messages to others' specific needs, and (6) the degree to which communicative goals and purposes are planned and structured.[6] Of all these variables, size probably has the biggest effect, since a change in size leads to all other changes.[7] Figure 2.1 shows how these factors affect communication.

According to the situational view, whenever two people interact in direct proximity, interpersonal communication is taking place. Before we decide whether or not this is a useful approach, let's look at a second way to define interpersonal communication.

Characteristics of Interaction		
number of persons	few	many
proximity of interactants	close	far
nature of feedback	immediate	delayed
communication roles	informal	formal
adaptation of message	specific	general
goals and purpose	unstructured	structured
Situational Levels:	Intrapersonal Small Group Public	
	Interpersonal Organizational Mass	

FIGURE 2.1
Situational characteristics and levels of communication

THE DEVELOPMENTAL APPROACH

According to the situational approach the interchange between a customer buying a new pair of shoes and the salesperson who hurriedly waits on him or her is just as interpersonal as the interaction between lovers trying to work out problems in their relationship. The **developmental approach** rejects this view, holding that interpersonal communication has a quality dimension. According to this approach only long-lasting reciprocal relationships in which interactants respond selectively and specifically to each other can be classified as interpersonal.[8] Thus, interactions between lovers would be interpersonal, but brief commercial interactions would not.

The most detailed explanation of the developmental approach is given by Gerald Miller and Mark Steinberg.[9] They argue that all dyadic relationships start by being impersonal. Only if certain changes occur do they become interpersonal. First of all, the rules governing the interaction must move from the cultural to the psychological level. Miller and Steinberg believe that three levels of rules guide our actions. **Cultural-level rules** are rules common to all members of a culture. For example, most Americans share rules for greetings and farewells. We know that it is appropriate to acknowledge another's presence when we meet, and we generally do it in similar ways: by smiling, nodding, or saying, "Hello." **Sociological-level rules,** on the other hand, are rules shared by members of specific groups within a culture. Soldiers, for example, have a unique greeting ritual, the salute. Lodge members may follow a sociological-level rule that tells them to greet their compatriots with a secret handshake. Finally, **psychological-level rules** are rules worked out by individuals. Some friends greet each other by slapping each other on the shoulder; others do so by hugging. Some use joking insults; others always begin an interaction with a compliment. There are no general cultural or group rules governing this practice.

People have always tried to control external forces through ritual use of symbols.

(Fred Kabotie, *Pueblo Green Corn Dance*)

Miller and Steinberg believe that communication becomes interpersonal only when the psychological level is reached. They also believe that other changes occur as relationships become interpersonal. For example, the kind of information people have about each other becomes increasingly unique; as a result, the level of knowledge they have about each other deepens. Interpersonal relationships are no longer based on stereotypes, and partners can predict each other's behaviors and motivations.

When we interact with a strange clerk in a shoe store, we have no background knowledge. We cannot treat the clerk individually, but instead according to the role he or she is fulfilling for us. Our relationship occurs at the surface level. It is *impersonal*, not interpersonal. When we interact with a friend, however, we have a shared background of experiences; we can sense his or her moods before anything is said; we know the person as an individual. Our relationship is *interpersonal* rather than impersonal.

Are you the same person when you are alone as when you are with others? (If a tree falls in a forest but no one is there, does it make a sound?) Is the person alone more "real" than the person interacting with others?

CRITICIZING THE SITUATIONAL/ DEVELOPMENTAL VIEWS

There are obviously advantages to both views. By focusing on *external* factors, the situational approach draws attention to the conditions surrounding communication. It tells us that context is important, and it allows us to divide communication into separate levels. The developmental approach, by focusing on *internal* aspects of relationships, reminds us that relationships vary in quality, evolving and changing over time. It emphasizes not just the external variables but how interactants actually feel and act toward each other.

Are there any disadvantages to these views? We would like to suggest that they may oversimplify the problem of defining communication contexts, either by overlooking important kinds of communication or by ignoring interactions between contexts. Let's look at each of these disadvantages.

The developmental view tends to restrict unnecessarily the meaning of interpersonal communication. According to the developmental view, only intimate relationships are of interest. While intimate relationships are extremely important, they are comparatively infrequent. Let's consider a typical day. Perhaps you decide to go to your favorite coffee shop for breakfast before renewing your license at the department of motor vehicles and then heading up to school. To get appropriate service you must communicate effectively with the person who waits on you and then with the motor vehicles clerk who goes over your paperwork. Once at school you must manage a variety of dyadic situations: You must deal with the person who steals the parking space you were patiently waiting for, the professor who wants to know why you're late, the clerk in the bursar's office who insists the school never received your check, and the fellow student who lost the notes she borrowed from you. While these interactions are neither intimate nor ultimately vital, they must be managed effectively and skillfully if you are to make it through the day. In each case you and another person are briefly connected by your mutual efforts to make sense of the world and of each other. In the developmental view, these kinds of relationships would not be given serious attention.

A disadvantage of the situational approach is that it ignores the complex relationships between different levels of communication. According to the situational view you are communicating either interpersonally or in some other way. No allowance is made for situations involving several levels simultaneously, nor is much said about the reciprocal effects of different levels on one another. In actuality, we often switch back and forth between levels rapidly. In talking to our boss, we may be operating in an organizational context, but we are also having a direct face-to-face interaction, as well as thinking to ourselves about the topic we are discussing. We are therefore engaged in organizational, interpersonal, and intrapersonal communication.

When you stop to think about it, determining what level of communication you are involved in at any given moment is surprisingly hard. Levels often blend in interesting ways. When new technologies are involved, simple distinctions seem even less applicable. Box 2.1 discusses one new form of communication that is changing all the rules by creating entirely new communication challenges.

Instead of thinking of interpersonal communication as separate from other forms of communication, we prefer to think of all communication as having an interpersonal element. While the clearest instance of interpersonal communication takes place when two people interact directly and personally, many other in-

teractions are partially interpersonal in nature. It may be useful to think of interpersonal communication as what philosophers and psychologists refer to as a "fuzzy set," a class that does not have clearly defined boundaries. Thus, *interpersonal communication takes place whenever two individuals, sharing the roles of sender and receiver, become connected through the mutual activity of creating meaning.* In addition, an interpersonal exchange may be brief or long-lasting, its content may be private or public, it may take place when two people are alone with each other or when there are others around, and it may be mediated or direct. What is important is that two people have formed a bond and that their interaction is mutual.

Forming Interpersonal Bonds

What does it mean to form an interpersonal bond? What happens to people when they share meaning? Perhaps the best way to answer these questions is to ask you to do a bit of imagining. Think of the last time you were completely alone. Try to picture yourself as clearly as you can. What did you look like? What were you doing? What was going through your mind? Now, imagine another person suddenly entering the scene and sitting or standing nearby. Picture your reaction. How did your relationship with yourself and with your surroundings change? What happened to you as a result of the mere presence of another?

CREATING INTERPERSONAL RELATIONSHIPS

Whenever two people become aware of each other (and awareness is the point at which interpersonal communication begins), at least two fundamental changes occur. First, they reorient. Second, their behavior becomes constrained. To

BOX **2.1**

Sex, Lies, and Cyberspace: Interpersonal Communication and Virtual Reality

In the past few years, perhaps no topic has captured our imagination more vividly than virtual reality. Experts and laypersons alike are not sure whether to laud or decry this new technology. For every person who believes virtual reality (VR) will expand human imagination and intelligence, there is someone else who views it as a drug that will destroy rational thought. For every expert who praises it as a new way to create community, there is another expert who believes VR will isolate us from one another.

But what, exactly, is VR? To answer that question, let's begin with a related concept, cyberspace. Cyberspace is the psychic "place" where humans interact with digital information. Cyberspace is where you are when you log-on to an electronic discussion group. It is the space through which your e-mail travels (and where lost or misplaced messages float indefinitely). It is the gateway you enter when you play an interactive computer game. Some people even say that you enter cyberspace when you make a simple phone call. Virtual reality is a special part of cyberspace, a place that seems particularly real and all-encompassing. When normal sensations are replaced by computer-generated information, so that we feel present in one environment while actually existing in another, distant environment,

we have entered VR. VR usually allows individuals to see and interact with virtual objects, and it is often networked, so that several people can enter a single virtual environment at once.

The architect who puts on a head-mounted display to walk through a new building before it is actually constructed is entering VR. So is the surgeon who sees into a patient's body to perform laparoscopic surgery, or the NASA scientist who guides a repair robot through virtual outer space. Author Howard Rheingold, who spent a year visiting visual worlds like these, gives us a sense of what VR feels like when he asks us to imagine "a wraparound television with three-dimensional programs, including three-dimensional sound, and solid objects that you can pick up and manipulate, even feel with your fingers and hands. . . . Imagine that you are the creator as well as the consumer of your artificial experience, with the power to use gesture or word to remold the world you see and hear and feel (16)." This is VR, and, he assures us, it is not fiction. The equipment exists today to enter such a world.

A technology as rich and powerful as VR has the potential to change many aspects of our lives, including interpersonal relationships. People who ponder the effects of VR on ftf (face-to-face) communication generally discuss two kinds of interaction: online communication, which currently exists, and virtual sex, for which the technology is not currently available.

We engage in online communication whenever we use e-mail or log-on to an interactive discussion group. Today electronic communication allows us to meet and talk with anonymous others at a distance and in relative safety. We are no longer constrained by the physical limitations of geography and time zones. We are also freed of conspicuous status markers and are no longer judged by our nonverbal characteristics. Because we can ignore or even recreate the body that is represented in cyberspace, it has been argued that online relationships are freer and more equal than real world relationships. Online interactions also allow us to escape real-world identities, presenting ourselves in any form we desire. It is fairly common, for example, for individuals communicating in cyberspace to "try on" a different gender, just to see what it is like to be perceived as male or female.

The ease with which we can take on virtual identities can, of course, lead to exploitation or manipulation. As philosopher Michael Heim points out, this is a serious concern. He believes that ftf interaction promotes loyalty and trust, and that "without directly meeting others physically, our ethics languish (102)." Online interactions may, he believes, amplify an "amoral indifference to human relations," because they are, by nature, less long-lasting and less deep than real-world relationships. Heim believes that as our personal autonomy is increased by electronic hookups, human interdependence and responsibility are decreased.

Interpersonal responsibility is certainly at issue in a second type of cyberspace experience, virtual sex. The name currently being used to describe the kind of VR system that will enable people to have sex with other people at a distance is "teledildonics," although "interactive tactile telepresence" might be a more accurate label. At least 30 years in the future, such a system is being visualized now. Individuals desiring to take part in this kind of virtual interaction will climb into lightweight body suits embedded with thousands of tiny sensors that can receive and send tactile information. The sensors will be so sensitive that the user will be able to feel the sensation of virtual silk or virtual skin. By donning a visual-display headset, users will perceive life-like visual representations of their own and their partners' body. Users may represent themselves accurately or may take on an artificial appearance, perhaps as a favorite movie star. After plugging into a telecommunication network, users will then be able to interact in whatever ways they like. "If you don't like the way the encounter is going," says Rheingold, "or someone requires your presence in physical reality, you can turn it all off by flicking a switch and taking off your virtual birthday suit (346)."

Although at this time VR sex is nothing more than a thought experiment, it is one that raises important questions. Will online sex (which asks so little of us in the way of caring or sharing) eventually affect sex in the real world? Will we come to prefer the convenience, ease, and safety of virtual interaction to its more emotionally complicated real-world counterpart? When sex no longer involves love and commitment, where will we turn for intimacy? Questions like these demand careful consideration. As Rheingold says, "Given the rate of development of VR technology, we don't have a great deal of time to tackle questions of morality, privacy, personal identity, and even the prospect of a fundamental change in human nature. When the VR revolution really gets rolling, we are likely to be too busy turning into whatever we are turning into to analyze or debate the consequences (350)."

SOURCES: Howard Rheingold, *Virtual Reality*. New York: Touchstone/Simon & Schuster, 1991.
Michael Hein, *The Metaphysics of Virtual Reality*. New York: Oxford University Press, 1993.

get a clearer picture of what it means to form an interpersonal relationship, let's look at each of these changes.

Reorientation

To orient is to locate oneself in time and space. To reorient means to change one's sense of location. People who are entirely alone often slip into a world of fantasy and daydreams. The mere presence of another person acts to bring them back to a more objective state. One of the first things that happens is a "rude awakening." Perhaps this is a survival mechanism, allowing the organism to sense danger. Regardless of why it occurs, one of the consequences of the presence of others is a heightened awareness of the world and of the self.

People who suddenly realize they are being observed exhibit other interesting changes. They sit up straighter, tense muscles that previously were relaxed, automatically rearrange their hair and clothing, and cease doing things that might reflect badly on them. Being observed seems to remind them of their physical appearance and behaviors. Psychologists refer to this as a state of **objective self-awareness.**[10]

The presence of others serves as a kind of mirror, reflecting back an image of self. If we find that self less than satisfactory, we correct our behaviors so as to present a more flattering image. This awareness of self is an extremely important characteristic of interpersonal bonds, and is a topic we shall discuss in much more detail later in this book. For now, what is important to remember is that interpersonal relationships show us who we are.

Behavioral Constraint

The presence of another not only gives us identity, it also acts to constrain our actions. When we interact with a stranger, we immediately try to predict what he or she is likely to do. This

prediction tells us what is possible within the interaction. It constrains our actions.

Behavioral constraint occurs in all relationships, even the most momentary. Have you ever seen a crowd crossing the street of a large city? Although hundreds of people pass one another in only a few seconds, they seldom collide. Seen in slow motion, their interaction is like an intricate dance. The "relationship" between them may last only a few seconds, but while it does their actions are coordinated.

William Wilmot gives an interesting illustration of the ways we are bound to others through communication.[11] The scene opens when Wilmot, sitting in a coffee shop, notices a young man staring intently at him. In order to avoid the stranger's stare, Wilmot turns away. When he glances nervously around he sees that he is still the object of observation. Finally, he rises and leaves, glaring at the young man as he exits. What is interesting is Wilmot's interpretation of this incident. Wilmot believes that an interpersonal interaction begins when there is a "perception of being perceived." As soon as two people become aware of each other, a relationship is formed, and as soon as that happens there is a corresponding loss of freedom. Wilmot believed that by staring at him, the stranger was pulling him into a relationship he did not want. He resented the fact that his behavior was being constrained by a stranger.

Of course, behavioral constraint is much more important in long-lasting relationships. When we form a relationship, we enter into an implicit contract, agreeing to abide by the rules we create together. Perhaps this is why so many people see commitment as a loss of freedom.

SENDING INTERPERSONAL MESSAGES

As soon as two people become aware of each other, they begin to send messages that allow the creation of interpersonal bonds. These messages may be intentional or unintentional, verbal or nonverbal, directed to matters of fact or focused on the participants and their relationship. While some of these messages are easy to identify, others are not as readily recognized even though these "invisible" messages play an important part in building interpersonal relationships.

Whenever we communicate, we communicate on at least two levels: the content and the relational. The **content level** is the overt and obvious meaning contained in a verbal message. When I say to you, "It's quite warm for this time of the year," I am generating content about the weather. At the same time, however, I am doing more. At the **relational level** I am sending messages about how I view you, how I want our relationship to progress, and how I want you to see me. How do I send these relational messages? Usually, through my nonverbal behavior. At the content level it's *what* I say that's important; at the relational level it's *how* I say it or *how* I act that counts. If, in the previous example, I talk about the weather in a friendly and open way, I indicate that I am outgoing, that I approve of you, and that I would like to make contact. If, however, I convey the message in a sneering and sarcastic way, I tell you that I do not like you, do not want to talk to you, and, perhaps, feel superior to you. These relational messages often accompany spoken content messages, but they can stand alone. If we return for a minute to the example of the stranger staring at Wilmot in the coffee shop, we see that what was upsetting about the interaction was that the stare was a silent, inappropriate, and somewhat enigmatic relational message.

We will return to the topic of relational messages throughout this book, particularly in Chapter 5, where we will analyze their importance in interaction. For now, we urge you to begin thinking about the inadvertent messages you may be sending to others. We want you to recognize that we build relationships through communication, and that this communication includes unspoken as well as spoken messages.

Posture, gesture, face — all reveal how we feel about ourselves and others. It's impossible not to send relational messages, although decoding them may not always be easy.

(Egon Schiele, *Seated Woman with Bent Knee*, 1917)

A Systems View of Interpersonal Communication

So far we have argued that whenever two people become aware of each other, an interpersonal bond is created. Another way to express this idea is to say that when people communicate they form an interpersonal system. To explore what it means to be part of a system, we will turn to a theory called **general systems theory.**

This theory arose when scientists working in many fields became aware that the same basic principles could be used to explain very different processes. Atomic structures, biological forms, and social patterns shared one thing in common: They could be described as systems.[12]

In simple terms a **system** is an organized collection of interdependent parts. Not every collection of parts is a system. The piles of rusted auto parts we see in a salvage yard are neither organized nor interdependent; they are a heap, not a system. The stores of chemicals on the shelf of a chemist's laboratory are not a system because they are isolated from one another. The people sitting in the sun in a public park are not a system because they are acting independently. Of course, all of the parts that make up these collections could be systems. If the auto parts were put back together into a functioning machine, they would form a mechanical system. If the chemist selected compatible chemicals and experimentally combined them in a test tube, a chemical system could be formed. And if the people in the park decided to get together to play a game of softball, a human system would be created.

CHARACTERISTICS OF HUMAN SYSTEMS

A number of systems characteristics can help us understand how relationships operate. The four most relevant to interpersonal communication are wholeness, interdependence, nonsummativity, and equifinality.

Wholeness

One of the things separating a system from a heap is that it has **wholeness** — that is, it operates as a whole, taking on unique properties and

characteristics. Systems act coherently. Although a car is made up of many parts, it isn't the parts we drive, it's the car. Although a team is made up of individual players, it isn't a single player who wins or loses, but the team. If we want to understand a system, we need to look at the unique ways in which the parts organize themselves and work together. What is important is the fact that the parts of a system are bound together into an entity that can be identified and observed in its own right.

Interdependence

When we say that the parts of a system act as a whole, we also imply that the parts have **interdependence.** Each part affects and is affected by every other part. A change in any part will be felt by all parts and by the system as a whole. Ecological systems are a good example here. We know that the physical environment is delicately balanced. To destroy or change one part is to make far-ranging changes in the nature of the whole.

Nonsummativity

Simply put, **nonsummativity** means that a whole is always more than the sum of its parts. Something emerges from a system that is much more complex than the individual parts. Water may be a combination of oxygen and hydrogen, but as an entity it is different from each element by itself. Similarly, when people join forces, they transform themselves into something more than what they were before.

Equifinality

A final implication of wholeness is that we cannot predict what will happen in a system by looking at how it began. Human systems are

Communication combines individual efforts in a unique whole. This friendship quilt, itself a product of interpersonal communication, is a perfect example of the blending of individual and group, private and public, efforts.

(Baltimore, 1848)

capable of self-regulation. They can meet the changing demands of the environment by reorganizing themselves. **Equifinality** means that a system is not bound by historical conditions: Two systems that start out at the same point may turn out very differently, while two systems that start out very differently may end up at similar points. The only way we can predict a system's operation is to examine the way it organizes itself and responds to its environment. The system is its own best explanation.

WHOLENESS IN INTERPERSONAL SYSTEMS

What has all of this to do with interpersonal relationships? Well, systems theorists argue that when people engage in interpersonal communication they create a system. This means their relationship takes on wholeness, interdependence, nonsummativity, and equifinality.

First of all, when two people communicate, the relationship they create is a unique and unitary whole. Each relationship develops its own characteristics; each is governed by a unique set of roles, norms, and rituals. This is why every dyad you form works in a slightly different way. Each relationship allows you to reveal a different aspect of your personality because you are part of a different whole.

When two people communicate interpersonally, they also become interdependent. This means that each affects the other. We often believe that we can enter a relationship without being affected by it. According to the systems view, this is impossible. We are always changed by our relationships with others, as they are changed by their relationships with us. And we are always in some way responsible for our interactions. Relationships are mutual creations. If they go smoothly it is because both parties coordinate their efforts effectively; similarly, if there are problems both members are responsible.

The fact that a whole is always more than the sum of its parts means that if we want to understand a dyad, we should try to analyze not what the members do when they are apart, but rather how they operate when they are together. Strict systems theorists believe that it is counterproductive to analyze individual personalities in order to understand interpersonal communication. Since individuals are constantly changing in response to each other, the best way to understand their relationship is to look at their behaviors when they are with each other. Relationships are defined by what people do, not by who they are.

Finally, the fact that relationships are equifinal means that it is difficult to predict what will occur in a relationship without looking at the way the system organizes itself and adapts to environmental pressures. Two couples, similar in background and education, with, as far as anyone can tell, a similar potential for happiness, may marry at the same time. One may stay together forever, building a strong, secure relationship, while the other may undergo a bitter divorce within five years. On the other hand, a third couple may marry who, in everyone's mind, is doomed to failure. Yet, somehow, the partners may remain a pair, managing to create a lasting relationship.

FEEDBACK IN HUMAN SYSTEMS

How do systems regulate themselves in order to adapt to their environments? They do so through the use of feedback. **Feedback** is the process by which a system compares its performance to a preset standard and uses this comparison to control its output. The standard example of a feedback mechanism is the household thermostat.[13] How does it work? A thermostat takes periodic readings of room temperatures and compares these to an initial setting. If the room temperature rises above the setting, the furnace is turned off, and heat is reduced. If the temperature falls below the set point, the furnace is turned back on. In this way a steady state is maintained: Information about the system's operation is fed back into the system and used as a control mechanism.

This kind of feedback is called negative feedback. It is designed to discourage system deviation; it is meant to keep the system from changing. When you check your weight daily to keep from gaining or losing too much, you are engaged in a negative feedback process. You are using information about your own behavior to control that behavior.

Of course, there are times when we do not wish a system to stay where it is. Rather, we wish it to increase or decrease its output. Feedback that encourages deviations is called positive feedback. A coach trying to encourage an athlete to break her previous record is using positive feedback. Information about performance is given to the athlete so that she can increase her speed rather than maintain it at a steady state. A person who wanted to get into the *Guinness Book of World Records* as the fattest man in the world would use positive feedback. Every day he would try to outdo his previous weight.

You may be used to thinking about negative feedback as feedback that is unpleasant or punishing, and positive feedback as feedback that is pleasant or rewarding. Don't let this everyday usage confuse you. We are using the terms in a more technical sense. Just remember that negative feedback discourages deviation from a standard while positive feedback encourages change.

Both feedback processes are found in relationships. If a relationship is going along well, the partners will try to protect it from change through negative feedback. They may know, for example, how much argument they can tolerate. When conflict escalates, negative feedback will keep it from getting out of control. At other times, however, positive feedback may encourage change. Trust, for example, often leads to more trust.

A relationship runs on information about itself. If that information is cut off, the relationship can no longer regulate itself and is in danger of becoming obsolete or running out of control. This is why the ability to give and receive feedback is such an essential part of communicative competence.

Relational Paths: Intimacy and Distance

Interpersonal systems rarely stay at the same point. As the parts of the system respond to one another and to outside pressures, the system evolves and changes. Much of a system's energy goes toward defining the nature of that change. When you and I form interpersonal relationships, we too are concerned with the path our relationship is taking. Some relationships will become long-lasting and intimate, characterized by mutual trust and dependence. Other relationships will exhibit a maximum amount of distance; members will remain courteous toward, but aloof from, each other. Most relationships will exist on some kind of middle ground. The path a relationship takes is often referred to as its **relational trajectory**.[14] In this section we consider how communication determines the paths relationships take.

INTERPERSONAL TRAJECTORIES: PRIVATE AND PUBLIC PATHS

In his excellent review of interpersonal bonding, Arthur Bochner tells us that there are two general relational trajectories. "On the one hand there is the type of social bond that gains 'coherence from a sentimental bond between persons who are essentially homogeneous'; on the other hand there is the type that integrates complementary differences into 'a practical organization in which mutual sentiments are unnecessary.'"[15] One way to label these two relational paths is to call the first private and the second public.

Private relationships are very much like the kind of relationship described in the developmental view. Over time they become more and more personal and unique. In a private relationship it makes a great deal of difference who our partner is. If we lose a friend or lover, we do not substitute someone else easily, for we are closely and interdependently connected. We are affected by each other in important ways, and our ties are very strong. In private relationships we make sense of each other by using unique, particularistic information about each other. In general, the rules of behavior we follow are individualistic, the product of negotiation. On the whole there is a good deal of sentiment involved in private relationships. These relationships are considered to be rewarding for their own intrinsic worth.

Public relationships are very different. The members of a public relationship are related in impersonal ways and very little change occurs over time. Members are substitutable. If the

TABLE 2.1 A relational dichotomy: private and public bonds	
Private	**Public**
In which we respond to the other in a personal and private manner	In which we respond to the other in an impersonal and public manner
Members are IRREPLACEABLE. It makes a difference who the other is.	Members are SUBSTITUTABLE. It makes no difference who the other is.
Members are INTERDEPENDENT.	Members are AUTONOMOUS.
Their way of knowing the other is PARTICULAR.	Their way of knowing the other is UNIVERSAL.
The rules governing behavior are INDIVIDUALISTIC.	The rules of governing behavior are NORMATIVE.
The tone of the relationship is SENTIMENTAL.	The tone of the relationship is PRACTICAL.
Rewards are primarily INTRINSIC.	Rewards are primarily EXTRINSIC.
Examples: sexual pairs, kinship pairs, marital partners, best friends	Examples: strangers, acquaintances, colleagues, work partners

clerk who waits on us is replaced by someone else, it will probably make very little difference to us. Instead of being interdependent, we are relatively autonomous. Our connections are slight and easily broken off. In public relationships we have little particularistic information about each other; instead, we attend to general class memberships to make sense of each other. The rules governing behavior are socially rather than individually determined — we are courteous and polite. Often the reason for the bond is practical rather than sentimental, and its rewards are extrinsic rather than intrinsic. Table 2.1 presents a model of differences between public and private relationships. We would like to make four points about this relational model.

1. *The two types of relationships we have described are extremes, and many variations are possible.* As you can see in Table 2.1, we have listed six dimensions that distinguish private and public relationships. Individuals working out a relationship must find a position on each

dimension. They must establish, for example, the extent to which they perceive a partner as important and unique as well as the amount of dependence that should characterize their bond. They must also determine how information should be exchanged and what kinds of rules will be followed during interaction. Finally, they must know how much emotional energy to invest and whether the relationship itself is of primary concern or whether it is simply a means to an end.

In a given culture some kinds of relationships will occur more often than others. For example, people in our culture expect honesty and openness in private relationships and guardedness in public relationships. Couples are expected to share everything, while strangers are to be told very little. Each of us, however, decides how far to go in following cultural norms. This means that although the culture may define only a few basic ways of relating, in reality there are as many kinds of relational paths as there are dyads.

2. *Over time, relationships will fluctuate and change.* Relationships are dynamic. There is constant movement and adjustment along each of the dimensions we have described. While marriage partners are generally dependent upon each other, the degree of autonomy and interdependence they require will vary through their married life. Constant readjustment of their positions will be necessary. Friends, too, must continually monitor their own behavior, deciding how much dependence and how much freedom should characterize their relationship.[16]

3. *Different skills and sensitivities are needed for different kinds of relationships.* Because we form many different kinds of bonds, we must learn a variety of skills. We need to know how to build private bonds through self-disclosure, but we need equally to know how to maintain a distance from others. Interpersonal competence is often a matter of knowing whether to employ public or private rules of behavior.

4. *Relational trajectories are defined through communication.* How do we settle on the path a relationship will follow? We define relational trajectories through communication. We constantly send each other messages (both verbal and nonverbal) about our relational expectations. Through a process of negotiation, we sift through these messages, deciding on a mutually satisfying outcome. Sometimes this process is relatively easy, as when two people in love follow the intimacy path. At other times it can be extremely painful, for example, when one partner wants the relationship to deepen while the other wants to maintain it at a more public level. Relationships are never stable. Defining and maintaining them takes a great deal of effort.

INDEPENDENCE VERSUS CONFORMITY: A BASIC INTERPERSONAL DILEMMA

One way to sum up the difference between private and public relationships is to say that private relationships allow us to exhibit uniqueness and independence while public relationships stress conformity and social solidarity. While humans need to feel connected to social groups, they also need to feel separateness. This is why both public and private relationships are necessary and why negotiating relationships is a serious matter.

We live in a society that tends to value the expression of personal individuality. Americans generally dislike dealing with people in terms of social roles. The idea of strangers bothers us; when we meet people, we try almost immediately to "get to know them." We want to interact on a friendly, informal, "first-name" basis right from the start.[17]

We carry this expectation into our long-lasting relationships, believing that over time relationships should increase in "personalness." A relationship that stays in the same place for any length of time is often described as "going nowhere." We expect the same degree of "progress" in our personal lives that we do in the business world. Occasionally this means that we try too hard too soon, not allowing relationships to grow at their own pace.

As a culture we tend to deemphasize public relationships, often losing sight of the fact that people have a need for distance as well as closeness. Public relationships are designed to give us that distance. They are meant to control and pace intimacy, keeping others from making personal demands on us or knowing us too well. Indeed, in public it is our place in the social structure rather than our individuality that defines us. We are identified by formal roles, and we are expected to act formally, following rules of courtesy.

While public relationships may seem undemocratic to some people, they have certain advantages. First of all, they affirm the social order. They remind us of social expectations and duties, making it clear to us that we are part of a collectivity. Second, they actually allow us to develop a sense of separateness. Psychologists tell us that without the ability to create boundaries between the self and others, we would

BOX **2.2**

Mind Your Manners: Some Social Functions of Etiquette

What do you think of rules of etiquette? Are they outmoded signs of a way of life that has disappeared? Are they ways of putting on a false front and deceiving people about your true feelings? Or do they serve some useful social purpose? Judith Martin, who makes her living as Miss Manners, author of advice columns and books on etiquette, believes that manners serve a useful function and that without social codes of behavior people cannot live a civilized life.

Martin recognizes that today most people distrust the idea of good manners. She traces this belief to the philosopher Jean-Jacques Rousseau, who felt that civilization destroys everything that is natural and good in people. She also finds this idea in the human potential movement's celebration of openness and authenticity as ways of life.

Martin believes codes of etiquette can be destructive. They can, for example, be used as a weapon in class warfare. But she also believes that manners are necessary for smooth social interaction. By heading off conflict, social codes allow people with irreconcilable differences to coexist. For Martin, individual freedom has to be tempered by the needs of society. This means that people cannot be free to do whatever they wish. Freedom and equality do not mean that everyone can be completely honest and exactly the same. For Martin, "a complete disregard of any distinctions, a total leveling of all hierarchies results in a kind of universal kindergarten where everyone wears the same playclothes all the time for all occasions and is expected to participate in show and tell all the time."

Martin recognizes that people today believe in being totally open and honest and establishing first-name relationships with as many people as possible. No longer is any distinction made between the ways we treat strangers and the ways we treat intimates. She feels there are dangers in this, one being that the techniques which work in the boardroom are being used in the bedroom. Everything is for sale. If you want to fall in love, she asks, what do you do? "You run a classified advertisement announcing a vacancy and you in-

have great difficulty developing a stable identity.[18] Public relationships also save us a great deal of psychological investment. Think what your life would be like if you were expected to "share thoughts and feelings, reveal intimate information and secrets, extend emotional support, and seek advice"[19] in dealing with everyone you encountered. On a purely practical level, it would be impossible. Although most of our important relationships will be private, there are advantages to public relationships. Box 2.2 gives one author's view of the impor-

tance of maintaining politeness in public and of the problems that can occur when we rush into intimacy.

The tension between the need for closeness and distance, the need to be recognized as a unique individual, and the need to be part of a social collective is fundamental. When we work out the nature of our relationships we are working out our answer to this dilemma. Because we believe this is a very important interpersonal tension, we shall return to it a number of times in the course of this text.

STYLISH SF seeks worldly SM for committed relationship, love, and laughter. Photo, please.
Box 556

SHARE THE FANTASY. MWM seeks adventurous female; tall, pretty, funloving, discreet, experimental. Life is short. Why not??
Box 557

GAY WJM. Intense, intelligent, intuitive, seeks nonsmoking monogamous partner to share interest in opera, French cooking, tennis, hiking, new experiences. Ready to take a chance again.
Box 448

clude a job description with the most detailed skill requirements." Friends and lovers are hired and fired with the same lack of emotion as employees.

While intimates are being treated like employees, strangers are treated as intimates. Nowadays, being on a first-name basis with your waitress ("Hi, I'm Cherry, and I'll be your server tonight. How 'ya doing?") and having your own personal banker ("You've got a friend at First

Federal") seems unavoidable. We no longer make any distinctions between the world of work (the public realm) and the world of home and family (the private realm). Martin points out a fundamental error in this kind of reasoning: While it may be the goal of business to move along and get things done, the goals of friendship and romance are to "repeat doing the same things and to like being where you are."

Martin believes people are confused about their obligations. She argues that we have to reestablish the dualism of the personal and professional realms so that everyone can have a reasonable portion of each. What do you think?

SOURCE: Judith Martin, *Common Courtesy.* New York: Atheneum, 1985. The text was originally delivered as an address at Harvard University under the title "The Question That Baffled Jefferson." An audiotape is available from the Harvard Forum.

ADDITIONAL READINGS

Martin, Judith. *Miss Manners' Guide to Excruciatingly Correct Behavior.* New York: Warner Books, 1991.
Baldridge, Letitia, *Letitia Baldridge's Complete Guide to the New Manners for the 90's.* New York: Macmillan, 1990.

Building Relationships: Levels of Relational Competence

In Chapter 1 we introduced you to our model of communicative competence. We suggested that in order to be a competent communicator, an individual must be able to (1) perceive the world accurately and sensitively, (2) set realistic and practical goals, (3) know when and how to follow social norms, (4) use message codes effectively, and (5) maintain individual identity. When individuals form interpersonal bonds, a new level of complexity is added. Not only must communicators be individually competent, they must be mutually competent. They must be able to adapt to each other in order to create a coordinated interpersonal system.

As Linda Harris points out, this is not always an easy task.[20] Some people hold very inflexible views of how relationships should operate. Although they can handle simple and familiar situations, they are unable to adapt to unusual episodes or unanticipated demands from their partners. Their solution to the problem of coordination is to force their partner to adapt or to "altercast" (that is, to choose a partner who agrees to play the "correct" interpersonal role). If two such inflexible individuals try to interact, and if their models of interpersonal relationships differ, the result is likely to be disastrous. Harris labels these people **minimally competent.**

Other people have been exposed to a wider variety of situations, so they have a more flexible relational model. They recognize the value of adaptability. They are willing to change in order to fit in if they sense that this willingness is reciprocal. Harris labels such people **satisfactorily competent.** They are a bit conservative, and their preferred manner of coordination is compromise: Each partner gives up a little in order to get something in return. Harris believes these people are most comfortable in familiar situations but lack the ability to work out problems in new and creative ways.

Other people are **optimally competent,** knowing when to adapt and when not to. They are aware of the way their interpersonal systems operate, and they can evaluate them objectively. These people are not afraid of change; they can handle relational problems creatively and effectively. Their system is maximally open.

What does it take to be optimally rather than minimally competent? First of all, it takes experience and flexibility. A person who knows only one way to do things will have trouble confronting new approaches; the more we learn about alternative ways of organizing relationships, the more flexible we can become. Second, relational competence involves the ability to use feedback effectively. We said earlier that interpersonal systems run on information. An individual unwilling to give or receive feedback is effectively restricting his or her ability to control the relationship. Talking about one's place in the system and the system as a whole is absolutely necessary for optimal competence.

Skill Building: A Preview

At the end of the next chapter, we begin focusing on specific skills that lead to interpersonal competence. While we don't pretend that the skills we've chosen form a complete list, we do believe that mastering them can help you improve your interpersonal competence. In this section we offer you a brief preview of each chapter and its skill-building focus.

Chapter 3 deals with nonverbal message competence. In this chapter we look at the silent messages we send to others. A problem area for most of us is knowing how to express our feelings clearly and congruently, using both verbal and nonverbal channels, so in this chapter we focus on the skill of emotional expressiveness.

Chapter 4 looks at verbal message competence, at how we use talk to build relationships. We also look at the skill of managing conversations, paying particular attention to the most difficult parts of a conversation, openings and closings.

Chapter 5 examines the relational messages that serve to define our bonds with others. It also looks at problematic sequences like spirals and double binds. We believe that many problem patterns could be avoided in relationships if partners had the ability to take each other's perspective and respond empathically. Too often, relationships dissolve because members are not able to see things from each other's point of view.

Chapter 6 examines interpretive competence by looking at the ways we perceive people, relationships, and social events. The skill-building section looks at one of the most important of all interpersonal skills, that of listening. When we think of communication, we often overlook listening and focus on the seemingly more active task of sending messages. In fact, listening is not passive, but rather is an extremely important part of good communication. For that reason it will be the first skill we discuss.

Chapter 7 focuses on role competence, on the social aspects that guide our communication. Often, society encourages us to act in mindless ways, to use tried-and-true social schemata rather than creative approaches to interaction. In this chapter we devote our skill-building section to overcoming stereotyped thinking and communicating creatively.

Chapter 8 talks about the development of the individual self and explains how our self-concept affects communication. We discuss the skill of self-disclosure in this chapter. While most authorities agree that people should reveal themselves to others, doing so is not easy. We look at appropriate and inappropriate ways of letting others know who we are and what we think.

Chapter 9 examines goal competence. It covers some of the ways we make interpersonal communication work for us. Some people have difficulty achieving their goals because they ask either too little or too much. In this chapter we discuss the important skill of assertiveness.

Chapter 10 talks about the family context. While there are many different skills we could focus on here, we believe that comforting skills and active listening are two of the most important. Family members rely on one another for support, and effective members need to know how to give that support.

Chapter 11 explains factors involved in building and maintaining intimate relationships. It also looks at the steps in the dissolution of relationships. Often relationships fail because members don't know how to handle conflict and stress effectively. Because they don't have the skill to fight fairly, their arguments destroy rather than improve the relationship.

Chapter 12 examines interpersonal relationships in the workplace, discussing the kinds of communication patterns that enhance professional relationships. The skill we emphasize here is negotiation.

Finally, Chapter 13 discusses ways in which culture and history influence communication. Every year our world becomes smaller and our chances of communicating across international boundaries increase. We'll end by offering some guidelines on how to make the most out of intercultural contact.

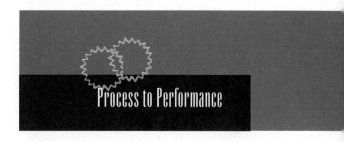

REVIEW TERMS

The following is a list of major concepts introduced in this chapter. The page where the concept is first mentioned is listed in parentheses.

situational approach (26)
intrapersonal communication (26)
interpersonal communication (26)
small-group communication (26)
organizational communication (26)
face-to-face public communication (26)
mediated public communication (27)
developmental approach (28)
cultural-level rules (28)
sociological-level rules (28)
psychological-level rules (28)
objective self-awareness (34)
content level (35)
relational level (35)
general systems theory (36)
system (36)
wholeness (36)
interdependence (36)
nonsummativity (36)
equifinality (37)
feedback (38)
relational trajectory (39)
private relationship (39)
public relationship (39)
minimal competence (44)
satisfactory competence (44)
optimal competence (44)

SUGGESTED READINGS

Borden, George A. *Human Communication Systems.* Boston: American Press, 1985. If you want to know more about systems theory, this is one place to start. In Chapters 2, 3, and 4, Borden offers a nice introduction to systems concepts. His endnotes also provide useful sources for further reading.

Gumpert, Gary, and Robert Cathcart, *Inter/ Media: Interpersonal Communication in a Media World,* 3rd ed. New York: Oxford University Press, 1986. The authors argue that the pervasiveness of modern media make traditional ways of thinking about communication obsolete. In this book they describe some of the effects of living in a mediated world.

Johnson, David W. *Reaching Out: Interpersonal Effectiveness and Self-Actualization,* 5th ed. Boston: Allyn & Bacon, 1993. If you're interested in learning more about the specific skills that lead to effective interpersonal interaction, you'll enjoy reading this book, which is full of exercises and quizzes that demonstrate or test interpersonal skills.

Stewart, John, ed. *Bridges Not Walls: A Book About Interpersonal Communication.* New York: McGraw-Hill, Inc., 1995. This reader contains a broad range of scholarly and popular articles taken from the fields of communication, philosophy, psychology, and education. It provides an overview of important issues and topics of interest in the area of interpersonal communication.

Wilmot, William W. *Dyadic Communication.* New York: Random House, 1987. Still one of the most intelligent and interesting discussions of dyadic relationships. Topics include self-perception, relational intricacies, and models of how relationships develop and dissolve.

Wood, Julia T. *Relational Communication: Continuity and Change in Personal Relationships.* Belmont, Calif.: Wadsworth, 1995. In this text, Wood focuses on how intimate personal relationships are developed and maintained. She blends theory with practical advice on how to improve relationships through effective interpersonal communication.

TOPICS FOR DISCUSSION

1. Think of a topic, say, a current event. How will communication about it change as communicators move from interpersonal to group, organizational, public, and mass communication contexts? Discuss changes in both the content and form of communication. Do you think there will also be changes in the reason the topic is discussed? Discuss the functions of communication at each level.

2. Think about a close personal relationship you have now. How did your communication change as you got to know your partner? Are there any times when you move back to the impersonal level? Do you believe couples shift between being impersonal and interpersonal, or do you believe that once a relationship is interpersonal, it stays that way until it dissolves?

3. Evaluate the advantages and disadvantages of the situational and developmental approaches. Which do you believe is the best way to think about interpersonal communication? Can you offer a third approach to the problem?

4. Think about how computers are changing the ways we communicate face-to-face. Do you communicate online often? If so, what have you observed about the special properties of this form of interpersonal communication. If not, what are your attitudes toward computer communication?

5. Think about the ways interpersonal bonds change self-awareness. List five people you encountered today. Did they make you aware of any aspects of yourself or your surroundings? What kinds of self-evaluations did you make on meeting them?

6. In what ways do others constrain the ways we behave? Think about the five people you listed in topic 5. Did you act the same way in front of each? Is this how you act when alone?

7. Think of an interpersonal system, for example, a sports team, a group of close friends, a family, or an interpersonal dyad you are now involved in. Apply the concepts of wholeness, interdependence, nonsummativity, and equifinality to these systems. What understanding do you gain by thinking of these collections of people as systems?

8. During a typical day, how much do you rely on feedback? Beginning from the moment you wake up, and continuing through the day, list ways you seek feedback (for example, looking in the mirror as you brush your teeth, looking at the nonverbal responses others give you when you greet them, and so on). Discuss what it might be like if you received no feedback cues from others in your environment. Is it possible for a system to exist without feedback?

9. Discuss some of the subtle ways others control us through feedback. Focus on nonverbal aspects. How powerful is nonverbal feedback from others in controlling your behavior?

10. Many social critics have suggested that our culture places undue emphasis on private relationships. Americans, they argue, are overly familiar. Discuss ways in which our culture encourages rapid development of private bonds (for example, the norm for clerks to tell strangers to "Have a nice day"). Discuss advantages and disadvantages of this push toward "instant intimacy."

11. Think of people you have known who fall into Harris's competence categories. Describe their behaviors.

OBSERVATION GUIDE

1. Observe a couple you know for about half an hour. Watch carefully for all of the ways, both verbal and nonverbal, the partners give and seek feedback from each other. Describe these feedback attempts as well as the kind of control each exercises on the other. How do they differ from each other in terms of control? How do they seek feedback, and how do they react to it once they have received it? What inferences can you make about their relationship?

2. Think of an interpersonal relationship that is important to you and that has lasted for some time. Graph it on the following chart developed from our model of private/public relationships:

Other is:

irreplaceable   *substitutable*

    1   2   3   4   5   6   7

We are:

interdependent   *autonomous*

    1   2   3   4   5   6   7

The information we use is:

particularistic   *universalistic*

    1   2   3   4   5   6   7

The rules we follow are:

individualistic   *normative*

    1   2   3   4   5   6   7

The emotional tone is:

sentimental   *practical*

    1   2   3   4   5   6   7

The rewards I get are:

intrinsic   *extrinsic*

    1   2   3   4   5   6   7

Has the relationship always had this profile, or has it changed over time? Were there key incidents that caused the profile of your relationship to change? Is it at the point you want it to be right now?

EXERCISES

1. As a class, discuss metaphors for interpersonal relationships. Complete the following sentence: Interpersonal relationships are like _____. Try to think of as many comparisons as possible; then look at what they tell you about the nature of relational bonds. What common themes can you uncover? Open the discussion by considering metaphors that are embedded in our language. For example, consider the following metaphors used to describe love: prisoner of love, bound together, tie the knot, get hitched. What is the central message behind these metaphors? What others can you come up with?

2. Choose a partner and decide who is to be sender and who is to be receiver. The sender should think of a recent personal experience that involved a problem in communication and recount that experience to the receiver. The receiver is to listen without giving any verbal or nonverbal feedback. If the receiver slips and gives feedback, start again. Once you have finished, reverse roles. Then discuss in a normal manner your experiences during this exercise. How easy or difficult was it to avoid giving feedback? How did you feel talking to someone who was not responding? In general, how important is feedback to interpersonal communication?

SENDING AND RECEIVING MESSAGES

The way we move our bodies communicates much about our mood, our interests, who we like and don't like, and much more.

(Albert Bloch, *Ragtime*)

3

Nonverbal Competence

If you've ever taken care of a small child, you're probably familiar with the following scene. While engrossed in a book or television program, you notice little Johnny slink into the room, hugging the wall, hands behind his back. He looks full-face in your direction, but only occasionally lifts his lowered eyelids. At the moment you give him your full attention, he blurts out, lower lip not quite quivering, "I didn't do anything!"

There is, of course, little doubt in your mind that something quite wrong has been done and that someone feels very guilty about it. The verbal denial only underscores your belief in the contradictory verbal and nonverbal messages being sent.

As we saw in the model presented in Chapter 1, accurate perceptions and knowledge of the self and the social system are not enough for effective communication to take place. We must be able to integrate perceptions and knowledge into appropriate verbal, nonverbal, and relational codes. In Chapter 4 we will look at the way we code messages verbally, while Chapter 5 will assess forms of relational communication. This chapter will discuss the variety of nonverbal channels through which coded messages can be sent and received.

Nonverbal messages are powerful, especially when they contradict verbal ones. But we often overlook the importance of more subtle nonverbal messages. Studies of small-group communication demonstrate that those who talk more often become leaders while those who actively listen and provide nonverbal feedback seldom get any credit for their contribution. Our inattention to nonverbals may have prompted British novelist John Fowles to remark, "The British mean far more than they say; Americans say far more than they mean."[1] We do, however, give some credit to those who work well in the nonverbal mode. People especially competent at reading others' nonverbal messages are labeled "intuitive," while those who send more nonverbals are called "expressive."

To make it in our culture, a person must first be articulate, then add in elements of intuition and expressiveness. (Clint Eastwood may be the exception here. He usually doesn't have to say anything to be effective.) We hope that by focusing on nonverbal codes first, you will become more aware of their function in everyday communication. You may already know a lot about diagramming sentences and increasing your vocabulary, but how many classes have you had on nonverbal communication?

We share a number of nonverbal signals with other species of animal. The marking of territories, threat displays when territorial bounds are violated, and relaxed, open-mouth expressions that signal approachability are examples of widely shared gestures rooted in a common biology, modified only by environment and culture. These rudimentary forms of communication preceded the evolution of the human brain's neocortex, which made language possible. The tendency to believe nonverbal messages when they contradict verbal ones (as in the opening example) may well be traced to the fact that nonverbal communication has a much longer evolutionary history. Language is, in the scheme of things, the "new kid on the block." Nonverbal communication, having been around, is like an old, trusted friend.

We also use nonverbal communication to initiate most verbal interactions. Breaking into a conversation often involves a complex dance of eye contact, head movement, preliminary gesturing, and vocalized throat-clearing if we do not want to be seen as rude. Greeting friends while walking across campus is preceded by a set of acknowledged approachability cues: eye contact, a flash of the eyebrows, perhaps even an abbreviated waving gesture. These nonverbal cues are not accidental; they are crucial regulators of conversation. For these reasons we think a good starting point for improving our ability to encode and decode messages is to attend to our own and others' nonverbal behaviors. They provide us with a context for interpreting many of the positive and negative connotations of messages. In this chapter, we will define nonverbal communication, describe what makes the nonverbal such a powerful

message system, examine in detail each of the nonverbal codes and how they function in interpersonal situations, and then summarize how we use verbal and nonverbal cues together to maintain or alter our interpersonal relationships. We will end the chapter with a discussion of how we can express ourselves better — especially our feelings — through nonverbal communication codes.

What Is Nonverbal Communication?

Suppose that as you are taking an exam, you notice that the person across the aisle keeps twitching his head and shoulders, then glancing quickly in your direction. Your eyes don't meet and nothing is said, but the other person has a very puzzled look on his face. Would you say that nonverbal communication has taken place?

Many scholars would say yes; others would say no. For the first group, all behavior has communicative potential and therefore should count as an instance of communication. In the preceding example nonverbal behavior has occurred and has been noticed by another person, so some information has been exchanged. Other scholars argue that we have to place some limits on what we call communication. If we don't establish limits, the term communication becomes too vague and loses its meaning. To counter this problem, two conditions are attached to nonverbal behaviors before they are considered acts of communication: There must be both some degree of intentionality and some level of consciousness on the part of either the sender or the receiver.[2]

One way to narrow the definition would be to stipulate that nonverbal behavior must be (1) perceived consciously by either the sender or the receiver, (2) intended as a message by the sender, or (3) interpreted by the receiver as intended. Thus, if the twitching behavior of the exam taker was an attempt to signal you for

Dance, which involves a complex synchronizing of body movements, is a form of both art and communication.

(Pieter Brueghel the elder, *The Wedding Dance*, c. 1566)

help, we might call it a poor attempt at communication, but an act of communication nonetheless. How would you know it was intentional? You might not know for sure, in which case you'd have to interpret it as an intentional attempt to get your attention and induce a state of guilt, so that you'll help him cheat. If the behavior was simply a sign of nervousness and didn't lead you to attribute it as having any message value, there is no reason to count it as an act of communication.

In a similar vein we can limit the realm of nonverbal communication to those behaviors that are consciously attended to by sender, receiver, or some third party. Frequently, we may not be aware of the nonverbal messages we send to others. As long as no one else is aware of such messages, there is no point in considering them to be communication. For instance, most people are not very aware of how their voice sounds to others. To some, a person whose voice has a nasal quality may sound like whining, while others won't consciously perceive the nasality at all. Those who notice the nasal quality may infer some attitude or personality trait. In this case a message has been received, or "leaked," even though it was not intended or interpreted as intentional.

In his research on the communication of emotion, Ross Buck makes a similar distinction between intentional and unintentional forms of nonverbal communication, but he argues that both forms occur simultaneously and are largely independent of each other. In Buck's view two radically different forms of communication coexist: a spontaneous and a symbolic communication system.[3] In many ways this distinction is more important than the distinction between verbal and nonverbal codes. In this section we'll discuss Buck's two forms of communication and then examine the communication power of nonverbal codes.

SPONTANEOUS COMMUNICATION

Spontaneous communication refers to a sender's nonvoluntary display of inner emotional states and a receiver's direct and immediate sensory awareness of those states. According to Buck it is a biologically based signal system that we share with other animals. When we communicate spontaneously, our nonverbal signs (such as gestures or facial expressions) are simply external manifestations of our internal emotions; they are not planned or intentional messages to others. Another person may, however, directly perceive these emotional signals if he or she is "tuned in" to them. It is possible for both sender and receiver to communicate in a purely spontaneous manner, where neither person consciously intends to send or receive the nonverbal signal. If you're like most people, the experience of happening upon a slithering snake will provoke an automatic sensation of fear, and the involuntary expression of that fear would probably register just as immediately and automatically to a friend walking a few feet behind you. In such a circumstance you would be communicating spontaneously, without ever intending to do so. George Herbert Mead once re-

ferred to this type of communication as a "conversation of gestures."[4]

SYMBOLIC COMMUNICATION

Whereas spontaneous communication occurs as a conversation of natural gestures, **symbolic communication** involves the use of arbitrary symbols, socially defined and intended to convey specific messages. While language is the clearest example of symbolic communication, many nonverbal cues are also used symbolically. When you want someone to know that you're glad to see him, you may "put on a happy face" to express that feeling. If you want to gain sympathy, you can produce a sagging posture and a hang-dog facial expression. Humans, unlike other animals, have learned to use symbolic communication to alter some spontaneous expressions. We can, with practice, learn to inhibit many of our natural expressions. For instance, deception involves the conscious control of gestures and facial expressions that would normally indicate emotions we do not want others to see or the manufacture of gestures suggestive of emotions we do not feel. These intentional uses of nonverbal cues are symbolic in nature. They are consciously encoded by senders and decoded by receivers who share the same set of conventional rules for their meaning.

Buck agrees that even though symbolic communication constitutes much of our human communication, spontaneous communication is still very much with us and perhaps more important than we realize. Much of our folk wisdom about "intuition," "animal magnetism," and good or bad "vibes" may be explained as spontaneous communication.

In summary, scholars disagree about how much of our nonverbal behavior can actually be thought of as nonverbal communication. Distinguishing between spontaneous and symbolic communication suggests that we can commu-

Children have a more difficult time disguising their feelings than adults do.
This young boy's posture and facial expression suggest that he is guilty as accused.

nicate nonverbally in two very different but equally powerful ways. Sometimes we use nonverbal cues intentionally and according to socially defined rules; at other times we connect with each other on an emotional level that we cannot verbalize or control.

THE POWER OF NONVERBAL CODES

Whether communicated spontaneously or symbolically, nonverbal behavior can evoke powerful messages. We need to be aware that we communicate in unintentional ways, but obviously we have the greatest opportunity to control and improve our use of symbolic (verbal and nonverbal) codes. While nonverbal messages often speak louder than words, they do not necessarily do so at all times. It is really a matter of matching the capacity of particular verbal and nonverbal codes with the nature of the social situation and our own self-identity and rela-

tional goals within that situation. To help us make such decisions, we need to understand some of the aspects of nonverbal messages that make them so powerful.

1. *Nonverbal codes are frequently given more credence and are more trusted than verbal forms of communication.* As we have noted, nonverbal codes have been in use longer than verbal ones. And since we live the first 12 to 18 months of life relying totally on nonverbal communication, it is little wonder that when in doubt, we tend to put our faith in the nonverbal message. Of course, this trust can backfire. Suppose you want to buy an insurance policy. The salesperson's nonverbal communication may seem to indicate a genuine concern for your welfare and may discourage you from reading the fine print of the policy because it's all "mumbo-jumbo." If you relied on the salesperson's nonverbal expression of concern, you might well be relying on the wrong code.

2. *Nonverbal codes are more emotionally powerful.* Nonverbal behaviors tell people about our emotional state. It takes a good deal of practice to hide our true feelings from others — and even then, close friends will often see through our attempts. When we want to convey how we feel about someone, language often fails us. Desmond Morris refers to the myriad gestures that express emotional bonding (interlocked arms, shoulder embraces, hand-holding) as "tie signs" that physically connect people in ways words cannot.[5]

3. *Nonverbal codes, while influenced by culture, do express more universal meaning.* Members of different linguistic groups must spend a lot of time and effort to learn each other's verbal codes, but they can communicate instantly by smiling or wrinkling their faces in disgust. The work of Paul Ekman and Wallace Friesen has shown a number of emotions to be expressed in the same way by members of different cultural groups.[6] Happiness, anger, disgust, fear, surprise, and sadness are all conveyed by using the same facial muscles in much the same way. There are differences, but they occur primarily in the rules that govern *when* it is appropriate to show the emotion in public or *how much* emotion should be displayed. Facial expressions are probably the most universal codes because of their prominence in face-to-face interaction. Other body movements and gestures have multiple and sometimes contradictory meanings within and across cultures, as we shall see later in this chapter. Most of these differences can be explained by Buck's distinction between spontaneous and symbolic communication. The more biologically based and spontaneous a nonverbal code is, the more universal its meaning. Nonverbal codes used in symbolic ways will express the localized meanings of a particular dyad, group, or culture.

4. *Nonverbal codes are continuous and natural.* Because gestures and body movements flow into one another without obvious beginnings and endings, they seem to be a more nat-ural part of our existence than words. Words are also strung together, but unless you mumble, your words don't slur into one another as nonverbals often do. Nonverbals are immediate — that is, they are physical extensions of our bodies, and their form resembles their message more than words' form does. A gesture signaling someone to "come here" imitates the movement of a body from a far place to a closer proximity. Words, perhaps because they can be written and stored away from the body, often seem more distant and more unnatural.

5. *Nonverbal codes occur in clusters.* Verbal communication is limited to a single channel at a time, but nonverbal communication operates in much the same way as recording studios use multitrack taping systems. Several channels are operating simultaneously and usually in concert. When different nonverbal codes send the same message, the impact is intensified. While you can repeat or rephrase verbal messages to achieve redundancy, it will take more time and still not mirror the intensity of the combined forces of touch and tone, facial expressions, body positioning and movement, and so on.

Given the unique capacity and power of nonverbal codes, we will now examine what they accomplish in everyday interactions.

The Functions of Nonverbal Codes: Three Ways to Use Them

We use nonverbal codes to achieve some very specific purposes. While researchers have proposed several ways to classify these functions, we have grouped them into three general types. Nonverbal codes may be used to (1) express meaning in and of themselves, (2) modify verbal messages, and (3) regulate the flow of interaction. Let's look at each of these functions.

In ancient Egypt statues such as this were commissioned for placement in the tombs of prominent officeholders. This statue is unique because of the way the woman embraces her husband, suggesting that she was the legitimate owner of the tomb.

(*Memy-Subu and His Wife*, Gizeh, c. 2420 B.C.)

EXPRESSING MEANING

Nonverbal messages are often used to convey how we feel about other people and how we see our relationship to them. Albert Mehrabian suggests that three fundamental dimensions of feeling are expressed through nonverbal communication: liking, status, and responsiveness.[7] It is easy to recognize that nonverbals express **liking** or disliking, as when people smile or turn up their noses at one another. **Status** is conveyed by nonverbal cues indicating how important or influential we think we are in relation to others. Staring at a subordinate may communicate snobbishness or dominance. **Responsiveness** indicates how aware we are of the other person and what level of involvement we feel with him or her. Bursting into tears or laughing heartily would indicate high responsiveness; a blank stare or an ever-so-slight chuckle would represent low responsiveness. In Chapter 5 we'll elaborate on the ways we send each other these relational messages.

MODIFYING VERBAL MESSAGES

While some nonverbal messages stand on their own, others work in conjunction with verbal messages. Nonverbals can complement, accent, repeat, substitute for, or contradict verbal messages. **Complementing** is the nonverbal elaboration of the verbal message. When friends say they are sick, their flushed faces, unsteady gait, and pained looks help us determine the extent of their illness. **Accenting** refers to nonverbals that underline or focus attention on a specific word or phrase. Pounding the table with your fist at the same time you say "I've had it!" makes that particular phrase stand out. Sometimes we give a verbal message and then try **repeating** it nonverbally to help the receiver process the total message. For instance, when someone asks a favor, we may say "Yes" and then nod our head to make sure the person knows our response was genuine. At other times we avoid the verbal response altogether, and the nonverbal serves a **substituting** function. A cold stare may say "No!" better than any verbalized refusal could. Some situations require substitution. Deep-sea divers cannot speak, so they rely on hand gestures and other body movements to indicate what they want one another to do.

You may frequently find nonverbal messages **contradicting** verbal ones. When they do, you have a choice to make. One of your professors may say she has plenty of time to go over a quiz with you, but if she remains standing, doesn't offer you a seat, and keeps fidgeting with her watch, you may question the sincerity of the verbal remark. As noted before, we generally believe the nonverbal message when a contradiction occurs. But, this is not always the case. Young children, perhaps because of their fascination with newly acquired language skills, often believe verbal statements, especially in cases of sarcasm.[8]

Other studies demonstrate that some people consistently rely on the verbal channel and others on the nonverbal channel when presented with contradictory cues.[9] One explanation for these channel preferences is that they are learned habits; another is that they are linked to patterns of left-right hemispheric dominance in the brain. The right hemisphere of the brain appears to be highly involved in processing spatial and holistic information, features prominent in most nonverbal codes. The left hemisphere, on the other hand, is better at processing verbal information. In most people, one hemisphere tends to be more active than the other and may affect the channels of communication to which we pay the most attention.

REGULATING THE FLOW OF INTERACTION

Finally, nonverbal codes function to **regulate** the flow of talk. When two people converse, nonverbals are primarily responsible for the smoothness of taking turns, avoiding long pauses, changing topics, even signaling when it is appropriate to end the conversation. In many professional contexts the function of nonverbal communication is simply the administration of

a service or task.[10] Thus, the nonverbal act of holding a patient's arm while the doctor administers an injection functions to make the task easier. A similar behavior in some other setting may function quite differently.

So far we have talked about nonverbal communication in general. We have defined nonverbal communication, seen what makes it such a powerful system, and identified three ways we use nonverbal cues. Now we turn to each separate channel of nonverbal communication. We call each of these channels a nonverbal "code."

The Structure of Nonverbal Codes: Seven Channels for Message Making

Nonverbal codes are structured in many ways. While a single message is almost always transmitted via more than one channel, we will discuss each code as if it stood alone. In this section, seven codes will be analyzed: proxemics, physical appearance, gaze, facial expression, kinesics, vocalics, and tactile communication (see Figure 3.1). Some scholars also include chronemics and olfaction as codes. *Chronemics* refers to the study and interpretation of time as message. Time is related to status in our culture. A doctor's time is considered more valuable than the patient's time, for instance. Rather than discuss chronemics as a separate code, we have chosen to emphasize the importance of timing as it relates to the other codes discussed. *Olfaction* has to do with the messages we attach to smells emitted by the body. Since humans rely on this code much less than other animals, and since there is very little research on how humans do communicate in this mode, we won't include it as a major nonverbal code.

As you read about each of the codes, keep in mind the functions that have been mentioned. Ask yourself how you could use each code to express a particular meaning, to modify a verbal message, or to regulate a conversation. The first code we will examine has to do with the way people use space.

PROXEMICS

Approaching other people is a more delicate proposition than most of us realize. Take the mundane matter of walking across campus or strolling through a busy shopping mall. As soon as visual contact is made or we sense that another body is nearby, we begin manipulating our own body movements and anticipating the movements of the other in order to avoid getting too close or bumping into one another. Ashley Montagu and Floyd Matson have pointed out that "there are virtually as many rules, customs, and conventions governing the conduct of 'sidewalkers' as there are for car drivers, the difference being that the sidewalk rules are unwritten and tacit and . . . completely unnoticed."[11] The next time you stop to talk to someone, notice how each of you shifts your body back and forth to establish a comfortable speaking distance. Watch when two people move from an open lobby area to a cramped, crowded enclosure such as a hallway, elevator, or cafeteria line. What actions result from this change in distance? People may actually stop talking or change to a more impersonal topic of conversation. Each of these situations is an example of how people use or adjust to changes in the spatial environment. Investigators call the study of messages sent in this mode **proxemics.**

How many ways do we use space to communicate? Architects design interior and exterior spaces to make personal, philosophical, or cultural statements. People grow hedges around the edges of their property to discourage trespassers. And perhaps the most powerful proxemic statements are made during conversation itself, by the simple measurement of how much distance we keep between ourselves and those we talk to.

Environmental Preferences

While each of us reacts to the environment in some unique ways, we are also programmed genetically and culturally to react in more similar ways. When we feel comfortable in a physical setting, we are more likely to communicate effectively. Or perhaps we should say, when we feel uncomfortable we communicate less effectively and may even attribute these negative feelings to the people in that environment. In a classic study Abraham Maslow and N. L. Mintz asked people in three different environments to rate the same group of photographs of faces (actually negative prints). One room was set up to be "beautiful," another "average," and the third "ugly." People consistently rated the photographs higher in energy and well-being in the beautiful room and lower in the ugly room.[12] This study supports the notion that the environment has a spillover effect on social interaction.

Other factors in environmental spaces can have a dramatic effect on our social behavior as well. Physical features of an environment (such as lighting, color, noise, and extremes in temperature) affect our preference for that environment.[13] In addition, more subjective perceptions (such as familiarity, novelty, and mystery) have been shown to affect whether we will approach or avoid an environment.[14]

According to Albert Mehrabian and James Russell, the combination of these environmental factors and our own predisposed mental sets produces emotional reactions along three dimensions: arousal-nonarousal, dominance-submissiveness, and pleasure-displeasure.[15] For instance, a visit to the Grand Canyon would probably give most people a moderate level of arousal, a submissive feeling, and a strong sense of pleasure, which combine to produce a sense of awe. For some people social conversation is very difficult in a bar or nightclub because they are unable to screen out all the background noise and flashing strobe lights. The level of arousal is so high for them that concentrating on talk is too difficult. Most of us feel more

FIGURE **3.1**
Seven nonverbal codes

dominant in those settings that are very familiar to us. We are more likely to tell someone what to do when they are on our turf, or territory, than when we are on theirs.

Territoriality

The concept of **territoriality** refers to the legal or assumed ownership of space. Lawrence Rosenfeld and Jean Civikly define territoriality as "the assumption of proprietary rights toward some geographical area, with the realization, at least for humans, that there is no basis for those rights."[16] Animals mark their territory by building nests, leaving excrement, and fending off intruders. Humans use a great variety of territorial markers, ranging from where they stop mowing the grass to the placement of personal photographs on otherwise institutional-looking desks.

Stanford Lyman and Marvin Scott have distinguished four types of territoriality in human interaction.[17] *Public territory* is owned by no one and accessible to anyone. City streets, park benches, and plazas exemplify this kind of territory. Each of these may, from time to time, become *interactional territories,* as when a softball team takes over a park to use as a practice field. Other spaces are designed for interaction. These include courtrooms and tennis courts. *Home territories* allow for an even greater degree of privacy. Strangers will rarely intrude on a space they consider to be someone else's home. This includes more than physical violations. A neighbor who constantly peers through your windows is considered rude and will usually not persist if you stare back. *Body territory,* the final classification used by Lyman and Scott, is more frequently referred to as personal space by other researchers.

Personal Space

The term **personal space** has been used to describe an imaginary bubble extending out from our bodies, an area considered to be almost as private as the body itself. We react strongly to movement into our personal space — only small children and intimate family and friends are allowed to enter this space without apology. Anthropologist Edward T. Hall has done the most to draw our attention to personal space and other forms of conversational distance.[18] In observations of middle-class Americans, Hall has distinguished four interaction zones:

- Intimate distance (0–18 inches). Reserved for lovemaking and very private conversations.

- Personal distance (18 inches–4 feet). The range at which one is comfortable with friends and acquaintances.

- Social distance (4–12 feet). Used for business transactions and role relations.

- Public distance (12–25 feet). Appropriate for public ceremonies, speechmaking, classroom lectures, and so on.

The actual distance at which you are comfortable talking to others may vary according to your personality and to age, sex, status, or cultural differences in relation to those you interact with. For example, Hall describes a visit to an apartment house in northern Germany. The house had a first-floor studio. From the front porch, the interior of the studio was clearly visible through a large window. While Hall was talking to a young woman on the porch, he could also see and be seen by an artist who was holding a conversation with another person inside the studio. Hall did not know the artist, so he largely ignored what was happening in the studio. A few minutes later the artist came outside and yelled at Hall for intruding without even a sign of greeting.[19] The difference was simply a matter of interpreting space. For the American there was enough space between the two pairs to allow them their separate activities. For the German his space had already been invaded.

Some people simply need more space than others. Unless you are aware of this, you may find yourself trying to move closer to others (to make yourself more comfortable) while they compensate by moving away (to reestablish their comfort zone). Hall points out one problem that may arise: "Since none of us is taught to look at space as isolated from other associations, feelings cued by the handling of space are often attributed to something else."[20] The most likely result is that you will form negative impressions of these people.

Research also demonstrates that those of the same age group stand closer to one another than age-discrepant pairs, and that male pairs space themselves farther apart than opposite-sex pairs, who usually space themselves farther apart than female pairs[21] Occasionally, the norms for personal space are violated without incident because one of the parties is viewed as a nonperson, as a mere object — for example, waiters, servants, and people in crowded elevators or stadiums.

Stop and think about the communicative functions that proxemics serve. We may use spatial distance or closeness to communicate feelings of liking, or to achieve some sense of privacy, or even to threaten or remind the other person of our status. Can you identify ways we use proxemics to regulate conversation or to modify the nature of our verbal statements? For instance, we may stand closer to someone we find physically attractive. Physical appearance is another code that often operates in conjunction with proxemics.

PHYSICAL APPEARANCE

Physical appearance alone can be a powerful message. Each culture defines its own prototypes of physical beauty as well as stereotypes about what physically beautiful or unattractive people look like. We will discuss first the message potential of the human body itself and then the artifacts we adorn our bodies with.

Characteristics of the Body

Facial features and beauty, color, length, and style of hair, skin color, the general shape of the body, and posture are among the physical features that people pay close attention to when they first make visual contact. The role of these features in communication depends on our awareness of them and the belief that the sender intended some message by his or her appearance. When a husband puts on a little weight and others notice this fact, communication may or may not be occurring. If you are his wife and you believe that body weight can be controlled, you may interpret his appearance as saying, "I don't care what I look like to you anymore. It's more important that I enjoy myself than that I look good for you."

The communication value of most natural body features is limited. Stereotypes aside, there is no message value in the natural color of one's hair or skin. Thus, we should pay attention to what people do to enhance, display, alter, or conceal their bodies. These are the real messages directed at us, because here the sender has some element of control.

Even so, we rely on these constant features a great deal in deciding with whom to communicate. Research demonstrates that most cultures have strong prototypes about physical beauty.[22] Many people believe that our own culture's prototypes are magnified by the media, influencing the evaluation of and desire to be with other people. One study involved college freshmen who signed up for a computer date to a dance. Pairs were actually matched at random rather than by interest or compatibility. When asked to indicate satisfaction with their date and desire to date again, physical attractiveness was the only predictor of either one.[23] Another study showed how physical attraction serves as a central trait in many of our implicit personality theories. A physically attractive person was consistently rated as more sociable, outgoing, poised, interesting, and sexually warm and responsive than an unattractive one.[24]

We tend to believe that physical beauty is intrinsic and interpreted the same way the world over, but Desmond Morris reminds us how temporary our prototypes are in his comparison of vital statistics of contestants in today's beauty pageants with carved figurines of past epochs:

If we consider [the Venus of Willendorf] as Miss Old Stone Age of 20,000 B.C., then, had she lived, her vital statistics would have been 96–89–96. Moving forward to 2000 B.C., Miss Indus Valley would have measured 45–34–63, and in the late Bronze Age, Miss Cyprus of 1500 B.C. would have registered 43–42–44. Later still, Miss Amlash of 1000 B.C. would have offered the startling proportions of 38–44–78, but Miss Syria of 1000 B.C., only a short distance away, would have measured an almost modern 31–26-36.[25]

While prototypes also exist for the ideal male physique, our point is simply to remind you of how temporary any ideal image is and to note that physical beauty standards vary across time and across cultures. Not only do people's evaluations of physical characteristics vary, but their assessments of material adornments do, too.

Clothing and Personal Artifacts

People go to great lengths to adorn their bodies. Fashionable clothing and accessories, tight or loose-fitting garments, hair color, earrings, and untied shoelaces are all forms of adornment.

Clothing has been long recognized as a way to communicate social status, group identification, and personality.[26] The popularity of books and magazine articles about what clothing to wear to job interviews and business meetings indicates our concern with the status implications of clothing. In one study, various styles of men's clothing were ranked for social status and then placed on models who had been independently ranked for status according to facial and head features alone. Invariably, higher-ranked clothing increased, and lower-ranked clothing decreased, the perceived status of the models.[27] In many large companies status distinctions are maintained by subtle factors such as suits made of more expensive fabric, while group membership is maintained by similarity in the basic type of apparel (professionals wear dark suits, staff wear simple dresses or shirtsleeves and slacks, maintenance personnel wear uniforms). People often identify with one another by wearing the same or similar clothes. The next time you visit an amusement park, watch groups of people and look for ways they identify with one another through clothing. The most obvious examples will be families where Mom, Dad, and all the kids are wearing T-shirts with the family's last name printed across the back. In what

other subtle and not-so-subtle ways do people say they are together?

Finally, dress may convey messages about the self, whether intentional or not. A friend reported turning down a good job offer because she didn't think the people she would have to work with were very stimulating. Her first impression was that "there was beige everywhere. Most of them wore two or three shades of beige, and their faces had a beige cast to them, and I would have to say their personalities were equally as beige." At other times physical appearance may be so eye-catching that the person becomes the focus of our visual field.

GAZE

Our eyes aren't just instruments for receiving stimuli; they are themselves messengers. Even the simple act of appreciating physical beauty requires that we proceed with caution. Erving Goffman has recommended that we "discipline our eyes" until we have mastered the skill of knowing how to look without appearing to be looking. For a fascinating view of how people in the late 19th century disciplined not only their eye behavior, but controlled their entire bodies to avoid social interaction, read Box 3.1. It demonstrates the extent to which we rely on visual cues to initiate conversation.

One of the first contributors to the literature on visual communication was Adam Kendon, who proposed that **gaze** served three primary functions in communication: (1) expressive, (2) regulative, and (3) monitoring.[28]

The Expressive Function of Gaze

Gaze plays an important role in the communication of emotions. Although identification of most emotions requires the decoding of complete facial cues, the eyes are especially expressive in conveying fear and surprise.[29] Likewise, gaze broadcasts interest in and liking of the

BOX **3.1**

The "Guarded Self": How to Avoid Being Seen in Public

Much has been written about the 19th-century movement of the young from American farms to cities. Most went in search of work at one of the many factories that sprang up during the industrial revolution. In any large-scale movement of people there are bound to be disruptions of the social order. Perhaps one of the central anxieties faced by these young urban immigrants was the adjustment from life in a community where people were under the watchful eye of neighbors who knew everything about them to an urban life where they were scrutinized by a steady flow of anonymous others. It is not surprising that agoraphobia (an irrational fear of open spaces, of going out in public) became widespread during this period.

John Kasson, in *Rudeness and Civility,* talks about the code of conduct that emerged as a way of managing such fears. "For men and women both . . . the glare of exposure could be overwhelming . . . embarrassment became a normal, even an essential, part of American urban life." Sensitivity to embarrassment was a direct conse-

quence of the lack of communal standards for behavior and a corresponding insecurity about one's own identity. The social webs that nurtured self-identity and held it in check were missing and nothing had emerged to replace them.

Enter the etiquette manual. "Etiquette is the machinery of society." said one New York advice-giver. "It prevents the agony of uncertainty. . . . If one is certain about being correct, there is little to be anxious about." Kasson suggests that etiquette was used as social armor against intrusion, that people needed ways to protect themselves from the scrutiny of others. The self-image of most urban dwellers appears to have been that of a "guarded self" whose maxim was "mind your own business." Body management and nonverbal communication were essential to the maintenance of such a public identity.

To fend off the unwanted gaze of others, advice writers taught the fine art of being inconspicuous. The genteel man or woman avoided flashy clothing; black became the fashion color of choice. Over time, the modern suit emerged for men—a dark, sober, anonymous uniform. In addition, men wore overcoats, full beards, and mustaches, essentially hiding the face and body from others. Likewise, women were advised to avoid "singularity" in their choice of clothing. They were also told to avoid excessive jewelry, strong perfume, or anything else likely to draw attention. In fact, the demand on women was considerably greater than on men. Women were admonished to avoid going out in public unless

other person, and researchers have found that people gaze more when they receive or want to receive approval, especially from someone who is higher in status.[30]

In addition, gazing can frequently create arousal in those being stared at. Imagine eating your lunch alone, enjoying your private thoughts, when you suddenly become aware

that someone is watching you. You glance in the person's direction, expecting him to look away, but he doesn't. How do you react? According to P. C. Ellsworth and to Miles Patterson, that depends on the attributions you make. If you sense that the other person's motives are harmless, or you find him interesting in some way, you will probably reciprocate by smiling and

here one could go too far. While it was proper to avoid staring or holding a glance too long, one had also to avoid the other extreme of appearing too shy or fearful.

It was not enough for people of the time to simply manage their own bodies. They were equally responsible for not looking at the indiscretions of others. Said one advice writer: "The rule is imperative, that no one should see, or, if that is impossible, should seem to see, or to have seen, anything that another person would choose to have concealed; unless indeed it is your business to watch for some misdemeanor." In most social situations, 19th-century people simply assumed that what they observed was none of their business.

absolutely necessary; there were many sectors of the city where an upstanding woman was a rare commodity. When they did venture forth, women were encouraged to travel by carriage rather than risk even a short walk. When walking could not be avoided, she was to step slowly in "a modest and measured gait," always staring straight ahead, never stopping. The rest of the body, for both men and women, was to be stifled. The hands should never touch the face, especially the nose, while in public. Chewing gum, eating, coughing, sneezing—literally anything that drew attention to the body was to be avoided. Perhaps the greatest act of self-discipline was the reining in of the eyes. Eye contact was seen as an invitation to social discourse, and so had to be guarded against with extreme caution. But even

SOURCE: John F. Kasson. "Venturing Forth: Bodily Management in Public," in *Rudeness and Civility: Manners in Nineteenth Century Urban America* (New York: Hill and Wang, 1990), pp. 112–146.

ADDITIONAL READINGS

Warren Susman, "'Personality' and the Making of Twentieth-Century Culture," in *Culture as History: The Transformation of American Society in the Twentieth Century.* New York: Pantheon Books, 1984, pp. 271–85.
Sarah Trenholm and Arthur Jensen, "The Guarded Self: Toward a Social History of Interpersonal Styles." Paper presented at the Speech Communication Association of Puerto Rico's annual conference, San Juan, December, 1990.

looking in that direction again later. If you attribute the other person's behavior negatively, you are more likely to compensate by turning away, giving a nasty look or leaving the other's presence.[31] We will have more to say about Patterson's work at the end of this chapter because it applies to how we react to a wide range of nonverbal cues.

Using Gaze to Regulate and Monitor Interaction

Gaze, along with other nonverbals, serves to regulate and monitor the other's reactions during conversation. Gaze first signals that we're available for communication. Averting our eyes says just the opposite. When you're in a hurry **67** and can't stop to talk, you may pretend not to see the other. Or you may simply opt for the "eyebrow flash"—a common sign of recognition that involves a look, a smile, a raising of the eyebrows, and a nod.[32] It may be used to acknowledge the other without committing yourself to conversation.

Once conversation has begun, eye behavior helps keep turn-taking and transitions flowing smoothly. The general pattern for Americans is to look more when they listen than when they speak, and to very rarely look at each other for more than a split second. Why do we follow this pattern? When we listen, gaze shows interest in what the other is saying and allows us to receive complementary or contradictory nonverbal cues. When we begin a speaking turn, we are busy concentrating on what we want to say and thus do not look at the other as frequently or as long.

Women, it seems, gaze more than men and are more uncomfortable when visual contact is cut off.[33] Some speculate that this is a function of traditional socialization, which teaches women to be more concerned with social affiliation. A greater difference has been noted in the gazing patterns of blacks and whites. Clara Mayo and Marianne LaFrance have shown that whites look more when listening and that blacks look more when talking and less when listening, just the opposite of whites.

> The White may feel he is not being listened to while the Black may feel he is being unduly scrutinized. Further, exchanges of the listener-speaker roles become disjunctive, leading to generalized discomfort in the encounter.[34]

Blacks use more "backchanneling" gestures; that is, they give more verbal and nonverbal feedback to a speaker while he or she is still talking. Because of this, it makes sense that a black speaker would look more while talking: He or she is simply trying to monitor the feedback others are giving. The fact that we use our eyes to monitor feedback has raised the question of where our vision is usually focused during interaction.

Looking versus Seeing

What do you focus your vision on when you talk to other people? Do you look into their eyes, in the direction of their eyes, or at the whole upper body? D. R. Rutter, in a comprehensive review of visual communication, makes a distinction between looking and seeing.[35] **Looking** refers to gazing in the direction of the other's eyes, whereas **seeing** is defined as visual contact with the whole person. Rutter argues that seeing is more important than looking when regulating and monitoring feedback. It was once thought that people used gaze to signal turn-taking. Now it appears that seeing the whole person is necessary for picking up other turn-taking cues such as nods and gestures. This relegates gaze to a lesser role in regulating interaction. Eye contact (mutual looking) plays an even smaller role. Some research suggests that eye contact happens so rarely that it is probably a random occurrence.[36] We encourage you to test these findings yourself. Keep in mind the distinctions between eye contact (mutual looking), gaze (looking), and seeing (gazing at the whole person). Which occur more often in your own conversations, and what functions do they appear to serve?

FACIAL EXPRESSION

One reason for getting a full view of the other person rather than gazing in the direction of the eyes is to pick up entire facial expressions, which may well be the single most important channel of nonverbal communication. People read a lot in our facial expressions. They infer some personality traits and attitudes, judge reactions to their own messages, regard facial expressions as verbal replacements, and, primarily, use them to determine our emotional state.

Since most of the research has focused on emotions, so will our discussion. We will examine how six universal expressions are created and controlled, and why we sometimes misread facial expressions.

Universal Expressions

The study of facial expression owes much to researchers Paul Ekman and Wallace Friesen. The comprehensiveness and quality of their work gives us confidence in their findings. They have demonstrated the universality of expression in conveying six basic human emotions [37] Regardless of culture, the emotional states of happiness, sadness, surprise, fear, anger, and disgust are communicated with remarkable similarity (see Figure 3.2). As Ross Buck would suggest, these facial expressions are recognized universally because they are part of our biological heritage, communicated spontaneously.

Ekman and Friesen identified three separate sets of facial muscles that are manipulated to form these six expressions. These muscles are found in the following areas: (1) the brow and forehead, (2) the eyes, eyelids, and root of the nose, and (3) the cheeks, mouth, most of the nose, and chin. Muscles in all of these facial regions combine in a particular way to produce a representation of a pure emotional state. For instance, surprise is announced by (1) the raising of the eyebrows, (2) the opening wide of the eyes, and (3) the dropping of the jaw and parting of the lips. Look at the other five emotions in Figure 3.2 and identify how they are expressed in each of the three facial regions. You may wish to consult Ekman and Friesen's book *Unmasking the Face* for further practice photos.

A key fact is that facial expressions are often short-lived. We rarely hold a look of surprise for long. If you can't believe the astronomical amount of your phone bill, surprise may quickly give way to disgust or anger. The person with you may see traces of both emotions on your face. The result is called a **facial blend.**

Since social interaction usually consists of rapid-fire exchanges, we are constantly changing expressions. What others see are usually blended expressions rather than pure emotional states.

But, you may be saying to yourself, people's facial expressions aren't always genuine. It is true that emotional expressions are universal, but *when* they are displayed is not. **Cultural display rules** often control this. We know that it is quite improper to laugh at someone who falls down, no matter how funny it strikes us. We are supposed to act surprised when an unannounced party is given in our honor, even though someone spilled the beans earlier. Business practice requires that salespeople show enthusiasm for vacuum cleaners, vegetable dicers, and other products that do not intrinsically excite them. Most people have personal display rules, ingrained early in life, such as "never show your anger in public." These are examples of the symbolic communication system inhibiting and modifying our natural or spontaneous expressions of emotion.

Women, at least in American culture, are generally more nonverbally expressive than men. This is also true with respect to facial expression. Most studies to date show adult women to have significantly more facial reactions and general facial activity than men.[38] Many people, regardless of sex, display a characteristic style of facial expression (see Figure 3.3). Withholders, for instance, may inhibit facial muscle so much that others marvel at how they can talk without moving their mouths.

But controlling the face is not quite so easy as we might think. Professional actors may be regarded as specialists in controlling their faces, but the rest of us don't fare so well. We give ourselves away to the perceptive observer by producing momentary **leakage cues,** unintended signs of our real feelings, which are largely but not completely masked in normal facial management. For example, when trying to maintain our composure in the face of the announcement that a coveted award went to another contestant, we let disappointment leak

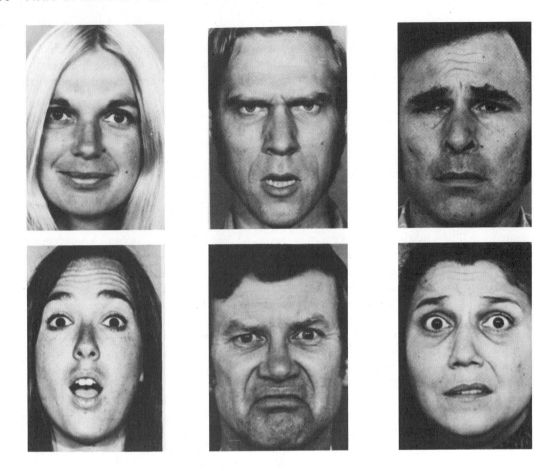

FIGURE **3.2**

The six universal facial expressions. Can you identify what emotion is being expressed in each of the photographs above? Researchers Paul Ekman and Wallace Friesen have studied facial expressions across cultures and have found these six (surprise, anger, happiness, fear, disgust, and sadness) to be universal.

Paul Ekman and Wallace F. Friesen, *Pictures of Facial Affect* (Palo Alto, Calif.: Consulting Psychologists Press, 1976).

out when we momentarily turn down the corners of the lips, quickly replacing it with "a stiff upper lip."

Misreading Facial Expressions

Even when people spontaneously express an emotional state, we may not perceive it. Norms regarding eye behavior are partly responsible. We look at the other person's face only about 50 percent of the time during conversation. Ekman and Friesen point out that this is due to more than just being polite and not staring at the other. Often we don't want to be burdened with the knowledge of how the other feels. This may reach comic proportions, as when a parent exasperated with a pouting child says, "I'm not looking at you!"

Withholder

This person's facial expression doesn't show how he feels. He isn't trying to deliberately deceive; he just shows very little expressiveness.

Revealer

Revealers tell all with their faces. They are very expressive and often say that they just can't help showing how they feel. You always know when a Revealer does or doesn't like the birthday present you gave her.

Unwitting Expressor

This person shows emotion without realizing it. He says things like, "How did you know I was angry?"

Blanked Expressor

Blanked expressors think they are showing an emotion when in fact they show little if any expression at all. They just have a kind of neutral look on their face at all times. They differ from a Withholder in that the Withholder usually knows that she is not expressive.

Frozen-Affect Expressor

The frozen-affect person constantly shows one emotion (such as happiness) when she is not experiencing that emotion at all.

Substitute Expressor

These people feel one emotion and think they are expressing it, but most onlookers would say some other emotion is being expressed. The person who feels angry but looks sad would be an example.

Every-Ready Expressor

This person almost instinctively shows the same emotion as his first response to any new event. Such a person may express surprise at good news, bad news, or the announcement that he has just been fired.

Flooded-affect Expressor

This person frequently displays more than one emotion. One of the emotions is characteristic of the person, similar to the Frozen-Affect Expressor. When another emotion is felt, it is mixed with the old characteristic expression. A person may look fearful, for instance, and thus show both fear and anger when he is angry.

FIGURE **3.3**

Do you have a characteristic style of facial expression? Paul Ekman and Wallace Friesen have identified eight different styles of facial expression in their research. Which one best fits you?

Adopted from Ekman and Friesen, *Unmasking the Face* (Englewood Cliffs, N.J.: Prentice-Hall, 1975), pp. 155–57. Illustration from Jim Harter, ed., *Men: A Pictorial Archive from Nineteenth-Century Sources* (New York: Dover, 1980), p. 3.

Other reasons for misreading the face include attending to competing verbal and nonverbal channels, not paying close attention to the context of interaction, and not knowing the target person's usual repertoire of facial expressions. When we are concentrating on what the person is saying or distracted by nervous gestures, we are likely to miss the momentary expressions that might reveal how the person really feels. Likewise, failure to perceive the context accurately may cause problems. When a friend or acquaintance is also your interviewer for a job, she may try to neutralize her expressions as much as possible so as not to show favoritism. If you think of her as a friend rather than an interviewer, you may read the expressionless face as genuine and think she doesn't want you to get the job. Finally, Ekman and Friesen suggest that you can improve the accuracy of your judgments by learning the idiosyncratic ways the other person uses facial expressions. This means making a concerted effort to record what the person does with his face in various situations, when you know for a fact that his reaction is or is not genuine. Facial expressions are, however, only one way we manipulate our bodies. We also communicate by managing other body movements known as kinesics.

KINESICS

The study of body movements such as gestures, posture, and head, trunk, and limb movements is known as **kinesics.** Facial expressions are also considered kinesics, but we have discussed them separately because of their overwhelming contribution in face-to-face interaction. At any rate, these kinesic behaviors help us determine when people consider themselves to be of equal or different status, when they are nervous, want to emphasize a point, and so on. Ekman and Friesen have proposed five categories of kinesic behavior: emblems, illustrators, affect displays, regulators, and adaptors.[39] We will look at each of these categories.

Emblems

Emblems are gestures that can easily be translated into verbal statements; there is widely shared agreement as to what they mean. When you doubt someone's sanity, you can indicate so by raising your hand to your temple and moving the forefinger in a circle. Almost every culture has developed different nonverbal symbols for saying yes and no. The way someone sticks out his tongue may indicate that he dislikes you (Rude Tongue), that he wants to be left alone (Concentration Tongue), or that he is flirting with you (Sexy Tongue).[40] In each case the placement or movement of the tongue is the crucial factor. One emblem that has had a very interesting history is the handshake. Box 3.2 describes the evolution of the symbolic meanings associated with this gesture.

Illustrators

Nonverbal behaviors that accompany speech, often emphasizing particular words or painting a picture of what is being said, are called **illustrators.** Hand batons are common examples. When people talk, they may raise a forefinger or wag it at the other person; hold their palms up, down, in front of them, or sideways; thrust their fist through the air, or clasp their hands together. None of these gestures has a meaning in and of itself, as an emblem would. Illustrators depend on, but also add an emphasis to, verbal messages.

Affect Displays

While emotions are communicated primarily via the face, **affect displays,** or postural and gestural cues, also work to convey how we feel. A child throws him- or herself to the ground and kicks arms and legs wildly in reaction to parental refusal. Such a tantrum is usually intentional and has a twofold purpose: It spontaneously expresses the emotion felt — rage — and is also a symbolic attempt to annoy or embarrass parents until they give in.

People may also synchronize their actions, consciously or not, to physically demonstrate an affective, or emotional, relationship among themselves. Children imitate the posture and gestures of their parents or heroes; people simultaneously lean forward to hear some choice gossip; and a group of "cool" teenagers mirror one another by leaning casually on one leg and resting their thumbs in their belt loops.

Regulators

Nonverbals that help control interaction flow are known as **regulators.** When you want to break into a conversation, you may use preliminary gestures such as leaning forward or tilting your head forward while raising your hand to a position where it may be used as an illustrator. What kinesic cues would you use to tell the other person that it is his or her turn to talk, or to hurry up, or to indicate that even though you have to pause to catch your breath, you have one more point to make before yielding the floor?

Adaptors

This final category includes any body movement designed to manage anxious, emotionally charged, or novel situations. **Self-adaptors** are manipulations of your own body: pressing a hand against your mouth, chewing your nails, crossing your arms, or brushing your hand through your hair. Since touch is often reassuring, we may touch ourselves to calm down or just to feel better. Self-touch may also indicate a desire to withdraw from interaction, to be left alone.

Object-adaptors are material objects used in the tension management process. Smoking cigarettes, tapping a pencil on your desk, caressing a stuffed animal, or chewing on a straw are exam-ples. Their only communicative value seems to be that they tell onlookers we're nervous or uncomfortable.

In summary, many kinesic movements (with the exception of emblems) may operate as unconscious messages on the sender's part. Habitual illustrators, regulators, and adaptors may either help or hinder our communication efforts. Since receivers are usually more aware of these gestures, we may be sending messages we don't want to send. But most people resist seeing themselves on videotape — perhaps we really don't want to know about our unconscious messages. Communication is hard enough without adding new pieces to the puzzle.

The nonverbal codes considered so far have been visual in nature. We now turn our attention to a code that is entirely auditory.

VOCALICS

Words are spoken through the medium of the voice, which has characteristics of its own, apart from the content of what is said. These characteristics are called **vocalics,** or paralanguage. *What* is said is frequently less important than *how* it is said. What we convey in our voices can accent, alter, or flatly contradict verbal meaning. For example, sarcasm is often a product of vocal inflection. Our investigation of the vocal channel will begin by looking at the qualities of the human voice that have message potential, followed by an examination of the role these characteristics play in impression formation and emotional expression.

Vocal Characteristics

While researchers have classified vocalic cues in several ways, we simply want you to be aware of the many components that make up the vocal system.[41] **Vocal qualities** include loudness, pitch, inflection, tempo, rhythm, intensity, articulation, and resonance. **Vocal characterizers**

One of the nonverbal gestures that we take for granted is the handshake. It is as common a form of greeting in cultures across the world as one is likely to find. It would seem that such a gesture would have a long history (it does) and a consistent one (it does not).

Historians are not sure when the handshake as a greeting originated. There is evidence that the gesture existed in 16th-century Poland, and was probably widespread in Europe much earlier than that. But from the 16th century to the early 1800s, the gesture lost favor and then returned in a different context and with a different meaning. The decline of the handshake began with the rise of courtly codes of civility among the elite in

France, Italy, and Spain. In courtly life, familiar greetings and leave-taking behavior took on the airs of hierarchy and sophisticated manners. The handshake was replaced by the gestures of doffing the hat, bowing, curtsying, and staying to the left of a person of higher rank.

As these codes of civility spread to the middle class, the control of one's body became a preeminent concern. Etiquette manuals, dance instructors, and tutors of all description taught individuals to keep their bodies erect, to walk properly in public, and to avoid gesticulating wildly or crossing the legs while in conversation. These gestures were widely known as the "science of conversing agreeably." But among all the etiquette books, one would not find any advice about shaking hands until a French manual in 1858 finally included the handshake, but restricted its use to the greetings of close friends. How did the gesture reemerge?

Historian Herman Roodenburg notes that the handshake could not make a comeback until the concern with manners began to relax a bit. Even the Dutch of the 17th century, widely acknowledged as an egalitarian society, did not practice the handshake as far as we know. In the meantime, the gesture began its comeback in the

---

are more specific sounds that we may occasionally recognize as speech acts themselves. Laughing, crying, moaning, yelling, and whining are examples. **Vocal segregates** are sounds that get in the way of fluent speech, including "uhs" and "ums," stuttering, and uncomfortable silences. The combinations of these cues produce the unique voice patterns of each person. You probably know someone whose voice is especially high-pitched or raspy or nasal or monotonic. How do these qualities affect your impressions of such people? People from different cultures or regions within the same culture usually differ from one another in characteristic ways. How do you react to those speakers whose vocal qualities differ from yours?

Messages in the Voice

The voice is often used to infer personality traits. When you talk to a stranger on the telephone, what image of the person do you form as you listen? David Addington's research on voice types and perceptions shows some of the more common attributions people make about the personality that goes with the voice. An example should suffice. A "breathy" male voice led listeners to infer that the speaker was young and artistic. The same characteristic in a female voice led to a stereotype of a more feminine, prettier, more petite, effervescent, yet shallow individual.[42] The accuracy of such impressions has never been proved. It's more likely that vo-

the handshake as a seal of reconciliation and the popular gesture of slapping hands to seal a business transaction in the marketplace. It was not long after these practices emerged that the Quakers began to use the handshake as a simple greeting that denoted a bond of friendship or brotherhood. Addressing each other as friends minimized the elements of hierarchy and class distinction that had previously been characterized forms of greeting in a culture preoccupied with manners and social status.

neighborhoods of 18th-century Paris and small Dutch towns. But it was not used as a gesture of greeting.

Roodenburg describes the semi-official "extra judicial" institutions that arose in these neighborhoods as a way of settling disputes without having to go before an official court of justice. Each neighborhood had its own informal commissaires who listened to each party and tried to find a way for them to reconcile. Usually one party would admit being in the wrong and would ask for forgiveness. The reconciliation was sealed by the parties giving each other "the hand of friendship." Roodenburg discovered similar rituals for settling disputes within the records of the Calvinist Church, and also noted the similarity between

SOURCE: Herman Roodenburg, "The 'Hand of Friendship': Shaking Hands and Other Gestures in the Dutch Republic," in J. Bremmer and H. Roodenburg, eds. *A Cultural History of Gesture* (Cambridge: Polity Press, 1991), pp. 152–89.

ADDITIONAL READINGS

Norbert Elias. *The History of Manners.* New York: Pantheon Books, 1978.
E. P. Thompson. *Customs in Common: Studies in Traditional Popular Culture.* New York: The New Press, 1993.
Richard L. Bushman. *The Refinement of America: Persons, Houses, Cities.* New York: Alfred A. Knopf, 1992.

cal cues are just one more aspect of our implicit personality theories. We factor in the vocal cues alongside others that then trigger a more complete prototypic impression.

We also use vocal cues to infer emotional states, especially when facial cues are unavailable or suspect. One review of the research on vocalics and emotion concluded that two emotions were most likely to be interpreted accurately: joy and hate. The hardest to communicate were love and shame.[43] The ability to judge emotions in the voice does vary, however. Some people are remarkably good at it while others can't make auditory distinctions or don't listen carefully. At certain times the context makes vocal cues more salient. In one study alcoholic

patients were more likely to seek additional treatment when a doctor made the referral in an "anxious" voice.[44]

From the auditory mode, which is one of the "distant" senses, we move to a consideration of the tactile mode, probably the most "immediate" sense.

TACTILE COMMUNICATION

From the time we are born, the nonverbal code of touch is extremely important. Studies of infants have shown how tactile stimulation triggers social, emotional, and even intellectual growth.[45] Advocates of the human potential **75** movement have stressed the need for adults to touch and be touched. In spite of this, we know very little about the role of touch as a message system. According to one reviewer, the research tends to emphasize only the positive role of touch.[46] Few investigators have studied how touch is used to dominate or threaten others. Yet we know from everyday experience that touching conveys a wide range of emotions and meanings.

Types of Touch

Touching may be the most ambiguous of the nonverbal codes because its meaning depends so much on the nature of the relationship, the age and sex of the other, and the situation, as well as where we are touched, how much pressure was applied, whether we think the touch was intentional or accidental, and how long the touch lasted. In addition, touch may be applied by brushing, patting, squeezing, stroking, embracing, slapping, kicking, and even tickling. The texture of touch may even be meaningful. Shaking hands with someone whose palm is sweaty is not very pleasant and may be interpreted as a sign of nervousness. The manner in which you place your hand on someone's arm may be the difference between reassuring or patronizing that person. The warmth or coldness of other cues, such as the tone of voice, may add meaning to being touched.

The Contexts and Functions of Touch

Touching may be used to signal aggression, status, friendliness, sexual interest, or simply to regulate interaction. But these meanings are mediated by context. Richard Heslin has classified the meanings of touch according to the relational context in which they occur.[47] The *professional/functional* context legitimates any kind of touch necessary to accomplish impersonal ends or services. Doctors and hair stylists are allowed to touch us in ways that other people

cannot. *Social/polite* relationships allow for a minimum of touching during greetings, goodbyes, and conversations. A handshake is acceptable, as is a brush on the arm to get another's attention. The meaning of other forms of touch in this setting is more difficult to determine. Brenda Major believes that touch may simultaneously communicate warmth and dominance, but that men and women pay attention to different aspects of the message. When an equal-status stranger initiates touch, men more often see it as an act of dominance; women see it as a friendly gesture.[48] Higher-status individuals seem to have more rights regarding touch. They can initiate touch more frequently, whereas a lower-status person rarely feels comfortable enough to reciprocate that touch.[49]

Friendship encourages a number of touching behaviors associated with liking. A shoulder embrace, a greater frequency of brushing the hand or arm, and a slight squeeze are examples of appropriate actions. In *love/intimate* relations, we find more hand-in-hand and arm-in-arm contact, more bodies leaning against one another, and more touching in general. Finally, sexual relationships forbid very few forms of touch. But even in sexual relationships, the meaning of touch may vary.

Heslin has proposed a curvilinear relationship between forms of touch and liking. In the initial stages of acquaintance, intimate touch is taboo and should lead to strong dislike. As a relationship becomes defined as loving or sexual, intimate touch becomes pleasurable. There is a danger, however, that the quantity of touching may lead to the view of the other person as a "sex object," reducing, sometimes drastically, the pleasure of touch. Although Heslin didn't include it in his scheme, we would add an *adversarial* relationship context. This could encompass professional wrestlers, some brothers and sisters, and normal folks during the course of an argument. You may grab someone by the shirt collar in an attempt to threaten her, or if things deteriorate, you may push or shove the person.

Touching is only one of many nonverbal codes. And, as we have reminded you all along, none of the codes stands alone. They operate as a complex, mixed-message system every time we interact with one another. How we can make sense out of and react to the total nonverbal package is the subject of the next section.

Balancing Nonverbal Codes: Compensating and Reciprocating

Most people in a crowded bus avoid looking at one another or limit their visual behavior to random glances. But what would you think if a stranger kept looking in your direction and, as seating opened up, moved closer to where you were sitting, and then offered someone else his seat and stood even closer to you, occasionally brushing his arm against yours? How would you react?

One way to view this stranger's behavior is to define his advances as increasing the physical and psychological immediacy or closeness between you. Our guess is that unless you were extremely attracted to this stranger, you would probably *compensate* for his behavior by distancing yourself in one or more ways. You might get up and change your seat, turn and look out the window, or bury your head in your newspaper.

We don't always avoid increases in nonverbal immediacy. Sometimes we *reciprocate* another's invitations. Is there any way to predict when we will compensate or reciprocate? Let's look at one theory that tries to account for these differences.

EQUILIBRIUM THEORY

Equilibrium theory presents one explanation of how the various nonverbal codes interact. It is the work of Miles Patterson and a number of earlier contributors whose theories Patterson has modified.[50] The first theory Patterson drew

from was Michael Argyle and Janet Dean's equilibrium model, which suggested that in any situation people establish a comfortable level of nonverbal intimacy by balancing various nonverbal cues. They maintain the normal level of involvement by **compensating** when something happens that increases the level of intimacy between them. During the course of developing a more personal relationship, they may escalate the level of involvement by **reciprocating** when the other initiates an increase in nonverbal intimacy. The proper balance of cues may be defined by cultural norms or negotiated by the two individuals.

The next time you shop at a mall, observe the seating patterns of strangers in the food court. Most strangers will not share a table, except under the most crowded circumstances. Note how they compensate to maintain equilibrium if forced to share. They'll sit on opposite sides and ends of the table. They may avoid interaction altogether, staring off in different directions. If they do talk, they are likely to make very limited and brief eye contact. If either engages in any intimacy behaviors — excessive staring, prolonged smiling, or intimate statements — the other will probably *compensate*. Equilibrium theory predicts that if one of these strangers increases the level of involvement beyond what was normal or comfortable, the other will compensate by reducing involvement in one or more codes (for example, if one moved closer, the other would avoid any eye contact). No doubt you've been in situations where something like this has happened.

But on other occasions you may have noted that increases in nonverbal involvement are matched by the other person. When someone cries and repeatedly looks up at you between sobs (in effect increasing the level of involvement), you may move closer to him, put your arm around his shoulder, and ask if you can help. In other words, you *reciprocate* by a further increase in intimacy. Equilibrium theory did not account for such reciprocity. To explain these two different reactions to the increase in nonverbal involvement, Patterson proposed that *changes in arousal* and *cognitive labeling* of that arousal change are important.

Many factors, including spontaneous communication, can cause a change in arousal, either by increasing or decreasing it. Being stared at or enclosed in an elevator with others may increase what was once low arousal, whereas being comforted and touched may decrease a high-arousal state. In addition, arousal may increase when the other person violates our expectations, causing us to become uncertain about what is going on. Once a change in arousal does occur, we go through a cognitive labeling process (symbolic communication) to determine if the emotion being felt is positive or negative. If we make a negative attribution (for example, fear or anger), compensation is the most likely response. If we label the arousal as positive (excitement or love), then the model predicts that reciprocity will occur. For example, suppose your good friend sneaks up behind you and tries to surprise you. She sticks her forefinger in your back and says, "Stick 'em up!" This behavior may startle or frighten you (a negative attribution), in which case you'll probably jump away and raise your arm for defense as you turn around. You would be compensating for the increased level of nonverbal involvement. The opposite reaction might occur if you recognized your friend's voice or expected some routine like this from her (a positive attribution). You might then reciprocate by turning around and embracing your friend.

COMPENSATING AND RECIPROCATING IN EVERYDAY LIFE

How well does equilibrium theory explain everyday interactions? We think you'll find that it can help you understand the give-and-take of nonverbal communication. One of the principal themes of this text is that communication is used to regulate the tension between feeling independent and feeling like a part of the social systems around us. When we feel closed in by a

relationship, we may compensate by reducing the level of nonverbal involvement. You can probably remember your early teenage years, when you desperately needed to present yourself as an adult, not a child. At that point in life, too much nonverbal involvement with parents, such as holding their hands or staying close to them while shopping, suggests that you are still a child. Compensation becomes a tool for establishing your own identity and your status as an adult.

Understanding the various nonverbal codes we have described is an important part of interpersonal communication. Even more important is understanding how they work in conjunction with one another and with verbal messages. Recognizing how people compensate and reciprocate for increases in nonverbal intimacy can help you manage your nonverbal communication more effectively.

The Interplay of Verbal and Nonverbal Communication

In practice, we seldom communicate solely through nonverbal channels. As we saw earlier, nonverbal codes are used to reinforce, repeat, or contradict verbal messages. At the same time, we often attach verbal labels to our own and others' nonverbal behaviors. The act of labeling is one way that we take nonverbal communication from the realm of the spontaneous to a clearly symbolic level. To illustrate, let's look at the interplay of the verbal and nonverbal in the experiencing of emotions.

Contrary to Ross Buck's assertion that most emotional communication occurs at an immediate and spontaneous level, some scholars believe that emotions, like other concepts, are socially constructed. James Averill, for instance, defines **emotions** as transitory social roles involving one's assessment of a social situation and experienced as passions rather than actions.[51] According to Averill, the experience of emotions like pleasure or anger involves more than a mere biological or intrapsychic reaction to a stimulus — it is largely dependent upon a system of sociocultural rules that indicate to the individual whether an emotion is proper or appropriate in a given situation. For instance, it is appropriate in our culture to cry at weddings and funerals, so we are much more likely to experience happiness or sadness in those circumstances. We are surrounded by situational cues that prompt our emotions. Yet we do not realize that our emotions are socially defined because part of the social definition is that emotions are passive — they "happen to us" rather than our choosing them. Most of us would rather believe we "fell in love" (uncontrollably) than admit we conspired to follow a socially defined pattern of interaction that eventually informed us that our feelings for each other could properly be called love.

The controversy may be more apparent than real. Buck argues that emotions *felt* are often but not always communicated spontaneously. Thus, emotions may be socially defined but experienced as inner states that are communicated via natural gestures. And of course, it is possible that emotional states are experienced spontaneously but either denied or modified by cultural display rules, which are socially defined. Perhaps we have become so sophisticated at symbolic communication that many emotions, once experienced at a purely spontaneous level, are now at least partially controlled by social definitions.

What is clear is that the communication of emotion is not always a straightforward process. Richard Buttny has demonstrated how we mix nonverbal affect displays and verbal labeling to hold others accountable for the experience of negative emotions.[52] He suggests that in conversation, relational partners often display and talk about emotions in order to fix blame or responsibility. The most obvious way we do this is by simply showing our feelings through vocalic cues, body posture, and silence or through verbal sarcasm. Another way is by verbally labeling our own negative emotions and implying that the other was somehow responsible. For example, simply stating that you are angry in the presence of a partner can frame events as problematic, as though the other somehow provoked your anger. Finally, we can ascribe a particular emotion to our partner and, in doing so, imply that his or her emotion is excessive, unjustified, or otherwise inappropriate. Note in the following exchange how Lori labels Scotty's emotion (she has just told him that she has to go home to Boston during fall break):

SCOTTY: (*with rising intonation*) I'm not gonna take . . . be able to take you to Boston, Lori.

LORI: I understand, we'll . . . we'll go another time.

SCOTTY: (*rapid pace, emphatic and rising intonation*) *What* other *time?*

LORI: In the spring . . . I'm gonna have my car up here . . . I'll bring it up after . . .

SCOTTY: Something will come up. (*audible outbreath*)

LORI: Oh *come on,* don't be angry.

SCOTTY: I'm not angry. . . . I just know . . . I . . . I *know* I just have the feeling that we're not going to get to Boston. . . . together.

LORI: We will go another time Scotty I promise we will go to Boston together . . .

SCOTTY: Lori? I'll put money on it . . . right now, that we will *not* go to Boston

LORI: (*marked increase in volume*) WE WILL GO TO BOSTON! WE WILL . . . BECAUSE WE CAN'T GO NOW WE HAVE *spring*time to go. . . . I wanted to go just as bad as you did Scott. . . .[53]

By telling Scott not to be angry, Lori is not only labeling his behavior but also framing it as an overreaction to their change in plans. Notice that despite his earlier emphatic statements, he denies being angry and seems willing to modify his emotion as disappointment. She might have been successful had she stopped, but her almost-too-easy insistence that there will be another opportunity seems to provoke a verbal betting gambit ("I'll put money on it"), a fairly clear display of anger.

As this example illustrates, the communication of emotion is a difficult and often unsuccessful enterprise. Even when friends are able to manage the occasional argument or nonverbal battle for dominance in the relationship, their characteristic differences in style and degree of nonverbal expressiveness will likely be an obstacle. Clearly, better understanding and communication of our own and other's feelings would help make relational life a lot easier. With that goal in mind, we turn our attention to some specific guidelines for improving our skills in this important area.

Skill Building: Communicating Feelings

Managing interpersonal relationships is never easy, but the management of emotional aspects of those relationships is doubly difficult. First of all, there are no simple guidelines. While we will focus here on skills such as how to better express your feelings and how to respond to the nonverbal displays and feeling statements of others, we cannot recommend their indiscriminate use. As much as openness is to be valued in relationships, there are times when emotional wounds are too painful to bear scrutiny. Likewise, some relationships or issues will not be significant enough to warrant bringing out all the heavy artillery to do emotional battle. And sometimes conversations that are direct and

forthright can be boring. Can you imagine what it would be like to flirt if all the suspense and ambiguity of meaning associated with it were stripped away?

However, for those times when you desire greater emotional openness in your relationships, you must have some strategies that will help you achieve your goals. Let's focus first on how to express your own feelings appropriately; then we'll look at how you can help others express themselves.

EXPRESSING FEELINGS

Most of us have not been taught how to express our emotions. In our culture, males in particular have difficulty expressing how they feel. The first step in improving our skills is to *become more aware of the emotions we do experience.* Ronald Adler suggests a diary procedure for monitoring your emotional communication.[54] Over a period of several days, you should record incidents in which you experienced a particular emotion such as anxiety, resentment, or pride. Then write a brief description of the situation (events surrounding the emotion), the way you expressed yourself verbally and nonverbally, and the consequences of your behavior (the end results — how others responded). Make sure you record specific nonverbal behaviors and verbal statements. This will indicate the extent to which you are actually expressing your feelings. After several days analyze your diary. Ask yourself which emotions you experience most often, how well you express what you feel, and how others respond to your behavior. By taking inventory in this way, you increase your awareness of your emotional experience and strengths and weaknesses in expressing those emotions.

Another way to increase awareness is to *actively seek feedback about your expressions of emotion from trusted sources.* Ekman and Friesen suggest that people are more internally aware of the specific nonverbal channels from which they have received the greatest amount of external feedback. We learn to pay attention to the nonverbal channels that others pay attention to. Buck calls this the "education of attention," one of the most significant ways we learn to manage our own nonverbal communication.

As you become more aware of your emotions, you can shift your attention to more constructive ways of communicating your feelings. You will want to keep in mind some simple principles to help develop those skills.

A key principle is to *express your feelings in a way that indicates your ownership of them*. Too often we speak of our feelings in impersonal terms, referring to them as if they belonged to the object of our perception or to some objective realm. "The painting isn't a very optimistic one, it depicts a depressing mood" or "Depression has set in again" are examples of failure to demonstrate ownership of feelings. Worse yet, we frequently blame others for how we feel. "You make me so mad" is one of the least constructive ways of talking about our feelings. While we have learned about emotions through a process that is socially constructed, the experience of those emotions belongs to us, not to anyone else. We can indicate ownership of our own feelings by using "I" statements that reflect the influence of both partners' behavior but concede ultimate self-responsibility for our own behavior. "I feel very lonely when you put in such long hours at the office" is much better than "You make me feel invisible." Notice that while the latter statement may have more dramatic impact, it lacks specificity and puts all the blame on the other, which is likely to provoke a defensive reaction, not a constructive one.

A final suggestion is to *match the form of expression with the situation and your own personal and relational goals*. We have three primary options regarding the communication of emotions. We can (1) avoid communicating altogether, (2) express our feelings directly, or (3) express our feelings in an indirect (equivocal) fashion. Each of these options has different consequences, depending upon the situation and our personal or relational goals. Direct expression is appropriate if the timing is right and if the emotion is one that needs to be expressed in order to achieve a personal or relational goal. If you want your friend to know that you value the friendship, a direct expression is probably the most effective way of saying it. On the other hand, avoidance or equivocal communication is sometimes more appropriate. Janet Bavelas and her colleagues define **equivocal communication** as messages that are ambiguous, uncertain, or open to more than one equally appropriate interpretation.[55] According to Bavelas we should express our feelings in an equivocal manner when all other choices would lead to negative consequences. For example, we are often confronted with a situation in which an expression of our true feelings would most likely hurt the other person. In some cases a painful truth may be the best thing for the long-term health of the relationship; but often it serves no real purpose. The equivocal response is one that expresses more than one truth or skirts the issue carefully. In Jane Austen's *Sense and Sensibility*, Marianne must find a way to state her honest opinion of her sister Elinor's lover without hurting Elinor's feelings:

> *Do not be offended, Elinor, if my praise of him is not in every thing equal to your sense of his merits. I have not had so many opportunities of estimating the minuter propensities of his mind, his inclinations and tastes as you have; but I have the highest opinion in the world of his goodness and sense. I think him every thing that is worthy and amiable.*[56]

Marianne's solution illustrates a classic way of balancing two important considerations: remaining true to her own sense of integrity and preserving goodwill in a relationship that is important to her.

REFLECTING FEELINGS

In addition to revealing your own feelings, it is also important to help others express theirs. Actively listening to and reflecting what you observe and hear is an important source of feedback to others. We can, for instance, *look for hidden feelings in others' behavior and carefully bring them to the surface.* "It sounds like you like him but can't bring yourself to say it" is an example of a typical reflective feeling statement. We can also *help others clarify their own feelings by pointing out any contradictory or ambivalent (equivocal) expressions.* Watching a friend open the gift you thought he or she would love can often present an opportunity for clarification. At first you notice the bright-eyed anticipation, the excited tone of voice — "Ohhhhh . . ." — and then carefully, with much less inflection, ". . . it's lovely. It's . . . it's just what I wanted." Being polite is, of course, the equivocal response, and you could just let it go at that and try harder next time. But if you really want to know what type of gift will please your friend, it is better to reflect the mixed feelings you heard and clarify them. You might say, "You seemed excited at first, but then a little dismayed. I'd really like to know if you're feeling disappointed."

It's also a good idea to *mention some aspect of the observed behavior first, then search for the feeling.* Consider Bryant, a student who has gone to see his professor about a group project. He has just admitted that his group wasted most of their in-class meeting time.

BRYANT: I didn't want to tell you about all this, I was afraid you'd get angry at me. Now you're telling me that you're not upset, but you're twisting the eraser off that pencil (*behavioral description*). I think maybe you really are mad at me.

PROFESSOR: (*recognizing his anger*) Well, I guess you're right. I am angry, but I hope you realize I'm angry with the whole group, not just you. It irks me that I provide class time for groups to meet and then students find a thousand reasons why they can't make it to class. I set aside time so you won't have to bicker about conflicting schedules and no time to meet, and then this happens. I'm angry at all of you, but I guess I should have realized this would happen.

Bryant bore the brunt of his professor's anger, but at least he helped the professor verbalize and understand his own feelings. Had he not reflected the professor's feelings, Bryant probably would have incurred most of the professor's wrath anyway. At least now, the professor knows what he was angry about and won't direct all the anger at Bryant. He may even be thankful that Bryant helped him recognize a problem in his class that needs to be addressed.

Finally, Lawrence Brammer offers some summary advice for reflecting the feelings of others. He suggests that you (1) read the total message — stated feelings, nonverbal body language, and content, (2) select the best mix of content and feelings to comment on and then occasionally interrupt to reflect those feelings, and (3) reflect the experience and then wait for the other to acknowledge your reflection before moving on.[57] In this way you make sure that the other is able and willing to handle a discussion of those emotions.

Remember, to become more skillful at emotional communication involves more than just learning how to say what's on your mind or showing how you really feel. If you take these principles to heart, you are another step closer to becoming a more communicatively competent person.

This chapter has emphasized the structure and function of nonverbal codes. Nonverbal communication is structured such that messages may be coded in at least seven or eight different channels. We have also mentioned some major functions that these codes serve: modifying the content of a message, expressing emotions, structuring relationships, and managing the flow of conversation. And we have provided some guidelines for improving the way you use and talk about nonverbal communication. Now it's up to you to apply those guidelines to improve your own nonverbal communication.

Process to Performance

REVIEW TERMS

The following is a list of major concepts introduced in this chapter. The page where the concept is first mentioned is listed in parentheses.

spontaneous communication (56)
symbolic communication (56)
liking (59)
status (59)
responsiveness (59)
complementing (59)
accenting (59)
repeating (59)
substituting (59)
contradicting (60)
regulating (60)
proxemics (61)
territoriality (62)
personal space (63)
physical appearance (64)
gaze (65)
looking (68)
seeing (68)
facial blend (69)
cultural display rules (69)
leakage cues (69)
kinesics (72)
emblems (72)
illustrators (72)

affect displays (72)
regulators (73)
self-adaptors (73)
object-adaptors (73)
vocalics (73)
vocal qualities (73)
vocal characterizers (73)
vocal segregates (74)
equilibrium theory (77)
compensating (77)
reciprocating (77)
emotions (78)
equivocal communication (81)

SUGGESTED READINGS

Paul Ekman. *Telling Lies.* New York: Norton, 1985. A very engaging look at the ways in which we use nonverbal communication to deceive and to read deception in others. Ekman carefully explains how research is conducted in order to demonstrate what's involved physiologically when we omit relevant information or fabricate a story. He also shows how willing we are to conspire with others so we will not detect their deceptions.

David McNeill. *Hand and Mind: What Gestures Reveal about Thought.* Chicago: University of Chicago Press, 1992. A highly original theory about the relationship between language and gesture. McNeill believes that gestures and language represent separate but simultaneous expressions of mental images or abstract ideas. As a result, both reveal different aspects of thought but also contribute to shaping that thought as well. While not the easiest reading, it is well worth the effort.

Montagu, Ashley, and Floyd Matson. *The Human Connection.* New York: McGraw-Hill, 1979. A very readable exploration into the nonverbal codes involved in approaching, meeting, signaling, and communicating with others.

TOPICS FOR DISCUSSION

1. In small groups discuss the advantages and disadvantages of the "limited" definition of nonverbal communication presented in the text (pp. 54–55). Decide for yourselves if we should include all nonverbal behavior as communication or whether some limits are necessary. Then try your hand at defining nonverbal communication.

2. The research in this chapter identifies facial expressions as the most universal of nonverbal gestures. Are there any other codes that you think might approach universal meaning (that is, that people from different cultures would interpret the same way)? Can you arrange the codes in order from most universal to least universal? What implications does this order have for interpreting and sending nonverbal messages in everyday interactions?

3. What are your own preferences in terms of personal space or conversational distance? How close do you like to stand when talking with friends, acquaintances, or strangers? Can you recall an episode in which conversational distance had a dramatic impact? What happened? How did you (or the other) respond to the violation of expectations? What was the outcome of the conversation?

4. Identify as many nonperson roles as you can (see p. 64). What do people say and do in the presence of these role persons that they would avoid if they met the same person in another setting?

5. Discuss the role of norms in nonverbal communication. Consider norms for two or three different codes. What are the advantages and disadvantages of following these norms? Can a person be too normal? How far can someone go in violating the norm before most people label her as abnormal? What positive outcomes can be achieved when norms are violated? When do norms become too limiting?

6. One study mentioned in the text pointed out differences in gaze between black and white Americans. Identify other ethnic, regional, or cultural groups you have interacted with and discuss the differences in nonverbal norms that you noticed. Can you think of appropriate ways to improve communication when such differences are apparent?

OBSERVATION GUIDE

1. Make your next trip to the zoo an investigation into nonverbal communication. Visit a large metropolitan zoo where you can observe primates and other species close to humans on the evolutionary scale. What similarities and differences do you see or hear? Organize your observations according to the various codes discussed in the text (facial, gaze, kinesics, and so on). What gestures seem to be used primarily for communication? What functions do they serve? Identify any gestures humans use that might have originated with earlier species. How has the meaning of such gestures changed?

2. Specify a particular block of time and try using nonverbal codes as a substitute for verbal ones. When people ask you questions, do not verbalize beyond unintelligible vocalizations such as grunts or groans. Vary the types of responses you make (vocalized only, facial only, combined responses, and so on). Keep track of your nonverbal codes for a couple of days and try to formulate some general principles about when substituting works best.

3. Observe people in naturally occurring conversations, recording the specific nonverbal codes used to regulate the flow of interaction. Which cues are more characteristic of smooth turn-taking? Which cues seem to cause awkward transitions or silences? Compare your observations with those of published research (your instructor can recommend journal articles or textbooks that summarize these behaviors).

4. It is a rare semester when students are not involved in at least one group project. Take advantage of these opportunities to observe non-

verbal interaction more closely. Take a few minutes during each meeting to observe how different group members communicate nonverbally. As unobtrusively as you can, record facial expressions, body posture and movement, gaze, gestures, and vocal characteristics. Also note the situation at hand so you won't interpret nonverbals out of context. What do these observations tell you about the interest level, status relations, and interpersonal competence of group members? What gestures are shared or imitated by other group members? What does this suggest about the bonding of group members together?

EXERCISES

1. Identify people you think are especially accurate in reading others' nonverbal cues or are very good at getting their message across nonverbally. These should be people who aren't members of your class. Formulate (in class) a set of interview questions to ask these people. You might want to ask what behaviors they attend to most often when they want to know what the other thinks or feels, and how they know when someone is deceiving them. For message sending, ask people how aware they are of their own nonverbals, which codes they use intentionally, and which they think are most important. Would they rather use verbal or nonverbal messages to give instructions or to convey emotions? You should think of other types of messages to ask them about. Interview a dozen people outside of class and compare the answers you get. Prepare a short presentation to the rest of the class, focusing on what you have learned about nonverbal communication competence.

2. Assemble groups of four or five. Have each person remove any cash, valuables, and "really embarrassing" items from their wallets. Place the wallets in a basket and give them to your instructor, who will redistribute the wallets to another group. Each group should analyze the contents of each wallet, writing down a brief profile of its owner. The profile should be based only on inferences made from the artifacts found in the wallet. It can include the person's sex, age, personality, appearance, interests. Once the profile of each wallet is written, enclose it in the wallet and return them to your instructor, who will return them to the original owners. Group members may then read the profiles written about them to one another or introduce one another to the class by reading the profiles aloud. Conclude the exercise by discussing the accuracy of the profiles and the particular artifacts that were most influential in communicating those impressions.

3. Divide the class into six groups. Each group is assigned one of the following communicative functions: (1) exercising social control, (2) regulating interaction, (3) expressing intimacy, (4) expressing emotion, (5) facilitating service or task goals, and (6) modifying the content of verbal messages. Each group should then compile a list of the ways each nonverbal code helps to accomplish that function. During the week group members should bring to class audiovisual examples of how this is done (family photos, magazine photos, film clips, audiotapes, and so on). Try to find both stereotypic and unusual examples to illustrate these functions. Groups could be given the last five to ten minutes of two or three class sessions to discuss what they have found and prepare a 10- to 15-minute presentation to the class. Presentations could be conducted the following week.

Language is the medium through which we express our deepest thoughts. In spoken form it connects us to one another; in written form it allows us to cross time and space and enter new worlds of words and ideas.

(E. K. F. Von Gekhardt (1830–1925), *The Students*)

4

Verbal Competence

On June 27, 1880, a remarkable woman was born. Although she graduated cum laude from Radcliffe College at the age of 24 and later became a famous author and lecturer, Helen Keller had to battle almost insurmountable odds. Many of you know her story. When she was a child she was struck with an illness that left her both blind and deaf for life. It was impossible for anyone to penetrate her dark and silent world. She developed a crude sign language, but she was constantly frustrated by her inability to communicate, often screaming and crying until she was exhausted.

All of this changed when Anne Sullivan became her teacher. Perhaps you recall the scene from *The Miracle Worker* in which the seven-year-old Helen first learns the meaning of language. She and Sullivan were in the well-house of the Keller home. Sullivan placed Helen's hands beneath the pump and spelled the word "w-a-t-e-r" into them. As she felt the cool liquid spill over her hands, Helen realized for the first time what words were. As she wrote later:

> *That living word awakened my soul, gave it light, hope, joy, set it free! . . . I left the well-house eager to learn. Everything had a name, every object which I touched seemed to quiver with life. That was because I saw everything with the strange, new sight that had come to me.*[1]

There are two ways to respond to this story. We can dwell on what Helen lacked and the obstacles she overcame. Or we can concentrate on what she gained that day at the well-house. What she gained was language, and with it history, literature, and culture. When she acquired language, she acquired access to the same symbolic world the rest of us inhabit. From that moment on, she didn't have to see or hear the world directly. She could share others' experiences.

This chapter is about what happens to each of us simply because we use language. It's about what language is, how it is put together, and how it affects us. We'll begin by defining **87** language, paying particular attention to the ways the verbal code differs from the nonverbal. Next we'll look at language structure, examining semantic, syntactic, and pragmatic levels. We will then consider how language affects our thoughts and behaviors. Finally, we'll look at ways of overcoming language confusion in order to increase message competence.

What Is Language?

In this section we will compare verbal and nonverbal codes and describe some of the power that comes to us through language

DIFFERENCES BETWEEN THE VERBAL AND NONVERBAL CODES

One of the major differences between verbal and nonverbal codes is that language is a digital code, while nonverbal is classified as analogic. Before we explain the differences between these codes, see if you can discover them for yourself by considering the examples shown in Figures 4.1 and 4.2. In the first figure, you see a drawing accompanied by a verbal description. Both the words and drawing describe the same subject, using different codes. The way the drawing conveys information is analogic; the way the written description conveys it is digital.

Now look at the second example. Figure 4.2 shows a braille translation of Helen Keller's description of her experience at the well-house. This is in a digital code. Above it is a still from *The Miracle Worker* in which actors convey Helen's experience analogically. As a third example, think for a minute about the difference between a sundial and a digital clock. A sundial shows time by reflecting the actual movement of the sun across the sky, while a digital clock displays separate numbers that change at fixed intervals.[2]

TOADS are found in almost every part of the world. Members of the family Bufonidae, they are squat and fat, have short legs and a warty skin. They secrete a poisonous substance from the parotoid glands behind the eye. They feed on the larvae of harmful insects.

FIGURE **4.1**
Analogic and digital representation of a toad

Try listing adjectives that describe the analogic examples. What do the movement of the shadow on the sundial, the gestures of the actors, and the lines of the drawing have in common? Next, try to describe the digital examples. What similarities are there between the digital readout, the braille letters, and the written words? If, for the first set, you came up with words like *natural, continuous, immediate, similar,* or *relational,* you have grasped the nature of analogic codes. If, for the second set, you chose words like *artificial, abstract, arbitrary, separate,* or *logical,* then you've discovered the essence of digital codes.

Analogic codes indicate meaning by being similar to what they convey. The actors' movements are like those of real people experiencing real emotions. The lines in the drawing trace the natural shape and form of the object they

FIGURE **4.2**
Analogic and digital representations of
Helen Keller's experience at the well-house

The desire to bind time by recording spoken communication is universal. The message in these hieroglyphs, written over 3,000 years ago, is accessible today to those who know how to break the verbal code.

(*King's Scribe Amenhotep and His Wife Renut*, c. 1275 B.C.)

represent. The movement of the shadow on the face of the sundial mirrors the passage of time. In analogic codes an expression and what it indicates are naturally connected. Many of the nonverbal behaviors we studied in Chapter 3 convey meaning analogically.

In **digital codes** meaning is conveyed symbolically. **Symbols** are units of meaning that are arbitrary and conventional. They're arbitrary because the relationship they have to the things they represent is artificial rather than natural. Consider the word *joy,* for example. The fact

that that particular combination of sounds and letters was chosen to represent the emotion is an arbitrary one. There is nothing particularly joyful in the word *joy.* The word stands for the emotion because people agreed that it should. Symbols are conventional, based on social agreement. We could easily change the meaning attached to the words in our language — if everyone within our language community agreed. Maybe the reason people react so emotionally to language changes is that such changes violate basic social contracts. At any rate, without knowing the conventions used to assign meaning to symbols, digital codes are impossible to understand.

We have seen that the way meanings are expressed differs in the two codes. The kinds of meanings they can express also differ. Analogic codes (especially those consisting of expressive behavior) seem to be best at conveying relationships and immediate emotional states. Digital codes are useful for more abstract, logical meanings. Assume that you don't know the story of Helen Keller. How much of it could you surmise by looking at the picture from *The Miracle Worker*? You could easily recognize that it involves two characters experiencing intense emotion. You might also understand what they're doing and what they feel for each other. What you could not understand is the history of their relationship or their interpretations of it. For this you would have to turn to digital reports.

CHARACTERISTICS OF THE VERBAL CODE

In Chapter 3 we listed some of the reasons nonverbal codes are so powerful. Language has a different kind of power. Four characteristics of the digital code distinguish it from the analogic code and allow us to act in otherwise impossible ways:[3]

1. *Verbal codes consist of discrete, separable units.* The structure of language is unique. It consists of units of sound and meaning that are discrete and separate. This fact gives language immense flexibility, for the units that make it up can be processed and manipulated more readily than those of the nonverbal codes. Words and sounds can be modified, combined in unique ways, and transmitted singly or in combination across time and space. They can be easily saved, stored, and retrieved. This is impossible in analogic codes. Although attempts have been made to break analogic displays into units and to write grammars describing their combinations, most have failed.[4]

2. *Language encourages us to create new realities.* One of the unique things about language is that it allows us to talk about absent or nonexistent things. Words don't need to have actual referents in the physical world. Of course, this is a mixed blessing. Language allows creativity, but it also allows us to deceive one another. In fact, Umberto Eco has defined language as "everything which can be used in order to lie."[5]

3. *Language gives us the ability to think in new and more complex ways.* Abstract nouns, logical words such as *and, or, all,* and *none,* and grammatical markers can't be expressed analogically. Such words allow the development of complex philosophical and mathematical systems. Language enhances our ability to think rationally and logically, although this doesn't mean we always do so.

4. *Verbal codes are self-reflexive.* Language can comment on itself; it allows us to talk about the way we talk. This quality is known as self-reflexiveness. It's what allows us to think about language and modify it when it doesn't work. Without this aspect of language, studying and improving communication would be impossible, for we would have no way to talk about it.

The Functions of Language

Stop for a minute and think of all the things you normally do with language. Think of as many examples as you can, like commenting on the weather, reminiscing with old friends, describing last night's NFL telecast, memorizing facts, cursing, making jokes, talking to yourself, writing poetry, telling white lies, cheering a team to victory. Clearly language isn't just a vehicle for exchanging facts and seeking information. In this section we'll list some of the functions of language.[6]

1. *Language is often used to conquer the silent and the unknown.* We all have a need to escape from silence. When alone in a dark or quiet place, we often talk simply to make noise. Somehow, unbroken silence can be oppressive and frightening — by talking, we defend ourselves against the unknown. We also conquer the unknown by labeling it. Things without names are threatening and mysterious. We can reduce them to more human and manageable proportions by naming them; perhaps we believe something that is named can be controlled. If so, we are not far from a belief in the magical qualities of language.

2. *Language allows us to express and control emotion.* Some talk may simply be an attempt to reduce inner tension. Many psychologists believe that we have a biologically based need to vent emotions. Shouting in joy or cursing in anger are examples of this function. Of course, language can also be used to inhibit emotion. For example, we can talk ourselves into calming down. In a classic episode of *The Honeymooners,* Jackie Gleason's character, Ralph Kramden, repeats, "Pins and needles, needles and pins, the happy man is the man who grins," and then counts to ten, hoping by the time he's finished he'll have forgotten what he was angry about.

3. *Language can reveal or camouflage our thoughts and motives.* What goes on within us remains hidden unless we choose to show it to others. We can discuss inner feelings directly or reveal them more subtly. Freud was one of the first to turn our attention to the meanings of linguistic errors or slips of the tongue. He called these errors *parapraxes* and believed they were caused by inner conflicts.[7] If, for example, a speaker were to say quite sweetly, "We'll do whatever I — I mean you — want," the substitution might indicate a hidden need for control. Although to the trained ear parapraxes reveal inner feelings, they are attempts to hide true desires and designs from both self and other. Of course, we can use language as camouflage more directly; we can hide behind overt lies, evasions, and half-truths.

4. *Language permits us to make and avoid contact.* Language connects us to others. The telephone company slogan "Reach out and touch someone" reflects this basic function. Telling someone "I just called to hear your voice" is using language to bridge distance. Of course, we can also talk to keep others away. A compulsive talker can avoid contact. Language can be a wall as well as a bridge.

5. *Language enables us to assert individual and social identity.* Each of us has a unique style; talk enables us to present it and thus an image of how we want to be perceived. At the same time, it also allows us to submerge ourselves in a group. Slang, jargon, and shared language games can signal social solidarity and a sense of belonging.

6. *Language may be used to give or seek information.* It almost goes without saying that language is an important medium for information exchange. It allows us to categorize and interpret the environment. Through language we can state, assert, describe, explain, and demonstrate the order we see around us. We also use language to gather information from others. Even seemingly trivial small talk, or *phatic communication,* can serve as social reconnaissance. Because survival is based on accurate predictions about the world, linguistic means of reducing uncertainty are essential.[8]

7. *Language allows us to control and be controlled by the world. Language is power.* It can be used to influence, regulate, persuade, or dominate. From making a good impression to brainwashing, we use language to control our world. Of course, language also controls us by affecting the way we perceive and think about the world. In many ways we are prisoners of language.

8. *Language can be used to monitor the process of communication.* As we noted earlier, language is self-reflexive; it allows us to *metacommunicate,* to communicate about the communication process. When two people discuss a topic of interest such as politics or religion, they are communicating. When they discuss their discussion, they are metacommunicating. Metacommunication occurs when we use language to check communication channels ("Did you understand what I said?"), regulate the flow of talk ("Wait a minute. Let me finish making this point"), or comment on language patterns ("I know I change the subject whenever you make a good point. It's just that I can't stand to be on the losing end of an argument").[9]

The Structure of Language: Three Levels of Meaning

Now that we know some of the functions of language, let's look briefly at how language is structured. Language can be analyzed on a number of levels.[10] The three we believe most important to the study of interpersonal communication are the word, the sentence, and the speech act. To understand and use language, we have to understand all these levels of meaning.

SEMANTIC MEANING: LANGUAGE AT THE LEVEL OF THE WORD

Actually, to be technically correct, we should use the term *morpheme* rather than *word*. A morpheme is a linguistic unit of meaning. Although in most cases morphemes are equivalent to words, some word fragments also carry meaning. For example, the *s* that tells us a word is plural has meaning in its own right. Therefore, a word like *dogs* is actually made up of two morphemes: the word *dog* and the plural morpheme *s*.

The study of meaning at this level is called **semantics.** While a full discussion of semantic meaning is beyond the scope of this book, we can at least begin by considering two kinds of word meanings: denotative and connotative.

Denotative and Connotative Meanings

Denotative meaning is public, conventional meaning. It is, in a sense, the meaning that was agreed upon when the language code was constructed. This kind of meaning belongs not to the individual but to the language system itself. To find out the denotative meaning of an unfamiliar word, we simply turn to an authoritative source such as the dictionary. That is why denotative meaning is often referred to as "dictionary meaning." **Connotative meaning** is private, often emotionally charged meaning. It becomes attached to words through experiences and associations. Here, individuals rather than the language system are the final authority. Consider the term *baseball*. Our dictionary tells us that its denotative meaning is

a game played with a ball, bat and gloves between two teams of nine players each on a large field centering on four bases that form the corners of a square 90 feet on each side, each team having a turn at bat and in the field during each of the nine innings that constitute a normal game, the winner being the team that scores the most runs.[11]

While this definition expresses (albeit awkwardly) at least part of the meaning of baseball, it seems curiously flat. There is more to meaning than what is in the dictionary. Part of what is missing is connotative meaning.

We chose this example because we, your authors, have very different attitudes toward baseball. For one of us, baseball is a neutral concept. That author can recall attending only one major league game (when a team called the Senators played in Washington, D.C.). If asked to identify famous baseball players, she could probably list only those whose names are associated with candy bars. For the other, baseball has much stronger and more positive meanings. As a child, he played baseball every day of the summer, using flour from the kitchen to mark out a diamond on a homemade playing field. He memorized batting averages and followed every aspect

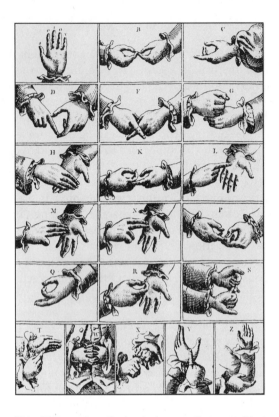

This 18th-century flysheet shows a finger spelling system used to communicate with the deaf. Although gestural, this code is actually digital. Can you think of other verbal codes that are not spoken?

of fellow Oklahoman Mickey Mantle's career. Even today he shows up at the office at the beginning of spring training wearing a Yankees baseball cap. For the two of us the term *baseball* has different connotations, as it does for each of you. There are as many connotations for a word as there are unique experiences with it.

The Importance of Semantic Competence

Mastering the semantics of one's language is important, for no one can communicate competently without an appropriate vocabulary. Peo-

ple who use words incorrectly may talk on for hours without realizing they are conveying messages they never meant.

Lack of semantic competence can also lead to feelings of isolation and rejection. Group membership is often associated with access to special words. If you have ever heard others talk in unintelligible technical terms, you know how incompetent and left out you felt. It's impossible to fit into a professional or social group without mastering the jargon that group favors.

Sensitivity to connotations is also an important part of semantic competence. Many arguments start because one party inadvertently uses a word that has negative connotations for the other. Calling a woman you do not know well "honey" or referring to her as a "girl" are good examples. While some women may not mind, others find this usage belittling. Words like *love* and *commitment* and *responsibility* also carry strong emotional charges. They can cause relational problems if individuals attach different meanings to them. To be fully competent, it is necessary to realize that words call up different reactions in each of us.

SYNTACTIC MEANING: LANGUAGE AT THE LEVEL OF THE UTTERANCE

Of course, words are rarely used in isolation; they usually occur in phrases or sentences. The study of the process by which words are combined and ordered into grammatical sequences is called **syntactics.**

Order as Meaning

It's important to be able to order words appropriately. Had the previous sentence been written, "Important it's words appropriately order to be to able," you would have been confused at the very least. Probably you would have decided that your authors were suffering from some kind of mental disorder. Part of a word's meaning is its relationship to the words that precede and follow it.

Although in English a single word may mean several things, context usually makes its meaning clear. *Port*, for example, means something different in the context of "No, not starboard, you fool! Port!" than it does in the context of "Please don't drop that bottle of priceless vintage port."

Consider the difference between the sentences "The ship sails" and "Ship the sails."[12] The words are the same, but their order differs. Meaning based on word order is called **syntactic meaning.** For a more interpersonal example, consider the two sentences "Sam wants to marry Claudine" and "Claudine wants to marry Sam." Although the words are the same, the meanings are not. And it could make a real difference to both Sam and Claudine whether one or both meanings are intended.

The Importance of Syntactic Competence

Strict rules govern sentence form. If we fail to abide by these rules, most people will react negatively. Syntax is thought to be a mark of social and economic status (which it often is) and also an indication of intellectual ability and moral rectitude (which it definitely is not). Syntax is a product of social learning, not native intelligence. We often believe that people who use "incorrect grammar" (grammar that violates our set of rules) are too "dumb" or "lazy" to use language "the right way," and we let this perception shape our impressions. At the same time, use of so-called incorrect sentence forms among a particular social group can demonstrate the solidarity of group membership. Members of the same social group frequently make the same grammatical mistakes: "We *was* going to her house" instead of "We *were* going . . ." The perceptions attached to syntactic communication determine competence.

PRAGMATIC MEANING: LANGUAGE AT THE LEVEL OF THE SPEECH ACT

In order to understand communication, it is necessary to go beyond the semantic and syntactic levels. Having a good vocabulary and knowing the rules of sentence construction will not guarantee adequate communication. We have to know how to use sentences in actual conversation. **Pragmatics** investigates language as it is used in actual interaction.

Language in Use

People don't generally talk just for the fun of it. When we use language, we use it to accomplish specific goals. The things we intend language to do for us are called speech acts.[13] Examples of **speech acts** are promising, questioning, threatening, praising, declaring, warning, requesting, and so on.

We said earlier that sentences can help us figure out the meanings of words. Speech acts can do the same for sentences. Knowing a sentence's meaning involves knowing its intended speech act. Let's say you've just written a poem. You're not sure how good it is, so you show it to a friend. Your friend reads it, thinks for a moment, and says, "I've never seen anything like it. It's unique." But what does this mean? Puzzling over the syntax and semantics of the sentence won't help you. In order to understand the message, you have to know what your friend was trying to do: compliment you, engage in literary criticism, or weasel out of saying anything at all. To be able to communicate, we must be able to assess the speech acts of others and formulate our own.

CMM: Interpreting and Producing Speech Acts

How do we know what speech acts mean? And how do we know when and how to use them?

A theory called the coordinated management of meaning (CMM for short) helps answer these questions.[14] According to CMM we know how to use language because we follow rules that tell us how to understand and produce speech acts. There are two kinds of rules in CMM theory: **constitutive rules,** which tell us how to recognize speech acts, and **regulative rules,** which identify, in a given context, the speech acts that are appropriate and inappropriate. Before looking at examples of these rules, let's consider how context affects communication behavior.

CMM theory tells us we have different rules for different contexts. What is appropriate in a heart-to-heart conversation is not appropriate at a formal dinner party. What is effective in showing a boss how responsible you are will not be effective in impressing a date. What works at home may not work at school. To communicate effectively, people must take into account the situation, their relationship, their self-images, and relevant cultural rules. Figure 4.3 shows the contexts that CMM identifies as important. The top portion of the figure lists the CMM contexts. As you can see, contexts are nested within one another, with higher levels including lower ones. Let's start near the bottom with the speech act. Speech acts make sense only when we understand the episode in which they occur. An **episode** is made up of a set of speech acts that fit together naturally. If you were to ask communicators, "What are you doing?" their answer would name the episode they're involved in. "Going for pizza," "shooting pool," "buying groceries," "having a barroom brawl," and "closing a big deal" are examples of episodes. Clearly, we expect different speech acts in different episodes — what is appropriate for the barroom may not be for the boardroom. If we know the episode in which an utterance occurs, we can fix its speech act more easily than if we hear it out of context. We'll also know which additional speech acts are appropriate and which would be out of place.

Another important context is the **relationship** between communicators. If you were to

ask communicators, "Who are you to each other?" their answer would identify their relationship: student-teacher, husband-wife, boss-worker, and so on. Relationships determine episodes. Episodes such as "discussing one's fears and hopes," "showing affection," and "borrowing money and clothes" are usually appropriate for the relationship we call best friends. But they are not particularly likely if the relationship is professor-student. If we know a speaker's relationship to us, we are likely to understand his or her meanings. We will also be in a better position to do or say the correct thing.

The next context is **life script,** or your sense of self. It answers the question "Who am I or who do I wish to be?" For example, a person at peace with nature and the universe enters into relationships, episodes, and speech acts that differ from those of an executive determined to make it to the top at all costs. The ways these two individuals interpret the world and the acts they consider legitimate are likely to be diametrically opposed. If we know who someone is, we're in a better position to understand that person's meanings and respond effectively to him or her. Finally, **cultural patterns** affect all other levels, since the groups we belong to determine the nature and function of talk.

Using Pragmatic Rules in Interaction

How does all of this work in practice? Assume you hear the words "You look terrible today" and you want to know what the speaker meant. To interpret the speaker's intended speech act, you must consult your set of constitutive rules. To pick the right rule, you must use contextual cues; words have different meanings in different contexts.

If the statement is uttered by a physician in the episode of "physical examination," you will probably decide to count the words as a medical diagnosis. If it is uttered by a friend in an episode of "joking around," you will interpret

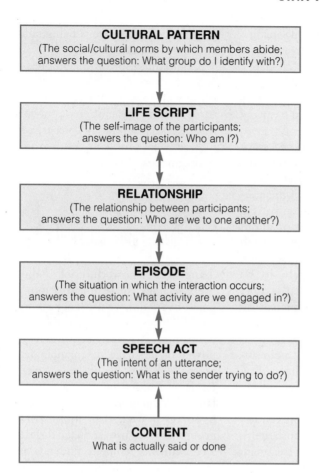

FIGURE 4-3
Levels of hierarchical meaning in CMM theory

	(Situation 1)	(Situation 2)	(Situation 3)
Cultural Pattern:	Middle-Class American	Middle-Class American	Middle-Class American
Life Script:	Educated Professional	Wild & Crazy Guy	Cold-blooded Egoist
Relationship:	Doctor/Patient	Pals	Rivals
Episode:	Medical Exam	Kidding Around	Business Meeting
Speech Act:	Diagnosis	Joke	Put-down
Content:	**"You look terrible today"**		

Each level adds meaning to levels above and below. Communication makes sense only in reference to the context in which it occurs.

it as the first move in a game of joking insults. Finally, if it is uttered in public by a subordinate who dislikes you, it may be seen as a "challenge to authority." Over the course of our lives, we build up a repertoire of interpretive rules that help us understand communication in a variety of contexts.

To respond to any comment, it is necessary to consult a regulative rule. Regulative rules tell you what speech acts are appropriate given your goals and your understanding of the context. In the case of the physical examination, your goal is probably to get information about your health. Your regulative rule set will tell you that insulting the doctor ("You think *I* look bad? Have *you* looked in a mirror lately, doc?") or asserting your authority ("That's quite enough. I'll see you in my office in half an hour") are not appropriate. Of course, these speech acts might be exactly the right thing to do if you are just joking around or if your authority is questioned. Your rule for the medical episode may read, "Given this context and my desire to get advice from my doctor, the proper speech act for me to perform is a polite request for further information." You then translate this speech act into something like "What treatment do you suggest?"

The Importance of Pragmatic Competence

Communicating appropriately isn't easy. Embarrassment results when contexts are misinterpreted or rule sets are inadequate. If you have ever burst into a conversation with some trivial remark, only to realize that you interrupted a serious discussion, you know how important it is to label episodes correctly. If you have ever come on too strong too soon with someone, you know how tricky reading relationships can be. If you have ever interpreted an innocent remark as a threat to self, you have seen the way life scripts affect perception. Part of mastering

pragmatic competence is being able to identify contextual levels accurately.

Communication is a complex, rule-bound process. If we learn to do it well, our relationships will be easy and rewarding. If we have trouble with pragmatic rules, the world can be a hostile place. In fact, it's been argued that many interpersonal problems result from differences in pragmatics.

Language, Power, and Politics

Language is a powerful tool. It allows us to express feelings, share information, and achieve goals. Every day we use language to control our worlds. But, if we're not careful, language can control us. In this section we examine the power of language to emancipate and to oppress. We'll begin by discussing one of the earliest formulations of the relationship between language, thought, and action, the Sapir-Whorf hypothesis. We'll then look at how different groups learn to use language differently and, as a consequence, come to understand themselves and their actions in unique ways. Finally, we'll look at some recent theories that emphasize the political dimensions of language use.

LINGUISTIC DETERMINISM: THE SAPIR-WHORF HYPOTHESIS

The influence of language on thought has been strongly articulated by two linguists, Edward Sapir and Benjamin Lee Whorf.[15] Their analysis of the effects of language on cognition, the **Sapir-Whorf hypothesis,** has two important parts. The first, **linguistic determinism,** says that language determines the way we interpret the world. In the words of Sapir, "we see and hear and otherwise experience very largely as we do because the language habits of our community predispose certain choices of interpretation."[16] The second part of their hypothesis, **linguistic relativity,** follows from the first. If language determines thought, then speakers of different languages will experience the world differently. Thought is relative to language.

Let's look at some evidence for this hypothesis. If you have studied a foreign language, you know that other languages often make distinctions that English doesn't. In English, for example, we simply say *you* when we want to talk to someone directly. In Spanish there are two forms of you, a polite form (*usted*) to be used with older persons, strangers, or those of high status, and a familiar form (*tu*). In Spanish it is grammatically necessary to mark that point in a relationship when participants change from being mere acquaintances to friends.

Not only do different languages tell us how to talk to one another, they also specify what to talk about. Different languages recognize different categories of experience. The words for colors are a classic example. In English there are seven basic colors in the spectrum (purple, indigo, blue, green, yellow, orange, and red). In Bassa, a Liberian language, there are only two: *hui* (which includes our purple, indigo, blue, and green) and *ziza* (which covers yellow, orange, and red).[17]

Another frequently cited example is the fact that Eskimos have many more words for snow than we do. These words enable them to talk about distinctions most non-Eskimos could not perceive. This doesn't mean that Liberians couldn't learn to make fine-color distinctions or that southerners could not learn to see different kinds of snow. It only means that it will be harder to do these things. Without a name for something, it takes longer to distinguish that thing from other things, and the distinctions are less stable.[18] Both the color and snow examples illustrate how our language separates things that are continuous in nature. The color spectrum is just that, a spectrum, not a collection of separate things. As Whorf tells us:

English terms, like "sky, hill, swamp," persuade us to regard some elusive aspect of nature's endless variety as a distinct THING, almost like a table or chair. Thus English and similar tongues lead us to think of the universe as a collection of rather distinct objects and events corresponding to words. Indeed, this is the implicit picture of classical physics and astronomy — that the universe is essentially a collection of detached objects of different sizes.[19]

Some American Indian languages preserve the unity of nature more fully than English. Sentences in these languages don't consist of nouns and verbs. If, for example, an English speaker were to see a light flash in the summer sky, he or she would say, "The light flashed." The action that took place would be indicated by a verb, while that which caused the action would be indicated by a separate noun and article. The Hopi speaker, however, would not divide what was seen into two parts. To the Hopi, the flashing and the light are one and are indicated by one simple "verb," *rehpi.*[20]

The Sapir-Whorf hypothesis tells us that English speakers don't normally see the world the same way Hopi speakers see it. While we may not be complete prisoners of our language, we are deeply affected by its structure. Every language encourages and aids its speakers in some endeavors while making other kinds of thoughts and actions more difficult. Box 4.1 illustrates how the Western Apache use language to comfort and counsel one another.

LANGUAGE, THOUGHT, AND ACTION: LANGUAGE AND NAMING

The Sapir-Whorf hypothesis argues that language shapes our understanding of the world. The results of this process can be both positive and negative. Language allows us to imagine new worlds and to reflect upon our own

BOX **4.1**

Speaking with Names: An Apache Language Ritual

For those of us who study interpersonal communication, language becomes most interesting when we see people using it to affect one another. Language is important not becauses it is an immensely complex abstract system, but because people use it to build interpersonal bonds. In an article titled "Speaking with Names," anthropologist Keith Basso describes how the Western Apaches of east-central Arizona use a specialized form of speaking to comfort, advise, and support one another.

Basso begins by describing the circumstances under which he first became aware of the language ritual known as speaking with names. A number of friends are seated together in the shade on a hot and dusty late afternoon. Present with Basso are Emily and Louise, Lola and her husband Robert, and their old yellow dog, Clifford. Louise is upset because her younger brother has become ill and has been taken to the hospital. Adding to her distress is the fact that earlier in the month her brother had inadvertently stepped on a snakeskin. Instead of seeking the services of a "snake medicine person" to perform a ritual cleansing, her brother laughed off the incident, thus showing disrespect for traditional teachings and putting himself in some danger of illness or death. Although it is not usual for the Western Apache to disclose personal details like this about their relatives, Louise has mentioned her fears. The following occurs in response. Lola is the first to speak, saying, "It happened at line of white rocks, extending upward and out, at this very place." After a long pause, Emily adds, "Yes. It happened at whiteness spreads out descending

to water, at this very place." After another pause, Lola breaks in, "Truly. It happened at trail extends across a long red ridge with alder trees, at this very place." Louise laughs softly as Robert, and then Lola, add, "Pleasantness and goodness will be forthcoming." Louise, much comforted, ends the interaction by turning to Clifford and asking, "My younger brother is foolish, isn't he dog?"

To most of us, the meaning of this bit of talk is puzzling. We understand the language but cannot fathom its social meaning. All we can tell is that its meaning was clear to the participants and its effects on Louise profoundly comforting. In an effort to understand the web of social understandings in which this conversation is embedded, Basso turned to a native informant, Lola. From her account he was able to piece together the meanings hidden below the words and sentences that had been uttered.

Lola began by explaining, "We gave that woman [i.e., Louise] pictures to work on in her mind. We didn't speak too much to her. We didn't hold her down. That way she could travel in her mind. . . . We gave her clear pictures with place names. So her mind went to those places, standing in front of them as our ancestors did long ago." To understand what Lola means, it's necessary to understand the importance of place names in Apache storytelling. Western Apache narratives are "spatially anchored" to specific locations, and these locations are labeled with descriptive place names. In form, place names provide not only a way of locating a place, but a point from which to view it. When speakers hear a place name, they imagine themselves traveling to that place and standing at the exact location as did their ancestors who first described that place. Place names evoke with surprising power and clarity all the ancestral events associated with a location. When Apache people practice "speaking with names" they are recommending that their listeners recall an ancestral story and apply it to their personal problems.

When Lola mentioned the first place name, she was trying to do a number of things. First,

thing of a risk, for the tale associated with it was off-color and humorous, concerning a young man who had to walk around clutching his crotch after he became infected because he violated a sexual taboo. Fortunately, Lola's strategy worked, and Louise laughed as she pictured the young man. Afterwards, Louise commented, "[The boy] was impulsive, He didn't think right. Then he got scared. Then he was made well again with medicine. . . . I've heard that story often, but it's always funny to see that boy holding on to himself, so shy and embarrassed (p. 240)." Robert and Lola, recognizing Louise's change in mood, then spoke to make the message of all these stories explicit by saying, "Pleasantness and goodness will be forthcoming." Louise closed the conversation by addressing the dog Clifford with a gentle criticism of her brother, a comment that told the others, in effect, "Nothing more need be said; you were polite and thoughtful not to criticize my brother, and I thank you for comforting me."

Basso's analysis is fascinating because it shows how much pragmatic meaning can be conveyed by a simple conversation. The ritual of speaking with names performed many functions: it produced a mental image of a location, evoked prior stories, affirmed the value of ancestral wisdom, displayed tactful attention to the face of the participants, signaled charitable concern, offered practical advice, transformed distressing thoughts, and healed Louise's wounded spirits. This example shows us how important a sensitive and caring use of language can be. Basso concludes, "Such powerful moments may not be commonplace in Western Apache speech communities, but they are certainly common enough—and when they occur, as on that hot and dusty day at Cibecue, robust worlds of meaning come vibrantly alive (p. 244)."

she was avoiding potentially embarrassing criticism of Louise's brother. She was also shifting attention to Louise herself and showing sympathy and concern. In addition, she was asking Louise to recall a particular story associated with the place name she chose. The situation that had happened at "line of white rocks extends upward and out" concerned a young girl who, while collecting firewood, slipped and was bitten by a snake. When her arm became badly swollen, a curing ceremony was performed. The girl then returned to her grandmother, affirming that she now knew how to "live right." When Basso asked Louise how she had reacted to the place name, Louise reported that her mind had instantly traveled to that spot and pictured vivid images of the girl. Louise had connected the girl in the story to her brother. Something bad had happened to the girl because she had ceased to think properly, but she was saved and learned from her mistake.

Emily's place name evoked a similar story concerning a young boy who was sick for a long time because he failed to follow ritual demands but who got better and remembered the lesson all his life. Again, Louise received intense images, reporting that she could hear the central character as he talked to his own children. The third place name, mentioned by Lola, was some-

SOURCE: Keith H. Basso, "'Speaking with Names': Language and Landscape Among the Western Apache," in George E. Marcus, ed., *Rereading Cultural Anthropology* (Durham, N. C.: Duke University Press, 1992), pp.220–51.

behaviors, but it also causes us to distort reality, create stereotypes, and lie. Let's consider some examples of how language affects everyday thought and action.

According to the Sapir-Whorf hypothesis, language allows us to make certain aspects of reality significant by naming them. Conversely, it allows us to ignore unimportant parts of reality by not naming them. Naming has important implications because it is easier to notice and think about a thing that has been named. Consider, for example, two terms that did not exist as part of our language until recently: *sexual harrassment* and *date rape*. Although the behaviors associated with these terms have existed for a long time, because they were not named they were not recognized. They lacked legitimacy, and their victims had no way of defining what had happened to them. Once the terms entered our language, it became possible to discuss these problems and work to put an end to them.[21]

In addition to naming things, language also gives things value. Many years ago, a group of theorists called symbolic interactionists pointed out that words consist of action plans. A word not only tells us that something exists but suggests how to think and what to do about it. Consider the object we refer to as a cat. To some it is a *pet*, to some it is merely *food*, and to still others it is a variety of *vermin*. The way we talk about it determines how we think about it and how we act toward it. Or, consider some of the common terms that refer to women: *babe, broad, lady, girl,* and *woman* have very different connotations and call for very different actions. The behaviors we are likely to use with a *broad* are very different than those we are likely to use with a *young lady* or with a *woman*.

GROUP MEMBERSHIP AND LANGUAGE USE: DISCOURSE AND IDENTITY

Our language habits affect not only how we see the world and how we act toward others, but how we view ourselves as well. People who belong to different groups develop different language habits, and these habits have important consequences for the way they think about themselves and the ways they live their lives. Gender and class are two groups associated with different styles of discourse. Box 4.2 gives an example of how both these factors affect language use.

Social Class and Discourse

British sociologist Basil Bernstein studied the way class membership is related to language usage.[22] He found that working-class language employs shorter, simpler, and more conventionalized grammatical forms, while middle-class syntax exhibits more variety and complexity. Middle-class speakers make more complex grammatical decisions; Bernstein refers to their code as the **elaborated code.** Working-class speakers tend to use grammar in more rigidly determined ways, employing commonly shared forms; for this reason he calls their language code the **restricted code.**

More interesting are pragmatic differences. Bernstein believes that the primary purpose of elaborated codes is to convey information. Elaborated-code speakers try to use language precisely, being careful to fill in all of the details a listener might need. Restricted-code users, on the other hand, emphasize the social aspects of language, using it as a tool for building social identity and binding the individual to the group. They assume listeners don't need to have background information spelled out. The following dialogue is a good example of a restricted code.[23] Gary and George are friends who are discussing their plans for the evening.

GARY: How's about Trucker's tonight?

GEORGE: A little stick, eh?

GARY: Why not?

GEORGE: Okay, mine or yours?

GARY: Oh no! Every man for himself . . . wife, you know.

GEORGE: (*to his new neighbor*) Why don't you come along too?

NEIGHBOR: (*with no idea of what he is getting himself into*) Sounds great!

Although our original source didn't give a direct translation into elaborated code, we can imagine that it would go something like this:

GARY: How would you like to go to our favorite country-western bar tonight, the one called Trucker's?

GEORGE: Do you mean to play pool?

GARY: Yes, why not?

GEORGE: OK, let's go together. Should we take your car or mine?

GARY: Oh no, we'd better go separately. My wife wants me to come home early tonight.

GEORGE: (*to the neighbor*) Why don't you come along too?

NEIGHBOR: (*understanding completely*) Sounds great!

As you can see, restricted codes are not well designed for use with outsiders. They rely heavily on shared assumptions and expectations, and they encourage social solidarity. They're often found in groups who are, or want to be, set apart from society at large. Prison inmates and adolescents are examples cited by Bernstein. The "dorm talk" college students use with roommates and friends may be another.

Elaborated codes, on the other hand, do little to emphasize group identity. They encourage a more distant approach to communication. While there is a correlation between code and class, code switching can and does occur. Bernstein's point is that the economic and social conditions associated with class make it likely that classes will use language differently much of the time.

Because of these differences, members of different classes may devalue one another's speech.

To restricted-code users, those with elaborated codes may seem cold and stilted. Restricted-code users may also feel embarrassed about their language, letting elaborated-code users define the value of their talk. One of the reasons Teamsterville men are so silent is that they view speaking as difficult and their own language style as "substandard." To elaborated-code users, restricted-code speakers may seem illogical and overly emotional, even, perhaps, uneducated or unintelligent. These differences can cause problems in cross-class communication. Think, for example, of how code differences might affect the relationship between a working-class child and a middle-class teacher.

Gender and Discourse

Gender also plays a part in language use. There have been many studies of male and female language patterns.[24] We will return to this topic in more detail in Chapter 7, where we discuss gender roles. For now, we will merely point out a few of the differences found in the kinds of discourse used by men and women.

First, men and women seem to have different vocabularies, in part because social rules focus their attention on different areas of experience. Women, for example, are reported to make finer color distinctions than men, while men have greater mechanical-technical vocabularies. It has also been suggested that women are more likely to use words such as *lovely, adorable, precious,* and *cute,* adjectives that some feel are trivial. Finally, women have been shown to use less intense words to express themselves.[25]

Second, there also appear to be syntactic differences. Women tend to use more tag endings (fragments such as "right?" or "OK?" tacked onto the end of sentences), qualifiers (words like *maybe* and *perhaps*), and disclaimers (sentences that ward off criticisms, like "Well, I may be wrong, but . . ."). While the use of these forms makes women seem more polite, it also makes them seem unsure of themselves.

BOX **4.2**

Talking Tough in Teamsterville: Male Role Enactment in an Urban Community

Talk is not valued the same in every community. Some cultures encourage talk while others inhibit it. But all develop strict rules about how to talk. In Teamsterville (the label for a blue-collar neighborhood in Chicago) talk is carefully regulated. The men in Teamsterville grow up with circumscribed ideas about the value of talk. Let's look at these ideas.

Teamsterville men know that talking in certain situations will cast doubt on their manliness. For example, self-disclosure or serious talk with

women or children is not considered manly. Responding to an insult or to insubordination by talking it out is definitely bad form. The Teamsterville man demeans himself if he responds to a challenge verbally rather than physically. Teamsterville men also avoid talking to status superiors. Talk with authority figures or strangers is mediated through professional speakers like local precinct captains, Catholic parish priests, or union stewards.

When does the Teamsterville man feel free to converse? When he is with his male friends. The place most appropriate for speaking is the street, sidewalk, and, to a lesser extent, porch.

Teamsterville men devalue talk in cases where other men would value it. Compare Teamsterville rules with those followed by white-collar suburbanites or black Americans in urban ghettos. In both of these cultures, being verbal is considered an advantage. The ghetto dweller takes pride in his ability to play word games like the dozens (see Box 13.1). The white suburbanite believes

---

Finally, there are pragmatic differences. Men's talk has been described as more direct and goal-directed than women's, while women's talk is often more polite and expressive. Of course, not everyone fits the stereotype. Traditionally, however, women have been taught to be more polite and indirect than men, while men's speech has been "more literal, direct, and to the point. It employs stronger statements and forms that tend to press compliance, agreement, or belief on the listener."[26]

Social and economic factors put varying pressures on us to use language to adapt to our assigned roles. As Barbara and Gene Eakins point out, "The damage comes when women and men cannot readily switch from one style to the other to meet the demands of the situation."[27] The damage also comes when men and women let the terms of their discourse define who they are, and when one style is considered superior to the other. As we have seen, restricted codes may be devalued, with the effect

being that restricted-code users feel uncomfortable expressing themselves in front of outsiders. The same may be true of women's language style. Feminist theorist Cheris Kramarae argues that women may sometimes express themselves with more difficulty than do men, simply because they have trouble fitting their own experiences into acceptable language forms or feel that what they have to say is not as important as what a man might have to say.[28]

Language, Domination, and Freedom

If language is so closely tied to thought and action, then it follows that whoever controls language controls thought and action. This position has been argued by a number of scholars who refer to themselves as **critical theorists.** They point out that whenever we choose words, we choose points of view as well. This choice may be an unconscious acceptance of the as-

It might be tempting for some of us to consider Teamsterville men as linguistically deprived. That conclusion, however, misses the point. All of us are constrained by cultural norms for using language. All of us feel comfortable speaking in some situations and with some people, and uncomfortable elsewhere. The meaning and value of communication is set down for us by our culture.

SOURCE: Gerry Philipsen, "Speaking 'Like a Man' in Teamsterville: Cultural Patterns of Role Enactment in an Urban Neighborhood," *Quarterly Journal of Speech* 61 (1975): 13–22.

that talking things out is an appropriate way of building relationships.

And the places for talk also differ by culture. Talk in an upper-middle-class suburb takes place in private, sheltered areas such as living rooms or backyards. Visitors are usually from outside a ten-block radius. Adults don't socialize on front porches or in front yards.

ADDITIONAL READINGS

Hymens, Dell. "Models of the Interaction of Language and Social Life." In *Directions in Sociolinguistics: The Ethnography of Communication.* John J. Gumberz and Dell Hymes, eds. New York: Holt, Rinehart & Winston, 1972.
Philipsen, Gerry. "Places for Speaking in Teamsterville." *Quarterly Journal of Speech* 62 (1976): 16–25.

sumptions that lie within our class or culture or it may be a conscious attempt to manipulate. Metaphors are one example. Compare the following two newspaper headlines: "Flood of immigrants pours into town" and "neighbors from across the border join hands with local business people." The effect is entirely different. The first portrays the presence of the immigrants as dangerous and potentially disastrous; the second represents them as a positive addition to the community. The headline writer may be unaware of the political implications of his or her word choices, but they are there nonetheless. The use of euphemisms is yet another example. When a military commander advocates using a "clean bomb" with a minimum of "collateral damage," it's easy to forget that he or she is talking about a bomb that is capable of wiping out whole cities and that the "collateral" damage being discussed is human life.

One of the things that happens when one group controls language is that the experiences of other groups may be ignored or devalued, either overtly (as when racist or sexist terms are common) or covertly (where the devaluation is more subtle.) Critical theorists believe that traditional ways of using language reflect and validate the experiences of dominant groups. One example of this line of reasoning is the feminist argument that traditional academic discourse values logic, abstract thought, argument, and convergent problem-solving, qualities more often associated with male experience than with female experience. Such discourse has little space for the more "female" qualities of emotional expression, concern for process, modesty, and caring.[29] When a subordinate group cannot find a way to express itself in the terms dictated by the dominant group, critical theorists say that group has been silenced. **Muted-group theorists** have suggested that women often feel less comfortable in public situations than do men. Women therefore "watch what they say and translate what they are feeling and thinking

Through symbols we can refer to the fantastic and mythical as well as the mundane.

(Detail of an imperial court robe, Chinese, T'ung Chih period, 1862–74)

into male terms. When masculine and feminine meanings and expressions conflict, the masculine tends to win out because of the dominance of males in society, and the result is that women are muted."[30]

Of course, not all language is harmful or oppressive. It is through language, after all, that we can discuss and critique these problems. Language can be reformed, and newer and fairer modes of expression can be developed. The efforts made to rid our language of sexist bias are a case in point.

Avoiding Sexist Language

Derogatory attitudes toward men and women can easily slip into language. In fact, it is often difficult to follow normal patterns of talk without reinforcing sexual stereotypes. In this section we'll look at a few of the many examples of sexism in our language and offer some guidelines for communicating in a more fair and equal way. It's important to keep in mind that this analysis looks at just one kind of oppressive language. Racist and heterosexist language patterns also bear the same kind of examination and analysis.

Let's begin with occupations. Occupations tend to be semantically classed as male or female. This is shown by the fact that when a person of the "wrong" sex enters a given occupation, we feel the need to mark that fact linguistically. A woman can be described as a "nurse" with no difficulty, but her male counterpart is usually referred to as a "male nurse." We indicate our surprise in the same way when we find a woman doing a "man's job." Thus, people talk about the new "lady mayor" or report they are seeing a "woman doctor."

Another kind of gender marker is the -ess or -ette diminutive form used in constructions like authoress, poetess, or sculptress. This usage often connotes that the individual being described is not as competent or powerful as her male counterpart. This form singles out women as special cases, as odd exceptions to the rule. We take a poet seriously, but there is something slightly humorous about a poetess.

Terms of address often contain subtle inequalities. It is quite common for a woman to be addressed by belittling terms in public contexts. Clerks or salespersons will much more frequently call a woman "honey," "sweetie," or "dear," than they will a man, who is most often addressed as "sir." And have you ever wondered why the marriage ceremony pronounces a couple "man and wife" rather than "husband and wife"? Wife, after all, is a relational term that defines the bride in terms of her new role, while man is an absolute term. To see this more clearly, consider how meaningless it would be to say, "I now pronounce you man and woman."

What are we to make of the fact that there are more than ten times as many sexual terms for females as for males, and that many of these terms tend to have negative connotations? Barbara and Gene Eakins tell us that "for women, the act defines the person: as slut, nympho, hooker, trick, whore, and so on."[31] This tendency to talk about women in physical terms is also reflected in our propensity to describe women's physical appearance more than men's. When Vice President Dan Quayle was nominated, the headline didn't read "Blonde cutie gets convention nod," but such ludicrous descriptions are often given of women. Eakins and Eakins cite a few examples:

> A woman running for political office is described as being "a petite grandmother with the figure of a twenty-year-old"; a lawyer being interviewed about her views on the Equal Rights Amendment is described as "well put together"; an artist exhibiting her paintings is portrayed as having a "low husky laugh" and "soft grey eyes"; an athlete is referred to as "a brown-eyed cutie." The women described are not candidates for Miss America or models. . . . They are women functioning in politics, law, the arts, and athletics.[32]

Another important way in which language discriminates is through use of the generic "man" forms. On the one hand, when we talk of "mankind" or say that "each person should examine his conscience," we supposedly mean both men and women. On the other hand, as Eakins and Eakins suggest, when someone uses masculine generics "in a general sense and another interprets the word as specifically masculine, there is a miscommunication and females are unintentionally excluded from the idea or statement."[33] Language reflects attitudes toward gender in many other ways. We refer you to Robin Lakoff's classic article "Language and Woman's Place" for an excellent overview.[34] We are not arguing here that language by itself causes sexism — the roots of sexism run much deeper than that. What we are suggesting is that

sexist language legitimizes and reinforces sexist thinking and that, without realizing it, we often talk in ways that are insulting and offensive to others. To avoid sexist speech, check yourself against the guidelines for nonsexist language given in Table 4.1.

Skill Building: Initiating Conversations

Throughout this chapter we have commented on the importance of becoming more competent in all aspects of language. To communicate effectively one must master semantics, syntactics, and pragmatics. While all are important, pragmatics probably plays the key role in interpersonal effectiveness. Language becomes important when we use it to make contact with others. And one of the best ways we make contact is through everyday conversation. Making casual small talk is not a trivial pursuit. It allows us to initiate and maintain relationships, to find out more about the world and ourselves. As noted previously, when a conversation goes well, we feel in tune with the world; when it goes badly, we feel awkward and isolated. In this section we'll look at a special conversational skill: knowing how to initiate conversation.

Talking with friends and colleagues is usually easy. We know and trust each other, and we've already worked out many of the rules of our relational cultures. Talking with strangers is often more difficult precisely because we don't know the rules and so don't know exactly how to coordinate our conversational moves. When we strike up a conversation with a stranger, we are attempting to change our relationship to that stranger, to move from the purely public end of the public/private continuum to the private end. Because a lot is at stake, we may, from time to time, become nervous and tongue-tied. A small amount of apprehension in talking to strangers

TABLE 4.1   Guidelines for the use of nonsexist language

Publishers urge writers to avoid the use of sexist language. Below is a summary of some of the concerns of the editors at Prentice-Hall and the examples they use to illustrate these concerns. In proofing a manuscript, authors are encouraged to ask themselves the following questions:

1. Are women and men described in similar ways or do the adjectives and modifiers used for women consistently create a negative impression?

Biased	**Unbiased**
Though a woman, she ran the business efficiently.	She ran the business efficiently.
Mrs. Acton, a statuesque blonde, is Joe Granger's assistant.	Jan Acton is Joe Granger's assistant.

2. Are people treated as human, or are all the portrayals done in terms of gender roles, giving readers the impression that only men do X and only women do Y?

Biased	**Unbiased**
Current tax regulations allow a head of household to deduct for the support of a wife and children.	Current tax regulations allow a head of household to deduct for the support of a spouse and children.
The line manager is responsible for the productivity of the department; his foremen, for the day-to-day work of the girls on the line.	The line manager is responsible for the productivity of the department; the supervisors, for that of the workers on the line.

3. Have you avoided the use of the generic masculine pronoun?

Biased	**Unbiased**
A person's facial expression does not always reveal his true feelings.	Facial expression is not always an indicator of a person's true feelings.
Sometimes a doctor will see his patients only in a hospital.	Sometimes a doctor will see patients only in a hospital.
The typical child does his homework right after school.	Most children do their homework right after school.

4. Have you avoided the use of the word *man* to mean all people and the use of *-man* words in general?

Biased	**Unbiased**
mankind	human race, people, humankind, humanity
man-made	manufactured, made, synthetic, artificial
the common man, the man in the street, the layman	the average citizen, the layperson, the nonspecialist

5. Have you used parallel treatment?

Biased	**Unbiased**
The men in the office took the girls to lunch.	The men in the office took the women to lunch.
man and wife	husband and wife
co-ed	student
the men and the ladies	the men and the women, the gentlemen and the ladies

6. Have you used gender-free titles?

Biased	**Unbiased**
chairman	chair, chairperson
congressman	member of Congress, representative
cleaning lady	cleaner
fireman	firefighter
mailman	mail carrier, letter carrier

is natural. Too much may signal the condition of communication apprehension, a kind of long-lasting interpersonal stage fright. People with high apprehension can overcome their fears if they seek help. Communication professors can often recommend a treatment program. Of course, you don't have to be a high-apprehensive to feel awkward in some interpersonal speaking situations — almost everyone has experienced periods of not knowing what to say. If you are like these people, the following guidelines should help make you a more confident conversationalist.

INITIATING TALK

Let's begin by looking at a hypothetical conversation between two strangers, Stacey and Stuart. As the scene opens, Stacey is trying to work up the courage to talk to Stuart.

STACEY: (I'm so bad at this kind of thing. I never know what to say. I hope I don't say something stupid.) Hi. Umm, uh, it's really raining cats and dogs out, isn't it? (Oh gosh. I can't believe I said "cats and dogs." He'll think I'm a complete idiot.)

STUART: (*smiles*) Yes. It never rains like this where I'm from. (She seems nice. I wonder if she's new here too.)

STACEY: Well, yes, it rains a lot here, especially in the rainy season. (I have no idea what to say next. All I want to do is get out of here.) Umm. (*long pause*) I have to go. Bye.

STUART: Bye. (What just happened?)

What did happen? Stacey made some simple mistakes that could have been avoided: Her self-talk was negative, she failed to pick up on free information provided by Stuart, and her conversational closing was awkward and abrupt. Below we'll explain these mistakes and look at

what Stacey could have done to turn this conversation around. Stacey believed that the conversation would be a disaster, and it was. Her expectations made the outcome inevitable, and the outcome only served to reinforce Stacey's view of herself as a poor conversationalist. If she wants to improve her conversational skills, her first step must be to change her expectations. Stacey's experience would have been quite different had she said to herself, "He looks nice. Since he's all alone, he'll probably be glad to talk to someone. If he is, I may make a new friend. If not, it's not the end of the world. At least I'll have tried." Like Stacey, we should *begin by relaxing and by viewing conversation in realistic, positive terms.*

Finding a Topic

Conversations may end before they begin for lack of a topic. Finding a topic, however, is really the easiest part of engaging in small talk. Most people don't expect a brilliant or original opening; they simply want a topic that can act as a springboard for further talk. Stacy's choice of the weather, while not highly creative, was not so bad. Experts in the art of conversation suggest there are three basic kinds of topics you can talk about: yourself, the other person, or the situation. In general, the latter is the best place to start.[35] Here are some examples of situationally generated topics:

(*in a health club*) Do you use the stairmaster often? What's the best program for a beginner?

(*in a classroom*) What have you heard about this class? Why did you sign up?

(*in a supermarket*) I saw you testing the watermelons for freshness. How can you tell if a melon's ripe?

(*in a private home*) I've been noticing your family photos. They're excellent. Did you take them yourself?

Most environments will suggest a topic, but if they don't the other person will. Here are some examples of topics based on what the other person is doing, wearing, or carrying.

I notice you're carrying a communication book. Have you taken interpersonal communication? What do you think of it?

Did you get your T-shirt in Beijing? What do the Chinese characters mean? When were you there?

I liked your comment in class today. What do you think people could do to conserve resources? Should the government be more involved?

I've been looking for a place to get my hair cut. Your cut is great, did you get it around here?

The third possibility, talking about yourself, should be used only in moderation. It's easier to interest others in talking about themselves than in talking about you.

We can sum up this discussion by suggesting a second guideline: *to find a topic, look to the situation or to the other person.*

Asking Questions

In the examples we've given so far, we've used questions. Asking someone else a question is one of the best ways to start up a conversation. Of course, questions should be used in moderation. You certainly don't want to make the other person feel he or she is under interrogation. Nevertheless, a single well-thought-out question is often a good starting point.

All questions are not equal. The perfect conversational question is one that is interesting and involving to the other without seeming intrusive. In general, open-ended rather than closed-ended questions are preferred. Closed-ended questions ask the respondent to choose a specific response. They usually ask for a one- or two-word answer, for example, "Do you like it here?" "Where are you from?" "How many miles do you jog?" Open-ended questions al-low the respondent free reign in answering and usually call for more elaboration, for example, "Why do you like it here?" "What was it like growing up in Philadelphia?" "How did you get involved in jogging?" The latter questions are more involving than the former. Thus, our third guideline for better conversation is *find an involving and interesting open-ended question to ask your partner.*

USING FREE INFORMATION DURING CONVERSATION

A good conversation doesn't stop after one question and one answer. A good conversation flows from one topic to another. An excellent way to get this to happen is to become aware of and use free information. **Free information** is extra information contained in a response, information that can suggest additional topics. In our example, Stuart provided free information to Stacey when he mentioned, "it never rains like this where I'm from." He was, in fact, telling her that he was new to the area and giving her a hint about where the conversation could go. Unfortunately, Stacey did not pick up on this information. If she had, they could have discussed their hometowns, their childhoods, and perhaps even places where they would like to live in the future.

It's important to listen carefully for free information. It is also important to help your conversational partners out by providing them with free information during your turn at talk. If a stranger asks you why you signed up for a class, you should go beyond a minimal response like "it fit my schedule" or "it sounded interesting." Better responses would be "because I'm working at two different jobs, my schedule is pretty tight. I like to schedule all my classes before noon" or "I'm a physical therapy major so learning to communicate effectively is pretty important, and the class sounded interesting." These responses can lead to long conversations on jobs and majors.

CLOSING CONVERSATIONS

The final step in carrying on a good conversation is to know how to close it gracefully. We have cultural expectations for conversational endings. If these are violated, the closing seems awkward and abrupt. Mark Knapp and his colleagues have pointed out that a good conversational closing does three things: (1) It signals inaccessibility by letting the other know that the conversation is nearing an end; (2) it signals supportiveness by showing appreciation for the conversation and hope for renewed contact; and (3) it summarizes the main topics of the interaction.[36] A good closing might go as follows: "I've got to go soon or I'll be late for work. I really enjoyed getting to talk to you about the music industry. If you'd like to hear my tapes, why don't you come by next Thursday. See you soon. Bye." Whether or not the relationship continues in the future, a closing such as this allows both parties to leave feeling good about themselves and their communication.

Process to Performance

REVIEW TERMS

The following is a list of major concepts introduced in this chapter. The page where the concept is first mentioned is listed in parentheses.

analogic code   (88)
digital code   (90)
symbol   (90)
semantics   (93)
denotative meaning   (93)

connotative meaning   (93)
syntactics   (94)
syntactic meaning   (95)
pragmatics   (95)
speech act   (95)
constitutive rule   (96)
regulative rule   (96)
episode   (96)
relationship   (96)
life script   (96)
cultural pattern   (96)
Sapir-Whorf hypothesis   (98)
linguistic determinism   (98)
linguistic relativity   (99)
elaborated code   (102)
restricted code   (102)
critical theorists   (104)
muted-group theorists   (105)
free information   (110)

SUGGESTED READINGS

Michael Agar, *Language Shock: Understanding the Culture of Conversation.* New York: William Morrow, 1994. This is a good-natured and highly readable book that explores the relationship between cultural values and language practice. Agar believes that language goes far beyond what you find in grammar books and dictionaries. Using examples from Austria, Mexico, India, and the United States, he describes the social aspects of language-in-use.

Joel Davis, *Mother Tongue: How Humans Create Language.* New York: Birch Lane Press, 1994. What is language? How did it come into being? How do we learn language? These and many other questions are answered in this intelligent and interesting work. In clear and simple language, Davis outlines the history of language, looks at languages around the world, and even discusses attempts to teach language to animals. This book is an excellent introduction to the field and will tell you everything you ever wanted to know about language and more.

Ray Jackendoff, *Patterns in the Mind: Language and Human Nature.* New York: Basic Books, 1994. There is a close connection between our nature as humans and our use of language. Jackendoff explores that connection in this interesting book on the psychology of language. A bit more challenging than the other books on this list, it is still lively and lucid, an excellent introduction to psycholinguistics.

Deborah Tannen, *Gender and Discourse.* New York: Oxford University Press, 1994. In this collection of essays, Tannen sets forth her theory of what it is like to be male or female and to talk to someone of the other gender. The five essays discuss, with examples, conversational strategies and their effects. Somewhat more "academic" than her popular books on male/female misunderstandings, it is still lively and readable, presenting a balanced, sensible view of gender and power.

TOPICS FOR DISCUSSION

1. It has been said that we live in a symbolic universe made up not of physical things, but of things that can be talked about. Discuss this statement. Think of things important to you that do not have physical existence.

2. In what kinds of communication situations is it most appropriate to use analogic messages? In what situations are digital codes a better choice? Try to think of instances in which using the wrong code could lead to interpersonal problems.

3. During spoken communication the verbal code is always accompanied to some extent by the analogic. Think of situations where the two codes could contradict or compete with each other. How could this problem be avoided or solved?

4. Have you ever been involved in a conflict that arose because of a disagreement in connotative meaning? What happened, and how did you resolve it?

5. Proper names often have strong connotations — we associate them with certain physical and mental characteristics. Do the following names have associations for you? If so, describe your idea of a Leland, Mary Ellen, Justin, Bambi, Tad, Kristine, Jane, and Billy Joe. Do you like your own name? If you could change it, what would you change it to, and why? If you marry, will you be willing to change your last name to that of your spouse? (Men, answer this one too.)

6. Discuss ways that your life script limits your communication. What kinds of talk would you avoid because such talk would say something negative about you?

7. Think of several different groups of people. If you wanted to impress members of these groups, how would your language change? Are there episodes you would either avoid or try to enact for each of these groups? Are there certain speech acts that would be off limits for one of these groups but not for the others?

8. What strategies do you use when you find yourself in a social situation with no rule sets to tell you how to act? How would you suggest a person go about developing rule sets?

9. How can language be used to increase social solidarity and group cohesion? Give some examples. What is your reaction to this kind of language use?

10. Do you believe that language can oppress groups within our culture? Why or why not? Are you in favor of making the kinds of language changes suggested in Table 4.1?

OBSERVATION GUIDE

1. Keep a diary of interactions for half a day. Begin by making brief notes every time you speak to someone, indicating what it was you

spoke about. Later, go back and indicate the function each fulfilled. Analyze how you typically use language. How much of your communication is spent in gaining or acquiring information? How much is spent in controlling or persuading others? Is your speech primarily expressive or instrumental?

2. Observe people talking in public places. Compare the topics discussed by all-male, all-female, and mixed couples. Compare the ways language is being used. Did you find any gender-related differences? If so, why do you think these differences exist, and how do you think they affect you?

3. Choose a recent conversation in which the outcome surprised you in some important way (examples: things turned out really bad; you didn't achieve the goals you sought; things went far better than you had anticipated; and so on). Write a brief description of the situation and your relationship to the other person. Then write the conversation in dialogue form as accurately as you can. Place descriptions of gestures, tone of voice, and so on in parentheses. Next apply the coordinated management of meaning (CMM) model discussed in this chapter. Identify how you interpreted the various message exchanges in terms of the following:

　a. the "speech act" as intended by the sender and/or interpreted by the receiver (the constitutive rule)

　b. the previous and subsequent acts influencing the production of each speech act (the regulative rule)

　c. your definition of the "episode" and how that influenced message choices or interpretations

　d. your view of the "relationship" in this situation and how that influenced message choices or interpretations

　e. the influence of your own "life script" on message choices or interpretations

Follow this up by "taking the role of the other person" and trying to determine how he or she

saw the same five elements (**a–e**). Discuss how this analysis could help you handle similar situations more successfully in the future.

EXERCISES

1. According to Hayakawa (in Chapter 3 of *Language in Thought and Action*), there are differences between facts, inferences, and judgments. To Hayakawa, a fact can be directly verified; it is a report of something we have seen, heard, or felt. An inference is a statement about the unknown made on the basis of the known, and a judgment indicates an expression of approval or disapproval. Discuss the extent to which the following statements involve facts, inferences, and/or judgments. (See pp. 44–45 of Hayakawa's book for additional examples.)

　a. She swore, threw the book across the room, and started to scream.

　b. He was angry.

　c. She is high-strung and bad-tempered.

　d. Overweight people should not wear stripes, plaids, or excessively bright colors.

　e. The grade-point averages of student athletes and student nonathletes are not significantly different.

　f. Athletes are just as smart as nonathletes.

　g. Poor people generally have lower morals than middle-class people.

　h. And Adam lived an hundred and thirty years and begat a son in his likeness, after his image; and called his name Seth. (Genesis 5:3)

　I. My lover is faithful to me.

　j. X is the best-looking guy in my class.

　k. The standard of living in the USA is one of the highest in the world.

2. Take a play, situation comedy, or soap opera script. For each line of dialogue, identify the speech act being performed. Indicate when a character switches from one speech act to another and when characters enter new episodes. Analyze how you would portray the character. What relationships does your character have with the others? How would you describe each character's life script? How would you say each line to make clear the meaning of the dialogue? How could nonverbal codes help to increase the effectiveness of your portrayal?

3. Below you will find a scale used to measure connotative meanings. According to Charles Osgood, its originator, whenever we come in contact with an object, we (1) evaluate its goodness, (2) judge its potency, and (3) decide how active it is. The first two items on the scale are evaluative; the next three measure potency; and the final three measure activity. By asking people to fill out this scale for any given concept, you can get a sense of what the concept means to them.

Semantic Differential Scale

Concept: _____

For each set of adjectives below, circle the number that best indicates where you would locate the meaning of the concept listed above.

good	1	2	3	4	5	6	7	bad
valuable	1	2	3	4	5	6	7	worthless
large	1	2	3	4	5	6	7	small
strong	1	2	3	4	5	6	7	weak
heavy	1	2	3	4	5	6	7	light
active	1	2	3	4	5	6	7	passive
fast	1	2	3	4	5	6	7	slow
hot	1	2	3	4	5	6	7	cold

a. Choose a partner. Think of a number of common activities and objects, for example, tennis playing, mountains, snakes, church, demolition derbies, marriage. Individually, fill out semantic differentials for each concept. Compare your semantic profiles. Discuss how you came to have these associations. How might your meanings affect your interpersonal relationships?

b. Take the name of any product, say, "oatmeal" or "potting soil." Ask at least 20 people to fill out a semantic differential scale on the product. Compile the average scores for the evaluation, activity, and potency dimensions. Now plan an advertising campaign for the product. You want to increase those dimensions of meaning on which your product is low. Come up with a plan to give the product more favorable connotations. How could music, color, camera movement, narration, and so on make your product appear better, more potent, and more active?

Through touch and posture, we send intimacy messages. The depth of our relational affection, trust, and inclusion is shown nonverbally.

(Gustav Vigeland, *Father, Mother, and Child*)

5

Relational Competence

The following encounter takes place at a company picnic. The hero is Johnson, who has been with the firm for only a few months. Hardly knowing anyone, he gravitates toward his immediate supervisor. While they are chatting, the vice-president for planning, Mr. Bigelow, comes up.

BIGELOW: (*ignoring Johnson and speaking directly to the supervisor*) Hope you didn't have any money on last night's game. Did I call it, or did I call it?

(*Our hero stands forgotten as his two superiors discuss the game. When a lull occurs, the supervisor remembers to introduce him.*)

BIGELOW: (*with obvious lack of interest*) Nice to meet you, Jackson.

JOHNSON: (*wondering if it is appropriate to correct a vice-president*) Very glad to meet you, sir. Actually, my name is . . .

BIGELOW: (*cutting in*) I've heard good things about you. Keep up the good work.

I'm always on the lookout for enterprising young men with fresh ideas. You'll find my door is always open.

JOHNSON: (*seizing his opportunity to offer a fresh idea*) You know, sir, one idea I've been considering . . .

BIGELOW: Right, fine. (*turning to the supervisor*) What we need is a drink. So how about those Mets! Think they have a chance?

(*Deep in conversation, the supervisor and vice-president move off toward the refreshments, leaving our employee feeling distinctly foolish. Just then, Johnson is hailed by a vaguely familiar figure whom he finally places as a fellow worker, Frazier.*)

FRAZIER: Hey Johnson, how ya doing? See you got to meet Mr. Big. Did he by any chance tell you (*imitating Bigelow*) "I'm always on the lookout for enterprising young men with fresh ideas"?

(*Both men laugh.*)

FRAZIER: Glad to see you. I read your report and, while I think you're dead wrong, I found it interesting. Let me buy you a beer while I give you the benefit of my experience. Your first mistake . . .

JOHNSON: (*surprisingly, beginning to warm up to Frazier*) Wait just a minute. What mistake? My plan is excellent. You're going to have to do some hard talking to convince me I'm off base.

The two men spend the next hour arguing, and Johnson leaves feeling he is finally being accepted in the organization.

How did it happen that Johnson felt better about himself when he was challenged than when he was complimented? Why was the cordial conversation with the vice-president less pleasant than the argument with the brash young coworker? In this chapter we'll try to answer these questions. We'll look at the kinds of relational messages we send and the way these messages affect us. We'll also examine the way relational patterns define and constrain interactions.

What Are Relational Messages?

In the previous situation two kinds of messages were being sent simultaneously: content and relational. **Content messages** consist of what is actually said about a topic. They are what we would transcribe if we were recording an interaction verbatim. In the situation with Mr. Bigelow, the content consisted of a compliment. In the conversation with Frazier, it was a criticism. In our scenario, however, something else was happening that was more important to Johnson than content. Relational messages were being sent. Let's discuss what relational

messages are, how they are sent, and what they mean.

THE NATURE OF RELATIONAL MESSAGES

Relational messages are cues that tell us what sort of a message a content message is to be taken as.[1] They let us know whether a statement is a put-down, a sincere overture of friendship, a sarcastic retort, or a joke. They indicate the speech acts behind the content. By telling us how to interpret a speaker's comments, they let us know what a speaker thinks of us. As Paul Watzlawick, Janet Bavelas, and Don Jackson point out, every message "not only conveys information but . . . at the same time it imposes behavior."[2] To understand how relational messages impose behavior, let's turn to another example.

You're at your high school reunion. An old rival sees you. She stares at you for a minute, looks at your brand-new outfit with thinly veiled amusement, and adjusts her impeccably tailored jacket. She glances briefly at her date, shrugs her shoulders almost imperceptibly, and drawls, "Great to see you. Care to join us?" Without saying anything directly, she has indicated her high opinion of herself and her low opinion of you. She has also indicated what she hopes you will do. The unspoken message is clear: "I'm inviting you to join us only because my manners are as well tailored as my suit. I hope, however, you will have the good grace to refuse."

Now let's rewrite the scene, this time supplying you with an old friend. She sees you, her eyes light up, and a big smile crosses her face. She gives you a hug, stands back, and looks you up and down. Keeping her arm around your shoulder, she guides you toward her date. "Great to see you. Care to join us?" This time you know you're sincerely wanted, and you accept with pleasure. Although the content message was the same, there was a world of difference on the relational level.

Relational messages are often subtle and complex, not readily deciphered by outsiders. The meanings in the scene are highly charged yet enigmatic. What do you think the relationship is between these three figures?

(Piazetta, *Il fiorellin d'amore*)

SENDING RELATIONAL MESSAGES

Relational messages are often conveyed indirectly and may therefore escape our attention. They are easiest to read when they signal a change in mood. For instance, when a parent, exasperated by his child's behavior, finally loses patience, the child usually responds to the relational shift. He can tell that this time, when Father says, "Go to bed," there is an additional relational message that says, "And I mean it!"

In most cases relational messages recede into the background. If a couple is getting along, their relational messages may acknowledge that fact, saying, in effect, "Our relationship is going fine. Let's keep it as it is." In fact, in most healthy relationships attention is directed to content, and relational meanings are scarcely noticed. Troubled relationships, however, "are characterized by a constant struggle about the nature of the relationship, with the content aspect of communication becoming less and less important."[3]

Relational messages are often sent unconsciously, through nonverbal channels. In their classic work on the subject, Watzlawick and his colleagues equate content messages with verbal statements, and relational messages with nonverbal behaviors. While people generally convey relational matters through unspoken dialogue, direct relational talk is possible.[4] When we tell people how much we care, or when we give them direct orders, the relational message is stated directly.

RELATIONAL MESSAGES AND RELATIONAL DEFINITIONS

When relational messages accumulate, they lead to **relational definitions**; that is, they give us an overall sense of who we are to one another. Relational definitions are mental models that label and classify relationships and specify how members should treat one another. As we get to know other people, we let them know what we think about them. We indicate the degree of affection we feel, the amount of attention we expect, and the kind of commitment we're willing to make. These messages define who we to one another and guide our behaviors.

For example, two individuals may arrive at the following relational understanding: "We are close but not intimate. We feel affection and trust but are not romantically involved. We are friends." Once they define themselves in this way, they will be bound by the norms and obligations of friendship and will try to act as friends should. Their relational definition will direct future behaviors.

The interpersonal literature describes relational definitions in a number of ways. Two of the most important equate relational definitions with cultures and with contracts.

Relationships as Culture

Culture, in its most general sense, is an acquired set of beliefs, attitudes, and values that people use to interpret their world and guide their actions. As we have seen in other chapters, cultural understandings are necessary for social harmony. While it isn't hard to grasp what culture is, it is hard to decide on the boundaries between cultures. Sometimes we use the term to refer to very large groupings (for example, Western versus Asian culture); other times we use it to refer to smaller groups (for instance, punk rockers or IBM employees). Julia Wood has suggested that if two people develop common orientations and behaviors, they can form their own **relational culture.**[5]

Like larger cultures, relational cultures guide members' perceptions of the world. Members of relational cultures create shared constructs, schemata, and scripts. They develop common language habits and codes of conduct. All the mechanisms that allow larger cultural units to develop work in miniature within relationships. Understanding a relationship, therefore, involves uncovering and analyzing these mechanisms.

Relationships as Contracts

The cultural metaphor is not the only way to think of relational definitions. A number of theorists, including Robert Carson, have used a contract negotiation metaphor to explain relationships.[6] When people negotiate a legal contract, they state what they expect to receive from one another, indicate mutual obligations, and outline any exceptions or contingency clauses. Carson tells us that the same thing happens implicitly during the negotiation of a **relational contract.** "The members of the dyad never quite state the 'rules' under which they are operating, but the rules are there nevertheless, and they are often followed in an utterly reliable fashion by both parties."[7]

A couple, Amy and Mark, might develop their contract in the following way. Amy tries out a behavior, perhaps by disclosing details of her past and expecting Mark to do the same. He, however, may nonverbally back off, change the subject, or refuse to respond. He wants a clause added to the contract: "There should be boundaries placed on what we discuss. Our pasts should be off limits." Amy may be willing to abide by this rule in most instances, but may wish to add the condition "when a self-disclosure can help us understand or solve a problem, then we should talk about the past." If Mark agrees, the amended version becomes part of their unstated contract.

When this rule is coupled with other rules concerning privacy and involvement, a general definition of the depth-superficiality dimension of their relationship is arrived at. Although Mark and Amy may not realize they have negotiated a contract and may not be able to list its rules, they can usually sum up their general understanding. For example, they may agree that "We respect each other's privacy." In Carson's terms they have negotiated part of an overall "master contract" that defines their relational identity. In Wood's terms one part of the relational culture has been specified. Whatever metaphor we use — culture or contract — the fact remains that couples build up all kinds of unstated rules, normative standards, role definitions, and relational labels.

Our definitions are often strongly influenced by outside sources. For example, we may try to follow religious or community-based images of "good" relationships. And whether we rebel against them or try to follow them, family models are also important to intimate bonds. Regardless of where our original definitions come from, when we enter relationships, we present them to our partners, and they are accepted, rejected, or modified.

The Content of Relational Messages

Only a few years ago the range of relational topics was assumed to be quite narrow, but current research shows that relational topics are much more varied and complex than first thought.[8] For example, Judee Burgoon and Jerold Hale have identified seven major and five minor **relational themes.** Their research indicates that we communicate about the following issues: dominance-submission, emotional arousal, composure, similarity, formality, task-social orientation, and intimacy.[9] Table 5.1 gives examples of these relational topics. We'll examine each in more detail.

SENDING DOMINANCE MESSAGES

Of all the relational messages identified, messages concerned with dominance have received the most attention. These messages focus on control, telling us "who has the right to direct, delimit, and define" the actions of a dyad.[10] They tell us who is in charge. It is common to talk about three types of dominance messages. Those that indicate a desire to take control or limit the action of others are called **one-up messages.** During conversations they often take the form of denials, disagreements, interruptions, topic changes, and the like. Messages that indicate a desire to give in or relinquish one's freedom are called **one-down messages.** Agreeing, acquiescing, giving up the floor, or allowing the other to direct the conversation are examples. Finally, statements indicating equivalence or failing to imply control are **one-across messages.**

Communication researchers often find it useful to code conversations in order to examine dominance patterns. Commonly, they indicate one-up messages with a (↑), one-down messages with a (↓), and one-across messages with a (→).[11] Coding dominance isn't difficult. To see for yourself, code the following dialogue. Be sure to consider how what is said relates to the rest of the conversation. To code the interaction, place the appropriate arrow next to each statement.

( ) ALLAN: Well, I'd say that you make most of the decisions about household matters.

( ) LOU: Yes, I guess I do.

( ) ALLAN: Sure you do. You have complete freedom because I trust your judgment.

( ) LOU: Yes, I . . .

( ) ALLAN: (*interrupting*) For example, when you decided to paint the den green, did I say anything?

( ) LOU: No. Sorry about that.

TABLE 5.1 Types of relational messages

1. **Dominance–Submission**
   "In this relationship I want to take control."
   "In this relationship I want to relinquish control."

2. **Emotional Arousal**
   "I am actively involved in and excited about what is happening."
   "I feel passive and unresponsive."

3. **Composure**
   "With you I am relaxed and in control of myself."
   "With you I am tense and out of control."

4. **Similarity**
   "We are like one another; we have something in common."
   "We are different; we have nothing in common."

5. **Formality**
   "Our relationship is guided by formal, cultural-level rules."
   "Our relationship is guided by informal, individual rules."

6. **Task–Social Orientation**
   "Our primary focus should be on the task at hand."
   "Our primary focus should be on each other and our relationship."

7. **Intimacy**
   "We are closely bound by ties of attachment and involvement."
   "We have little attachment; we are not close."

   a. **Affection–Hostility**
      "I feel positive emotions toward you."
      "I feel negative emotions toward you."

   b. **Trust**
      "I know that you won't hurt me."
      "I fear that you will harm me."

   c. **Depth–Superficiality**
      "I wish you to know personal things about me."
      "I wish to keep myself hidden from you."

   d. **Inclusion–Exclusion**
      "I wish to be with you."
      "I wish to be distant from you."

   e. **Intensity of Involvement**
      "You are a central focus of my thoughts and feelings."
      "You are of no interest to me."

Adapted from Judee K. Burgoon and Jerold L. Hale, "The Fundamental Topoi of Relational Communication," *Communication Monographs* 51 (1984): 193–214.

We've made your task easy — the control pattern here is not subtle. Allan's comments are all one-ups. Even though he says that Lou has control, his style belies his words. He takes control of the conversation, interrupts Lou, and finishes Lou's sentences. Allan is clearly saying, "I'm the one in charge." Lou is clearly in the one-down position and appears to be saying, "Go ahead. I'll follow your lead."

Talk, of course, isn't the only way to indicate dominance. Many behaviors demonstrate control. The executive who picks up the chalk at a meeting and stands in front of the blackboard signals a desire to direct the group. Conversely, the person who takes an inconspicuous seat in the back of the room may be trying to avoid taking control.

INDICATING EMOTIONAL TONE

In the Burgoon and Hale system, two themes indicate emotion: emotional arousal and composure. *Emotional arousal* refers to how responsive we are to others; it lets others know whether we are excited or bored. People generally find it easy to read arousal cues. And often arousal is contagious. Talking to someone who is excited can increase our excitement level, while trying to tell a joke to an apathetic listener can dampen our enthusiasm. As Burgoon and Hale point out, arousal messages can "run the gamut from highly manic activities to complete passivity (as when sleeping)."[12]

Composure, the other common emotional theme, indicates self-control. It shows we're capable of calmness and detachment, that we won't give way or fall apart. Sometimes such an attitude can seem cold, for it says, in effect, "I can control my emotions and act with poise. Nothing you do will cause me to react emotionally." In most cases, however, we value those with composure and draw on their strength. Although composure and emotional arousal may seem to be simple opposites, Burgoon and Hale believe they are separate relational dimensions,

Status and dominance are relational messages conveyed in many ways. Posture, facial expression, costume, and position all indicate clearly which of these three figures has the highest status.

for "it is possible for someone to be both highly aroused and highly controlled (as when expressing contempt) or nonaroused and uncomposed (as when showing restless boredom)."[13]

SHOWING SIMILARITY

Similarity, another important relational cue, has powerful effects on attraction and credibility.[14] Although we often hear that opposites attract, research shows that it is more often the case that birds of a feather flock together. People generally seek out others who are similar in appearance and actions to themselves. If you doubt this, ask yourself how willing you are to communicate with someone whose behavior is totally different from yours or what your first reaction is to people who look strange. Most people find it difficult to deal with the odd or unusual.

DEFINING EPISODES

Because we need to know what kinds of rules to follow, we usually scan episodes for *formality* cues. In formal episodes we stick to general, cultural-level rules of conduct, while in informal episodes we can deviate from these rules and act more naturally.

In shared-work situations we must also decide on the level of *task-social orientation* we wish to maintain. We need to let our partners know whether we intend to stick to business or have fun. For example, assume you have been assigned a very attractive lab partner in a tough science course. You must decide whether to concentrate on work or spend time getting to know your partner. This involves some fairly tricky relational negotiations, for if you set the wrong tone, both task and social outcomes can be adversely affected.

INDICATING INTIMACY

The relational message with the greatest potential to define a relationship is probably that of *intimacy.* Intimacy messages are central to the growth and development of interpersonal trajectories. Whether our goal is to create a private relationship or to maintain distance, we must control intimacy cues. Perhaps because they're so important, intimacy cues are often hard to express directly. We sometimes become tongue-tied when we try to convey closeness and concern.

Intimacy messages are complex. Burgoon and Hale have wisely broken intimacy down into subcategories, each describing a different dimension of attachment and involvement. Some of the most vital intimacy messages are those that signal *affection-hostility.* Very early in our lives we learn how to identify anger and love. Children become adept at knowing how far their parents can be pushed before affection turns to annoyance. Messages along the affection-hostility dimension are easy to decode, perhaps because they are usually conveyed through a number of channels working in concert.

Another key intimacy dimension is *trust.* People who are trusting are open to risk; they let others know how vulnerable they are and willingly place themselves in positions where they may be hurt. People who are trustworthy won't exploit others' vulnerabilities. We know that relationships don't progress very far toward intimacy unless those involved are both trustworthy and trusting.

Depth-superficiality is another intimacy dimension. It indicates the extent to which partners are willing to give each other access to personal information. In intimate relationships participants engage in self-disclosure. Those who refuse to open themselves to others indicate that they prefer to keep the relationship at a nonintimate public level.

Closely related to depth-superficiality is the *inclusion-exclusion* dimension of intimacy. Messages that fall along this continuum indicate a willingness to associate with others. People generally described as "warm" or "welcoming" are indicating inclusion. Those described as "cold" may be giving off exclusion messages.

Finally, intimacy is signaled by *intensity* of involvement. If you are intensely involved with someone, he or she is central to you, the focus of all your attention. If you are uninterested, unwilling to listen, or inattentive, involvement is minimal.

Intimacy, then, is a complex blend of many factors that can combine in different ways. When people are in love, for example, all of the positive aspects of intimacy work together. Lovers convey affection, trust, openness, closeness, and intensity of involvement. This, however, is only one form of intimacy. Many other combinations are possible. For example, people are sometimes bound together by mutual hostility. Intimacy is not an all-or-nothing affair. To indicate the kind and degree of our intimacy, we send many relational messages.

In our own ways we are always sending relational messages. The way we stand and move, as well as our facial expressions and gestures, let others know what we think of them and want from them. We even send relational messages when we engage in mediated communication. A hastily scrawled note on the back of an envelope sends a different message from a beautifully written letter on scented stationery. In fact, we can even send relational messages over e-mail, as Box 5.1 illustrates.

How Relational Messages Affect Us

One of the most important aspects of relational messages is that they affect receivers' self-concepts. When we tell others how we feel about them, we can either enhance or diminish their feelings of self-worth. Let's look at some different types of relational messages and see how they affect identity.

CONFIRMING AND DISCONFIRMING MESSAGES

One of the best explanations of the relationship between interpersonal communication and self-concept is given by Evelyn Sieburg. She argues that whenever we communicate with people, we present to them a version of ourselves.[15] Their response invariably tells us something about the success of this self-presentation. Responses that make us value ourselves more are known as **confirming messages.** Those that

make us devalue ourselves are known as **disconfirming messages.** Although each dyad is unique, Sieburg felt it was possible to identify responses that confirm and disconfirm most people. Table 5.2 defines and gives examples of these responses.

To understand these responses better, let's look again at the scenario that opened this chapter. Johnson, the new employee, was anxious to make a good impression on his boss by presenting the best self possible. Bigelow's responses served to disconfirm him in several ways. By failing to acknowledge Johnson's presence, Bigelow was being impervious. He told him, in effect, "You are not worth noticing." By failing to match his tone of voice to his cordial words, he confused Johnson. Bigelow's words and actions were incongruous.

Bigelow also interrupted Johnson, cutting him off in mid-sentence. Furthermore, he changed the subject when Johnson began to talk. Because Bigelow minimally acknowledged Johnson's contribution before he took the conversation in another direction, his response was tangential rather than totally irrelevant. Bigelow's tendency to hide behind impersonal clichés was also disconfirming because it kept Johnson at a distance. About the only thing Bigelow did not do was become tongue-tied and flustered, a response that would have signaled incoherence. No wonder Johnson felt unhappy about the meeting. He felt he was being told, "You are unimportant and unworthy."

One of the reasons Johnson liked Frazier was that Frazier used no disconfirmations. Although he disagreed with Johnson, he did so in a way that said, "You are a worthy opponent. I may not agree with you completely, but I respect you." As you can see in Table 5.2, a number of responses lead people to value themselves more. These confirming responses include direct acknowledgment, agreement about content, supportive feedback, clarifying responses, and expression of positive feeling. All of these are ways to improve another's self-concept.

BOX **5.1**

Netiquette: Common Courtesy Online

Some people manage to be annoying whenever they open their mouths. No matter what the topic, their relational messages are negative. The bore who talks about topics no one else cares about, the bully who takes up more conversational space than is appropriate, the nonlistener who breaks in with questions that have just been answered, or the attacker, who turns every conversation into a conflict, are just a few of the people we meet everyday, people who can bring a pleasant conversation to a standstill. People like this lack relational manners, the social agreements that we all need to follow whenever we engage in a complex cooperative activity like communication.

Common courtesy is necessary whenever and wherever we communicate — including cyberspace. In *Netiquette,* Virginia Shea presents an etiquette manual for the information age, a guide to making friends and avoiding *faux pas* while navigating the net. For, in virtual worlds, just like in the real world, courtesy and concern for others are necessary for building effective relationships.

Although most of us have heard of the Internet, we may still be confused about what it actually is. Basically it is a "network of networks," a way to connect to other people anywhere in the world. In 1994, 25–30 million people had access to the Internet, and this number is growing daily. Access allows a user to retrieve information, send electronic mail to anyone else who is connected, share opinions through electronic discussion groups, and even play fantasy adventure games known as "MUDs." Shea mentions several reasons people communicate via computer: online communities can put people in touch with experts, let us find others with shared interests, and even allow us to deal with individuals we can't stand in person.

When communicating online, people often act in ways they would never act in the real world. Shea tells us that on the net, "it's frighteningly easy to forget that your correspondent is a person with feelings more or less like your own (35)." Normally polite people think nothing of sending cruel or offensive messages, perhaps because they can't see their partners' reactions. For Shea, the Prime Directive of Netiquette is to *Remember that those are real people out there.* One way to do this is never to say anything on the net that you wouldn't say to a person's face. Not only is this rule designed to protect the feelings of others, it is to one's own advantage. Remember that communication on the net is written, and chances are your words are stored somewhere where they can come back to haunt you.

Whenever we communicate, we put demands on other people's time. This is equally true in cyberspace, where there is a limit to the system's bandwidth, the information carrying capacity of communication channels. When you send a copy of a message to everyone on your mailing list rather than to those who are really interested, or when you accidentally post the same message several times, you are imposing on others. Shea asks you to *Recognize the fact that you are not the center of cyberspace.*

Although you may not be aware of it, you are creating an impression every time you post a message. Although you will not be judged by your clothes, or age, or beauty, you will be judged by the quality of your writing as well as by the content of what you say. Shea urges people to brush up on spelling and grammar, and to *Know what you're talking about and make sense.* Bad information spreads even more quickly on the net than it does in real life, so take responsibility for your assertions.

People who are new to the net, newbies, inevitably make mistakes. If you are a veteran user, *Be forgiving of other people's mistakes* by using private e-mail to inform them of their errors. Posting a criticism in front of the entire discussion group is publicly embarrassing and a sure way to start conflict. If you are a newbie, try not to waste time by asking stupid questions, questions you could have answered yourself with a little effort. Most discussion groups have FAQs (Frequently Asked Questions) that can give you the basic knowledge that others in the group share. Get a copy and read it before posting any messages. Newbies should also send messages that are appropriate to a given discussion group. Don't, like the man Shea describes, ask a discussion group of feminists for tips on how to pick up women. One way for you as a newbie to avoid common errors is to *Lurk before you Leap*; that is, before you post any messages, read the comments of others, getting a feel for the norms and interests of group members.

Violating the rules we've just discussed is a sure fire way to start a flame war, a series of escalating attacks in which individuals express their anger with one another. Flame wars can destroy a discussion group. Prolonged or uncontrolled flaming is not only mean-spirited and hurtful, it can get you a bad reputation in a discussion group. If you don't want your correspondents to pull out their "bozo filters" or put you in a "kill file" (ways to screen out your messages automatically, making you a cyberspace pariah), then avoid gratuitous flaming and *Help keep flame wars under control.* This means not posting flame-bait (messages that will inevitably make others angry) or responding to it. If you inadver-

tently flame (posting spelling or grammar corrections is sure-fire flame-bait), apologize as soon as possible.

Although the originators of early online communities envisioned a democratic society where people would help and support one another, the net seems to have as many villains as any other community. We have all heard of pedophiles who roam the net luring children into sexual discussions or actual meetings. In addition, people have used the net for personal and sexual harassment. Although soliciting onscreen sex talk (an activity called net.sleazing) is acceptable in some MUDs, it is unacceptable in many other contexts. You should always be aware of where you are in cyberspace. If you wander into a place that makes you feel uncomfortable, leave. If someone acts offensively in your space, report the behavior to the systems administrator who can ban the sender from the system.

A more complex problem is the tendency of users to create false identities. While this is expected in MUDs, it is inappropriate in other contexts. Shea states, "long-term misrepresentation of oneself in romance discussion groups or chat areas, where the purpose of the interaction is to form a serious relationship, is definitely not acceptable (84)." So too is online cheating. Pursuing a romantic relationship with two online partners at the same time is definitely bad form. According to Shea, "you owe your online friends the same standards of honor and honesty as your nonvirtual friends." Remember that all communication has real consequences. The relational messages we send in cyberspace are just as significant as those we send during face-to-face interaction.

SOURCE: Virginia Shea, *Netiquette.* San Francisco: Albion Books, 1994.

TABLE 5.2 A taxonomy of confirming and disconfirming messages

Disconfirming responses	Definition	Example
Impervious	When B fails to acknowledge, even minimally, A's message	A: Hi! B: (continues working, ignoring A)
Interrupting	When B cuts A's message short	A: So then I . . . B: Nice chatting with you. Bye!
Irrelevant	When B's response is unrelated to what A has been saying	A: So then he left me. B: I'm thinking of going to Bermuda on break.
Tangential	When B acknowledges A's message but immediately takes the talk in another direction	A: I just don't know what to do. B: Gee, too bad. Have you seen my new car?
Impersonal	When B conducts a monologue or uses nonimmediate, cliché-ridden, overintellectual language	A: How can I improve my grade, professor? B: Adequate classroom performance is a function of cognitive and affective integration.
Incoherent	When B's response is rambling and difficult to follow	A: Tell me what's wrong. B: Well, un, see, it's a . . . gosh, hard to say.
Incongruous	When B's nonverbal and verbal messages are contradictory	A: Are you angry with me? B: No. Of course not. Why should I be? (said sarcastically)

Confirming responses	Definition	Example
Direct acknowledgment	When B reacts directly to A's message	A: Can we talk? B: Of course. Come over.
Agreement about content	When B reinforces opinions offered by A	A: I've definitely noticed a change in Joe lately. B: Yes. I have too.
Supportive	When B expresses understanding and reassurance to A	A: I feel just awful. B: I understand. I think you did the right thing.
Clarifying	When B tries to clarify A's message	A: I'm not sure what to do about it. B: So you're confused and upset, is that it?
Expression of positive feeling	When B expresses positive feelings about A's message	A: No, I think we should tell him about it. B: Now I know what you mean. Good idea!

Adapted from Frank E. X. Dance and Carl E. Larson, *Speech Communication, Concepts and Behavior* (New York: Holt, Rinehart, & Winston, 1972) pp. 141–43.

PARADOXES AND DOUBLE BINDS

Contradictory messages are called paradoxes, and repeated exposure to them can cause us to doubt the validity of our own perceptions. There are two kinds of paradoxes that can damage the self-image: paradoxical definitions and paradoxical injunctions.[16]

In **paradoxical definitions** speakers present themselves in contradictory ways. A classic example is the statement "I am a liar." If the speaker is really a liar, then the statement must be true. But a speaker who describes himself truthfully cannot be a liar. If this is confusing, you have the idea. Paradoxical messages always confuse us; they challenge our belief in rationality and consistency. And what is oddest about them is that although it is the speaker who is being illogical, it is the receiver who feels confused and disconfirmed. Any time a message is delivered that defines a relationship in contradictory ways ("I am your friend but I don't want to be around you," "I respect your ideas but I can't support them"), it can be considered to be a paradoxical definition.

Another kind of paradox, a **paradoxical injunction,** gives us an impossible order, one that must be disobeyed in order to be obeyed. "Stop giving in to me" is a good example. If you obey the command, you are giving in. If you refuse to give in, you are giving in because you are obeying the injunction. Other examples are "Dominate me!" "Be spontaneous," "Disagree with everything I say," and "Love me for myself, not because I ask you to." While paradoxes may be fun to think about if you like brainteasers, during interaction they are much less benign. They undermine our belief in logic and put us in a situation where we're damned if we do and damned if we don't.

Imagine that you are a child whose mother says to you, "I want you to be more affectionate." But when you show affection by trying to touch her, she stiffens and backs off. Or you are a young adult whose father tells you, "I want you to be independent and have a life of your own." But when you do strike out on your own, he develops severe chest pains. Such a situation, where there is no "correct" response, is called a **double bind.**[17] In a true double bind, (1) the relationship between the two people involved must be an intense and important one; (2) the "victim" must be presented with a contradictory injunction; and (3) he or she must have no way of escaping, either by recognizing the paradoxical nature of the message or by withdrawing from the interaction. The victim must react, although reacting "correctly" is impossible.

Imagine being the victim of a habitual double bind, with no way of returning to a more logical world. After a while, this kind of treatment could make you question your own sanity. You might begin to act in ways normal people would consider "crazy." Even mild cases of contradictory behavior can be upsetting. Some people habitually use sarcasm and jokes so that we're never really sure what they think of us. For most of us, this is disquieting, because we can't be sure whether we are being accepted or not. These kinds of messages are also double binding.[18]

Pragmatic Patterns and Relational Sequences

While we react strongly to others' relational messages, our own are often invisible. How, then, can we diagnose communication problems? The only real way is to pay more attention to our own actions. You may recall from Chapter 3 that pragmatic communication patterns refer to the way we use speech in everyday interactions — speech acts, episodes, regulative and constitutive rules. By uncovering repetitive sequences of behavior, we can often discover why our relationships are going the way they are. In this section we'll examine the influence of patterns of behavior on interpersonal relationships.

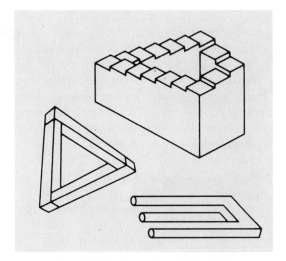

For most people inconsistencies and paradoxes are vaguely unsettling. Although the impossible figures drawn here fascinate us, they also confuse and disconcert our sense of reality.

LOOKING FOR MEANING IN PATTERNS

Before we begin discussing pragmatic patterns, there are three points to consider. All three have been implicit in our previous discussions.

1. *Relational definitions are created not by a single individual, but by both members of a relationship working together.* The fact that one person has a domineering personality does not necessarily mean that she will be a dominant member in all her relationships. Her partner has a great deal to do with how dominance-submission patterns get worked out.

2. *To understand relational definitions, we need to become aware of patterns of behavior.* In relationships certain sequences of acts become favored and repeated over time. To diagnose a relationship, we need to uncover these patterns of repeated acts.

3. *It is generally unproductive to blame individuals for the way a relationship progresses.* Although participants often blame the patterns they do recognize on their partners, it is more productive to place any blame on co-created patterns.

These points are part of a perspective developed by researchers known as the **Palo Alto group**.[19] These researchers, primarily psychotherapists, wanted to learn why some relationships were so destructive. They felt the answer could be found in communication patterns. While our interest is with a more normal range of behaviors than those investigated by the Palo Alto group, the insights they provide can quite easily be applied to everyday interaction.

PATTERNS VERSUS PEOPLE: THE LOCUS OF DYADIC COMMUNICATION

The Palo Alto group argues that when people enter a relationship, it is the relationship itself that most affects them, not their individual personalities. With some people we are relaxed and happy; with others we are at our absolute worst. Does this mean our personalities change when we are with different people? The Palo Alto group says no. What changes is our communication system. To understand relationships, we must understand the behaviors that make up the dyadic system.

But how do we go about looking at behaviors that are usually invisible? What should we look for? First, we should look at sequences rather than individual acts. Unless we know how an individual act is connected to other behaviors, we cannot understand its relational meaning. Let's take an example. Suppose you hear a laugh. Can you assume that it means someone is happy? Of course not. It all depends on what happened before. The laugh may have been an appreciative response to a good joke. Or it may have been a scornful response to a desperate request. The smallest unit to carry relational meaning is not a single act,

These women don't have to say a word to indicate their smug, narrow-minded approach to life. Their relational messages clearly convey their attitudes.

(Grant Wood, *Daughters of Revolution,* 1932)

but at least two acts in sequence, or what is called an **interact.**[20]

To understand a relationship fully, we must often look at a number of interacts. Let's assume that the laugh we heard followed an apology. To understand this interact's relational meaning, we must connect it to other interacts. Perhaps the following scenario applies. Lee habitually gets mad and insults Adam. When this happens, Adam usually responds by threatening to leave Lee, who, terrified that Adam will make good on the threat, begs for forgiveness. At that point Adam scornfully laughs at Lee, which causes the whole process to start over. The laugh takes on a sinister aspect in this scenario, for the sequence clearly is a disturbed one. Of course, this unpleasant pattern is not the only explanation for the apology-laugh. Perhaps when tired, Lee acts irritable but usually realizes it and apologizes immediately. Adam, understanding this, laughs good-naturedly to let Lee know everything is OK. A very different meaning can now be assigned to the laugh. The point here is that

we can understand and control relationships best by looking for patterns. If necessary, we can then intervene to break the pattern.

THE PROBLEM OF PUNCTUATION

Even among people who can identify dysfunctional patterns, there is often a stumbling block to changing them: the tendency to punctuate sequences inappropriately. In grammar, punctuation marks are ways of dividing words into units that belong together. In punctuating a sentence, we use a capital letter to show where it begins. In a relational sequence **punctuation** serves essentially the same purpose: It lets us know when the sequence begins.

Let's consider an example that occurs often in real life, although the position of husband and wife may be reversed. A couple is locked in a pattern in which the wife, feeling ignored, nags her husband. The husband responds to this attack by withdrawing. The more he withdraws, the more she nags, and the more she nags, the more he withdraws. They are enmeshed in a self-perpetuating pattern.[21]

Even if they recognize what's going on, they may spend all their energy arguing over who started it. The wife punctuates the sequence by saying it was the husband's fault. The husband punctuates it by saying he withdrew only because she began it all by nagging. Of course, none of this does any good; the conflict only worsens.

TYPES OF PATTERNS

Although each dyad works out its own relational patterns, some occur with enough frequency that they can be labeled and described. Common relational patterns include (1) complementary and symmetrical, (2) evolving, and (3) unwanted repetitive.

Complementarity and Symmetry

One of the easiest ways to classify patterns of interacts is to consider whether they are similar or different in relational meaning. When the acts in a sequence are relationally opposite, we have what is called a **complementary pattern.** A sequence characterized by a repeated pattern of one-ups followed by one-downs would be so labeled. A pattern consisting of acts that are similar is called a **symmetrical pattern.** If such a pattern consists entirely of one-ups, it is considered to be an example of **competitive symmetry.** If it includes only one-downs, it is **submissive symmetry.** Look at the following conversations and see if you can tell which is complementary, which is competitively symmetrical, and which is submissively symmetrical.

Conversation 1

JOAN: Let's begin by defining the problem.

JANE: OK, that's fine.

JOAN: We'll make a chart showing all the negative forces.

JANE: Sounds good. Should I . . .

JOAN: No, I'll do it. Hand me that paper.

JANE: OK.

Conversation 2

JOAN: Let's begin by defining the problem.

JANE: We did that last time; we don't have time now.

JOAN: We need to review it. I'll make a chart . . .

JANE: You can do that later. Anyone have any solutions?

JOAN: Wait a minute! Who made you the expert?

JANE: Don't be a jerk!

Conversation 3

JOAN: How would you like to begin?

JANE: Whatever you suggest is just fine.

JOAN: I'll agree with whatever you say.

JANE: No, really, you decide.

JOAN: I'd be happy to go along with what you think.

JANE: I really have no preference.

It's not very difficult to label these conversations. Conversation 1 is complementary. Joan takes control and Jane acquiesces. Their control behaviors are opposite and therefore complement each other. Conversation 2 is characterized by competitive symmetry. Here both Joan and Jane want to direct the activity. Such a conversation may signal a fight for leadership. Conversation 3 illustrates submissive symmetry. Although the two seem agreeable, they are actually in a contest to see who can force the other to take control.

Is one sequence better than the others? Not really. Although the complementary relationship shows the least amount of disagreement, it's not necessarily the best. Habitual complementarity can trap participants in rigid roles. When we are young, it is natural for our relationship with our parents to be complementary. But how natural would it be if we still let Mom and Dad make all the decisions when we were 30?

While on the face of it symmetrical patterns seem to be negative, since they are characterized by struggle, there are times when they can be positive. The clash involved in competitive symmetry can sometimes motivate partners to be more creative. And sometimes the willingness to give in characterized by submissive symmetry can signal care and concern. What is unhealthy is any pattern so rigid it cannot change. If, for example, a dominant member in a complementary relationship becomes ill and can no longer make decisions, it may be necessary for the submissive member to take over. If the members cannot make the switch, severe problems of adaptation are possible.

Evolving Patterns: The Problem of Spirals

Over time, relational roles may become more and more extreme. When the actions of each party intensify the actions of the other, we have a **spiral**.[22] Spirals often arise where there is competitive symmetry. Assume you and a friend are competing for a prize. The harder you work and the better you do, the harder she works and the better she does. As you near your goal, you redouble your efforts, and she does the same when it looks like you are about to win. While healthy competition may lead you to reach your potential, unchecked competition may spiral out of control and become an obsession.

There are times when intensifying a relationship makes it better. If by showing affection you increase a friend's confidence so that he acts more lovable, you will probably feel even more affection. The relationship can develop in a positive direction. This is a progressive spiral. Unfortunately, the opposite can occur. If, for example, you lose trust in a friend, that friend may decide that it is useless to act in a trustworthy manner. He may therefore violate your trust, and the relationship will degenerate. This is a regressive spiral.

William Wilmot believes that most relationships are characterized by alternating spirals that fluctuate between being progressive and being regressive. He argues that most couples place limits on how high or low a spiral can go. When a spiral reaches one of these limits, it must change directions or the relationship will dissolve. Our nagging wife and withdrawing husband cannot keep up their regressive spiral for long. It will have to reverse if they are to stay together [23] Box 5.2 further discusses how spirals define roles and looks at some of the social mechanisms for restraining runaway escalation.

Unwanted Patterns: Controlling URPs

If relational patterns are negotiated, you would think that people would steer clear of destructive sequences. Unfortunately, many patterns are undesired and undesirable. In **unwanted repetitive patterns (URPs)** participants feel out of control. Have you ever known someone who just rubbed you the wrong way? Every time you got together, a fight would inevitably ensue. If so, you have experienced an URP. In most URPs the following conditions will occur: (1) A clear sequence of alternating messages will inform each participant exactly what comes next; (2) the URP will be recurrent; (3) it will occur regardless of topic or situation; (4) the sequence will be unwanted; and (5) the participants will both share the perception that it could not be avoided. They will feel a compulsion to see it through to its conclusion.[24]

BOX **5.2**

Schismogenesis: Patterns of Role Differentiation in a New Guinea Village

In the 1930s, anthropologist Gregory Bateson first described the complementary and symmetrical interaction patterns we have discussed. At the time, he was working among the Iatmul tribe of New Guinea, one of whose characteristics was extravagant competitive exhibitionism by the men, accompanied by passive admiration by the women. Bateson was interested in understanding this extreme behavior, which clearly placed a strain on its practitioners.

To explain the progressive differentiation in roles he observed, he coined the word *schismogenesis,* meaning an escalation in the intensity of a behavior caused by one's partner's reactions. He noted that schismogenesis could be complementary (as when exhibitionism was increased by admiration and admiration by exhibitionism) or symmetrical (as when rival moieties, or tribal

subdivisions, competed in bullying novices during initiations).

Bateson felt that schismogenesis, unless restrained, could destroy relationships. He also felt that it could develop in all long-term interactions between intimates. He noted that the result of uncontrolled schismogenesis was hostility, inability to empathize, and mutual jealousy. After long-term complementary schismogenesis, partners feel disgust for each other's behavior.

One of the most interesting parts of Bateson's discussion centers on cultural mechanisms for restraining schismogenesis. Bateson suggests a number of them:

1. Adding a small amount of complementary behavior to a symmetrical relationship may stabilize role differentiation. Conversely, adding symmetry to an essentially complementary relationship can ease tension. For example, if management plays basketball once a year with labor, this small dose of symmetry may ease feelings of difference.

2. A couple experiencing complementary schismogenesis may try to change its topic by focusing on different behaviors. A couple acting out a dominance-submission pattern may convert that pattern to nurturing-weakness, a more acceptable kind of role differentiation.

It is not completely clear why URPs occur. They appear to be an immediate reaction to "triggering" messages. Participants respond automatically, without considering the consequences. They touch off simplistic, almost childish, responses in each other. Perhaps these responses are somehow connected to core beliefs about the self.

What can be done about URPs? The first step is to recognize them for what they are and to try to overcome the tendency to punctuate them inappropriately. The next step is somehow to break the sequence. Wilmot offers five suggestions for stopping spirals that seem applicable to all kinds of URPs.[25]

1. *Change your behavior.* For example, if a partner is afraid of commitment and your insistence is only making her more fearful, perhaps you should stop asking for commitment and instead treat the relationship more casually. Wilmot suggests that if doing more of the same doesn't work, doing less of the same might.

2. *Use third parties.* Friends, counselors, or relatives can all provide new perspectives and break problem patterns.

4. The groups or individuals experiencing schismogenesis may be united in opposition to a common enemy. We know, for example, that during war, nationalist sentiment overcomes internal political rivalries.

5. Hierarchical organization may ease the strain of complementary relationships by allowing an individual to dominate the group below while being submissive to the group above. For example, the husband who is powerless at work can dominate his children.

6. Inverse schismogenetic patterns may restrain one another. For example, love, a positive escalation of emotion, may counteract rivalry, a more negative emotion.

SOURCE: Gregory Bateson, *Naven*, 2nd ed. (Stanford, Calif.: Stanford University Press, 1958).

ADDITIONAL READINGS

Bateson, Gregory. *Steps to an Ecology of Mind.* New York: Ballantine, 1972.
Watzlawick, Paul, Janet Beavin Bavelas, and Don D. Jackson, *The Pragmatics of Human Communication.* New York: Norton, 1967.

3. Refocusing symmetrical rivalry may also be effective. For example, true hostility may be shifted to mock aggression. Box 13.1 gives a good example of this process.

3. *Reaffirm your relational goals.* If your partner is very important to you, try to recall how the relationship developed and what your original goals and commitments were. If the person is a casual acquaintance, think about why it is necessary for you to work together. Discuss this with your partner.

4. *Try to spend either more or less time with the person.* You may succeed in breaking the pattern either by sharing more of yourself or by taking time out to be alone.

5. *Try changing an external situation.* Maybe a change of location, even a vacation to-

gether, may succeed in upsetting relational habits and providing new patterns of behavior.

Skill Building: Empathy and Perspective-Taking

This chapter has emphasized how relational messages influence the way people interpret the content in each other's messages and, over time,

135

define the nature of their relationship. While relational messages are occasionally verbalized, we have seen that most of the time they are conveyed nonverbally and indirectly. Since relational messages are often communicated spontaneously, the ability to manage them hinges on our becoming more aware of those relational messages we send to and receive from others. Such an awareness can be developed by improving the skills of empathy and perspective-taking.

Traditionally, social scientists have defined empathy in one of two ways: (1) as an individual's ability to experience how another person feels or (2) as the ability to predict accurately another person's verbal descriptions of herself, her situation, or her own emotional state.[26] We prefer to separate these definitions, referring to empathy as the ability to spontaneously identify with another on a direct emotional level and perspective-taking as a more cognitively oriented appraisal of how the other perceives himself, his situation, and his emotions. These two skills are closely related but not identical. Empathy is probably experienced and communicated at a spontaneous level; perspective-taking is more symbolic in nature.

While empathizing with another certainly helps us understand that person's feelings, empathy alone will not necessarily result in effective communication. Perspective-taking is often required to see the situation more completely and respond appropriately. An example may help clarify this distinction. Let's suppose that your best friend, Samantha, has been rather depressed lately. You know her so well that even when she tries to cover it up, you sense how she feels. In fact, you are so in tune with her that after only a few minutes of interaction, you feel as depressed as she does. You clearly empathize with her, but your getting depressed is not quite the prescription for cheering her up. Empathy alone does not provide much comfort. On the other hand, if you engage in perspective-taking, you are attempting to see the situation from her vantage point and make some sense of it. You

try to identify what aspects of the current situation she has focused on, what goals she might have had in mind, what from her perspective must have gone wrong, and why she reacted as she did. In short, you're not just feeling as she feels, but trying to cognitively understand what the whole situation looks and feels like to her. In doing this, you also take into account such things as how she views your relationship and what she expects or hopes a good friend will do in a situation like this. As a result, you might realize that what she needs is your understanding and your gentle reassurance that things will improve. The last thing she needs is the burden of having to help *both of you* recover from depression. Keeping the distinction between empathy and perspective-taking in mind, let's look at some ways that we can improve both of these skills.

Perhaps the single most important thing you can do is *remind yourself to pay attention to the spontaneous emotional expressions of others.* Tests of nonverbal receiving ability indicate that people vary widely in their sensitivity to the nonverbal cues of others. However, researchers have also discovered that when instructed to pay attention to nonverbal cues, most people improve significantly.[27] The implication should be clear — empathy (sensing another's emotional state) results from being aware of his or her nonverbal indications of emotion, but we have to remind ourselves to be attentive. No one else is going to do it for us.

Empathic ability can also be improved if you *communicate in a more expressive manner yourself.* Ross Buck has argued that empathy is not really an individual skill because it is strongly influenced by the expressive communicative qualities of both sender and receiver. According to Buck, "by being expressive, a person encourages the other to reciprocate, so that an expressive person in effect goes through life leaving a trail of emotional expression in his or her wake, while a nonexpressive person leaves the reverse."[28] If our own expressive behavior prompts others to be more expressive and we pay attention to the wider range of nonverbal cues they display, we should be more accurate in reading others' emotional state. Greater empathy will be the result.

Empathy is important in that it provides an emotional connection and a motivation to understand and help others. But greater cognitive awareness of another's point of view requires more than just an emotional connection. It requires us to infer how the other person's social-cognitive framing of a situation differs from our own.

One important way we can enhance perspective-taking ability is to *resist our own egocentric tendencies to define the other's experience in our own terms.* This means we must be able to suspend our own view of a situation before we can see another's perspective on the same situation. It may be useful to take inventory of the personal constructs, stereotypes, scripts, and rules that we typically associate with a particular situation and then explore alternative ways of defining that situation. Interacting with people whose ethnic or social background differs from your own is another way to gain a different vantage point. Make it a practice in such conversations to place your own opinions and perceptions on hold and listen carefully to how others talk about events and people. Try to identify how the other's cognitive framework (personal constructs, scripts, attributions) differs from your own.

You can also increase your perspective-taking ability if you *ask others to verbalize their perspectives and then probe for details.* While this may be awkward in some situations, it simply represents an extension of the normal process of getting to know someone. People regularly share their opinions with one another but do not always explore one another's views in much detail. Since most people are willing to talk about their own egocentric views of the world, why not take advantage and learn as much about their perspective as you can?

The more you practice perspective-taking, the sharper your skills will be when you need them.

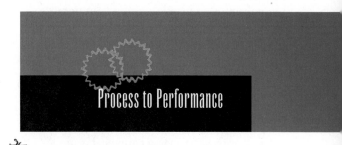

Process to Performance

REVIEW TERMS

The following is a list of major concepts introduced in this chapter. The page where the concept is first mentioned is listed in parentheses.

content messages   (118)
relational messages   (118)
relational definitions   (120)
relational culture   (120)
relational contract   (120)
relational themes   (121)
one-up message   (121)
one-down message   (121)
one-across message   (121)
confirming message   (125)
disconfirming message   (125)
paradoxical definition   (129)
paradoxical injunction   (129)
double bind   (129)
Palo Alto group   (130)
interact   (131)
punctuation   (131)
complementary pattern   (132)
symmetrical pattern   (132)
competitive symmetry   (132)
submissive symmetry   (132)
spiral   (133)
URP   (133)
empathy   (136)
perspective-taking   (136)

SUGGESTED READINGS

Bateson, Gregory. *Steps to an Ecology of Mind.* New York: Ballantine, 1972. Bateson is one of our most original thinkers. This is a collection of his ideas about communication and interaction. It's impossible to read Bateson without gaining insights.

Bavelas, Janet Beavin, Alex Black, Nicole Chovil, and Jennifer Mullett. *Equivocal Communication.* Newbury Park, Calif.: Sage, 1990. This book analyzes the social functions of ambiguous communication and argues that being equivocal is not always bad.

Coupland, Nikolas, Howard Giles, and John M. Wiemann. *'Miscommunication' and Problematic Talk.* Newbury Park, Calif.: Sage, 1991. This book contains a series of scholarly articles on problematic talk and misunderstanding. Topics include miscommunication in medicine, in intercultural encounters, in complex organizations, as well as problems at the person-machine interface.

Cupach, William R. and Brian H. Spitzberg. *The Dark Side of Interpersonal Communication.* Hillsdale, N.J.: Erlbaum, 1994. The authors believe that it is important for us to understand how people deal with communication that is "difficult, problematic, challenging, distressing, and disruptive." They include articles on topics such as paradoxes, deception, invasion of privacy, and abusive relationships.

Laing, R. D. *Knots.* New York: Vintage Books, 1970. A fascinating look at some of the "psychologics" that lead us into relational binds and paradoxes.

Wood, Julia T. *Relational Communication: Continuity and Change in Personal Relationships.* Belmont, Calif.: Wadsworth, 1995. In this text, Wood focuses on how intimate, personal relationships are developed and maintained. She blends theory with practical advice on how to improve relationships through effective interpersonal communication.

TOPICS FOR DISCUSSION

1. Why do you think people prefer to use nonverbal codes rather than verbal codes to express relational messages, especially since nonverbal codes are often less explicit and harder to decode accurately? Could there be some advantage to ambiguous coding?

2. Most of the time relational codes go unnoticed. When and under what conditions do people pay attention to relational codes? See if you can construct a theory of some of the factors affecting this process.

3. Review the relational themes in Table 5.1. Discuss how each of the nonverbal codes discussed in Chapter 3 can be used to convey each theme.

4. Analyze the way relational themes are conveyed by students and teachers in classroom contexts. Be specific.

5. Imagine you are on a job interview. What kinds of impressions would you like to convey? What relational messages would it be most appropriate to send? How could you convey these messages most effectively in an office setting during a 20-minute screening interview?

6. It has been argued that many traditional patterns of male-female interaction (men holding the door for women and paying for dates) are relational messages indicating dominance. What is your opinion?

7. Research has shown that women are often more sensitive to subtle relational cues than men are. Why do you suppose women have traditionally been more subtle and men more blunt in their relational messages? What implications does this have for cross-sex interactions?

8. Evaluate the metaphors of culture and contract as descriptions of the way people define relationships. Are these useful ways to think of relational development? In what ways do they break down?

9. Build a model describing how couples reach consensus on relational definitions. What factors are involved? What steps take place?

10. Try to come up with a list of suggestions to stop URPs.

OBSERVATION GUIDE

1. Think of a situation in which you were disconfirmed by someone. Describe the disconfirmation. How did you feel about it? How was the situation resolved? Now think of a situation in which you felt confirmed. What was done or said to give you that feeling?

2. Have you ever been in an URP? If so, describe the pattern in detail. What was the sequence? How did you feel? What did you do about it? If the URP was resolved, how was this accomplished? If it was not resolved, what do you think might have worked? If you have never been in an URP, you have probably observed one. Answer the same questions as previously about an observed URP.

3. Think of a current relationship. What is your relational definition? How did you arrive at it? What kinds of agreements and norms characterize the relationship? Think of a rule that took some negotiation and describe this process. If the negotiation process was easy, what made it so? If difficult, why? What could have been done to ease the situation?

EXERCISES

1. Take a play, a recording of a favorite TV show, or a tape of a real-life conversation. Working with a partner, choose a segment and code it, using the following system:[29]

Dominance	(↑ +)	: An attempt to severely restrict the freedom of the other.
Structuring	(↑)	: An attempt to control the other while leaving him or her some options.
Equivalence	(→)	: An attempt at mutual identification or equality.
Deference	(↓)	: A willingness to follow while retaining some freedom.
Submission	(↓ +)	: An extreme willingness to be led by the other.

Discuss the coding until you agree. If possible, record your discussion on a portable tape recorder. What kind of pattern do you see? Is it complementary or symmetrical or mixed? How would you sum up their relationship? (To make this even more interesting, go back and listen to the tape of your own interaction. Together, analyze the control dimension that occurred between you during this exercise.)

2. This exercise is designed to give you practice in sending and receiving relational messages. Begin by forming groups of four or six. Turn to the 12 relational themes identified by Burgoon and Hale. Take a pack of 3 X 5 cards and print the names of each relational theme on a separate card, making cards for both positive and negative expressions of a theme (that is, make one card for dominance and another for submission, one for affection and one for hostility, and so on).

Now shuffle the cards and deal an equal number to each member. The person who begins chooses a card from his hand and acts out the relational message. The only words that can be used are the letters of the alphabet recited in order. As a player acts out the message, each member of the group should write on a scrap of paper the message being conveyed. After all members have made their guesses, they should compare answers.

Award five points to the player if he manages to match at least one group member; award five points to all who guessed correctly. Once the points have been awarded, the current player discards the card that was played, and the next person acts out one of her cards. Continue until all the cards have been played. In case of a tie, have the players involved play a runoff round.

Discuss how difficult it was to convey the messages. Are you an emotionally expressive person? Why or why not? Are you sensitive to others' messages? Why or why not?

3

INTERPERSONAL PROCESSES

Perception involves a complex array of social constructions. We shape and are shaped by what we perceive in others and the world around us.

(M. C. Escher, *Still Life with Reflecting Sphere*, 1934)

6

Interpretive Competence: How We Perceive Individuals, Relationships, and Social Events

A friend of yours has arranged for you to be interviewed for an important position with the company she works for. In fact, she will be one of the interviewers. She has, of course, informed you that she cannot show any favoritism and will conduct the interview in a rather formal, businesslike manner. You are told that the interview will be held over coffee at a local restaurant and that two or three of the company's representatives, including your friend, will be there. You are to arrive promptly at 3:00 P.M., your friend says, and you may as well wait in the lobby until she gets there. Naturally, you are more than prompt, you're 15 minutes early. You hang around the lobby, feeling more nervous with each passing minute.

Finally, as three o'clock comes and goes, you sneak a peek inside the restaurant. Here is what you see: Your friend is already seated at a table with two other people, a male and a female. All three are dressed in business suits. The two women are having wine, and the young man is sipping a cup of coffee. Your friend is talking quite seriously with the young man who, quite

frankly, looks a little nervous. The other woman is looking around the place, as if expecting someone. You begin to worry. Maybe you misunderstood your friend's instructions. She glances away from the man but doesn't see you. At last you decide that they must be waiting for you. So you check yourself in the mirror and start walking toward their table. As you approach, you hear your friend say to the other woman, "Chris, do you have anything else you'd like to ask Mr. Gannon?" Suddenly, your friend notices you. She looks a little surprised, then acts very coolly toward you, and hesitates as if not sure what to do next. Before you read on, take a few minutes to answer the following questions: (1) How would you define the situation or describe what's really going on among the four participants? Which behaviors did you focus on to help you decide? (2) What kind of people are involved? What impressions do you have of each one? (3) How are the participants related to one another? (4) How can you explain their behavior? Write down anything else you perceive to be important in this situation. **145**

TABLE 6.1 The four social cognition questions

For any given conversation or social interaction:

1. How does each participant view the situation? What type of event or activity does each think he or she is participating in?

2. What impressions do the participants have of each other?

3. What kind of relationship have the participants enacted? Do they both view the relationship as having the same status (for example, friends or casual acquaintances)?

4. What explanations do the participants provide to account for their own and each other's behavior?

The four questions you have just considered are all concerned with **social cognition,** the study of the cognitive structures and processes that influence our perceptions of people and social events (see Table 6.1). Social cognitions enable us to categorize people and make sense of social interactions. The stereotype is one of the most common types of cognitive structures that influences how we communicate with others. When we meet someone new, we often classify him or her as a member of some group (for example, a BMCWM—Boring Middle-Class White Male) and then form expectations based on our experience with other members of that group. Stereotypes and other forms of social cognition can be helpful or harmful, but they are inevitable. We humans have an insatiable appetite for categorizing. In this chapter we'll look at many of the ways people categorize social life in order to make sense of it.

Before discussing specific social cognition factors, we'll talk briefly about why social cog-

nitive processes are an important part of communication. Then we'll look at what the structural features of social cognition are and how the perceptual process works. Finally, we'll detail the four major social cognition processes: (1) sizing up the situation, (2) sizing up people, (3) sizing up relationships, and (4) explaining interpersonal behavior. The chapter will conclude with some suggestions for improving one of our most significant perceptual skills: listening. Once you understand how these processes work and how you can manage them in your own interactions, you will have increased your own level of interpretive competence.

Why Is Social Cognition Important in Interpersonal Communication?

It may seem strange to spend an entire chapter on social cognition in a book about interpersonal communication. After all, social cognition—how we perceive people and events—seems to be an internal process, more in the domain of psychology than communication. This distinction, while important, is also misleading. Each of the social sciences contributes significantly to the understanding of the others. In our case the knowledge of how we categorize social phenomena helps us understand and, ideally, improve how we communicate. Social cognition and interpersonal comunication relate to each other in at least four ways. Not only does the way we categorize our social world affect how we receive messages, what actions we will think are appropriate, and how much we will be able to control our own communication (or have it control us), but the way we categorize people and contexts can change as a result of communication with others. In this section we'll explore each of these four relationships between social cognition and interpersonal communication.

SOCIAL COGNITION AND THE RECEPTION OF MESSAGES

Our observations are influenced by our frame of reference (mental state, past experiences, biases, and so on). This frame of reference then affects which of the many messages in our environment we pay attention to. If you are hungry and thinking about food, your frame of reference will predispose you to notice the smell of onions on a friend's breath, the picture of a hot dog on a billboard, and the familiar jingle of a fast-food restaurant on the car radio. If you expect to meet someone described to you as a "comedian," you will probably focus more on the funny things that person says and either forget or be surprised by the serious remarks you hear. Since we cannot possibly pay attention to every message sent our way, the ones we do receive are greatly affected by our cognitive frame of reference.

Researchers have shown that people can be "primed" to perceive ambiguous stimuli in ways that are consistent with the particular social cognition that was activated.[1] A cognitive structure can easily be primed by an item in the newspaper or by something someone says to you. For instance, Jim Smith is a member of many different social groups (American, middle class, urbanite, male, model railroad enthusiast, computer hack, parent, and so on). At any given moment only one or two of these social identities is likely to be foremost in his thinking. The arrival in the morning mail of new issues of *Model Railroader* and *Personal Computing* may surreptitiously prime him to interpret messages all day long from a hobby-oriented frame of reference. His wife's simple inquiry, "What would you like to do this evening?" might be seen as a unwanted demand on his free time — time that could be spent pursuing one of his hobbies.

Likewise, the removal of a previously salient social category can alter how we receive messages. In their review of changes in the social life of children, Tory Higgins and Jacquelynne Parsons note the important effect that entering school has on children's judgments of one another. Age-segregated classrooms sharply reduce the child's contact with peers who are younger or older. This change in social experience tends to make age a less salient social category. As a result, children begin to pay more attention to and judge each other more in terms of personal characteristics.[2]

SOCIAL COGNITION AND ACTION

The ability to communicate in an appropriate or effective manner also rests on the frame of reference we have in any given situation. Our actions are based on our perceptions. We produce messages that we think will be appropriate depending upon how we "see" the situation; who the other person is, what she is doing, what we think her motives are, what our own goals and sense of self are, and what type of relationship we believe we have with her. If, in his conversation with a car salesman, Jon perceives him to be "an elderly gent," Jon will probably act in ways consistent with his social cognitions or beliefs about the elderly. Believing that older folks are always on the verge of senility, Jon may think he can outfox the salesman and get a much better deal on a new automobile. Note how Jon's behavior would probably change if his stereotype of an older salesman included beliefs such as "older and wiser," "shrewd," "has heard it all before," and so on.

SOCIAL COGNITION AND CONTROL

Because perceptions channel action, our ability to exercise control over our own communication is directly linked to our awareness of social cognition processes. Many times we limit our message-sending options because we miss the relevant cues in the environment or from the

This 19th-century engraving, entitled *Puzzle-Brain Mountain,* demonstrates how people can have multiple interpretations of the same object or event. If you look at the drawing in a straightforward fashion, you probably perceive a mountain landscape; turning the picture on its side will reveal the outline and features of a man's face.

other person that could "activate" a more appropriate cognitive framework. We fall easily into the same old cognitive ruts and assume that we know all there is to know about the situation. When we do this, we will act in a mindless manner that inevitably gets us into trouble. Witness the couple that regularly spends entire evenings watching whatever happens to be on TV. The script becomes the frame of reference for their actions together ("If it's Tuesday night, we must be watching . . ."). They may each believe that watching TV is what the other wants to do. As a result, they do not explore other options for relational activities, such as going out for the evening, playing a game, or having a conversation. When we are conscious of our frame of reference or try to see a situation from more than one frame, we can increase the number and quality of message options available to us.

The type of mindless interaction described previously has been studied extensively by social psychologist Ellen Langer.[3] Langer notes that human creativity is a result of the mindful activity of creating new categories or distinctions in the world around us. However, once we forge a new category, it tends to take on a life of its own and we become "trapped by our own categories." We are then like "projectiles moving along a predetermined course."[4] The more mindless we are, the less control we have.

Greetings are a common form of mindless interaction. How many times have you communicated as automatically as Pat does in this crowded, noisy hallway:

PAT: Good morning, Chris. How's it going?

CHRIS: Good . . . I guess. Actually, things could be better. Are you . . .

PAT: (*continuing down the hall, calling over his shoulder*) Fine, thanks.

CHRIS: (*trying to catch Pat's eye*) Could we talk when you get some time?

PAT: (*walking away*) Yeah, good to see you, too. Take care.

Notice how Pat assumes that Chris's responses will follow the typical greeting ritual ("Hi, how are you?" "Fine, and you?" "Good, thanks.") and doesn't really listen to confirm what Chris actually says. We tend to interact unthinkingly in many situations. The reason for the frequency of mindless interaction is that we overlearn situations so thoroughly that we are essentially following scripts. In fact, much of our interaction is scripted — we are able to predict what will happen next with considerable accuracy (we'll have more to say about such scripts later in this chapter). Charles Berger and William Douglas argue that we pay close attention to our own and others' behavior only under rather specific conditions, such as when (1) novel situations occur for which no script exists, (2) external factors interrupt a scripted interaction, (3) scripted behavior requires more effort than usual, (4) the outcome of a situation is not what we expected, or (5) multiple scripts

come into conflict.[5] In most circumstances we act without being all that aware of what we're doing.

In many cases such mindless interaction may actually be quite efficient. If we stopped to think about everything we do, our interactions would be filled with more hesitations and awkward pauses than usual. But a steady diet of mindless interaction can remove control of communication from us. We then run the risk of not learning from successful communication encounters because we can't remember what happened. And of course, bad habits are repeated endlessly when we aren't aware of them.

COMMUNICATION AND CHANGES IN SOCIAL COGNITIONS

The relationship between social cognition processes and communication is not one-way. Just as our cognitive frame of reference influences how we send and receive messages, the messages we exchange with others can influence our own and others' cognitive representations of the social world. This fact is perhaps most obvious with small children. A child learns to use the social categories taught to him or her by parents. Several researchers have demonstrated the important effects that the style of parental communication has on a child's development of social-cognitive abilities. For example, parents with a *power-assertive* style are more likely to use their authority and specific rewards and punishments as disciplinary strategies ("Do this because I said so."). On the other hand, parents with a *person-centered style* typically try to explain their actions to the child, identifying reasons and motives. Research suggests that the person-centered style enhances the child's social-cognitive development because it teaches the child to consider the perspectives of others, an ability that leads to better understanding of others' intentions, motives, and feelings.[6] Thus, it appears that how we communicate does affect the social cognitions that other people develop.

As adults our interactions with others can also change the way we categorize people and social events. Think about what happens when, for instance, you join a new social circle or organization. Part of the socialization process is learning to talk like the other people in the group, which in turn means thinking in the same terms (using the same social categories) as they do. When a person joins the sales or marketing staff of a large national manufacturer, his or her concept of the "customer" will change in remarkable ways. People will no longer be seen as just consumers, but as 18- to 32-year-olds, upwardly mobile achievers, emulators, experientials, inner directeds, or the societally conscious. These are terms that Madison Avenue uses to describe different consumer lifestyles.[7] They are also concepts that serve as focal points for designing sales pitches.

The Structure of Social Cognition

Before we can fully understand how our social cognitions influence the way we communicate, we need to have a basic understanding of how social cognition processes work. In this section we begin with a brief description of how cognitive psychologists believe the mind functions to form categories and what factors promote the use of one category over another. Then we describe some of the particular cognitive structures related to social perceptions.

HOW THE MIND WORKS

Most cognitive psychologists today believe that the human brain is more than just a simple "recorder" of stimuli within the environment. The brain plays a highly active "organizing" role in interpreting incoming information. Inputs from the environment are received as sensory stimuli (hot or cold sensations, light waves, sound waves, and so on) that travel along neural pathways to the brain. The brain itself is composed of tiny structures or nodes linked together by associational paths. These interconnected pathways can be thought to be creating "mental models" of what we experience. When we encounter a new or ambiguous situation, the incoming stimuli are compared to previously stored models. If the current stimuli closely match a recent or frequently activated model, that structure or model is likely to be activated again. The cognitive model then serves as a guide by processing additional stimuli in line with our expectations. In fact, our perceptions are often distorted because the brain imposes the mental models on the stimuli, organizing them to be more in accordance with the model.

Think about the path you take to work or school every day. If you had to draw a map of how to get there, you would not suddenly recall every turn in the road or every signpost along the way. You would forget landmarks and features that did not fit your mental model. It's not the real landscape between home and office that you rely on, it's the mental shorthand you've developed that would guide your drawing of the map. Our social perceptions function in much the same way. We each have mental images of different "types" of people, for example. If our initial impression of someone closely resembles our cognitive model of a "preppy" person, we are likely to perceive that person as having many of the characteristics stored in our cognitive model, even though the person did not actually demonstrate those characteristics. We might remember the person as wearing penny loafers, for instance, even though he or she was not.

TYPES OF COGNITIVE STRUCTURES

Many different kinds of cognitive structures influence our social behavior. Cognitive psychologists have created the term *schemata* as a general label for these mental models. A **schema** is a

A prototype of one person's "best example" of a category of people or objects. Robert Bechtle's painting illustrates his idea of the prototypical American family.

(*'61 Pontiac*, 1968–69)

cognitive structure that helps us process and organize information.[8] It is, in effect, a coherent set of expectations that enable us to comprehend and make sense of novel events.[9] Presumably, schema and other forms of social cognition operate outside our awareness, making it difficult to observe them directly. Researchers study schema by exposing people to social events and then testing how they remember what they have experienced. The assumption is that "people do not *reproduce* from memory what *was* but at least partly *reconstruct* what *was* based on what *must have been*."[10] The difference between what actually happened and how it is remembered is taken to be an indication of the expectations associated with a cognitive schema. So far, researchers have identified four basic types of schemata that we think are relevant to interpersonal communication: prototypes, personal constructs, stereotypes, and scripts.

Prototypes help us to categorize objects, people, events, or relationships. They answer the question "What is it?" A **prototype** is an organized set of knowledge that reflects the best example of a category of persons, objects, or events.[11] Thus, we each have our own prototypical image of a used-car salesperson (person prototype), the qualities of a good friend (relational prototype), or the type of conversation that makes a good first impression (event prototype).

A *person prototype* refers to the characteristics we associate with a given category of persons, such as nerds, preppies, valley girls, or jocks. No two individuals we might categorize as "yuppies" are identical, yet we have a mental image of what a typical one looks or acts like. The more any person matches the prototype, the easier he or she is to classify. Prototypes help us "identify" what kind of person we are dealing with by matching appearance, behavior, and perceived qualities to a known prototype. Most of us probably have a cognitive prototype of a "friendly person" that we use to help us decide whether or not to strike up a conversation with a stranger. If the stranger's appearance, eye contact, and overall demeanor match our "friendly" prototype, we will be more likely to pursue a conversation.

A *relational prototype* is a cognitive mechanism that stores and organizes knowledge (expectations and beliefs) about a particular type of interpersonal relationship. Every time we interact, we use a prototype to guide our own message production. If we want to maintain a friendship, for example, we will behave in accordance with the relationship rules we associate with the prototype of a "good friend" and avoid behaviors that we think of as merely "casual friends." If our desire is to move the friendship even further, let's say toward that of "best friends," we will rely on our conception of behaviors that fit that prototype.

An *event prototype* registers our beliefs and expectations about a type of social episode. We associate different behaviors as typical of a fraternity party versus a dinner party. For instance, we may expect beer to be served at one and wine at the other. Or we may expect people to act in a more spontaneous and raucous fashion at one and to act dignified and reserved at the other, and so on.

A **personal construct,** on the other hand, allows us to describe things in greater detail and make judgments about them. Constructs are mental yardsticks for deciding how two things are similar yet different from a third thing.[12]

They answer the questions "What are its characteristics?" and "What do I think about it?" For instance, you might judge members of the Hell's Angels and Guardian Angels to be violent and dangerous in contrast to members of the California Angels baseball team. Another person might perceive the Guardian Angels and California Angels to be positive role models, with the Hell's Angels serving as negative role models. The terms *violent, dangerous,* and *positive* versus *negative* role models are examples of personal constructs. We will look at other examples of constructs in person perception later in this chapter.

Stereotypes are closely related to prototypes, but they are not the same thing. A prototype categorizes people; a stereotype goes beyond categorizing to the level of prediction. A stereotype is simply a set of beliefs about the probable behavior of members of a particular group.[13] Stereotypes have a certain sense of "allness" to them, as if every member of a group always behaves like other members. Thus, stereotypes answer the question "What can I expect it to do?" You might stereotype a Doberman pinscher as an attack dog, expecting it to take your leg off if you get too near. Stereotypes may or may not be accurate. They may outlive their usefulness and they may be unfair to individuals, but they do make the world more organized and predictable. Culture is a major source of stereotypes, many of which are prejudicial to members of fringe groups. We will explore communication patterns related to prejudice in Chapter 13.

Scripts are guides to action. A script is defined as a "coherent sequence of events expected by the individual either as a participant or as an observer."[14] Scripts answer the questions "What can we do together?" "How shall I proceed?" and "What do I do next?" Many scripts — such as attending a traditional wedding or going to a Catholic mass — are well defined and make it easy for us to know what to do next. Unscramble the following list of behaviors associated with a "restaurant" script, and place them in the usual sequence:

TABLE 6.2 What Do Cognitive Schemata Help Us Do?		
Type of Schema	**Helps Us To:**	**Example**
Prototypes: Person prototypes Relational prototypes	Identify what kind of person, relationship, object, or event we're dealing with	Person prototype: valley girl, nerd, gearhead Relational prototype: All-American couple, bosom buddies
Personal constructs: Physical constructs Role constructs Interaction constructs Psychological constructs	Define the characteristics of a person, object, or event	Physical: thin-bulky Role: helper-helpee Interaction: talkative-quiet Psychological: optimistic-pessimistic
Stereotypes	Develop expectations for the behavior associated with a person or social event	Blondes have more fun; Greeks are stuck-ups; engineers are boring
Scripts	Know what to do in a particular situation	"Greeting script," "first-date script," a "knock-down, drag-out fighting script"

- The waiter takes your order.
- You pay the bill.
- You go to the salad bar.
- You look at the menu.
- You leave a tip.
- The hostess seats you.
- The waiter brings your meal.
- The waiter brings water.
- You ask about the special.

Chances are you know the script pretty well. What other situations do you know that are highly scripted? Can you identify the sequence of events? Which ones are crucial? Which ones could be omitted without ruining the performance of the script?

Prototypes, constructs, stereotypes, and scripts are all extremely useful cognitive schemata. Each type of schema directly affects our communication with others. We interact differently with different types of people or in different types of relationships. We may even have a cognitive script for "how to test the best-friend potential" of a relationship. Such a script might suggest that certain best-friend behaviors ought to occur before others. For example, an invitation to go on an all-day shopping spree might precede spending a weekend at the family's lake retreat, since the first is of shorter duration, limited to a single activity, and doesn't involve contact with one's family. As we interact, we use personal constructs to make mental notes about the relational implications of each other's messages. Some of these impressions may even alter our prototypic expectations, changing the way we use the prototype in future interactions. Once we have formed a basic impression of a type of person or relationship, stereotypes help us estimate how the other is likely to behave, and we can plan our own communication accordingly.

The Perceptual Process: An Overview

There are two ways to think about the relationship between events and our perceptions of them. One view is that physical reality just happens and our senses, as long as they are not impaired, simply record what is out there in a more or less objective fashion. This suggests that we are *passive* receivers of incoming stimuli — much like the windshield on your car collects insects and dirt particles that happen to come its way. Most theorists, however, believe that perception is an *active* process. Our minds are constantly working to fill in missing information or link events and experiences together in ways that make sense to us. We could never make sense of television programs, for example, if perception was a passive process. Our mind has to actively categorize commercials as irrelevant to the story line, as well as manage a whole host of technical conventions such as fade-ins and fade-outs to simulate the passing of time, blurred images that suggest a dreamlike state, and so on. The work our brain performs in helping us perceive the world amounts to a full-time occupation. In this section we'll explore how we actively structure our environment, attending to some elements while ignoring others and interpreting and organizing all that we perceive.

CREATING STRUCTURE, STABILITY, AND MEANING

We construct our own reality by structuring, stabilizing, and relating the stream of stimuli around us in meaningful ways.[15] Normally our culture provides us with a number of ways to structure events. We are not born into a world totally devoid of meaning. But most of the meaning is social — conventions and agreements created by the members of social groups. For instance, every culture finds its own ways to structure the passage of time. In our culture a "day" is broken down into smaller units of hours, minutes, and seconds. But we do not perceive every unit of time objectively. On some occasions, such as watching the end of a close basketball game or timing the 100-meter dash, we structure time into seconds and even hundreths of a second. At other times we structure time so loosely that hours may go by without even registering. We may forget to eat or go to class because we're wrapped up in a good book or involved in a conversation with an old friend we haven't seen in years. We simply don't perceive the passage of time.

During the course of a baseball game, the home plate umpire has to structure and restructure a strike zone for each batter. There is no such thing as an objective strike zone (the area over home plate and between the batter's armpits and knees, through which a pitched ball must pass in order to be called a strike). The pitcher, catcher, and batter each see a different strike zone as well. For each of them, the stimulus of a pitched ball and a batter's reaction will be categorized as a ball or strike, a fair or foul ball, and so on. Each is likely to structure the stimulus somewhat differently from the other players or the umpires.

People perceive objects as stable and unchanging. The next time you watch television, pay close attention to the size of the images on the screen (and thus on the retina of your eye). When the camera shot is a close-up, a person's face may be as large as the entire screen. As the camera fades away, the head gets smaller. Yet you have no trouble assuming that it's the same person with the same size head; you don't think the person's head is constantly expanding and contracting. You are actively processing the stimulus so that it appears stable in size. The point is that the actual image on the retina of the eye is not stable — it keeps changing in size — but we perceive it as stable.

Finally, we relate events or stimuli to one another in ways that have meaning for us. When you develop a headache, you probably try to relate its occurrence to something else in the environment. The jackhammer outside your window, the glare of your computer screen, or the presence of someone you despise at your birthday party may all be leading candidates for the cause of your headache. Actually, none of these may be responsible, but the perception that they are meaningfully related will influence your behavior — to close the window, turn off the computer, or try to leave the party. Medical researchers engage in the same process of trying to relate environmental stimuli and the body's physiological responses in meaningful ways. They just use more sophisticated theories and statistical models to decide what is "meaningful."

Studies show how ingrained the process is even when no apparent order or meaning exists. In one study, a tape recording of indistinct vowel sounds was presented to people with the following instructions: "This is a recording of a man talking. He is not speaking very plainly, but if you listen carefully you will be able to tell what he is saying. I'll play it over and over again, so you can get it, but be sure to tell me as soon as you have an idea of what he is saying." Surprisingly, people had little trouble identifying intelligible verbal content, unaware that it was entirely their own creation.[16] We humans want to experience meaning and order in everything that we see and hear, so much so that we frequently create it by altering our perceptions of stimuli.

Culture plays a key role in structuring our perceptions. We are all taught conventional ways of perceiving people and objects. In fact, culture is what makes social cognitions "social." Every individual is capable of making cognitive distinctions; but most of our cognitions are social — they are derived from interaction with other people who learned them from still other people. Like most cultures, we typically assume that our own way of life is at least a little "better" than most; we judge people from other cultures in terms of how they differ from our own. Studies have shown that even watching a film involves perceptual skills that are culturally learned. Box 6.1 reveals how filmmakers try to manage our perceptions by relying on their understanding of the perceptual process plus a number of conventional techniques (for example, using a musical score to simulate fear, happiness, or other emotions). In what ways do we use similar props or "arrange" scenes to influence how other people perceive us? In some respects we are all cinematographers using our knowledge of people's perceptual tendencies to alter their impressions of us. Some of us just understand the process better than others.

It should be clear by now just how much of a role we play in our own perceptions of objects, events, and people. The process can be arbitrarily broken down into a series of steps, even though they may often occur simultaneously. Let's look at how we expose ourselves and selectively attend to some stimuli, add previous knowledge or expectations regarding that stimulus, and integrate what we see, hear, or feel into an organized whole.

SELECTIVE EXPOSURE AND ATTENTION

There is no shortage of stimuli in everyday life. Regardless of whether the situation is a solitary activity or a communicative event, we are exposed to many more stimuli than our brain can possibly process. Sometimes we go out of our way to expose ourselves to stimuli. **Selective exposure** refers to placing ourselves in or avoiding situations where we will be certain to encounter a specific stimulus; thus, we tend to encounter only stimuli that we want or expect to encounter. Visiting another country, enrolling in foreign language or anthropology courses, and listening to international broadcasts on short-wave radio will expose you to stimuli not

BOX **6.1**

Perception Goes to the Movies: How Cinematographers Influence What We See

A

Filmmakers are faced with the challenge of communicating their visual message through a limited medium. The "big screen" is only a two-dimensional rectangle, with a dominant horizontal shape. Every scene in a film has to be conveyed within this frame. To create the appearance of depth or extreme heights, a feeling of suspense, or emotional arousal, directors and cinematographers must know quite a lot about the perceptual processes of the audience. They must determine how we are likely to interpret and react to the placement and movement of elements within the frame, the effects of lighting and color, different camera angles, and so on. What do cinematographers know about us that enables them to achieve their intended effects?

Whether their knowledge is implicit or explicit, filmmakers understand a number of perceptual principles that have become the basis for a conventionalized code of filmmaking. For one thing, they know that our attention is most likely to be drawn to the central portion of the screen. We expect elements within the frame to be balanced, with dominant elements near the center, or slightly above center in the case of most medium

shots. When a director's purpose is to achieve realism, most shots will be balanced in this way, since that is what he or she knows the audience expects. The result is unobtrusive. But when a sense of drama is needed, the "norm" is usually violated. Dominant figures or elements may be placed near the edge of the screen, perhaps even fading out of the picture.

To create a sense of dominance or power, important elements may be emphasized by placing them in the top third of the screen. Sometimes this is done subtly by focusing the camera clearly on a character in the center third, leaving another character slightly out of focus. The result is a "reminder" of who is really in control (see Photo A). Also, by using a low camera angle, a figure on the screen may appear more dominant or menacing, as it looks down on us or on other characters or objects.

experienced by many Americans. Turning off the TV and avoiding caffeine are also ways of selecting what stimuli you are exposed to.

Once in an environment, we will selectively attend to some stimuli and ignore others. **Selective attention** refers to our active participation in determining which of the many stimuli pre-

sent we will actually perceive. As you read this, stop and try to process as many stimuli as you can. Check all of your senses. What background noises can you bring into focus (for example, the stereo, the television, the humming of the refrigerator)? What can you feel that you were not aware of moments ago? What can you see in

The opposite effect can be achieved by placing characters in the lower portion of the frame. Characters placed this way look especially vulnerable or helpless, and even more so if the rest of the screen is empty or stark in contrast to the lonely figure at the bottom of the screen. A bird's-eye camera view (directly overhead of the action) is disorienting to the viewer, since we rarely see such a view in ordinary life. Scenes constructed in this fashion are often used to portray a theme of fate or destiny.

In our culture we also expect forward movement to be conveyed from left to right. By showing movement "against the grain," a filmmaker can create a feeling of tension in the viewer. Downward motion can be used to invoke a sense of danger or vulnerability.

Bright or dark color, as well as special lighting, can dominate a frame. Our attention is drawn to brighter colors and lighted areas of an otherwise dark screen (see Photo B). Darkly lit scenes and dark colors may symbolize doom for the characters involved. Color may also be used to balance other compositional features in the frame. A dominant shape on one side of the screen might be compensated for by a bright color on the other side.

These conventions are but a few of the tricks of the trade that cinematographers rely on to communicate through film. Each is based on research in perceptual processes. Can you think of other ways that filmmakers try to manage what you see on the screen?

SOURCES: Giannetti, Louis D. *Understanding Movies.* Englewood Cliffs, N.J.: Prentice-Hall, 1976.
Nichols, Bill. *Ideology and the Image.* Bloomington: Indiana University Press, 1981.

your field of vision if you really concentrate? Now you have some idea just how much there is to be processed at any given moment. Imagine not being able to block out some of these sights and sounds in order to return to the task of reading this chapter; it would be impossible to concentrate on the task at hand.

Fortunately, we can tune in and out the stimuli we receive. To a certain extent, this process is outside our awareness. Some environmental features seem to demand our attention. For instance, brightly colored moving objects generally catch our attention more readily than do dull, stationary ones; extremely tall persons stand out in a crowd; potholes on highways are hard to ignore because they are such a contrast to the relatively flat road surface. At other times physiological states may influence what you perceive. People who suffer from allergies such as hay fever notice more pollen in the air, selectively tune in when the pollen count is given on the evening weather report, and rarely pass over an ad for allergy medication.

While these examples make it appear that our attention is dictated by external affairs, we do exercise a great deal of control over what we perceive. We pay more attention to things that interest us or things that we are mentally prepared to see or hear. The fact that your best friend drives a brown, banged-up Chevy Impala may set you up to notice every brown Chevy Impala that crosses your path.

Past experiences, present motivations, and future goals all play a role in what we choose to attend to out of the myriad of stimuli in the world.

INTERPRETING AND ORGANIZING STIMULI

Once a stimulus has caught our attention, we must classify it in some way and relate it to other known stimulus categories. First, let's look at how we interpret what we perceive.

Interpreting Objects

When you were an infant, the entire world was new to you. Every object within sight needed to be touched and studied carefully, so you could figure out what to do with each one. By now, you perceive most objects as already interpreted. Once you were not so sure. The process of interpreting is done so quickly that we usually don't realize it. When driving to work or school, you immediately interpret a stimulus that is red, octagonal, and attached to a 10-foot pole alongside the road. Stop signs are familiar objects to drivers. But what if you suddenly see a small, brownish blur darting in front of your

car? Can you categorize it as quickly as you do a stop sign? It may have been a squirrel, a puppy, or a brown paper bag. At times like these you are a little more aware that you are interpreting reality as much as seeing it. If we occasionally have difficulty interpreting concrete objects, imagine the problems we face when interpreting something as abstract as the communication behavior of another person.

Organizing Stimuli

The stimuli we do attend to and interpret do not exist in isolation. As we saw earlier, we relate various stimuli in ways that will make them more meaningful. Our brain actively processes stimuli using many of the cognitive structures we identified earlier: prototypes, personal constructs, stereotypes, and scripts.

Take, for example, the driver who sees the brownish blur moving onto the road in front of her. How might she organize this particular stimulus in relation to other stimuli in the environment? Let's look at several possibilities, given what she perceives in her immediate environment as well as her cognitive frame of mind. If she noticed the shopping center she just passed, she might be more likely to assume that the blur is a wadded-up paper bag from the grocery. On the other hand, if she just left home after walking her dog, the recently activated cognitive schema of "dog" might lead her to see the blur as a puppy. Or suppose that earlier that morning she cleaned her back porch, repotting the tomato plants that had been dug up by squirrels. Not only would the cognitive prototype of "squirrel" be activated, but the personal constructs of "dirty," "rotten," and "good-for-nothing" might also be activated. If this were the case, she might not try very hard to avoid hitting the blur — unless, of course, she endorses a lifestyle that includes a cognitive script about what happens to people who abuse animals. In other words, our perception of a single stimulus is always colored by the way in which we organize that stimulus in relation to other stimuli and cognitions.

Look at Nikolaus Braun's *Street Scene in Berlin* for a few moments; then look away and try to recall as many objects or scenes as you can. This exercise will give you some idea of just how selective your attention and recall can be.

(Nikolaus Braun (1900–1950), *Street Scene in Berlin*)

During the organizing step of the perceptual process, we not only arrange stimuli together, we also envelope them with our past experiences, preconceptions, and beliefs about the stimulus person, object, or event. We do this by imposing our cognitive schemes on the world we see. A popular song captures this tendency with the phrase "What a fool believes, he sees." We would amend this statement by removing the word "fool." We are all influenced by our cognitive schemata. To see how these schemata affect interpersonal situations, we return to the four social cognition processes mentioned at the outset of this chapter.

Four Processes in Interpersonal Perception

To interact with others successfully requires a wealth of social knowledge. You must be able to perceive the information in your social environment accurately enough to know which of the hundreds of schemata in your memory bank are the best ones to pull out of the vault. This is, of course, a very complicated operation. Cognitive psychologists are just beginning to understand how we do it. We have tried to simplify the problem by highlighting four perceptual processes that people engage in before, during, and after social interaction. These include identifying (1) what the situation is, (2) who the other person is, (3) who you are and what kind of relationship between self and other is implied, and (4) why things unfold the way they do. Let's examine each of these processes more closely.

SIZING UP SITUATIONS

The more we know about the particular situations in which we interact with others, the more likely we are to produce effective messages. We propose three useful ways to manage situations: (1) identifying episodes, (2) knowing scripts, and (3) perceiving potential consequences of following scripts.

Orienting Ourselves: Episode Identification

At one time or another, we have all been in situations where we didn't know what was going on or what to do. Visiting a foreign culture or being initiated into a sorority or fraternity are examples of situations that are not very well defined for us. Knowing the situation can make interactions much easier. In its simplest form a situation is "a place plus a definition."[17] When we enter a place, our first task is to orient ourselves or get our bearings. One way to do this is to ask the simple question "Where am I?" We find ourselves in a variety of places every day: in the car, at home or work, in the shopping mall, at the zoo, church, or bus station, and so on. Where we are determines to a large extent what we can do socially. But identifying the place alone is not enough. For instance, a church building can serve as a place for worship, weddings, ice cream socials, even bingo. To communicate appropriately requires that we recognize the physical and social cues that de-

fine the episode or activity that is taking place. Each culture has an array of social episodes or activities for its members to follow. For the individual, **social episodes** are "internal cognitive representations about common, recurring interaction routines within a defined cultural milieu."[18] Some typical social episodes? Having a big family dinner, attending a parent-teacher conference, planning a party, gossiping. How do we know which episodes to enact? Often we have a particular episode in mind when we initiate a conversation with someone. Perhaps you know someone who likes to "pick fights" or tease a brother or sister in order to get him or her riled up. Often enacting an episode is a process of negotiation — one person suggests an activity, only to have the other counter with another option, as in this conversation:

LAURA: I noticed that Kmart is having a sale on lawn mowers.

BUD: This is the only evening I'm free all week. I don't want to spend it shopping for a lawn mower. Besides, the Battle of the Mack Trucks is going on at the fairgrounds tonight.

Social interaction is a continuous dance in which participants accept and decline each other's invitations to enact different episodes. For instance, when two old friends have a chance meeting on the street, the question "Can I buy you a drink?" is an invitation to engage in the episode of "talking over old times." Refusing the drink because you are not thirsty would be missing the point — it would reflect a failure to recognize the other's definition of the situation.

Using Scripts to Guide Interaction: Open, Closed, and Defined Episodes

When people play out an episode, they may also follow a script. As we have seen, a script is a highly predictable sequence of events. Some classroom learning episodes are highly scripted;

others are not. For example, you may be able to predict (from experience) that every Wednesday morning your history professor will call the roll, hand out a quiz, collect the quizzes, lecture for 20 minutes, and end the class with a humorous anecdote. The more predictable the sequence of events, the more scripted the interaction is. Another class may be taught so differently that you never know for sure what will happen in a given class period. Both examples are classroom episodes, but only the first one follows a clearly identifable script.

Scripts and episodes are useful guides to interaction. Identifying the episode narrows the range of possible actions and reactions. Knowing the script makes social life even more predictable. Michael Brenner has proposed that the vast majority of social episodes fall into one of three types: closed, open, and defined.[19]

Closed Episodes When a situation is almost completely scripted, it is a **closed episode.** Rules for proper behavior are well known in advance and govern the flow of interaction. Rituals such as greetings and religious observances are closed episodes. Many business organizations tightly script interactions by training their personnel to follow carefully devised sets of procedures. If you've ever applied for a loan at a bank, you have probably participated in a closed episode. You have a standard set of questions you want answered (the loan rate, fixed or variable, length of repayment, and so on) and so does the loan officer (income, collateral, address, credit references, and so on). Other, less formal, interactions are also somewhat scripted. An episode of "small talk" has a limited range of topics, although the sequence in which these topics are discussed may vary.

Open Episodes When participants enter a situation without any preconceived plan or with a very general one, they are involved in an **open episode.** In such situations there is greater freedom to create new forms of interaction and to change episodes midway through. Episodes such as "hanging out with friends" are some-

times scripted, but not always. When almost anything can be introduced as a topic of conversation or an activity to perform, the episode is an open one. An orchestra performing a John Philip Sousa march is clearly following a musical script, but a group of musicians having a "jam session" is not. The freedom to improvise or break the rules is typical of an open episode. Some open episodes may be unsettling, since there is no clear idea of what should be done next. Perhaps you have been in situations where nobody seemed to know what to do. We know of an instructor whose routine on the first day of class was to walk into the room, assume the lotus position on top of his desk, and say nothing for the first half of the class. His point was to show how communication is used to define ambiguous situations. Eventually, students would begin talking to one another, trying to figure out what he was doing. From the students' point of view, this was an open episode.

Defined Episodes While closed episodes are known to be such in advance as a result of expectations, many situations are defined "in progress" as participants follow their own personal goals and plans to achieve a working consensus. Even so, the consensus is often temporary — definitions of the situation may fall apart as quickly as they develop. A **defined episode** is an open episode in which the participants are trying to negotiate some closure. The difference is that open episodes are experienced as creative and liberating; defined episodes are competitive attempts to control the activity. Brenner suggests that defined episodes are often ambiguous and unstructured interactions because each partner may be proposing alternative directions for the episode. For example, a not-very-good salesperson might initiate a "sales episode" but eventually succumb to a clever-but-unwilling-to-buy customer's definition of the situation as "shooting the breeze." A romantic evening can be spoiled quickly when a candlelight dinner becomes redefined as an episode of "stilted conversation" or "talking about the kids." In closed relationships people

Our individual traits are minimized in many social situations so that our behavior will conform to social expectations. Note how Cezanne emphasizes the card players' concentration on the game—so intent are they that their individual personalities are suppressed.

(Paul Cezanne, *The Card Players*)

may spend a lot of time just deciding what episode to enact next. We know of four friends who, in the course of one evening, proposed over 20 different activities for that evening. Needless to say, they ended up doing nothing but talking about what they could be doing. Chances are none of the persons involved planned to spend the evening that way, but our observations lead us to believe that these two couples frequently end up playing this "what do you want to do tonight" episode.

Although we may think that closed episodes are too limiting and value open ones for the freedom they provide, stop and think how chaotic social life would be without any well-defined or scripted episodes. The important thing, of course, is that we recognize the types of episodes others propose so that we can accept the invitation or decline gracefully.

Identifying Consequences of Episodes and Scripts

Sometimes it is just as important to perceive the possible outcomes of a situation, like the chess player who sees several moves ahead, as it is to properly label that situation. We can avoid detrimental outcomes if we can see them coming. Salespeople often use the tried-and-true "yes technique" to set up unwitting customers. They ask questions that seem unrelated to selling their product, such as "Are those lovely photographs of *your* children?" or "I've had a hard time catching you at home. You must work awfully long hours." The customer's automatic "yes" in response to each question or comment establishes a habitual pattern that could cost a lot of money at the end of the episode.

Following a script can lead to positive or negative outcomes. Sometimes we know the script so well that we can tell our friends what they are going to say next. If we finish the sentence for them, they may be gratified that we understand them so well or offended that we cut them off. Another negative consequence is that scripted interactions can become boring or even damage a relationship if repeated too often. Researchers who study marital conflict patterns often comment that couples get caught up in "conflict scripts" that neither person intended to start but both felt compelled to see to the bitter end once the episode began. And as we have already seen, expecting the interaction to follow a script can prevent us from perceiving important messages the other may be sending our way. Following the script can also limit creativity, but only if we remain tied completely to the script. Minor alterations, improvisations, and other forms of playing with the script can add some spice to everyday interactions.

SIZING UP PEOPLE

As we interact, we come to an understanding of what other people are like. Knowing how to size up the individual is another way to reduce our uncertainty about communication. In studying the process of impression formation, researchers have discovered several factors that

influence our judgment. We will discuss four of these factors: (1) the use of personal constructs, (2) implicit personality theory, (3) self-fulfilling prophecies, and (4) cognitive complexity.

The Use of Personal Constructs to Judge Others

Earlier in the chapter, we identified personal constructs as mental yardsticks for evaluating objects, events, and people. Here we focus on how we use those constructs to form impressions of those people we communicate with. Since constructs are "personal," no two people will use them in exactly the same way. You and I may both observe Bill eating a sandwich in two bites, mustard dribbling down his chin. You may think he is "aggressive" while I argue that he is "messy" and "impolite." What we see in others is a combination of their actual behavior and our personal construct of their behavior. These constructs say as much about you and me as they do about Bill.

Even though we each use different constructs to judge others, we do use them in similar ways. Steven Duck has noted a typical pattern in the use of four different kinds of constructs.[20] The four types are:

- Physical constructs (tall-short, beautiful-ugly)
- Role constructs (buyer-seller, teacher-student)
- Interaction constructs (friendly-hostile, polite-rude)
- Psychological constructs (motivated-lazy, kind-cruel)

Our initial impressions are frequently based on physical attributes — we take stock of how people are dressed or how attractive they are. These are quickly followed by the formation of role constructs as we try to make sense out of each other's position in the social world. As we talk, we may focus attention on interaction constructs, or aspects of the other's style of communication. Finally, we use these observations to infer what makes the other tick (psychological constructs) — we begin to guess at motivations and build a personality for the other. When we reach this last stage, we have gone beyond simply interpreting what we see and hear; we've begun to assume that we know things about the person that we can't see.

Implicit Personality Theory: Organizing Trait Impressions

We don't simply form isolated opinions of other people; rather, we organize all of our individual perceptions into a more complete picture by filling in a lot of missing information. One of the ways we do this is through what is referred to as an **implicit personality theory.** This is the belief on our part that certain individual traits are related to other traits. If we observe a trait that we think is part of a cluster, we will assume that the person also has the rest of the traits in the cluster. Each of us has our own notions of what traits go together. For some, the traits (or constructs) "intelligent," "quiet," and "friendly" may cluster together.[21] If we observe behavior that we interpret as friendly and quiet, we may then attribute intelligence to that person without any firsthand evidence. The formation of trait impressions depends on several factors: (1) the perception of central traits, (2) the order in which traits are observed, and (3) the influence of prototypes and stereotypes.

Central Traits   Some traits may carry more weight than others in forming impressions and can be described as central traits. When present, a central trait changes the way we perceive the whole cluster of traits. In a classic study, social psychologist Harold Kelley presented two groups of students with the following list of adjectives describing a new instructor they were about to meet. One group was told the new in-

structor was "*warm,* industrious, critical, practical, and determined"; the other group was told the instructor was "*cold,* industrious, critical, practical, and determined."

Which description do you think led students to form a more favorable impression? If you said the first description, you are in agreement with most of the students in this study. The central trait (warm-cold) changed the way the perceiver judged the other traits, which in turn affected the overall impression.[22]

Primacy versus Recency Effect   Another factor that makes some traits stand out is *when* they are first perceived. The tendency for first impressions to be lasting ones is known as the **primacy effect.** When more recent observations change our initial impression, we have the **recency effect.** Which effect is more likely to prevail? Generally, the primacy effect rules — we tend to form impressions quickly and hold on to them. For example, you attend a social mixer and see Pete, whom you do not know, placing a whoopee cushion on the chair of some unsuspecting person. You surmise that he must have gone to a lot of trouble to bring the cushion and waited anxiously for the right moment to play his practical joke. You quickly form an impression of him as a "clown," and you are not overly impressed by such people. Your impression is likely to stick, especially if you later hear him laughing at someone who recoiled from a piece of plastic vomit. Even if he spends the rest of the evening in a rather docile mood, your impression is unlikely to change. Psychiatrist Leonard Zunin estimates that the first impression is formed solidly within the first four minutes of interaction with a stranger, followed by a decision to continue or terminate the episode.[23]

Prototypes and Stereotypes   Prototypes and stereotypes may also affect the emerging impression. Physical traits or key words and phrases used by a person may be so similar to our image of the prototypical "sales manager type" that we have trouble describing that person in any other way. Furthermore, if you have an associated stereotype that all salespeople have loose morals and tell offensive jokes, you can flesh out a complete impression in a matter of a few seconds. Once the impression is formed, you may only notice behaviors that are consistent with the image and ignore those that do not fit. Suppose someone other than Pete leaves the party with the whoopee cushion in tow. Objectively, this may call into question your belief that Pete planned a series of practical jokes for the evening. But you will probably not give it much thought now that you are convinced you know what kind of person he is. In this way we reinforce stereotypes even in the face of contradictory evidence.

A recent study illustrates what people who employ different prototypes will do with the same basic information about another person. Researcher Randy Wood had students imagine that they were observing a "deceptive scenario" in which a smooth-talking used car salesperson was selling a car known to be a "lemon" to an unsuspecting customer. Wood asked his student observers to read several cue cards, each of which described a different deceptive behavior such as "excessive fidgeting," "talks slower," "overly friendly," "looks away," and so on. Students were to rank order the behaviors from those least likely to be observed in this situation to those most likely to be observed. Interestingly, Wood found that people had significantly different expectations, indicating the existence of several different types of deceptive communicators rather than a single prototype. Expectations were grouped into four different types. The first type was defined by cues such as fast-talking, overly dominant, excessive smiling, overly dramatic, and attentive — cues suggestive of a very *high intensity* level. Other students expected the salesperson to be *overly tense* and focused on cues such as excessive fidgeting, looking away, and frequent body shifts. A third group relied on a prototype with a central trait of *vagueness* — friendly, dominant, forced smile, but vague in communicating content. And yet a fourth group expected to observe the salesperson as one who was relaxed,

friendly, and who communicates exceptionally well — in other words, one *highly skilled* at deception. In another deceptive scenario, these same students used different prototypes than they did in the salesperson situation. This suggests that individuals may have a variety of schemata even for the same general type (e.g., a deceptive person) and that they match them to different situations in different ways.[24]

Interpersonal Self-Fulfilling Prophecies

Another important perceptual tendency is the **self-fulfilling prophecy**. Unlike the more passive implicit personality theory (in which traits are associated in the mind), the self-fulfilling prophecy involves both perception *and* behavior. It starts when one person — the observer — believing something to be true about another person — the target — begins acting toward the target as if the belief were fact. This action prompts the target to behave in line with the observer's expectations. If you believe your friend is "touchy," you are likely to avoid sensitive topics and be more hesitant in what you say. The effect of your behavior? Your friend becomes oversensitive because *you* are acting oversolicitous. Unaware that you helped create the prickly atmosphere, you say to yourself, "My God, it's true. You can't say anything to him."

Cognitive Complexity: Factors Affecting Impression Formation

Not everyone forms impressions in the same way. Observers differ in the number and quality of personal constructs they use to evaluate others. A **cognitively complex** person's system is greater in number of personal constructs (*differentiation*), includes more abstract psychological categories (*abstraction*), and has more elaborate ways of relating various constructs (*integration*).[25] A cognitively simple person has fewer, less abstract constructs about people and views those constructs as relatively isolated impressions. Let's look at an example comparing the two extremes.

Suppose Pat and Chris observe Marvin on several occasions. They are both present when Marvin (1) cheats on an English test, (2) takes charge and gets everyone out of a burning building, (3) refuses to help with a charity car wash, (4) helps a friend study for a difficult math test, (5) embarrasses another friend by pointing out her faults in front of a large group of people, and (6) always gives blood when there is an opportunity.

If you want to test yourself, you might write down your own impression of Marvin before reading on. Then come back and read the impressions that Chris and Pat formed.

To Pat, Marvin is "tall and handsome, but extremely selfish, difficult to get along with, and not trustworthy." When reminded of some of the positive things Marvin has done, Pat shrugs and says, "It's just a front. The real Marvin is a cheat."

To Chris, "Marvin seems selfish when he is unsure of himself, but quite selfless when he knows he can help out. Marvin is also very outspoken and direct — he says what is on his mind. If he believes in a cause, he'll support it. If he doesn't think it's important he won't give it the time of day." Chris sums up Marvin's behavior as being motivated by his insecurity: "If he didn't worry so much about being noticed, he wouldn't make himself look so bad. He has real potential."

Why are these two impressions so different? Pat uses fewer, more concrete constructs (for example, "tall and handsome") and ignores much of the information that doesn't fit with the emerging impression. If this impression is typical of her reactions, Pat's construct system is a relatively undeveloped one. Contrast that with Chris, who demonstrates a fairly high level of cognitive complexity. By integrating the apparent contradictions in Marvin's behavior, Chris has arrived at a more subtle understanding of Marvin, recognizing situational constraints as well as psychological motivations.

Research has shown cognitively complex persons to be more accurate in processing information about others, better at placing themselves in the role of the other person, and more patient in weighing most of the evidence before formulating a complete impression.[26] Less complex individuals tend to either stick with their original impression and ignore contradictory information or to change the impression to fit the most recent information they have.[27] They lack the ability to integrate the constructs they use into a more complete image of others.

Considering the differences between more complex and less complex persons, you might get the impression that the more complex, the better. Actually, it depends on the situation and the other person. Imagine Pat and Chris talking to each other. They would probably drive each other crazy. Pat would claim that Chris thinks too much and analyzes everybody. Chris would charge Pat with making snap judgments. In general, complex persons are more versatile in social situations and better at cross-cultural adaptation (as we will see in Chapter 13). But a cognitively complex person is not necessarily a "better" person. Like any of us, such a person can abuse his or her abilities by being unethical, insensitive, and so on.

SIZING UP RELATIONSHIPS

As we read the situation and form impressions of the other, we also face the perceptual task of determining what relevant aspects of self fit the situation and how the emerging relationship between self and other should be interpreted.

Self-Monitoring: Deciding Who to Be

We will consider the self-concept and communication in much more detail in Chapters 7 and 8; for now, it is important to realize that our

Body type is often taken to be a cue for personality, yet such attributions vary according to culture. Japanese artist Hokusai depicts thin people as energetic and tense; his fat people seem more relaxed and cheerful.

self-concept is frequently connected to our definition of the situation. Just as we form impressions of others, we form and present images of ourselves to others. The awareness of images of self and the ability to adapt these images to the situation at hand has been referred to as **self-monitoring**.[28] A high self-monitor tends to read the social situation first and then present an appropriate face, as opposed to simply presenting a consistent image of self in every situation.

Mark Snyder characterizes the difference between a high and low self-monitor in the form of the question each might ask in defining the situation.

The high self-monitor asks, "Who does this situation want me to be and how can I be that person?" In so doing, the high self-monitoring individual reads the character of the situation to identify the type of person called for by that type of situation, constructs a mental image or representation of a person who best exemplifies that type of person, and uses the prototypic person's self-presentation and expressive behavior as a set of guidelines for monitoring his or her own verbal and nonverbal actions. [The low self-monitor asks] "Who am I and how can I be me in this situation?"[29]

Instead of calling on a prototype to guide his or her actions, the low self-monitor behaves in accordance with an image of his or her "real" self.

To test yourself, make a short list of five or six very different social situations you frequently take part in. Write down how you typically behave in each situation, or better yet, have someone observe you in each of those situations and write down what you do. Then compare your actual behavior to Snyder's self-monitoring questions. Do you normally present a consistent self-image, or do you alter your self-presentation for each situation?

Our culture often sends us mixed messages. For instance, we are told to "be ourselves" and "remain true to self," messages that seem to endorse the low self-monitor's position. On the other hand, research demonstrates that being adaptable (being a high self-monitor) is one of the keys to social success. It is probably best to recognize that either extreme can be limiting. If we always try to maintain a consistent self-concept, we will be less versatile and probably less human because we won't experience the full range of human emotions and potentials. But if we are always changing to fit the situation or someone else's conception of us, we may compromise important standards and values. The best course is to ask ourselves which is more important in a given situation — being adaptable or being consistent. On one occasion it may be important for you to exert your individuality and violate the family rule that "everyone comes home for Christmas." The next year you might pass up a wonderful ski trip just to be home and fit in again.

Defining Relationships: Self in Relation to Others

When people interact, each presents an image of self to the other. These images are, however, usually quite fluid. We are responsive to the feedback of the other and begin quickly to negotiate a definition of the relationship between self and other. Thus, one important perceptual process is the identification of the type of relationship that applies in a given situation. Office workers at a company picnic may perceive that the superior-subordinate relationship with the

boss no longer applies during a game of softball. As long as the boss sees things the same way, there is no problem. But what if the boss assumes he or she is still in charge and wants to pitch? The difference in perceptions may lead to negative feelings that were never intended.

A wide range of relationship labels are available to us. We can be casual or long-time acquaintances, friends, close friends, almost friends, just friends, coworkers, neighbors, bowling partners, platonic lovers, husbands and wives, ex-husbands and -wives, blood brothers or sisters, business associates, straight man and funnyman, roommates, counselor and advisee, master and slave, even student and teacher. The list could go on.

Once a relational label is firm in our mind, it tends to limit our perception of what we can do together. Most American couples who have just begun dating probably don't even think about drawing up and signing prenuptial agreements about finances, children, property, and so on. These actions are not perceived as having anything to do with "real" romantic relationships.

Several studies have demonstrated the existence of relational prototypes. In the same way that we have mental images of typical personalities, we also form cognitive models of the best example of a romantic relationship or a good friendship. Sally Planalp found that prototypes students held of the student-professor relationship seemed to be guided by their expectations about the respective rights and obligations that each party has in different situations. Planalp had students read three conversations between a professor and student: (1) a student asking to add the professor's class, (2) a student asking to make up an exam that had been missed, and (3) a student requesting a change of grade for the professor's class. Different students read different versions of the conversations, some in which the professor made dominant, neutral, or submissive statements and others in which the student's statements varied in terms of dominance or submissiveness. One week later, students were asked to identify whether the conversation they had read the week before contained the dominant, neutral, or submissive statements. As expected, students "remembered" (incorrectly) having read statements that were more in line with prototypical expectations than they were with the actual dialogues the students had read.[30]

Robert Carson has used the term **master contract** to refer to the worked-out definition of a relationship that guides the recurring interaction of any dyad.[31] This means that as relationships develop, perceptions that were originally guided by a prototype eventually give way to an understanding based on verbalized agreements or silent acceptance of established patterns of behavior. We will have much more to say about relationships in the remaining chapters of this book. For now, it is important to recognize that identifying what type of relationship you're involved in may be just as crucial as knowing the situation or forming a useful impression of the other.

EXPLAINING BEHAVIOR: ATTRIBUTION THEORIES

When all is said and done, we are frequently left with the question "Why did he (or she) do that?" or "Why did I do that?" Most of the time we are quick to offer some type of explanation. If we think we understand what motivated our own or another's actions, we have reduced some uncertainty and made our world a little more predictable. Theories concerned with how the average person infers the cause(s) of social behavior have been called *attribution theories*. Before we examine some of these theories, let's look at a typical conversation and try to explain each person's behavior.

Imagine that you've been visiting your friends Angela and Howie for a few days. You are sitting at the kitchen table with Howie when

Angela comes home from work. She looks very tired. The following conversation ensues:

HOWIE: (*looking up from the plastic model car kit he has been putting together*) Hi, honey. How was work?

ANGELA: (*after saying hello to you, she scans the room*) Howie! You haven't done the dishes yet? They're left over from last night. Can't you do anything you're asked to do?

HOWIE: It's been a busy morning. I just haven't had time.

ANGELA: No time! You don't have a job. You're not looking for work. And you can't find 15 minutes to do a dozen dishes?

HOWIE: I've been looking through the classifieds, for your information.

ANGELA: Did you send out any resumes?

HOWIE: No, not really . . .

ANGELA: Here we go again. Do I have to physically force you to sit down and write letters of application and send your resume out?

HOWIE: I'll do it. I'll do it.

ANGELA: You'll do what? The dishes or the resumes? . . .

How would you explain the communication behavior of your two friends? Is Angela the kind of person who constantly nags and belittles others? Or did Howie provoke this tirade? What other explanations could there be?

Attribution theorists have discovered several different ways that you and I infer the causes of each other's behavior. We will look at two of the more prominent attribution theories — correspondent inference theory and covariance theory — and see how they explain our perceptions of Angela and Howie's interaction.

Children learn who they might (or might not) become by imitating the activities and behavior of their parents.

Making Correspondent Inferences

When we observe another person's behavior, we generally attribute that behavior to one of two types of causes: internal dispositions or external situational factors. Anytime we explain someone's actions in terms of his or her personality, motivation, or personal preferences, we are making an *internal attribution*. For instance, you might believe that Howie's behavior stems from his innate laziness. When we perceive behavior to be the result of social pressure, unusual circumstances, or physical forces beyond the individual's control, we are making a *situational attribution*. What if you knew that Angela had just arrived home from work, where she had been informed that she was in danger of losing her job due to impending budget cuts? You might perceive her behavior as being caused by temporary frustration or anxiety, not

her personality. In their **correspondent inference theory**, Edward Jones and Keith Davis have focused on the conditions that lead people to make dispositional attributions. They have discovered that we are more likely to make a dispositional judgment if we perceive the actor as making a choice between two or more courses of action that are nonnormative or that have noncommon effects [32]

A choice is *nonnormative* when no strong social expectations exist or when the behavior goes against the grain of those expectations. For instance, if a police officer suddenly starts dancing while directing traffic, his behavior is nonnormative, that is, not typical of most police officers. Observers are more likely to explain his actions in terms of his personal disposition. Telling a lie presents an interesting case. Lying is, for the most part, an undesirable behavior (nonnormative) in our culture. If we catch someone in a lie we usually consider it a reflection of character. But we make an exception in the case of "white lies." Ellen's response to her dinner host that the overcooked corned beef was "tasty" is more socially acceptable (normative) than describing it as "rubber dipped in water" (nonnormative). We would probably explain the latter statement as indicative of Ellen's personality more than we would the first one.

Two alternatives have *noncommon effects* if they differ significantly in the kinds of outcomes they will produce. For instance, Kate tells you that she has decided to take in a movie this evening. You would probably attribute her behavior to different causes if you knew what her other options were. If she had considered a movie as opposed to renting a video, watching television, or going out to eat, you would not have much reason to make a dispositional judgment. All of those choices would have a common effect: Kate would be entertaining herself. On the other hand, if she chose to go to a movie instead of to church, you might perceive the outcome as differing in terms of a religious commitment. If she goes to church, you perceive her as religious; if she goes to the movie, she is less religious. In this last case, because Kate's options had different, noncommon effects, you are more likely to infer that the choice reflects a personal (internal) disposition.

How would correspondent inference theory explain our perception of the conversation between Angela and Howie? Did you notice any nonnormative choices or noncommon effects operating to influence your attributions? We generally think that people who have a close relationship will greet each other warmly when they first see each other at the end of a long day. Howie did so, but Angela's initial remark about the dishes may have struck you as nonnormative. She seems to have lashed out at Howie right from the start. But what about Howie's behavior? If he is out of work, we are likely to see his putting a model kit together as a choice between work and play — a choice that entails noncommon effects. Furthermore, our culture is still not particularly tolerant of men who are not working, regardless of the reasons. It appears that aspects of both Angela's and Howie's behavior provide us with reasons for making internal attributions.

Using Covarying Information

Another attribution theory is the covariation model proposed by Harold Kelley.[33] **Covariance theory** takes into account the types of information we gather in order to attribute a cause to someone's behavior. Kelley and other researchers have suggested four types of causal attributions we tend to make. We can attribute a person's behavior to the following:

- The actor (the person who performed the behavior)

- The target (the stimulus object or person the behavior is aimed at)

- The circumstances (the physical setting or social context)

- The relationship (the master contract governing actor and target when they interact)

You will notice that the first of these factors is an internal attribution while the other three are more situational. Which of these causal attributions we will make depends on three types of information available to us: consensus, consistency, and distinctiveness.[34]

Consensus refers to the belief or perception that given the same set of social circumstances, most people would behave in a similar manner. It is an answer to the question, "Would most people do that in this situation?" If the answer is "yes," we have high consensus; if it is "no," we get low consensus. When episodes are highly scripted and most people follow the script, we are likely to explain their behavior by pointing to the expectations of the situation. Conversely, when a person acts differently than our expectations for that situation, we tend to attribute blame to the person.

If we observe a person who behaves in the same way across a wide range of situations, we have information leading to high consistency. **Consistency** has to do with similar behaviors performed by a single individual over time. It is an answer to the question, "Does this person act this way all or most of the time?" If Angela blows up once in a while, we give her the benefit of the doubt and attribute it to the situation. If she always seems to find a bone to pick, her highly consistent behavior would probably lead us to invoke her personality as the prime cause.

A judgment of high **distinctiveness** is rendered if we think something specific to the current situation elicited this behavior from the actor. "Did this person's behavior occur because of a particular stimulus or person involved?" If Howie's behavior or some other element of the situation led to Angela's outburst, we wouldn't blame her for it. On the other hand, if we can't find anything particular that seemed to elicit her behavior, she ends up taking the fall (an internal attribution).

Kelley's covariance theory suggests that we are more likely to attribute behavior to *the person* when we perceive low consensus, low distinctivness, and high consistency. With any other combination of information or perceptions, we will be more inclined to assume the situation or target shaped the person's behavior.

Look at Angela and Howie again. If we believe that some people get upset about dirty dishes and others don't (low consensus), and that Angela does not get angry very often (low consistency), but that Howie's actions caused her behavior (high distinctiveness), then Kelley's theory predicts that we would not likely blame Angela for the way she behaved (an internal attribution), but that she was reacting to circumstances (a situational attribution).

Identifying Attributional Biases

If all the causes of behavior we attribute were clearly logical and made use of all the relevant information, our social lives would be much easier to manage. Unfortunately, we humans are notoriously irrational at times. A number of perceptual biases affect how we arrive at causal attributions. We rely on some of these biases when we have no prior knowledge of the persons being observed, and at other times the biases just override whatever knowledge we do have.

Personality Bias Toward Others   The most common bias is to explain other people's behavior in terms of their personality dispositions. [35] We are especially prone to this **personality bias** when we observe strangers. We just naturally assume that a stranger who throws a shoe at the television screen lacks self-control or is mentally unstable. The bias is even stronger if the person's behavior is contrary to our expectations.[36] Since we expect people in a restaurant to be eating or drinking, we probably think that only a buffoon would start singing in that setting. Rarely do we look for other explanations —

such as the possibility that someone offered him $50 to do it or that the woman he was with accepted his proposal of marriage. Cognitively complex individuals may be less susceptible to this bias, perhaps because of their tendency to engage in role-taking. When we try to see a situation from the other person's point of view, we may see more situational or relational causes.

Situational Bias Toward Self   When we're asked to explain our own behavior, the story is somewhat different — we're more likely to rely on **situational bias.** If I throw a shoe at the television, I can explain that it was because of tension built up at the office, a stupid call by the referee, or the loose morals of television producers. There are several reasons why we tend to attribute our own behavior to situational factors. In the case of negative behavior, blaming it on the situation can serve as an excuse or justification for that behavior. Another reason is that we simply have more information about our own past and present experience than an observer would. We know if we've had a bad day; an observer probably doesn't. Finally, our visual vantage point makes a difference. When we behave, we don't see ourselves performing the action. What we do see is other people and external circumstances. It's much more likely that we will reference the situation as the cause of our behavior.

Bias Toward Groups   In addition to these two biases, perceived group membership also produces a bias. We explain the behavior of members of highly stereotyped *out-groups* (groups we do not belong to) differently than the behavior of *in-group* members (such as our own friends, associates, or ethnic group). In general, researchers have found that we attribute positive behavior by in-group members to their personal dispositions, while negative behavior is explained in terms of situational factors. We explain the behavior of out-group members in exactly the opposite manner. Positive behavior is explained away as situationally produced, while negative behavior is seen as the product of personality or group culture.[37] For example, suppose you are watching a close friend play in a tennis tournament when she screams at the referee for calling her shot out of bounds. You turn to the person next to you and say, "She's been under a lot of pressure lately. I think she just needed to blow off some steam." Moments later, her opponent (from an arch-rival institution) heatedly disputes another out-of-bounds call. "Why do they let people without manners play this game?" you think to yourself.

Why are we so prone to discriminate in favor of friends and against members of other social groups? We usually think of friends as being similar to us in many ways, but apparently perceive them to be even more similar when compared to an outsider. This in-group/out-group comparison seems to set in motion a role-taking process in which we identify closely with the in-group member and view things from his or her perspective. As a result, we often seek a situational account for the behavior. In contrast, we tend to view the out-group member with very little empathy or understanding. This makes it easier to assume the person would behave negatively regardless of the situation.

Bias Toward Cultures Culture also plays a significant role in producing attributional bias. Our culture is a very individualistic one. As a result, we have a greater tendency to believe that the individual person is responsible for his or her behavior. In collectivist cultures such as Japan or India, situational attributions are more common.[38] A *collectivist culture* is one in which group goals have a higher priority than individual goals; loyalty to the group is usually expressed by behaving according to the rules in different situations. Thus, in collectivist cultures people are more aware of situational constraints and less aware of individual differences.

How can knowledge of these causal schemata and attributional biases help improve interpersonal communication? The first step is to realize that our past interactions with a person

influence how we decide to communicate in the present. To a large extent, what we remember about past interactions is stored in the form of attributions. If you have a tendency to explain interactions in terms of single causes (such as personal or stimulus attributions), your communication may frequently take the form of complaining about or blaming the other. You may even do this without realizing it. It may be beneficial to sit down occasionally and evaluate how you've been explaining the events that have happened in your important relationships. Another effective way to improve our own and others' interpretive competence is to use and respond positively to reflections and interpretations (see Box 6.2)

Building Skills: Becoming a Competent Listener

This chapter has focused on the ways we process information about social situations and the people involved in them. This processing of information leads to perceptions that strongly influence the way we communicate with others. With a growing awareness of these perceptual processes, we will be better able to improve interpersonal communication.

How can we turn this knowledge into practical social skills? There are many ways to increase our perceptual competence. One of the keys is to keep in mind the four social cognition processes introduced in this chapter: sizing up situations, people, and relationships and explaining behavior. It is important to remember that each of us sizes up things differently because we rely on different personal constructs, prototypes, stereotypes, scripts, and causal schemata.

One way to better learn these concepts is to *spend some time observing people in social situations.* People-watching can be a fascinating

BOX **6.2**

Interpretive Competence: Making Sense By Using Reflections and Interpretations

The process we have dubbed as interpretive competence is all about making sense out of social situations, the people involved, and the messages they send or give off. One way to improve interpretive competence is by practicing two feedback tools that make possible interpretations more obvious. When we use these two talk tools, others can confirm or re-direct our interpretations, if need be. Psychologist Gerald Goodman suggests two specific "talk tools" — reflections and interpretations — that help produce better sense-making. *Reflections* are feedback messages that attempt to mirror or register another's meaning. There is no bid to add new meaning or analyze or judge; we just try to re-present the other's message in a somewhat condensed version. It's trying to get the essence of what another means. A good reflective statement is the kind that elicits a response like "exactly," or "absolutely."

One easy way to learn how to provide reflections is to listen to group discussions and think of ways to summarize the different points of view being expressed. Goodman calls this a *roundup reflection.* Here's an example from an episode of *Donahue.* A 20-minute debate on parental discipline of children has been relatively one-sided, with both the panel expert and most of the audience expressing the sentiment that parents should be more assertive and less permissive with their kids. A number of different points have

been made about being tired of kids talking back to their parents, the parents feeling inferior to "experts" (e.g., child psychologists), or feeling guilty for possibly damaging a child's self-esteem, and even the idea that a good smack now and then gets and keeps a child's attention. Phil Donahue, consummate talk show host, sums several minutes of talk with a concise reflection that rounds up the fragmented comments: "It's as if we're almost afraid of our own children . . . afraid to assert our own authority . . . everything is the parent's fault and there's a lot of guilt inflicted on them."

Donahue's summary statement crystalizes the sentiment and also implicitly invites others to express an opposite point of view, which they do. But the dissenters, who argue that kids need more reassurance, that guilt is a way of making parents more aware, that physical punishment indicates a lack of communication skills, and can easily lead to reliance on absolute force, are being shouted down by the majority. Once again, Donahue draws out the essence of the minority argument: "In some quarters of this room is the suggestion that if we use words like "firmness, reasserting control," what we allow some parents to do is . . . use absolute force without any kind of sensitivity toward the wishes of a child . . . Force works only for a little while. . ." As Goodman notes, Donahue's use of roundup reflections "brought balance to the issues."

Interpretations, on the other hand, are attempts to remake another's message, to add new meaning, and to redirect the process of sense-making. Interpretations are much more assertive than reflections. As a result, they are risky ventures, but they demonstrate that interpretive competence is as much a process of constructing meaning as it is one of discovering it. Interpretations can actually help another person see his or her actions in a new context — they can add new meaning to one's understanding.

Goodman illustrates this with a lengthy phone conversation between long-time friends Jean and Claudette, both single and in their thirties, complaining about the lack of nonsexual relationships with men of their own age:

CLAUDETTE: I've never even had those *semi*-friends that some women make out of men.

JEAN: That's been true all the years I've known you, Claude. I've always seen you that way. But it's been so easy for you to attract all sorts of lovers. You beat us all at capturing men.

CLAUDETTE: Big deal — all I have to do is make myself up and catch their eye . . . But why can't men see us as more than just their sexual conquest? . . . Am I to blame 'cause I was born beautiful? (*they both laugh*) But really, what the hell did I do to deserve this treatment?

JEAN: (*mock cowgirl drawl*) Not a thang, honey. Pretty little thang like you . . . (*Back to regular voice*) Uh, maybe you *can* do, you know, something about the way you talk to men. Claude, I have to tell you, over the years I've seen you contribute to the problem just the way you communicate. . . . it might be partly your fault that guys look at you as sexually available.

Goodman notes that Jean offers two interpretations in this brief excerpt from their conversation. The first is her classification of Claudette as highly successful at developing sexual relationships with men. It's meant and taken as a compliment. The second interpretation is considerably more risky. Jean suggests to Claudette that she is partly to blame for not having male *friends* because she communicates in a way that suggests she wants a *sexual* relationship. The conversation continues with Claudette resisting but not necessarily rejecting Jean's interpretation. While no definitive conclusions are drawn, Jean has successfully created new meaning for Claudette to ponder. In this example, Jean has not only made sense of Claudette's original message, she has also sized up her friend and gently offered Claudette another way of sizing up her own situation.

SOURCE: Gerald Goodman. *The Talk Book: The Intimate Science of Communicating in Close Relationships* (Emmaus, Pa: Rodale Press, 1988).

ADDITIONAL READINGS

Cherney, Marcia, and Susan Tynan. *Communicoding*. New York: Donald I. Fine, 1989.

pastime. Find public places where you can watch people without drawing attention to yourself. Watch films, read novels, and ask friends how they handle different situations. Then try to explain what you see and hear in terms of the ideas presented in this chapter.

Another important practice is to *flex your perceptual muscles before, during, and after your own social interactions.* By flexing your muscles, we mean taking the time to check your perceptions of people and situations to see if they're really appropriate. If you wanted to ask your boss for a raise, it would make sense to plan your strategy in advance and think about what you wanted to say. We're simply suggesting that you take one more step and consider how your perceptions of yourself, the boss, your relationship, and the timing of your request might lead you to alter your message. You should also anticipate how your boss is likely to perceive these same factors. After the conversation you should assess which of your perceptions were accurate and which might have led to some misunderstanding. No doubt this will be difficult at first. You will feel self-conscious and perform awkwardly until the practice becomes second nature to you. But in the long run you will develop the ability to better understand your own habits. Such understanding is the first step in altering undesirable habits.

But none of these practices is more important than developing the social skill of listening. We spend roughly 70–80 percent of our waking hours engaged in some form of verbal communication. Of this, only 30 percent is spent talking while 45–50 percent is devoted to listening to someone. Yet studies reveal that the average person is not a very good listener. We retain only about half of what we hear immediately after an interaction, and within 48 hours retention is a mere 25 percent.[39]

Not only is listening a skill that we need to improve, it is the one skill that can help us better manage social cognitions. Listening is, in effect, trying to understand messages in terms of the other's cognitive framework instead of our own. If we consider what another person thinks, feels, and perceives as a relatively unknown world, then listening is the best (perhaps the only) way to tap into that world and explore it. Until we explore how other people view things, we have little hope of understanding either them or our interactions with them. Listening is probably the single most important communication skill. When we fail to listen, we usually apply our other verbal and nonverbal skills inappropriately.

TYPES OF LISTENING

Listening is defined in many ways. One of the most complete definitions is offered by Charles Petrie: "the composite process by which oral language communicated by some source is received, critically and purposefully attended to, recognized, and interpreted (or comprehended) in terms of past experiences and future expectancies."[40] We would like to broaden Petrie's definition a bit by suggesting that listening involves receiving information from *all* of our senses. Many of the messages we assign meaning to are visual. We listen to more than spoken words.

Most experts on listening emphasize that it has many purposes.[41] Sometimes we listen simply to discriminate between stimuli. For example, we struggle to identify a scary sound heard in the middle of the night; we listen carefully to determine whether our guests are coming "today" or "Tuesday"; we try to decide whether our boss's smile is sincere or feigned. This kind of listening is called **discriminatory listening** and is basic to all other forms of listening. We succeed in this kind of listening by recognizing a stimulus.

Sometimes we listen for the sheer pleasure of the activity. For instance, we listen to our favorite records or tapes; we hear and see a stage production of a new play; we watch a classic movie and appreciate the director's cinematic skill. In all these cases we are engaging in **appreciative listening.** Here we succeed if we experience the stimulus in desired ways.

Much of the listening we do involves receiving and remembering new information. For example, we listen as our accountant explains what the new tax laws mean; we concentrate as our child tells us what he wants for his birthday; we watch and listen as a friend directs us to her home. In these situations we are involved in **comprehensive listening.** We try our best to understand a speaker's meaning as accurately as possible. We succeed if we can accurately recreate the intended meaning and hold it in memory.

We also listen to make judgments. For instance, when we see a commercial, we listen to determine whether to buy the product; when we hear a politician talk, we must decide whether we support her views; when a friend asks to borrow money, we try to evaluate our chances of being repaid. This is **evaluative listening.** We go beyond comprehension; we make judgments about the intentions and competence of a source and about the completeness of the information. Here we do not succeed by simply understanding the appeal; success involves making sound decisions about it.

Finally, we listen to help others. When a child cries uncontrollably, we try to comfort and calm him; when a friend's most important relationship breaks up, we lend a sympathetic ear; when an acquaintance needs to talk out a decision, we help uncover options. In these cases we are taking part in **empathic listening.** Here our goal is to help someone else. We succeed when they are better able to understand or cope with a problem.

DEVELOPING LISTENING SKILLS

Each of these kinds of listening involves different skills. At their annual conference in 1984, members of the Speech Communication Association adopted a list of skills essential for two of the major types of listening: comprehensive and evaluative.[42] To listen *comprehensively* requires the following essential skills:

- Recognizing main ideas
- Identifying supporting details
- Recognizing explicit relationships among ideas
- Recalling basic ideas and details

To critically *evaluate* what a source is saying requires an additional set of skills:

- Attending with an open mind
- Perceiving the speaker's purpose and organization of ideas
- Discriminating between statements of fact and statements of opinion
- Distinguishing between emotional and logical arguments
- Detecting bias and prejudice
- Recognizing the speaker's attitude
- Synthesizing and evaluating by drawing logical inferences and conclusions
- Recalling the implications and arguments
- Recognizing discrepancies between the speaker's verbal and nonverbal messages

While all types of listening are important, the one most closely related to improving interpersonal communication is *empathic,* or therapeutic, listening. It is especially important when emotions are involved. To improve empathic listening requires many of the same skills for comprehension, plus the following four important guidelines or rules:

1. *Respect the other's point of view.* To respect another's point of view means that we must want to listen; we have to care about what the other person thinks and feels. This is especially difficult during interpersonal conflicts because we become so preoccupied with our own ideas and emotions that we don't take time to think about our partner's views. We are also quick to dismiss what others say if it differs from what we believe. We tend to close down the perceptual process when encountering something we disagree with. It is essential to explore the other's point of view rather than avoid it.

2. *Make sure you fully understand what the other has said before responding* Most people spend more time preparing their own messages than listening to others' statements. This leads to the rule of understanding before you speak. Think how many times you have interrupted someone before he or she was finished in order to make an objection or correction. As a result, you may think you disagree when you don't. Interruptions rob you of information and serve to disconfirm others.

3. *Check your understanding by paraphrasing.* Once you think you understand what the other is saying, you should check it out by paraphrasing. To **paraphrase** is to state in your own words what you think the other person means. Paraphrasing isn't a matter of repeating what has just been said. Instead, you should describe your understanding of the comment in your own way. If a friend says to you, "I hate my physics class. Everyone is smarter than I am. I know I'm going to fail. I don't know why you hang around with a dummy like me, anyway," check to make sure you understand what your friend is really trying to say. A paraphrase might go something like this: "Let me see if I understand. You're having trouble in class and it's making you doubt your competence. You're afraid I'll think you're dumb if you do badly." In social cognition terms you're trying to recognize the personal constructs the other is using or the script he or she seems to be following.

Most people's first instinct is to comfort rather than paraphrase. "Nonsense, you'll do fine. Don't worry" is a good response only if your friend is not serious. If she is really upset, such a response dismisses her fears, saying in effect, "You have no right to feel the way you do." A paraphrase allows you to make sure you know what is bothering her. When you're not used to doing it, paraphrasing can seem odd. Try to vary the opening line of a paraphrase. It sounds trite and awkward to start off every statement with "What I think I hear you saying is . . ."

4. *When paraphrasing, make sure you express relational as well as content meaning.* In many interactions feelings are more important than words. If your partner says, "You know, you forgot my birthday, not that it's that important, really," you should check out the feeling behind the statement. Some people have difficulty expressing feelings overtly, so they hint instead. A good listener will try to read between the lines and will help others say what they really mean.

While listening to others means trying to see the world from their point of view, we must not become completely other-centered. To improve our perceptual awareness we must also listen to ourselves. We can employ the same skills by focusing inward to discover the world as we have constructed it. Ask yourself questions as to why you seem more comfortable in some situations, with certain people, or in specific types of relationships. Don't simply accept your first explanation; try paraphrasing your own views. You may discover that you really feel different or you may convince yourself that there are other ways of looking at the circumstances or people involved.

This chapter has provided you with a lot of information about the perceptual process and some of the cognitive schemata that people use to make sense of their social world. We have tried to simplify what you need to know by structuring this information around four cognitive processes that influence interpersonal communication: how we size up situations, people, and relationships and how we explain the causes of social interaction. Finally, we have suggested how you can improve your listening skills in order to better understand your own and others' cognitive frameworks. Understanding social cognition processes is the first step to improving interpersonal communication because so much of the meaning we assign to messages depends on our *perceptions* of the social context and the persons involved.

Process to Performance

REVIEW TERMS

The following is a list of major concepts introduced in this chapter. The page where the concept is first mentioned in listed in parentheses.

social cognition   (146)
schema   (150)
prototype   (151)
personal construct   (152)
stereotypes   (152)
scripts   (152)
selective exposure   (155)
selective attention   (156)
social episodes   (160)
closed episode   (160)
open episode   (161)
defined episode   (161)
implicit personality theory   (164)
primacy effect   (164)
recency effect   (164)

self-fulfilling prophecy   (165)
cognitive complexity   (165)
self-monitoring   (167)
master contract   (169)
correspondent inference theory   (170)
covariance theory   (171)
consensus   (171)
consistency   (171)
distinctiveness   (171)
personality bias   (172)
situational bias   (172)
discriminatory listening   (176)
appreciative listening   (177)
comprehensive listening   (177)
evaluative listening   (177)
empathic listening   (177)
paraphrasing   (178)

SUGGESTED READINGS

Csikszentmihalyi, Mihaly. *Flow: The Psychology of Optimal Experience.* New York: Harper & Row, 1990. An intriguing book with the powerful thesis that human happiness is largely the result of fully attending to the physical and sensory nature of the task at hand such that we forget everything else in order to concentrate our efforts. The book has many implications for improving interpretive competence.

Judson, Sylvia Shaw. *The Quiet Eye: A Way of Looking at Pictures.* Washington, D.C.: Regnery Gateway, 1982. First published in 1954, this simple but elegant little book encourages the kind of contemplation that fosters interpretive competence. In the author's own words, it is meant to "communicate a sense of affirmation, of wonder, of trust. This is a spirit alien to much of the art of our insecure time, but one which I am confident will some day return."

Langer, Ellen J. *Mindfulness.* Reading, Mass.: Addison-Wesley, 1989. A highly readable and enlightening look at the ways in which our social categories trap us and make us victims of our own constructs. Langer describes many of her own research studies on various aspects of "mindless behavior." She conducts research the way novelists write stories. In one study, she recreated a nursing home retreat environment to simulate the year 1959 in order to study the ability of mindful behavior to reverse the detrimental effects of aging.

Hall, Edward T. *Beyond Culture.* Garden City, N.Y.: Anchor Books, 1977. An extremely insightful and highly readable book about the role of culture in structuring our perceptions of reality and everyday events.

Watzlawick, Paul. *How Real Is Real?* New York: Random House, 1976. A wide-ranging look at the ways animals, people, and governments manage reality through ritual, perceptual tendencies, and the use of disinformation. The implications for communication are thoroughly explored.

TOPICS FOR DISCUSSION

1. Look again at the conversation between Angela and Howie on page 169. Can you identify messages that you think either person might have selectively attended to? Are there any messages that either one seemed to ignore? Can you think of conversations you have been involved in where you or another person selectively attended to or ignored important messages? What should we do when we think another person is attending to the wrong message? How can we become better at recognizing our own tendencies in this regard?

2. To communicate effectively, we suggested that you have to accurately perceive the situation, yourself, the other, and the relationship between you and the other. In small groups, have each person identify one or more scenarios in which an individual has misperceived the situation, person, or relationship. TV sitcoms frequently are based on circumstances like these

and may be a good source to get you started. After you've identified several situations, discuss the kinds of attributions we might make in each situation.

3. The posters you have seen of the Nerd, the Valley Girl, the Preppy, and the Yuppie are all examples of person prototypes. Identify as many other prototypes of persons as you can. Talk about the characteristics that cluster to form each prototype. Can you do the same thing for situations or relationships?

4. To make sure you understand the difference between a prototype and a stereotype, take some of the prototypes mentioned in Topic 3 and identify common stereotypes associated with each one. Are all of the stereotypes negative ones? Which stereotypes seem more useful? In what way?

5. Examine your own implicit personality theories. Based on your experience, what traits seem to go together naturally? Why do you think they are associated? What traits are central ones that would drastically change your overall impression of a person?

6. The examples of self-fulfilling prophecy in this chapter generally present it as a negative perceptual tendency. Does it have to be? Can you think of a time when positive perceptions of others changed their behavior? Discuss what you could do to change a negative self-fulfilling prophecy midway through a situation.

7. Master contracts are working agreements that govern dyadic relationships. Think of a specific relationship in each of the following categories: (1) student-teacher, (2) parent-child, (3) romantic dyad, (4) best friends, and (5) coworkers. Now try to identify what the master contract of each relationship is. Then identify ways that contract limits your perception of things you can do together or limits the range of messages you can use to influence each other.

8. Think about the last major argument you were involved in. Explain why the other person behaved the way she or he did. What type of attributions did you make? Did you use prior information concerning consensus, consistency, or distinctiveness? Now try to generate reasons why you could have made one of the other three types of attributions.

OBSERVATION GUIDE

1. Watch a half-hour episode of a situation comedy or other television program that consists primarily of dialogue. If you can, audio- or videotape the program so you can play it back several times. Choose an interesting segment, such as a misunderstanding, and write down the essence of each message exchanged. Then write down the perceptual factors that best account for why that message was produced or interpreted the way it was.

2. Conduct your own study of attributions. Look for newspaper or magazine accounts of some event that two or more people perceived differently. A good example is Mia Farrow's and Woody Allen's differing accounts of the problems leading to their break-up. Write down a brief description of the situation, the behavior in question, the actor's account, and the target's explanation. What biases do you find in the results? Are they consistent with those reported in this chapter? If not, can you explain the differences?

EXERCISES

1. This exercise is designed to measure the way you construct your interpersonal world and form impressions of others. It is based on George Kelly's Role Repertory Construct Test. The end result will be a list of several of your own *personal constructs*. Follow these steps:

a. Look at the following list of role titles and place in the blank the name or initials of someone you know personally who fits that category. Choose a *different* person for each category. If you can't think of anyone for a particular role, then name some other impor-

tant person in your life and describe the role he or she plays in relation to you.

Role Category	Name or Initials of Person
1. Mother	____
2. Father	____
3. Boyfriend (or girlfriend)	____
4. Brother (or someone like a brother)	____
5. Sister (or someone like a sister)	____
6. Best same-sex friend	____
7. Best opposite-sex friend	____
8. A teacher you like	____
9. A teacher you dislike	____
10. Most intelligent person you know	____
11. Someone you pity	____
12. A boss or superior	____
13. Someone who threatens you	____
14. A new acquaintance	____
15. Yourself	____

b. Now think about three of the persons you listed (your mother, sister, and someone who threatens you) and compare them. Try to think of some important ways that two of them are alike but different from the third person. For instance, you might say that two of these people are friendly while the other is more cold-natured. On a sheet of paper, list as many "constructs," or similarities and differences for these three people as you can. Your list might look like this:

friendly-cold-natured

good-looking-unattractive

talkative-quiet

c. Repeat step b for each of the following role sets:

1. Father, your boss, a new acquaintance

2. Boyfriend, best same-sex friend, best opposite-sex friend

3. Liked teacher, disliked teacher, yourself

4. Brother, sister, most intelligent person

5. Best opposite-sex friend, mother, sister

6. Girlfriend, father, mother

Your list should be rather long by now. This should give you a pretty good idea of the personal constructs you typically use to form impressions of others. Compare your constructs with those of your classmates. How similar or different are they? Which constructs that other people use seem unimportant to you? Why do you think people see the world so similarly or differently?

2. Throw an impression-formation party. As a class, design a set of 5–10 questions that you can ask strangers in order to get to know them a little better. Then assign several class members to interviewing teams (one interviewer and one camera person). If you can, secure a portable video camera unit and videotape interviews with people of different ages and ethnic or social backgrounds. Make sure you film each person for about 10–15 seconds before you begin asking the questions (we'll explain why later). If you cannot get video equipment, use audiotape recorders and take several snapshots of each person. Bring the recorders and/or snapshots to class on the designated day. Replay the videos in class, stopping once before any verbal communication takes place and then again at the conclusion of the interview (or look at the snapshots before you listen to the audiotapes). Have each person in the class write down his or her impressions, based first on the nonverbal cues alone, then on the total verbal-nonverbal image. Compare your impressions and talk about the perceptual factors that affected those impressions.

We are all social actors, performing for others —
and for ourselves.

(Jean Pezous (1815–85), *Portrait of Charles Deburau*)

7

Role Competence:
Adapting to Social Expectations

A very young child does not know what an "address" is. He knows that he has a home and that he lives there with his sister and his dog, and he may even be able to repeat "47 Pratt Street" when his grandparents ask him where he lives. But he doesn't understand the idea that his home has coordinates and can be located in relation to other people's homes.

Slowly, however, the idea of "address" takes shape. The child learns to differentiate his friends' homes from his own. He knows what it means to go to Grandma's or to visit cousins in New York. Eventually, he will understand much more. He will learn to locate the homes of everyone he knows on a map. Where formerly a letter to a cousin was simply addressed "To Kerry," now the envelope carries quite specific directions: "1200 Elm Street, Newfield, New York, U.S.A., The World, The Solar System, The Universe." The child becomes fascinated with the world and his place in it. As sociologist Peter Berger tells us, "This locating of oneself in configurations conceived by strangers is one of the important aspects of what, perhaps euphemistically, is called 'growing up.'"[1]

Berger points out that as children mature they continue to accumulate addresses — ones locating them on a social rather than a geographical map. "I'm seven years old"; "My dad and mom are divorced"; "I go to second grade, but I'm not very good at spelling"; "My mom is a secretary"; "When I grow up I'm going to learn to fix cars and drive a Trans-Am." As children learn their position on the social map, they also begin to understand just what they can expect out of life and what life expects out of them. They adapt themselves to a larger social system. What this adaptation means for identity and for communication will be the topic of this chapter and the next. In this chapter we will look at some of the ways society shapes and controls us. In the next chapter we will consider how, despite these social pressures, we manage to create an identity that is uniquely ours.

185

Being Part of the Group: Following Social Rules

One of the fundamental facts about us is that we are social animals. The fantasy of the loner, living a solitary life and answering to no one, may fascinate us, but most of us will spend our lives following rules others have made. To live a "civilized" life means we must be willing to live up to the expectations of others. The competent communicator is one who follows social rules. In this section we'll look at what social controls and pressures to conform we are exposed to and examine how social roles work and how they constrain our communication.

SOCIAL CONTROL AND CONFORMITY PRESSURES

Why does society place such a high premium on conformity? One reason is that in order to operate effectively, members of social groups must coordinate their activities. Each member must complete assigned tasks and follow rules. Since we belong to many social groups, we are subject to many levels of social control. Berger asks us to think of ourselves at the center of a series of concentric circles, each representing a system of control. These circles represent social coordinates; they stand for the "many forces that constrain and coerce one."[2]

The forces that constrain us are many. Formal economic and legal sanctions control our actions in obvious ways. In addition, more subtle pressures affect us: the desire to uphold the standards and moral customs of our community, our fear of ridicule, our fundamental need for inclusion. Whatever the reason, we are, to a large extent, what our culture wants us to be. Anthropologist Ruth Benedict expresses it this way:

The life history of the individual is first and foremost an accommodation to the patterns and standards traditionally handed down in his community. From the moment of birth the customs into which he is born shape his experience and behaviour. By the time he can talk, he is a little creature of his culture, and by the time he is grown and able to take part in its activities, its habits are his habits, its beliefs his beliefs, its impossibilities his impossibilities.[3]

While we feel that individuals have a bit more room to maneuver than Benedict allows them, we also believe that a large part of who we are and how we communicate is determined for us by social norms. One of the most powerful limits to our freedom comes from social roles.

THE NATURE OF SOCIAL ROLES

Every day we face new situations. If we had to stop and decide how to act in each case, we'd have a difficult time of it. Luckily, we act appropriately without very much thought. This is because we know implicitly how someone in our position should behave: We have learned what sociologists call a role, one of the strongest forms of social control.

To understand what a role is, we have to begin by understanding the concept of position. A **position** is a social label that tells people who we are, what our duties and rights are, and where we stand in comparison to others. Some of the positions a society recognizes are occupational (butcher, baker, candlestick maker). Others refer to placement in the family (grandparent, parent, son, or daughter). Still others indicate age, sex, prestige, or associational groupings.[4] In all cases positions indicate location on the social map.

Positions are not just empty titles. People are expected to take their positions seriously. Children and adults do not amuse themselves in the

We learn what to expect out of life very early; our families supply us with information about position and role.

(Pablo Picasso, *Family at Supper,* 1903)

same ways. A professional politician and a professional wrestler will address their publics differently. Each position carries with it a set of behavioral guidelines. These guidelines are what we call **roles**: sets of expectations that govern how persons holding a given position should behave. We know several things about roles: (1) They are learned; (2) they are general; (3) they affect our identities; and (4) most of us play multiple roles.

1. *Roles are learned.* We aren't born with a knowledge of roles. We learn to meet social expectations in much the same way we learn to ride a bicycle or play the accordion. We learn by observing others, by receiving instruction, by practicing, by experiencing praise or criticism. All of the principles that affect learning in general affect role acquisition. Box 7.1 shows one of the many ways we learn roles: through imitative play.

2. *Roles are generalized guidelines for behavior.* While roles give us a general idea of how to perform in a given position, they don't spell out every move. We are often left to our own devices when it comes to working out the details of our performances. Most college students, for example, need time to figure out how

to be a student. Being a student entails more than enrolling for classes; students must act, dress, and even think in particular ways. Freshmen or returning students may have a hard time of it at first, since these issues are rarely addressed in the college catalog. A role is a generalized and idealized model for behavior, not a fully developed script. Competent role performance, therefore, involves experimentation, improvisation, and adjustment.

3. *Roles affect beliefs about self.* It takes time to learn a role, but after a while the strangeness wears off. Eventually, people stop noticing their roles. A first-year teacher, for example, may initially feel ambivalent about her authority. But it will probably not be too long before she begins to believe in a teacher's right to instruct and discipline. She may even begin to consider rebellious students as unruly or ungrateful. Similarly, a soldier newly promoted to the rank of officer may be slightly embarrassed by accompanying signs of deference. He will soon become accustomed to being saluted, however, and will begin to resent insubordination.

Enacting a role over a prolonged period may affect one's personality and identity. **Role rigidity** occurs when a role takes over one's identity. Most experts believe it is psychologically necessary to separate self from role. People whose commitment to a single role is too rigid tend to lose perspective. They may find it increasingly hard to relate in any other way. Teachers, for example, may become so used to the role of instructor that friendly conversations turn into lectures. Military officers may treat their children like little "noncoms."

4. *People have multiple roles to play.* People fill a number of positions simultaneously. This means they must be nimble in moving between roles. An intern in a hospital, for instance, must be a number of different people: At work he or she is a doctor; at home, a husband or wife; at a party, a friend or neighbor; and at town council meetings, a citizen. Our intern must be sensitive enough to recognize the varying demands of each role and flexible enough to adapt to them,

for each role calls for a slightly different form of communication. Meeting the communication demands of all of these situations involves a great deal of role versatility. The number of roles an individual can successfully play is called a **role repertoire.** Clearly, the larger the role repertoire, the more communicative flexibility one has.

Most of the time people switch roles easily. Sometimes, however, they experience **role conflict.** This occurs when two or more roles make opposing demands. Workaholics, for example, often find that professional and personal demands conflict. Attention directed to family concerns is attention taken away from their businesses, and vice versa. Resolving this kind of dilemma is no easy matter; it may ultimately lead to painful choices.

Role conflicts also occur in times of social transition. In the period before an old role has become obsolete and a new role fully accepted, people are often pulled in opposite directions. Our changing understandings of what it means to be male or female and current redefinitions of the shape and purpose of the family are good examples.

Choosing Our Roles

If it is true that we play multiple roles, how do we decide who to be in a given situation? How, indeed, do we know who we are? George McCall and J. L. Simmons address this question in their role identity model.[5] In order to get through life, they believe, we have to decide which identities to assume. In a sense we are like circus performers, juggling commitments and role demands, trying not to slip off the tightrope that defines our passage through life.

While we have many role identities, some are more important than others. What determines the salience of a role? McCall and Simmons believe there are three sets of factors: (1) the degree of support we receive for playing a role,

(2) the amount of commitment we feel toward it, and (3) the kinds of rewards we receive from it. Let's look at each of these factors.

SOCIAL SUPPORT AND ROLE IDENTITY

If those around us support our efforts, we are more likely to embrace a role than if they ridicule us. It is a fact of life that we are constantly being evaluated. Assume, for instance, that you dream of becoming a marathon runner. If your family and friends give you support and encouragement, you will go on with your dream. If they laugh at your lack of speed and stamina, you may not believe enough in yourself to keep on.

The Looking-Glass Self

A number of social scientists besides McCall and Simmons have stressed the importance of social support in defining and maintaining a role. Charles Horton Cooley, for example, believes that others act as mirrors, reflecting back at us who we are and how we're doing. Cooley expressed this idea in a two-line poem: "Each to each a looking glass/Reflects the other that doth pass." The **looking-glass self** is the self that comes to us from others.[6] Think about it for a moment. No matter how strong-willed and self-assured you are, if everybody you encounter treats you as incompetent, you will question your abilities. Or even worse, suppose everyone ignored you completely. You'd probably begin to wonder if you were dreaming. It would be like looking into a mirror and failing to see your reflection.

Social Comparison Processes

Social support is essential to most of us. Why? Leon Festinger in his **social comparison theory** gives one reason.[7] He believes that people have

a basic need to know how they're doing; they need to know how their opinions and abilities stack up. Since it's hard to find objective scales to measure beliefs and talents, most of us must turn to other people for feedback.

We don't turn to just anyone, however. People who are similar to us provide us the most useful comparisons. A beginning tennis player would be foolish to compare herself with Martina Navratilova; it would make more sense to look at another beginning player. Similarly, college students gain little insight from knowing they're more educated than kindergartners; they need to know how they rate against other college students. Most of the time we compare ourselves with those we believe are in our league or who are slightly better than we are. Because our need for social comparison is so strong, most of our associations will be with people who are similar.

What Festinger is suggesting is that the need for social comparison leads to conformity pressures. We choose as friends people who are similar enough to reinforce role identities. If unexpected changes in identity are discovered in a relationship, efforts will be made to reestablish similarity. Have you ever been shocked and disappointed when a friend turned out to hold unexpected opinions? If so, you probably exerted subtle pressures to change your friend back into someone you felt more comfortable with. Have you ever been uncomfortable because your abilities were above or below your friends'? Some people will pretend to be better than they are, while others will play dumb, just to fit in. We try to be what our comparison groups tell us we should be.

COMMITMENT AND ROLE IDENTITY

The amount of material and the number of psychological resources invested in a role also determines how significant it will be. Perhaps you have always admired a runner. Ever since you were a child, you wanted to be like her. Your commitment will be so great you may persevere

They Just Like to Be Not the Same as Us: Play Patterns and the Development of Sex Role Identities

In *Boys and Girls: Superheroes in the Doll Corner,* elementary scool teacher Vivian Gussin Paley describes how kindergartners' play contributes to sex role development. Paley tells us that by kindergarten age, children have a strong need to define what it means to be boys and girls. Younger children are not concerned with gender. Three-year-olds, for example, fail to distinguish between male and female behaviors. A three-year-old playing the role of a policeman may also cook the food and feed the baby, while one playing a mother may put on a man's vest and hat. Boys may tell you they are fathers and girls that they are mothers most of the time, but occasionally they will say the opposite without feeling uncomfortable.

Around the age of four, children begin to play gender-based roles more frequently. Girls start enacting family dramas, assigning themselves the roles of mother, baby, or sister and preferring that boys be fathers, plumbers, carpenters, or firemen. Although the girls are sometimes willing to exchange their domestic roles for those of Wonderwoman or Supergirl, it is the boys who specialize in being monsters or superheroes.

By age five or six, gender-based play is firmly established. Not only do the children fantasize sex-based roles, they invent rituals to separate themselves. Although society helps to create the shape of play by providing Barbie dolls and Star Wars action figures, the children themselves often elaborate on gender themes in creative ways. In the group Paley observed, for example, boys hopped to get their milk, while girls skipped to the paper shelf.

What does typical play look like in a kindergarten class? Let's watch the boys play in the doll corner. Jeremy begins. He drags the play oven to the middle of the floor, announcing, "This is the computer terminal." The other boys quickly begin arranging the rest of the spaceship. Andrew talks into a silver dress-up slipper, "Pilot to crew, pilot to crew, ready for landing. Snow

even in the face of discouraging feedback. This effect will be doubly strong if you've made a financial investment, say, by buying expensive running shoes and hiring a coach. Commitment and investment are important factors in determining role salience.

Daryl Bem offers a theoretical explanation of why commitment and investment make certain role identities more salient.[8] His **self-perception theory** maintains that one way we learn about who we are is through self-observation. Bem believes that often it is hard for us to tell directly what we are thinking and feeling. In order to get a clearer idea of our emotions or attitudes, we observe our external behaviors. What we see ourselves doing often helps explain ambiguous emotions or attitudes.

This theory may seem odd to you. Most people think they have direct access to emotions and attitudes. Bem's point, however, is that internal sensations are often hard to identify. Think about it for a moment. How do you feel when you're in love? Does your heart race? Do your palms sweat? Does your breathing rate increase? Now think about what you experience when you are scared to death. Aren't the sensations pretty similar? One way to tell the difference is to observe external cues. If these sensa-

Paley notes that the stories boys and girls tell at this age are also very different. Girls tell stories of "good little families" of kings and queens, princes and princesses. Boys prefer tales with bad guys. Paley once asked the girls why boys never told stories about princes. The girls responded that princes are too "fancy" for boys. Boys like characters who are rough. One of the kindergartners, Charlotte, summed up the discussion: "Here's what I think. They don't want to be fancy because girls do. They just like to be not the same as us."

planet down below." Suddenly the boys sight Darth Vader. Andrew takes two sticks, runs over to the paint corner, and asks Mary Ann for red paint to transform them into light-sabres. Then, before rushing into battle, he says gallantly, "Thanks, miss; I won't forget this."

Meanwhile, the girls have decided to build a zoo from blocks. They take four rubber lions and name them Mother, Father, Sister, and Baby and place them in a two-story house. Paley observes, "Girls tame lions by putting them into houses. Boys conquer houses by sending them into space."

SOURCE: Vivian Gussin Paley, *Boys and Girls: Superheroes in the Doll Corner* (Chicago: University of Chicago Press, 1984).

ADDITIONAL READINGS

Paley, Vivian G., *Bad Guys Don't Have Birthdays: Fantasy Play at Four.* Chicago: University of Chicago Press, 1991.
Paley, Vivian G., *You Can't Say You Can't Play.* Cambridge, Mass.: Harvard University Press, 1988.
Stein, Sarah Bonnett. *Girls and Boys: The Limits of Nonsexist Childrearing.* New York: Scribner, 1983.

tions occur during the middle of a crucial job interview, it is probably fear you are feeling. On the other hand, if they occur during an intimate candlelight dinner, love is the likely culprit.

Bem also believes external cues give us information about our attitudes and values. If we observe ourselves spending a great deal of time and effort doing something, we will probably decide it is important and worthwhile. People often say things like "I must really like the food here; look at how much I ate," or "It must have been a great party; I stayed till dawn," or "I spend all my time training for the marathon; it must be the most important thing in my life right now." The more time, effort, and money we spend on something, the more likely we are to believe we value it.

REWARDS AND ROLE IDENTITY

Both intrinsic and extrinsic rewards also determine how important a role becomes to us. The average person who runs a marathon is unlikely to be motivated by extrinsic rewards, for runners are not usually highly paid. A runner may receive important intrinsic rewards, however. Amateur runners often feel a sense of pride in

Others act as mirrors, allowing us to see ourselves. Their response gives us a sense of who we are.

(Pablo Picasso, *Girl Before a Mirror*, 1932)

accomplishing what few others can do. This feeling of competence goes a long way toward strengthening role allegiance. On the other hand, a runner who fails to complete a race, who experiences painful leg cramps, and who is going broke paying entrance fees may reconsider the importance of running.

McCall and Simmons believe that all of the factors we have discussed interact to determine reactions to roles. Throughout our lives we try on the different roles society presents to us. Those that fit are retained, while those that don't are rejected until we build up a repertoire of roles we're willing to play.

How Social Roles Affect Communication

The reason roles are of interest to us is that they affect our communication with one another. Embedded in every role are instructions for how to talk and what to talk about. In this section, we investigate how roles guide interactions. We start by looking at one very significant role, gender. We then take a more general look at how all of the social roles we play turn us into performers.

GENDER ROLES AND COMMUNICATION

In Chapter 4 we briefly touched on the fact that males and females may use language differently. Here we'll look in more detail at some of the ways gender roles affect interaction. As we will see, there has been a lot of interest in this topic, and researchers have investigated a number of ways in which males' and females' communication differs. Quite substantial differences in both verbal and nonverbal behavior have been found.

Gender and Verbal Behavior

Before we look at research results, stop and test your knowledge of gender differences by answering the following questions: Who do you think talks more, men or women? Who chooses topics, and who changes them? Which sex is more direct, and which more polite? What do men like to talk about, and what interests women?

If you relied on stereotypes, it probably wasn't hard for you to answer these questions, for our society has strong images about what male and female talk is like. First, women are supposed to talk more than men. The stereotype tells us that women chatter away while their strong, silent partners hide behind their copies of the *Wall Street Journal,* trying to stem the flow of talk by automatically responding, "Yes, dear." Second, women have a reputation for a different kind of talk: more hesitant, more polite, and more trivial. The stereotype tells us that when men do deign to talk, their talk is direct, forceful, and concerned with important topics. Let's see what the case really is.

Flow of Talk   It's hard to understand where women's reputation for gabbing comes from if we look at their behavior in mixed-sex dyads.

In truth, when men and women talk to one another, most studies show that men talk more than women. Not only that, men are much better than women at controlling talk. Studies also show that men are more successful in interrupting than are women. In one study men successfully interrupted women 28 out of 29 times, while women were able to "cut in" in only 17 out of 47 attempts. Another study investigated the kind of interruptions that men and women use and found that men tended to interrupt to state opinions, while women interrupted to ask questions. Finally, there is evidence that men control topic choice more than women do.[9]

The picture provided by this research is certainly not of women as nonstop talkers. Where, then, does the stereotype come from? Laurie Arliss speculates that it may be based on our notions of how people behave with same-sex friends. Women report that talk is an important activity for building friendships and show a greater preference for "just talking" with their female friends, whereas male friends seem to prefer engaging in more structured activity.[10]

Type of Talk   As we saw in Chapter 4, men and women have different vocabularies because they are encouraged to focus their attention on different parts of the world. Women's greater ability to make fine color distinctions and men's greater knowledge of mechanical-technical words are clearly related to traditional social roles rather than to any innate differences. Men's use of intense language (men are often permitted to "curse a blue streak," women have less freedom to do so) can also be traced to social roles.[11] As men and women grow up, they are reinforced for using certain words and punished for using others.

Women and men differ from one another not only in word choice but in verbal style as well. A number of researchers describe what they call the **female register,** a style of talk associated with women. A speaker using the female register uses more **qualifiers** ("Perhaps," "Maybe"), more **disclaimers** ("This may be a

Masks disguise and create identity. This royal mask, made in the early 16th century at the Court of Benin (Africa), was used to placate spirits. Although some of us may wear actual masks only at Halloween or costume parties, all of us wear social masks most of our lives.

silly question, but . . ."), more **tag questions** ("It's that way, right?"), more **polite forms** ("If it wouldn't be too much trouble . . ."), and more **intensifiers** ("It's really exceptionally nice out"). What is the result of using or not using a female register? On the positive side, using the female register shows politeness and concern for others' opinions. On the negative side, it may make the speaker appear subordinate and uncertain. Barbara and Gene Eakins sum up the differences in register between males and females by saying that women's speech avoids

"imposing belief, agreement, or obedience on others" and that it is "person-centered and concerned with interpersonal matters." Men's speech, in contrast, is more apt to involve "straight factual communication" and is more "literal, direct, and to the point."[12]

In addition to the directness/politeness dimension, men's and women's language also differs along an instrumental/expressive dimension. Talk concerned with getting things done, usually through an exchange of factual information, is **instrumental talk.** If a student needed to be directed to the registrar's office, it would be instrumental to say, "It's on the second floor of Job Hall. Make a left as you leave the office and follow the corridor through the next three buildings. Then take the stairs next to the reception area." Talk concerned with feelings is **expressive talk.** If you were to say to the same student, "You look like you're having a terrible day!" or "Cheer up; I'm sure everything will be fine," you would be using expressive talk. In general, women's speech uses more person-oriented expressive talk, while men's speech is more fact-oriented and instrumental. Although there is nothing wrong with either kind of talk, insisting that men use one form while women use another in a kind of verbal division of labor can rob both genders of flexibility. Eakins and Eakins feel that this kind of gender-based difference becomes a problem if men and women find that they cannot switch registers to meet the demands of a situation but must remain one-sided and narrow in their communication.[13]

Not only is the way men and women talk different, what they talk about also appears to vary, or at least that is the traditional assumption. If the topic is fashion, or children, or romance, we assume the speaker is female; if the topic is sports, politics, money, or sex, we assume the speaker is male. Early studies did find this kind of difference. But today, it looks like some changes are taking place. Arliss tells us that today's men are talking more about their relationships with women, that both males and females talk more about work, and that both feel freer to talk about sexual experiences.[14]

Gender and Nonverbal Communication

Communication differences between men and women are not limited to talk. Gender differences have also been found in facial display, gaze, use of personal space, and touch. First of all, women tend to be more presentationally expressive than men. It is more appropriate for women to show their emotions than it is for

When women and men are brought up with different values and communication styles, the outcome can be misunderstanding and conflict.

(Roy Lichtenstein, *Forget It! Forget Me!,* 1962)

men, although this depends to some extent on the emotion being displayed. In general, women are rewarded for positive emotions, like smiling. They are also given permission to show sadness and fear. However, they are not expected to display anger too forcefully, for then they will seem "unladylike." The opposite is true for men: Anger is manly, while tears are not. If women mask anger with tears, men mask sadness with anger.

As with verbal differences, the gender of one's interactional partner is important in nonverbal displays. We find, for example, that the largest amount of mutual gaze occurs between female partners, with mixed dyads second, and all-male dyads last. This same pattern holds for spatial proximity and touch. Females touch one another more and stand closer to one another than do members of male-female dyads, while males interacting with other males stand farthest apart and engage in the least amount of touch. We should add that touch behavior is complicated by type of touch. Men are allowed more aggressive touch than women, while women's touch is expected to be more affiliative than that of men. And, when it comes to sexual touching, men are still expected to initiate, and women to respond.

The nonverbal picture seems to suggest that men display more nonverbal forcefulness and power than women. Just as men control more of the talk in an interaction, they also control more space. Their gestures are larger and more expansive, and the territory given up to them is larger.

Gender Differences and Culture

What do these differences mean? Where do they come from? The answers are by no means clear, but we can speculate. Certainly, one of the reasons men and women talk and move differently is the cultural stereotypes that surround them from birth. The first thing that happens to most American babies is that they are wrapped in either a pink or a blue blanket, just as the first question asked by friends and relatives is "Is it a boy or a girl?" And from the moment the answer is given and the child properly classified, a different set of expectations is placed upon him or her. The child spends a lifetime either meeting these expectations or trying to overcome them.

While every culture has gender roles, not every culture defines gender in exactly the same way. In our culture, as we have seen, women are considered the expressive sex. In other cultures, women are the sensible, down-to-earth types, and men are emotional and expressive. Even within a single culture, definitions of gender roles change over time. This is certainly true of America, as box 7.2 shows.

COMMUNICATION AS PERFORMANCE

Of course, gender is not the only role that affects interaction. Children and adults speak differently, as do members of different occupations and members of different social groups. When we take on a role, it is almost as though we are handed a script which maps out our social performances for us. Roles tell us how to play our parts in the social drama of everyday life.

Creating the Ideal Character: Face Work

Like stage actors, social actors want to make an impact on an audience. We want to create characters who will be admired and accepted. McCall and Simmons believe that "one of man's most distinctive motives is the compelling and perpetual drive to acquire support for his idealized conceptions of himself."[15] Gaining the approval of an appreciative audience is one way to acquire support for the idealized self, and one way of doing this is to create a character who embodies the values of society.

Sociologist Erving Goffman uses the term face to describe the part of self presented to others for their approval.[16] As we mentioned in Chapter 1, an individual's face embodies social values; it is an approved identity. **Face-work** is effort spent in presenting face to others. Although the term face may seem odd at first, Goffman is actually following common usage. For example, we say that a person who violates social values has "lost face." We describe efforts to avoid embarrassment as "saving face." And some college students refer to time spent impressing others as "face time."

During communication we present face by taking a **line.** Our lines consist of the verbal and nonverbal behaviors we use during a performance. We must be very careful to take appropriate lines. If we act in ways that aren't "in line" with our position on the social map, others will reject us. The middle-class social climber who tries to pass as a member of the social register or the rich industrialist who tries to relate to his factory workers by acting like "one of the guys" are both out of line. Both will be ridiculed.

During communication we must be careful to preserve our own face and protect that of others. Not only must *we* make a good impression, we must help *others* to make a good impression too. If, for example, we are at a formal dinner party and one of the other guests commits a faux pas, we generally look away, politely pretending not to see that he or she is using the wrong fork. If the social error committed is so obvious that it cannot be ignored, we may try to redefine or diminish it. If our guest unknowingly insults the hostess, we may treat the comment as a joke.

In actively working to maintain our own face, we try to steer clear of situations we feel we can't handle. If someone brings up a topic we're ignorant about, we may change the subject to avoid embarrassment. If we inadvertently offend someone, we can save face by apologizing for our insensitivity or by offering to make amends.

Goffman believes that interpersonal communication is a risky business. We must continually be on our guard for threats to face and line.

> An unguarded glance, a momentary change in tone of voice, an ecological position taken or not taken, can drench a talk with judgmental significance. . . . There is no occasion of talk so trivial as not to require each participant to show serious concern with the way in which he handles himself and the others present.[17]

The image presented by Goffman is that of nervous individuals doing their best to avoid disaster. While Goffman may exaggerate the dangers of interpersonal communication, there is certainly some truth to the idea that we are motivated by social approval. Unless you're a completely free spirit, you're probably careful

not to do odd or embarrassing things in public. And unless you are completely uncaring and insensitive, you try to keep others from making fools of themselves. Stop and think about it for a minute. You may be surprised to find how much communication centers on protecting face and line.

Getting Ready for the Play: Other Aspects of Self-Presentation

When we go to a play, we expect costumes, lighting, and sets. When we interact in everyday life, we also expect a proper background.

Sets, Costumes, and Props Goffman divides the arena where our everyday performances take place into two parts.[18] The public part, the stage, he calls the **front.** There are two aspects to front: setting and personal front. **Setting** includes all of the scenery and props that make the performance possible. **Personal front** involves costume, makeup, physical characteristics, gestures, and the like.

When our front is creatively designed, we can give an effective performance. If we don't maintain a convincing front, however, our performance may crumble. Executives of major corporations know the value of sumptuous surroundings. They spend a great deal of money on impressive office furnishings and artifacts, in the belief that a visitor who spies an original Picasso on the mahogany wall of the reception area is bound to be impressed by their power and wealth. If they're also wearing a $1200 suit and are surrounded by a large and respectful entourage, the effect will be increased. Their front acts as a frame for the business drama about to unfold.

All of us are viewed against the backdrop of our own front regions. If our personal surroundings are warm and inviting, we're likely to make friends easily. If we have to communicate in a cold and forbidding atmosphere, we will have to work harder to overcome its ef-

BOX 7.2

When Is a Man a "Real Man?"

Like most of the concepts encountered in this book, "manhood" is a social construction, a human invention that carries with it a long and varied history. Acknowledging that fact makes the search for what is universally "male" a rather futile one. In examining the evolution of American manhood, historian E. Anthony Rotundo tells us that the concept has passed through at least three significant historical rewrites.

Colonial men, who were thought to be more virtuous and sexually restrained than women, defined themselves primarily as heads of households and emphasized their duties to family and community more than any individual achievements they might have accomplished. Reason and control of the emotions were considered traits of manliness. Rotundo refers to this era as an age of *communal manhood*.

In the early years of the 19th century, this view began to give way to a concept of *self-made manhood* as the new market economy merged with a still relatively young republican form of government. As the market philosophy of individual interest began to take hold, a man's identity and social status as a person who had achieved success in business and politics began to mirror the economic philosophy. Ambition, rivalry, dominance, aggression, and freedom from authority

defined "the new man." Even so, these new passions were not unambiguously praised. A man had to demonstrate that he had these desires under control.

Slowly, toward the end of the 19th century, another transformation began to take shape. The felt need to control the passionate side of manhood began to disintegrate. Competitiveness and toughness were exalted as ends in themselves, while the male body's appearance and athleticism became important components of manhood. Rotundo calls this the emergence of *passionate manhood*. These passionate tendencies became so strong that many men exchanged what would today be called love letters.

Rotundo's examination of the transition from boyhood to manhood in the 19th century reveals some fascinating communication practices that marked the move from one social role to another. For most middle-class boys, the first three to four years of life were lived in the largely female world of the home (including the wearing of female-style gowns). Mothers instilled in their sons the strong moral values of good character (self-restraint and self-denial) that would later be needed to control the passions that dominated the marketplace world of adult men.

By the age of six, boys found freedom from a female world perceived as constraining in the free play of their peers. This "boy culture" was wild, careless, primitive, violent, and almost totally devoid of adult supervision. Rotundo describes it as "mutual nurture combined with assault and battery." Their play was dominated by rituals that emphasized the values of stoicism (suppressing feelings of pain or tenderness), daring (high risk-taking), loyalty, the mastery of new skills, competition, and most of all — independence. The worst fate for a young boy was to

physical assaults of boy culture with verbal assaults that taught them the value of a quick wit, a good argument, and abstract thinking — all skills they would need in the workplace. In transition to the world of romantic love, these young men developed romantic friendships that would today be easily mistaken for homosexual relationships. They frequently slept in the same bed, sometimes held each other for warmth as well as an expression of affection, and confided in each other in great detail about their personal hopes and fears. Since females were largely an enigma to young men, their male friendships served as a kind of rehearsal for marriage that allowed them to test feelings of intimacy without a lifelong commitment at stake. Such romantic relationships were widely accepted among both young men and young women. For women, these types of relationships would last throughout life; for young men, they represented but a passing phase on the road to manhood. In fact, these same highly charged emotional relationships in youth became rather stoic and distant friendships in adulthood.

called a "mama's boy." It meant that he stayed too close to the values of home. In contrast, young girls remained in the confines of the home, under the watchful eyes of their mothers and older sisters.

The transition from boyhood to manhood was anything but clear-cut. Young men struggled mightily with the twin uncertainties of love and career. "Boy culture" did little to prepare them for either, so they had to turn to each other for support. They did so by creating their own clubs and organizations in which they debated, ate, drank, and sang. In effect, they replaced the

SOURCE: E. A. Rotundo. *American Manhood: Transformations in Masculinity from the Revolution to the Modern Era* (New York: Basic Books, 1993).

ADDITIONAL READINGS

Henley, N. M., and C. Kramarae, "Gender, Power, and Miscommunication," in N. Coupland, H. Giles, and J. Wiemann (Eds.) *Miscommunication and Problematic Talk.* Newbury Park, Calif.: Sage 1991: pp. 18–43.

J. T. Wood. *Gendered Lives: Communication, Gender, and Culture.* Belmont, Calif.: Wadsworth, 1994.

Often the settings in which we live come to define us. Communication possible in a tenement may be impossible in a penthouse.

(Millard Sheets, *Tenement Flats*, c. 1934)

fects. The way we set the scene for encounters can affect their outcome. You might find it interesting to analyze what your surroundings say about you and how they affect the ways that you communicate.

Backstage Behavior If actors had to remain on stage for more than a few hours, they would probably lose touch with reality. Luckily, between acts they can retreat backstage, where they are no longer on call; they can relax and be themselves. The private area where social actors can escape the critical eye of their audience is called the **back region.** "The faculty lounge, the members-only club, the executive washroom, and the rehearsal studio are examples of back regions."[19] Goffman believes that dedication to role is not always absolute; most of us need a place where we can slip out of our roles and simply be whoever we want to.

The back region answers our need for privacy. By entering it, we escape the rigors of role enactment. But what if we don't have a physical space to flee to? Then we must rely on psychological space. We find a way to let others know the roles we are playing do not completely define us. Goffman calls this **role distance.**[20] Every situation we enter, he says, puts demands

on us. Occasionally, we resent these demands and try to let others know that there is more to us than meets the eye.

Goffman did much of his research in the medical community, where roles are very well defined. The role of intern is a particularly demanding one. Although interns are expected to be dedicated to their profession, an intern's status in the hospital isn't high. Interns may therefore feel the need to exhibit role distance. There are a number of ways they can do this. They can use a slightly amused facial expression designed to show the absurdity of their position. They may take longer than necessary to obey a request, forcing others to ask twice. They may flirt or joke, reminding those present of other roles in the outside world. This borderline rebellion allows them to fight back without actually violating role demands. Think back to your school days. How did you and your classmates rebel against your status as schoolchildren? We're willing to bet you used similar tactics.

Ensemble Acting Most plays are not one-person shows — the success of the performance depends on teamwork. Social actors are in much the same situation. Along with roles come **role sets,** others who help put on a given performance. The role set of a defense attorney includes clients, prosecuting attorneys, judges, law clerks, and office staff. The role set of a rock star may include band members, agents, managers, bodyguards, roadies, an astrologer or two, and, perhaps, groupies. These are the people who make performances possible. With them, individuals can become stars; without them, they convince no one.

Members of a role set must exercise loyalty, discipline, and circumspection.[21] A politician's family is a good example of a role set. One of their functions is to back up the candidate's performance, presenting an image of wholesomeness and dedication. They must be careful not to give away the act by revealing the candidate's flaws. They must stay in character, never deviating from the party line and never showing anything but delight with their lot in life. And they must never hog the spotlight by seeking personal publicity. According to Goffman, being a particular kind of person is not necessarily a personal matter; it involves a high degree of teamwork.

It is clear that the members of a role set must work together. If members refuse to coordinate their acts, chaos is likely. There are several ways to ensure a cohesive performance. One is to choose relational partners who will play their parts reliably. The politician who chooses a spouse merely to further a career uses a method called **altercasting.** While most of us are not that cold-blooded, we often choose friends who will support our definition of self. Morris Rosenberg has said, "Friendship is the purest illustration of picking one's propaganda."[22]

Another technique we can use to ensure smooth performance is that of **mirroring.**[23] Mirroring is the flip side of altercasting. Here we achieve coordination by following the lead of our partner. While both altercasting and mirroring can assure a coordinated performance, they are not very satisfying, since in either case it is one partner who makes all of the decisions. A more satisfactory technique, from the relational point of view, is **mutual negotiation.** Here both partners work together to construct roles that are mutually satisfactory. To do this successfully we must have the kind of maximal competence we discussed at the end of Chapter 2.

COMMUNICATION AND STORY-TELLING

Whereas Goffman sees humans as performers in a social drama, other theorists view humans as storytellers. **Narrative theorists** believe that we make sense of our world by making up and sharing stories about it. These stories may be addressed to ourselves, for example, when we create a personal identity by constructing an autobiography, or they may be directed to others. Families, businesses, even whole nations, share stories that reflect their sense of who they are and "provide a communal focus for individual identity."[24] The social roles we choose to play are reinforced and maintained through narrative forms including legends, stories, jokes, and myths.

Storytelling begins at a very young age. Vivian Paley has written a number of charming books that describe how children play. In *Bad Guys Don't Have Birthdays,* she shows how children work out their own personal fears and conflicts and learn to cooperate by making up stories as they play.[25] In constructing stories about good guys and bad guys, Care Bears and monsters, children make sense of their lives, figure out their place in their families, and express their needs and concerns.

As adults we continue to tell stories, both in private and in public. Psychologist Jerome Bruner has written about the importance of the autobiographies we create for ourselves. Bruner agrees with other narrative theorists that reality is not immediately given but instead socially constructed. He argues that we understand our own identities by telling stories about ourselves. These stories, once constructed, can determine how we live our lives. They become so real that they begin to "achieve the power to

In public settings, surface features define us. We reveal our social roles but hide the individual selves that lie within.

(Edward Kienholz, *The Beanery,* 1927)

structure perceptual experience, to organize memory, to segment and purpose-build the very 'events' of a life." Bruner believes that, in the end, "we *become* the autobiographical narratives by which we 'tell about' our lives."[26] What Bruner means is that as we experience life, we constantly think about and reinterpret it. Over time, we begin to take these interpretations as absolute facts, and we may even start behaving like the characters in our stories. A person who views himself as a victim may begin to act like a victim, whereas someone who sees herself as a bold and courageous character takes on that identity. If you were to write out the autobiography you have created in your mind, what form would it take? Would it be a comedy, or a drama, or a farce? What would its major themes and moral lessons be?

Although autobiographical narratives can be idiosyncratic, they usually follow the storytelling conventions of the author's culture. In creating individual identities, we are actually following social guidelines. The social aspects of narrative are more clearly seen when we look at group narratives. Families, for example, often create stories that they tell and retell over the years. Often these stories embody family values. For example, a story about how Dad walked ten miles through the snow to get to school is designed to teach children to value the advantages they have and to admire hard work and perseverance. Stories can also establish family roles. The story about how naughty Jane was and what a little angel Tommy was suggests that Jane is the "black sheep" of the family, while Tommy is the model child.

Larger groups also use stories and jokes to build cohesion and socialize members. In large businesses, certain stories become part of the corporate culture. Stories about how great the founder of the business was give voice to the values of the organization. Jokes let employees know what kinds of behaviors are permissible and what kinds are ludicrous. Even countries use narratives to build social cohesion and construct shared versions of reality. At a national level, we often participate in mythic storytelling. A **myth** is an anonymous shared story of "origins and destinies." National myths explain the nature and goals of a country and reflect the qualities and values admired by its citizens. Politicians may retell and add new elements to national myths in order to appeal to voters. President Reagan, considered one of the most effective communicators of his time, used mythic storytelling repeatedly. The story he had to tell was one that appealed to many Americans looking for national identity and validation. To Reagan, America was a "chosen nation, grounded in its families and neighborhoods, and driven inevitably forward by its heroic working people toward a world of freedom and economic progress . . ."[27] This is an enormously appealing and self-justifying story, but it is, of course, only one of the stories that can be told about America. Other Americans, with different experiences and different belief systems, construct stories with different sets of heroes and villians.

Narratives allow individuals, group, and nations to make sense of the world. Much of our understanding of who we are, what we are here for, and how we should behave is communicated to us in story form. It's a good idea to pay attention to the stories you hear everyday. They are more than just ways to pass the time. They are cultural constructions that shape our lives.

Skill Building: Becoming More Mindful

In both this and the previous chapter, we've stressed how easy it is to let routines take over our communication. We've seen that people perceive the world and others in it by filtering

their perceptions through socially constructed schemata. We've also seen that there are many pressures on us to play socially approved roles and to follow socially appropriate scripts. What this means is that it is possible to get through life on automatic pilot, to carry out our lives in a mindless way.

There are some benefits to mindless action. When we rely on distinctions from the past, we don't have to stop and think about everyday activities. When we automatically follow social roles, we can easily fit in. Life seems very simple when we are acting mindlessly. At the same time, acting mindlessly presents some real dangers. When in a mindless state, we lack creativity, exhibit emotional and cognitive rigidity, and find it impossible to adapt to new communication situations. Our relationships lack flexibility and originality. In this section we'll look at some ways you can gain more control over your perceptions and actions by becoming more mindful. This basic interpersonal skill will allow you to create more rewarding relational cultures.

MINDFULNESS AND OPEN-MINDEDNESS

Mindfulness and mindlessness are basic cognitive states. According to psychologist Ellen J. Langer, **mindlessness** is a state of reduced attention. The individual is trapped in categories devised in the past. **Mindfulness,** on the other hand, is a state of "alert and lively awareness" involving active information processing and encouraging the creation of new categories and distinctions.[28]

The mindlessness/mindfulness dichotomy is similar to Milton Rokeach's distinction between closed- and open-mindedness. Rokeach believed that people could be categorized according to the rigidity of their cognitive systems. For Rokeach the basic characteristic that defined a person's openness is "the extent to which the person can receive, evaluate, and act on relevant information received from the outside on its own intrinsic merits, unencumbered by irrelevant factors in the situation, within the person, or from the outside."[29]

Closed-minded people, when compared with those who are open-minded, tend to be less able to learn new information. They have more difficulty discriminating between information and the source of that information so that they tend to accept whatever authorities say is true. They also tend to have problems in resolving conflicts, refusing to compromise because they equate compromise with defeat.

While followers of Rokeach have often treated open- and closed-mindedness as relatively enduring personality characteristics, Langer emphasizes that mindfulness and mindlessness are mental states and that people can be encouraged to switch from one to the other. She argues that mindlessness is not a personality characteristic, that we are all capable of both mental conditions.

Langer also denies the common belief that it is easier to be mindless than mindful. Psychologists used to believe that we resist mindful activity because being mindful takes too much effort. Langer proposed that "effort is involved in switching from a mindless to a mindful mode, analogous to the force required to change the direction of a moving object," but that the mindful state, once we have switched into it, is no more tiring than the mindless state. Being mindful can be effortless and even energizing.[30]

INCREASING MINDFULNESS

When we are in a mindless state, we are, by definition, unaware and uncritical. The first step in reducing mindlessness, then, is to *become aware of the extent to which perceptions and behaviors are socially determined.* Most people fail to realize that their perceptions and behaviors are largely socially constructed. The social rules we

follow as a matter of course seldom have the "feel" of rules. We believe our behavior is freely chosen rather than socially controlled.

Unfortunately, much of our conduct is triggered by habit. We eat not because we're hungry but because the clock says it's noon. We go to a party not because we particularly want to but because all of our friends are going. We dress appropriately because it wouldn't be right not to. When we do all of these things, we are letting the social situation control our responses. In order to become more mindful, we must *become aware of the contextual triggers that govern our behavior.* There may, in fact, be nothing wrong with following social rules, but we can't decide until we recognize that these acts are rule-governed.

When we are in a state of mindfulness, we can critically evaluate our options. We may decide to follow the norms and act out our roles, or we may decide to transcend the system; what's important is that we make a conscious decision. One test you might want to apply in deciding whether to conform to social expectations is to tack a "because clause" onto a description of your behavior. You should say to yourself, "I'm going downtown tonight because . . ." If you can't think of any good reason for your action, maybe that action bears more thought.

Often we do things in noncreative, rigid ways because we come to premature closure. Once we've thought of one way to do something, we don't go further and try to think of other possible ways to do it. This closure can occur in our process of enacting role requirements or in our efforts to solve problems. For instance, a teacher may teach the same way he or she has always taught without bothering to ask if there's a different way to teach. Or a group may make mediocre decisions because the members stop as soon as they've found a solution without asking themselves whether it is the best solution. What both of these examples suggest is that we should make a real effort to *examine thoughts and actions critically, looking for new solutions and perspectives.*

One way to increase creativity is to make sure that we *don't engage in self-censorship or premature cognitive commitments.* One of the biggest blocks to creativity is our fear of being judged. We hold back potentially interesting ideas and commit to dull but safe solutions because we're afraid original ideas and actions may seem silly. This tendency to self-censorship is so strong that we must often use artificial means to change it. Techniques such as brainstorming, where individuals are encouraged to express all ideas no matter how insignificant or ridiculous they may at first appear, are specifically designed to help us overcome our own fear of creativity. While brainstorming is often used in formal organizational contexts, it can be used by single individuals to solve interpersonal problems. Remember that to get along with someone else, you must be flexible, adaptable, and creative. In relationships don't be afraid to try something new.

Another way to increase creativity is to *take multiple perspectives.* Much of how we react to the world we learned as children. As we grow up we learn to take on new perspectives so as not to be trapped in childish patterns. But even as adults we can benefit from trying our best to see the world in as many different ways as possible. Piper and Langer did an interesting study in which they asked people to watch a soap opera from several different perspectives — that of a politician, a director, a psychologist, a lawyer, a doctor, and a child.[31] This mindful viewing allowed subjects to see the characters as more complex and less stereotypic than did a control group of mindless, single-perspective viewers. Subjects got more out of the show when encouraged to take multiple perspectives. The same might be true of real-life experiences if we were to work hard at seeing things in multiple ways.

All of us could benefit by spending more of our time in a mindful rather than a mindless

state. The best way to do this is to become more aware of the situations in which we act mindlessly and to be critical of our own behaviors.

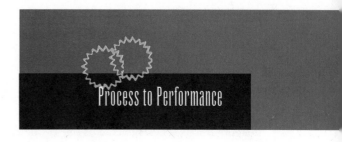

Process to Performance

REVIEW TERMS

The following is a list of major concepts introduced in this chapter. The page where the concept is first mentioned is listed in parentheses.

position (186)
role (187)
role rigidity (188)
role repertoire (188)
role conflict (188)
looking-glass self (189)
social comparison theory (189)
self-perception theory (190)
female register (193)
qualifiers (193)
disclaimers (193)
tag questions (194)
polite forms (194)
intensifiers (194)
instrumental talk (194)
expressive talk (195)
face (196)
face-work (196)
line (196)
front (197)
setting (197)
personal front (197)
back region (200)
role distance (200)

role set   (200)
altercasting   (201)
mirroring   (201)
mutual negotiation   (201)
narrative theorists   (201)
myth   (203)
mindlessness   (203)
mindfulness   (203)

SUGGESTED READINGS

Benedict, Ruth. *Patterns of Culture.* New York: Penguin Books, 1946. Benedict is one of the most famous of the early cultural anthropologists. In this classic she explores the relationship between culture and personality.

Goffman, Erving. *The Presentation of Self in Everyday Life.* Garden City, N.Y.: Anchor Books, 1959. Goffman is not easy reading, but he is well worth the effort. If you take the time to read him slowly and thoughtfully, you'll find insights on every page. But watch out — Goffman can be addicting. After reading him, you won't view the world the same again.

Hewitt, John P. *Self and Society: A Symbolic Interactionist Social Psychology,* 5th ed. Newton Highlands, Mass.: Allyn and Bacon, 1991. If you want to explore the complex relationship between self, society, and communication, then you need to understand a school of thought known as symbolic interactionism. This is one of the easiest introductions to this important field.

Paley, Vivian G., *Bad Guys Don't Have Birthdays.* Chicago: University of Chicago Press, 1991. Paley observes and reports on the fantasy play of nursery school children in this amusing and fascinating book. As she traces the stories the children cooperatively create, she demonstrates how narrative can be used to banish fears and build connections.

Wood, Julia T., *Gendered Lives: Communication, Gender, and Culture.* Belmont, Calif.: Wadsworth, 1994. Wood explores the impact that gender has on our lives. Topics include gender and friendships, gender in business and professional relationships, and gender and the media. This text is lively, comprehensive, and current.

TOPICS FOR DISCUSSION

1. In *Invitation to Sociology,* Peter Berger tells us: "Where human beings live or work in compact groups, in which they are personally known and to which they are tied by feelings of personal loyalty . . . , very potent and simultaneously very subtle mechanisms of control are constantly brought to bear upon the . . . deviant." Think about some of the ways social groups control their members. How many can you identify? Don't forget mechanisms like ridicule, gossip, ostracism, and disapproval. How effective are these mechanisms? Why do you think they work?

2. To what extent are we "creatures of our culture"? Do you agree with Benedict that our possibilities and impossibilities are predetermined by culture? Can you think of examples of why this might or might not be true?

3. What career are you interested in? If you aren't already in that career, what kinds of role changes do you anticipate undergoing when you enter that arena? Can you think of ways this role transition can be made easier?

4. What advice would you give to a high school student who will be entering your school next semester? What do you believe he or she would need to know to be able to "fit in" and assume the student role as defined at your school? What does this tell you about the "ideal" student role identity at your university?

5. Discuss specific social norms designed to help others "save face." Can you describe any situations you've been in where you had to help another save face? What did you do? How did you feel?

6. Although we didn't discuss it explicitly in the text, Goffman says there are times when we engage in aggressive face-work — actions designed to make us look good at the expense of others. Has anyone ever done this to you? How did you handle it? In general, what are some of the ways people engage in aggressive face-work?

7. Discuss some typical "lines" college students use to impress one another. Which are the most successful? Which are the least successful?

8. Box 7.1 discusses male-female sex roles. What is your reaction? If you had children, would you try to prevent or limit the amount of traditional sex role socialization they received or would you encourage it? Does it make a difference what toys and games a child plays (with) when young? Were you raised with traditional or nontraditional sex roles?

9. Do you believe that women and men have different communication styles? If so, what impact do you think these differences have on the way we lead our lives? Do you think images of manhood and womanhood are changing today? If so, what social forces are causing these changes?

10. How important are gender roles to your personal identity? When do you find yourself most influenced by gender roles? When do they seem least relevant? Do you ever put them aside?

11. Think back to the stories that are told at the family celebrations you attend. What values and lessons do they contain?

OBSERVATION GUIDE

1. How controlled are you by simple social norms? How willing are you to sacrifice face or line? Choose a simple social norm and violate it. Don't do something outrageous that would offend others; simply do something that is slightly odd or atypical. For example, wear an article of clothing that is not quite appropriate. Or sit by yourself instead of joining your friends as you usually do. Carefully note reactions. Be specific. What kinds of pressures were placed on you? Describe your own feelings about doing this. Was it hard to do? Did you feel awkward and uncomfortable? Are you too much or too little affected by social norms? Relate this experience to the social comparison process.

2. Analyze your own style of self-presentation from a dramatic point of view. Think of a particular communication incident where you were trying to make a good impression. What face were you trying to present? What line did you take? How did your setting and personal front either help or hinder you? Describe in detail all relevant props, furnishings, and costuming decisions. Was this a solo performance, or did you count on others to help you put on your front? If the interaction was successful, how much was attributable to front? If the interaction didn't quite work out, how would you redirect it if you had the chance?

3. Collect the stories and jokes you hear during the next few days. Write them out so that their details are clear to you. Now analyze these stories in as much detail as possible. Try thinking of yourself as an anthropologist or folklorist who has stumbled upon a collection of stories from a foreign culture and is trying to reconstruct and make sense of that culture. What lessons and values are implicit in the stories? What does that tell you about the culture from which they were collected? Did any parts of their content surprise or even offend you? Why?

EXERCISES

1. Working with a partner, list all of the roles you have assumed during the last week. Try to determine the communication expectations for

each role. Write out at least three rules of communication behavior for each role you identify.

2. Work with an opposite-sex partner. Plan a skit showing a male-female interaction embodying typical sex roles. Present it to the class, but take the sex role opposite to your own; that is, if you are male, play the female part, and if you are female, play the male part. As a class, discuss the portrayals. What behaviors were used to portray the opposite sex? Were the portrayals accurate? How did you feel while portraying your part, and why? Was this hard or easy? Embarrassing or fun?

Many artists have an acute sense of their own identity. Vincent van Gogh painted some 24 self-portraits during one two-year period in Paris. What do you think are the costs and benefits of so much self-reflection?

8

Self Competence: Establishing Individual Identities

"Don't call me that! My name is Toby," says an irritated three-year-old, responding to his father's attempt to dub him with some clever nickname. The act of naming carries great social significance for us. As we learn to categorize the world around us, we also learn our place within it. Our name usually sets us apart from other human beings and is one of the most significant ways that we remind ourselves of our uniqueness — of our individuality. In fact, new theories about the evolution of the human mind and of language suggest that the very things that make us human, such as self-consciousness and personal memory, are not necessarily innate. These abilities seem to be derived from the use of language itself during the very early years of childhood.[1] Our own American culture and language use in particular recognize and emphasize the uniqueness of the individual person.

Interpersonal communication influences the development of this unique personal identity. Since we cannot "see" ourselves (except in mirrors, in photographs, and in our mind's eye), we rely on others' impressions of us and feedback to us to form our own opinions of self. As this sense of self begins to develop, we are confronted with one of the most enduring dilemmas of social life: whether to conform to social expectations and present ourselves as "one of the group" or to deviate and be seen as an individual who stands "apart from the crowd." When we conform to standard roles and rules, we are taking on a **social identity** defined by and borrowed from society; when we resist standard roles or make our own rules, we are forging a **personal identity**. To be fully human means to develop and express the self in terms of both social and personal self-identities. In the previous chapter we looked at forces that encourage conformity and the development of our social identities; in this chapter we explore the factors that foster independence and individuality, or personal identity.

The tension between conformity and independence is probably felt to some extent in all cultures, but it is particularly strong in our culture. In collectivist cultures such as Japan and China there is a greater tendency to conform to social expectations — expressions of individuality are seen as disrespectful and self-centered.

Pressures to conform are present in our own culture as well. Chapter 7 demonstrated that people adapt to the social roles and situations defined by their culture. The starting point for social life is the inheritance of complex signs and symbols from previous generations. The family you were born into had already established roles, rules, and customs long before your arrival, as did the schools, churches, political parties, and other institutions you may have joined later.

We begin this chapter with a brief historical overview of how the modern image of ourselves as unique individuals came about. This is important because we have a very strong tendency to think of "the self" as being a fundamental aspect of human nature, as something that has always existed regardless of culture or the passing of time. Once we understand that the concept of self is a historical construct, we will spend the bulk of this chapter looking at how researchers today have defined and studied the concept of self, how it changes over a lifetime, and how it relates to our interpersonal communication practices.

The Self in History

The concept of personal identity or self-concept is a recent historical development. During most of recorded history, people defined themselves according to their place or rank in society (lord of the manor, servant, merchant, peasant, and so on). Certainly people recognized their own individual existence, and frequently thought of themselves as having "souls," but they did not dwell on the unique differences between one soul or self and another. The first recorded use of the word "conscious" to denote awareness of internal thoughts and sensations dates from the late 16th century, while the word "self-conscious" doesn't make its appearance until over a hundred years later.[2] Several historians have observed that a cultures changes, so does

the language that describes the self.[3] Different historical eras, it is argued, generate their own "modal selves." A **modal self** refers to an idealized type of person whose existence is viewed as essential if the prevailing social order within a culture is to maintain itself.[4] This conception of self also rests on the assumption that when cultural change occurs, it almost demands a change in the types of people who inhabit the culture. For instance, the kind of person who knew his place and drew his identity largely from being the "head of a household" fit very well in the hierarchical society of colonial America. We might call the modal self of that time a "communal self" because playing out the role you were dealt by gender and birth was essential in recreating the moral and social order.

The cultural vision of self began to change as the Industrial Revolution and the new American democracy took hold. Prior to the revolution in machinery and methods of work, most people worked from their homes. The home and the workplace were one and the same. The concept of a private self apart from the community had little significance since everything one did was closely scrutinized by family and community leaders. But the proliferation of shops and factories caused a division between public and private spheres: The public arena became the world of commerce and politics, and the home a refuge from that world. In a world where men left the home to work and where the household was becoming more of a feminine domain, it was difficult to sustain the male identity as "head of the household." In addition, the new economy required employees who were punctual, loyal, honest, and hard-working. These requirements were the driving force for the creation of what historian Warren Susman has called a "culture of character" and a corresponding modal self defined by various attributes of *character: being conscious of duty, a good citizen, honorable, moral, well-mannered, and a doer of good deeds.*[5]

Late in the 19th century, another transformation occurred. The modal self built around character began to give way to the even more individualized concept of *personality*. Where a self-image based on character was accomplished by living up to a well-defined social standard of morals and values, a self-image defined by having a personality meant to be *different, fascinating, stunning, magnetic, creative, dominant, or forceful*.[6] How did this shift in modal selves happen? Susman believes that several factors were at work, but two stand out. One is the fact that more and more Americans moved to urban areas to find work. There they lived constantly in a crowd, and developed the need to feel significant or different from everyone around them. In diaries, journals, and advice books of the time, people repeatedly stressed that "personality is the quality of being Somebody."[7] A second major change was a move from a producer to a consumer society. A person of good character fit in well in a society that needed to make things, but not in an economy more and more designed around people "buying things." With an image of self as a unique personality, one would be more inclined to buy accessories and decorate the home in a way that reflected his or her individual traits. By the beginning of this century, all the elements were in place to support our modern notion of who we are. As you see in Box 8.1, some believe that we are in the midst of another great social transformation, and that our image of the self as a stable, enduring personality is beginning to crumble around the edges.

Self-Concepts: Gaining Independence from Social Roles and Rules

As we saw in Chapter 7, a smoothly running society depends on our following socially assigned roles and rules. We also saw that roles do not totally define us. We exercise some choice in the matter of adopting which of several possible roles to play in any given situation. We play some roles more frequently than others and

may become very good at a few of them, internalizing them as part of who we are. But we also distance ourselves from some roles and avoid others as much as possible. The *choices* we make concerning what roles we play and how we play them reflect a growing independence from our cultural inheritance. This independence from cultural rules eventually culminates in one or more rather stable self-concepts, which we use to determine when we should conform to social rules and when we should resist following them. In order to understand how self-concepts emerge and stabilize, we need first to define them.

WHAT IS THE SELF-CONCEPT?

In our modern era, the **self-concept** is defined as each person's own subjective view or image of him- or herself as a person.[8] While we often use the terms *self-concept* and *personality* interchangeably, they are not the same thing. Most scholarly definitions of **personality** assume each of us exhibits organized, enduring, and characteristic ways of behaving *as measured by psychological tests*. The difference? Personality refers to how psychologists see us; the self-concept refers to how we see ourselves. Although others (including researchers) are entitled to their own opinions about us, and may disagree with one another about what kind of person we really are, our self-concept remains our own private view of ourselves. In the first part of this chapter, we take a self-concept approach to understanding the mutual influence of interpersonal communication and personal identity. Later in the chapter, we consider research conducted from the personality perspective.

Self as Subject and Object

Our understanding of what the self-concept is and how it develops owes a great deal to a group of social scientists who refer to themselves as *symbolic interactionists*. Perhaps the

BOX 8.1

The Saturated Self: Will You Still Be You Tomorrow?

Social psychologist Kenneth Gergen believes that we have already entered an era of profound social change. In his book, *The Saturated Self,* he contends that modern transportation and communication technologies (e.g., international travel, television, telephones, electronic mail) are propelling us toward a new type of self-consciousness, which he labels a postmodern or *populated self.*

Noting that communication defines social reality, Gergen argues that different historical eras produce different kinds of self-identities. The modern era (dating from the late 19th and early 20th centuries), with its rational, scientific viewpoint that constructs the world as composed of fundamental, essential properties, makes it natural to think of the self as a thing-in-itself, as a fundamentally stable entity. And as long as most relationships are based primarily on face-to-face or written communication, and most of those relationships last a lifetime, the self-identities formed and maintained through social interaction with well-known others are likely to seem very stable indeed. As a result, most people in Western cultures think of themselves as having a "true self," a stable interior identity that remains essentially consistent despite changes in fads, location, relationships, and so on.

But Gergen, and many others, believe that the modern era may be coming to a close. A crisis in the social and natural sciences has raised doubts as to our ability to know anything objectively. Many scholars now believe that even the language with which we express our so-called objective viewpoints does not reflect or mirror reality; it is tainted through and through with social and ideological bias. Moreover, Gergen points to the "enormous proliferation of relationships" that new technologies make possible. We are much more likely than previous generations to have friends and acquaintances all over the geographical map. Many of these relationships will be fleeting, but nonetheless provide opportunities to interact with "different" others and to try on new self-identites. Radio, television, and newer forms of electronic communication have dramatically expanded the range and variety of relationships we are able to witness and participate in. We no longer form our opinions (or self-identities) based solely on an immediate audience of parents, peers, and local community values. It is not uncommon for people to think of themselves as having relationships with media celebrities, or to actually talk with them on television call-in shows. The combination of computer desktop publishing and electronic modems gives people the chance to "become direct agents in their own self-multiplication" (the capacity to have a significant presence in more than one place at a time).

Conversations with unknown others via the Internet or 900 numbers is now a 24-hour-a-day possibility. Gergen believes that these new forms of relationship are accelerating at the same time that traditional relationships are undergoing radical transformation. He describes all-too-typical family interactions as "microwave relationships" because of the vastly differing schedules of parents and children that make the family sit-down

Our personal identity is actually a collection of selves that we monitor and use in different situations.

(Pablo Picasso, *The Red Armchair*, 1931)

dinner a rare event. Such relationships are being defined by "intense heat for the immediate provision of nourishment." The idea of spending "quality time" with our children is one indication that the amount of time devoted to such relationships is changing.

Gergen calls this the social saturation of identity. With a greater variety of relationships, either fleeting or in a constant state of disruption, stability in relationships and in personal identities will become harder and harder to maintain. The result is "a populating of the self" with many different possible identities, many of which contradict each other. As more voices enter the fray, the question "Who am I?" becomes more difficult to answer. The self that seems rational within one set of relationships may seem absurd from another viewpoint. While this splitting of the self in many different directions makes us candidates for a permanent identity crisis, it may have some liberating features as well.

One possibility that Gergen envisions in the emerging postmodern self is a greater emphasis on relationships over individual concerns. Instead of asking, "How should I live my life?" we may be more inclined to wonder, "What will my family will do with its life?" or "How will my marriage go today?" or "How will my team of coworkers get by this week?" While it seems odd to make relational terms the center of attention and to push the self to the periphery, neither social unit is more "natural" than the other. For most of human history, the community or social group has been the dominant social unit. The ideology of individualism has risen to prominence only in the last three centuries, and even then, only in Western cultures. If Gergen is right, the next hundred years may be very interesting indeed.

SOURCE: Kenneth J. Gergen. *The Saturated Self: Dilemmas of Identity in Contemporary Life*. New York: Basic Books, 1991.

ADDITIONAL READINGS

Giddens, Anthony. *Modernity and Self-Identity: Self and Society in the Late Modern Age*. Stanford, Calif.: Stanford University Press, 1991.
Lash, Scott, and Jonathan Friedman, eds. *Modernity and Identity*. Oxford: Blackwell, 1992.

best-known of these theorists was George Herbert Mead, who emphasized the importance of language and gesture as symbols that give us the unique ability to exercise control over our own conduct and, ultimately, to develop a consciousness of self. Symbolic interactionists use the term *self* in two very distinct ways.[9] First of all, the self refers to a *process* of alternating between two states of consciousness: the self as "subject" and the self as "object." When a person is in the subjective state of consciousness, she is acting toward other people or events in an immediate, spontaneous, and impulsive way. From the objective perspective, a person imagines herself as others might see her.

Mead believed that we are constantly alternating between the subjective and objective perspectives, sometimes behaving without much reflection, at other times attending to the feedback of others in order to "get outside of the self" and see how others view us. He believed that this ability is what enables us to exercise self-control. We must be able to see ourselves as others do if we hope to alter our own behavior. And we come to know ourselves indirectly — that is, through the eyes of others — only by imagining how others respond to us.

While Mead emphasized that the self is really a process, symbolic interactionists (as well as most of us) also use the term *self* to refer to one of the results of that process: namely, that humans often view the self *as an object or entity in its own right.* Just as we can perceive an object such as an automobile as having specific attributes (for example, sleek styling, comfortable features, good gas mileage), so we come to view ourselves as having stable features (such as a hot temper, consideration for others, or a willingness to take risks). The tendencies to view self as process and as product generally hold each other in check. If we viewed the self-concept as something that changes with every new interaction, we would never develop any sense of self as a stable and whole person. On the other hand, if we viewed the self-concept as a finished product, we would severely limit our ability to

change or try on new identities. Fortunately, most of us do not have to deal with these questions very often. Our self-concept, even while adapting to the subtleties of a new situation, almost always feels as if it hadn't changed at all. This is because the self-concept is complex and ambiguously defined — ambiguous enough to allow room for change *and* stability.

The Ambiguous Self

Even though we like to think that we have one true self, we actually have several selves. These self-concepts may be influenced by several factors: (1) the accuracy of various perceptions, (2) the expectations placed on us by ourselves and others, (3) social context, and (4) relational context.

The Accuracy of Various Perceptions Our self-concepts are not entirely or even primarily of our own making; they are the products of social interactions with others. As a result, we all experience ourselves as objects and form impressions of our own identity; so does every person with whom we interact. Since perceptions of the self are subject to the same biases as the perceptions of others discussed in Chapter 6, the "self" will always be defined a little differently by every perceiver. In other words, there will always be some degree of uncertainty about whose perception of self should be considered the most accurate. For instance, a professor delivers what seemed to her to be an excellent lecture. She feels quite competent and satisfied with her presentation of self. Immediately after the lecture, however, two students imply that the lecture was hard to follow, while another complains about fellow students sleeping or passing notes and talking during the lecture. Each of these perceptions represents different evaluations of the professor's self-identity. We may try to ignore them, but we are always aware that others' perceptions of our "self" may not match our own.

Expectations The clarity of the self-concept may be further clouded by the variety of expectations placed on us by ourselves and others. The professor views her teaching and research to be equally important aspects of her role, but she knows that students expect her to make a greater commitment to teaching and advising. Meanwhile, she isn't quite sure how to square the dean's public statements that teaching is a top priority with his tendency to deny tenure to excellent teachers who have not published enough research articles. Furthermore, she feels that her husband and certainly her children expect her to forgo writing lesson plans and grading papers at home to spend more time with them. In the midst of all these competing demands and expectations, is it surprising that she questions her priorities and often wonders who she is or is supposed to be?

Social Context Differing role and relational expectations and conflicting feedback about the self makes defining the self a tenuous activity at best. To further complicate matters, the move from one social situation to another often encourages us to enact a different self-concept. Some situations seem to require that we be a particular kind of person, while others permit us to be ourselves (that is, whichever self we might prefer to be at the moment). A highly scripted or *closed* episode (see Chapter 6), such as a debate contest, requires that the participants present themselves as informative, aggressive, and contentious; the bus ride home consists of several *open* episodes (talking about the tournament, eating dinner at a diner, enjoying one-on-one conversations) that grant them greater leeway to choose other self-concepts to display. Mark Snyder and William Ickes have demonstrated that personality traits are better predictors of behavior in situations that are not very scripted; when the situation is highly scripted, one's personality seems to be subdued.[10] Presumably, we perceive ourselves differently in such situations and alter our behavior accordingly.

Each of the factors discussed here makes defining the self in terms of even a handful of traits or descriptive qualities quite difficult. This ambiguity leads most of us to describe ourselves with rather general terms like "friendly" or "outgoing." However, these terms have considerable flexibility when applied to different situations. Being friendly to neighbors can involve relatively simple acts such as exchanging greetings or loaning our tools; it usually requires greater energy and a wider variety of behaviors to be perceived as friendly at a social mixer. Even so, we often move from one episode in which we act in a friendly and outgoing manner to another in which we may be nasty and cantankerous. Why don't we perceive ourselves to be schizophrenic when this happens?

One of the reasons that we do not feel any great anxiety about assuming or discarding a different persona is that many of our self-concepts are so firmly entrenched in different situations that it does not *feel* as if we are behaving out of character. When we behave according to the rules and roles of a given situation, our behaving *appropriately* absolves us of any need to explain why we acted the way we did. We need only account for our behavior when we (or someone else) perceives it to be a deviation from the norm. And when we do deviate from expectations, we often justify breaking the rules by invoking a particular self-image that we want to maintain ("I know you hate blind dates, so I didn't tell you someone else was coming to dinner. I guess I'm just a matchmaker at heart"). So we tend not to recognize contradictions in our portrayals of self as long as they are appropriate to the situation, and we reinforce the idea of a unified self whenever we do deviate from social routine.

Relational Context There is yet another explanation for our ability to monitor several self-concepts and still believe in an essential unity of the self. We employ different self-concepts in different types of relationships, but we do not necessarily feel any tension between these selves. We are able to compartmentalize our relationships in such a way that we do not perceive any incongruity between how we act as the tyrannical boss or the loving husband. Charles Horton Cooley explained how we come to view the self differently in the presence of different people. You may recall Cooley's *looking-glass self* introduced in Chapter 7. Cooley identified three essential elements in the self-concept: (1) how we think we appear to the other person, (2) how we think that person judges our appearance, and (3) how we feel about ourselves in reaction to the other's perception of us. Note the similarity in the views of Cooley and Mead. Cooley shows how we might come to feel that we are not the same person from one relationship to another when he says that "we are ashamed to seem evasive in the presence of a straightforward man, cowardly in the presence of a brave one, gross in the eyes of a refined one, and so on."[11] Perhaps if we met all three of these people in the space of five minutes we would feel a little uncomfortable with who we really are. But we ordinarily have some breathing space between encounters that enables us to shift gears and establish an appropriate persona.

While interacting with very different kinds of people can occasionally test our sense of self, this is not always the case. Our self-concept can appear to us as relatively stable when we are equally comfortable in a variety of different relationships. For instance, a person may feel just as comfortable being "herself" with her parents as she does with her best friend. In each case, however, she perceives herself in somewhat different ways. With her parents she sees herself as independent, serious-minded, and caring. With her friend she may still see herself as caring, but also as witty, playful, and carefree. "I am occasionally serious with my friend, but for the most part I am like a kid who never grew up; for my parents I grew up years ago to avoid being treated like a child." The type of relationship we have with another person inevitably affects who we are in that relationship.

In spite of the fact that we behave differently in various relationships, the limited range of those relationships can reinforce our sense of a stable self-identity. Several researchers have noted that the choices we make in terms of whom to spend time with and what types of situations to enact can provide consistent feedback to reinforce a single, preferred self-concept. Anthony Greenwald has drawn an analogy between the self and a totalitarian political organization, in that we can be so intent on the survival of a particular image of self that we surround ourselves only with people who reinforce that image and pay attention only to feedback we want to hear.[12]

Public and Private Self

Self-concepts can also differ in terms of a public or private orientation. How we think of the self when we are in public or "on display" for others to see is a **public self-concept.** These aspects of self are readily apparent when we play a social role that allows some self-expression. Sports commentators sometimes refer to athletic teams as reflecting their coach's personality. In such cases the coach has imbued the role with one of his or her public self-concepts. It is also possible to derive a public self-concept from one of the social roles that we play frequently and associate closely with our identity. Many people internalize the roles they play at work and see themselves as primarily a police officer, teacher, social worker, or salesperson. A role has been internalized when a person continues to function in that role outside its original or appropriate context. For instance, a father may police his children as if he were still captain of the precinct; a wife may lecture her husband as if he were a student in her class; a social worker may meddle in the affairs of the neighbors as if they were cases on file in the office.

Most of us probably think of a **private self-concept** as somehow closer to the real thing. These are the aspects of self that aren't so readily apparent to casual passersby or even to relatively close friends. Perceptions of our own psychological traits, personal values, and most frequent emotional states head the list of candidates for how we describe our private self. One tendency in this regard has been reported by William McGuire and his colleagues as the **distinctiveness postulate.**[13] According to this research we tend to encode as features of the self-concept those aspects of our own appearance or behavior that are unusual in some way. For instance, one study showed that schoolchildren were more likely to describe themselves in terms of their birthplace, their sex or ethnic background, their hair and eye color, or their height and weight if any of these features were different from the majority of their classmates.[14] This again shows the important role situation and others play in our definition of self. Chances are that as the people around us change, so will various facets of our self-concept recede into the background (because they are not unusual anymore), only to be replaced by new ways in which we find ourselves to be distinct from those around us.

Self-Esteem

Another aspect of the self-concept is our characteristic level of **self-esteem.** While our self-concept is an image of self as a particular kind of person, self-esteem refers to the positive or negative feelings we associate with our self-images. When a person has a high level of self-esteem, he or she is more perceptive, more confident, and more likely to express personal attitudes even if unpopular. Such a person also tends to make friends more easily.[15] People with low self-esteem want the approval of others but are usually so preoccupied with and down on themselves that they fail to interpret other people's behavior accurately. More specifically, they often fail to recognize when another person is being friendly and may even look for signs that the other is uninterested or does not like them.[16] As

a result, they forget to be sociable and friendly, which helps produce less fulfilling social relations and reinforces their low self-image.

Now that we have some idea what the self-concept is and how many versions of it may exist, we want to look at how it develops in individuals from infancy to adulthood.

HOW DOES THE SELF-CONCEPT DEVELOP AND CHANGE?

Although many psychologists and parents will argue that a newborn baby shows signs of uniqueness, few will argue that we are born with a full-fledged sense of personal identity. The self-concept is constructed message by message, act by act, one reaction after another. The social construction of a personal identity takes a good deal of time and is no easy matter. We do know something about the process by which we gain our autonomy from the environment around us, try on various identities, and finally adopt and modify some of them for our very own. Let's examine this process as it unfolds in childhood and then trace it into adulthood.

Development in Childhood

Earlier in this century it was believed that a newborn baby was something like a blank slate that could be written upon, a lump of clay that could be shaped almost exclusively by the social environment into which it was born. We now know that an infant is fully equipped to use most of the same senses that an adult does, and that the infant can also distinguish the human face from other visual cues, identify the sound of its own mother's voice, and make many other distinctions. In spite of these remarkable capabilities, the human infant has a long way to go before we can consider it to be a fully developed person with a unique self-identity.

Psychologists Michael Lewis and Jeanne Brooks-Gunn have described the process in

The distinctiveness postulate suggests that we see ourselves in terms of how we are different or unusual from those around us.

(*Mr. Patrick O'Brien — The Irish Giant,* 18th-century engraving)

which infants begin to develop a sense of self.[17] Several features of biological inheritance, cognitive development, and the social environment conspire to make a sense of self possible. First of all, infants, like the rest of us, are highly attracted to the image of other infants. An infant finds her own reflection in a mirror to be quite fascinating and will watch herself or another infant far longer than she will watch an adult image. Second, within the first three months of age, the infant begins to recognize a cause-and-effect relationship between her own movements and the corresponding movements of her own image in a mirror. She recognizes that when she moves her hand, the image in the mirror moves its hand! But the sense of self experienced here is but a fleeting one. Only after acquiring the concept of *object permanence* at around eight months does the infant recognize that her own

body and its mirror image are enduring entities. She can now hold in her mind the knowledge of an object (a toy, her mother, or her self) without necessarily seeing or touching it. Finally, sometime after the first year, the infant develops the ability to categorize objects, people, and events. One set of social categories that emerges are self-categorizations.

Self-categories emerge along with other types of social cognitions such as those related to the perception of others (see Chapter 6). Like our own knowledge of others, the infant's knowledge is developed through interactions with other people. Undoubtedly, the infant has more specific knowledge of his or her primary caregivers, but soon learns to distinguish self and others in terms of some simple categories. Lewis and Brooks-Gunn believe that three particular categories are important in the child's early knowledge: familiarity, age, and gender. By three months, an infant can distinguish his or her mother's face from that of a stranger. Recognition of the father and of siblings, grandparents, and others as familiar takes place shortly thereafter. This marks an initial distinction between familiar and unfamiliar others and is crucial to the formation of relationships with these significant others. A key element associated with familiar others is the expectation of *patterned interaction,* which creates a sense of continuity. The self cannot be experienced as an entity that continues over time until others are experienced in that way.

By age 9–12 months, self-recognition begins to take shape as the infant learns to differentiate between a photograph of him- or herself and one of another infant the same age. At 16–18 months, most infants can also recognize gender differences, as they respond differently to same- and opposite-sex baby pictures. Of those 18-month-old infants who have verbal labels for "mommy" and "daddy" or "boy" and "girl," 80–90 percent apply them correctly to pictures of children and adults. While the issue of gender stereotyping remains a controversial one among adults in our society, there is little doubt that by the time a child is able to speak, he or she has acquired substantial knowledge about his or her own gender and will incorporate that knowledge as a foundation for elaborating a sense of personal identity.

Jerome Kagan argues that a more wholistic sense of self begins to develop around the age of two and becomes increasingly articulated from that point.[18] Kagan believes that the child's self-awareness hinges on two complementary developments in childhood. The first is a growing awareness of the self as a separate entity with intentions, feelings, standards, and the ability to achieve goals. The two-year-old can recognize a picture of herself, can talk about her own actions as she performs them, and is aware of her own ability to influence the actions of adult caregivers. By three years of age, a sense of possession develops that indicates the child conceives of a self that can possess objects and control them. This sense of self is initially just the realization of a separate body, but in time, and especially with the acquisition of language, the child begins to use the linguistic label "me" to refer to her own momentary desires and later to refer to herself as the source or agent performing some behavior.

The interpersonal relationships between infant and primary caregivers are a key factor in nurturing personal identity. For a child to develop a sense of "intention" with himself as the agent of intention requires that he first be able to accomplish an objective and then to infer that he meant to do so. But how does the child learn what his own intentions are? Andrew Lock argues that infants acquire this sense of mastery by gradually taking over control of their own actions from the caregivers.[19] Initially, the caregiver performs all or most of an activity during interaction with the infant. For instance, Lock points out how a mother will act as puppetmaster while helping the child play with a formboard. She will place a piece on the board, just about to fall into its hole, and then manipulate the child's hand so that it knocks the piece in place. Eventually, the child begins to perform the actions on his own, but he has learned what to do as part of a relationship. Only later will his actions seem to be his own. As Russian psychologist L. S. Vygotsky puts it:

Every function in the child's cultural development appears twice: first, on the social level, and later on the individual level; first between people (interpsychological), and then inside the child (intrapsychological).... All the higher functions originate as actual relations between human individuals.[20]

Thus the child's relationships and interpersonal communication with significant others play a central role in the development of the child's sense of self. Recalling our earlier discussion of the historical emergence of uniqueness as a self-concept, it should be clear that if a belief in personality did not first exist on the societal level, it would be unlikely to develop at the individual level. We believe in the self as a stable, unique entity because of the scaffolding built by parents and culture.

The central role of the primary caregiver is even more important in Vittorio Guidano's view of self-development.[21] Guidano believes that the degree of attachment achieved between infant and caregiver creates a stable interpersonal context that is essential for the gradual attainment of self-identity and that also promotes in the child a sense of competence. Within Western culture at least, researchers have shown that it is difficult for a child to form a secure attachment with more than one person "because attachment figures tend to be arranged in a hierarchical order with the principal figure at the top."[22] This suggests that the child develops much of his or her self-identity in the context of a unique personal relationship. For Guidano the *uniqueness* of the infant-caregiver relationship becomes the basis for eventually viewing the self as unique. This relationship acts as a cognitive template for pulling together otherwise fragmentary information about the self into an organized whole. Once again, the uniqueness developed *between* people becomes the source of uniqueness eventually identified as *within* the individual.

In infancy the child's attachment to a primary caregiver creates an identification of self and caregiver as one. As infancy gives way to childhood, Guidano believes that the development of a genuine self-identity requires a "turning away" from the source of identification. Initially, the child manages this by inferring the attachment figure's attitudes and the behavioral patterns, motivations, and emotions felt within that relationship as aspects of his or her own self-perception. Throughout childhood the sense of self is intricately tied to the emotional bond between child and significant others.

Only during adolescence, with the advent of logical/deductive cognitive abilities, does the self-concept begin to be internalized as a set of abstract qualities and values. As Guidano points out, the identification with one's parents remains largely at a tacit level, however. An adolescent is likely to view his parents' values as ridiculous and irrelevant to himself, until he discovers years later that his beliefs are remarkably similar to those of his parents.

During much of childhood, the sense of self is also affected by specific interactions in which role-playing is either encouraged or discouraged. While this happens throughout childhood, it becomes more crucial once the child is capable of **symbolic role-taking.** This skill involves learning to assume a role mentally without having to do so physically. At this point a world of selves is opened up to the young child, a world limited only by the power of his or her imagination. Communication with others is also enhanced as the child can now begin to see what the world might look like to other people. As the child tries on various roles, the significant others in her world are constantly reacting to her performances. Some role presentations meet with overwhelming approval, others earn a reprimand, and still others get mixed reviews or some other ambiguous response. In effect, these interactions take the form of the parent telling the child, "That's you!" or "That's not you!" And since the parents are seen as Godlike authorities by the young child, she seldom doubts that the parents' feedback is accurate. Repeated episodes of role-play followed by parental (and later peer) confirmation or disconfirmation certainly go a long way in establishing a sense of who one is or is not.

Development in Adulthood

By now it should be clear that our self-concepts develop slowly over many interaction episodes with both significant others and relative strangers. As we move through adolescence and into adulthood, our self-concepts seem to stabilize. As a result of repeated interactions and consistent feedback, we begin to think of our self-

Our fascination with the question of who we are is an endless source of amusement, at least in our culture.

(Albrecht Dürer, *Self-Portrait at Age Twenty-two,* 1493)

these various identities back to us, how is it that we maintain a stable sense of who we are? William Wilmot explains yet another way we stabilize our identity by referring to the **residual self**.[23] As Wilmot sees it, we enter every social transaction with some kind of self-concept, derived from our past experiences in similar situations, present expectations, and any future consequences we foresee. Thus there is always a "residue" of our past identities in every encounter. If we project essentially the same residual identity in a new situation, and others offer their approval of that identity, then little or no change takes place in the self-concept. For example, Horace thinks of himself as a "nice, friendly guy" when it comes to meeting new people. He makes new friends easily, and his old friends tell him he's too nice for his own good. He attends a social gathering where he engages in a half-dozen pleasant conversations with strangers, all of whom seem genuinely pleased to have made his acquaintance. His self-concept can remain intact.

At other times, however, the self we project may not be reinforced. We may sense that others see us quite differently than we see ourselves. When this happens, we are likely to find some way to incorporate both views, and we leave the situation with a slightly "new" residual self. Suppose Horace, the socialite, attends another gala event and acts the same way he always does when meeting strangers. This time people don't warm up to his friendly conversations. He overhears one person call him "Mr. I. M. Friendly" while another labels him "a fraud." Horace leaves this encounter with a slightly altered self-concept. He still thinks of himself as friendly but now maybe a little too sugar-coated.

Some writers refer to this event-by-event building of the residual self as a "biographical" or "historical" self. In other words, even though we may present a different self in every interaction, the one fact that ties all the selves together is that they emanate from the same physical self. Thus, no matter which self we present — as

identity in more and more limited terms. Yet it would be a mistake to think that we enter adulthood as a finished product. In some very subtle ways we continue to change and yet remain much the same person in our own minds. Subtle changes can occur as a result of what we call the residual self, self-perception, and self-talk.

Changes in the Residual Self If the symbolic interactionists are correct, then the reflections of self in the mirrors held up by others always have the potential to alter our self-identity. If we appear as a different person to our various circles of friends, and if they reflect

long as it seems appropriate, is approved by others, and does not consciously conflict with another important aspect of our self-concept — our sense of who we are will probably remain stable. In fact, Anthony Greenwald has identified three cognitive biases that help to preserve the sense of a stable identity: egocentricity, beneffectance, and cognitive conservatism.[24]

The first bias, **egocentricity,** refers to the fact that we have a better memory for information that is highly relevant to our conception of self. If you see yourself as a "genius," you're more likely to remember SAT scores and comments about how good your ideas are or how well you play Trivial Pursuit. You may forget comments about such mundane matters as burning the brownies or not picking your clothes up off the floor.

A second bias, **beneffectance,** enables us to perceive ourselves as more responsible for positive outcomes and less responsible for negative ones. Thus, our friend Horace could reconcile the reactions to his friendly self-concept by taking credit when being friendly pays off and invoking the maxim "You can't please everyone" when it does not.

Finally, as we look back on our lives, we tend to apply the principle of **cognitive conservatism,** seeking out information that confirms our own self-concept and revising our own biographical memory so that it fits better with our present self-concept. You can test this principle yourself by writing a brief autobiography sometime when you are down on your luck, and then writing another one when you are feeling on top of the world. Then compare the two when your self-concept is on a more even keel. This principle suggests that you would interpret the same events quite differently depending on how you saw your self at the time you wrote about them.

Changes Through Self-Perception   Cognitive biases, such as those just discussed, help reinforce our self-concepts. But on occasion, simple observation of our own behavior leads to the development of new self-concepts. As

you may recall from Chapter 7, Daryl Bem proposed his **self-perception theory** to explain how many of our self-definitions come about and are changed. Bem suggests that we come to know who we are by observing our own behavior "after the fact" and then inferring what kind of person we must be.[25] Suppose you're cleaning your apartment and notice that your garbage can is full of paper and aluminum cans. On a whim you decide to take them to a recycling center. Later that day as the temperature drops below zero, you think about turning the heat up but decide against it. Finally, you catch yourself just as you are about to toss a gum wrapper out of your car window. You put it in the ashtray instead. As you take stock of your behavior, you may be led to the conclusion that you are fast becoming a "conservationist." This may also happen when friends point out aspects of your behavior that you have overlooked. In effect, you may say to yourself, "I did give money to the college fund. I do stop to help people who have flat tires. I must be a charitable person."

Changes Through Self-Talk   Sometimes we talk ourselves into altering our self-concepts. Some people spend considerable time in self-reflection, prayer, or just talking to themselves. These internal dialogues can be persuasive and are often directed at self-improvement. Through symbolic role-taking, we can imagine ourselves as being another person or having a totally different personality. We can produce one or more ideal self-concepts and convince ourselves to try them out. Box 8.2 illustrates a very interesting form of what we might call non-self talk. In the practice of Zen meditation, the goal is to talk oneself out of the need to rely on a self-concept at all.

As we have seen, the development of a self-concept is a complex process of transforming our early identification with primary caregivers into attributes of our own, learning social roles and adopting some of them as our own, and internalizing the feedback of others into a more comprehensive sense of self. As we grow up, our parents and peers encourage us to play some roles more than others and to spice them up by adding in elements of our own emerging personality. We also try to distance ourselves from social roles so that we are not totally defined by them. The process continues into adulthood, although there are a number of ways we convince ourselves that we have a consistent or stable self-concept. The end result is that we think of ourselves as "unique individuals," unlike anyone else.

Self-Concepts and Interpersonal Communication

Although we have argued that self-concepts and interpersonal communication mutually influence each other, we have not said much about how perceiving ourselves as having a stable self-concept influences the way we communicate with others. One major function of the self-concept is that it acts as a guide, channeling what we perceive, how we should act, and what we remember. Although cognitive psychologists have only recently shown renewed interest in studying the concept of self, their efforts have shed some new light on how various self-concepts influence our perceptions and our behavior. In this section we will look at the influence of three aspects of self-concepts: (1) self-schemata, (2) life scripts, and (3) self-handicapping strategies. We'll also briefly discuss the relationship between self-identity and communication behavior.

SELF-SCHEMATA

It must be obvious by now that each of us has not one but several self-concepts. You probably think about your self in somewhat different ways when you are at work, with your parents, alone, or with an intimate friend. Even though they are different, these various self-concepts are related. Cognitive psychologists have been investigating the ways people organize their self-concepts. They refer to **self-schemata** as cognitive structures that organize and guide the processing of self-related information.[26]

People use different organizing principles to make sense of their collection of self-concepts. Hazel Markus has identified several of them. For some people, independence or dependence is the central principle in their self-schema; for others, masculinity or femininity may be dominant.[27] Whatever the organizing principle, it affects how we perceive ourselves and our social world. For instance, someone whose self-schema is based on the organizing principle of "being competitive" is likely to remember more incidents in which she was competitive and fewer in which cooperation occurred. Evidence also suggests that such a person is likely to hold the view that "everyone is competitive" as a way of justifying her own competitiveness.

LIFE SCRIPTS

Sometimes an organizing principle becomes elaborated into a **life script,** or a relatively fixed way of thinking about the self and relating to others. Eric Berne originated the concept and defined four very general life scripts: "I'm OK, You're OK," "I'm OK, You're not OK," "I'm not OK, You're OK," and "I'm not OK, You're not OK."[28] Each of these scripts represents a basic view of self and others and influences how we perceive social situations. Barnett Pearce and Vernon Cronen offer an extended definition of a life script as "that repertoire of episodes that a person perceives as identified with him/herself."[29] The life script of a practical joker, for example, would entail a number of episodes such as "hiding things from people," "placing a thumbtack or whoopee cushion on another's chair," and other, similar escapades.

BOX **8.2**

Zen and the Art of Selflessness: "What Is Your Original Face Before Your Mother and Father Were Born?"

Our culture values people as isolated, separate individuals. We spend a great deal of our time reflecting on who we are. But not every culture attaches so much importance to the individual and ego involvement in social life. In fact, in Japanese Zen Buddhism, practitioners strive to eliminate self-identity altogether, to achieve a sense of *mu,* or nothingness. They reject the idea that a person's essence or being can be an object of thought.

The ideal of personal activity in Zen is "non-doing," or what some call a "state of no-mind." According to T. P. Kasulis, the author of *Zen Action, Zen Person,* it is the ability to be "unself-consciously responsive," or in harmony with the surrounding social context and interpersonal relations. Lao-tzu, the founder of Taoism, once suggested that the ideal person was like water —

responsive and yielding, but not fatalistic. By yielding (or being in harmony with the situation), water follows its path and eventually wears away the rock obstructing it (thus it is not fatalistic).

Of course, this philosophy is quite complementary with much of Japanese culture. Social situations are highly defined in Japan, so that knowing one's role and being in harmony with the situation is much easier than it is in our own culture. The self is defined to a much greater extent by social relationships with parents, children, husbands and wives, and in-laws.

All these important relations or "between-nesses" are stripped away when a person enters a Zen monastery. The result, if Zen training is successful, is a person whose self-definition has been essentially erased, since there is little sense of a private self to begin with. Rinzai, a well-known Zen master, refers to this achievement as becoming "a true person of no status."

According to Zen philosophy, the self is a social fiction that gets in the way of truly experiencing life. Kasulis describes the process of writing at his desk, including the pen, paper, and other paraphernalia around him: "These are not merely things in my experience; they *are* my experience. My self does not relate to these things, my self is these things." Contrary to our Western view of a person apart from, yet moving through,

SELF-HANDICAPPING STRATEGIES

While most people no doubt adopt life scripts that they believe will result in positive public images, on some occasions a life script can be used as an excuse for a potentially negative self-presentation. A person who fears that he won't be capable of performing a new dance step may decline an invitation to dance by invoking his life script of "A real man doesn't . . ." He may thus be using his life script as a **self-handicapping strategy.** In their research on this

subject, Steven Berglas and Edward Jones defined a self-handicapping strategy as a technique for manufacturing protective excuses ahead of time to prevent possible failure in the future.[30] The research has shown that some people will talk or act in ways that protect them from bearing the brunt of future failures. They'll offer excuses in the event that they fail an exam, make a mistake in a financial report, or miss a crucial free throw. Supposedly, the excuse planted ahead of time ("I had to work," "Company came over," "The old wrist is acting up

predominantly public — and observable in relationship to others. Like a chess piece without a chessboard or a rulebook to play by, the solitary person has no meaning. Kasulis contrasts the two views in the following example of two people exchanging apologies: For Westerners, the discourse would go something like this:

> A: *Oh, excuse me.*
> B: *Oh no, excuse me.*

For the Japanese, the emphasis would be not on the individual who is responsible, but on the relationship, or the "betweenness" of the two:

> A: *The indebtedness does not end.*
> B: *Oh no, the indebtedness goes this way.*

There is little doubt that the self is one of our many socially constructed realities. But for us, it is one that seems so natural we can hardly imagine living without it. For a Zen person, the self is *the problem* that distorts perception of events and relationships. The Zen master poses the problem in one of the most popular koans in Zen training: If identity is so fundamental, "What is your original face before your mother and father were born?"

SOURCE: T.P. Kasulis, *Zen Action, Zen Person* (Honolulu: University Press of Hawaii, 1981).

one context after another, the Zen view is that an individual is a person only insofar as he or she is *in* one of these contexts. Private feelings may exist, but the individual's meaning as a person is

again") takes the heat off the individual and places the blame on the circumstance.

SELF-IDENTITY AND COMMUNICATION BEHAVIOR

Research on self-schemata, life scripts, and self-handicapping strategies demonstrates the pervasive effects of how we view ourselves and how those views can influence interpersonal communication. In fact, the relationship between our self-identity and our actual communication behavior is a reflexive one. That is, the residual self we bring to a situation shapes the way we communicate, and in turn, the way we communicate can influence and revise what we think about ourselves.

For example, a young woman enters her boss's office during her first week on the job to talk about how to approach her first real client. She has had considerable sales experience in a previous position with another company. She sees herself as an "aggressive and competent

In Greek mythology, the young Narcissus fell in love with his own reflection and pined away until he was turned into the flower that bears his name.

salesperson." This identity shapes the way she communicates with her boss. She walks into the office with confidence, engages in a little small talk, and then proceeds to lay out her plan for snaring the client. Along the way, however, she uncharacteristically stumbles over her words, forgets a major step in her proposal, and almost knocks the boss's coffee cup off the desk. While these behaviors do not completely shatter her competent salesperson image, they do crumble it a bit around the edges. The feedback she receives from observing her own behavior plus the boss's reaction modifies her self-identity; she won't see herself in quite the same way the next time she enters the boss's office.

This reflexive relationship between self-identity and communication should make us realize that our self-concept is always under construction, and therefore subject to change. Remem-

ber, one of the most troublesome of human traits is that we create or reify social realities (like the self, the government, and so on) and then forget that we created them in the first place. We aren't stuck with our personalities — we just tend to rebuild the same ones time after time. We can, in cooperation with those around us, alter who we are.

This tendency to view our self-concept as something beyond our control is often reflected in what we call the personality perspective on social behavior. Next we turn our attention to research that has focused on communication-related aspects of personality that are also believed to influence how we communicate.

Individual Differences and Interpersonal Communication

At the outset of this chapter, we drew a distinction between research into the self-concept and the personality, respectively. The self-concept is usually measured by asking an individual to describe his or her private view of self, allowing the individual to highlight what aspects of self are perceived as relevant to a given situation. An assessment of personality, on the other hand, is typically based on an individual's response to a series of questions generated by researchers and deemed by them to be an important predictor or explanation of behavior.

Since most of the research on personal dispositions and communication behavior has used personality measures, we report some of those results in this section. Our own bias is that self-concept measures are a better indicator of the link between personal identity and interpersonal communication for two reasons. First, self-concepts are probably "activated" by the individual's perceptions of a given situation or relationship, and the individual is usually in a better position than the researcher to describe his or her own perceptions. This means that even though a person scores high on a particular measure of personality (say, assertiveness), that aspect of self may not be highly relevant in a given context (waiting in line to see a movie) or within the rules of a specific relationship (a best friend). Second, personality tests are often wrongly regarded as the final word in describing the ontological status of the individual. The idea that "If I scored high on the Machiavellian scale, then I must be Machiavellian" seems inadequate to describe the complexities of a given human personality.

Nonetheless, research conducted from the personality approach can be both interesting and informative if placed in proper perspective. Sometimes an aspect of one's personality may be tacitly influencing behavior, even though the person is not consciously aware of it. Some research indicates that implicit or nonconscious motivations (such as personality traits) are better predictors of spontaneous behavior, whereas consciously attributed motivations (such as the self-concept) better predict how we will respond when we anticipate a particular situation.[31] As you read this section of the chapter, keep in mind that specific findings are most likely to apply when a particular personality orientation has been activated and is represented as a self-concept.

Like the self-concept, personality traits have been shown to influence how we communicate verbally and nonverbally. In this section we review the research on five communication-related personality traits: (1) communicator style, (2) rhetorical sensitivity, and (3) communication apprehension, (4) attachment style, and (5) intimacy motivation.

COMMUNICATOR STYLE

The concept of **communicator style** has been defined by Robert Norton as "the way one ver- bally, nonverbally, and paraverbally interacts to signal how literal meaning should be taken, interpreted, filtered, or understood."[32] Norton identifies nine prominent communication styles that not only color the meaning of messages but establish personal identities as well. One's style may be dominant, dramatic, contentious, animated, impression-leaving, relaxed, attentive, open, or friendly. Table 8.1 defines and provides examples of each style.

A style is usually established by the simple repetition of behaviors associated with that particular style. Others soon begin to expect the person to interact that way on a regular basis. A person who repeatedly turns a clever phrase or states her observations in offbeat ways may be regarded as having an impression-leaving style. The more she uses that style, the more likely it is that others will associate it with her personality. She doesn't always have to be clever or offbeat to maintain the style. Once established, it is likely to affect the expectations of those who know her. You may hang around just in case she says something striking.

According to Norton, people don't usually rely on a single communicator style, but instead develop what might be called a "style profile" — a combination of style variables. One person may tend to communicate by blending a dominant style with a friendly and attentive style. Another may be equally effective combining a dominant style with some aspects of the impression-leaving and contentious styles. You might want to inspect Table 8.1 and see if you can discover your own style profiles. Which one style or combination of styles do you use most frequently with your best friend? When interacting with your instructors or an employer? Can you identify situations in which the style you use may not be the most effective one? Think of a particular situation, such as telling a friend about one of your recent accomplishments. To what extent do you conceive yourself in terms of a particular communicator style in that situation? Which style does your

TABLE 8.1 Communicator styles and their manifestations	
Communicator style	**Verbal and nonverbal manifestations**
Dominant	Tends to come on strong, take charge of social situations, speak frequently, and otherwise control conversations.
Dramatic	Likes to act out the point physically and vocally. Tells jokes and stories and often exaggerates to make the point. Speech tends to be picturesque.
Contentious	Loves to argue, quick to challenge others, precise about defining things, and often insists that others show proof to back up their arguments. Once wound up, hard to stop.
Animated	Expresses self nonverbally: constantly gestures, using a wide variety of facial expressions; face and eyes usually reveal emotions and feelings.
Impression-Leaving	Says things in a memorable fashion. People usually don't forget such a person easily.
Relaxed	Comes across as calm and collected during interaction, especially under pressure. The rhythm and flow of speech is rarely affected by feelings of nervousness.
Attentive	Listens to others very carefully and lets them know it by giving nonverbal feedback such as eye contact and nodding. Shows empathy and can usually repeat back exactly what others said.
Open	Readily reveals personal information. Openly expresses emotions.
Friendly	Gives positive feedback to recognize, encourage, and reinforce other people.

Derived from Robert Norton, *Communicator Style: Theory, Application, and Measures* (Beverly Hills, Calif.: Sage, 1983), p. 64–72.

self-concept encourage? Which ones does it prohibit or discourage? A useful exercise is to practice using different communicator styles until you can turn them on and off at will. Then you can manage your style rather than having it manage you.

RHETORICAL SENSITIVITY

In the view of Donald Darnell and Wayne Brockriede, there are three basic types of communicators: (1) Noble Selves, (2) Rhetorical Reflectors, and (3) Rhetorical Sensitives.[33]

The Noble Self

The person who has a self-schema that emphasizes consistency above all else is a **noble self.** Darnell and Brockriede defined these people as ones who "see any variation from their personal norms as hypocritical, as a denial of integrity, as a cardinal sin." A Noble Self who has an organizing principle of honesty may struggle frequently with issues such as how to respond to a friend who asks, "Do you think I'll get the job?" or "How do I look?" The Noble Self will feel a strong obligation to say exactly what he thinks, no matter how it affects the other person.

The Rhetorical Reflector

At the other extreme are **rhetorical reflectors,** persons who "have no Self to call their own. For each person and each situation they present a new self."[34] This kind of person is most concerned about being "appropriate." She will follow the social rules of the situation or will try to be the kind of person the other wants her to be. In response to the friend's question, "How do I look?" the Rhetorical Reflector will say what she thinks you want to hear.

The Rhetorical Sensitive

In contrast to these two extremes, the **rhetorical sensitive** has a much more complex self-schema. Roderick Hart and Don Burks characterize this kind of person as an "undulating, fluctuating entity, always unsure, always guessing, continually weighing . . . the values, attitudes and philosophical predispositions of others."[35] Once he understands the complexity of the situation, the other, and the self, he "swims in a sea of probabilities" before actually communicating. Such a person

- Realizes that there is no "single self," that any situation will require one of several selves

- Avoids communicative rigidity and does not try to be overly consistent or arbitrarily follow social conventions

- Avoids forming messages without regard for the other, yet doesn't simply try to placate others

- Realizes that there are times when an idea should not be communicated

- Seeks a variety of ways to communicate ideas and feelings.[36]

Being rhetorically sensitive requires that we think about the way we communicate before, during, and after we interact with others.

It should be clear from this discussion that a rhetorically sensitive communicator is one who can monitor situations, determine which self would be most appropriate, enact an effective communicator style, and make any necessary adjustments. No doubt we would judge such a person as highly competent. And of course, now that we know what to do, we can work at becoming rhetorically sensitive ourselves. All we need to do is practice. There may, however, be one major obstacle in our path that practice alone will not overcome: a debilitating anxiety known as communication apprehension.

COMMUNICATION APPREHENSION

Communication apprehension refers to "an individual's level of fear or anxiety associated with either real or anticipated communication with another person or persons."[37] According to the research of James McCroskey, as much as 20 percent of the U.S. population can be categorized as highly apprehensive.[38] Most of us are anxious about communicating in one situation or another: public presentations, job interviews, first dates. Being apprehensive in these situations is fairly normal. Those people who are highly apprehensive tend to feel anxious in a wide variety of communication situations, including talking to people they already know.

When communication apprehension strikes, the results are very predictable. All our knowledge about communicating effectively goes out the window. For instance, even though we know that a more dramatic communicator style would grab an audience's attention and give us a better chance of being heard, the feeling of fear strangles our expressiveness. Fortunately, researchers have discovered several facts about this anxiety that make it much more manageable.

Communication apprehension is not an innate disability, but a learned reaction to physiological arousal. When we're called upon to perform an important task, the body begins pumping more adrenalin into the blood to provide energy. Physically, we feel an increase in arousal; cognitively, we label that arousal as fear.[39]

The fear of communicating can be overcome, first by labeling the arousal as energy rather than fear, and then by focusing on the potentially positive rather than negative outcomes of any communication transaction. Although you shouldn't expect an overnight transformation, you can begin to approach communication situations with a different perspective, one that puts you (and those you interact with) in mutual control of social forces, rather than letting the forces control you.

ATTACHMENT STYLES

Another communicative predisposition grows out of our early relationships. Researchers have investigated different **attachment styles** that develop in infancy but continue to influence communication and relationship behavior throughout life.[40] As we saw earlier in this chapter, infants form an early mental image of self and other based on interactions with primary caregivers. Attachment theory holds that infants develop different styles of attachment depending upon the positive or negative nature of these mental images. Kim Bartholomew has elaborated on four styles of adult attachment that stem from these early interactions. If the images of self and other are both positive, a **secure style** of attachment emerges that fosters highly sociable behavior. The individual becomes comfortable with both intimacy and autonomy. When both images are negative, however, a more **fearful style** results. The child with a low regard for self is more dependent on others for acceptance, but may have trouble gaining favor because of a lack of trust in others. Hypersensitive to social approval, but fearing rejection, he or she is likely to avoid social situations and close relationships. Desiring intimacy, but seemingly un-

able to achieve it, one who is fearful of attachment is often anxious and ambivalent around others. A third style results when a person has a low opinion of self, but a generally positive view of others. Bartholomew calls this a **preoccupied style.** Like someone with a fearful style, this person is highly dependent upon others who will reinforce feelings of self-worth. When a preoccupied person finds someone who makes him feel good, he can become very obsessive about the relationship. Finally, a person with a **dismissing style** tends to deny any need for attachment. Such a person has a very positive self-image, but a markedly low opinion of other people. As a result, she values her autonomy and asserts that relationships are not all that important, preferring to spend time and energy on the more impersonal arenas of work and individual leisure pursuits. Compared to the people who exhibit the three nonsecure styles, those with secure styles are much more likely to have romantic relationships that last longer, and to report greater satisfaction and stronger perceptions of intimacy, commitment, and trust in those relationships.[41] They also tend to engage in more expressive and supportive behaviors, less verbal aggression or withdrawal when interacting with others.[42]

INTIMACY MOTIVATION

The need for intimacy has been studied in a way that mirrors our concern in this chapter about the personality/self-concept distinction. D. P. McAdams defines the **need for intimacy** as a "recurrent preference or readiness for experiences of close, warm, and communicative exchange with others — interpersonal interaction that is seen by the interactants as an end in itself, rather than a means to another end."[43] Research suggests that the need for intimacy is a largely nonconscious preference for spending time in dyads as opposed to group situations, and for engaging in higher levels of eye contact, smiling, and laughter that seems to promote self-disclosure in others.[44] Those high in the need for intimacy also engage in a greater percentage of interactions with women.[45] These people seem to have an almost intuitive sense of how to carry off a socially intimate performance.

Judy-Anne Craig and her associates measured another form of this need that reflected people's conscious concern for achieving intimacy. They referred to this as a *self-attributed need for intimacy*. They found that this orientation led people to engage in a greater number of total interactions with many different people rather than just close dyadic partners. They speculated that this conscious awareness of self as needing intimacy was more focused on achieving an *outcome* (making a friend, self-disclosing to further a relationship, and so on) rather than being engaged in a less conscious *process* that naturally exhibits characteristics of intimacy.

It should be clear by now that the way we think about ourselves can either limit or expand our ability to communicate. We cannot over-emphasize the importance of giving ourselves options for communicating in a world where the only question about change is how fast it will occur, not if or when. To manage our communication in such a world requires that we increase our awareness of the self we present to others and discover ways to balance the tensions between conformity and individuality. We conclude this chapter by exploring how we can put our knowledge of self-concepts to work for us.

The self-concept is always under construction. Even in our quietest moments, self presentations may be made to an imagined audience or defined in part by the particular scene or stage directions we believe to be appropriate.

(Edward Hopper, *Compartment C, Car 293*, 1938)

Skill Building: Improving Competence Through Self-Disclosure

Feeling good about ourselves — having a good self-image — is an essential component in effective interpersonal communication. It is difficult to appear competent if you do not feel competent. It is hard to like others and be liked by others if you do not like and respect yourself. While the development of your self-concepts was hardly under your control as a child, at this stage you are not a finished product. You have just as many opportunities as an adult to surround yourself with the kind of people who will hold up the mirror for you and help you fashion a general life script and self-concepts appropriate to various situations and relationships. Just as your parents played a key role in providing a stable environment for the development of your childhood self-concept, the significant others in your current social networks (and those in your future) play, and will continue to play, key roles in helping you become a well-rounded, communicatively competent adult. Meeting new people and negotiating changes in our ongoing relationships means that our self-concepts always remain under construction. Knowing this should lead us to further develop any skills related to presenting and managing the self. One of the very important and often misunderstood communication skills that we need to master is self-disclosure.

WHAT IS SELF-DISCLOSURE?

Self-disclosure is usually defined as any information you reveal about yourself that others are unlikely to discover from other sources. This covers a wide range of territory, from the simple revelation that you like country music to the highly risky disclosure that you spent six months in a juvenile detention home as a teenager. When and how we choose to reveal aspects of our personal history can make a lasting impression on others — to our benefit or to our detriment. Our disclosures can strike a chord of empathy in another person or cause him or her to recoil from us. Disclosures are often risky, and when they are, they place us in a vulnerable position. For example, admitting that tears welled up in your eyes during a particularly sad movie scene may cause a new acquaintance to perceive you as overly emotional, out-of-control, or weak. But exposing vulnerability by such disclosures is one of the very few ways that people in our culture establish trust with one another. Without trust, solid friendships and close, intimate relationships are not possible; without one or two of these relationships, there is no support system for ongoing elaboration of our system of self-concepts.

There is a danger, of course, that some people will go to extremes, becoming avid self-disclosers in hopes of developing hundreds of close relationships. A frequent problem for very

lonely people is that when they get the opportunity to disclose, they overdo it. You have no doubt been victim to grandpa's stories about the good old days or to a new acquaintance who took you seriously when you said, "Tell me a little about yourself." These types of episodes are called *flooded disclosures* because the individual needs to "get it all out" and may not think he or she will ever get another chance. Most of us (especially males) don't have to worry about going too far — we are underdisclosers, typically revealing far less than our relational partners would like to hear. Another typical problem is *premature disclosure,* which occurs often in a dating context. Because of a person's strong desire to make a good impression and get to know the other, the individual reveals intimate details too quickly and unexpectedly and not in the normal flow of conversation. The result is the opposite of what was hoped for: The individual is often perceived as troubled or deviant, and is not seen as attractive or likable.[46] Researchers have been studying the process of self-disclosure, and some of the general principles they have formulated can help us manage our self-disclosures and avoid some of the pitfalls just described.

MASTERING THE RULES OF SELF-DISCLOSURE

Learning to self-disclose, like most communication skills, requires an understanding of the communication process and a careful balance between conforming to socially appropriate rules and occasionally breaking the rules in creative ways. First, let's look at some of the general rules that should guide your use of self-disclosure.

1. *Make sure that disclosures are appropriate to the topic at hand and fit the flow of conversation.* This rule is so general that it could apply to any message, not just self-disclosures. But it is also a rule easily overlooked. Conversation between two new acquaintances is supposed to reduce anxiety, not cause it. That's why we usually follow the rules of small talk and say things that are safe. We want to make a good impression, so we try to sprinkle the conversation with interesting information about ourselves, but such revelations need to fit the conversation. If what we reveal to another person seems a little weird or poorly timed, it's all that other person has to work with in making a judgment about us. Once we become acquainted, we tend to get sloppy in applying the rule. You might decide ahead of time to reveal something at the next opportunity and then force the disclosure in an irrelevant way or at an inappropriate time. If it's important for the other to know and the conversation isn't moving in that direction, you can always steer things a bit. You can, for instance, nonchalantly move a discussion about last night's episode of *Roseanne* to a previous episode that dealt with an issue that reminds you of something you did two years ago (which was what you wanted to reveal in the first place). The key is to make the flow of topics as natural as possible. If you force it, the other will probably feel that he or she has been set up. Once a relationship gets on its feet, you can relax the rule a bit. As long as someone feels comfortable with you, that person can deal with an occasional disclosure out of the blue.

2. *Begin with safe, nonrisky disclosures.* When disclosures do not involve high risk, you put less of yourself on the line should the disclosure fail to leave the desired impression. The safest disclosures are *descriptive* ones that reveal factual information about yourself (your hometown, your major, occupational plans). While safe and nonthreatening, however, these disclosures are not always the most captivating. Ideally, you want your initial disclosures to be safe but a little tantalizing. They can say to the other, "There's a lot more to talk about . . . when we're both ready." You should realize, however, that even descriptive disclosures say a

lot about you. The revelation that you plan to be an accountant implies a lot (even if stereotypic) about your personal qualities, future lifestyle, and so on.

3. *Disclose in small doses.* To avoid the problem of burdening another person with a flood of unwanted disclosures, it is usually best to reveal a glimpse of yourself here and there. Flooded disclosures may make us feel good ("Whew, it feels great to get that off my chest"), but they seldom sound as good to the embattled listener ("Ouch, stop! Please stop, I can't take any more!"). Small doses keep things manageable and also give the other person an opportunity to disclose, which leads to the next principle.

4. *Match the level and amount of the other's disclosure.* Otherwise known as the "norm of reciprocity," this rule monitors the process of opening up by making sure the relationship does not become a one-sided affair. It's easy to get caught up talking about ourselves and forget to give the other person a chance. By matching disclosures, we virtually guarantee that we both approve of the way things are going. If the other person's disclosures become briefer or revert to an earlier level of safe topics, that's a good sign that he or she isn't ready to move on. It also indicates that you should slow down the pace of your own disclosure. For some people, too much disclosure can be overwhelming. It's not that they don't like you or want to know more about you, they just need to catch their breath and let things unfold more slowly. The matching principle is probably the single most important rule of disclosure because it reveals the state of the relationship between two people.

5. *Remember that style of disclosure is as important as substance.* How you disclose your feelings and opinions and how you receive another's disclosures can encourage or discourage the whole process. Your nonverbal manner itself should signal openness and reinforce the verbal message. Trying to self-disclose in an in-

direct manner ("beating around the bush") may suggest that you feel uncomfortable, don't really trust the other person, or have to be very careful how you say things. Any one of these nonverbal messages could undermine the attempt at verbal openness. Likewise, showing little enthusiasm for the other person's disclosure attempts can reduce the chances for further disclosure. Barbara Montgomery's research on open communication indicates that most people pay more attention to the style of disclosure than to the actual content being revealed.[47]

   6. *Reserve your most important disclosures for significant, ongoing relationships.* People who self-disclose indiscriminately do not understand that self-disclosure is an integral part of what makes intimate relationships so special. The escalation of disclosure from small, reciprocated, safe topics to largely unrestricted and risky revelations requires the safe confines of a trusting and committed relationship. As we saw earlier in this chapter, strong bonds of attachment serve as the primary context for nurturing a stable personal identity that is open to change. While on rare occasions people successfully reveal a great deal about themselves to total strangers, such as pouring out their soul to a fellow passenger on a five-hour train ride, such occurrences are not the norm. They generally occur as a result of unusual circumstances (will never see the person again, seeking out the help of a professional counselor, and so on).

While these rules serve as general guidelines for managing self-disclosure, you may discover that sometimes you want to risk breaking one of these rules. Because creative efforts are often appreciated in our society, you may occasionally be successful in such ventures. One way of increasing your chances in these situations is to use aligning actions to manage perceptions of deviance from the norm. An **aligning action** is a statement that tries to minimize the perceived deviation from the norm by pointing out special

circumstances or reasons why the deviation should take place. Imagine that you've just arrived at your fifth freshman orientation session on your second day on campus. The host pairs you off with yet another student to get acquainted. (You've only been through this routine about 150 times already.) Under these circumstances you might say something like, "You'll forgive me, I hope. I've only met a hundred people in two days and we've said the same things to each other a hundred times over. I'm sure you've experienced the same thing. Maybe you wouldn't mind if we talked about something more substantial than all the parties we've attended?" Chances are the other person does feel the same way and would gladly agree. Without the aligning action, however, you could have launched into an episode of flooded disclosures and probably scared the person away for good.

As this chapter has stressed, our identities are constructed in the process of communicating with others. This means that to be ourselves we must manage others' impressions of us through the messages we exchange with them. One of the best ways to do this is by increasing our repertoire of message options: verbal and nonverbal strategies, a working vocabulary, the range of communicator styles we can use comfortably, and so on. In the following chapters we'll encounter a number of communication tactics that will serve us in this regard. The important thing for you to do at this point is to make a commitment to yourself to develop your ability to use a wide range of communication strategies. You might begin now by making a list of some specific communication behaviors or skills that you don't perform as well as you'd like. Seek out opportunities to work on these skills so that you can add them to your repertoire and call on them when you need them. By doing so, you will be building the kind of identity that is adaptable enough to enjoy the best of times and survive the worst of them.

Process to Performance

REVIEW TERMS

The following is a list of major concepts introduced in this chapter. The page where the concept is first mentioned is listed in parentheses.

social identity   (211)
personal identity   (211)
modal self   (212)
self-concept   (213)
personality   (213)
public self-concept   (218)
private self-concept   (218)
distinctiveness postulate   (219)
self-esteem   (219)
symbolic role-taking   (222)
residual self   (223)
egocentricity   (224)
beneffectance   (224)
cognitive conservatism   (224)
self-perception theory   (224)
self-schemata   (225)
life script   (225)
self-handicapping strategies   (226)
communicator style   (229)
noble self   (230)
rhetorical reflector   (231)
rhetorical sensitive   (231)
communication apprehension   (231)
attachment style   (232)
secure style   (232)
fearful style   (232)
preoccupied style   (232)
dismissing style   (232)

need for intimacy   (232)
self-disclosure   (234)
aligning action   (236)

SUGGESTED READINGS

James Lincoln Collier. *The Rise of Selfishness in America.* New York: Oxford University Press, 1991. An excellent historical review of how the obsession with the self-concept and related notions of literary and artistic expression, leisure pursuits, and various forms of vice sprang full-force in American life during the late 19th and early 20th centuries. Collier's sketch of the emerging entertainment industry and its influence on self and selfishness is intriguing.

Kenneth Gergen. *The Saturated Self: Dilemmas of Identity in Contemporary Life.* New York: Basic Books, 1991. Kenneth Gergen, one of our most prolific researchers on the self-concept, chronicles the historical evolution of the self from the romantic self of the 19th century to the modern self of the early 20th century, and now the emerging saturated self of the postmodern era (see Box 8.1). This is a book that will challenge one's taken-for-granted views of the self.

Cushman, Donald, and Dudley Cahn, Jr. *Communication in Interpersonal Relationships.* Albany: State University of New York Press, 1985. This book focuses on interpersonal communication as the major force in developing, presenting, and validating individuals' self-concepts. No other book we've seen emphasizes the role of self-concept as much as this one.

Berne, Eric. *Games People Play.* New York: Grove Press, 1964. A highly readable book about the influence of life scripts and game-playing on interpersonal relationships. By identifying these games in your own relationships, you can determine whether the self-concepts these games reinforce are really worthwhile.

TOPICS FOR DISCUSSION

1. Think of five or six different interpersonal situations in which there are clear role requirements: teacher-student, doctor-patient, and so on. Now think of several real people you know who play those roles. Draw distinctions between those communication behaviors, rules, and obligations that are role-related and those that emanate from the self-concepts of the individuals involved. What potential advantages or disadvantages occur when people add self-expression to their social roles?

2. Discuss the distinctiveness postulate in terms of what makes you distinct from your various groups of friends, family, and other acquaintances. Compare the ways in which you behave differently in one group versus another. To what extent are you really a different person to each group? How does the distinctiveness postulate help account for this? Are some distinctions more important than others (for example, sex, age, height, weight, attitudes, personality, and so on)?

3. Self-perception theory suggests that we often behave first and then decide what kind of person we must be, based on observations of our own behavior. Can you think of examples of this happening to you? Have you ever pointed out behaviors to a friend that led him or her to revise a self-concept? In what ways do we block out perceptions of our own behavior in order to protect a self-concept?

4. Do you agree or disagree with the statement that we do not have one "real" self, but many selves? What do you think are the strongest arguments for your point of view? How would you convince someone who held the opposite point of view?

5. Talk about the advantages and disadvantages of each of the three types of communica-

tors: Noble Self, Rhetorical Reflector, and Rhetorical Sensitive. Are people really distinct types or are there some aspects of self that we try to maintain consistently (Noble Self)? When would the Rhetorical Reflector be a positive and healthy self-concept?

OBSERVATION GUIDE

1. For this exercise you will rely on the observations of at least two other close friends. This is called the 20-Questions Statement Test. The objective of the exercise is to discover aspects of your self-concept that are "consistent" or at least apparent to both yourself and several of your friends. You should write down 20 two- or three-word statements about yourself by completing the following phrases:

　　a. "I am. . ."
　　b. "I like. . ."
　　c. "I have done. . ."

Ask your friends to complete the same statements about you. Now compare lists, identifying those self-concept statements that appear on all or most of the lists. What similarities or discrepancies surprise you the most? Are most of the statements self-identifying ("I am. . ."), evaluative ("I like. . ."), or behavioral ("I have done. . .")? What does this tell you about your self-concept(s)? Conclude your observations by writing a brief analysis of your self-concept in each of the relationships involved. Why do you think you appear the way you do to each person?

2. Visit a day care center or early childhood learning center, or observe a series of mother-infant interactions. Look for examples of self-concepts in development. Record examples of verbal or nonverbal communication that reflect the child's awareness of his or her own intentions, motivations, or sense of self. Watch how adult caregivers structure interaction or conversation to lead a child to a greater sense of accomplishment or self-awareness. Ask questions of the older children, such as, "Who's your favorite hero?" or "Who do you like to be when you play?" What do their answers tell you about their developing self-concepts? What behaviors or roles are reinforced by playmates or attending adults? Ask your instructor if you can present some of your findings to the class.

EXERCISES

1. This exercise should be conducted in groups of four. Initially, two people will role-play a conversation while the other two act as observers. Later you will reverse roles. The objective of the exercise is to improve your ability to enact a wider range of communicator styles. You should follow the steps below. Step **a** may be done prior to class to save time.

a. Individually, write down your own ideal communicator style profile for meeting new people. Write down how you would like to come across in terms of the styles described in Table 8.1. Also write down a style you feel is very difficult for you to enact and a situation in which you would like to be able to use this style.

b. Decide who will role-play and who will observe first. One observer should record the behavior of role player 1, and the other role player 2. Observers should make a list of the nine communicator styles and write down examples of each style they witness during the role-play. Plan to provide feedback at the conclusion of the role-play.

c. The first role-play is a conversation between two strangers. After exchanging greetings, you will hold a two-minute conversation about your choice of topics: sports, movies, careers, campus or world events, and so on. Throughout the conversation, role players want to enact their ideal communicator style profile. Don't tell the observers what that style is, just try to come across in the preferred manner. Begin the conversation.

d. After a couple of minutes, cut the conversation off and let the observers provide feedback to each role player. Compare style observations with what the role player was trying to do. Suggest ways to improve the enactment of each aspect of the style profile.

e. Switch roles and repeat steps **b, c,** and **d.**

f. If you have time, continue the exercise by working on the difficult situation and style profile that each person has written down. Conclude the exercise by talking about how you can improve your range of styles in actual situations.

2. Bring to class examples of media messages that reinforce how people in our culture think about the self, in terms of either their social or their personal identities. Look for examples in magazine advertisements, television commercials, song lyrics, newspaper advice columns, radio or TV talk shows, and so on. In what ways do these messages affect how we see ourselves? Is there any truth to the argument that a society (in our case, a consumer society) creates the kind of people (in our case, consumer-oriented selves) it needs to keep the system going?

Interpersonal influence is as old as the human race.
For good or bad we are often persuaded by those
closest to us.

(Albrecht Altdorfer, *The Fall of Man*, c. 1535)

9

Goal Competence: Interpersonal Influence

Everyone thought Paul was headed straight for success. At college he had been an above-average student, motivated and bright. He had a small but close circle of friends and a good relationship with his family. In fact, his parents were so proud of him that they gave him a trip across the country as a graduation present. Because they knew their son made friends easily, they weren't surprised when he called them from San Francisco to tell them he was going to explore the coast with some kids he'd met. Before hanging up, Paul told them he loved them and promised to call in a week. That phone call was the last any of Paul's friends or relatives heard from him until, six months later, a private detective found him wearing saffron robes and selling flowers on a street corner in Seattle. Like thousands of other young Americans, Paul had joined a cult.

Paul's family and friends were stunned and confused. What had happened to cause such a radical change in Paul's behavior? What techniques of mind control could so rapidly turn a normal boy into a true believer? Had Paul been, in fact, as normal as he seemed, or did he have some fundamental psychological flaw that everyone had overlooked? Who was responsible for what happened?

When a young man like Paul makes such a "radical departure," it is natural to be alarmed and to look for explanations.[1] In some cases, the results are tragic. Members of some cults are subjected to psychological or sexual abuse or worse. But in other cases, the results are not as negative. People who join the more mainstream cults often find belief systems that help them make sense of the world. For them, the decision to join turns out to be a positive one. In fact, many cult recruits are ordinary people, reasonably well balanced, well educated, and well brought up. And the techniques used, far from being mysterious forms of brainwashing, are actually fairly ordinary modes of interpersonal influence.[2] Box 6.1 describes what goes on during cult conversion, looking specifically at techniques used by the Unification Church.

BOX 9.1

Moon for the Misbegotten: Methods of Cult Conversion

Enough first-person accounts of conversion experiences now exist to allow us to piece together the techniques cults use to recruit new members. You may be surprised to discover how simple and yet how effective these methods are. What is clear is that they depend very heavily on the creation of interpersonal bonds. The account given here is based on experiences of former members of Rev. Sun Myung Moon's Unification Church, but similar methods are used by many cults.

The first step in recruitment is for a cult member to approach a target of about the same age and background. The recruiter, usually attractive and friendly, strikes up a conversation, inviting the target to a picnic or similar social event. There an attempt is made to determine whether the target's beliefs and values make him eligible for further influence. No direct identification of the cult or overt proselytizing takes place at this time.

If the target seems suitable, he is invited to a retreat, usually in a beautiful, secluded area outside the city where contact was first made. No pressure is exerted. It is important that his decision to accept be voluntary. Once at the retreat, he is cut off from all the hassles of the outside world; there are no TVs, radios, or telephones, no difficult decisions to be made. He is surrounded by attractive role models who seem sincerely happy, vital, energetic, and unconditionally accepting both of one another and of him. The atmosphere and activities are reminiscent of a summer camp. Simple games (dodgeball, tug-of-war, red rover) immerse him in competitive group play. Traditional songs and rhythmic chants and cheers evoke an elementary school atmosphere where simple obedience, pleasure, and belonging are key.

Group beliefs are expressed in simple language incorporating popularly accepted values such as unity, peace, and love. Teachings take the form of truisms, tautologies, and comforting but difficult-to-pin-down slogans ("When you possess the egoless ambition which is not centered on the self, you have many shields around you; you will be safe no matter what you do"; "Love is everywhere and has every motivation"). If the target tries to question these beliefs, members show concern and deep disappointment, urging him to suspend judgment and wait for enlighten-

---

As you will see, the methods used to recruit members are not very different from the methods you and I might use to make new friends, convince a candidate to accept a job with our firm, or persuade a member to abide by club bylaws.

Much of our communication is goal-driven. While our goals may not be as single-minded and our strategies as systematic as those of the people who sought Paul's conversion, they are nonetheless important. We communicate for

specific reasons: We want others to accept our ideas, to enter into relationships with us, or to see us as we want to be seen. Competent communicators achieve these ends by anticipating others' reactions. They know that in our everyday interactions we affect one another in profound and important ways and that communication is a basic tool for controlling the world around us.

In this chapter we'll focus on the ways in which we use communication to affect one an-

ment. Afraid of offending his "hosts" and of being excluded from the love of the group, he seeks meaning and understanding. This effort at self-persuasion is met by the return of group acceptance and affection.

The need to belong is a key to understanding the recruitment process. Cult members create a perfect interpersonal relationship in which everything is shared: food, clothes, love, faith. For the period of commitment, the target becomes part of that relationship, experiencing the innocence and security of early childhood.

What happens to cult members? It has been estimated that 90 percent decide to leave after about two years. Many see the experience as beneficial. Although they abandon the cult, few of those who leave of their own volition have bad feelings about their stay. Instead, they take with them lasting values, which they integrate into their new lives.

Eileen Barker, who interviewed many members of the Unification Church, believes that those who join have not been irresistably brainwashed. She tells us that the potential Moonie is not a gullible fool who accepts any argument unquestioningly. He or she is usually an idealistic achiever, someone with a strong sense of service and duty who can find no other way to contribute to society and who becomes swept away by the excitement of discovering answers to puzzling religious questions. She also believes that people who join cults are no more likely to become mindless robots than their peers who commute to work everyday. "They will develop in a number of ways, both emotionally and intellectually, and while they may miss one set of opportunities and experiences, they usually have the opportunity to enjoy many other, often remarkably wide-ranging and challenging experiences. But they will also find that they are presented with a wide range of problems, disillusionments and disappointments, and the majority will, without the need of outside intervention, leave . . . within a couple of years of joining (258–59)."

SOURCE: Saul V. Levine, "Radical Departures," *Psychology Today* 18 (8) (August 1984): 20-27, and Eileen Barker, *The Making of a Moonie: Choice or Brainwashing?* (London: Basil Blackwell, 1984).

ADDITIONAL READINGS

Lofland, John. *Doomsday Cult: A Study of Conversion, Proselytization, and Maintenance of Faith.* Englewood Cliffs, N.J.: Prentice-Hall, 1966.
Stark, Rodney, and William Sims Bainbridge. *The Future of Religion: Secularization, Revival and Cult Formation.* Berkeley and Los Angeles: University of California Press, 1985.

other. We'll begin with a brief discussion of the importance of symbolic role-taking and social sensitivity in strategic interaction. Then we will examine some basic needs that motivate human action and some theories that explain how recognizing these needs can help us be more effective communicators. We will also look at the importance of identity management in goal achievement. Finally, we'll review some basic strategies individuals use to get others to comply with requests.

Communication and Strategic Interaction

The field of speech communication has traditionally been concerned with the study of strategic interaction — with explaining how people use communication to affect one another and to achieve their ends. Communication is, after all, a process of creating reality. It is important that we understand how realities are created and that we have some control over those we create. This means that we must master the instrumental uses of talk. In this section we'll examine several issues related to interpersonal communication and then consider symbolic role-taking and social sensitivity.

INSTRUMENTAL, RELATIONAL, AND IDENTITY ISSUES

Ruth Anne Clark and Jesse Delia have suggested that whenever we talk we simultaneously address three different issues. One is the *instrumental issue.* When we are acting instrumentally, we are attempting to achieve a specific goal, trying to get something done through talk. In most cases the instrumental issue is our primary focus. At the same time that we are behaving instrumentally, however, we are also offering a commentary on our interpersonal relationship — we are working to create a relational culture. This is what Clark and Delia refer to as the *relational issue.* Finally, a third issue is being addressed: the *identity issue.* Each sentence that we utter "contributes to the definition of the situational identities of the interactants."[3]

During different interactions, different issues are at stake. When our major objective is to convey information or to argue a position, we focus on instrumental talk. When our major concern is to let others know what we think about them or to forge a relationship, then our talk is a vehicle for relational issues. Finally, when self-presentation is at stake, we address the identity issue. What complicates this picture is that, even though one issue may achieve prominence, the others are also simultaneously being presented. Indeed, the three are so interrelated that each affects the other. If, for example, you want to persuade someone to agree with you, you must be able to marshall effective arguments and present them convincingly. You must also be able to create a good impression and build rapport. Your most brilliant argument

will be ruined if your relational and identity messages are negative. Or take the case of a physician whose concern is to explain to a patient the importance of remaining on medication. The physician's instrumental message can be undermined if he or she fails to build trust or to confront the patient's fears.

Competent communicators must be able to balance all three issues. First, they must have a clear understanding of their instrumental goals. Second, they must be able to take their receivers' perspectives, adjusting their messages to these perspectives. Third, they must be socially sensitive, adapting to the interaction as it unfolds and realizing that influence is a process of creating shared understanding. And finally, during this entire process they must be sensitive to the relationship they are creating and to their own and their partners' identities.

SYMBOLIC ROLE-TAKING AND SOCIAL SENSITIVITY

Two of the most important skills associated with effective instrumental communication are symbolic role-taking (or perspective-taking as it is often called) and social sensitivity. We can see their importance by looking at the development of persuasive ability in children. Very young children have difficulties in bridging the gap between their intended meaning and others' interpretations. Their first attempts at making their needs known are very crude. They often assume that others can read their minds, and it does not occur to them that they must spell out their needs. Later, the child begins to understand the importance of telling a caregiver exactly what he or she wants. At this stage the child makes simple requests but fails to offer any support for them. Eventually, the child comes to understand that a request should be accompanied by a reason and that the best reasons are framed in terms of others' needs.

Role-taking is necessary not only for children but for adults as well. Clark and Delia suggest that the goal-competent communicator must be able to identify major objections that prevent others from complying with requests. One of the hardest things for people to do is to understand why others disagree. Our ideas often seem so evident to us that we automatically assume they will seem that way to others. The goal-competent communicator is able to anticipate another's reaction.

In addition to role-taking, the goal-competent communicator must also be socially sensitive and have at his or her disposal a flexible repertoire of persuasive strategies. The individual who knows only one way to achieve a goal will be unable to adapt successfully to a wide range of communication interactions. Conversely, the individual who can think of many different lines of reasoning and can cast an argument in different ways will be better able to adapt a message to an individual receiver.

Understanding Others' Needs

In our discussion so far, we've indicated that to influence others you must be able to understand their needs and goals — you must be able to take their perspective into account. This is no small task, because human needs are complex and varied and not easy to predict. Still, some widely shared needs and some general theories of influence seem to apply across many situations. In this section we'll investigate ways that you can influence others by meeting their need for rewards, consistency and stability, and self-respect.

THE NEED FOR REWARDS

Why do people engage in some behaviors while avoiding others? For some the answer is simple: People act so as to maximize rewards and minimize punishments. Actions associated with pos-

itive stimuli will be repeated, while actions associated with negative stimuli will be avoided. People who hold this view of motivation are called learning theorists.

To understand their position, let's begin with the concepts of stimulus and response. A **stimulus** is any unit of sensory input; a **response** is any unit of behavior. When a doctor tests a patient's reflexes, the tap of the hammer is the stimulus; the knee jerk that follows is a response. Learning theorists believe that all behavior consists of stimulus-response chains following one another in a neverending series.

Let's look at an example. It's time to take Rover for a walk. Rover's owner, Mrs. Walker, removes his leash from the closet. Rover hears the clank of the chain and rushes toward the door, knocking over the water dish in his excitement. Mrs. Walker cries, "Rover, just look what you've done! No walk for you, you bad dog," as she hauls out the mop. Rover slinks off with a hangdog expression. "Never mind. It's not your fault. Let's go out," Mrs. Walker sighs, and she retrieves the chain. Rover barks, runs around in circles, and wags his tail so hard he scatters trash all over the kitchen.

Let's look at all this from Mrs. Walker's standpoint. Going to the closet for the leash is a behavior, and therefore a response (R). It is followed by Rover's accident with the water dish, which serves as a stimulus (S) for her actions of scolding and mopping (R's). Rover's guilty reaction (S) prompts Mrs. Walker to reassure her pet (R). From Rover's viewpoint, everything is reversed. The rattling of the leash is a stimulus (S) that causes Rover to run into the water dish (R). The spilled water and the owner's scolding (S's) let him know he is in trouble and had better show contrition (R). And so it goes. Each action and reaction continues the chain of stimulus and response.

A reasonably intelligent person (or dog) soon realizes that the consequences of behavior can be either pleasant or painful. Learning occurs when an organism actively discriminates between positive and negative stimuli, seeking out those that are rewarding and avoiding those that are punishing. It follows that people are influenced by the rewards and punishments associated with their behavior.

There are several models of learning; classical conditioning, operant conditioning, and social learning are three of the most important. The classical conditioning model focuses on what happens before a response (the S-to-R relationship), while the operant conditioning model focuses on what happens after a response (the R-to-S link). Social learning modifies both by taking into account the nature of the human being involved in the S-R chain.[4] Let's look briefly at each model, as well as at social exchange theory.

Classical Conditioning and Learning

Certain stimuli naturally result in certain responses. For example, most people wince when they get an injection. There is nothing very surprising about this. What is more surprising is that the response to one stimulus can be transferred to another. Just reading about getting a shot or just passing a doctor's office may be enough to make some people cringe. When two stimuli are paired so that the response to one (the natural or unconditioned stimulus) becomes attached to another (the conditioned stimulus), **classical conditioning** has taken place.

Many of you no doubt are familiar with I.P. Pavlov's experiments in classical conditioning.[5] Pavlov knew that without any conditioning, laboratory dogs salivate when given meat powder. The unconditioned stimulus of meat powder is naturally followed by the unconditioned response of salivation. His experiments demonstrated the effects of associating a new stimulus, a ringing bell, with the meat powder. After a number of trials the bell alone (the conditioned stimulus) began to cause the dog to salivate. The dog learned to respond in a new way. Figure 9.1 gives another example of classical learning.

Classical, or associational, learning plays a large role in interpersonal situations. Many responses to others are based on associations. It's not unusual to feel instant dislike for a stranger simply because he or she reminds you of someone from your past. It's also not uncommon to let responses to context color your impressions. You may dislike people you meet under trying or uncomfortable conditions, while you may be overly impressed with those you meet in luxurious surroundings.

People respond positively to stimuli associated with rewards. That's why advertisers pair their products with attractive stimuli. And it's why movie stars like to display themselves in glamorous surroundings. Think back to Paul and the cult members. His initial experience was very pleasant. Members were friendly and fun-loving and wholesome. In many ways, being with them must have been like being a carefree child again; living at their farm must have been like being back at summer camp.

Operant Conditioning and Learning

Associational learning is not the only way rewards and punishments affect people. Actions are also controlled by their consequences. According to **operant conditioning,** if a response's consequences are rewarding, the response will be repeated; if punishing, it will cease.[6] Controlling the consequences of an action is called **reinforcement.** Parents reinforce their children by making sure that treats follow good behavior and punishments follow bad. If you were ever "grounded," you were the target of operant conditioning. Figure 9.1 compares operant and classical learning.

Behaviors occur because of the reinforcements that follow them. But what kinds of stimuli provide the best reinforcement? The answer isn't easy. While money and power are effective reinforcers in our culture, even they don't work with everyone. The only way to

Classical Conditioning

situation: As a child, every time Tim made funny faces, his friends and relatives laughed and he felt good. Clowning was associated with praise and laughter.

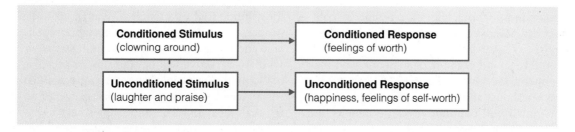

Operant Conditioning

situation: In high school, Tim enters the talent show; audience response determines his future responses.

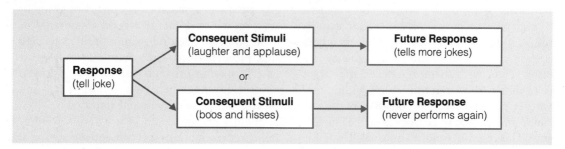

Social Learning

situation: Tim observes the success of a famous comedian; he imagines himself becoming famous, too. He imitates his hero.

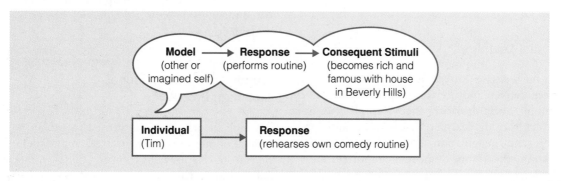

F I G U R E **9.1**

A comparison of three learning theories

know whether a reinforcer will be successful is to try it. If it increases or decreases a target behavior, it is a reinforcer. If it has no effect, then it's not.

For most schoolchildren, a teacher's scoldings are negative reinforcers, while a teacher's praise is positive. But not always. The class clown is a good example of someone who may be encouraged by disapproval. The more the teacher shouts and scolds, the more likely it is the clown will continue. Because people find different stimuli appealing, the first step in operant conditioning is to find out what stimuli will be effective reinforcers.

Acts of interpersonal approval or disapproval, called **social reinforcers,** are usually potent forms of influence. Social reinforcement plays a large part in the cult conversion experience, as it does in everyday life. Cult members dispense smiles and praise freely whenever a visitor agrees with them, but when the target shows doubt, these reinforcers are withdrawn. In order to keep receiving positive reinforcement, a prospect may censor his or her uncertainty. This reaction is not so unusual. Think for a minute about what happens when people you value criticize or tease you. You probably change your behavior. It takes a very unusual person to keep on doing things that others obviously dislike.

Social Learning

So far we have looked at learning that results from active exposure to positive and negative stimuli. **Social learning theory** emphasizes indirect learning, learning that involves anticipation and imagination.[7] According to social learning theory one of the most important ways we learn is by observing others being rewarded or punished. This kind of learning is called **modeling** or **vicarious learning.** What happens to someone else shows what may happen to us. If a schoolchild sees a classmate punished for acting out in class, she learns that such behavior

leads to trouble. If she sees her friend gain popularity as a result, however, she may decide to follow suit.

Not all models are equally influential. We are most influenced by models similar in attitude, gender, or age. In addition, models who are reliable and competent, who are of high status, or who are attractive will have greater impact. Finally, the more people we see being rewarded for a given behavior, the more likely we are to try that behavior.[8] These principles help to explain why cult recruiters are so successful, for they are usually young and attractive.

Another way people learn is by rewarding themselves when goals are met. This is called **self-reinforcement.** A person who tells himself "As soon as all my work is done, I'm going to treat myself to dinner in a good restaurant" or "I'm going to keep rehearsing until I can play this piece perfectly, no matter how long it takes" is using principles of social learning to control his own behavior. Punishments and pleasures may be actively self-imposed.

A final way we learn is as a result of symbolic representations of consequences. Social learning theory is based on the belief that humans are thinking beings. Through our ability to reason, we can imagine an action's consequences. We can also respond to others' persuasive arguments. Rewards and punishments mediated through thought and talk are a powerful mode of control.

Learning and Interpersonal Exchange Processes

Learning theories have been used to explain a number of interpersonal processes, among them the reasons relationships form and dissolve. **Social exchange theory** is a learning model that states that if given a choice between two relationships, we will choose the more rewarding one.[9] Most people give up on relationships when the punishments begin to outweigh the pleasures. In general, people avoid costly relationships although they may endure a short string of losses if they believe they'll get a return on their investment in the long run. According to social exchange theory while every successful exchange may not involve a large profit, it should at least allow us to break even.

Every interaction involves relational messages, or cues indicating how a specific message should be interpreted. In exchange theory, objects or actions that carry relational meaning are called **relational currencies.**[10] Gifts, favors, time, access rights, and so on are all examples. Even food can carry relational meaning. When you visit home after an absence, a special meal may be prepared. What is significant is not the food itself, but the affection conveyed by the action.

Exchange can be very complicated. Like economic currency, relational currency can become devalued or inflated over time, partners can fail to agree on appropriate exchange rates, and relationships can even go bankrupt if the exchange is mismanaged. If, for example, one of the parties feels she is doing all of the giving and receiving nothing in return, trouble can result. If Melanie was brought up in a family that expresses love through expensive gifts and Carlos wasn't taught to value material goods, there may be conflict. She will think he doesn't respect or care for her, while he may think her shallow and grasping. Neither will get adequate rewards, and the relationship may fail. When we think of the effects of rewards and punishments on behavior, we must remember to include relational currencies.

THE NEED FOR STABILITY AND CONSISTENCY

Is all behavior a result of learning? Some say no, believing that our primary need is not for rewards but for cognitive consistency. These people believe that internal contradictions are deeply troubling. When confusions and inconsistencies occur, people do their best to return to a state of consistency. Theories based on this supposition are called consistency theories.[11]

Maintaining Relational Balance

According to **balance theory** we feel comfortable, or balanced, when valued others agree with us on important issues.[12] When people we like oppose us or when people we dislike take our side, we are confused and uncomfortable. This state of discomfort is called imbalance. The typical situation described by balance theory involves a person (P), another person (O) who is related to P, and a stimulus (X) about which both P and O have opinions. If P's relationship to O and X is out of balance, P will try to change it. Figure 9.2 describes ways a P-O-X relationship can be either balanced or imbalanced.

Let's consider the relationship between Peggy (P), Oscar (O), and the stimulus heavy metal rock music (X). If Peggy and Oscar are friends, and if both like this kind of music, then their relationship is balanced — there is a positive relationship between all three elements of the triad. This state of affairs is illustrated in the first of the balanced states diagrammed in Figure 9.2. Under these conditions Peggy will be happy with her relationship to both O and X.

Unfortunately, not all relationships are balanced. If Peggy detests rock music on aesthetic or moral grounds, knowing that her friend Oscar likes what she hates will cause discomfort. Her relationship with O and X will be out of balance. She can correct this in three ways: (1) by changing her attitude to Oscar, (2) by changing her taste in music, or (3) by trying to convert Oscar. While pressures toward balance may be very mild if one's relationship to O or X is trivial or inconsequential, they can be quite powerful if the relationship is important. For example, when we discover a close friend acting dishonorably, the strain may be severe. Something has to be done to get things back in balance.

situation: A person (P) holds either a positive or negative attitude toward another person (O) and toward a stimulus (X). O also holds an attitude toward X, and P is aware of O's attitude.

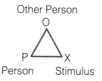

Other Person

Person   Stimulus

Balanced States

The P-O-X relationship is stable; P need take no action.

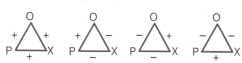

Unbalanced States

The P-O-X relationship is unstable; P must restore balance.

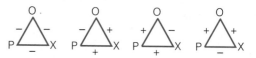

To restore balance P can:
1. change own attitude toward O
2. change own attitude toward X
3. try to change O's attitude toward X

FIGURE **9.2**
Balance theory

Balance theory explains why we are attracted to similar others and accounts for some conformity pressures. Consider Julie's statements in the following dialogue:

JULIE: That was a pretty good movie, wasn't it?

JEFF: Well, I don't know, I thought it was kind of slow.

JULIE: Oh, well, yes, it was slow. But the acting. . . ?

JEFF: A bit stilted.

JULIE: Oh. Yeah. I guess it could have been a lot better.

Julie wants Jeff to like her, so when they disagree, she amends her statements. Her desire for balance makes her easily influenced. As long as her attraction to Jeff remains high, she will make every effort to agree with him.

In general, balance theory tells us that people who are liked and admired have a great deal of influence over the attitudes of others. Advertisers, of course, have always known this; celebrities are paid huge sums of money for endorsing products. But the effect is not limited to the world of advertising. The principles of balance theory are very relevant to interpersonal situations. Have you ever agreed with others just to get them to like you? Have you ever threatened to leave someone unless he or she changed?

Achieving Congruity

According to balance theory, there are only three ways to reduce inconsistency: We change our attitude toward X *or* we change our attitude toward O *or* we try to change O's attitude toward X. But are those really all the possibilities? Think about it. If a friend says something you don't particularly like, isn't it possible that you might change your attitude toward both your friend *and* his idea? You might like him a bit less because his views aren't what they should be, but you might also like the idea a bit more because he thought of it. And wouldn't your response depend on how good a friend he was and on the issue of disagreement? If your best friend likes lime sherbet instead of orange, it is unlikely you will resolve the imbalance by dropping him. Balance theory doesn't take these factors into account. **Congruity theory,** however, does.[13]

Every day speakers make statements about objects. Sports figures endorse products, judges rule for or against defendants, politicians take stands. Congruity theory allows us to predict the effects of these statements; it lets us know whether these statements will damage or increase the source's credibility.

Let's say that an average citizen reads in the morning paper that a presidential adviser has been indicted for fraud. Since the citizen already has a mild aversion to the adviser, this news doesn't bother her. She gets upset, however, when she reads that the president, whom she admires and respects, has decided to stand behind the adviser. According to congruity theory, when a well-liked source says something positive about a disliked object, a state of cognitive discomfort called incongruity occurs.

To reduce incongruity, both the attitude toward the president and the attitude toward the adviser will have to change. The amount of change will not be equal in both cases, however. The most strongly held attitude will change less, while the weaker attitude will change more. Since our newspaper reader reveres the president and only mildly dislikes the adviser, her attitude toward the adviser will change more. This case is illustrated in Figure 9.3.

Congruity theory allows us to compute the actual amount of attitude change that will occur. Congruity theory calculations always use a scale ranging from –3 (indicating a strong negative attitude) to +3 (indicating a strong positive attitude). Let's assume that the original rating of the president is +3 and that of the adviser is -1. As you can see in Figure 9.3, there are four scale units between the two attitudes. Change will be

inversely proportional to the original positions, so the president's rating will go down one unit and the adviser's will go up three units. Our citizen now rates both the president and the adviser at +2. The adviser has gained credibility, while the president has lost. For those of you who are mathematically minded, Figure 9.3 gives a formula that can be used to compute congruity in this and other situations.

The ability to make predictions based on scale ratings is a valuable one for professional pollsters, political consultants, and marketing executives. In the average interpersonal situation, however, attitude scales aren't often used. What is important in interpersonal interactions is knowing that in cases of incongruity, attitudes toward both source and object are likely to change. Every time you advocate something that displeases your friends, their opinion of you decreases a bit; every time you associate yourself with things they approve of, their attraction toward you increases. It is useful to remember that your attraction is always fluctuating as a result of the attitudes you reveal. Only if you are very well liked can you get away with advocating unpopular views. People who stand by their views in the face of disapproval often pay a high price in terms of popularity.

Congruity theory also explains changes in attitudes as a result of group conformity pressures. If one close friend advocates a position you dislike, you will increase your liking for that position only a small amount. If another friend also favors the position, however, it becomes a bit more attractive. If all your friends agree, you may finally reach the point of approving wholeheartedly of the idea.

Reducing Internal Dissonance

Our final consistency model is **cognitive dissonance theory.**[14] The most general of all the consistency models, it maintains that whenever a person becomes aware of holding a cognition inconsistent with other cognitions, there will

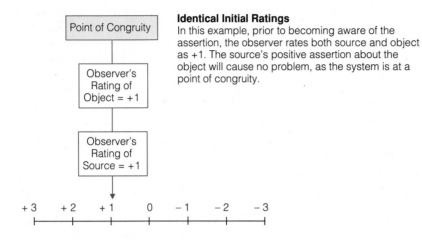

Identical Initial Ratings
In this example, prior to becoming aware of the assertion, the observer rates both source and object as +1. The source's positive assertion about the object will cause no problem, as the system is at a point of congruity.

Unequal Initial Ratings
In this example, prior to becoming aware of the assertion, the observer rates the source as + 3 and the object as –1. The source's positive assertion about the object will cause incongruity. The observer must adjust attitudes to point of congruity, + 2.

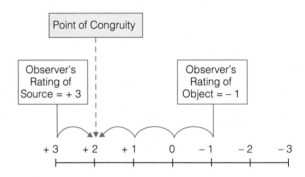

To restore congruity the observer must decrease liking for source and increase liking for stimulus. Amount of change will be inversely proportional to initial rankings.

Congruity point may also be computed by using the following formula:

$$R_o + \frac{|A_o|}{|A_o| + |A_s|} A_o + (d) \frac{|A_s|}{|A_o| + |A_s|} A_s$$

Where R_o = congruity point for object, A_o = initial attitude to object, A_s = initial attitude to source, d = direction of assertion, +1 if positive, –1 if negative. A bracket around a symbol indicates absolute value (value without + or – sign). Note: Example is for case where assertion is positive; with negative assertions, congruity occurs when ratings are mirror images (for example, + 2, – 2 indicate congruity when source speaks against object).

FIGURE 9.3
Congruity theory

be pressure to reduce the inconsistency. This pressure is called *dissonance.* Dissonance always occurs as a result of a decision between alternatives.

Let's say that upon graduation you have a choice between two jobs. One is in Albuquerque, New Mexico, a city that intrigues you. The other is in a suburb of Buffalo, New York. You decide on the latter. How you feel about this decision will depend on all of the cognitions you hold about the two jobs and the two cities. Some cognitions will be consonant, or consistent, with your choice of the Buffalo job, for example, believing that the Buffalo job provides opportunity for advancement. Some beliefs may be dissonant, or inconsistent, with your decision, for example, hating cold weather. Still other beliefs will be irrelevant; liking Woody Allen movies or believing yourself to be an honest person has little if anything to do with the decision.

According to dissonance theory the dissonance you feel after any decision is a function of the number and importance of the perceptions you hold about that decision. This relationship is illustrated in the following formula:

Amount of dissonance after decision =

$$\frac{\text{\# of dissonant cognitions} \times \text{their importance}}{\text{\# of consonant cognitions} \times \text{their importance}}$$

If there are a number of career advantages to moving to Buffalo, if the only dissonant element is a dislike of cold weather, and if climate is not very important, then dissonance will be low. If, however, you have a lot of objections to the Buffalo move and each is very important, then dissonance will be high, and you will have to do something to reduce it.

There are several ways to reduce dissonance. The most obvious is to turn down the Buffalo job and move to the Southwest. If that is impossible, you can manufacture cognitions consonant with your decision. You can convince yourself that housing costs in Buffalo are very

low, that it has a good orchestra and exciting professional sports teams, and that its location near the Canadian border will give you easy access to international travel. At the same time, you can reduce dissonance even further by thinking unpleasant thoughts about Albuquerque. You can act as your own change agent by providing yourself with positive information about your decision and negative information about alternatives.

How does this apply to influence? Let's look at an example. Perhaps you want to persuade a friend to stop smoking. If you point out that it makes no sense for someone who values good health and dislikes wasting money to smoke, perhaps your friend will reduce the ensuing dissonance by giving up cigarettes.

Dissonance can lead to interpersonal influence in another way. Most people don't like their actions to violate their beliefs. If they act in ways contrary to their attitudes, they may reduce dissonance by changing their beliefs. This influence strategy is known as **counterattitudinal advocacy.** For example, one way to encourage kids to take more pride in their country might be to involve them in an essay contest. While at first they may think of patriotism as "corny," by the time they finish researching the subject, writing their compositions, and delivering them with enthusiasm, their private beliefs may change to match their public actions.

The effects of counterattitudinal advocacy will be stronger if it is voluntary, if a lot of effort is involved, if the sponsor is not particularly attractive, and if the reward for participation is not great. In all these cases there are no external justifications to explain away compliance. As a result, the only way to reduce dissonance is through attitude change. If we do an unpleasant task for a large reward, we can always rationalize our behavior by saying, "I hated it, but I needed the money." If, however, we work long and hard for free, the only way to make sense of our actions is to say, "Actually, I liked doing it." This principle explains why we

created by an action, the more likely the internal attitude will change.

Reducing Uncertainty

According to some theorists in our field, the need for consistency explains a lot about how and why we communicate.[15] They believe people have a basic drive to reduce uncertainty. The more uncertainty we experience, the less we can predict events. In a situation of total uncertainty or randomness, purposeful action would be impossible. Communication provides a means of reducing uncertainty. Through communication we gather information about the world. The need to live in a predictable and consistent universe is one of the chief reasons we communicate.

THE NEED FOR SELF-RESPECT

We have nearly finished our discussion of the forces that motivate action. There is one more we should look at briefly, however, one already discussed at some length in Chapter 7: the need to present a proper face to the world. A number of theorists hold that people need to respect themselves and be respected by others.

In his **value theory** Milton Rokeach tells us the self-concept is a powerful guide to behavior.[16] Each of us has an identity we try to live up to. For Rokeach, the clearest reflection of people's identities is their values. A value is simply a belief that some goals and paths to goal achievement are better than others. For example, some people believe that altruism is more worthwhile than self-interest; they therefore act with kindness and charity. Others believe it is important to achieve personal success. They may value ambition and material security above everything else. Table 9.1 lists some of the values Rokeach believes are basic to all people. If you

Characteristics attributed to sources can enhance or inhibit their ability to persuade. When source and message "match," influence will be high.

value things we have to work hard for. The fraternity or sorority that is the hardest to get into and has the most difficult initiation ceremonies is often the most popular. The commitment we make voluntarily will be more lasting than one made under duress. This is why cult members try to convince recruits that their decision to join is voluntary. The stronger the dissonance

TABLE 9.1 Terminal and instrumental values	
Terminal values — **preferable end states of existence**	**Instrumental values —** **preferable modes of conduct**
A comfortable life (a prosperous life)	Ambitious (hardworking, aspiring)
An exciting life (a stimulating, active life)	Broad-minded (open-minded)
A sense of accomplishment (lasting contribution)	Capable (competent, effective)
A world at peace (free of war and conflict)	Cheerful (lighthearted, joyful)
A world of beauty (beauty of nature and the arts)	Clean (neat, tidy)
Equality (brotherhood, equal opportunity for all)	Courageous (standing up for your beliefs)
Family security (taking care of loved ones)	Forgiving (willing to pardon others)
Freedom (independence, free choice)	Helpful (working for the welfare of others)
Happiness (contentedness)	Honest (sincere, truthful)
Inner harmony (freedom from inner conflict)	Imaginative (daring, creative)
Mature love (sexual and spiritual intimacy)	Independent (self-reliant, self-sufficient)
National security (protection from attack)	Intellectual (intelligent, reflective)
Pleasure (an enjoyable, leisurely life)	Logical (consistent, rational)
Salvation (saved, eternal life)	Loving (affectionate, tender)
Self-respect (self-esteem)	Obedient (dutiful, respectful)
Social recognition (respect, admiration)	Polite (courteous, well-mannered)
True friendship (close companionship)	Responsible (dependable, reliable)
Wisdom (a mature understanding of life)	Self-controlled (restrained, self-disciplined)

Terminal values are associated with life goals; instrumental values define appropriate means for achieving these goals. Both guide action.

Reprinted with permission from Milton Rokeach, *Beliefs, Attitudes, and Values* (San Francisco: Jossey-Bass, 1968). Copyright 1968 by Jossey-Bass.

were asked to rank these, which would you consider the most important?

Rokeach believes people can be influenced by appeals to their value systems. If, for example, bravery is high in your hierarchy of values, you may undertake very foolhardy actions in order to avoid being labeled a coward. You may be highly influenced by challenges or dares. If you believe that stealing is wrong, anticipated guilt may stop you from shoplifting. Values are key parts of our life scripts. One of our strongest motivations is to remain true to what we believe is right.

Not only do we need to be true to private images of self, most of us also need to present favorable public images. Young children may begin smoking in order to appear older and more sophisticated to their peers. They may even get together and practice until they can smoke without feeling sick or looking foolish. For them, smoking is a form of self-presentation. What kind of interpersonal appeal will discourage them? Probably not rational arguments about health hazards. A better approach might be to convince them that smoking is unattractive and unsophisticated, that it makes them look silly and juvenile.

Value theorists believe that people often engage in unrewarding and inconsistent behaviors simply to act out a valued life script. The "macho" man, for example, may have to do a lot of unpleasant things to prove himself. Think about it. Have you ever sacrificed rewards because getting them would involve violating a value? Have you ever done things that were irrational and inconsistent in order to act out a social role? If so, you may agree with value theory.

SUMMARY: CHOICE AND MOTIVATION

As we have seen, learning theories hold that people are motivated by the rewards and punishments accompanying their behaviors, consistency theories state that people need to make their belief systems stable and consistent, and value theories tell us that people act so as to create favorable images. But which theory is right? It's possible that they all are. At various times we may try to fulfill all of these needs. Daniel Katz believes that people form and maintain attitudes for several different reasons.[17] He identifies four functions of attitudes: adjustment, knowledge, value expression, and ego defense. The first three correspond pretty closely to learning, consistency, and self-validation theories, respectively. The last reflects the individual's need to defend the ego from psychological threat and is based on psychoanalytic theory.

Katz makes two important points about motivation. The first is that people are motivated at various times by various forces. Although Katz doesn't explain why our motivations shift, it's possible that people have different motivational schemata that guide actions. When the reward-punishment schema is uppermost, we tend to judge an action in terms of gains and losses. When a value schema is in place, we take a more noble stance. And when the consistency schema is being used, we try to act rationally. If this is true, then part of being a successful change agent involves calling up the correct schema in our audience. There are things a persuader probably can do to switch a target from concern with reward attainment to concern with value exemplification. Think about it. What would you do to change the focus of a target's attention from self-interest to self-sacrifice?

Katz makes a second point worth considering. Different methods must be used to change different kinds of attitudes. If a behavior is driven by a need for adjustment, then it can be changed by promises or threats. If it helps the individual maintain a stable worldview, then rational arguments should be used. Katz tells us that interpersonal influence must be flexible and varied.

Identity and Influence: Source Characteristics

While an understanding of target needs plays a major role in interpersonal influence, it's not the whole story. As we've seen, a source always makes some identity declaration during interaction. Communication scholars have known for a long time that not all speakers are equally persuasive and that who the speaker is may be as important as what he or she says. While Aristotle was the first to recognize that a speaker's character, knowledge, and goodwill are a significant part of persuasion, others since him have noted the importance of the attributions receivers make about sources.[18] Think of all the ways we have of describing persuasive speakers; we refer to their credibility, expertness, dynamism, charisma, and the like. Clearly, the characteristics a public speaker manages to convey to an audience provide him or her with a great deal of power. Source characteristics are probably even more important in the interpersonal context, where the relationship between sender and receiver is a close and personal one. Let's examine these ideas more closely.

POWER AND INTERPERSONAL INFLUENCE

Power and influence go hand in hand. A powerful person is one who can control a situation, and this control can come in many ways. John R. French and Bertram Raven believe there are five kinds of power: reward, coercive, expert, legitimate, and referent.[19]

A source perceived as controlling rewards has **reward power.** The employer determining who gets a raise, the political boss deciding on the next candidate for governor, the guy in the bar standing drinks for his buddies, or the teenager lending out the latest albums are all wielding reward power. When people own things we want or need, they become important to us, and their importance is in direct proportion to our need. Control of physical or emotional resources is a prominent aspect of power.

Of course, the ability to dispense rewards is not the only base of power. The person who can inspire fear has **coercive power.** Most people comply with the requests of an armed criminal or a burly bully. On an interpersonal level, fear of being excluded or unmasked can lead to psychological coercion. People often rule with threats as well as promises.

Sometimes a source is influential because he or she has special knowledge or skill. This influence base is called **expert power.** In an age in which it is impossible to know everything, people must rely on specialists. We seldom question

the recommendations of physicians or engineers or scientists.

While intelligence and training are significant sources of power, sheer attractiveness can also lead to influence. The people we admire have **referent power.** Rock stars have their groupies, gang leaders their faithful lieutenants, and teenagers their adoring kid brothers and sisters. In each case these figures embody some moral or physical attribute others admire. Imitation is not only the sincerest form of flattery but an indication of interpersonal influence.

Of course, sometimes the actual characteristics of a source are not as important as his or her symbolic characteristics. When people become representatives of social institutions, they take on **legitimate power.** Most law-abiding citizens obey a police officer without question. Compliance has almost nothing to do with the officer's personality or ability; rather, he or she represents the power of the state and therefore has the "right" to control actions. While you may question the fairness of a particular assignment your professors make, you seldom question their right to make assignments. The academic setting legitimizes teachers' requests.

SELF-PRESENTATION STRATEGIES

Having a power base is all very well, but it counts for nothing unless others know about it. Power is largely a matter of attribution. How, then, do you make sure others know you're powerful? One way is by employing self-presentation strategies to translate power bases into observable behaviors. Edward Jones and Thane Pittman have described five methods of strategic self-presentation used in interpersonal influence situations: ingratiation, intimidation, self-promotion, exemplification, and supplication.[20]

According to norms of reciprocity, we generally like those who like us. It is hard to mistreat people who appreciate us; indeed, we often feel we owe them something in return. This

Teachers influence and control in many ways. All of the power bases
discussed by French and Raven may be used at some time or other. How
do teachers show legitimate, reward, coercive, referent, and expert power?

(Winslow Homer, *The Country School*, 1871)

suggests that we can influence others by appearing to like them and by being pleasant and friendly. This strategy is called **ingratiation**. The ingratiator uses charm, helpfulness, and flattery to control others.

While many people are sincerely nice, the ingratiator is strategically nice. In practice this is somewhat tricky. If the ingratiator is too nice, the target will become suspicious, and the strategy will backfire. The classic case of the ingratiator is the "yes man" who tells others whatever they want to hear in order to curry favor. While this is an extreme behavior, most of us have been taught that we should be pleasant if we want to influence others. As the saying goes, you can catch more flies with honey than with vinegar.

People who use **intimidation** aren't at all concerned with being nice. Instead, they want to appear dangerous. We generally give in to people who get ungovernably angry or violent. Young children often throw tantrums to get their way, while older people bully and threaten. Sometimes the destruction the intimidator threatens is self-destruction. Having an asthma attack or a dizzy spell whenever we are crossed is one way of controlling those around us.

Self-promotion is another strategy. Self-promoters want to be perceived as competent. They emphasize expert power. Others are so impressed with their training and experience that they have little choice but to agree. The dilemma facing the self-promoter is how to present an impressive list of credentials without seeming to

American artist George Bellows was fascinated by evangelist Billy Sunday, whose charismatic style caused havoc in his audience. Sunday embodied the influence strategy of exemplification.

(George Bellows, *The Sawdust Trail,* 1916)

BOX **9.2**

Caveat Emptor: Techniques of Confidence Tricksters

Professional confidence tricksters rarely use a "hard sell" when setting up their marks. In fact, it is often the mark who begs to be let in on the deal, believing he's putting something over on the con artist. Con artists know that getting their targets to persuade themselves is their most effective technique. Two things are essential in a well-run con game: The mark must believe it's possible to get something for nothing, and the con must seem absolutely trustworthy. How do con artists manage to make their marks believe their unbelievable tales? By knowing the mark's weaknesses and by putting on a credible front.

One of the most imaginative and stylish of all confidence tricksters was "Count" Victor Lustig. Early in his career he managed to sell the Eiffel Tower, not once, but twice! Throughout his life he assumed many identities and created many unusual "business opportunities" for gullible investors.

A classic example was the "money machine" he sold to a hardheaded businessman for $25,000. In the winter of 1925–26, Lustig turned up in Palm Beach hoping to find the perfect mark, someone whose greed was equaled by his need for status. Lustig's first step was to acquire an appropriate front. Hiring a chauffeur-driven Rolls-Royce, he checked into an expensive suite at one of the finest hotels and waited. Before long, opportunity presented itself in the person of Herman Loller, a self-made millionaire frustrated by his lack of social importance. To someone like Loller, knowing a cultured European aristocrat was extremely flattering. As they became friends, Loller confided some business setbacks. Lustig reluctantly revealed that he, too, had had money problems but that they had been solved by his "money-making machine," a box that would duplicate any paper currency so accurately that no bank could tell the difference. To "romance" the story, Lustig revealed that the machine had originally been developed by the Germans to undermine Allied currencies during World War I. It had fallen by chance into the hands of a Rumanian friend. It was, of course, the only one of its kind in the world.

brag. One way is to ensure the aid of a friend who can enthusiastically describe the promoter's accomplishments, allowing the promoter to look modest and slightly embarrassed. While self-promotion can be carried to extremes, most people try to appear as competent as possible. We all like to look as though we know what we're doing, especially in public situations. Every time we attempt to build credibility, we are engaging in mild forms of self-promotion.

Another way to influence is through exemplification. Exemplifiers control others by personifying the values they admire. They project so much integrity that others feel either admiration or guilt. Think of the influence wielded by religious prophets or saints; they are extreme examples of exemplifiers, people whose goodness is power.

Most of us don't go that far, although we do use exemplification in many influence situations. The child who acts like a "little angel" to impress his folks, the student who asks the teacher for extra reading assignments, and the employee who is always willing to work late if the boss

bers on one bill to make it identical to the other. He calmly suggested that Loller take each bill to a bank to make sure it was genuine.

Loller was hooked. He begged for a copy of the box. Lustig demurred. When Loller offered $25,000, he reluctantly gave in. Loller was so taken by Lustig's story that when the box failed to work, he convinced himself that he was operating it incorrectly. It was almost a year before he began to suspect and went to the police.

If you feel that Loller must have been particularly gullible, consider the fact that Lustig pulled off the same scheme again, selling his machine to a sheriff for $10,000 and the chance to escape from jail. It appears that people will believe just about anything if they really want to.

Loller begged for a demonstration. Lustig showed him a beautiful mahogany box into which he placed a $100 bill. Six hours later, he removed two damp bills, identical to the last detail. They looked perfect, as they should have, since both were completely genuine. Lustig had merely altered the threes and eights of the serial num-

SOURCE: Colin Rose, ed., *The World's Greatest Rip-Offs* (New York: Sterling, 1978).

ADDITIONAL READINGS

Mackay, Charles. *Extraordinary Popular Delusions and the Madness of Crowds.* New York: Farrar, Straus & Giroux, 1932.

Wade, Carlson. *Great Hoaxes and Famous Imposters.* Middle Village, N.Y.: Jonathan David, 1976.

needs her are all using this presentational strategy. Of course, exemplification doesn't always lead to popularity. Students have highly uncomplimentary labels for other students who try to impress teachers; exemplifiers make everyone else look bad in comparison.

The final strategy outlined by Jones and Pittman is called **supplication.** Here the presentation is that of helplessness. The supplicator appears so weak and defenseless that others feel a duty to act as protector. Not so long ago, women were taught that men resented strong women. Advice columns urged women to play dumb if they wanted to get a man. Women had to pretend to be bewildered by machines, too weak to carry anything heavier than a handbag, and too scatterbrained to balance a checkbook. A competent man would then step in and solve all of the problems. Through helplessness women achieved a certain kind of influence. Most of that has changed now, and most people feel the change is a healthy one, for the supplicator often pays the price of diminished self-worth. People who play helpless for too long, whether male or female, may come to think of themselves as helpless, and that is not a particularly good feeling. "Learned helplessness" is the label given to people who have actually lost particular abilities or skills because of fear or long-term supplication.

While all of these strategies can be unhealthy if carried to an extreme, we probably all use modified forms of them. Think about it for a minute. When you want something from someone, do you ever use these techniques? Probably. They are common ways of influencing others. You might find it interesting to consider whether you know people who are ingratiators, intimidators, self-promoters, exemplifiers, or supplicators. Most of our students have no difficulty thinking of examples from among their friends or acquaintances.

INFLUENCE AS SELF-PERSUASION

We hope we haven't given you the impression that influence is something a source does to a target. We don't want you to think that clever sources have complete control over their targets. Keep in mind that sources can set up conditions that will enhance influence, but it is receivers who ultimately convince themselves. Box 9.2 (page 260) gives a good example of how receivers participate in their own persuasion.

Cognitive response theory stresses the large part played by the receiver during the influence process. It states that during persuasion, receivers generate cognitions about the messages they hear. Receivers search their cognitive files for preexisting attitudes, knowledge, and feelings and try to make sense of a source's message in light of what they already know. Messages supported by prior beliefs will probably be accepted; unsupported messages may have a negative or boomerang effect. Influence targets are active generators of information rather than passive receivers. In a real sense we cannot influence others; we can only hope they will influence themselves in ways we want them to.

Like all communication, influence is an active transaction between source and receiver.

Planning Persuasive Messages: Compliance-Gaining Strategies

In the previous pages we looked at general explanations of social influence. But how is all of this translated into communication? When faced with actual influence situations, what does the competent communicator do? If you were in situations like the following, what influence strategies would you use?

Your aunt who lives nearby and with whom you are close has a large basement with a finished recreation room. You have a very tiny apartment and would like to have a big party in your aunt's basement. However, she can be finicky about cleaning and sometimes minds noise.

You are going away for a weekend and need someone to take care of your cat. You have spoken to your neighbor, Marty, once or twice in the past year. He seems to be home most weekends. You want him to feed the cat while you are gone.

Your car has stalled out and the battery is dead. You need to call the service station to get your car jumped but do not want to leave the car. A teenager approaches. You want her to call the service station and report where you are.[21]

These situations represent just some of the cases studied by researchers interested in an area of interpersonal influence known as **compliance gain.** These researchers have spent a great deal of time trying to understand the conditions in which communicators will use different kinds of message strategies.[22] In this section we'll look at what kinds of message strategies are available and how they are structured.

KINDS OF MESSAGE STRATEGIES

A number of social scientists have compiled lists of compliance-gaining strategies. One of the earliest, and perhaps the best known, was developed by Gerald Marwell and David Schmitt. They believed that there were at least 16 ways a communicator could get someone to respond to a request.[23] Table 9.2 describes these strategies. Others have described similar but slightly different sets of strategies.[24] While no one completely satisfactory list has been developed, certainly there are many ways to gain compliance from others.

The success of these strategies seems to depend on the situation. Research suggests that intimacy (how close source and target are to each other), dominance (what their relative feelings of power are), resistance (whether the target will comply easily or resist the request), rights (how justified the request is), personal benefits (whether the request is selfish or altruistic), and consequences (what the long-term effects of the request are) will affect choice of a strategy.[25] Certainly this makes sense. We don't ask a friend for a relatively inconsequential favor the same way we ask a stranger to do something that will involve a great deal of effort. You might find it useful to look at Table 9.2 and ask yourself if you have ever used any of the strategies. Try to figure out when and with what kind of people you use a particular technique. Which have been the most successful for you, and why?

THE STRUCTURE OF REQUESTS

Recent studies have examined the kinds of strategies most often chosen. Although evidence is sketchy, apparently people avoid the more complex strategies and favor direct, positive requests. One study found that appeals to altruism ("Do it for me") and promises ("I'll do you a favor one day") were the most frequently used strategies and that subjects don't generally choose negative sanctions.[26]

The same study also looked at the ways people structure their requests. It concluded that most messages making a request consist of two basic parts. The speaker begins by establishing a reason for making the request and then politely asks if the target is willing to comply. Both of these techniques help to define the request as reasonable rather than as an arbitrary order. How would you respond if someone said to you, "Go get me a glass of water"? In most situations this would seem rude. You probably will respond more positively to a message that establishes need ("Gosh, I'm thirsty") and asks rather than orders ("Would you mind getting me some water?"). It is important to include components that define the nature of the communicative speech act.

A competent communicator must also be aware of the face needs of the target. Messages vary depending on the extent to which the sender takes account of the positive and negative face of the receiver.[27] "Positive face" attempts acknowledge the need of the target to be liked and appreciated and are indicated by the presence or absence of greetings, gossip, and reference to the relationship. Compare "Hi, how are you doing? Remember Tim? Well, he sends his regards. You know, I would really appreciate it if you could do me a favor" with "Hello. Would you do me a favor?"

"Negative face" techniques acknowledge the target's desire to feel autonomous and uncoerced. The competent communicator softens a request by indicating uncertainty as to the outcome and a reluctance to impose. Compare "Would you mind?" or "Please let me know if it's an imposition" with "Do it!"

Messages may also vary depending on the extent to which the source tries to enhance her

TABLE 9.2	**Sixteen methods of gaining compliance**
1. Promise	*(If you comply, I will reward you)* You offer to increase Dick's allowance if he increases his studying.
2. Threat	*(If you do not comply, I will punish you)* You threaten to forbid Dick the use of the car if he does not increase his studying.
3. Expertise (positive)	*(If you comply, you will be rewarded because of "the nature of things")* You point out to Dick that if he gets good grades he'll be able to get into a good college and get a good job.
4. Expertise (negative)	*(If you do not comply, you will be punished because of "the nature of things")* You point out to Dick that if he doesn't get good grades he won't be able to get into a good college or get a good job.
5. Liking	*(Actor is friendly and helpful to get target in "good frame of mind" so that he will comply)* You try to be as friendly and pleasant as possible to get Dick in the "right frame of mind" before asking him to study.
6. Pre-Giving	*(Actor rewards target before requesting compliance)* You raise Dick's allowance and tell him you now expect him to study.
7. Aversive Stimulation	*(Actor continuously punishes target, making cessation contingent on compliance)* You forbid Dick the use of the car and tell him he will not be allowed to drive until he studies more.
8. Debt	*(You owe me compliance because of past favors)* You point out that you have sacrificed and saved to pay for Dick's education and that he owes it to you to get good enough grades to get into a good college.
9. Moral appeal	*(You are immoral if you do not comply)* You tell Dick that it is morally wrong for anyone not to get as good grades as he can and that he should study more.
10. Self-feeling (Positive)	*(You will feel better about yourself if you comply)* You tell Dick he will feel proud if he gets himself to study more.
11. Self-feeling (Negative)	*(You will feel worse about yourself if you do not comply)* You tell Dick he will feel ashamed of himself if he gets bad grades.
12. Altercasting (Positive)	*(A person with "good" qualities would comply)* You tell Dick that since he is a mature and intelligent boy, he naturally will want to study more and get good grades.
13. Altercasting (Negative)	*(Only a person with "bad" qualities would not comply)* You tell Dick that only someone very childish does not study as he should.
14. Altruism	*(I need your compliance very badly, so do it for me)* You tell Dick that you really want very badly for him to get into a good college and that you wish he would study more as a personal favor to you.
15. Esteem (Positive)	*(People you value will think better of you if you comply)* You tell Dick that the whole family will be very proud of him if he gets good grades.
16. Esteem (Negative)	*(People you value will think worse of you if you do not comply)* You tell Dick that the whole family will be disappointed (in him) if he gets poor grades.

Reprinted with permission from Gerald Marwell and David R. Schmitt, "Dimensions of Compliance-Gaining Behaviors: An Empirical Analysis," *Sociometry* 30 (1967): 357–58.

own face. A source who needs to borrow money may make some attempt to show she isn't a deadbeat. The person who says "I need to borrow 50 bucks" may leave us in doubt as to our chances of being repaid. The person who lets us know "I have some money saved, but I need another 50 bucks for the down payment. I get paid at the end of next week. I wonder if I could borrow. . ." is more likely to be successful. In influence situations, as in all others, concern with face is an essential aspect of communicative competence.

Interpersonal Influence and Goal Competence

Interpersonal influence is a complex process that takes a great deal of sensitivity and awareness. In order to persuade others, the competent communicator must understand the theoretical principles underlying social influence processes. These principles are not hard to apply. There are certain basic ways to enhance influence that cut across all theories. First of all, communicators should be aware of their own bases of power. Others respond to us according to the attributions they make about us; we want those attributions to be favorable. The persuasive speaker should build credibility; the interpersonal communicator should present himself as attractively as possible.

Second, it is important to frame appeals that take into account the needs and desires of others. If we know people are motivated by rewards, we can convince them by offering rewards. If we know they are troubled by inconsistency, we can show that our proposals will lead to stability. If we understand their values, we can appeal to them. The competent change agent matches technique to receiver needs.

Third, we should realize that if we can get receivers to influence themselves, our work will be done for us. Encouraging a target to behave in ways related to our proposals is a cardinal influence principle. If we can get someone to try our product, to act on our ideas, to testify to our beliefs, we have gone a long way toward persuading him or her. Only the incompetent communicator sees persuasion as a one-way process.

In summary, competent communicators must be sensitive to the context, to their own self-presentations, and to the target's needs and vulnerabilities. They must then be able to translate this sensitivity into rhetorically acceptable message forms. While we cannot list all of the ways to do this, we can urge you to observe what works and what doesn't and to form your own theories of interpersonal influence.

Skill Building: Becoming More Assertive

Ellen has had a long week and needs some privacy. She wants to write some letters, watch a video, and just relax. Just when she's settling in, her friend Scott knocks on the door. He's had another fight with his girlfriend and, for the third time this week, wants Ellen to analyze his relationship. Ellen likes Scott a lot, but she's tired of playing counselor. Although she'd like to tell Scott to leave, she doesn't know what to say. After all, he's upset and she really wasn't doing anything important. So she sighs and spends the evening attending to his needs rather than to her own. Later she feels disappointed with herself and resentful of Scott. Ellen has a problem in being assertive.

In many ways Steve is the opposite of Ellen. When people like Scott ask him for help, he's likely to insult them, yelling at them to get out and leave him alone. Although his style is very different from Ellen's, Steve and Ellen share a problem in being properly assertive. Neither Ellen nor Steve knows how to attain goals effectively. Ellen is nonassertive; she gives up when she should stand up for her rights. Steve is aggressive; he is inappropriately abusive when he perceives his rights as being threatened. Both need to learn how to express their needs clearly and firmly in a way that shows respect both for themselves and for others. In short, both need to learn how to be assertive.

While you may not share either Ellen's or Steve's interpersonal styles, you too may sometimes have problems in being assertive. Regardless of how confident you are most of the time, in some situations you probably find it hard to achieve your goals. Ask yourself if you find any of the following behaviors difficult: expressing your viewpoint when others disagree, expressing negative emotions when you honestly feel them, expressing positive feelings like affection or empathy, disagreeing with authority figures, asking people to explain things you don't understand, making requests, or denying a request from someone you care about. If you do, you may benefit from becoming more assertive.

The first step in improving your ability to get your needs met is to *know the difference between nonassertive, aggressive, and assertive responses*. **Nonassertiveness** is a dysfunctional behavior in which individuals do not stand up for their rights when those rights are infringed upon. It is "self-denying, generates anxiety and negative feelings toward oneself and others, and leads to strained interpersonal relations." **Aggressiveness** is a dysfunctional behavior in which individuals ignore the rights of others by using offensive and hostile behaviors. It "generates negative feelings — such as guilt, remorse, fear of consequences, and alienation — causes constant confrontation with others, and leads to shallow emotional ties." **Assertiveness** is "standing up for one's own rights, without infringing upon the rights of others. It is adaptive

behavior because it is functional in a given context, is self-enhancing, generates positive feelings toward oneself and others, and leads to smooth interpersonal relations."[28]

Suppose Elisa borrowed Jodi's notes and did not return them as promised. Now Jodi needs them and wants Elisa to bring them to her. Elisa is busy and says she'll do it tomorrow. A nonassertive response would be, "I really need them tonight. If it's too much trouble, I guess I can take the bus over to your house and pick them up." An aggressive response would be, "Elisa, I'm sick and tired of your thoughtlessness. This behavior is so typical of you. Just don't expect me to ever do you a favor again. In fact, don't bother to talk to me again." An assertive response would be, "Tomorrow will be too late. I've set aside time to study tonight. I know you're busy, but I'm sure you can spare the half-hour it will take to drive over. I'll expect them by seven."

To improve your ability to achieve goals, take time to *examine your attitudes toward your own and others' rights.* The key to assertiveness is standing up for your rights without violating those of others. It takes some thought to find the ideal balance point between self-respect and respect for others, especially when rights come into conflict. If you're not sure whether you are overstepping your rights or selling yourself short, talk it over with a friend.

Talking with a friend brings us to another way of becoming more comfortable with assertive behavior: *Get feedback about your behavior.* One way to judge your behavior is to try to look at it from the outside. If, for example, you are in a restaurant where the service is terrible, and you're not sure whether to complain, ask yourself what a reasonable person would do in the situation. If you agree that a reasonable person would complain, then go ahead. You can also get feedback by directly asking others. If an employee has come in late for the third time in a week, you can check your behavior by asking a friend to listen to what you intend to say and evaluate its assertiveness. You can even get feedback from your employee. "I'd like you to make sure you get here by eight. When you're late, it inconveniences the rest of us, because we have to wait to get into the office. Do you think this is an unreasonable demand?"

If assertiveness is something you'd really like to work on, *consider keeping a diary in which you record responses to problem situations.* If you decide to keep a diary, record what triggered the situation, how you felt, what you actually said or did, and what you would like to have done. The written record should provide you with a clearer idea of situations that cause you problems, and by writing down what you wish you'd said, you can practice assertive behaviors. In addition to writing down appropriate responses, you can actually *rehearse correct responses by role-playing them.* Unfamiliar responses are more difficult than those that are familiar. If you're not used to being assertive, you need to rehearse until assertive responses become natural. And when you do handle a situation just as you wanted to, *give yourself self-reinforcement.* Congratulate yourself, let a friend know what you did, or even give yourself a treat. You've mastered a new skill and you deserve to be rewarded.

Finally, *know that sometimes you may choose not to be assertive.* Not everyone is reasonable, and not everyone will respond appropriately to your decision to be assertive. Sometimes you may decide not to be assertive. Harold Dawley and W. W. Wenrich tell us

✗ *the governing factor in your decision should be the evaluation of the seriousness of the potentially negative consequences of your assertive behavior. If in a particular situation you believe that the liabilities of an assertive act far outweigh the possible rewards, you may choose — and wisely so — not to assert yourself. But the key word here is "choose."* [29]

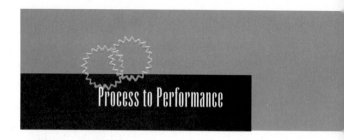

Process to Performance

REVIEW TERMS

The following is a list of major concepts introduced in this chapter. The page where the concept is first mentioned is listed in parentheses.

stimulus **(245)**
response **(245)**
classical conditioning **(246)**
operant conditioning **(246)**
reinforcement **(246)**
social reinforcer **(248)**
social learning theory **(248)**
modeling/vicarious learning **(248)**
self-reinforcement **(248)**
social exchange theory **(248)**
relational currencies **(249)**
balance theory **(249)**
congruity theory **(251)**
cognitive dissonance theory **(251)**
counterattitudinal advocacy **(253)**
value theory **(254)**
reward power **(257)**
coercive power **(257)**
expert power **(257)**
referent power **(257)**
legitimate power **(257)**
ingratiation **(258)**
intimidation **(258)**
self-promotion **(258)**
exemplification **(260)**
supplication **(261)**
cognitive response theory **(262)**
compliance gain **(262)**
nonassertiveness **(266)**
aggressiveness **(266)**
assertiveness **(266)**

SUGGESTED READINGS

Cialdini, R. B. *Influence: Science and Practice,* 2nd ed. Glenview, Ill.: Scott Foresman, 1988. A lively, entertaining, intelligent discussion of the "tricks" compliance professionals use to manipulate and persuade others. If you want to learn how to protect yourself from being fooled by professionals, you should definitely read this book.

Lofland, John. *Doomsday Cult: A Study of Conversion, Proselytization, and Maintenance of Faith.* Englewood Cliffs, N.J.: Prentice-Hall, 1966. A participant observer's firsthand account of the beginning of the Moon cult.

Mackay, Charles. *Extraordinary Popular Delusions and the Madness of Crowds.* New York: Farrar, Straus & Giroux, 1932. People will believe anything, and in this fascinating book, Mackay traces the history of some of the world's most bizarre beliefs.

Zimbardo, Philip G., Ebbe B. Ebbesen, and Christina Maslach. *Influencing Attitudes and Changing Behavior.* Reading, Mass.: Addison-Wesley, 1977. This book introduces major theories of persuasion in social psychology. For the beginning student, its interest will probably lie with the case studies, including Zimbardo's analysis of the 1974 Patty Hearst kidnapping case. (He was an expert witness at the trial.)

Whetten, David A., and Kim S. Cameron. *Developing Management Skills: Gaining Power and Influence.* New York: Harper Collins, 1993. This practical book offers advice on how managers can increase their ability to influence employees.

TOPICS FOR DISCUSSION

1. Think about the ways household products are named (Tide, Mr. Clean, Fab, Biz, Lestoil, and so on). Analyze the kinds of associations the manufacturers hope you will make. Think also about packaging and presentation. Discuss the effectiveness of this influence ploy.

2. If you are a parent, what kinds of reinforcers work with your children? If you are not, think back to the ways your parents used reinforcement principles to control you. What techniques were used, and how effective were they?

3. You may have gone to a school that used a token economy as an incentive to learning. If so, share your experiences. If you did not, do you think it is a good way of influencing children? (In a token economy kids are paid tokens for good behavior; these tokens can be redeemed for treats or privileges.)

4. What do you think of the economic model used in social exchange theory? Do you think it's a good way to describe relationships? If not, why not? If so, can you extend the metaphor?

5. Modeling theory states that we pick things up by watching others. Have you been influenced by models since you came to college? If so, who were your models, what did you learn from them, and why were they successful?

6. When you were very young, what media figures (TV or radio or books) served as models for you? What effect did they have on you?

7. Have you ever experienced the kind of pressures described by balance theory, for example, finding yourself disliking a friend because of his or her beliefs? How did you resolve your imbalance? Does balance or congruity theory come closer to describing the way you resolved the situation?

8. Think about the last fairly important decision you made. Did you do anything to avoid dissonance, such as rationalizing your decision or exposing yourself only to information that told you you were right? Describe what you did to protect yourself from dissonance.

9. Think of the person you most trust. What personal characteristics give that person credibility? What suggestions would you give the average person who wanted to increase his or her credibility?

10. Refer to the situations that open the section on compliance gaining (p. 262). What techniques would you use in each situation to get the person to comply? Describe specifically what you would say or do.

OBSERVATION GUIDE

1. Schools are in the business of influencing people. What are some of the ways the institution you now attend tries to influence you? How did they get you to come? How do they control you once you're here? How will they affect you once you are an alumnus? Don't forget things like architecture and interior design of dorms and classrooms, layout of campus, college handbooks and advertising materials, peer influences, course selection, and so on. How successful is this influence?

2. Analyze your own power. When you want others to do things, how do you go about it? What bases do you use? How could you improve and increase your power bases? Outline a plan to become more powerful.

3. Observe people you know who are ingratiators, intimidators, self-promoters, exemplifiers, and/or supplicators. Describe in detail how they go about achieving power. Describe your feelings about them. Do you find yourself using any of these techniques? What is the outcome?

EXERCISES

1. Bring a number of popular magazines containing advertisements to class. Form small groups and look through the magazines to find examples of each theory of influence. Keep looking until you have uncovered uses of all three learning theories, of each of the consistency theories, and of value theory. A single ad or article may use several theories at the same time. Once you have found examples, report to the class. Which of all the examples do you think was the most effective? Why?

2. Form groups of four or five. You have just been hired to mount a campaign to improve the image of the city of Mudville. Think of the worst city you can imagine; Mudville is at least that bad. Its civic leaders have decided to try to improve the morale of its citizens and the image it projects to the rest of the world. Your group is to come up with a public relations campaign. Report your plan to the rest of the class, explaining the theories behind each technique. (Make up any information about Mudville itself that you feel you need.)

3. Choose a partner. Individually rank the terminal and instrumental values given in Table 9.1. Give a rank of 1 to the value most important to you personally, a rank of 2 to the second most important value, and so on. Once you have finished, think about what these rankings say about you. Are you altruistic or egoistic? A realist or an idealist? Discuss your rankings with your partner. Explain why you feel the way you do. (This is also a good exercise to do with people who are close to you. It will allow you to examine one another's value structures.)

4

RELATIONAL CONTEXTS

Henry Moore's sculpture Mother and Child captures the elusive idea of family systems. Except for the fact that we physically inhabit separate bodies, it is seldom clear where the psychological boundaries around self and other family members begin and end.

(Henry Moore (1898–1986), *Mother and Child*)

10

Family Interaction Patterns

We are a family that has always been very close in spirit. Our father was drowned in a sailing accident when we were young, and our mother has always stressed the fact that our familial relationships have a kind of permanence that we will never meet with again. I don't think about the family much, but when I remember its members and the coast where they lived and the sea salt that I think is in our blood, I am happy to recall that I am a Pommeroy — that I have the nose, the coloring, and the promise of longevity — and that while we are not a distinguished family, we enjoy the illusion, when we are together, that the Pommeroys are unique. I don't say any of this because I'm interested in family history or because this sense of uniqueness is deep or important to me but in order to advance the point that we are loyal to one another in spite of our differences, and that any rupture in this loyalty is a source of confusion and pain.[1]

So begins John Cheever's short story "Good-bye, My Brother." This description of the fic-

tional Pommeroy family is striking in its portrayal of the mixed emotions of family life. Here is a man who views his family as close, permanently bonded, and loyal. At the same time, he admits it is undistinguished, built on illusion, and not a frequent subject of his thoughts.

Families are indeed a varied lot. They can be as quiet and inconspicuous as the Pommeroys or as public and powerful as the Kennedys. Even people who have no shared bloodlines often consider themselves family. Organizations as varied as churches, clubs, even businesses describe themselves as "one big happy family." Politicians haggle over whose party best represents "traditional family values."

From the perspective of this book, the family is a social construction, both a product of communication and a context in which communication takes place. In fact, it is one of the richest sources of communication patterns that we have. In order to better understand the impact the family has on our communication, in this chapter we'll examine the family as a system, its historical evolution, and some of the communication patterns found within the family system. **273**

Maintaining Family Ties

As you read this chapter, you may find yourself looking for some magic formula, some specific set of communication patterns or skills that will enable you and your family to reach the zenith of family life. You should know by now that you won't encounter any such formula in this book. The interpersonal communication patterns that lead to success or failure are many, and their creation and variety should be a source of celebration as much as sorrow. In fact, many family therapists and researchers agree that the myth of the "ideal family" is a problem in itself.[2]

What is the myth? You probably know it well. The ideal family inhabits a home where stress rarely occurs. Members of the family can and do talk to one another about almost anything, regardless of differences in age, sex, or viewpoint. They smile comfortably at one another even when they disagree. They don't yell or scream. They hug a lot. They listen to one another with ears pricked for maximum reception — something an expert might call "total listening." They frequently sit and look at one another for long periods of time — just thrilled to be a family unit. They indulge in practical jokes and other forms of good, clean fun. In short, they play, pray, stay, say "hey," and are A-OK together.

So maybe we exaggerate a little. But the fact is that "normal" families don't always get along. They have built-in differences in perspective and conflicts of interest. There are typical stages in family life that produce crisis points. Outside interests of family members and socioeconomic changes require adaptation and change by the family as a unit. Yet for all the difficulties any family must face, it is perhaps the best-equipped social unit in society. Families are conservative by nature, providing a buffer between a rapidly changing society and the individual's need to maintain a stable identity. The family, even a troubled one, can provide a sense of perma-

nence in an otherwise changing world. The family is our first "social reality" and the source of many of the communication patterns and types of relationships we will repeat later in life. Virginia Satir has characterized the family as a "factory" where different kinds of people are made.[3] It is the family as a factory that we wish to investigate here.

As a producer of persons, communication patterns, relationships, and other social realities, any family can be judged as doing its job very well or quite poorly. In some cases the results may appear to speak for themselves, as when one family turns out several productive citizens while another family consistently produces social deviants. In most cases the results are mixed, and many other socioenvironmental factors have to be considered. Rather than identify any one "ideal" family type, this chapter will describe the family as a system of elements that operate together, producing communication patterns that enable its members to either adapt to, or resist, outside influences and typical crises within the family system. Once you understand the processes underlying family interaction, you should be a better judge of your family of origin (the family that produced you) as well as any family you help produce in the future. In fact, once you understand the patterns of interaction that were forged in the family you grew up with, you may be surprised to find yourself repeating many of those same patterns in your current intimate relationships (see Chapter 11). Let's begin by looking at the system of relationships we call a "family."

The Family As a System: Structure and Function

In describing the family as a "system," it may sound like we have given in to the technology of our times, making something full of life seem dull and mechanical. This is, of course, not our

Individuals and subsystems within the family.

(Marisol, *The Family,* 1962)

goal at all. On the contrary, thinking about the family as a system brings it to life, provides new insights, and gives us a vocabulary for talking about family communication. In Chapter 2 we introduced the basic concepts of systems theory: open and closed systems, wholeness, interdependence, nonsummativity, and equifinality. You may wish to review that discussion before you read on.

Scholars differ on the precise definition of what a family is. Some prefer to emphasize the traditional values of our culture and define the family in terms of marriage and biological kinship. We prefer to use a somewhat broader definition that includes groups of people who think of themselves as "family" even though they may not be related by blood or marriage. Kathleen Galvin and Bernard Brommel define the **family** as "a network of people who live together over long periods of time bound by ties of marriage, blood, or commitment, legal or otherwise."[4]

Family rules and interactions may be observed at the level of the whole unit ("As a family, we always had a big Sunday dinner at Grandma's — she was the only one with place-settings for 24") or at the level of one of its many subsystems ("Annie and Chris always fought over whose turn it was to do the dishes"). **Subsystems** may vary from the husband-wife, parent-child, or brother-sister dyad to temporary coalitions formed by one group of family members against another.

Something to remember about a family as a system is that each family member is one of its parts. And even though each part is a unique individual, he or she is also a functioning component of the whole system. As in any mechanical system, there must be some working order among the individual parts. In a human system we would call the working order between any two parts their "relationship." The various working orders developed by the entire family could be called the **family structure.** The structure of the family keeps it functioning smoothly, coordinating the efforts of its various subsystems. The family system can also be analyzed in terms of its **family functions,** that is, the services it provides for its members and the society at large. The most obvious functions of a family are to provide socialization, food and shelter, and emotional support for its members. For society, the family serves as a major means of passing on cultural beliefs to succeeding generations.

Finally, every human system goes through a process of **evolution.** No family system remains static. The evolution of the system refers to how the family adapts to the developmental changes and personal needs of its members as well as to the changing social and economic needs of the culture. We will look at each of these aspects of the family system in turn.

FAMILY STRUCTURES

A family may have as many different structures as it has events or issues to deal with. There may be a power-authority structure for dealing with family discipline problems, a decision-making structure for determining how the family will manage impending changes or make use of its free time, and perhaps an interaction network that indicates which family members are more likely to talk to one another about problems, share secrets, or form coalitions in order to increase their influence. In each of these structures family members play different roles and relate to other family members in unique ways. These roles and relationships are built up as members repeat patterned episodes of communication.

Power-Authority Structure

Each of us learns a great deal about how to handle and express authority by observing how it worked in our own family. Ronald Cromwell and David Olson define **power** in the family as the "ability (potential or actual) to change the behavior of other family members."[5] In most families power is legitimately held by one or both parents. Parents are allowed to discipline their children, but not vice versa. However, as most parents know, children quickly develop their own power bases. Little Johnny knows that putting on his "cute face" will usually make his father laugh rather than punish him, and he also knows that crying will wear his mother down until she allows him to have some ice cream.

Some families establish very clear lines of authority, others allow individual members to determine how much influence they want to exert. Basil Bernstein refers to the first type of family as having a **positional structure**; the second type he calls a **person-oriented structure.**[6] In a positional family, lines of authority are hierarchically arranged. In a traditional family, power may ultimately rest with the father. In his absence the mother takes charge, and in her absence temporary power is passed on to the oldest child, and so on. Some research indicates that positional families make greater use of restricted language codes (see Chapter 4). In other words, there are limited opportunities for children to

verbalize their own opinions, since they don't have much influence. Person-oriented families, on the other hand, rely to a much greater extent on communication as a means of influence. All members of the family are usually allowed to state their opinions and to defend or explain their actions prior to any discipline. As a result, these families teach their children to use elaborated language codes, a skill that enables them to adapt to a wider variety of social circles. Not every family can be labeled as positional or person-oriented. Bernstein describes the two types as being at opposite ends of a spectrum. Your family probably falls somewhere in between. Later in this chapter we will find out how a family's authority structure influences the development of a child's cognitive and communicative abilities.

Decision-Making Structure

In some families the power and decision-making structures may be almost identical. This would be the case if the parents make all of the family decisions, set the rules, and are the only ones who enforce them. In person-oriented families, however, a variety of **decision-making structures** are possible since children are allowed greater opportunities to influence one another and their parents. In any given person-oriented family, a more verbal and expressive child or spouse may play a larger role in decision making than less verbal members.

As part of its decision-making structure, a family is likely to develop a particular decision-making style or use a different style to handle different kinds of decisions. Ralph Turner has identified three common family decision-making styles: consensus, accommodation, and de facto.[7] Perhaps one of them fits your family. The least common, but most admirable, style of decision making is **consensus.** A family reaches consensus when its members try to make a unanimous decision, seeking input from all members, negotiating differences of opinion or values, and finding a solution that everyone feels is satisfactory. This method requires a great deal more talk than the other two styles. In many cases true agreement among family members is an almost impossible task. However, the process of trying to reach consensus may well be more important than the actual outcome.

A more common style of decision making is **accommodation,** a process in which less articulate or less dominating members of the family give in to those who hold the power or are more persistent. Decision by vote is a form of accommodation. Turner suggests that members usually accommodate because they don't see the value of further discussion. They see the "handwriting on the wall" and figure it isn't worth their time to argue when others leave no room for negotiation. In the long run this style may have a negative impact on family life, especially if the same few members are allowed to dominate decision making and "discussion" becomes a meaningless term. Using this style also tends to avoid conflict, which means that problems may not be aired and tensions may resurface more often. However, this need not always be the case. An accommodating style can be managed successfully if everyone gives in on occasion, so that each family member has a sense of being able to influence the rest of the family when an issue is important to him or her.

When neither of the first two methods works, many families resort to de facto decision making. A **de facto decision** is one in which a single member of the family acts alone or the matter is decided by events, usually after a period of unproductive discussion. A typical example of this style occurs on family trips. A 20-minute discussion about where to stop for lunch seems to be resolving nothing. After passing a dozen fast-food restaurants, the driver finally pulls over in exasperation: "We're eating here!" Or a sign along the interstate warning "Last services for 50 miles" makes the decision for them.

No doubt one of these styles characterizes the way most families make decisions, yet you may find that your family has one or more unique patterns of communication when making decisions. If you can describe that pattern

and its outcomes (who it favors, how satisfactory it is to most family members, and most important, what quality of decisions it produces), you will be in a better position to understand and change the process when necessary.

Interaction Structure

Another way to look at the structure of the family is to describe the communication channels that are most frequently used within it. Some family members may spend more time with one another; some may talk to one another more than they do to other family members. The typical patterns of interaction within a family (who talks to whom most frequently) are its **communication network.** The structure of family networks may vary a great deal. A family with a *centralized* network has a single member who interacts a great deal with all the members and may or may not pass information along to the rest of the family. This central member acts as a go-between, keeping family members in touch even though they may not actually speak to one another very often. In an extended family a parent or grandparent may play this role. Sons and daughters living away from home may phone their parents rather than one another, since they know they'll find out what's happening that way.

Families that are highly cohesive tend to reflect a decentralized network, one in which frequent interaction is likely to occur among all or most family members. Extended families of this type may have large phone bills, since everyone wants to hear the news from the source. When something exciting happens to one member, he or she shares it with everybody, not just the central figure.

Look at the diagrams of different communication networks in Figure 10.1 and see which one best represents your own family network. In fact, your family may have more than one network. Many families alter their communication patterns in order to deal with different situations or events. Since individuals have different

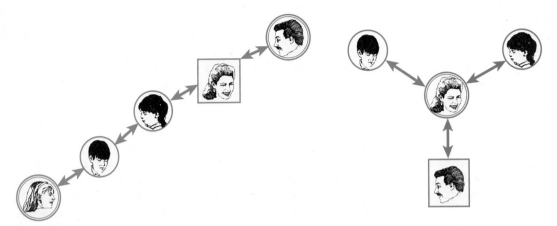

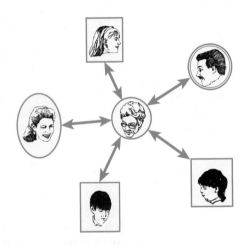

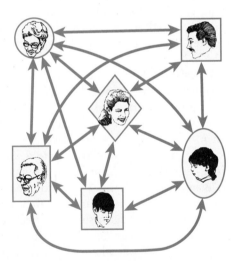

THE CHAIN NETWORK. Family members relay messages to one another via a series of other family members. It is typically used when members see each other occasionally but are rarely all together at once. Messages are, however, prone to distortion as they are passed along.

THE "Y" NETWORK. A centralized network where one member serves as a "gatekeeper," allowing some but not all messages to be exchanged among members. One parent may monitor the children's requests of the other parent, or an older child may summarize her sibling's desires to the parents.

THE WHEEL NETWORK. A highly centralized network found in families that communicate through one key figure. Most members do not talk directly to one another. They find out about each other from the central figure.

THE ALL-CHANNEL NETWORK. The most decentralized network of all. It is characteristic of families that spend a lot of time together as a unit and in separate dyads. All or most of the communication channels are open and utilized.

FIGURE **10.1**
Four family communication networks

likes and dislikes, one or more members may be automatically left out of the network when certain types of information are being exchanged. The prudish sister who thinks gossip is a form of evil is more likely to be the subject of the family rumor mill and less likely to hear about it. The brother who eschews sports is not included in the summer-long discussions of the pennant race, even though he may often be within earshot of those discussions. Younger children, especially, are often told to go outside and play when a family problem has to be dealt with. They are not yet a part of the problem-solving network.

Let's take a look at some of the structures we've been talking about in a hypothetical family, the Clicks. At the simplest level the family role structure consists of a father (Bic, age 38), a mother (Barbara, age 36), an elder daughter (Brenda, age 15), a middle son (Buck, age 12), and the "baby" (Binky, age 6). The power structure in this family is a positional one, with the father and mother having the most influence, followed by Brenda, with less influence exerted by Buck and Binky. Although no one has ever stated the power structure, the children "know" that Mother is more likely to enforce rules regarding table manners and foul language, whereas Father makes sure everyone does assigned chores. In the parents' absence Brenda is allowed to enforce rules, but she cannot actually punish her brothers.

The decision-making structure is a little different. When important decisions are made, such as where to go on vacation, everyone gets to make a pitch for where he or she would like to go. Buck has developed the habit of researching his places of interest (this year he wants to visit several historical museums and see a Red Sox game), so he is often more persuasive than his brother and sister. Although the parents tend to rule out some places because of expense or distance, a family decision is usually reached by majority vote. Most family decisions are made this way. (This decision style reflects a mix of consensus and accommodation.)

Finally, the interaction structure in the Click family is an interesting one. Brenda is very close to her father, primarily because she's interested in his work as a race car mechanic. She's always asking him questions about how things work. She's also very protective of Binky and hates Buck's guts. Buck is the isolate in the family. He reads a lot about history and loves baseball. He talks extensively about his interests, but not to anyone in particular. If pressed, he would say he gets along with Binky better than anyone else in the family. Binky is his mother's favorite. They frequently form a coalition in the family decision-making process. The three Click family structures are depicted in Figure 10.2.

The structured relations of the Click family are not necessarily typical of most families. Every family establishes its own patterns and means for handling recurring situations. You may want to analyze your own family's structures and see whether they've changed since you were younger.

Characteristics of Family Structures

Family structures evolve over time as family members establish and repeat patterns of interaction. These structures have a number of characteristics in common, including the differentiation of members into roles, the creation and maintenance of boundaries, and the coordination of subsystems.

Role Differentiation In a given family structure, members perform different tasks in relation to one another. In an efficient family structure these roles are complementary. When a parent disciplines, a child is supposed to obey. This ideal isn't always achieved, of course, but the system won't function very well if the ideal is rarely achieved. Tension often arises in families when two members compete for the same roles, as when one parent intentionally counteracts the authority of the other: "I don't care what your mother said, you can't go!" The

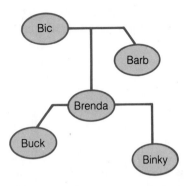

a. Power–Authority Structure
A Modified Chain Network

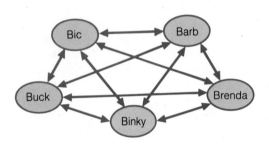

b. Decision–making Structure
All-Channel Network

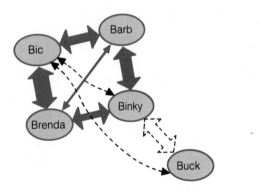

c. Interaction Structure

FIGURE **10.2**
Three family structures — the Click Family

point here is that there must be enough complementarity of roles for the system to function, yet not so much specialization of roles that the family cannot adapt to the absence of the member who usually plays a particular role.

Boundaries According to Salvador Minuchin, a noted family therapist, a family must establish and maintain clear boundaries among its members and between itself and the outside world. The **boundaries** of a subsystem consist of "rules defining who participates and how."[8] Inside the family there are often physical boundaries such as separate bedrooms, toys, or clothing, and corresponding rules for who is allowed to enter such spaces and play with or wear such belongings. Parents may even impose boundaries on themselves to give their children room to breathe or grow or simply to avoid being overwhelmed by demands. Not interfering as two younger children settle their own dispute or telling them "I can't help you out — you'll have to solve this problem yourselves" is an example of setting boundaries. It says, in essence, "No adults allowed."

Likewise, families may regulate the extent to which the outside world is allowed to penetrate the family's day-to-day world. David Kantor and William Lehr identified three basic types of families that differed largely in how they deal with the society at large.[9] An **open family** is one that encourages its members to experience a wide variety of social life and then share those experiences with the rest of the family, providing a constant source of new ideas. This kind of family adapts to changes in the culture and is typified by the prototypic parent/chauffeur rushing children off to dance class, piano lessons, baseball practice, and the movies before taking in an adult education course at the local community college. The boundaries between family life and the rest of life are quite flexible, each influencing the other.

A **closed family** reacts to the larger society with a little more suspicion or indifference.

"The family that plays together stays together" is a maxim that expresses the values of the closed family. Many outside activities are restricted or participation is monitored very closely by the authority figures in the family. At any rate, family always comes first in relation to outside activities. Boundaries are often reflected in different sets of rules — one for appropriate behavior with family members, another for behavior in the presence of strangers.

In contrast to the close-knit relations and high degree of sharing in both open and closed families, the third type of family is much more independent and unpredictable. This type may go months without much interaction among family members and then suddenly spend the next three weeks in constant companionship. Plans for a family get-together may be made and then changed several times because of the fluctuating interests of family members. Because life is so unpredictable in such a family, Kantor and Lehr called it a **random family.** The boundaries in random families are not very clearly drawn and may be a frequent source of misunderstanding and dispute.

Minuchin describes the boundaries of a family system along a continuum that ranges from "enmeshed" at one end to "disengaged" at the other extreme.[10] An **enmeshed system** is one that sacrifices the autonomy of its members in order to experience a great deal of cohesion. Family members feel close to one another, but the family doesn't develop clear boundaries around each person's identity. As a result, privacy and independent thinking are discouraged. A **disengaged system,** on the other hand, promotes independence at the risk of not developing a sense of family loyalty. The boundaries around individual subsystems are too rigid, and in the extreme case members are unable to provide each other with social support. It is important to remember that these boundaries may be true of the family as a whole or that individual subsystems in the family may be enmeshed or disengaged.

Coordination of Subsystems In one sense, family life isn't much different from life in the corporate world. This is especially true of a large or extended family. Just as businesses are organized around teams of individual employees with different skills trying to coordinate their efforts to produce a product, so a family unit is organized into subsystems of individuals whose efforts must be coordinated in order to produce its products (reasonable facsimiles of persons, values, chores, and so on). Later in this chapter we'll look at the typical communication patterns of the various family subsystems. For now, it is important to realize that these subsystems do overlap and have to be coordinated. The husband-wife dyad cannot act in isolation. Whatever spouses do as husband and wife will also influence their roles in the parent-child subsystems they are a part of. A prime example of this is reflected in the tension many parents feel about both spouses working and being away from their children. While the parents may be convinced that they need the money, they may be equally concerned about how the children will handle (and interpret) being left alone or with a sitter. Careful explanation may be necessary in order to enable these subsystems to adapt to the change without damaging the more permanent family relationship.

THE FUNCTIONS OF THE FAMILY

The structured relationships that emerge through repeated episodes of communication do so for a number of reasons. When we examine the reasons for these communication patterns, we are really asking what their function or purpose is within the family unit. Communication within the family works in two very broad ways: (1) Internal functions keep the system running and serve the individuals who make up the family unit; (2) external functions or services are provided to the larger society. We shall look at each of these in turn.

John Biggers' mural, Family Uniity, talks to us of family structure and the importance of ancestral ties in African-American culture. Notice that the women are shown bearing a house on their shoulders, indicating their central connection to the home. Biggers employes elements of West African iconography to express his unique cultural experience.

(John Biggers, detail of *Family Unity* mural, 1979–1984)

Internal Functions

Families provide such basic necessities as shelter, warmth, and care. In addition, the family may also fulfill the following psychosocial functions: socialization, intellectual development, recreation, and emotional support.

Providing Care   The human infant is one of the most helpless creatures on the face of the earth. Unable to provide for himself, he exists in an extended state of dependence on adults. Thus, the most basic needs such as food, shelter, clothing, and caretaking become the first function that the family fulfills. This function has the status of moral, if not legal, obligation in most societies. In the United States the courts may take a child away from his parents if he is not adequately cared for.

Socialization   Beyond simple provisions, the family is also one of the primary teachers of what it means to be human, male or female, moral or immoral, polite or impolite. As children we learn what sort of behavior is deemed appropriate for boys and girls as a result of the sexual stereotypes provided by our family. The results of socialization are so ingrained that by the time we are near adulthood, many of our patterns of thought and behavior seem "natural" to us and are hard to change. A child who is socialized to be patriotic may have a hard time understanding how anyone could not show respect for our national symbols. We have a friend whose mother required her children to stand at attention every time they heard the national anthem, regardless of whether they were at a parade or watching a baseball game on TV. Many of us have been socialized in similar ways.

Intellectual Development   Many parents spend a great deal of time, money, and anxiety to make sure that their children have ample opportunity and rewards for academic achievement. The learning environment is loaded with educational toys, magazines, and special cable TV selections. Communication often takes the form of reciting the ABCs, counting, or responding to a battery of questions: "What's your name? How do you spell it? Where do you live? What's your phone number?" Kindergarten is preceded by educational day care, and so on. At the other extreme, many parents neglect early intellectual development, hoping the schools will do the job later on. Or they openly reject it, saying things like "I hope my child doesn't grow up to be smart. Who needs it?"

Recreation   Play is one of the major forms of childhood activity. Every family has its own repertoire of family games and traditions. Not every family plays together, but they can find ways to just "do nothing" together, which is essentially what the recreation function is all about.

Emotional Support   Probably the most important of the internal functions is the ability of the family to provide a sense of belonging — love, affection, kinship, companionship, acceptance, and inner resolve. This is especially important in terms of individual self-esteem, in which the strength drawn from the family serves as a springboard for confidence in dealing with the external world.

A number of social critics have lamented the fact that many of the functions once provided primarily by the family are now being taken over by the larger society (child care, schools, nursing homes, and so on). Christopher Lasch argues that, as a result, we expect the family to be primarily a refuge of emotional support.[11] Such an overemphasis on any one function may be asking too much of the system.

External Functions

The family serves the culture as much as it serves its individual members, in two primary ways: (1) passing cultural values to its younger members and (2) accommodating cultural change.

Transmission   The family is the first and perhaps the most important transmitter of cultural values from generation to generation. Parents relay the cultural myths and guidelines they learned when they were young by reading the same stories, legends, and fairy tales to their children. They perform the same function when they reinforce the values their children glean from television. Many people overestimate the influence of TV programs on young children and underestimate parents' ability to influence how children interpret what they see and hear. Parents play a vital role in this process. The attitudes and values that children hold are directly related to those of their parents, at least early in life and usually for much longer.

Straw polls taken in fourth-grade classrooms invariably show that children vote for the same presidential candidates as their parents. Parents are the ultimate authorities from a child's perspective, and the ultimate message from parents to children is how to belong to their own social circles and the larger culture. Every culture teaches its young to be patriotic, to value their own way of life in comparison to other cultures. In our own culture this means that parents must pass on values such as liberty, the pursuit of happiness, and, usually, material wealth, democratic rule, religious freedom, individualism, expansion of horizons, and so on.

Accommodation In addition to the passing on of unchanging cultural values, the family also encourages its members to adapt to many of the changes that any society goes through. Our own culture has undergone major social changes in the last 25 years. The role of women has been redefined, civil rights have been granted, or at least promised, to many minorities, and battles for freedom of sexual preference rage on. But these changes become real only when major social institutions such as the family, the church, and the corporation begin to accommodate them. In the family, old rules about what is women's work or which toys and games boys and girls should play with are gradually replaced. Now is a good time to assess how your own family has or has not adapted to some of these major cultural changes.

On a more mundane level, families ensure cultural change by competing with other families in the pursuit of a more elaborate lifestyle. "Keeping up with the Joneses" is an American middle-class tradition. American technology creates computers and video recorders; American families accommodate by purchasing them and making changes in daily routines and lifestyles so that they get their money's worth. Eventually, these superficial changes may result in changes in one or more family structures. For instance, the child who masters a computer language may be consulted more frequently and earn a more prominent position in the family's decision-making hierarchy.

The degree to which family life is separate from or integrated into a local community also teaches children about their proper roles as citizens. It is significant that much of the social interaction in our neighborhoods has moved from front porch stoops and parlors to family rooms and backyards in the past few decades. Box 10.1 shows how some architects and social planners are rethinking the isolation of American families in the traditional suburb.

The Evolving Family: Calibrating Change

Families are not static social units. From the time two people decide to marry or start a family, they can expect change to play a major role in their affairs. Some of these changes are highly predictable; others are not. The successful family will be the one that learns to manage the typical stresses and strains of family life. The chances of being successful can be increased by understanding the dynamics of change and by developing some useful coping strategies. Let's look at each of these processes in more detail.

THE DYNAMICS OF CHANGE IN THE FAMILY

The sources of change in family life are many. Among the most predictable changes are those associated with the family life cycle and stressful contact with outsiders. In addition, there are unpredictable crises such as illness or death, divorce or desertion. Each of these events may cause either a temporary or long-term upheaval in family structures, rules, and the boundaries drawn among family subsystems.

The Family Life Cycle

Over the years researchers have pieced together the typical stages of the family life cycle. These stages represent the most likely sequence of events in family life. Most scholars would agree with the following seven **life cycle stages** adapted from the work of David Olson and Hamilton McCubbin.[12]

- *Stage 1:* Young married couples without children

- *Stage 2:* Families with preschoolers

- *Stage 3:* Families with school-age children

- *Stage 4:* Families with adolescents

- *Stage 5:* Launching families — sending young adults into the world

- *Stage 6:* The empty nest — life after the children

- *Stage 7:* Retirement years

While each of these stages is highly predictable (assuming a couple does have children), the degree of stress and strain associated with each stage will vary from family to family. The more a young couple anticipates how their life may change with the birth of a first child, the easier the transition may be. Many people now make elaborate plans for retirement; others wait until they "get the golden parachute" before concerning themselves with the inevitable changes. Knowing what's ahead may not make for completely smooth sailing, but it does help one to prepare psychologically for impending changes. Talking about such changes in advance helps a family to negotiate and coordinate the future rather than react to events as they happen.

Perhaps the most significant change in a couple's life is the onset of the first pregnancy. For most people this stage represents the transition to being a family. Researchers have found that even in the most egalitarian of relationships, the birth of the first child engenders a return to more traditional sex roles. In part this is due to the lack of role models for being egalitarian parents — and so we typically fall back on our own parents (who were likely to be traditional mothers and fathers) as role models. In two recent studies couples who defined their relationship as egalitarian and companionate had the greatest difficulty adjusting to the birth of their first child. On the other hand, couples whose relationship already had clear sex-role divisions found the adjustment to be much smoother.[13] In another study J. H. Meyerowitz and H. Feldman found that having a baby tended to improve the relationship between spouses during the early weeks following birth. After five

weeks, 85 percent of couples said things were "going well" in their own relationship. Within four months, however, the percentage dropped to 65 percent. At the same time, many of the husbands had taken on most of the family decision making, and both spouses reported a decline in the amount of time spent talking to each other.[14] Further cementing a return to traditional roles, many women reported that their pregnancy helped them to feel more accepted by their husbands and even their own parents.[15]

Another key transition period in the family life cycle is the "launching period" — when young adult children go away to college, move to their own apartment, or get married and leave home. In most marriages this is a characteristic low point in marital satisfaction, spousal companionship, and consensus on roles within the marriage.[16] One of the most significant factors during this period is the void that departing children create in the family system. Stephen Anderson characterizes the changes with the following example:

> *The physical departure of a child whose day-to-day familial role included the regulation of emotional distance in the parents' relationship (for example, misbehavior when marital tension rises, serving as referee during conflicts, or as a coalition partner supporting one parent against another) could precipitate the need for parents to deal more directly with one another or to triangulate another child into the vacated role.*[17]

In comparing families in which a child left home for college versus families in which the child stayed home and commuted to a local university, Anderson found that perceptions of the amount of personal communication between spouses actually increased when the child commuted but decreased when the child went away to school.[18] Presumably, this result was due to the continued presence of the son or daughter as an indirect source of communication between parents.

BOX **10.1**

A Better Place to Live: How the Built Environment Shapes Family and Community Life

Winston Churchill reportedly said, "We shape our buildings and then they shape us." Social scientists have for some time documented the effects of overcrowded homes, the lack of privacy, the aesthetic design of rooms, lighting, decor, and many other features of the environment on human perception and behavior. And now, archictects are beginning to take seriously the design of neighborhoods that foster interaction among members of a community. Given what we know about the mutual influence of people and their environment, it's surprising that we don't exercise more control in shaping the homes and communities that shape us.

In *A Better Place to Live,* author Philip Langdon has chronicled what is wrong with the design of typical American suburbs and what a handful of architects and developers are doing about it. Langdon argues that suburban living not only has contaminated the environment (e.g., excessive automobile emissions), but has also been bad for us as individuals and as communities. The suburban mode of life fragments people and communities because it separates where we live from where we work, shop, and play. It also raises the cost of living unnecessarily. The average two-car family must work three months — after taxes — just to support its annual automobile expenses. Furthermore, most suburbs are exclusively residential, with few parks or other public places where people can congregate and interact.

Grocery stores and other daily amenities are generally located well beyond walking distance on congested commercial strips. The overall effect is that most suburbs are not inviting enough for people to make a permanent commitment to live in them. High turnover results as nearly one-fifth of Americans change their address each year. It is no wonder that people are reluctant to develop relationships with transient neighbors. The lack of socialization within a community can lead to a sense of isolation, which erodes mental stability (Etzioni, 1991) and places additional strain on marriage partners who have no one to turn to but themselves to satisfy their varied social needs.

For the past decade, architects Andres Duany and Elizabeth Plater-Zyberk have been designing new urban communities along the lines of the 19th-century small town. They call on city governments and town planners to follow several principles of neighborhood design that will encourage social interaction and turn neighborhoods into safe, full-functioning communities:

- Each neighborhood should have an identifiable center that will attract people and a well-defined set of boundaries that enable people to identify "the neighborhood" without totally separating them from other neighborhoods.
- The neighborhood should be small enough (a quarter-to-half-mile radius) for people to walk from the center to the edge in 5–10 minutes. (A neighborhood that is walkable promotes interaction and gives people a sense of ownership.)
- It should contain a mixture of different sizes, prices, and types of housing to accomodate people of different income levels and different stages of life. Houses should be in close proximity to one another (on relatively small lots). This enables a wider range of diversity and fulfills developer Henry Turley's admonition that "democracy assumes — no demands — that

we know, understand, and respect our fellow citizens."

- Each neighborhood should have a network of interconnected streets and sidewalks that make it easy to get from one place to another without getting lost or feeling fearful. Duany and Plater-Zyberk argue that streets should be seen as outdoor "public rooms" so people can enjoy spending time in them. To make the streets more amenable to humans, garages would be moved to the back of the lot, making them accesible from alleyways.
- Each neighborhood should have a number of "civic" buildings (a meeting hall, a church, a school, a day care center, etc.) where people can congregate.
- The best neighborhoods should also have what sociologist Ray Oldenburg calls "third places" (cafés, pubs, beauty parlors, etc.) where people can socialize without feeling compelled to invite others home with them.
- More small businesses should locate within or near neighborhoods so people can work close to home. Alternatively, larger corporations should continue the trend of allowing many employees to telecommute from their own home.

These principles are being applied in towns and cities across the country. Seaside, Florida is one example of a walkable community. Most of its streets are a narrow eighteen feet wide and paved with a brick-like material that forces motorists to slow down. Every house has a generous front porch and is located close enough to the sidewalk to encourage small talk with passersby. Streets are laid out in a grid pattern, but are anything but dull-looking. Langdon describes them as "visual knockouts" because of the narrow, steepled houses that line them and the frequent pavilions, gazebos, and sculptures that break up the flow. Charleston Place in Boca Raton, Florida has garden courts and brick walkways with rose-covered walls between backyards. Its "outdoor public rooms" are so inviting that residents can be seen outside on every block during the evening hours.

Communities designed for interpersonal communication ultimately support family life by providing safer neighborhoods and a wide ranging support system. When parents and children feel less isolated from the social world around them, they may not have to solve all their problems within the confines of the home — and who knows — they may be a bit less likely to get on each other's nerves.

SOURCE: Philip Langdon, *A Better Place to Live: Reshaping the American Suburb.* (Amherst, Mass.: University of Massachusetts Press, 1994)

ADDITIONAL READINGS

Oldenburg, Ray. *The Great Good Place: Cafés, Coffee Shops, Community Centers, Beauty Parlors, General Stores, Bars, Hangouts, and How They Get You Through the Day.* New York: Paragon House, 1991.

Etzioni, Amitai. *A Responsive Society: Collected Essays on Guiding Deliberate Social Change.* San Francisco: Jossey-Bass Publishers, 1991.

Lappé, Frances Moore, and Paul Martin DuBois. *The Quickening of America: Rebuilding Our Nation, Remaking Our Lives.* San Francisco: Jossey-Bass Publishers, 1994.

The study of changes in communication patterns across the family life cycle is in its infancy. These initial results suggest that many interesting discoveries await us.

Stressful Contact with Outside Sources

Just as the family life cycle produces change from within the family unit, so may other factors impose change from the outside. Every family member belongs to numerous groups and social institutions, all of which may produce stress that is brought home. The most obvious of these institutions are the school and the workplace. When a parent loses a job or a child is sent home from school for disciplinary reasons, the effect reverberates throughout the family system. Even more subtle stresses, such as a bad day at the office, may precipitate an argument between the spouses, which may be overheard by a child, who thinks it is her fault that her parents argue. Likewise, an entire family may experience stress from a neighborhood that disapproves of their barking dog or the junkyard appearance of their property.

One of the most basic functions of the family is taking care of its young, which helps to establish a basis for trust.

Illness or Death of a Family Member

Every family has to anticipate the developmental changes inherent in the family life cycle as well as the impact of everyday contact with the outside world. But other crises such as death, major illness, or handicap are not so predictable. In one sense the crisis stage is inevitable; every family knows it will suffer loss in some form. But few families can prepare themselves in advance for such crises. There is a strong taboo in our society against talking about death. Perhaps it is a tribute to the power of the verbal code. We are afraid of the "magical" aspect of language, that words let loose may somehow escape our control and unleash dark forces.

Our unpreparedness, combined with the emotional pain, makes the family system especially vulnerable during such crises. In addition, the physical loss or diminished capacity of a family member means that the system must change — someone else must function in the roles formerly played by that person. This is rarely an easy adjustment. The loss of a spouse may require that the remaining spouse get a new job, be both mother and father to the children (or, if the children are older, the spouse may become dependent on them), or force the oldest child to take over household and babysitting chores, and so on. Some members of the family may resent anyone who tries to fill the shoes of another ("You're not my mother — you can't replace her!"). In some cases the cohesiveness of the family may suffer, especially if the deceased member was the primary source of affection. In other cases a slightly disengaged family may strengthen its bonds as everyone pulls together to offer reassurance and keep the system functioning.

Divorce or Separation of Family Members

Another major crisis in family life involves the deterioration, temporary or more permanent, of the relationship between two or more family members. Although the term divorce is usually reserved for the termination of a spousal relationship, it could just as easily be applied to any relationship within the family. Two older brothers who have not spoken to each other in years, a runaway child, a son or daughter who marries just to get away from home — all represent a breaking of ties that bind. In each case the crisis requires a readjustment in the family system. Most divorces, especially those involving children, are essentially a matter of redefining relationships rather than a total termination. In today's society, termination of a marriage does not usually result in the termination of parenting roles. Ex-spouses tend to maintain some kind of relationship, even if it is indirect contact where the children serve as the channel for communication. Even so, a recent study shows that few ex-spouses have frequent contact with each other, and what contact there is tends to be less than harmonious. While most ex-spouses agreed that their relationship should be based on norms of politeness, 41 percent of them admitted that they did not treat their ex-spouse as well as they should.[19]

Ex-spouses who have coparenting status rarely talk to one another or about their children. This prompted one researcher to redefine coparenting as "parallel parenting" in which

there is little if any consistency in the rules and in disciplining the child from different parents.[20] The lone exception to this trend seems to be in some dual-career families in higher socioeconomic circles.[21] Apparently, in situations where the woman is financially self-sufficient and does not have to rely on the ex-spouse for support, the relationship with the ex-spouse is more harmonious. This allows both parents to put their relationship behind them and concentrate more on their roles as parents.

Is there a predictable pattern that families follow in dealing with unexpected losses such as death or divorce? According to a number of scholars, there is. Kathleen Galvin and Bernard Brommel have synthesized the work of these scholars into four basic **crisis stages.**[22]

- *Stage 1:* Shock resulting in numbness or disbelief, denial

- *Stage 2:* Recoil stage resulting in anger, confusion, blaming, guilt, and bargaining

- *Stage 3:* Depression

- *Stage 4:* Reorganization resulting in acceptance and recovery

These stages are normal, perhaps even necessary, for a successful adaptation to changed circumstances. At each stage communication is crucial, if only for family members to express the emotions of denial, anger, and depression. Obviously, they can express these feelings to one another, but it may also help if their social network of friends and acquaintances lends a supportive ear. Well-meaning friends may avoid the family in their time of grief or distress, cutting off valuable assistance. What should you say in such situations? The best evidence suggests that a simple expression of sympathy and a willingness to listen are the best responses. Knowledge of the typical stages the family is going through should help you to understand (and not judge) what you hear.

STRATEGIES FOR COPING WITH CHANGE

Since nothing is as permanent as change, it is wise to start developing strategies your family can use in managing its own life cycle as well as handling unexpected events.

Anticipating Change

Everyone develops a basic philosophy or outlook on life. Some people expect their lives to be settled by the time they are 25 or 30. They expect to develop a routine and live that way ever after. Others are frightened by such prospects. While we do not advocate a chaotic lifestyle with no goals, expectations, or ritualistic patterns, we do suggest that you come to terms with the fact that just when you think you've got it all together, a major change is probably right around the corner. One way to improve your forecasting ability is to read extensively about individual and family life cycles. These changes happen to most families, and it is unlikely that yours will be the exception.

Encouraging Family Cohesiveness

Families that develop and maintain at least a moderate amount of cohesiveness are more likely to survive stressful times than those that become too disengaged. When members lose touch with one another, providing emotional support in crisis situations becomes more difficult. Most families probably think of themselves as having strong bonds simply because they are family. Clichés like "Blood is thicker than water" and "Family comes first" reinforce the cultural stereotype of what it means to be a family. Yet a family needs to exhibit *observable* signs of cohesiveness — interdependent behavior patterns — that it can call on in times of need. Look for evidence of cohesion in your family's everyday interaction. What family rituals seem important to all or most members? What activi-ties will members sacrifice if a family emergency arises? If some family members are away at college or live in another city, how regular are the phone calls or letters? These kinds of interdependent actions are probably the best indicators of cohesiveness.

Maintaining Adaptability

Family interaction can easily get into a rut, following routine patterns of decision making, assignment of chores, times and places to talk, and so on. When a family encounters stress or the loss of a member, some of these routines may actually become dysfunctional. A family that has always emphasized logical thought in its decision making may be unable to think clearly in an emotional crisis. Logic may not even be the best course of action in such situations. To be adaptable means that a family system has *alternative* ways to handle even the most routine problems.

How can you encourage adaptability? One way is to force the family to deal with minor changes on occasion. Successful management of small problems can increase coping power in the face of larger ones. Another simple activity is to ask family members to think of new solutions to typical problems, even while "the old way" is still working. In business these are called contingency plans, and it is considered a cardinal sin not to have any.

Building Social Networks

The old adage "no man is an island" could be applied to families as well. A family may be quite self-sufficient in good times and may have tremendous inner resolve during tough times, but it never hurts to have the support of neighbors, church members, or friends of the family. In troubled times nothing may seem very stable within the family unit, and that's when a stable social network (of which the entire family is a member) can serve as a safety net. Members of this network can provide a perspective that is often missing in a time of stress.

Families in History

Earlier in this chapter, we talked about the myth of the ideal family. Today many fear the loss of traditional family values and lament the statistical death of the nuclear family. Taking into consideration a 50 percent divorce rate, the high rate of teenage pregnancies, the increasing number of single-parent and stepfamilies, and the fact that almost one-fourth of all American households are single individuals, we seem to have cause for great concern. But if we consult our own history, we find that the family has undergone several radical transformations that easily rival what we are witnessing today.

In *Domestic Revolutions,* historians Steven Mintz and Susan Kellogg recount three such transformations in what could be called the modal, or most frequently occurring, type of family structure and lifestyle. Beginning with colonial times, the *godly family* gave way in succession to the *democratic family* of the early 19th century, and the *companionate family* of the mid-20th century.[23]

The **godly family** of the colonial era has also been described as "a little commonwealth" because every facet of social life was centered in family activity — the family was a microcosm of the larger society. The family household was the site of economic production, a place of religious instruction, and as head of the household, the father was its legal and political representative to the wider community. Family relations were very formal and the authority structure was unquestionably patriarchal and hierarchical. The male head of the household had sole possession of the family's resources of land and expertise in a craft or trade. As a result, he could command the respect and deference of his chil-

dren, who were considered to be miniature adults in need of discipline more than nurture. Child-rearing was but one of many functions of the family, and a secondary one at that. Infants could be "put out" to wet nurses for breast-feeding so the mother could devote more time to household chores. Older children were frequently sent to live with other families where they could be more properly disciplined. The entire community supported family descipline in this way. Given the strong Calvinist belief in original sin, moral instruction to rid the child of evil influences was much more important than any notion of building the child's self-esteem. But by the end of the 18th century, a new industrial economy was gearing up to weaken the father's all-encompassing authority and signal the end of the godly family.

In its place, a new **democratic family** structure developed. This new modal family was less formal, less hierarchical, and more tender. As work moved outside the home, the family became a more private institution. Marriage and parenting acquired a startling new emotional significance as the home, no longer a microcosm of society, became a protective shell keeping the cut-throat world of work at bay. Children were now recognized as unique individuals in need of love and attention, as well as preparation to be successful citizens and laborers. Child-rearing became the full-time job of the mother, who assumed more of the moral authority within the home. The goal of a mother shifted from breaking the will of a sinful child to shaping his or her character to face the temptations of life. The goal of a wife was to reform her husband, who faced constant temptation in the public sphere, and to promote moral reform of the society as a whole. Box 10.2, which portrays the bankrupt moral society of urban London a hundred years earlier, illustrates the need for moral reform that became widespread in the era of the democratic family.

The values of self-denial and character development defined the democratic family. But family values would undergo another domestic revolution in the early 20th century with the

BOX **10.2**

Childhood in the 18th Century: What Shapes the Family That Shapes Us?

William Hogarth, artist and political satirist in early 18th-century London, is said to have produced "the most significant single body of hard facts about English manners of his age." His drawings, published in the popular broadsheets of London, were well known. At the time, London was a collection of merging villages, not yet the great metropolis it would become in the 19th century. Hogarth's sympathies were with the oppressed lower classes, beleaguered servants, and innocent children corrupted by the city. His satire was directed at the whole social structure (customs, laws, government, and church) that failed to protect the children who were sent from the countryside to find work. He saw the family, and especially the child, as victims of a corrupt society — one he hoped the moral commentaries in his drawings

would help reform. According to art historian David Kunzle, "Hogarth's perception of the child was as an essentially parentless creature in a society which reneged upon parental responsibility within both the private nuclear family and the public family formed by social institutions." A good deal of his work as an artist was devoted to criticizing a society that allowed such things to happen.

One of Hogarth's most important ventures was a series of five drawings, produced in 1730, known as *A Harlot's Progress.* This box shows the first and last of these drawings, depicting Hogarth's view of the treatment of the family and

Figure 1
William Hogarth, *A Harlot's Progress, Scene I*

emergence of the **companionate family.** Paralleling and promoting the shift from a self-concept based on character to one celebrating personality (see Chapter 8), the companionate family extolled the virtues of spouses as "friends and lovers" and parents and children as "pals."

Permissive child-rearing practices were believed necessary to foster self-expression, self-fulfillment, and mutual happiness. Smaller family sizes and the abundant wealth of the nation made it possible for many (but certainly not all) to invest heavily in the idea that one's children

Figure 2
William Hogarth, *A Harlot's Progress, Scene V*

variety of lecherous characters abounds (note the man in the doorway, hand in his pocket, believed to symbolize a Colonel Charteris, who was on trial for rape at the time of this drawing).

In the intervening scenes Kate "progresses" from the role of servant girl to that of a prostitute, is arrested and sent to a women's prison, where she receives inadequate care. In the final plate (Figure 2) she has died a premature death, leaving an illegitimate child (center, in front of the coffin). The young child, alone and ignored by the "mourners," is no doubt doomed to a miserable life himself.

its members by the very social institutions created to support the people. In the first plate (Figure 1) we see an innocent young country girl, Kate Hackabout, arriving in London to stay with her cousin Tom and find work as a servant. But there is no family to meet her or protect her from the procuress (foreground) who seeks out and lures young women into prostitution. Note the other young girls in the wagon (background), who are under the watchful eye of a minister, seemingly protected from harm. The inadequacy of the church is seen, however, as the minister offers no assistance to the young Kate. Meanwhile, a

What Hogarth has shown us in these remarkable renderings is the role of larger social forces (whether corrupt or not) in shaping family life at a given point in history. We might do well to look at our current social structures (patterns of work, legal system, government intervention, therapy professions, and so on) and contemplate how they shape roles and communication patterns within the various forms of the family as we know them today.

SOURCE: David Kunzle, "William Hogarth: The Ravaged Child in the Corrupt City," in *Changing Images of the Family*, ed. Virginia Tufte and Barbara Myerhoff (New Haven: Yale University Press, 1979), pp. 99–140.

should experience a better lifestyle than that of the parents.

In contrast to the rather clear modal families of the past, Mintz and Kellogg describe our modern era as "a society without a clear unitary set of family ideals and values." It is likely that we are in the midst of yet another historical transformation, but it is not yet clear whether a single modal type of family will take center stage, or what roles, characteristics, and values will define it. In the section that follows, we will do our best to make sense of the research on the family communication patterns that characterize our own time.

Family Communication Patterns

Without adequate communication, family structures of any age would fall apart, internal and external functions would be impaired, the continuity of culture would be disrupted, and the idea of "family" would devolve into a useless social concept. In this section we want to direct our attention to many of the communication patterns that keep modern families functioning, as well as some that threaten to tear at the fabric of family life. Some of these patterns are characteristic of the family as a whole; others are typical of subsystems within the family unit.

INTERACTION PATTERNS IN THE FAMILY AS A WHOLE

Family systems interact in ways that make their life together more than the sum of the individual members. Two broad categories of interaction will be considered: (1) the creation of specific rules to guide family communication and (2) the development of more general family themes and identities.

Family Communication Rules

For a family to function adequately, the behavior of its members must be at least partially coordinated. This coordination can be achieved through the establishment and enforcement of family rules. You may recall that in Chapter 4 we introduced two types of communication rules: regulative and constitutive. You will find that family life is full of both types.

Regulative Rules These rules serve as guides for action. Regulative rules describe what

kinds of actions define one as a member of the family. From an individual or a family perspective, these rules may be seen as *obligatory, prohibited, appropriate,* or *irrelevant.* As you read the following examples, think about the regulative rules that operate in your own family.

An obligatory rule is one that is usually verbalized as "you must" or "we have to." Some obligatory rules are blatant: "As long as you live under this roof, you will keep your room clean" or "Always be on time. Nothing is worse than being late." Others are the result of subtle, often nonverbal, example-setting and reinforcement: "From the time we were very young, we always hugged and kissed each other before bedtime. No one said you had to, but Mom got this hurt-puppy look on her face if you forgot."

Most children probably think the world is populated with rules for what you "can't" or "shouldn't" do. "Don't raise your voice to me — or your father!" "Don't you dare go out of this house looking like that!" These rules generally describe behavior that may be OK for members of other families, but not this particular family. Occasionally, a rule statement may be a combination of *obligation* and *prohibition:* "I want you to be honest with me — but you don't have to tell me everything you do!" A wide variety of family rules can be described as simply *appropriate.* These rules don't carry the force of an obligation but are deemed "good" behavior for a family member. Being polite to strangers and sharing toys with a brother or sister might be considered appropriate actions. Any time a behavior is met with a response like "That was a good thing you did. I'm very proud of you," it probably reflects a rule or guide for appropriate communication.

Finally, some regulative rules are *irrelevant* as far as family membership is concerned. Those actions a person performs that neither embarrass other family members nor evoke a response of pride can be considered irrelevant. For some families a child's participation in extracurricular activities at school might be thought of as simply filling time; for another family it might be an obligation.

Constitutive Rules   While regulative rules guide action, constitutive rules determine meaning. For some families a given behavior or communication pattern may have positive connotations, while others view the same pattern as negative. The following statements are examples of family members offering *interpretations* of behavior: "Helping your brother with his chores means that you care," "Talking to strangers is dangerous," "Going to X-rated movies is a sin," and "A real man stands up for himself." Constitutive rules may have implicit regulative rules associated with them. When a person says, "Making snide remarks is a sign of disrespect," he or she is probably implying that you shouldn't make snide remarks to people. But that may not always be the case. If someone is acting stuffy, you may follow the regulative rule "A stuffed shirt deserves no respect."

Think for a moment about the constitutive rules that distinguish your family. Are there actions that your family interprets differently than most? What regulative rules are associated with them? Make a list of which rules in your family are well known by everyone, which ones are unwritten, and which ones cause the most misunderstanding or conflict. Are there some things you can't talk about as a family? Are there other things that, while taboo in most families, are discussed openly in your own?

Family Themes and Identities

The family communication rules we just looked at apply to specific behaviors and instances. When we look at the overall pattern of family rules, we are likely to discover some general themes that influence the specific rules we follow. **Family themes** are recurring attitudes, beliefs, or outlooks on life shared by the entire family. Many families thrive on competition, subscribe to a particular set of religious beliefs, or view "togetherness" as the key to a happy life. Some families are anxious; they worry about everything. In contrast, other families have an overall outlook that "life is a gamble;

take a risk." This family theme influences many of their everyday rules. They have fewer prohibitive rules than most families, and they always make themselves available for new experiences.

When family themes are prominent and the family unit is cohesive, a **family identity** emerges. Just as each individual develops a self-image, so members of the family share a group image, a sense of who they are as a unit. When you hear family members describe themselves as "fun-loving," "high achievers," or "responsible citizens," they are putting into words the constructs or images that govern their behavior as a group. We know an extended family that has labeled themselves as "sojourners" because none of them stays in one place very long. One member moved his family three times in one year. Another has moved from New England to the Southwest and back five times in six years. Most family members start getting "itchy" after two years in the same place.

Based on interviews with members from a wide variety of families, journalist Jane Howard summarized ten characteristics of "good families." As you read her list you'll notice specific family themes, rules, roles, and communication practices. According to Howard, good families:

- *have a chief, heroine, or founder.* This person is the magnet who draws family members together and inspires someone in the next generation to carry on the family traditions.

- *have a switchboard operator.* This person always knows what everyone is doing and keeps the others posted.

- *are cohesive but not stifling.* Membership in the family means a great deal to all, but does not prevent members from pursuing outside interests.

- *are hospitable.* Their homes are places where other people's children like to spend time.

- *deal directly with their problems.* Members do not avoid confrontation or hope problems will go away. They find a way to work through conflicts.

- *prize their rituals.* They celebrate holidays, special events, and everyday life in unique and sometimes cornball fashion. Members anticipate the regular Sunday brunch or the summer reunion at the lake.

- *are openly affectionate.* Members share how they feel about one another, although in a wide variety of ways.

- *have a sense of place.* Whether it is "the old country," "the old homestead" or a new home housing old family symbols, members share a definite sense of belonging tied to those symbols.

- *build connections to posterity.* Through children or extended family, members see themselves as linked to something purposeful and enduring.

- *honor their elders.* Respect for the family heritage is embodied in intergenerational communication.[24]

How would you describe your own family's identity? What makes yours a "good" family? What themes or communication rules are associated with the family identity?

INTERACTION PATTERNS IN FAMILY SUBSYSTEMS

Every family consists of one or more subsystems. In this section we will describe several different family dyads, including the husband-wife, the parent-child, and the sibling subsystem.

The Husband-Wife Subsystem

The first subsystem in a family is the husband-wife relationship. Prior to the birth of the first child, this relationship is the focus of family life.

Studies indicate that the quality of communication between the spouses is the single best predictor of satisfaction with the marriage.[25] How much satisfaction they experience depends, in part, on what type of marital relationship they negotiate and how they handle recurring issues such as control, togetherness and freedom, and expression of affection. Mary Anne Fitzpatrick and her colleagues have studied how congruent couples are in their relational definitions along three conceptual dimensions: autonomy-interdependence, conventional-nonconventional ideology, and conflict engagement-conflict avoidance. As a result four very different types of couples have emerged from these studies: traditionals, separates, independents, and separate traditionals.[26]

Traditional couples are highly interdependent, share conventional views of marriage and family life, and engage in conflict on a fairly regular basis. They are also very expressive in their communication styles, and sharing information is a high priority with them. **Separate couples,** on the other hand, tend to be more autonomous — spouses give each other more room, they aren't as expressive, and while they hold fairly conservative views on marriage, they don't feel as strongly about their views as traditionals. In addition, they tend to avoid conflicts as much as possible. They deal with conflict situations by taking on complementary roles — one person decides what to do, and the other follows. **Independent couples** differ from the others in that they subscribe to more nonconventional values and views about relationships. They are not as autonomous as separates, but are only moderately interdependent. Spouses are very expressive emotionally and do not avoid conflict with one another. In fact, independents have the highest levels of self-disclosure observed among all couple types. Fitzpatrick reports that 60 percent of the couples she has studied fall into one of the first three types. The remaining 40 percent are "mixed types," which means that the couples disagree in their definition of the relationship or

Degas, who knew the Bellelli family, captured their dynamics in this portrait. Posture, costume, touch, facial expressions — all reveal alienation between husband and wife, as one of the daughters attempts to bridge the gap. Try analyzing snapshots of your own family. Do they reveal relationships?

(Edgar Degas, *La Famille Bellelli*)

in their views about marriage. **Separate/traditional couples** are the most distinct of these hybrid types. Spouses have the most conventional sex roles of all types, self-disclose very little, ask fewer questions, and yet score consistently high on all ratings of marital satisfaction. One study reported that wives in this type of relationship have a more accurate understanding of their husbands than in any other type.[27] Of the four types, traditionals and separate/traditionals seem to be the most satisfied with their mar-

riage, while independents and separates report the least satisfaction.

Regardless of the type of relationship, research indicates that satisfaction with the marriage tends to level off over time, and especially after the birth of the first child. The decline in satisfaction is usually compensated for by the satisfaction derived from the new role as a parent.[28] Research, as we have already seen, shows a marked increase in traditional values and sex-role stereotyping once children arrive on the scene.[29] Thus, the transition to parenthood may lead to changes in the spouses' definition of their relationship. Another potentially detrimental change with the advent of parenthood is that partners begin to spend more time in parental roles and less time with each other. Family therapists often advise spouses to check their talk when they are finally alone to make sure that, even then, they don't talk about the children. Ask yourself what rules you think a family should establish to increase the likelihood that the parents will have at least some "alone time" as a couple.

The maintenance of a positive husband-wife subsystem depends in part on what they do talk about when they are alone. We have already seen that the type of relationship spouses have affects their willingness to self-disclose and their frequency of communication. Research also indicates that, in general, men and women perceive the importance of certain types of communication quite differently. Linda Acitelli reports that husbands tend to value "talk about their relationship" only when they perceive it to be necessary (for instance, to resolve a conflict). Women, on the other hand, value relationship talk even when things are going smoothly.[30] This preference by men to avoid routine relational talk and women's preference for it can place a strain on the husband-wife relationship, especially when so much interaction time is devoted to children and other matters.

Furthermore, wives tend to have much more vivid memories of significant relational conversations or events such as a first date or a recent argument. This can lead wives and husbands to misconstrue that such events were less important to the husband. However, the research showed no relationship between ratings of an event's importance and ability to recall the event in vivid detail.[31]

There is also evidence that how spouses communicate depends on generational and life-span influences. In a study of the conversations of young, middle-aged, and retired married couples, Paul Zietlow and Alan Sillars found that middle-aged and older couples were generally less expressive than younger couples.[32] Younger couples used communication as an outlet for releasing tensions and also as a vehicle for negotiating needed role changes. The middle-aged couples also communicated to adjust roles but seemed less urgent in their need to confront conflicts. Older couples demonstrated a uniquely cordial style of interaction (characterized by casual conversation and small talk) when conflicts were not very important to them, but were noticeably bitter and complaint-oriented during conflicts. They seldom communicated to resolve conflict as the younger couples did. The older couples were seen as subscribing to a vision of the spousal relationship as one that "can minimize conflict and, at the same time, create incompetence in addressing those conflicts which are not resolved by conformity to external role standards."[33]

While some of these patterns reflect generational differences in values and relational definitions, the importance attached to conflict issues may well reflect different stages of the family life cycle for these couples. Younger couples tend to be faced with many more adjustments, especially if children are involved. Thus, they may have to confront more conflicts than older couples. In contrast, the middle-aged and older couples, having weathered many storms, could afford to be more relaxed and less expressive about conflict issues.

The Parent-Child Subsystem

The function of the parent-child subsystem is one of mutual socialization. An infant needs to be cared for, be offered emotional support, and have appropriate behavior shaped through an imaginative blend of example and discipline. There is no question that the messages parents send a child influence the development of the child's personality and moral code. What parents struggle with is trying to determine precisely which communication patterns will lead to the desired outcomes.

Transmission of culture: A Japanese grandmother teaches a teenager
the tea ceremony.

Experts differ widely in their specific advice to parents, and even a sampling of different views would be beyond the scope of this book. What does seem to be generally agreed upon is that affection and support messages are the first priority of parenting, with control and discipline a close second. Research suggests that to gain the compliance of a child, a basic bond of *affection* must be established first. **Support messages** from parents such as praising, approving, encouraging, and showing affection are linked to higher levels of self-esteem in children and greater conformity to authority.[34] Desmond Morris has suggested that all children under two years of age need basic care and unconditional love; when they reach age two, restrictions and discipline should begin.[35]

The forms of discipline available to parents are not much different from the compliance-gaining strategies introduced in Chapter 9. In the parenting literature they are referred to as **control messages**: power assertion, love withdrawal, and induction.[36] **Power assertion** refers to a parent's use of physical coercion, unexplained demands, restricted privileges, and so on. Consistent use of coercion tends to make children feel rejected by their parents and leads to aggression, dependency, and less internalization of moral standards. **Love withdrawal** also involves a strategy of threatening negative consequences if the child fails to comply. Love withdrawal occurs when a child's failure to obey results in a parent withholding expressions of affection, ridiculing the child, or displaying the proverbial cold shoulder. **Induction** is the strategy of reasoning with a child about his or her behavior in an effort to help the child *understand* why they should follow certain rules ("You can't play with the train because you might break it") or why a given behavior is wrong or hurtful ("How would you feel if Sally did that to you?"). Most parents use a mixture of all three types of discipline. In fact, researchers have known for quite some time that any type of discipline can be effective when the overall relationship between parent and child is warm and affectionate.[37] Researchers have been particularly interested in the effects on a child's moral reasoning capabilities when one disciplining strategy is used more frequently than the others. In their review of this research, Gene Brody and David Shaffer found that greater parental use of inductive strategies is closely associated with a child's ability to internalize ethical standards and apply them even when parents or other authority figures are not present. Frequent use of power assertive strategies, on the other hand, tends to produce an external moral orientation, where the child is more responsive to the probability of rewards or punishments and less likely to internalize and think in complex ways about moral issues. The results when parents use love withdrawal have been more problematic, with no clear indication of its effect on moral reasoning.[38]

Interestingly, mothers appear to the primary disciplinarians in most families. Given their less active role in actually dispensing discipline, effective fathers seem to influence their children's moral development more indirectly as "competent role models" whose moral values rub off on their children.[39] Another possibility is that fathers tend to specialize in power assertive strategies but use them sparingly while mothers do the bulk of the disciplining using more inductive strategies. The evidence for such a view stems from the fact that many mothers of father-absent children use more power assertive strategies, presumably because they have to do the work of both parents.[40]

There is also evidence that parental use of inductive strategies not only influences a child's social-cognitive and moral reasoning, but also directly affects the child's own communication skill development. Children of mothers who used inductive, person-centered strategies are more effective than children of position-

centered or power assertive parents at a host of communicative tasks, including persuading others, giving instructions, taking the perspective of the other, and offering comfort to someone who is distressed.[41]

Obviously, inductive strategies are unlikely to work until a child is old enough to respond to them with some degree of understanding. And as children get older, other influences besides the parents (television viewing, peer culture, other adult role models) begin to make inroads. By this point, parents hope that their children will have internalized the family's values at least to the extent that they influence the child's choice of friends and how they respond to alternative values expressed on television or by teachers and other adults. One area of concern for many parents is establishing regulative rules regarding the amount and type of TV programming a child is allowed to watch. Also related is the generation of constitutive rules regarding the meaning and morality of televised violence and sexual behavior and the distinction between reality and fiction. Several studies have examined the role of television as a source of conversational topics between parents and children and the role of parental mediation or explanation of television form and content to children. **Parental mediation** refers to a parent viewing television with the child, discussing specific programs before or after they are seen, and talking about TV in general. Roger Desmond and his colleagues have identified three general categories of parent-child talk about TV: (1) *criticism,* in which parents make evaluative comments about specific programs or commercials, (2) *interpretation,* in which parents explain TV as a medium or calm a child's fears about violence or unusual behavior observed, and (3) *rule making and discipline,* in which parents encourage the viewing of certain programs, as well as limiting others.[42] In regard to rule making, these researchers report some interesting results. A child's comprehension of what he or she watches is closely related to the type of parental mediation that occurs. The ability to distinguish reality from fiction, for instance, was enhanced when (1) the family controlled television viewing, (2) both positive and negative rules were enforced, (3) strong discipline was utilized, and (4) the amount of TV watched was relatively low. In addition, comprehension of specific program plots was related to the adherence to TV rules, positive communication between mother and child, and frequent explanations of TV content by parents. Since viewing television is often associated with greater passivity, the researchers suggest that "one of the most important functions of family mediation may be to elevate some children's amount of invested mental effort or attention during viewing."[43]

As adolescence approaches, parent and child often experience a great deal of apprehension about and stress in their relationship. Increased influence by peers and attempts to establish a more autonomous relationship with parents often result in strained interactions. But new studies demonstrate that these difficulties do not reflect the total relationship between parent and child. William Rawlins and Melissa Holl report that adolescents tend to view both parents and friends as important conversational partners, but target them for discussion of very different topics and needs. Parents are seen as important sources on issues that require a historical perspective — something the parent has been through before and would know about. On the other hand, if input is needed regarding current issues or problems, adolescents turn to their friends. Another important and encouraging difference was the perception that although parents are seen as more judgmental than friends, they are also seen as more caring. There is a realization that parental criticism usually emerges from a real concern for the child.[44]

Another interesting change in parent-child relationships occurs during the launching years. Stephen Anderson found significant gender differences when a son or daughter leaves home. Mother-son communication improved after the son went away to college, whereas the mother-daughter relationship was better if the daughter remained at home and commuted to college.[45] Anderson hypothesizes that the son's departure

from home gave him enough distance to reestablish a stronger familial bond. In contrast, daughters were better able to manage the mother-daughter relationship and establish their own identity at the same time.

As we noted in a previous section of this chapter, the companionate family that dominated the earlier part of this century seems to be undergoing a new transformation. New family structures, such as a blended family with one stepparent and/or one or more adopted children, have introduced new elements into parental communication practices. Mark Fine and Lawrence Kurdek found that in stepfamilies, the biological parent and the step-parent often follow very different parenting scripts. Biological parents engage in, and believe they should engage in, more parenting behaviors than their stepparent counterpart. Differences occurred in regard to control (disciplining behaviors), but were especially strong in terms of showing warmth. The authors surmised that natural parents, because of their greater biological investment in the child, were much more likely to spend time with and communicate support to the child.[46] These findings demonstrate the ambiguity that continues to abound regarding appropriate roles in newly emergent family forms.

The Sibling Subsystem

Sibling relationships are perhaps the most interesting relationships in a family. When siblings are young and close in age, they are a primary source of imagination and ingenuity. Twins frequently create their own private languages, and other siblings are almost as imaginative. An older sibling may socialize a younger brother or sister almost as much as her parents. Mix in a little sibling rivalry and you have relationships as rich as any other.

Siblings are peers and thus have a more egalitarian relationship with one another than with their parents. Since they can be more assertive with one another, siblings usually are. Their interaction is characterized by physical aggression and other forms of antisocial behavior. As children get older, they mature and engage in more social behavior, cooperating to play games and so on. Cooperation increases more between same-sex siblings than it does between brothers and sisters, due no doubt to emerging sex-typed identities. Younger children tend to imitate one another a lot, but this behavior also decreases more between opposite-sex siblings as they grow older.

Several other age- and sex-related tendencies have been borne out by research: Younger children tend to like and revere their older siblings, and their liking is not reciprocated to the same degree; older brothers and younger sisters tend to have the most conflict-ridden relationships; and the older sister-younger brother relationship usually has the least conflict.[47]

Like other subsystem relationships, the sibling relationship changes over the life span. A. Goetting summarized these changes as occurring in three stages: (1) childhood-adolescence, (2) early and middle adulthood, and (3) old age.[48] During all three periods siblings tend to provide one another with companionship and social support, although physical proximity is greater during the childhood period. In childhood an older sibling is likely to function occasionally as a caregiver and to teach social and other skills to the younger sibling. In adulthood the frequency of interaction may decline, especially if siblings are geographically separated, but relationships are often maintained via telephone and family reunions. In their review of research on sibling relations, Victor Cicirelli and Jon Nussbaum note that even when interaction is sparse, adult siblings maintain a symbolic relationship by identifying with one another and recalling shared incidents.[49] Older siblings tend to provide services to one another such as occasionally lending money, baby-sitting one another's kids, sharing concerns, and caring for elderly parents. Finally, in old age, the relationship may take on greater significance as friends and other family members die. Older siblings also help one another review life events and face current ones. The range in types of elderly sibling relationships is also interesting. D. T. Gold characterized five types of relationships as intimate (14 percent), congenial (30 percent), loyal (34 percent), apathetic (11 percent), and hostile (11 percent), respectively.[50] The percentages reveal the relative strength and importance of sibling relations as people get older. It is also interesting to note that sisters are an increasingly important target of interaction for both males and females as they age. Cicirelli and Nussbaum speculate that the greater expressiveness of females and their traditional role as nurturers lead both males and females to seek out sisters for emotional support and physical aid.

Clearly, communication patterns within the various family subsystems change in number, frequency and function over time. Even so, family relationships have a kind of permanence seldom experienced outside the family. Indeed, most romantic relationships develop outside the family boundaries but soon become enmeshed within the extended family via marriage and childbirth. We often take for granted the closeness and emotional support that family members traditionally provide one another. But we have only to be reminded of the pain of child abuse, abandonment, and other forms of family violence to realize that the ideals are not always achieved. Acknowledging the dark side of family life should encourage us to develop the communication skills necessary for building and sustaining positive personal and family relationships. To assist in that endeavor, let's revisit the model of communicative competence introduced in Chapter 1.

Communicative Competence and the Family

As you may recall, we defined communicative competence in Chapter 1 as consisting of five subskills: interpretive, role, goal, self, and message competence.

FAMILY AND INTERPRETIVE COMPETENCE

Interpretive competence involves attention to context. When we are mindful of how a current family conversation or dispute relates to the family's history, its important rituals or values, and its place within a larger kinship or community network, we exhibit interpretive competence. In Chapter 6, we discussed cognitive schemas such as relational prototypes and scripts. These operate in families as well. Family members often develop similar prototypes of how a family should interact, but these may be countered by peer group and media influences. Whatever our prototypes of the ideal family, even if they are myths, they establish expectations and channel what we desire to happen. When actual interactions do not live up to the ideal, we can be unreasonably harsh critics of our family unit. In addition, our expectations (and those of other family members) are subject to change, especially in these turbulent times when the companionate family ideal appears to be evolving toward some as yet unknown new modal family. Questions arise in such a microwave world. Should we judge older rituals and scripts as out of date and in need of modification? Do we cling to the companionate ideal and judge our current patterns of interaction in light of its values? Attention to these issues helps us assess the appropriateness of family identities, rules, and disciplinary strategies as well as the significance of everyday roles and conversations.

FAMILY AND ROLE COMPETENCE

Families have much to teach us about role competence. We tend to think of roles as "job descriptions" and being able to play them competently as simply learning a few sets of rules and skills. Yet if we take the concept of the family system to heart, we will realize that the roles we play are interlocked and thus always changing. Systems theory tells us that there is no husband role without a wife, no child without a parent role, and no way to be a brother or sister without someone cast in the opposite role. Family therapists tell us that problems in families never belong to individuals alone, but are symptoms of the roles parents and children play in relation to one another. Acting out the role of "rebellious teenager," for instance, often involves a triangle of roles: an overinvolved mother, an underinvolved father, and the rebellious son or daughter.[51] Just as professional actors must master ensemble relationships to pull off a successful part, developing role competence within the family means learning all the parts different members play and how they are interwoven. Knowledge of typical communication patterns associated with different role relations and the realization that alternative patterns can be negotiated help us become more proficient at role competence.

FAMILY AND GOAL COMPETENCE

The range of possible family types, roles, rules, and communication strategies offer us plenty of goals to pursue within the family context. We may want our family to be more like the "good families" described by Jane Howard or desire greater involvement of family members in the neighborhood or community. But identifying goals for family communication and achieving them are two different things. Sometimes we have to be more realistic about what's possible. While we might prefer to live in a community like Seaside, Florida (see Box 10.1) where the physical environment is designed to harmonize families and neighborhoods, we have to make do with the families, houses, and communities in which we actually live. It might be surprising to know that on average, people living in the Bronx, New York have more positive feelings and greater hope and faith in what the future holds for their families and communities than people of far greater wealth and social status living in Beverly Hills.[52] Achieving our goals for better family communication is more likely when we approach them realistically — improving one interaction at a time, one relationship at a time.

FAMILY AND SELF COMPETENCE

As Virginia Satir puts in, our families are "peoplemaking factories."[53] The communication patterns established early on between the primary caretaker and an infant do much to shape the self-concept, self-esteem, cognitive development, and even the attachment style by which the child will relate to others much later in life.[54] Not only are the foundations for self competence laid in infant-parent communication, the process of self-development continues throughout the family life cycle. Self-identity is influenced by communication patterns in sibling as well as intergenerational relationships. In turn, emerging or faltering levels of self competence feed back into the family system. An individual's problems affect the entire family system, often in complex ways. As we change, the family system must adapt and reconfigure itself.

FAMILY AND MESSAGE COMPETENCE

Our families are also laboratories for message making. We not only learn the meanings associated with verbal, nonverbal, and relational acts at home, we are also given the opportunity to try out new words and gestures and test the relational implications of new communication strategies before attempting them in the larger social world. A brother or sister is often the first to hear and critique a request for a first date or an apology soon to be offered to a friend. Parents listen patiently while we polish a speech for a fifth-grade class or rehearse lines for the school play. In daily interaction with family members, we test compliance-gaining strategies, practice gender displays, and learn how to give or receive feedback. It is not, of course, just practice. As we saw in Chapter 5, relational messages in families

have serious consequences. Family members are sometimes victims of "double binds" in which a spouse or child simultaneously receives confirming and disconfirming messages and doesn't know how to respond appropriately. Message competence is both learned and tested within the family.

In many ways, our families affect our communicative competence. For almost all of us, the family will be a lifelong context in which we operate. Sometimes soothing us, occasionally antagonizing us, family members remain a significant part of our lives long after the family of origin gives way to the creation of a new family unit through marriage and childbirth. Family members are often our line of last resort when things get tough.

In closing this chapter we turn our attention to one of the skills that enables family members and friends to count on one another in times of need: the skill of comforting.

Skill Building: Communicating to Comfort

One of the most essential forms of communication within the family is the emotional support function. Parents provide emotional support when they show affection for and acceptance of their children and each other. This not only fosters cohesiveness within the family unit but also serves as a key component in a child's development of a positive self-image and feelings of self-worth. Many of the communication skills associated with this function (such as active listening, empathy and perspective-taking, and expression of feelings) have been discussed in earlier chapters. Another closely related skill is that of comforting one another during times of emotional upheaval and distress. Keep in mind that while this skill is essential in spousal and parent-child relationships, it is helpful in other contexts, such as developing and maintaining friendships and intimate relationships, as well.

Brant Burleson defines the act of **comforting** as trying to alleviate, moderate, or salve the distressed emotional state of another person.[55] There are numerous ways to offer emotional comfort, but researchers have identified several important distinctions among the messages that most people use and the ones that tend to be successful. We have drawn three general principles from this research to help improve your competence when trying to comfort others.

The first step in successful comforting is to *adopt an other-centered approach.* This means that you must listen carefully to understand how the distressed other sees his or her situation and what feelings he or she has experienced. Your response will be more sensitive if you acknowledge the validity of the other's viewpoint and feelings ("I know how much you wanted your relationship with Jeff to work out. It really hurts when you put so much into a relationship only to see it fall apart"). In contrast, most people become speaker-centered and either give advice ("Why don't you try. . . ") or tell the other how he or she should feel ("You can't let things get to you like this. You've got to be tough"). In one study researchers asked bereaved parents and spouses what kind of comforting messages they found to be most "helpful" and "unhelpful." Giving advice, minimizing their feelings, encouraging their recovery, and forced cheerfulness topped the list as unhelpful messages. In contrast, simply expressing concern, providing an opportunity to ventilate feelings, and just being there were seen as most helpful.[56]

Another way to comfort effectively is to *compose messages that are evaluatively neutral.* This strategy involves describing the other's feelings and the situation giving rise to those feelings in general rather than specific terms. Thus, you should avoid mentioning too many specific details or evaluating the personalities involved. In comforting a friend who just broke up with her boyfriend, you will probably inflict more pain if you mention how difficult it must have been to return his ring or to give up some cherished ritual (spring break vacations) that the two shared. Negative evaluations such as berating the boyfriend ("He was no good for you") are usually ineffective as well. Keeping things at a general level shows that you care; getting too specific implies a kind of opportunistic voyeurism — as if you can't wait to explore what went wrong.

You can also improve comforting messages by trying to *help put events and feelings in perspective for the other.* This is probably the only form of advice-giving that a distressed person will tolerate because it may help the person better understand his or her own feelings. Sometimes this means offering alternative explanations of the events that have taken place. If a friend feels that she didn't do well in a job interview, you can, after acknowledging her feelings, propose that she look at it as a learning experience. If she can identify aspects of the interview that didn't go well, she'll know what to work harder on next time. Or you can reverse the perceptions. Maybe the interview was not successful because it was not a company in which she could fully display her talents. Perhaps she prevented a greater calamity down the road: working for a company that would not appreciate her. Because stressful situations are often emotionally overwhelming, Burleson suggests that many distressed people fail to develop cognitive explanations of their feelings — explanations that might produce some psychological distance from the emotional trauma.

James Applegate has proposed that in attempting to provide comfort, people use strategies that differ in terms of how much of the perspective and feelings of the other are acknowledged and elaborated on. The least effective strategies are those that condemn, deny, or ignore the feelings and perspective of the other. Somewhat better are those strategies that at least *implicitly* recognize the other's perspective and feelings by diverting attention to other topics, simply acknowledging how the other feels, or attempting to "explain away" those feelings. Finally, the most sophisticated and successful comforting strategies *explicitly* confirm the other's feelings, elaborate on or explain the feelings, or help the other gain another vantage point regarding those feelings.[57] Most people, most of the time, tend to use denial or implicit strategies rather than the more explicit strategies, even though research has confirmed that the more explicit strategies are perceived as more effective.[58]

Comforting messages seem to work best when we take the perspective of the other and demonstrate an acceptance of his or her feelings. While the skills involved in comforting are demanding, we can, with patience and practice, learn to be more competent at providing solace and encouragement to those whose well-being is important to us.

Throughout this chapter we have identified some of the structures, functions, and communication patterns that typically emerge in American families. Knowledge of these patterns is certainly a good first step in improving your ability to function effectively as a member of your family. But your family is bound to be different in some ways from the "norms" described here. Thus, it is essential that you develop the ability to recognize and describe the patterns of interaction that your family actually follows. This task may take a considerable amount of your time, but it will be worth it. You might keep a journal in which you write down the communication behavior you observe in all of the subsystems of your family as well as those times when you are all together. Try to abstract the communication rules and family themes present in the observations you have recorded. Try to predict the evolution of your family system by imagining how things might change at the next step in the family life cycle or in the event an unexpected crisis occurs. Once you have described the way things are in your own family, you can begin to explore other al-

ternatives. Ask friends how they handle similar situations in their families. Next time you read a novel or watch a film, pay attention to scenes involving families. What rules, themes, or identities do they project? What we are suggesting here is not an easy assignment. But it may well be the best way to improve your knowledge and your ability to help create or revitalize your own family.

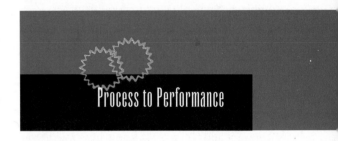

Process to Performance

REVIEW TERMS

The following is a list of major concepts introduced in this chapter. The page where the concept is first mentioned is listed in parentheses.

family (275)
subsystems (275)
family structure (275)
family functions (275)
evolution (275)
power (276)
positional structure (276)
person-oriented structure (276)
decision-making structure (276)
consensus (276)
accommodation (277)
de facto decision (277)
communication network (277)
boundaries (280)
open family (280)
closed family (280)
random family (281)

enmeshed system   (281)
disengaged system   (281)
life cycle stages   (284)
crisis stages   (289)
godly family   (291)
democratic family   (291)
companionate family   (292)
family themes   (295)
family identity   (295)
traditional couples   (296)
separate couples   (296)
independent couples   (296)
separate/traditional couples   (297)
support messages   (299)
control messages   (299)
power assertion   (299)
love withdrawal   (299)
induction   (299)
parental mediation   (300)
comforting   (305)

SUGGESTED READINGS

Rubin, Lillian. *Families on the Faultline: America's Working Class Speaks about the Family, the Economy, Race, and Ethnicity.* New York: Harper Collins, 1994. Rubin, a sociologist and psychotherapist, interviewed nearly 400 working-class men, women, and children. Updating her classic work *Worlds of Pain* (written in 1976), she paints a portrait of working-class families whose shattered dreams have given new impetus to psychological and political divisions based on race and ethnicity. While she does not focus specifically on communication, Rubin clearly shows how the social and economic changes of the past twenty-five years serve as a backdrop for family and community interaction.

Mintz, Steven, and Susan Kellogg. *Domestic Revolutions: A Social History of American Family Life.* New York: The Free Press, 1988. This book chronicles the transformations of family life from the godly family of the colonial era to the radically diverse family types of the 1980s. The authors trace developments in families of the white middle and working classes, American Indian, and African-American cultures.

Coontz, Stephanie. *The Way We Never Were: American Families and the Nostalgia Trap.* New York: Basic Books, 1992. In this social history of the family, Coontz places current concerns about the family into historical perspective. Demolishing myths about the family, she discusses such topics as parenting, privacy, love, sex roles, feminism, and sex.

Nichols, Michael P. *The Power of the Family: Mastering the Hidden Dance of Family Relationships.* New York: Fireside Books, 1988. Nichols, a family therapist, brings systems theory to life by demonstrating how a fictional teenage son's rebellion is linked to the behavior of every member of his family. Nichols takes a variety of issues ranging from sibling rivalry to divorce and shows how the issue reverberates throughout the family system. A highly readable introduction to the complexities of family life.

Galvin, Kathleen, and Bernard Brommel. *Family Communication: Cohesion and Change.* New York: Harper Collins, 1991. An excellent introductory text, written for courses in family communication. This very well-written book will get you up-to-date on the latest research and put it all in perspective.

Chavis, Geri Giebel, (ed.). *Family: Stories from the Interior.* St. Paul, Minn.: Graywolf Press, 1987. A wonderful collection of short stories organized around the themes of husband-wife, mother-son, mother-daughter, father-son, father-daughter, and sibling relation-ships. Authors include Willa Cather, John Updike, John Cheever, Gwendolyn Brooks, and many others. Reading these short stories is a great way to test your ability to recognize family communication patterns in action.

Satir, Virginia. *Peoplemaking.* Palo Alto, Calif.: Science and Behavior Books, 1972. A book that truly blends theory about families with practical, engaging activities that any family can use to better understand itself. It is written in a lively style and intended as a workbook for families interested in changing some of their rules and family structures.

TOPICS FOR DISCUSSION

1. As a class, offer your own perceptions of the "ideal" family. How do your versions differ from the one described on page 274? Is there any harm in the fact that real families rarely live up to the ideal?

2. Discuss the appropriateness as well as the benefits and negative consequences of allowing children to be influential in the family decision-making structure. Is it better, for instance, that children "be seen and not heard," or for them to be treated as small adults with somewhat equal input and negotiating power? What other issues are at stake here?

3. How can families balance the tensions of enmeshment and disengagement as discussed on page 281? How do members of your own family signal when they need to be alone or in the company of others? Is it possible to designate "alone time" or "together time" for different family subsystems and the whole family? Discuss the value or harmful consequences of separate vacations for family members.

4. Another way to enhance discussion about family life is to identify the ways that families achieve each of the functions listed on pages 282–284. Discuss positive and negative communication patterns associated with each function.

5. As mentioned in the text, some critics believe that too many family functions have been taken over by other social institutions. Schools have the major responsibility for intellectual development and even socialization. Day-care personnel or baby-sitters feed, clothe, and play with our children. This leaves the family with the primary function of giving emotional support. What are the risks of having the family "specialize" in only one or two functions? Does it place too much of an emotional burden on family members, especially when other activities and functions become "foreign" to the family?

6. Starting with the descriptions of couple types on pages 296–297, try to logically deduce the type of family (open, closed, or random; enmeshed or disengaged) that each couple type is most likely to produce. Is this a viable way to predict the evolution of a family? Why or why not?

OBSERVATION GUIDE

1. Write a brief paper describing the evolution of your own family. Start as far back as possible, relying on interviews with older members of your family (grandparents, great-aunts and -uncles, and so on). Try to determine which family themes have survived the generations and which ones have characterized each successive generation.

2. Observe different television families — single-parent, extended, nuclear, and blended (those created by adoption or remarriage). Look for common threads. Which commonalities are essential to the concept of "family" and which ones are just currently fashionable?

3. In the same vein as the previous activity, choose a fictitious television or film family and study several episodes of family interaction. Identify the family themes, regulative and constitutive rules, and other recurring communication patterns in evidence in the family and its subsystems. Compare the fictitious family with your own and other families you have known. Which themes, rules, boundaries, or patterns are unrealistic? Are TV families similar to or different from real ones? What expectations do

TV families engender in real ones? Are there any dangers in the depictions of families on television?

EXERCISES

1. a. Divide the class into several groups, varying in size from two to six. Each group will be a family unit for the duration of one week. Either the group or the instructor can decide who will play the roles of mother, father, oldest child, and so on. You may want to assign different ages to each of the children.

b. Once roles are determined, the "parents" should meet to discuss the values and rules that they want to use as guides to raising their children. At the same time, the siblings may meet and develop their own personas for the week.

c. Next, each "family" should meet as a group to plan two or three outings for the coming week. These may include trips to the park, shopping excursions, a family dinner. Plans should be tailored to fit the ages of the children. Childless couples will, of course, plan their own events. These outings should be planned and carried out during the week.

d. Parents should make the "rules" for the week clear to each of the children. Some parents may insist that a child phone one or both of them for permission to go out at night, for example. (The instructor may wish to set some ground rules to prevent abuse. For instance, role playing might be limited to specific hours of the school day.) In the spirit of the exercise, family members should reluctantly follow some of the rules they don't like and, on occasion, try to see what they can get away with.

e. Each family member should keep a journal of thoughts, feelings, and observations of communication in the family. A short paper might be required in which family structures, functions, identity, rules, decision-making style, and so on are evaluated and commented on. A class discussion at the end of the week should be enlightening.

2. Divide the class into seven groups. Each group is responsible for researching one of the stages in the family life cycle and making a ten-minute report to the rest of the class. Research could focus on identifying (1) the major issues in each stage, (2) typical communication patterns, and (3) the most common family problems. Groups can use skits, role-plays, and other audiovisual means for depicting family communication in each stage.

11

Intimate Relationships: Creating Dyadic Identities

A young man approached the instructor of his interpersonal communication class and revealed the following dilemma:

I've dated the same woman several times, and it seems like we've got a pretty good thing going. I mean, we talk about things pretty openly and we get along really well. But last week she stumped me. We were talking along and she said something about what a "goofy relationship" we have and then she laughed pretty hard. I asked her what she meant, and she said, "Oh, nothing, really; sometimes we just strike me as being funny together." For the life of me, I don't get it. If we really have such a good relationship, then I guess she's just joking and I should take it in stride. But maybe she's trying to tell me something. Maybe the so-called joke is her way of telling me she's not so hot on this relationship anymore. Should I believe what she says or what I think she means? I sure wish I knew.[1]

This young man's experience is not unique. At one time or another, most of us have been in a similar situation. We have faced those awkward moments in a relationship where we're not sure which carries more weight: the messages being exchanged at the moment or the definition of the relationship we thought we had prior to that exchange. As students of communication, we realize that relationships are constantly being defined and redefined through the communication process. We know that in the beginning of a relationship most of the messages we exchange are based on cultural scripts or limited knowledge of the other's social status and group memberships. To get to know someone on a personal level is a more complicated process.

In this chapter we want to explore how we move relationships away from the public level and toward the more personal. We'll begin by briefly examining how intimate relationships have evolved historically, then we'll define intimacy as we think of it today and its two major forms: friendships and romantic couples. Next we'll look at two ways these relationships can be created: through conscious planning and rational awareness of relational messages or through a slower, less conscious process of creating interdependence and other conditions for intimacy. Then we'll investigate the various ways people are attracted to one another over time, culminating in a review of the typical stages of development, maintenance, and decay in friendships and then in romantic relationships. We will also examine what it means to be communicatively competent in our close personal relationships. Finally, we'll consider two important communication skills that help us keep a close relationship together: managing conflict and stress.

Have People Always Had Intimate Relationships?

To even ask this question may seem puzzling to many. We feel certain that people, no matter what culture or century they lived in, must have always felt the basic human emotions of love, closeness, and sharing intimate secrets. How could it be otherwise? But historians have long known that what counts as love, intimacy, or closeness has varied significantly from one place and time to another. Howard Gadlin chronicled the changing meanings of "intimacy" from colonial America to the modern era. He noted that colonials thought of intimacy in terms of physical rather than psychological closeness.[2] Married couples interacted with one another in a way that we would find aloof and disconcerting. Richard Sennett tells us that in 18th-century Europe, people courted one another using a fixed system of ritualized lines. The same "phrases" were used from one affair to the next, as though they had no particular meaning for the specific partners involved.[3] Romantic

love, with its emphasis on knowing the innermost thoughts of a partner, seems clearly to have been an invention of the 19th century (see Box 11.1).

Communication theorist Timothy Stephen has speculated that the modern tendency to define close relationships as *jointly created worlds of shared meaning* would not have made sense in earlier eras where basic values, beliefs, and lifestyles were widely shared and men and women had distinctly different roles to play in society. Under those conditions, a relationship based on the creation of a "unique dyadic world" would likely have been seen as a threat to the stability of the social order. But as our society became more pluralistic, the need to choose among alternative value systems and self-identities has created the conditions for close relationships that serve as a bond for reinforcing those values and identities.[4] This brief look at the history of intimacy should help us realize that the types of relationships we value today have not always been so important to people. That realization should serve as a reminder that in the future, intimate relationships may take yet another historical turn. Let us keep that in mind as we examine the process of forming close relationships in our own time.

How Are Intimate Relationships Formed Today?

Intimate relationships normally begin just like any other social relationship — governed by rules and conventions of politeness, by the adoption by each person of a culturally provided face and line, and so on. But at a certain point these impersonal roles and rules are abandoned and replaced by a new, more personalized system of interaction. How does this happen? What are two people moving toward when they begin to create a private interpersonal relationship? Let's turn our attention to how private relationships develop.

DEFINING PRIVATE BONDS

In Chapter 2 we outlined how private bonds tend to differ from public ones in our culture (summarized in Table 2.1). It might help to think about each of the dimensions mentioned as *criteria* by which we judge a relationship to be more or less intimate. For instance, we said that private relations tend to place a greater emphasis on *who* the persons involved are (irreplaceable criterion), and on *how* they structure their everyday lives around shared activities (interdependence criterion), share more unique information about themselves (particularistic criterion), negotiate unique rules to guide their relationship rather than follow social norms (individualistic rules criterion), allow emotion and affection to play an important role in their interaction (sentimentality criterion), and finally, derive more rewards from the relationship itself as opposed to what the relationship can do for each person individually (intrinsic reward criterion).

We do not believe that every intimate relationship will fulfill all of these criteria or that the criteria represent some sort of ideal of intimacy. But we do conceptualize modern intimacy as exhibiting more of these criteria, more frequently, than public relationships do. For instance, people, such as members of a surgical team, who work together on tasks that are highly interdependent, may actually spend more hours in a day together than each spends with significant others. However, they probably wouldn't classify their work relationships as intimate unless they also exhibited several of the other criteria mentioned above. We can define **intimacy** in our own time as a unique bond created by two people through some combination of highly interdependent actions, individualized rules, and personal disclosures, and viewed by both parties as relatively affectionate, intrinsically rewarding, and irreplaceable.

A central feature of all relationships is that they are not static. Thus, an intimate relationship may be more or less interdependent or sentimental or individualistic from day to day, or even from moment to moment. In fact, many intimate relationships dissolve. In one study college students were asked to identify and report on their closest relationship. Nine months later, 42 percent of these close relationships had crumbled.[5] As for those relationships that do survive, we might even say that they are created and re-created by repetition of familiar episodes with consistent roles and rules. They may also be renegotiated and changed through the introduction of new episodes or modified roles and rules. For example, two friends constantly rebuild their relationship by engaging in favorite episodes such as "going to the movies," "cross-country skiing," or "exchanging recipes" with each other. A married couple may reaffirm their intimacy through regular episodes of "recounting the day's events" and "talking about future plans." Or they may increase their intimacy by adding some new episode such as "camping in the woods" to their repertoire. Or they may shift the basis of their intimacy. They may become more autonomous (he takes cooking classes and a separate vacation; she joins a fitness club and starts "bowling with the girls") and compensate by increasing the amount of self-disclosure with each other.

From these examples we should realize that an intimate relationship isn't something we make and then put on a shelf to look at and admire. Relationships are a lot like driving the same way to work or school every day. We know there are other routes, but we continue to follow the familiar path. In the same way, we keep rebuilding the same relationship day in and day out by engaging in the same familiar episodes. Intimate relationships, then, only seem stable to us because we repeatedly glue together the familiar parts (interacts, episodes, and so on) or replace them with new ones that are similar in some way. And frequently, they aren't very stable at all, as events signal

BOX **11.1**

Cupid's Shuttlecock: Individualism and Romantic Love in 19th-Century America

One of the most important developments in interpersonal relations during the 19th century was the rise of romantic love. In colonial times, love was considered a duty that often followed rather than preceded marriage; in the 19th century, love became a necessary condition for marriage. By the early 1800s, the heart was playing a large part in the formation and maintenance of intimate relationships. In *Searching the Heart,* Karen Lystra describes romantic love as it occurred in the 19th century and shows how falling in love depended on, and at the same time strengthened, an individual sense of self.

Prior to the 18th century, people tended to define themselves in terms of their social roles. Little attention was given to the personal qualities that made someone a unique individual; self-consciousness and emotional analysis were not encouraged. By the late 18th and early 19th centuries, people were beginning to define themselves quite differently. They believed that they had within them a romantic self — an inner identity that transcended social roles. The romantic self was a kind of "anti-role" consisting of what was left when all social conventions were stripped away.

Becoming aware of the romantic self was a necessary part of developing the individuality needed to adapt to modern society. Falling in love was one way of exploring and strengthening that self, for romantic love was related to self-examination and disclosure. Indeed, the single most important characteristic of romantic love was the pressure lovers felt to reveal themselves to one another. Lovers felt an obsessive need to unmask themselves — to share their true selves and real feelings. In many cases, this was an unfamiliar process, for people were not yet used to self-analysis. Nevertheless, writers of love letters constantly urged their partners to express inner feelings. As they responded to this demand, lovers learned to analyze their thoughts and emotions. In discussing one 19th-century lover, Lystra writes, "though he was not on a deliberate quest for personality, the process of romantic love . . . propelled him into a self-development that expanded his conscious interior life (37)."

The demand for self-disclosure was in many ways at odds with the outward self-restraint and moral seriousness demanded in the public sphere. The same people who refused to display any emotion in public expressed intense feelings in private. Love letters from the period show that

changes on some or all six of the dimensions of intimacy.

In our culture the most common types of intimate relationships tend to be romantic couples, friendships, and family members. In a study of college students' closest relationships, Ellen Berscheid and her colleagues found that nearly half identified a romantic relationship, while 36 percent nominated a friendship and 14 percent mentioned a relationship with a family member.[6] Since we discussed family relationships in the last chapter, we will devote most of this chapter to a discussion of friendships and romantic couples.

FRIENDSHIPS AND ROMANTIC RELATIONSHIPS

On the surface the differences between friendships and romantic relationships seem obvious. Rules for sexual behavior mark the distinction

falling in love was a highly emotional process involving self-criticism followed by tender reassurance. One partner would reveal faults and flaws ("I am mean, sometimes wickedly mean and unworthy of the pure love of yourself"), where-

upon the other would offer reassurances ("[you are] the most perfect and fascinating woman I have ever known.") Lystra believes these reassurances fostered partners' self-esteem, building a healthy sense of self.

Another characteristic of romantic love was a sense that lovers shared an identity. So strong was this identification, that lovers often described themselves as halves of a single whole. This mutual identification encouraged them to explore the personalities of those they loved and to develop an almost modern sense of empathy.

In the 19th century, lovers were highly emotional, and their letters showed extreme fluctuations between jealousy, despair, and joy. "I have been a shuttle-cock of Cupid ever since you left," says one 19th-century lover, "now writing in misery, now exultant with happiness." For most lovers, suffering authenticated love, making it deeper and truer. When apart, lovers would think constantly of their loved one, in ways that might seem obsessive to us today.

Romantic love fulfilled a unique function in the 19th century. To Victorians who felt adrift in the competitive world of urban capitalism, it offered security and affirmation. And by falling in love, people learned to explore and celebrate the individual self.

SOURCE: Karen Lystra, *Searching the Heart* (New York: Oxford University Press, 1989).

for some people. For others, mutual expressions of passionate love indicate romance, whereas friendship is based on strong liking or companionship. Others think of romance as short-lived, giving way to friendship if the relationship is to last. Try your own hand at defining the difference between friends and lovers. It's not as easy as you might think.

There probably are other, more subtle differences such as our expectations about where each type of relationship should fall on the six di-

mensions we've mentioned (how much sentiment should be expressed, how much and what type of interdependence is allowed, and so on). For example, some theorists argue that behavioral interdependence among friends is normally voluntary; they don't usually make demands on each other's time without asking first.[7] In a marriage such interdependence may be expected and even taken for granted. Thus, while both types of relationships may be considered intimate ones, they tend to differ in one major respect.

As relations develop over time, friendships tend to retain their voluntary nature, while romantic relationships show a tendency to build obligations and commitments into their bond.

Even within the same type of intimate relationship, such as marriages, we know that people work out their relationships in vastly different ways. For instance, any one intimate relationship might be characterized as highly irreplaceable, interdependent, and sentimental; moderately individualistic and intrinsic; not especially particularistic. In such a relationship neither person may be able to conceive of living with anyone else, even if one partner died. They may do almost everything together, from working in the same office to attending the same social events to going to bed at the same time. They may be very expressive in their affection for each other.

Or they may have both grown up in a subculture that dictated most of the rules for how partners are to relate to one another and thus developed only a few rules that are truly unique to their own relationship. They may also have been taught to marry the right kind of person for reasons of social status or economic security, and so they derive as many extrinsic rewards from the relationship as they do intrinsic ones. And finally, they may enjoy talking about topics that many of us would consider impersonal, such as world and civic events, the weather, and what's on television, so much so that they spend little time talking about and revealing private attitudes and feelings. And they may be very satisfied with their relationship.

INFLUENCES IN DEFINING INTIMACY

We have defined intimacy as a flexible concept, fluctuating along several dimensions of behavior and meaning. We have also seen that the meaning of intimacy changes from culture to culture, from family to family, and from time to time within cultures and families. Let's look at the influence of family and cultural messages on how we define our own intimate relationships.

Family Messages

In the last chapter we discussed some of the types of long-term relationships that couples develop. Such relationships are often influenced by family interaction patterns learned earlier in life. Thus, each of us may bring into a relationship quite different impressions of what intimacy means. Perhaps you can recall verbal or nonverbal messages you heard as a child that suggested to you what "ideal" relationships were like. These differing perceptions of intimacy no doubt influence how we come to define any current relationships.

Recent Cultural Messages

Likewise, our views of what intimate relationships should be like can be influenced by changing cultural messages. In a review of popular magazines from the 1950s to the early 1970s, Virginia Kidd chronicled a major shift in perceptions of and advice given about interpersonal relationships.[8] The 1950s and early 1960s vision of relationships was described by Kidd as a single standard of self-sacrifice and avoidance of conflict (Vision I). Every effort was made to keep your partner happy. This view eventually gave way to a second vision in the late 1960s, one in which self-sacrifice was replaced by self-fulfillment and conflict avoidance was replaced by a norm of open expression of feelings, friendly or hostile (Vision II). A follow-up study in 1993 by Diane Prusank, Robert Duran, and Dena DeLillo found that a third vision had made its way into women's magazines since the 1970s.[9] Vision III seems to suggest a middle-ground approach to the choice of self or other orientation by encouraging sensitivity, and negotiating when and how to be open while still protecting the partner's feelings. Couples are advised to schedule time for discussing different issues, such as how frequently to have sex and how to achieve equality in the relationship. Table 11.1 (page 318) identifies some of the major differences in these three visions.

THE CREATION OF INTIMATE RELATIONS

Some researchers believe that intimate relationships develop because, like the Marines, people are constantly looking for a few good ones. The process is portrayed as resembling shopping for a good pair of shoes. You keep trying pairs on until you find one that fits. This approach assumes that people are highly cognizant of their own behavior and the implications of their interactions with others. Other social scientists point out that intimate relations often seem to just happen and can't be predicted very well in advance. The conventional wisdom here is that you just never know when love is going to hit you. Furthermore, many relationships develop slowly, almost imperceptibly, mixing elements of both the personal and impersonal. Both views are probably true at times, since communication patterns and their meanings are often seen more clearly in retrospect.[10]

Planning for Intimacy

Some analyses of how intimate relations develop attribute a lot of strategic planning to the partners involved. Initial interactions are described as "auditions for friendship," and interactants are thought to be consciously evaluating each other's behavior in light of how well the other matches some ideal partner. In this view most of the communication between two newly-mets is in the form of testing the other's credentials for intimacy: "Are you my type?" "Do you measure up to my standards?" "Here, take this test. Let's see if you can pass it."

But how frequently or to what extent do we actually test the intimacy potential of a new relationship? Certainly we sometimes take stock of our lives and realize that our intimate relations are few and far between. First semester, freshman year may be one of those times. We meet dozens, even hundreds, of new people, only a few of whom will become close friends. We may be very conscious of how we select them and

they select us. Dating is another example of the kind of situation in which we may be highly aware of the potential of a relationship. We are taught to use the dating game as a means for finding the right person; it is not usually seen as an end in itself, an activity to be enjoyed outright. The cultural messages we receive may encourage us to be more aware of the process. In our culture the number of self-help books on achieving intimacy suggest that it is a prized possession. We may start to look at relationships as "commodities" — products to be purchased. If we adopt this view, we may indeed pay more attention to our shopping habits, making sure that we're good consumers of relationships.

In summary, there do seem to be occasions when we are highly aware of the intimacy potential of a new relationship. We may even plan encounters in advance, hoping that the relationship will move in the direction of intimacy. But there is no indication that we are always so conscious of where a relationship is going. In fact, many relationships survive for years on a relatively impersonal basis before they develop toward intimacy.

Conditions for Intimacy

Intimate relationships are not always planned; proposals are not always rehearsed. There is not always a pursuer and a pursued. But neither does an intimate relationship spring itself on the parties in full-fledged form. The development of such a relationship is part of the communication process. But for one reason or another, the partners involved have not perceived (or have ignored) the intimacy potential in the messages and activities they have shared. Researchers point to a number of factors that may be combined and either gradually or suddenly make us aware of a relationship's potential for intimacy.

One of these factors, **physical proximity,** simply increases the likelihood that two people will communicate more frequently with each other. This factor alone seldom leads to intimacy, unless there are few other people available

TABLE 11.1 A comparision of interpersonal ideologics in two eras		
Vision I **1950s–early 1960s**	**Vision II** **mid-1960s–early 1970s**	**Vision III** **mid-1970s–late 1980s**
SINGLE STANDARD is the norm for relational behavior, defined in terms of appropriate male-female behavior.	CHANGE is the norm for relational behavior; model marriage is a myth.	PREDICTABLE CHANGE is the norm for relational behavior; relationships go through phases.
Relational meanings are PRECONCEIVED.	Relational meanings are FLEXIBLE, negotiable.	Relational meanings are NEGOTIATED within certain boundaries.
Deviation from norms is akin to EMOTIONAL PROBLEMS.	Deviation from norms can be seen as CREATIVITY, a way to negotiate new types of relationships.	Deviation from norms reflects GROWTH of INDIVIDUAL SELVES; knowledge of own and other's self can help the relationship adapt to these changes.
Competence is creating an image resembling the cultural IDEAL.	Competence is OPENNESS; relationships are a way to express the unique self.	Competence is TAKING CARE OF THE RELATIONSHIP, balancing concern for self and others.
Major prescriptions for communication		
SELF-SACRIFICE — make others happy.	BE YOURSELF — express your own feelings.	FOCUS ON THE RELATIONSHIP — make it work through negotiation.
AVOID CONFLICT or causing discomfort; conflict is negative.	COMMUNICATE. Failure to communicate is negative; "Suffering is not the worst thing in life . . . indifference is."	SHARE YOUR FEELINGS, BUT SEEK PERMISSION FIRST. Draw boundaries around when and where to deal with conflict. Schedule time for it.
TOGETHERNESS. Simply being with each other is most important; "You won't even want a night out alone."	AUTONOMY. Togetherness is important as long as it doesn't interfere too much with own freedom.	EQUALITY. Couples achieve their own sense of balance in the relationship. This balance is defined by the couple, not easily understood by outsiders.

Adapted from two sources: Virginia Kidd, "Happily Ever After and Other Relationship Styles: Advice on Interpersonal Relations in Popular Magazines, 1951–1973," *Quarterly Journal of Speech* 61 (1975): 31–39; Diane Prusank, Robert Duran, and Dena DeLillo, "Interpersonal Relationships in Women's Magazines: Dating and Relating in the 1970s and 1980s," *Journal of Social and Personal Relationships* 10 (1993): 307–320.

for interaction. More often, proximity sets the stage for other factors to interact. Perhaps one of the most common and often overlooked sources that lays the groundwork for possible intimacy is the frequency of **shared episodes.**

An episode is shared when two people engage in an activity that neither could do alone. Thus, when two people work closely together, or go mountain-climbing together, or engage in any shared activity repeatedly, they increase their interdependence. At first, partners develop behavioral interdependence. Their initial investment is simply an exchange of coordinated behaviors. Harriet Braiker and Harold Kelley point out that the normal pattern of development in close relationships is a movement from (1) behavioral interdependence to (2) the creation of rules and norms for joint action to (3) interdependence in personal attitudes and characteristics.[11] This suggests that establishing behavioral synchrony, while it does not in any way guarantee intimacy, certainly paves the way for future development should it be desired or encouraged.

Earlier we mentioned that dating is usually seen as a precursor to a more serious relationship, although it could be viewed as an end in itself. Parents and teenagers often view the process differently. A teenager, seeing the date as just an activity, tells her parents not to worry, "It's nothing serious." The parent, perhaps intuitively recognizing the potential of such behavioral interdependence, admonishes, "Don't go out with anyone you wouldn't want to marry."

Other situational factors can influence movement toward intimacy. Times, places, and dates can affect how we feel and create what Mark Knapp calls a "state of **intimacy readiness.**" Valentine's Day, spring fever, and the senior year of high school or college all qualify as intimacy producers.[12] Likewise, finding yourself in a situation that is normally defined as intimate may induce feelings of intimacy. You go to a dance with several friends and acquaintances; as the evening wears on, most of your friends drift off, leaving you alone in the company of the only other person in your party — one who happens to make an attractive partner. Fate strikes

again — with consequences no one could have predicted. In these circumstances it doesn't matter so much who the partner is — what matters is that there is a partner. The relationship may be off and running before you've even had a chance to assess it.

Romantic feelings are another situational factor that influences movement toward intimacy, perhaps the most common factor in our culture. Most of us require that "falling in love" feeling before we legitimize a relationship as intimate. In their analysis of romantic love, Warren Shibles and Charles Zastrow identify three primary components: (1) an event that brings two people together, such as a date; (2) positive self-talk, an inner dialogue in which you convince yourself that the other is attractive; and (3) an emotional response or feeling of arousal (increased heart rate, nervous excitement, and so on).[13]

Interestingly, the absence of one component changes the nature of the feeling. Arousal and attraction without the event lead to romantic fantasies; the event and arousal without the attraction produce avoidance; the event and attraction but no arousal suggest friendship but not love; and so on. The most fascinating component, however, is the emotional response. A number of studies have demonstrated that any emotion, including love, consists of two things: physiological arousal and a cognitive label, such as love, hate, fear. The cognitive labels are produced by cultural and social definitions of the situation.[14] In one study, three groups of men experienced different levels of arousal before viewing videotapes of women they were told they would get to meet. Those who had higher levels of arousal were more attracted to beautiful women and more repulsed by less attractive women than those men who had been exposed to lower levels of arousal.[15]

Regardless of the type of intimate bond or our level of awareness about how it was created, researchers have long known that intimate relations rarely get off the ground without some form of attraction. People who find each other attractive communicate more frequently, giving

In intimate relationships, we do not always need a reason to be together.

(John Singer Sargent, *Paul Helleu Sketching with His Wife,* 1889)

their relationship the opportunity to develop in a more personal direction.

Interpersonal Attraction: Opening the Door

We may "like" a lot of people, that is, develop a positive impression of them through self-talk, without ever pursuing a more personal relation-

ship with them. In some cases this may be "liking from afar" (without any interaction to speak of); in other cases we may continue to interact with a person on a cultural or sociological level. Richard Sennett has referred to this type of interaction as **civility,** or "an activity which protects people from each other and yet allows them to enjoy each other's company."[16] We are likely to be attracted to a lot of people in this way. Many of the same factors that attract people to form civil, impersonal relations also lay the groundwork for more personal relationships should both partners desire to pursue one.

In fact, one theory of attraction suggests that we begin almost immediately to evaluate others as potential friends or romantic partners. From the entire pool of people we meet, we begin a process of "filtering out" those who have little potential and taking a closer look at those who show promise. Let's discuss this theory in more detail.

DUCK'S FILTERING THEORY OF ATTRACTION

Steven Duck's **filtering theory** of attraction explains when and how we use the verbal and nonverbal cues of others to determine their attractiveness as a relational partner. He suggests that people use a distinct and sequentially ordered set of criteria to evaluate each other's attractiveness.[17] We assess the attractiveness of a new acquaintance and of people we have known for some time differently. Attraction is determined by different criteria as a relationship moves in a more personal direction. These criteria act as filters, sifting out those people who are not likely to fit in one of our social circles. According to Duck the sequence of filters goes something like this: (1) sociological or incidental cues, (2) other pre-interaction cues, (3) interaction cues, and (4) cognitive cues.

Sociological or Incidental Cues

The first criterion of attraction is that people must have an opportunity to observe each other. Thus, such factors as the proximity of homes or work sites, the frequency of interaction, and the expectation of future encounters encourage the development of attraction.

Other Pre-Interaction Cues

Once we know that we're likely to meet a person again, we begin to scrutinize his or her behavior from afar. Physical cues such as height, weight, beauty, clothing, and other surrounding artifacts become useful as a basis for attraction. These cues may be used to infer the person's social status, income, and lifestyle. Perceptions of how similar or different we are may be inferred, but they are limited in scope. We may, however, use this information to determine whether we want to initiate a conversation and what topics of conversation might be appropriate.

Interaction Cues

Much more information becomes available to us once interaction begins. The topics of conversation we both enjoy, the length of time each person talks, smoothness of turn-taking, as well as duration of eye contact and interaction distance, may all be cues that help us determine liking. Some behaviors of the other may turn us off immediately, while others may take several interactions to evaluate. According to Duck the more we interact, the less important the sociological and pre-interaction cues will become as a basis for attraction.

Cognitive Cues

Eventually, interaction behaviors enable us to form impressions of the other's attitudes, beliefs, and personality. Once these are formed, attraction is more likely to be based on assessments of these cognitive characteristics than on group memberships, clothing, or specific behaviors.

INTERPERSONAL MAGNETS: FACTORS THAT PULL US TOGETHER AND PUSH US APART

The filtering process we have just described tells us how people assess attractiveness in a very general way. A lot of research has been conducted on more specific factors that draw people together and create attraction or repulsion between them. This research finds that people

are often attracted to each other for one or more of the following reasons: perceptions of physical beauty, important similarities, reciprocated liking, complementary needs, and anticipated costs or rewards. We will look briefly at what this research suggests about the interpersonal dance of approach-avoidance.

Physical Beauty

As filtering theory suggests, **physical beauty** is often the most important basis for attraction *initially*. In Chapter 3 we talked about physical appearance as a nonverbal code. We also noted that most cultures identify prototypes of male and female beauty, which influence our perceptions of physical attractiveness. This information suggests that we would most likely pursue relationships with those people we consider the most physically attractive. However, several research studies support a slightly different view, called the **matching hypothesis.** According to this research the decision to interact and pursue a more personal relationship is often based on

the perception that we are relative equals in terms of physical attractiveness.[18] Many people assume they don't have a chance with someone they think is better-looking than themselves. As a result we often evaluate the attractiveness of both self and other to see if we match up.

Similarity

How many times have you heard it said that "birds of a feather flock together" or that two people are "kindred spirits"? Common sense tells us that people are attracted to each other because they have key **similarities:** They like the same food, the same politics, and the same kind of people. They share many of the same personality traits. Most of the research that has tested the similarity hypothesis finds some measure of support for it.[19] Even so, a clear understanding of the relationship between similarity and attraction has been elusive. For all the ways that two people can be similar, there are just as many, if not more, differences between them. In fact, recent research suggests that the most important similarities related to attraction may be outside our awareness altogether.

Brant Burleson and his colleagues have found that similarities in cognitive complexity (see Chapter 6) are strongly related to attraction. In one study, married couples were much more similar in their levels of cognitive complexity than randomly generated pairs of males and females.[20] In the same study, the married couples were tested for similarity in their ability to accurately perceive the intentions of their partner during a discussion of a marital problem. Interestingly, couples who possessed similarly low skill levels were equally satisfied with their relationships as were the highly skilled couples. Burleson believes the results indicate that similar levels of cognitive and communicative ability lead to enjoyable interactions. For highly complex and skilled individuals, engaging in accurate and sensitive communication and feeling understood may be a good test of a valued relational ability. For less skilled individuals, concern about innermost feelings and nuances of meaning may be seen as "obsessive, boring, and hair-splitting." Similar results were found in studies of friends and dating partners, where similarity in value attached to emotional forms of communication (ego support, comforting, and conflict management) predicted attractiveness of partner and satisfaction with the relationship.[21]

Reciprocal Liking

We are often attracted to another person for the simple reason that he or she has demonstrated **reciprocal liking,** or an interest or observable liking for us first. Several studies confirm that expressed liking will usually be reciprocated.[22] If you think about it, it's only natural to like those who like us. After all, if someone is capable of recognizing what a wonderful person you are and enjoys *your* company, she must be a half-decent person herself. Likewise, the person whose face registers disgust when he sees you enter the room is likely to elicit the same response from you.

Some research shows that expressed liking may often be enough to offset initial perceptions of dissimilarity. Benjamin Broome found college students to be more attracted to a foreign student who was quoted as saying Americans were easy to get along with, well informed, and interesting to talk to.[23] In this case the expressed "liking" was for Americans in general; it wasn't even directed at the target.

While the reciprocal-liking hypothesis may seem natural, it doesn't always hold up. Under some conditions we tend not to respond positively to those who show liking for us. The basic premise of the reciprocal-liking hypothesis is that each person likes himself. If, however, a person has a negative self-image, he may have a hard time convincing himself that others really do like him and may view expressions of liking as polite insincerity. This may be called the Groucho Marx syndrome ("I wouldn't join a club that would have me for a member"). Such a person thinks there must be something *wrong* with someone who would like him. Also, the expression of liking must be situationally appropriate. If there is any indication that the behavior of the other is patronizing or manipulative in some way, we may not reciprocate.[24]

Complementary Needs

According to psychologist William Schutz, each of us has differing degrees of three basic interpersonal needs: inclusion, control, and affection.[25] As a relationship develops, the degree to which one person's needs match or **complement** the other's may make them more or less attractive to each other.

The **need for inclusion** refers to how strongly we desire to be in the presence of other people. Obviously, there are times when each of us wants to be alone, but some people may have a greater need for privacy. Schutz described such a person as an *undersocial.* Likewise, an *oversocial* person is one who seems to constantly need people around. This need takes two forms: (1) the need to include others in your own activities — a reaching out to others — and (2) the need to be included in activities initiated by others — as when others invite you to join their group or club. For a pair's inclusion needs to be complementary, they must be fairly similar.

The second interpersonal need, the **need for control,** refers to a characteristic desire to control the behavior of others or have others control our behavior. The person who likes to control others is called an *autocrat;* someone who prefers to let others decide is labeled an *abdicrat.* Control needs are complementary when one person likes to take charge and the other doesn't mind or actually prefers that someone else be in control. Since most people prefer to have some degree of control in their relationships, control needs often have to be worked out through negotiation.

Finally, people may differ in their **need for affection.** This refers to the degree to which an individual feels she must express affection or closeness to others or have others express affection for her. This differs from inclusion needs in that we may like to have a lot of people around us but feel no particular motivation to get very close to them. Or we may not care for the company of a lot of people but want to be very close to those few we do include in our social circle. Obviously, when two people's needs for affection differ greatly, they won't be able to fulfill those needs for each other. As a result, attraction may wane when such needs go unfulfilled over a long period of time.

Costs and Rewards

According to one perspective on attraction, people exchange resources as they interact. These resources are often referred to as relational currencies (see Chapter 9) and may be economic in nature (money, goods, services, and so on) or more or less *intimate* (time, friendship, love, and so on).[26] The outcome of any exchange of resources between two people can be viewed in terms of losses and gains. According to exchange theory, as interpersonal communication takes place, the ratio of costs to rewards derived by each person is a good predictor of how attracted each person will be to the relationship. One of the difficulties in testing this hypothesis has been identifying what communication behaviors and episodes are most rewarding or costly to a particular individual *prior* to interaction. It is still possible, of course, that people do base their attraction for one another on this kind of analysis, at least some of the time.

Other Sources of Attraction

Researchers are unlikely to ever identify all of the sources of attraction that bring people together. Attraction may be based on important qualities of conversation itself (above and be-

yond what it suggests about underlying similarities, complementary needs, and so on). We can only speculate that such factors as humor or witty repartee, nonverbal behavior reminiscent of a previous relationship, and a host of other idiosyncrasies may be frequent bases for attraction. It may be a good idea to try to identify the things that you find most attractive about the content and manner of *talk* experienced in the various relationships you have already established.

Remember that the factors we have isolated as leading to attraction aren't as static as they may sound. Interaction affects our perceptions of similarity, complementarity, costs and rewards, and so on. We create these factors *in talk.* We cannot overemphasize this fact. Two people may have similar needs, but unless they make each other aware of their similarities, there is no basis for attraction. Self-perception theory (see Chapter 7) suggests that we may communicate with others in such a way that we later determine we *must* like them. Some research confirms that this frequently happens when people disclose personal information to relative strangers.[27]

As we interact with people, we may discover a number of ways we are attracted to one another that could serve as a basis for developing a more personal relationship. Next we turn our attention to how relationship development typically takes place.

The Closer the Better: Revealing Self to Other

As the filtering theory of attraction suggests, being attracted to someone initially doesn't automatically move the relationship toward intimacy. Even though a person meets all the criteria for being an attractive "casual acquaintance" or "conversational partner," there may be little evidence that he or she would be "a good

TABLE 11.2 A comparision of two models of relationship development		
Friendship development (Rawlins)	**Stage**	**Romantic development (Knapp)**
Role-limited interaction	1	Initiating
Friendly relations	2	Experimenting
Moves toward friendship	3	Intensifying
Nascent friendship	4	Integrating
Stabilized friendship	5	Bonding
Waning friendship	6	Differentiating
—	7	Circumscribing
—	8	Stagnating
—	9	Avoiding
—	10	Terminating

Adapted from William K. Rawlins, "Friendship as a Communicative Achievement: A Theory and an Interpretive Analysis of Verbal Reports," unpublished dissertation, Temple University, 1981, and from Mark L. Knapp, *Interpersonal Communication and Human Relationships* (Boston: Allyn and Bacon, 1984).

friend" or "romantic partner." For relationships to move in the direction of intimacy, qualitatively different communication patterns must be initiated and repeated. Researchers studying these changes in communication generally refer to the development as occurring in stages. In this section we will describe the typical stages of relational development, first for friendships and then for romantic couples, paying close attention to the communication patterns that typify each stage. Table 11.2 offers a comparison between the stages of development for friends and the stages typical of romantic relationships.

STAGES OF DEVELOPMENT IN FRIENDSHIP

The study of friendship has been sorely neglected by social scientists — romantic relations seem to have garnered most of the attention.

Nonetheless, interest in how friendships take shape is increasing. One of the most comprehensive models of friendship development has been proposed by William Rawlins.[28] A typical friendship progresses through six stages: (1) role-limited interaction, (2) friendly relations, (3) moves toward friendship, (4) nascent friendship, (5) stabilized friendship, and (6) waning friendship.

Role-Limited Interaction

Friendships start out like any other relationship. Initial interactions are characterized by the adoption of social roles and rules such as those described in Chapter 7. We have described these as public interactions governed by the rules of civility. Although some friendships may be forged quickly as the result of participation in an unusual set of circumstances (for example, life-threatening situations or isolation from others), these are the exceptions.

Friendly Relations

As we indicated earlier, role interactions can be carried out in a number of ways. An adviser-advisee or employer-employee relationship may be characterized by businesslike attention to detail or may include overtones of positive sentiment. In completing a loan application, there is no *necessity* that banker and client exchange humorous anecdotes or friendly chit-chat. In many such situations the friendly behavior pattern is to be enjoyed in its own right; it is not necessarily an invitation to further friendship. Nonetheless, friendly relations do establish the groundwork for a potential friendship to be built.

Moves toward Friendship

When people interact in roles, their behavior is dictated by cultural rules and their reason for being together is "obligated" to a large extent. We would consider it rude and outrageous if a loan officer suddenly complained of being tired and cut short our banking transaction. Yet it is this very obligation of role playing that is a barrier to friendship and other intimate relations. Rawlins suggests that one of the fundamental defining elements of friendship is its voluntary nature. Friends may, with much greater success than the loan officer, complain of tiredness and be released from an ongoing activity. In the moves-toward-friendship stage, invitations to engage in episodes that are less role-bound are extended and voluntarily accepted. Many of these activities may be short in duration so neither party feels obligated to continue the interaction. Third parties may be included to avoid undue strain in these tentative explorations. Other activities may proceed in a kind of open-ended time frame. Since participation is voluntary, either party may decide when he or she

wants to conclude the episode; neither party has a right to place demands on the other's time. "Going to a movie with several others" is a good example of a short-term third-party episode. The possibility of extending the evening at a favorite watering hole typifies the open-ended time frame.

Qualitative changes also occur in the content of interactions during this stage. Rawlins' research indicates that people begin creating "jointly constructed views" of the world during this phase. Talk may initially focus on similarities in attitudes and values and gradually change to explorations of differences in opinions. When consensus results in the altering of viewpoints held prior to interaction, a jointly constructed view emerges. Friendship is often characterized by voluntarily spending time together and enjoying highly relaxed forms of nonverbal communication.

Nascent Friendship

Once moves toward friendship become repetitive, a pair may begin to think of themselves as "becoming friends." Friendship is crystallized in this stage. Significant changes in communication take place. Role interactions that once characterized the relationship are now seen as inappropriate. Rawlins refers to this as the development of "negative norms" — forms of communication that are now out of bounds. Even though the voluntary nature of friendship remains a constant feature, emerging friends often *choose* to participate in a wider range of activities and topics of conversation.

Stabilized Friendship

The establishment of friendship is rarely celebrated in our culture. There are few, if any, bonding rituals such as "becoming blood brothers." As a result, the bonds of friendship are often very fragile. Verbal legitimacy may be obtained by calling each other "friend," but the meaning of the term is weakened by overuse. Casual acquaintances often call each other friends, in spite of the fact that they know very little about each other. Immigrants to this country often have difficulty adjusting to how loosely we use the term. "I'm having 20 *friends* over for a party — why don't you join us?" is a real contradiction in terms for many non-natives.[29]

How, then, do we know when a relationship has become a stable friendship? Most writers emphasize the importance of developing trust. Obviously, trust doesn't just materialize at a single stage of relational development. The process unfolds slowly, involving two related types of behavior. **Trusting behavior** refers to any behavior that increases one person's vulnerability to another. Anyone who voluntarily enters a dangerous situation with another person or reveals very personal information to another is engaging in trusting behavior. Police officers routinely place themselves in the trust of their partners. **Trustworthy behavior** is a response to trusting behavior that protects the vulnerability of the other. A friend who lets a secret slip out to a third party has failed to exhibit trustworthy behavior. The development of trust is a delicate process and takes considerable time as friends expose their vulnerabilities one by one, often with extreme caution.

Another way that individuals maintain friendships is through assimilation of each other's attitudes and beliefs. In other words, we sometimes adjust our own beliefs to be more in line with those of our friend. One study, however, revealed a tendency in cross-sex friendships to estimate the other's opinion on an issue by assuming that they agree with us more than they really do.[30] This suggests that we may maintain stability under somewhat false pretenses.

Many people distinguish among types of friends or levels of friendship. Paul Wright differentiates *superficial* friendships, in which partners enjoy each other's company, from more *developed* friendships based on mutual concern and recognition of the other's uniqueness and irreplaceable qualities.[31] While researchers seldom agree about the precise number of levels of friendship, a common distinction is to differentiate among casual, close, and best friends. Casual friendships fall into the superficial category, while close and best friends would qualify as more developed relationships. People generally have several close friends but only one best friend.

Robert Hays asked college students to keep a daily record of their interactions with one close and one casual friend for a week. He found that close friends interacted more frequently, across a greater range of settings, and perceived their talk to be more exclusive and more emotionally supporting than did casual friends. Having fun and feeling relaxed with each other were strong predictors of relational progression.[32]

Suzanna Rose and Felicisima Serafica studied the strategies that different types of friends used to keep or end their relationships.[33] For casual friends frequent interaction was an important aspect of maintaining the relationship. A lack of interaction, whether by design or happenstance, seems to threaten such relationships. The maintenance of close and best friendships was more dependent on the quality of interaction, especially demonstrations of affection. Such relationships were more likely to end if arguments, betrayals, or boredom lowered the level of perceived affection. Interestingly, less frequent interaction was more threatening to close than to best friends. As one woman put it: "You have to work harder at a close friendship than a best one. It requires more effort. You can't take a close friend as much for granted."[34]

Waning Friendship

Like any relationship, a friendship does not maintain itself. It requires effort on each person's part to keep in touch and to explore new activities and interests. Friendships may begin to wane as a result of neglect, lack of support

Friendship is often characterized by voluntarily spending time together and enjoying highly relaxed forms of nonverbal communication.

from significant others, major violations of trust, deviance from important relational norms, competing demands on time, and a host of other possible factors. In terms of communication patterns, a waning friendship may be revealed by a growing increase in restraint where candor once existed and in autonomy where togetherness was once the rule. When this is undesirable, we should probably be concerned but avoid overreacting. Most friendships will go through periods like this. We all have friends who seem to disappear — no cards, no letters, no phone calls — only to resurface months later, fill us in on all the news, and go on as though there had been no interruption.

Many of the stages and communication patterns in friendship development are similar to those encountered in relations we define here as romantic couples — dating partners, spouses, long-term live-in partners. In fact, many couples describe themselves as "best friends" in addition to being romantically involved. Yet there are essential differences in the way romantic relationships develop and the communication patterns that constitute that development. We will look at these relationships next.

STAGES OF DEVELOPMENT IN ROMANTIC COUPLING

Romantic relationships progress in many of the same ways that friendships do, and the same issues of trust, candor-restraint, and autonomy-togetherness have to be worked out. Since we have already discussed many of these issues, our review of the stages of development for romantic pairs will be somewhat brief. We'll try to point out the major differences between relationships that are moving along a friendship trajectory as opposed to those on the romantic path.

Although many models of the development of romantic intimacy are available, we will use one of the more popular ones, developed by Mark Knapp.[35] Five stages depict the "process of coming together": initiating, experimenting, intensifying, integrating, and bonding. While these stages may not reflect the development of every romantic relationship, they do describe a typical path. Later we will look at the process of relationships coming apart.

Initiating

This stage is similar to the "role-limited interaction" stage of friendship. Communication at this point largely consists of greetings and other types of contact required by the situation. The first day on a new job or the first day of a new semester present us with numerous opportunities to initiate relationships. Communication is extremely stylized to allow people to interact with little knowledge of one another. Initial filters of attraction may be applied and judgments of communication competence made.

Experimenting

If a relationship survives the initial contact, the pair may continue to use standard formulas of interaction to engage in small talk. People who are skilled at initiating and maintaining conversations (see Chapter 4) manage relationships at this level quite competently. Small talk and other interaction rituals enable a person to present a desired self-image, form impressions of the other, and isolate similarities for further exploration. A norm of politeness rules these interactions.

For most of the 20th century, the experimenting phase has been the domain of males. It was generally assumed that a male would make the first move to initiate a date. (However, this was not the case in the 19th century. See Box 11.2 for an historical exception to the rule.) In today's climate of equality, of course, female-initiated dating has made a return. But with what results? In a recent study, 90 percent of the males questioned had been asked out on a first date by a female. In less than half the cases, however, was a second date initiated by the female. It appears that once a dating relationship begins, subsequent dates are either mutually negotiated or initiated by the male. In spite of that fact, males had positive perceptions of a female initiator (versus a woman who waited to be asked out or hinted to the man). The direct female initiator was perceived as more flexible, truthful, extroverted, more of a feminist, and more socially liberal.[36] The researchers speculated that the perception of the female-initiator as a feminist may change the nature of the script a male draws upon to guide actions on a first date.

Flirting is another interesting way in which both males and females experiment with relationship potential. However, flirting behavior is easily misinterpreted. This was illustrated in a study where students completed a questionnaire measuring their beliefs about flirting and were then shown one of eight different versions of a conversation between a male and female student waiting outside a professor's office. In four of the video segments, a male initiated the conversation and exhibited nonverbal cues characterized as "friendly," "flirting," "seductive," or "neutral." In the other four versions, a female initiated the conversation. No matter how intimate the nonverbal display, when the man initiated the conversation, he was rarely perceived as seductive or promiscuous. For the female, on the other hand, the mere fact that she initiated the conversation was enough for her to be perceived as "somewhat seductive." The authors concluded that perceptions of the female would probably be even stronger had the setting been in a bar or some other "marketplace" location.[37] Thus, flirting behavior, while clearly an option as a tool for experimenting, still appears to be problematic in terms of the gendered messages drawn from its occurrence.

Yet another strategy employed during the experimenting phase is the use of affinity-seeking "tests" designed to measure how well others like us and whether we should try to advance the relationship to the intensifying stage. Robert Bell and John Daly found seven classes of **affinity-seeking strategies** that people use to produce greater liking.[38] Table 11.3 summarizes these strategies. The use of such strategies points out how important our own communication behavior is in generating liking — a key ingredient if a relationship is to progress. The researchers also found that personality characteristics such as assertiveness, communication apprehension, and communicator style influenced which strategies people used and what degree of success they had. High self-monitors and highly assertive and responsive individuals were aware of more strategies and also used more strategies than most

BOX **11.2**

Playing the Dating Game: A Social History of Courtship

In every culture and in every age, people meet and fall in love. When it happens, it seems to be the most natural thing in the world. In reality, falling in love is not as personal and spontaneous as it appears to be; rather, it is part of a culturally constructed courtship system that is connected to social as well as individual concerns. In *From Front Porch to Back Seat,* Beth Bailey examines the history of this system in America and shows its connection to issues of power, money, and gender identity.

In the late 19th century conventional heterosexual courtship took the form of "calling." When a young woman reached marriageable age, she was allowed to receive male callers in her home, under the watchful eye of a chaperone. The entire calling system was controlled and regulated by women and took place in their sphere. Only if he were expressly invited by a young woman or her mother, was a young man allowed to pay a call. It was considered highly unsuitable for a man to force his attention on a lady by initiating contact.

By the mid-1920s an entirely new system of courtship — the date — had emerged. Although the word "date" was originally associated with prostitution (making a date was a code for buying sexual favors), it soon became an accepted term for a new courtship pattern. Couples who dated no longer sat together in the front parlor of a private home. They went out to theaters, restaurants, and dance halls. This move into the public sphere gave couples unprecedented freedom. It also transformed power relations between the sexes. Men, who controlled the public sphere, now controlled courtship, and women were forbidden to take the initiative. According to mid-20th-century advice manuals, girls who "usurped the right of boys to choose their own dates," who refused to respect "the time-honored custom of boys to take the first step," would "ruin a good dating career." Bailey argues this role-reversal occurred because "going out" cost money — men's money. Both men and women recognized that dating involved an economic exchange. A young man with lots of money could afford a beauty queen; a poorer man had to settle for a less attractive partner. Expensive flowers or fine restaurants were symbols that said "for the man, 'See what I can afford,' and for the woman, 'See how much I'm worth.'"

Bailey points out that the rise of dating coincided with the rise of consumption and competition as cultural ideals. Whereas courtship was about marriage, dating was about competition. Before World War II, American youth used dating

people, while people who were highly apprehensive about communicating had a very limited repertoire.

Intensifying

Most relationships don't move beyond initiating and experimenting. As in friendship,

intimates-to-be make overtures to each other that signal a new intensity to their interactions. Knapp notes a number of changes in verbal communication patterns: increased informality in forms of address, increased use of the pronouns we and us, the creation of private codes and verbal shortcuts, and so on. But these do not occur overnight. The process involves a good deal of testing. Affinity-seeking strategies,

as a way to demonstrate popularity and self-worth. One won the dating game by the number, variety, and quality of the dates one could get. While no girl wanted to date a "semigoon" or "spook," even an unappealing date was better than nothing. At dances, popularity was measured by the number of different partners one danced with. To be left with the same partner for more than one dance was a girl's worst nightmare and a source of embarrassment to her escort whose own worth fell if his date was not a sought-after commodity.

After World War II, couples began to value stable and safe relationships rather than conspicuous popularity. Nevertheless, competition was still involved. Young people felt great pressure to make the "best catch" possible. A 13-year-old who did not date was considered a "late bloomer," and by 15, teens were expected to have "steadies." The college woman who reached graduation without her MRS degree often felt her education had been wasted. No one wanted to be left behind in the marriage sweepstakes.

Regardless of whether young people went steady or dated multiple partners, the relations between the sexes remained the same. Girls were advised to demonstrate submissiveness, never to take the initiative, and to avoid seeming to be smarter than their boyfriends. As a teenage boy from Shaker Heights said, "I don't mind if a girl knows more than I do . . . I just like her to act like she knows a little less."

Today the values and assumptions associated with dating seem slightly ridiculous. Since the sexual and feminist revolutions courtship has changed dramatically. Modern relationships are characterized by more freedom and equality as well as by more uncertainty and complexity, as couples work out difficult issues of independence, control, and gender identity.

SOURCE: Beth L. Bailey, *From Front Porch to Back Seat: Courtship in Twentieth-Century America* (Baltimore: The Johns Hopkins University Press, 1988).

for instance, are subtle ways of indicating our own relationship-readiness, but to determine the feelings and perceptions of the other requires even greater subtlety. Research shows that talking about the state of a relationship is generally taboo, so people resort to more indirect tests. Leslie Baxter and William Wilmot call these "secret tests." Apparently, when a relationship has "romantic potential," partners rely most frequently on indirect suggestions, separation tests, endurance tests, and triangle tests.[39] **Indirect suggestions** include such things as jokingly referring to the relationship in more serious terms and flirting. This allows the initiator a chance to see how the other responds. If he or she takes it as a joke, things likely will remain at the more superficial level. **Separation tests** involve such things as not seeing the other for

TABLE 11.3 Affinity-seeking strategies		
Strategy type	**Sample strategies**	**Definition/example**
Control/visibility	Personal autonomy	Presents self as independent, free thinker
	Rewarding of association	Presents self as capable of rewarding other; give gifts
	Assumption of control	Takes charge of situations
	Dynamism	Acts lively and animated
	Presentation of interesting self	Presents self as someone interesting to know
	Physical attractiveness	Tries to look and dress as attractively as possible
Mutual trust	Trustworthiness	Presents self as honest and reliable
	Openness	Discloses personal information
Politeness	Conversational rule-keeping	Adheres closely to cultural rules for politeness.
	Concession of control	Allows target to assume control of relational activities
Concern/caring	Self-concept confirmation	Compliments, helps target feel good about self
	Elicitation of other's disclosure	Encourages other to talk about self
	Listening	Listens actively and attentively
	Supportiveness	Sides with target on issues
	Sensitivity	Acts in warm, empathic manner
	Altruism	Assists others in current activities; does favors; runs errands
Other involvement	Facilitation of enjoyment	Tries to maximize positiveness of interaction
	Inclusion of other	Includes target in own social groups
	Nonverbal immediacy	Signals interest in other through variety of nonverbal cues
Self-involvement	Self-inclusion	Arranges environment to come in closer contact
	Influence perceptions of closeness	Uses nicknames; talks about "us" to alter perceptions
Commonalities	Pointing out of similarities	Emphasizes things the two have in common
	Assumption of equality	Treats other as social equal; avoids one-up games, snobbery
	Comfortable self	Acts comfortable and relaxed around other

Based on Robert Bell and John Daly, "The Affinity-Seeking Function of Communication," *Communication Monographs* 51 (1984): 91–115.

brief or extended periods of time (to see if the other makes contact or seems to have missed us), whereas **endurance tests** increase the costs associated with the relationship to see if the other is willing to remain. Asking a person to go out of his or her way to do a favor is an example. Finally, **triangle tests** include going out with others to test for jealousy and mentioning someone else you think the other might be interested in to see his or her reaction.

James Tolhuizen also studied strategies that partners use to transform a casual dating relationship into a more serious and exclusive one.[40] While many of the same affinity-seeking strategies used during experimenting were also employed at this later stage, Tolhuizen found a greater tendency for partners to talk about and negotiate relational issues, to make direct requests for a more serious relationship, and to show affection through more casual touching, verbal expressions of affection, and increased sexual intimacy. Although there were very few gender differences, females did engage in more relational negotiation and more often waited for the male to press for greater commitment. In most situations the person who wanted a more serious relationship used a combination of strategies, usually coupled with increased contact or reward-giving.

Integrating

At this stage, partners in romantic couples begin to organize their everyday lives around each other. Interdependence becomes more and more visible to others. As with friendship, jointly constructed views of the world emerge, plans are made with the other in mind, and social circles begin to overlap. In fact, one study of romantic relationships demonstrated just how important communication with the other's social network is. Malcolm Parks and Mara Adelman interviewed 172 college students, asking how frequently they talked to their dating partner's family and friends and how much those people supported the relationship. Interviews three months later showed that those who were more involved with their dating partner's social network were more likely to still be dating. In addition, they also felt they had a better understanding of their partner's behavior, attitudes, and feelings.[41]

Integrating may occur in a number of other ways. Some people make small purchases together that become common property. Others may change some of their habits so they can spend more time together. For example, a divorced mother invites a potential stepfather to have dinner with her and her children. Integration can also be achieved symbolically. Leslie Baxter defines **relational symbols** as "concrete metacommunicative 'statements' about the abstract qualities of intimacy, caring solidarity. . . which the parties equate with their relationship."[42] She describes five types of symbols that couples often associate with their relational identity and how they are used:

- *Behavioral action symbols:* interaction rituals, games, nicknames, or inside jokes that are frequently and exclusively used by the couple

- *Events/times:* references to the first date, first kiss, or a particular weekend that holds significance for the couple

- *Physical objects:* gifts that signify important steps in the relationship

- *Symbolic places:* references to places that have special meaning

- *Symbolic cultural artifacts:* songs, books, or films the couple views as "their own"

Many of these relational symbols are used as integrating mechanisms to indicate the exclusivity of the relationship, seclusion from the outside world, shared activities, and growing intimacy. In short, they signal partners' integration as a couple.

Integrating the lives of two separate individuals is no easy task. The process is fraught with difficulties, and most relationships must endure a lot of conflict to survive this far. Many people find their differences are too significant to encourage further development. As a result, they terminate the relationship or reestablish a greater degree of independence and lessen the intensity of their involvement. For those who forge ahead, the role of interpersonal conflict is crucial. Social scientists are gradually learning the significance of conflict in the development of close relationships. Avoiding conflict may prevent people from discovering potentially rewarding aspects of a relationship. Overreacting to conflict or mishandling it can make continuing the relationship painful. Successful management of conflict often leads to greater understanding and commitment to a relationship.

Bonding

Once two people's lives have become intertwined to their mutual satisfaction, private commitments are often formalized. The bonding stage is really one that institutionalizes the relationship. At some point, the two parties have a serious discussion about their level of commitment to each other. Robert Fulghum calls this **covenant talk** — "two people working out what they want, what they believe, what they hope for each other."[43] While marrying, buying a house together, or making some other public commitment cements the bond and gives it a public image, Fulghum advises couples to pay more attention to their covenant talk because it's "the real wedding." Although the typical intimate relationship in our culture reaches the bonding stage by integrating two selves through reciprocated self-disclosures, this is not an absolute necessity. Close bonds are frequently created among members of sports teams, youth gangs, musical groups, and groups supporting some cause. These group members may feel bonded out of a sense of brotherhood or sister-

During the integration and bonding stages, friends and lovers signal the nature of their relationship to the world, often through nonverbal means.

(Pablo Picasso, *The Lovers*, 1923)

hood, as opposed to knowing very much about one another's personal feelings or psychological profiles. Some unique professional dyads, such as ice-skating duos, dancers, and trapeze artists, develop a kind of intimacy based more on complex behavioral interdependence than on knowledge of the psyche. Yet we would be hard-pressed to classify these relationships as simply based on sociological or cultural knowledge of each other.

Although relationships don't stop developing at this point, there is often a "honeymoon" period in which the emotional bond between two individuals seems to carry the day. This period rarely lasts very long, but let's hope it will last long enough for us to introduce the next section of the chapter.

Two Close for Comfort: Maintaining Identity in Intimate Relationships

Once the bonds of friendship or romance are viewed as a long-term involvement, a new issue comes into play. Partners must negotiate how each can reestablish a sense of identity and more clearly define the boundaries between the self and the relationship to promote harmony. In this section we'll focus on these issues, as well as examine the stages a deteriorating relationship passes through.

BALANCING SELF-IDENTITY AND RELATIONAL IDENTITY

When two people form a close relationship, they give much of themselves to it. Accommodations are made by both parties so that the new relationship can fit into their already busy lives. Other relationships may suffer from lack of attention, as may some personal pursuits. Obviously, what's given up is replaced by much that is new and exciting and that promises to offer future rewards. At the same time, the bonding process can frequently lead to a feeling of being engulfed by the relationship. Intimates, especially those who live together, spend many of their nonworking hours in close physical proximity. And for those who subscribe to the "openness in communication" school of thought, the psychological intimacy can be overwhelming. The self-identity can get lost in the shuffle.

How do people deal with the problem of investing themselves in an important relationship while maintaining a strong sense of self? This is probably the major issue in managing close relationships. Some people react by becoming virtually self-less, contributing most of their

energy to the relationship. Others place the emphasis on self-growth, maintaining close relationships so long as they don't stifle that growth.

Most of us, however, must learn to creatively manage the tension between self-identity and relational identity. Researchers characterize this tension in friendship as one of learning how to balance (1) the need to be expressive versus the need to be protective, (2) the need for autonomy versus the need for togetherness and (3) the need for predictability versus the need for novelty.[44] We think these three tensions are at the heart of long-term romantic relationships as well.

The Expressive-Protective Dialectic

When two people learn to trust each other, they're usually more willing to disclose both positive and negative personal information. The focus on trust reveals what William Rawlins calls **expressive-protective dialectic.** Friends share a desire to be expressive, to reveal personal thoughts and feelings. At the same time, however, too much openness may reveal areas of vulnerability. This leads to a need to be protective of each other's weaknesses. Protectiveness works in two ways. First, there is a need to protect the self. Each of us has vulnerabilities or old wounds we don't like to open. A relationship that extols the virtues of total openness may put undue stress on us. Second, we must be sensitive to similar vulnerabilities in our close friends. This means learning not to pry into certain areas.

Candor and restraint are both necessary to maintain a stable relationship. In fact, Rawlins argues, friends have to negotiate "necessary conditions for closeness." This tension is experienced on a topic-by-topic basis as friends and lovers decide which issues are ripe for candid disclosure and which are best handled with restraint.

The Autonomy-Togetherness Dialectic

This issue isn't limited to friendships, but it is an especially sensitive issue since the bond of friendship is such a voluntary one. The **autonomy-togetherness dialectic** states that friends must be careful not to assume that the other will automatically participate in any given activity. They cannot always take each other's time for granted. However, it's awkward to repeatedly ask each other about activities that we do together on a routine basis. The ability to balance this tension is the hallmark of good friendships. This tension also exists within romantic relationships. In fact, it may be more crucial because the amount of time spent together is usually much greater. Each partner in a relationship should realize that the more time they spend together, the greater the need for freedom is likely to become. And since no two people are alike, one partner may reach that threshold more quickly than the other.

These relational issues, themes, boundaries, and patterns are worked out by couples in much the same way that families work them out (see Chapter 10). In fact, our family of origin may contribute a great deal to what we see as the possible ways to work out these tensions.

The Novelty-Predictability Dialectic

A major aspect of developing a relationship is establishing regular patterns of interaction that the couple comes to view as distinctively its own. According to the **novelty-predictability dialectic,** over time, the relationship takes on a life of its own and partners become quite predictable to each other. With this level of predictability comes the risk of boredom or the feeling that the relationship has turned stale. In a study of this phenomenon, Leslie Baxter found that most couples prefer the basic nature of their relationship to remain predictable but would like their conversations and daily activities to reflect greater novelty.[45] "You never

surprise me anymore" is a good sign that the daily routine is too predictable.

Working Out Dialectic Tensions

Baxter also studied how couples managed these three strains in their relationships. She found that all three dialectics were present across the stages of a developing relationship. Couples managed these tensions by utilizing six different strategies:

- *Selection:* The couple opts for one of the extremes. You may recall from Chapter 10 that "separates" in married couples chose to spend much of their time apart (preferring autonomy over togetherness).

- *Cyclic alternation:* The couple cycles through periods of togetherness, followed by another period of autonomy (or cyles of highly predictable, then novel activities).

- *Topical segmentation:* The couple chooses autonomy or closedness in some activities, togetherness or openness in other arenas.

- *Moderation:* The couple might compromise or dilute both polar extremes. For instance, small talk that is open but superficial would dilute the pull toward either openness or closedness.

- *Disqualification:* The couple manages the tension through equivocal or indirect means, for example, by hinting at problems rather than discussing them openly.

- *Reframing:* The couple transforms the issue so that it is viewed as having a different level of meaning. Autonomy could be redefined as enhancing the time spent together (and no longer defined as the opposite of togetherness).

Baxter found that a majority of couples managed the autonomy-togetherness dialectic

The success of long-term relationships often depends on how well a couple works out basic relational dilemmas such as autonomy or togetherness.

through cyclic separation, while segmenting or moderating openness-closedness. Segmentation was also frequently applied to manage the predictability-novelty issue. Couples tried to introduce novelty at the level of their activities while maintaining predictability in talking about their relationship, remaining faithful, and so on. Couples also went through periods of interacting predictably, then introducing some novelty (cyclic alternation).

A lot of couples balance candor-restraint tensions, almost unconsciously, by mismanaging interpersonal perceptions. Partners buffer themselves by occasionally using ambiguous or tangential communication. For example, they often talk around the edges of an issue they disagree on. They may phrase their views in such a way that the other can interpret some agreement if so desired. As long as the issue isn't crucial to their everyday interaction, they can

engage in restraint. The success of long-term relationships often depends on how well a couple works out basic relational dilemmas such as autonomy or togetherness.

In an insightful review of research, Allan Sillars and Michael Scott identified several perceptual biases that develop and are reinforced in intimate relationships.[46] Specifically, they found that individuals in intimate relationships tend to (1) perceive their own relational communication (such as instigating conflict) as more positive than their partner does, (2) overestimate the similarity between their own and their partner's attitudes, (3) differ in their perceptions of who makes important family or relational decisions, and (4) describe relational problems in general rather than specific terms (for example, referring to each other's general traits rather than focusing on specific behaviors). These tendencies frequently lead intimates to blame each other for conflicts and to attribute their partner's behavior to personality traits, and their own behavior to situational factors.

Sillars and Scott offer some interesting explanations for these perceptual biases. For one, they argue that *familiarity* increases our confidence that we understand our partner's feelings and attitudes. This confidence, based initially on self-disclosures and efforts to understand, may soon expand to areas that haven't been so thoroughly investigated. Thus, we only *think* we understand each other. Mind reading, often referred to as a cardinal sin in interpersonal relating, may actually serve an important function from time to time.

Emotional involvement is also a leading candidate for perceptual bias according to Sillars and Scott. Intimates are at once each other's "most knowledgeable *and* least objective observer."[47] Overall, positive sentiment for one's partner may bias interpretation of messages in the direction of **assimilation,** or greater presumed agreement than actually exists. On the other hand, during periods of stress or conflict, messages may be interpreted on the basis of **contrast,** or greater presumed disagreement. Likewise, research indicates that when people experience emotional stress, their abilities to process information decline and they rely on more simplistic, stereotypic ways of thinking. Obviously, this can lead to perceptual biases.

When these tensions are not adequately balanced, relational maintenance becomes difficult. How, then, do we maintain close personal relationships? We do so by engaging in mundane, but ultimately significant daily routines with one another. We talk about nothing as though it were important, we anticipate and perform a request before the other has to ask it, or we read the Sunday papers without speaking. Sometimes, when these routines reflect too much togetherness or too much openness or too much predictabilty, we counter them by introducing or responding to behaviors that enhance the opposite poles of autonomy, closedness, or novelty. Sometimes, we intentionally or unintentionally misread or misunderstand one another in order to maintain the perception of agreement or balance in the relationship. And sometimes we are unable to keep the changes within the boundaries we desire and it becomes clear that the relationship is starting to decay.

Next we turn our attention to the stages that characterize this process of decline. As we describe these stages of coming apart, remember that they aren't necessarily irreversible. Relationships are frequently rebuilt after short periods of decay. Naturally, rebuilding becomes more difficult when deterioration is the result of long periods of neglect or extremely painful conflicts and violations of trust.

STAGES OF RELATIONSHIP DISSOLUTION

Mark Knapp's model of relational change includes five stages of deterioration: (1) differentiating, (2) circumscribing, (3) stagnating, (4) avoiding, and (5) terminating. Steve Duck describes the process a bit differently by focusing on the locus of action as it moves from the internal thoughts of a single person (*intrapsychic phase*) to interaction between the partners (*dyadic phase*) to announcements to the wider social network (*social* and *grave-dressing phases*).[48] In addition, new research demonstrates that the sequence of relationships coming apart as depicted by researchers fits very closely with the prototypic sequence of events that people associate with de-escalating relationships. James Honeycutt, James Cantrill, and Terre Allen found that individuals tend to agree on the rank order sequence of the 11 behaviors as indicative of a relationship coming apart (see Table 11.4).

Differentiating

When relational partners begin to remind each other that they are separate individuals and that

TABLE 11.4	Prototypic behaviors in de-escalating relationships	
Knapp's stage of deterioration	**Duck's phase of dissolution**	**Prototypic behaviors in de-escalation**
Differentiating		
Circumscribing	Intrapsychic	1. Stop expressing intimate feelings
	Dyadic	2. Disagree about attitudes, opinions
		3. Argue about little things
		4. Verbal fighting and antagonizing other
Stagnating	Social	5. Spend less time together
Avoiding		6. Avoid other in public settings
		7. Trial rejuvenation
		8. Talk about breaking up
		9. Become interested in others
		10. Start seeing others
Terminating	Grave dressing	11. Final breakup

Males ranked "arguing about little things" before "disagreeing about attitudes and opinions" and placed "spending less time together" before "verbal fighting."

Source: James Honeycutt, James Cantrill, and Terre Allen, "Memory Structures for Relational Decay: A Cognitive Test of Sequencing of De-escalating Actions and Stages," *Human Communication Research*, 1992, 18, 528–582.

they have other concerns besides their relationship, they have begun the process of differentiating. Often episodes of differentiating are triggered by seemingly innocuous events. A close friend — we'll call her Mary Ann Marker — described receiving a piece of junk mail shortly after her marriage to a man named Jones. The letter was addressed to "Mary A. Jones." At first she didn't realize who the letter was meant for. When reality sank in, she said, it almost destroyed her identity. She didn't know who she was. She promptly informed her husband that

she wanted to keep her maiden name. The emergence of two-career families, with the necessity of dealing with competing time constraints and goals, has made this stage more commonplace than it might once have been. This stage may be more accurately referred to as a stage of relational maintenance, since most intimate relationships cannot avoid periods of differentiating. Many couples may engage in a repetitive cycle of breaking up and making up, as partners move from bonding to differentiating, back to integration and bonding, and so on.

Circumscribing

Deterioration becomes more serious when intimates begin to restrict their communication with each other on a regular basis. This may occur as a result of major violations of trust or increasing uncertainty about the quality of the relationship. Sally Planalp and James Honeycutt studied events such as deception, changes in personality or values, competing relationships or extramarital affairs, and confidence betrayal — all events that increased uncertainty about the relationship. Over one-quarter of the relationships ended as a direct result of such an event. Another one-third felt that their relationship was never as close after the event took place.[49] Knapp indicates that conversations in this phase are shorter in duration, limited to safe topics for fear of touching a raw nerve, and almost totally devoid of any new self-disclosures. The only time a couple seems happy is when the partners are putting up a front for their friends.

Much of the dissolution of the relationship at this point can be internal to one partner. Steve Duck describes an *intra-psychic phase* in which one partner begins to doubt the other or finds him or her lacking in terms of relational performance. The partner considers the costs associated with withdrawing from the relationship as well as the positive benefits in pursuing alternative relationships before coming to the conclusion that he or she would be justified in breaking off the relationship. There may also be aspects of what Duck refers to as a *dyadic phase* of confrontation over relational transgressions or failures. The partners may make attempts at repair or reconciliation, which if successful result in a new commitment or bond. If these attempts are not successful, the parties may openly discuss their intentions to sever the relationship.

Stagnating

This stage is apparent when both members have developed such an expectation of unpleasant and unproductive talk that they feel there is little left to be said. Relationships that are based primarily on extrinsic rewards may continue for many months or years at this stage. While there is little interaction between partners at this stage, Duck indicates that some partners enter a more active *social phase* in which they initiate gossip and offer their respective accounts of the impending doom to select members of their social networks. By doing this, they signal to each other that the relationship is inevitably coming to its end.

Avoiding

Physical avoidance soon follows. The partners begin rearranging their lives to avoid the necessity of face-to-face interaction. Separate bedrooms, different work shifts, and trial separations are examples of the behavior characteristic of this stage. The pain of interaction simply isn't worth it anymore.

Terminating

The final stage of interaction prior to physically and psychologically leaving a relationship consists primarily of talk that prepares each person for the impending termination. Often situational factors are responsible for the death of a relationship, as when one party has to move to another city or a college senior has to leave friends behind. Even under these conditions, people frequently disassociate themselves from their friends a few weeks before the move is made. Presumably, this makes the actual termination easier.

Duck aptly defines this as a *grave-dressing phase.* Talk takes the form of emphasizing benefits of the future ("It's off to the real world. Several interviews. Things are looking great!") or denouncing the past ("I'm getting out of this stinkhole. Four years — what a waste!"). Post-

I wish that Stanley and I could like each ~~other~~ when we are together - But we don't.

Patty
Brann

The statement under the photograph — written by the woman pictured — aptly describes the situation.

Photo by Jim Goldberg

mortem retrospection can even be somewhat positive as partners take stock of what they once had, but this is usually tempered by the need for each partner to tell publicly his or her own version of the break-up story. Odds are high that each will claim responsibility for initiating the break-up and attribute significant blame to the other party.

Many organizations schedule "exit interviews" when their employees leave the company, in hopes of finding out why they quit and what can be done to prevent others from following the same course. This wise practice has not yet become routine in interpersonal relationships. Perhaps a few valuable lessons could be learned if we adopted such a policy.

Managing the stages of relational growth and decline calls for considerable communicative competence. Let's look more closely at how we can improve our competence in relationships.

Communicative Competence and Intimate Relations

Many scholars believe that our modern era has been dominated by an **ideology of intimacy,** although some think this may be changing.[50] Such an ideology implies that intimacy, or psychological closeness, is the yardstick by which we should measure all of our relationships. Relationships in which we have not yet shared personal information are often referred to as "mere" acquaintances or "superficial" relations, as though they have not progressed very far. We saw that ritual introductions to strangers can feel remarkably like "auditions for friendship." Our expectations for close friendships and romantic relations are so naturally tied to sharing intimacies that we often regard low levels of intimacy as indications of a stalled or failed relationship. The assumptions we make about intimate relationships will affect how we process information, play out our roles, establish goals, define the self, and construct messages. In turn, all of these communicative competencies will influence how a particular close relationship develops over time. Let's look at how intimacy and the various forms of communication competence are related.

INTIMACY AND INTERPRETIVE COMPETENCE

Interpretive competence involves our ability to pay attention to and integrate important contextual information such as social setting, time, appropriate relational prototypes and scripts, and so on. As this chapter has shown, friendships and romantic relations tend to develop in a somewhat scripted sequence of phases. Knowledge of these typical phases and ability to recognize relational message cues that signal potential for movement from one phase to the next are important components of interpretive competence. Perhaps the greatest indication of our perceptual competence is our ability to pick up subtle cues and attend to the feedback of the other. No one wants to be too obvious or to be seen as begging for a more intimate relationship. A classic case of perennial misreading of perceptual cues involves the characters of Sam and Diane from the sit-com *Cheers.* Despite their obvious attraction for one another, they work from very different prototypes of what an intimate relationship ought to be like. Sam expects an enjoyable physical relationship and a quick jaunt through the phases of relationship development. Diane, on the other hand, wants charm, wit, and intellectual stimulation to accompany their path to psychological intimacy. A good deal of the humor in the show was based on the reliable fact that each would interpret the other's "scripts for intimacy" as entirely the wrong way to do it.

INTIMACY AND ROLE COMPETENCE

The roles that we expect a friend, lover, or marriage partner to play and the roles that actually evolve in a relationship are often quite different. Gender roles obviously play a big part in close, heterosexual relations. Competence in this regard reflects our ability to adapt our roles to one another. Our culture creates expectations that gender roles in marriage, for instance, should be relatively equal in terms of who does the housework, gets the meals, and who is allotted free time for leisure pursuits. Yet in the vast majority of cases, even where they work outside the home, women still perform a disproportionate share of household duties while males assume and get more leisure time once the workday is completed.[51] The unresolved tensions surrounding such role definitions can be a real test for a close relationship. Likewise, role definitions in friendship can influence perceptions of intimacy. If one partner has a role expectation that a best friend will drop everything in order to attend to a friend's need and the other views being physically present as a voluntary act, role competence will not likely be displayed in the case of a minor crisis. In this way, role competence in relation to intimacy is not only relationship-specific, but may also be situation-specific. We can work to improve our role competence by talking about our expectations or deciphering each other's expectations from discussions about past relationships. We can also probe for reasons when a partner seems disappointed in us. Often disappointment is related to unfulfilled role expectations. Role negotiation is never easy in close relationships. The dialectic tensions discussed in this chapter reflect deep-seated role expectations about appropriate levels of autonomy, openness, and novelty in a relationship. Role competence requires an ability to recognize when a relationship is experiencing too much autonomy, for instance, and to respond with behaviors that will enhance togetherness.

INTIMACY AND SELF COMPETENCE

As we have already seen, the construction of a highly enmeshing relational identity can sometimes threaten our sense of self apart from the relationship. The fluctuations in sacrificing or empowering the self as seen in the transition from Vision I to Vision II type relationships (see Table 11.1) demonstrates how we have culturally dealt with this dilemma. With the emergence of Vision III in the late 1970s, we appear to have found a way out. By promoting both mutual self-development and working on the relationship as important goals, we try to enhance both rather than choose between them. Of course, these admirable goals are easier stated than achieved. The odds of maintaining or building self competence are enhanced when we choose relational partners who are similar to ourselves, especially in terms of social skills or cognitive complexity, as Burleson's research discussed earlier in the chapter suggests. However,

given our propensity for selecting partners on the basis of physical attractiveness or social approval of others, we may frequently place ourselves in relationships where the balance is harder to achieve.

The typical phases of relationship development and our modern emphasis on falling in love may also make things more difficult. While there is great pleasure in the feelings associated with romantic love, the high expectations of oneness, togetherness, and emotional arousal actually create the inevitably temporary honeymoon state. This letdown makes the reassertion of self interest appear as the first step down the road to dissolution. In fact, our tendency to view relationships as ever-changing (going through stages) while holding to a concept of self as essentially stable (the true self) may make us feel that we are compromising self every time we enter a relationship. Perhaps this explains why so many are afraid to commit themselves to a close relationship. Self competence cannot be viewed in isolation from the other elements of our model of competence.

INTIMACY AND GOAL COMPETENCE

Failure to identify specific relational goals is one reason why close relationships do not always turn out the way we would like. Knowing that we want a good or close relationship is often too ambiguous. The better we understand what we want out of a relationship, the more likely we are to translate the goal into effective messages. When we encounter a relational problem, such as a conflict or a serious transgression, our tendency is to focus first on what we need to *do* in order to manage the conflict or whether to reveal, conceal, or confront the other about the broken promise. Focusing too quickly on the message or action itself means we will probably do whatever we have done in the past in similar situations and usually involves a limited range of options and unpredictable or unsatisfactory outcomes.

Taking the time to ask ourselves what we want as an outcome can lead to more precise or more creative message choices. For instance, knowing how much and what kind of autonomy you want in a relationship helps you better decide which activities to pursue and which to decline. By not assessing your relational goals adequately, you may solve the immediate situation only to realize that what you really wanted was to redefine the relationship itself.

INTIMACY AND MESSAGE COMPETENCE

Clearly achieving intimacy is affected by the messages we intentionally and inadvertently use to entice, enthrall, manipulate, mollify, adulate, anger, help, or hurt one another. We demonstrate message competence when we express ourselves in ways that our relational partner can comprehend and that also reflect an understanding of the social situations, roles, goals, and desired self-images in which we carry out our relationship. In the *Cheers* episode involving Sam and Diane's first kiss, they both eventually size up their social situation and each other as simultaneously attractive and repulsive. They have to work with each other in an unequal role relationship, they assess each other's social backgrounds as inferior to their own, their self-concepts are opposite in many ways, and they have radically different goals for their lives. And yet, each finds the other to be fascinating, puzzling, and a real challenge to understand or perhaps conquer. In terms of message competence, they read specific nonverbal cues signalling attraction accurately enough, but have difficulty translating them into what the other sees as appropriate verbal and relational lines of action. In a scene where they confront their feelings for one another directly, Diane responds to Sam's question, "Don't you think we should kiss?" by psychoanalyzing. She comments that a relationship will never work if it starts out by one per-

son asking permission to kiss the other. Sam, unaware that his verbal message has already "ruined the moment," presses on: "Yeah, let's just skip the kiss and hit the sack."

Message competence depends a great deal on the other competencies, but does not necessarily follow from them. We may know exactly what needs to be done to repair a faltering relationship, for instance, but fail miserably due to our inabilty to find the right words or demonstrate nonverbally just how earnestly we want to change. How do we improve message competence in close relations? One way is to pay closer attention to our partner's reactions to the words and actions we already perform. We may discover emotional trigger words (or actions) that have predictably positive or negative effects. For those situations that can be anticipated, rehearsing what we want to say and imagining how the friend or partner might react can be helpful. Another way to improve our message making is to practice particular skills such as those discussed at the end of most chapters in this text.

Managing intimate relationships requires a variety of perceptual and communication skills. At the outset we must present ourselves in a favorable light and develop our repertoire of positive relational messages and affinity-seeking strategies. Through the subtle use of secret tests, we can better judge when to pursue a relationship and when it might be better to hold off. The relationships we do pursue can be integrated and solidified by developing meaningful relational symbols. As a relationship matures, we must carefully negotiate ways to handle the inevitable tensions of autonomy-togetherness, candor-restraint, and predictability-novelty. The maintenance of such relationships also depends on our ability to confront major problems that we are unable to handle through subtle hints and suggestions. This makes the management of conflict one of the most important communication skills for partners in an intimate relationship. We turn our attention now to this crucial skill.

Skill Building: Managing Interpersonal Conflict and Stress

Even in the best of relationships, we occasionally go through periods of conflict and stress. Conflicts are a normal and expected part of everyday life. While communication can't magically erase basic differences in values, goals, and expectations, it can help us manage relational problems if used realistically and skillfully. In this section we'll look at some rules for getting the most out of conflict. We'll consider what the positive aspects of interpersonal conflict are, discuss how conflict is often mismanaged, and look at how you should go about communicating during a conflict episode.

POSITIVE ASPECTS OF INTERPERSONAL CONFLICT

In general, **interpersonal conflict** occurs whenever goals are blocked. Interpersonal conflict occurs when the goals or actions of two people are incompatible, that is, whenever they cannot negotiate a mutually satisfactory outcome.[52] While conflicts can make us angry and irrational, they are not always bad. Well-managed conflict should be welcomed rather than avoided, for it can be healthy for a relationship. Here are several specific positive characteristics of conflict.

1. *Conflict means interdependence.* Conflict is a sign that two people are involved in each other's lives. If people were entirely autonomous, they could not experience conflict. The fact that people fight means that they still care.[53] While repeated conflict may be a sign of relational disintegration, fighting means a relationship has not entered the stagnation stage. When conflicts are successfully managed and resolved,

the aftermath is often an increase in cohesion — many partners feel closer after a well-managed conflict.

2. *Conflict signals a need for a change.* While change can be frightening because it disrupts familiar patterns, it can also be healthy. Without the ability to adapt, a system will eventually run down. Conflict is an opportunity to become more adaptable and creative. A productive conflict allows participants to find new ways of relating to each other.

3. *Conflict allows problem diagnosis.* Many people tend to deny rather than acknowledge problems. Overt conflict can provide information about mutual needs and expectations. It also acts as a safety valve by keeping problems from building up. A relationship in which no conflict ever occurs is unnatural. Its members may be engaging in unrealistic denial.

MISMANAGED CONFLICT

One of the reasons we fear conflict is that most of the time we manage it very badly. Let's look at some of the things we all do that make conflict destructive rather than productive. One way to mismanage conflict is to try to escape it. Individuals or couples undergoing intense conflict may sometimes experience "a mental paralysis which leads to no action at all."[54] They appear uninterested and unconcerned although they are really experiencing intense emotion. The ultimate outcome may be literal escape — the partners walk away from each other and allow the relationship to dissolve. While it may be inevitable that a relationship will end, escape doesn't give it a chance to succeed.

The opposite way of mismanaging conflict is by being too aggressive. Instead of ignoring the problem, the couple fights. While fighting isn't necessarily a bad thing, there are destructive ways to fight. George Bach and Peter Wyden discuss several.[55] One way to ensure that a fight will be harmful is to time it badly. Try not to begin a fight as your partner walks through the door after a busy day or right before dinner guests are scheduled to arrive. People should be prepared to deal with conflict; adequate time should be set aside for the process.

Fights should also be kept up-to-date. If a fight is continually postponed, it may get out of control when it does occur. Failing to confront problems as they crop up is known as **gunny-sacking.** It's as though you stick all of your grievances into an old gunnysack, which gets heavier and heavier until finally it bursts.

Gunnysacking can lead to another unfair tactic, **kitchen-sinking.** In a kitchen-sink fight every possible argument (everything but the kitchen sink) is thrown in. For example, Mary and Janet, two neighbors, may start arguing because Janet hit Mary's garbage cans while backing out of her driveway. In the course of the fight, however, they will use any weapon they can lay their hands on. Janet may call Mary a troublemaker, and Mary may counter by calling Janet selfish and reckless. Janet will then up the stakes by calling Mary's children names, and Mary may respond by insulting Janet's husband. And so on. Before long, the original topic has been forgotten; the goal now is to draw as much blood as possible.

Another unfair tactic mentioned by Bach and Wyden is labeling, or **stereotyping.** If Janet were to say to Mary, "Of course you're inconsiderate. New Yorkers always are," she would be guilty of stereotyping, a practice that will only lead to more conflict.

EFFECTIVE FEEDBACK DURING CONFLICT

Simply avoiding negative tactics is not enough. To manage a conflict successfully, you should also express yourself clearly and directly, letting the other person know exactly what you are feeling. In the skill-building sections of both Chapters 3 and 4, we stressed how important it is to know your own feelings and express them

directly and clearly. Here we offer some specific guidelines for feedback during conflict.[56]

1. *Own your own message.* Let's say you are extremely annoyed with your mate over his or her failure to cut the grass. Instead of working in the yard as promised, your partner has settled down in front of the TV to watch roller derby. Which of the following is the best way to bring up your feelings? Should you say, "You know, it doesn't really bother me, but the neighbors are beginning to complain. Everyone on the block thinks the grass is too high"? Or should you say, "I'm angry. You promised to cut the grass, but you haven't done it"?

If you're the one who is angry, it is dishonest to attribute the anger to someone else. Besides, telling someone that "everyone" agrees that he or she is inadequate leaves that person feeling defensive and helpless.

2. *Don't apologize for your feelings.* If you keep apologizing, you put all the blame on yourself. Would you take the following comment seriously? "I'm sorry, I hate to bring this up, and I probably have no right to feel this way, but it kind of bothers me when you talk like that."

3. *Make your messages specific and behavioral.* Your partner needs to know exactly what is upsetting you. Of the following two statements, which is best? "I think you've got a really rotten attitude" or "You just interrupted me. It makes me angry because I feel that you aren't interested in hearing what I have to say." Most experts agree the second gives more information and is therefore more helpful. Changing one's entire attitude is a pretty tall order; being careful not to interrupt is a much easier task. Often people simply don't realize they've been doing something offensive, and they are happy to change when they get specific feedback.

4. *Make sure your verbal and nonverbal messages match.* If you try to appear calm and controlled while telling someone how angry you are, you are sending a mixed message. Similarly, if you use sarcasm to express your feelings, you disconfirm your partner. "I just love it when you do that" said in a sarcastic and biting tone is confusing and ineffective feedback.

5. *Avoid evaluating and interpreting your partner.* What can someone do in response to a statement like "You are just about the most egotistical, narcissistic person I've ever met"? Very little, except to feel inadequate and insulted. Instead of describing a behavior, you have attacked a person.

CONFLICT CONTAINMENT

When conflict gets too large, it spins out of control. One way to keep it manageable is by **fractionating,** or breaking it up into small, easily managed units. Trying to change everything overnight isn't the answer. Working on one small thing at a time is.[57] Let's say you're in one of those momentary states when everything looks bad, when you hate your entire life. Try to fractionate your feelings. If you find out that you dislike your job, hate your neighborhood, and are less than thrilled with your social life, work on these problems one at a time. If you and your boss aren't getting along, sit down and try to list your grievances in simple, behavioral terms. Now you have an idea of where to begin. Through a process of negotiation, you may be able to reach agreement about how to resolve your conflict.

One technique that helps in fractionating is **negative inquiry.**[58] If your boss tells you she's unhappy with your performance, instead of becoming defensive, try asking for as much information as possible. Say something like "Could you tell me exactly what I'm doing that is below standard?" After she responds, go one step further: "Is there anything else you can think of? Are there other things I could do to improve my performance?" You show your willingness to improve and you gather useful information at the same time.

It's also important to plan your approach to conflict and to analyze each conflict after the fact. Conflicts are usually stressful, and we know that under stress our thinking becomes very simplistic and stereotypic. That's why you should evaluate conflict strategies when your thinking is clearest.

There is no magic cure for relational problems, but there are ways to manage them more effectively. In this chapter we've emphasized the positive aspects of conflict and we've looked at some of the things that can go wrong when our communication gets out of control. In the skill-building section at the end of the next chapter, we'll return to this topic. We'll give you some hints on how to choose an appropriate conflict style and how to improve your negotiating skills.

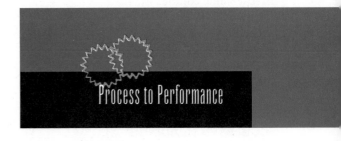

Process to Performance

REVIEW TERMS

The following is a list of major concepts introduced in this chapter. The page where the concept is first mentioned is listed in parentheses.

intimacy (313)
physical proximity (317)
shared episodes (319)
intimacy readiness (319)
romantic feelings (319)
civility (320)
filtering theory (321)
physical beauty (322)
matching hypothesis (322)
similarity (322)

reciprocal liking   (323)
complementary needs   (323)
need for inclusion   (323)
need for control   (323)
need for affection   (324)
trusting behavior   (327)
trustworthy behavior   (327)
affinity-seeking strategies   (329)
indirect suggestions   (331)
separation tests   (331)
endurance tests   (333)
triangle tests   (333)
relational symbols   (333)
covenant talk   (334)
expressive-protective dialectic   (335)
autonomy-togetherness dialectic   (336)
novelty-predictability dialectic   (336)
assimilation   (338)
contrast   (338)
ideology of intimacy   (342)
interpersonal conflict   (345)
gunnysacking   (346)
kitchen-sinking   (346)
stereotyping   (346)
fractionating   (347)
negative inquiry   (347)

SUGGESTED READINGS

Cupach, William, and Brian Spitzberg, eds. *The Dark Side of Interpersonal Communication.* Hillsdale, N.J.: Lawrence Erlbaum, 1994. This volume investigates the mysterious and seedy underworld of interpersonal communication. Topics range from messages that hurt to relational transgressions to physical and psychological abuse. Also included are chapters on deception, parental privacy invasions, and the dark side of "normal" family interaction.

Rubin, Lillian B. *Intimate Strangers: Men and Women Together.* New York: Harper & Row, 1983. This intriguing book is a compilation of case study interviews conducted by the author. Using a combination of cultural

factors and psychoanalytic theory, Rubin offers a fascinating explanation for why male-female relationships are difficult to manage. Differing male and female perceptions of intimacy are explored in detail.

TOPICS FOR DISCUSSION

1. Discuss the intimate relationships that you most admire. These may range from those of parents to friends to those depicted in novels or films. Of course, be sure to evaluate the "reality" of any fictional relationships you discuss.

2. To what extent do you think people plan for intimacy or just respond to conditions for intimacy? Do you find yourself using initial interactions as auditions for friendship? If so, what do you look for? What tests or experiments do you use to discover intimacy potential? What risks are involved?

3. Is involvement in a friendship as voluntary as Rawlins suggests? If so, are voluntary activities a major distinction between friendships and romantic relationships? What other differences in communication distinguish friends from intimate couples?

4. When are people most likely to be in what Knapp calls a state of intimacy readiness?

5. How can we best resolve the contrary notions that "birds of a feather flock together" and "opposites attract"?

6. What sources of attraction, other than those mentioned in the chapter, can you identify? Using filtering theory as a guide, when do you think each of the sources of attraction you've identified, plus those in the chapter, are most salient?

OBSERVATION GUIDE

1. Choose a close friend or romantic partner and enlist his or her cooperation in observing your communication together. Tape record or write out in dialogue form some of your conversations. If you write them down, do so as soon as possible after the conversation occurs, making sure you both agree about the substance of the conversation. Try to record the language used as accurately as possible. When you have recorded two or three conversations, analyze them in order to determine (1) what stage the relationship appears to be in, identifying specific communication behaviors as support, and (2) what communication behaviors tend to maintain the relationship in that stage or encourage further development or differentiation.

2. Keep a journal for one week and record examples of how you handle the three dialectic tensions (expressiveness versus protectiveness, autonomy versus togetherness, and predictability versus novelty) in each of several important and intimate relationships. Review these entries at the end of the week and ask yourself whether you handled them successfully. Write down some things you could have said or done to improve your management of these three tensions.

EXERCISES

1. Bring to class as many examples of cultural messages about attraction and ideal images of intimate relationships as you can find. These can include magazine and television advertisements, personal advice columns or talk shows, music videos or lyrics. In small groups take some of these examples and rewrite or revise them to fit Vision I of Virginia Kidd's relational ideals (see Table 11.1). What other visions are possible? Create ads or responses to advice column questions that would reflect these different visions. Talk about ways to evaluate and respond to cultural messages.

2. Your instructor will give you a copy of William Schutz's FIRO-B scale to complete before coming to class. This scale measures the interpersonal needs for control, inclusion, and affection. In class your instructor will create several dyads, some pairing people with very different scores on the different needs, others pairing people who are similar on one need or another. Role-play the situations below assuming that you and your partner have an intimate relationship:

a. deciding whether to establish separate or joint checking accounts

b. establishing rules for when and how often nights out with the "guys" or "girls" will be allowed

c. deciding what forms of public displays of affection you should engage in

You may think of other situations as well. Then discuss as a class the impact of interpersonal needs, complementarity, similarity, and the negotiation of differences in needs.

Work relationships are an important part of our interpersonal worlds. Without open communication, we can feel alienated and alone.

(Edward Hopper, *Office at Night,* 1940)

Professional Relationships: Communicating with Colleagues and Other Strangers

"Let's do lunch" can be dangerous. At least it was for Peter G. Peterson, Lewis Glucksman, and Wall Street's oldest continuing investment banking partnership, Lehman Brothers Kuhn Loeb. The story that follows, condensed from a *New York Times Magazine* article by Ken Auletta, demonstrates the severe consequences when executives fail to maintain civil relations and resort to ineffective means of communication.[1] Peterson and Glucksman were co-chief executive officers at Lehman Brothers, Peterson having elevated Glucksman to be his peer only a few weeks prior to the disastrous luncheon. Peterson was proud of the fact that he had made an executive out of the rough-edged Glucksman.

Their differences were notable. Peterson was Ivy League, knew the Washington elite, and had been a successful executive with several other companies. He knew how to move among the upper crust. Glucksman, on the other hand, had worked his way up the corporate ladder over 21 years with the firm. He put in long hours and

was a visible manager of the everyday affairs of the company. He took care of the inside; Peterson dealt with the outside clientele. Glucksman had come from a lower-middle-class family and resented what he thought was Peterson's snobbish, condescending attitude.

At the heart of their problem was a shared dislike for each other's role in the company. Glucksman was a "trader," Peterson a "banker." In the investment business a trader buys and sells securities and must think fast and make firm decisions. A banker enjoys the luxury of a more relaxed, longer-term view of the business, advising clients, setting up mergers, and so on. Bankers refer to "lowly traders," while traders think of bankers as "haughty." Neither is very fond of the other, but both are needed for the business to function.

Things came to a head at a luncheon where Peterson was asked to make a presentation. Peterson arranged for Glucksman to be invited also. But at the luncheon Peterson was seated at the head of the table, next to the host. Glucksman was relegated to an inconspicuous side seat, which made him irate. Further irritated by what he considered to be a name-dropping presentation, Glucksman began making noisy distractions with his silverware and the movement of his chair. To make matters worse, Peterson tried to include Glucksman in the presentation, and Glucksman responded by talking for several minutes, angering Peterson.

Glucksman reportedly left the luncheon in a rage, determined to oust Peterson. He was successful because of his support from company insiders. But ten months later, the company was faltering so badly that it had to be sold. The fall of Lehman Brothers was complete.

Why would two extremely capable executives let the friction between them ruin their company? Why couldn't they come to terms with their differences and respect each other's efforts? How often does this kind of problem lurk behind the mergers, failures, and losses of companies we read about every day? We hope that your own professional pursuits do not come to such bitter ends. And while we can't promise to provide you with infallible means of communication, we do think that this chapter will help you understand the world of public, or professional interpersonal communication a little better. Here you will find research and suggestions on communicating in everyday social transactions, in professional dyads, in small work groups, and across the organizational chart.

Interpersonal Communication in Public Situations

In Chapter 2 we argued against the developmental view of interpersonal communication because it limits the kinds of relationships we should be concerned with. This view encourages us to focus exclusively on more intimate rela-

tionships, where psychological-level rules are used to interpret and react to message exchanges. As we said earlier, only a handful of our relationships can be considered friendships or intimate relations. We simply don't have the time or the need to develop every relationship into an intimate one. This means that most of our relationships remain in the impersonal, public sector of social interaction. To better understand how public interpersonal situations work, let's consider a little history on the subject. Then we'll examine who participates in public and professional situations, and what criteria might exist for measuring success in such interactions.

THE PUBLIC REALM IN HISTORY

The public realm of impersonal roles and civil communication has been a far more important place in other historical periods than it seems to be today. As we have already seen, earlier eras were less individualistic and more communal (Chapter 8). Public spaces were designed for interaction of the people. The 15th-century Italian architect Leon Battista Alberti wrote, "The People, by thus meeting frequently together at publick Feasts, might grow more humane, and be closer linked in Friendship one with another. So I imagined our Ancesters instituted publick Shows in the City, not so much for the Sake of Diversions themselves as for their Usefulness."[2] Public life in the Rennaisance and throughout much of history was highly "theatrical" and intended to result in feelings of benevolence, goodwill, expansiveness, jubilation, generosity of spirit.[3]

In fact, the rising influence of print in the 18th century was seen as a threat to public discourse. Because reading meant spending time in isolation from others, it was not uncommon to hear diatribes against mad, fantasizing writers and readers. Historian Warren Leland believes this anxiety that reading and writing might minimize the significance of oral discourse led to an ironic explosion between 1650 and 1800 of more than 200 essays, manuals, and books urging a more conscious use of conversation.[4] When performed correctly, conversation was seen as a sifter of Truth. One writer noted that "The primitive and literal Sense of this Word [conversation] is. . . to *Turn round together*; and in its more copious Usage we intend by it, that reciprocal Interchange of Ideas, by which Truth is examined, Things are, in a manner, *turned round,* and sifted, and all our Knowledge communicated to each other."[5] The assumption, now challenged by modern communication theory, was that language contained the Truth, and that in speaking, the Truth would win out. Certainly, the American Revolution was sparked by much oral debate among ordinary citizens. But too much solitary reflection or private, nonpublic discourse raised the threat that fantasy would obscure the Truth. Conversation performed without care could be equally harmful. The 17th century witnessed the rise of coffeehouses and salons in France and England devoted almost exclusively to the practice of public conversation. Of course, the next three centuries observed the slow evolution of a private sphere, first within the home and later within the self-concepts of persons themselves. With that evolution, private forms of conversation began to dominate. Today, the public sphere has receded in importance to the point where there are fewer and fewer public spaces where serious conversation among strangers or acquaintances is likely to take place. Nonetheless, truncated forms of public communication do still exist in our neighborhoods, workplaces, and via the ever increasing numbers of interactive electronic media (as you may recall from Box 2.1 and Box 5.2).

PARTICIPANTS IN PUBLIC INTERACTIONS

The list of public relationships today includes all your casual acquaintances; the neighbors with the picket fence; those crazy coworkers at the factory; your egotistic supervisor; representatives of your friendly federal, state, and local governments; your barber or hair-care professional; the clerks who sell you shoes, clothing, groceries, and lottery tickets; your doctor, dentist, and lawyer; as well as the dozens of total strangers you encounter every day. Now, you may feel that your interactions with these people are inconsequential and not worth the time it takes to read this chapter. If so, we urge you to reconsider, and we encourage you to think about some of the basic considerations in any public interpersonal situation.

CRITERIA FOR MANAGING PUBLIC INTERACTIONS

To make public situations work, people invent standardized ways to interact without feeling too uncertain, investing too much of their private selves in the transaction, or disrupting the social order of things. We have identified the following criteria that seem to govern public interactions: (1) The interaction should involve appropriate roles and scripts; (2) interactants should be respectful of each other; (3) interactions should enable both participants to achieve their practical goals; and (4) interactions should allow some room for the expressive behavior of individuals.

Enacting Roles and Scripts

Becoming personally familiar with every sales clerk, stockboy, or cashier we encounter would be impracticable and inefficient. To save time, protect our privacy, and make social interaction more predictable, members of our culture have worked out scripts and roles for most conceivable public interactions. Recall that a script (discussed in Chapter 6) is a highly predictable sequence of behaviors or events; it tells us what should happen next in a given situation. Roles (discussed in Chapter 7) define the expectations each person has of the other; they tell us who

Showing respect for one another has been the hallmark of civil relations in cultures the world over.

(Paul Klee, *Two Men Meet, Each Believing the Other to Be of Higher Rank,* 1903)

should perform each part of the script. A cashier would be baffled if you offered to pay for a shirt you had not yet picked out (because you messed up the sequencing of the script). Likewise, you cannot ask the sales clerk to "try the shirt on and see if it fits" (because that's not part of the sales clerk's role). Any interaction is more difficult when you don't know the roles or the lines of action, but public interactions are virtually impossible without them.

Showing and Deserving Respect

Even though our private lives are shielded from those we interact with in public encounters, we are still people and not simply automatons. In fact, the hallmark of social interaction is the giving and receiving of respect. Rom Harre, a noted social psychologist, argues that "the deepest human motive is to seek the respect of others."[6] Role interactions can become dehumanizing for one or both persons involved, but

they need not. Very few social roles are designed to belittle those who play them. The problem usually arises because people don't understand the complementary nature of social roles — for example, no one can properly be identified as a doctor without having patients. Likewise, role interactions may go bad when a culture develops a misguided sense of individualism. According to some observers our culture has been experiencing a long-term trend toward narcissism — a kind of self-interest that devalues any relationship that doesn't help a person get in touch with the private, personal self.[7] When this happens, a large portion of the social world (strangers and casual acquaintances) becomes unimportant to us, unless we can quickly transform them into intimates. The result is a lack of respect for the vast majority of people we come into contact with.

When social roles are properly valued, respect is achieved by the use of some subtle social mechanisms. Erving Goffman has identified two such mechanisms that help people maintain deference or respect: avoidance rituals and presentational rituals. He has also shown that in order to be worthy of the respect of others, a person must show proper demeanor.[8]

Avoidance Rituals   People show respect by purposely allowing one another the right to privacy. **Avoidance rituals** refer to the cultural norms for appropriate personal distance as discussed in Chapter 3. You may have experienced discomfort when an overeager salesperson pounces on you as you enter a store and hovers too close, even though you protest, "I'm just looking, thanks." Another avoidance ritual is the use of formal titles and surnames rather than first names, a sign of respect that many fear is disappearing from the American sense of etiquette. Younger people seem to prefer the informality of first names and associate the use of formal address with snobbery or aloofness. Older Americans, on the other hand, are often offended at such familiarity. Can you think of other ways that people avoid trespassing on one another's privacy? Which ones do you think are most acceptable today?

Presentational Rituals   Avoidance rituals show respect by identifying out-of-bounds role behavior. **Presentational rituals,** according to Goffman, show respect in a more positive vein. These rituals include salutations, compliments, provision of minor services, and invitations to participate in group activities. Notice how each of these rituals shows respect in a typical morning at the office. Upon arrival at work, coworkers greet one another in a friendly manner, but they don't take a great deal of time to do so ("Good morning, Mr. Whitmore," "How are you, Ms. Pendergrass?" and so on). If one of them has been away on vacation, the greeting is usually much more expressive ("Well, what do you know! Look who's back from the tropics. Did you enjoy your vacation?") and a little longer in duration. This doesn't mean the parties are better friends; it is simply a matter of showing respect. To greet the returning vaca-

tioner in the same way that you greet the associate you saw yesterday would be disrespectful, as though his or her absence was not recognized. Even when you dislike the other person, the show of respect simply maintains civility.

Throughout the day colleagues may compliment one another on the way they are dressed, or how they handled a client, or for the promptness in providing needed information. Or they may symbolize respect by providing small, unrequested services such as pouring an extra cup of coffee or delivering an important piece of mail. Finally, respect can be shown by including everyone, even the office lowlife, in group activities. If a few people are stopping off for drinks after work, an invitation to anyone in earshot is an appropriate sign of respect. The invitee should be allowed to decline: It is the invitation, not the acceptance, that symbolizes respect.

Goffman notes that avoidance rituals and presentational rituals are in constant tension. To invite a colleague or acquaintance to join you is trespassing on his or her right to privacy. "A peculiar tension must be maintained, for these opposing requirements of conduct must somehow be held apart from one another and yet realized together in the same interaction: the gestures which carry an actor to a recipient must also signify that things will not be carried too far."[9] Thus, the importance of offering invitations without expecting compliance, doing small rather than large favors (that might imply escalation of the relationship), and not overdoing the greeting ritual should be recognized.

Demeanor   To be civil means that you show respect toward others and behave in a manner deserving of respect. Every culture defines the qualities of a decent person a little differently, and cultures change over time. Goffman identifies the characteristics of **demeanor,** or of a properly "housebroken" human being: discretion and sincerity, modesty, sportsmanship, reasonable command of the language, control of body movements, control of emotions, appetite, and desires, and poise under pressure.[10] Perhaps you can add or delete items from this list to capture the state of proper demeanor people expect in today's world.

Giving Priority to Practical Goals

People interact in public for one of two primary reasons: to accomplish some practical end such as the purchase of goods and services or simply to enjoy the company of others through role playing. Our top priority is often the practical. We go to the market to buy food and related items, not to visit with the personnel. This criterion may seem so obvious that it need not be mentioned, yet you have no doubt encountered people who have temporarily forgotten the purpose of a transaction. A customer who wants to return a defective product may get so annoyed at waiting in line that he barks at the clerk (whose ultimate goal is to provide customer satisfaction). In turn, the clerk reacts to the customer's rude behavior by saying, "I don't have to take this, sir. You can return your product when you get a new personality!" The customer storms away, shouting the equivalent of "I will never shop here again!" Only later do they both realize that they failed to achieve their practical goals.

Making Room for Expressive Behavior

The other primary reason for public interaction is often overlooked. We usually assume that practical goals are the major reason for interacting with people we don't know very well. But Richard Sennett suggests that for most of our history, people have reveled in the opportunity to "playact" in public.[11] **Playacting** simply means to try on new roles, to be someone you've never been before, to hide behind a mask and enjoy the company of strangers. Many public places exist where such behavior has a higher priority, but there are fewer now than in the past. People congregate and get lost in the crowd at concerts, sporting events, and large New Year's Eve parties. In these places people can increase their repertoire of identities and can literally be anybody they want to be. We can still playact to a certain degree in groups of strangers, as when one stranger convinces another to join in an impromptu dance during Mardi Gras. Friends are more likely to engage in some scripted routine from a favorite movie, and do it in front of a group of strangers as a form of entertainment. In short, some public interactions allow us the opportunity (at least) to be expressive, to enjoy life, to act the fool, and to give others some enjoyment by participating with us or playing the role of audience.

Now that we have seen some of the criteria that govern public interactions, we want to look more closely at interactions in the context of work. First, we'll describe patterns characteristic of professional dyads. Then we'll investigate the interpersonal communication processes in small work groups and large organizations.

Interpersonal Communication in Professional Dyads

On average, people spend nearly one-third of their adult life at work. And over half of the jobs in the United States are now categorized as information-processing and/or as providing services to the general public.[12] In these sectors of the labor market, communication has a very high priority. Surveys of corporate leaders reveal that the two skills most desired in new recruits are writing and speaking skills.[13] Also high on the list is the ability to deal with people on a one-to-one basis. The work situations in which people need to apply these skills vary a great deal, but we have grouped them into three broad categories: (1) interactions between su-

The Moulin Rouge, a Parisian dance hall and cabaret, was immortalized by the French artist Toulouse-Lautrec in over 30 paintings. Note how the artist was able to capture the diversity of the clientele. How does interpersonal communication change when we move into public contexts?

(Henri de Toulouse-Lautrec, At the Moulin Rouge, 1892)

pervisors and subordinates, (2) interactions between people in professional helping relationships, and (3) interactions between employees and the general public. After outlining these working role relationships, we look at one of the most difficult relationships to manage in the workplace — a workplace romance.

COMMUNICATING IN THE SUPERVISOR-SUBORDINATE RELATIONSHIP

Most organizations rely on some type of formal hierarchy of authority, where some members have legitimate rights over others. These rights include the assignment of work, supervision, and evaluation of job performance. Research indicates that supervisors spend roughly one-third to two-thirds of their time in direct communication with their subordinates, usually providing information about organizational policy and practices, the goals of the company, job instructions, rationales behind instructions, or feedback about performance. Subordinates, for their part, tend to provide their superiors with information about themselves, job-related problems, tasks that need to be done, current work, and information about policies and practices requested by the supervisor.[14]

Status Differences in Communication

The key attribute of the supervisor-subordinate relationship is that of status. Since supervisors have higher status by virtue of their position, they also seem to have initiation rights. Supervisors are freer to start and stop discussions and to interrupt a subordinate; superiors can also choose to stand closer, touch casually, and use an informal mode of address; for a lower-status employee to reciprocate would be a sign of disrespect. In addition, superiors regularly expect subordinates to disclose information that makes them potentially vulnerable. For example, if you admit to your boss that you find it difficult to work with another employee, such information could be interpreted negatively and could affect your chances for a raise, promotion, or good evaluation. Given these problems, it is little wonder that supervisors and subordinates are often wary of one another.

Yet research also confirms that developing an effective relationship with your supervisor is one of the best predictors of job satisfaction.[15] How can you build a quality supervisor-subordinate relationship? Obviously, the supervisor is in the best position to set the tone for the relationship. He or she can make a concerted effort to avoid the negative effects of the status barrier. The subordinate can also do a lot by maintaining respect for those of higher status without sacrificing personal integrity. As you read about the keys to supervising effectively and directing communication upward, try to think of ways that status differences help or hinder communicative efforts.

Effective Supervisory Communication

In a comprehensive review of research on supervisor-subordinate communication, Fredric Jablin reports that more research has been focused on characteristics of effective versus ineffective supervisors than on any other topic.[16] The most complete list of characteristics related to effectiveness was provided by Charles Redding.[17] He suggested that better supervisors

- are more "communication-minded" — they enjoy talking with subordinates

- are willing to listen and take appropriate action in response to employees' suggestions and complaints

- tend to "ask" or "persuade" employees more frequently than "telling" or "demanding" them to do things

- are sensitive to subordinates' feelings and ego-defense needs, careful to reprimand in private, and so on

- are more open in passing information along to subordinates, giving advance notice of changes, and explaining rationales behind policies and regulations

There are problems with simple lists like this one, however. A number of situational factors can influence effective leadership. Take the characteristic of being open with subordinates, for instance. As we shall see, the organizational culture socializes its employees (supervisors and subordinates alike) to use particular communication styles and avoid others. A manager with an open style of communication may not last long in a "closed-mouth" organization. In addition, Jablin has shown that subordinates are more likely to respond to an open style when their supervisor is less involved in organizational politics.[18] Perhaps subordinates don't trust a superior who is likely to move on up the ladder as much as they do one who "stays home" and seems more loyal to his or her subordinates. Also, such politicking may actually increase the perceived status differences between superior and subordinate. Furthermore, the maturity level of an individual or group of subordinates can alter a supervisor's style. A supervisor is more likely to be successful by being demanding and less open with a group that

Work has become increasingly dependent on good communication skills to coordinate the division of labor.

demonstrates few work-related skills and a low motivation level. We will have more to say about that in our discussion of group leadership a little later in this chapter.

Directing Communication Upward

By now you know that interpersonal communication is a two-way street and that a supervisor cannot be successful alone. For their relationship to be a good one, both supervisor and subordinate must work hard to create and maintain it. What can you do as a subordinate to build a good working relationship? You can start by (1) drawing some distinctions between natural role differences and dysfunctional role differences between yourself and your superior and (2) recognizing the tendency toward upward distortion.

Natural and Dysfunctional Role Differences **Natural role differences** arise from the fact that job descriptions differ. Supervisors have to be concerned about how policies and procedures affect their entire unit, not just one person. They're in a position of having to satisfy their superiors, other departments, perhaps even outside suppliers or customers. You aren't in that position and so your perspectives are likely to differ. This is good in many ways; it frees you from a lot of concerns and allows you to concentrate on your own responsibilities.

Dysfunctional role differences, on the other hand, are perceptual and behavioral differences that hinder productivity. Researchers call disagreements or misunderstandings about crucial organizational issues "semantic-information distance." Frequent disagreements about specific job duties and the amount of authority a supervisor has are not uncommon. These kinds of differences need to be discussed and settled rather than allowed to drag on, slowing down productivity and souring the relationship. In addition, supervisors and subordinates both have a tendency to overestimate what the other knows or remembers about specific issues. As a result, acting on such assumptions can often lead to misunderstanding and trouble.

Upward Distortion   A problem that needs to be dealt with by every person in a position of reporting to a supervisor is the tendency to distort information that is passed along to the superior. Studies show that this **upward distortion** is most likely to occur when the news is negative or places the subordinate in a bad light. It is only human nature to present the best image possible, especially when the other person has a lot of influence over your future. Nobody wants to be the one to tell the boss that his or her new work procedure is a functional failure, that it takes more time and causes more mistakes than the old way. Research also suggests that subordinates who have advancement aspirations, who don't feel very secure in their jobs, or who don't trust their superiors are the most likely to distort information.[19] This tendency can be overcome, however. Superiors often put less stock in positive messages received from subordinates and view negative reports as more accurate. In one study supervisors stated that their most effective subordinates were also the ones most willing to report bad news.[20] Perhaps there is not so much truth to the old proverb about killing the messenger who bears bad tidings. Or perhaps it is a good idea to test the waters first by reporting some very "minor" bad news.

COMMUNICATING IN THE HELPING PROFESSIONS

In times of emotional or physical stress, we often turn to friends for help. When the strain becomes too great or we become physically ill,

professional help is needed. Our discussion of the helping professions is two-pronged. Some of you may be considering careers in one of these professions and want to know what message-sending and -receiving skills will be most beneficial. Others may be more concerned with receiving the best professional care. You are more interested in knowing what to expect and how to improve the care you receive through effective communication. There is a growing interest among communication scholars in investigating the communication patterns between professional helpers and their clients. We will look briefly at interactions in two general types of professional relationships: therapeutic and health care dyads.

Client-Counselor Interactions

A formal therapeutic relationship exists any time an individual seeks out a professionally trained helper who is paid for his or her services. Psychiatrists, social workers, family therapists, the clergy, employment counselors, advice columnists, academic counselors, and parole officers make their living as professional helpers. On occasion, bartenders, prostitutes, teachers, and private detectives also find themselves in the position of offering advice or consoling a client. And, on a more informal basis, friends often provide one another with a therapeutic ear.

Carl Rogers, one of the pioneers in the study and practice of therapeutic communication, outlined three elements of communication that have become axiomatic in modern therapy: warmth, genuineness, and accurate empathy.[21] **Warmth** refers to messages that convey support and encouragement and create a positive environment for exploring problems and solutions. A therapist exhibits **genuineness** when she shows that her concern for the client is uppermost in her mind. Equally important is **accurate empathy,** the ability to listen and understand the feelings and emotions expressed by the client.

Loyd Pettegrew and Richard Thomas conducted a study comparing clients' perceptions of the communicator styles used by their therapists with other people's perceptions of an untrained friend or acquaintance they had turned to for help. They found that friends and therapists alike whose behavior was perceived as friendly, attentive, relaxed, and impression-leaving and who presented a good communicator image created the most positive therapeutic climate.[22] "Informal helpers" were seen as more friendly and genuine, but also as more dominating and contentious, than their professional counterparts. The formal therapists were, however, viewed as more attentive and relaxed. Pettegrew and Thomas explained these findings by noting the differing expectations that people have of friends versus therapists. "Perhaps the client implicitly knows that the therapist's interest in him is of a professional nature and is, therefore, less concerned with the therapist providing friendly cues."[23] Friends can be more dominating and argumentative because "the helpee holds a greater latitude of acceptable behavior for the informal helper, while assertive or argumentative behavior from formal helpers might jeopardize their professional relationship with the client."[24]

The strongest similarity between effective informal and formal therapists was their ability to accurately empathize — to understand the feelings and emotions of the helpee.

Patient-Health Care Provider Interactions

Relatively speaking, only a small percentage of Americans turn to professional therapists to improve their mental health. But when our physical health is at stake, we rarely hesitate to seek out members of the medical profession. In this context we are likely to interact with doctors, dentists, nurses, technicians, receptionists, medical records personnel, hospital administrators, and a host of others. Most of the research to date has focused on interactions of primary-care doctors and nurses with their patients. Those are the types of interactions we will focus on as well.

Communication between health care providers and patients is usually aimed at one of four primary goals: (1) diagnosing patients, (2) counseling patients about appropriate treatment, (3) gaining the cooperation of patients in subscribing to recommended treatment, and (4) educating patients about the nature of an illness, its causes, symptoms, and so on.[25] As this list indicates, the communication between these specialists and their patients is largely one-sided. Several studies confirm that doctors talk more than patients, ask nearly twice as many questions, and give more commands.[26]

Consumer advocates argue that this trend needs to be tempered. They suggest that patients should ask questions and insist on explanations for treatments they don't understand.[27] Several factors, however, discourage this kind of frank communication on the part of the patient. First of all, physicians are accorded such high status and viewed as so highly credible that patients feel unqualified to question or dispute them. Furthermore, many professionals and patients alike assume that the technical language of medicine is beyond the comprehension of the patient. Little effort is made to bridge the gap. Finally, the medical interview is highly scripted (opening greeting, reasons for visit, symptoms/physical examination, diagnosis, treatment/medication/testing, appointment for next visit), and scripted interactions are highly resistant to change, because people assume that's the way it is.[28]

Knowing that these patterns exist, health care professionals and patients are mutually responsible for altering them when they prove unsatisfactory. Doctors and nurses should be sensitive to the reluctance of patients to question or ask for further explanation. And patients must overcome the passive nature of their role, remembering that doctors are primarily advisers, not dictators.

COMMUNICATING WITH STRANGERS: CUSTOMER RELATIONS

Another common interaction is the one that takes place between customers and clerks. These roles are sometimes called "boundary-spanning" roles because the individuals who fill them interact primarily with people who are not members of the work organization. Typical roles include sales representatives, purchasing agents, public relations personnel, real estate agents, table servers, delivery persons, postal clerks, bank tellers, financial advisers, and so on.

In some ways these relations are more difficult to manage because the status distinctions are not so clear-cut. Supervisors and subordinates know who the ultimate authority is, and professionals are expected to know more than those who seek their help. But the customer-clerk relationship has not been so neatly defined. Some customers view the role of a clerk as essentially a servant, and many businesses instruct their personnel to put the customer first. Other people recognize the relationship as one of mutual dependency and grant customer and clerk fairly equal status. Still other customers place themselves in a submissive role to the salesperson ("When you get the time, could you please show me the Nikon 35mm camera? I would really appreciate it. Thank you ever so much. No, that's OK, I'll wait").

In spite of these differing assumptions about the nature of customer relations, there are some general guidelines. Perhaps the most important thing for a salesperson to remember is that different customers respond to different approaches. Just as in other contexts, here people have learned different rules for appropriate or preferred interaction with sales representatives. When shopping, some like to browse and don't want to be bothered by salespeople — and they give off unmistakable nonverbal cues: not making eye contact, turning away from approaching salespeople, and so on. Other people desire special attention and will wait for the clerk to approach them, demonstrate merchandise, or offer advice. Asking questions about their preferences is a subtle way to find out whether advice is desired. A clerk must always be sensitive to the customer's nonverbals — they will tell you if your rules are not their rules.

Most customers will respond to simple, courteous behavior and a pleasant but not overly friendly manner. In positions where repeat business is important, a clerk should find out the customer's name and remember to use the appropriate form of address (Mr., Ms., Dr., and so on). Many salespeople go out of their way to provide regular customers with a little extra attention, such as a card or phone call in advance of a sales promotion. That little extra often results in customer loyalty.

MANAGING THE OFFICE ROMANCE

Traditional wisdom has held that business and pleasure do not mix. For most of this century, organizations have discouraged the pursuit of romantic relationships in the workplace. Many companies had strict policies forbidding both husband and wife from working for the organization or at least from working in the same unit. But such attitudes are changing, primarily because people have relaxed their attitudes about sexual activity in general, more women have entered the workforce, and the organization has become more central to many people's lives.[29]

In the past, when romance flourished in the office, organizational policies often called for one partner (usually the woman) to quit or be transferred. The rationale usually focused on the perception that working intimates might allow their romantic problems to affect their work, or that such relations would serve as a distraction to other workers. In addition, it has often been charged that employees might use romance, or sex at least, to further their chances of career success. James Dillard conducted a study in which he asked both participants and observers of office romances to describe the motives for such a relationship and its effect on the workers'

Customer relations are often impersonal and sometimes unfeeling.
Note the bureaucrats hiding behind rules and regulations in this eerie
evocation of modern organizational life.

(George Tooker, *Government Bureau*, 1956)

productivity. Surprisingly, he found that only 17 percent of participants and observers thought the relationship had a harmful effect on the employees' job performance. The majority (62 percent) felt that the relationship made no difference at all, while 21 percent thought the relationship actually had a positive effect on performance. The most disturbing (but not surprising) finding was that gender bias remains alive and well. Females who were perceived to be using the relationship to enhance their careers were the subject of negative talk on the organizational grapevine. On the other hand, males who were perceived as forming the relationship because they were really in love were greatly admired by grapevine participants.[30]

Patrice Buzzanell asked 326 members of many different organizations how they had experienced romantic relations at work and how they managed them. She found that those who had actually participated in an office romance were much more positive about the relationship than those who had not had one. In terms of managing the relationship, Buzzanell discovered that when romantic partners were careful to maintain their professional demeanor and patterns of information sharing with coworkers, their relationship was either ignored, supported, or encouraged by others.[31] Some writers on the subject have asserted that the negative consequences of office romance are more pronounced in organizations that restrict the emotional

BOX **12.1**

"Sorry, I'm Not Apologizing": Conversational Rituals between Women and Men at Work

Much of our everyday conversation is ritual. We repeatedly ask others how they are doing without any expectation that they will take us literally and give a full account of their recent medical history. We say and hear things in a mindless fashion, because what's really important is that our words serve as a social lubricant. What we say is far less important than the fact that we are still talking to one another. Deborah Tannen, in her book *Talking From 9 to 5,* says that while we often exchange significant content messages about the work we do, "the meat of the work that has to be done is held together, made pleasant and possible, by the ketchup, relish, and bun of conversational rituals" (41). When a ritual is recognized, both parties know not to take the words literally. Problems arise, however, when cowork-

ers use different rituals and fail to recognize the appropriate category of talk. One example is the ritual use of the words "I'm sorry."

The British are well known for "saying sorry." They say it to each other perhaps 20 or 30 times a day. When a London sidewalk is crowded and people inadvertently bump each other, a near chorus of "sorry" can be heard. Its function is merely one of maintaining a sense of decency while being jostled about on a busy street. In America, saying "I'm sorry" can easily be misunderstood, especially in the world of work where most of the jostling has to do with image and status. To be successful in business, women have been frequently advised to avoid apologizing and other forms of so-called "powerless speech." Softening criticism with praise, thanking people for routine services, and asking others for opinions instead of asserting your own are forms of speech often seen as submissive. They are also behaviors that women tend to engage in more than men. Misunderstandings often occur because men fail to recognize them as ritualistic, and women do not realize that men will take them literally.

Tannen tells of a well-known columnist who gave her a private phone number, only to have Tannen lose it. When asked if she would provide

expressiveness of their employees, forcing them to sneak around, act guilty, or exhibit sexual tension.[32] The preoccupation with not getting caught may affect their work more than the problems in the relationship itself. Some have argued that relaxing concerns about romantic relationships at work will provide a better context for all kinds of male-female relationships. When colleagues are not worried about how a cross-gender relationship will be perceived, they may be more likely to form close platonic friendships and more effective working relationships with the opposite sex. Box 12.1 certainly illustrates the need for males and females to better understand one another's communication tendencies.

Interpersonal Communication in Groups and Organizations

In addition to the dyadic situations we've discussed, an employee must learn to communicate effectively with small groups of coworkers and find ways to plug into more specialized com-the number again, the woman instantly responded with "Oh, I'm sorry—it's . . ." In this case, and in many others, "I'm sorry" is not really an apology; it's a way of saving face for the other person or expressing regret or understanding. In the same way, saying "thank you" even when the other person has not provided any service, can be a ritualized way of closing a conversation. But all rituals depend on mutually shared assumptions. If women at work often say they're sorry and men never do, the imbalance probably reflects ritual versus literal interpretations.

Women tend to use compliments and give praise at work much more than men do at work, but are reluctant to criticize directly. Men, on the other hand, like their criticism straight and tend to keep quiet when someone is doing a good job. The result: men often miss the indirect criticisms given by women and women feel ignored or taken for granted because they are seldom told if they are doing a good job. Another ritual difference is the kind of small talk used as conversational filler. Women, according to Tannen, often complain about problems in relationships as a way of showing that they are on equal footing (neither is perfect). If taken literally, this kind of talk can be interpreted as chronic complaining. Equally confusing to some women is the ritual sports talk

banter engaged in by most men, and increasingly, by many women.

While there are gender differences in conversational style and ritual use of language, the important point is that taking ritualistic language literally can lead to problematic perceptions of others. Since we tend to be unaware of many of the ways that we ourselves use language ritually, it should not surprise us when we interpret the rituals of others in a literal fashion. And since the American workplace was shaped largely by the language rituals of men, it may still take us a while to learn and appreciate the full range of rituals available to us.

SOURCE: Deborah Tannen. *Talking From 9 to 5: How Women's and Men's Conversational Styles Affect Who Gets Heard, Who Gets Credit, and What Gets Done at Work* (New York: William Morrow & Company, 1994.)

ADDITIONAL READING

Charles Conrad. *Strategic Organizational Communication: Toward the Twenty-First Century.* Orlando, Fla.: Harcourt Brace, 1994. See especially Chapters 12 and 13 on strategies of accomodation in managing gender, race, and ethnic diversity in organizations.

munication channels that flow throughout the organization. Let's begin by investigating the communication patterns of small work groups; then we'll examine communication within the larger organization.

INTERPERSONAL RELATIONSHIPS IN SMALL GROUPS

Small groups exist in organizations for many reasons. Many groups are formally created as permanent functioning bodies within the organization: Departments, committees, and work groups within departments are examples. The tasks of these groups may include decision making, problem solving, information sharing, and performance of integrated work routines. On occasion temporary (ad hoc) groups are organized to produce new policies, redesign procedures, or smooth out problems between organizational units. Alongside these formal groups, employees form their own informal groups for sharing information and establishing acceptable work norms.

Regardless of the type of group, many of the dynamics of group interaction will be the same. Every group will evolve specialized roles for its **365** members, norms and sanctions to govern group interaction, and some forms of social cohesion to keep the group together. Of all the roles in group interaction, the leadership role has gained the most attention from laypersons and experts alike.

Leadership and Dyadic Linkage

In most organizations the leadership role in a task or decision-making group will be formally assigned. As a leader you will be expected to motivate, direct, evaluate, correct, and work with the group in an efficient manner while ensuring high-quality production. What makes for effective leadership? For years researchers thought that leadership could be predicted by identifying the **personality traits** of leaders. They hoped to discover the consistent stuff of leadership: intelligence, charisma, sociability, and so on. But the correlation between personality and leadership has proved elusive. After more than 750 studies, the attempt to construct a profile of leader characteristics has been largely written off, and researchers have turned to other approaches.[33]

Today, **leadership** is more and more viewed as a communicative achievement. Leaders are thought to be "managers of meaning" who invite others to share in defining and building a shared vision of the group or corporate future. Leadership is the product of a leader-follower relationship, not the act of a single individual. Many organizations have redefined the role of managers, moving away from the notion of a manager as one who controls, supervises, or tells others what to do. In today's "team-based" organization, a manager is more often thought of as a resource person — someone who has the responsibility of locating and providing support knowledge and materials so that employees can perform their jobs at a higher level of excellence. Max DePree, chairman of the board at Herman Miller, an innovative furniture manufacturer, describes the role of leader as "a servant" whose

only success is the performance of the followers. For DePree, the qualities of leadership are all relational. A leader has an awareness of the human spirit that fosters integrity, intellectual curiosity, comfort with ambiguity, the courage to trust followers, and the realization that to lead one must be present — available to listen and talk with employees.[34]

Leadership can be seen as a group relationship as well as a series of dyadic relationships. **Dyadic linkage theory** takes on the conventional business wisdom that leaders should treat all of their subordinates in the same manner to avoid giving the impression of playing favorites or treating some employees unfairly. However, some research calls this view into question. The dyadic linkage model of leadership suggests that every dyadic relationship is unique in some ways and that effective leaders adapt their style to fit the person. This means that, as a leader, you might use a more autocratic style with those subordinates who respond well to direction, prodding, or an occasional kick in the pants. Likewise, you would be prudent to give more latitude to highly competent, go-it-on-their-own employees, and to use a more participatory, equal-status style with workers who perform the most critical functions in your unit.

In short, leadership requires sensitivity to followers' needs and a rather flexible package of communication options. Think about your most recent work experience. Imagine yourself as the leader of that group. How would you adapt your leadership style to each individual member? What would you do to motivate each one?

Membership and Identity

As important as leadership is, one should never forget to cultivate good group relations with coworkers. Work units are the heart and soul of most organizations. When a unit doesn't function well, the effect usually ripples throughout the organization. There are several aspects of group communication that you should become aware of and use to improve or maintain group relations. This includes the development of complementary roles, effective group norms, and a cohesive group identity.

Group Role Repertory Experts agree that for a group to work well together, members must take on different roles and reinforce one another for role performances. Most also agree on five specific roles that are most essential: task leader, social leader, information provider, tension releaser, and devil's advocate. The important thing to remember here is that in playing group roles, members need to achieve a delicate balance of complementarity and duplication. In other words, group interaction is most effective when the role each person plays complements rather than competes with the roles of other group members. For instance, when Gibson provides the group with information about projected sales figures (information provider), Gerber questions the validity of the figures (devil's advocate). In turn, Gibson provides additional information about how the figures were arrived at. Their actions are complementary because together they have increased the group's confidence that the information they have is accurate; they have advanced the group toward its goal. Sometimes role behavior is not complementary. When an argument gets out of hand, Gruber (tension reliever) breaks the tension with a joke. If Gerber follows with another joke, his behavior is competing with Gruber's, not complementing it (unless, of course, the first joke failed to ease the tension successfully).

Role specialization can be taken too far, however. Group members need to be able to play a variety of roles to cover for a group member who is absent or not up to par on a given day. It might be helpful to think of group members as having primary and secondary roles. Primary roles are the ones they play most frequently; secondary roles are the ones they are capable of performing when the regular performer cannot. It takes time for roles to develop in a new group, so you should expect competition for leadership

and other key roles to take place until members find their niche. Roles that are not assigned formally will develop as a result of the positive or negative feedback the group provides to each member's communicative efforts.

Group Norms Group roles refer to behavioral expectations the group has for specific individuals. Group norms, on the other hand, are expectations the group has of *all* its members. Without norms a group has no identity, no way of distinguishing itself from all the other work groups in the organization. And it has no way of governing the behavior of the whole group. A group can develop norms for high or low productivity, or members may establish a pattern of pulling practical jokes on one another.

Communication is the key to establishing good group norms and maintaining them or changing outdated ones. Members of effective groups tend to talk to one another about the standards they follow and reinforce one another for performing well. The job satisfaction of individual workers has been traced to their working with colleagues who express positive attitudes about their jobs.[35] Most groups have key members, sometimes known as "opinion leaders," who are the most influential in changing the norms. A good leader will seek these people out when he or she wants to change the internal standards of a work group.

Group Cohesion While roles and norms are necessary for effective group functioning, cohesiveness makes group life enjoyable and fulfilling. It provides members with a more complete sense of group identity and a sense of belonging. Simply defined, **cohesion** refers to the degree to which group members like one another and want to remain in the group. There are a number of factors that relate to cohesion: the expression of similarities in attitude, beliefs, and values; the use of group-related pronouns such as we, us, and ours instead of yours and mine; the development of trust; inside jokes, unusual rituals, traditions, or stories; survival of

Communication in the workplace is sometimes restricted to nonverbal forms due to environmental restraints (noise, physical separation, and the like). Yet strong relationships are often developed by workers in situations similar to that pictured.

(Jacob Lawrence, *Builders No. 1*, 1970)

difficult times together; and so on. When a group begins to exhibit this kind of behavior, it is becoming more cohesive.

As much as cohesiveness is valued, experts point out the pitfalls of becoming too cohesive. When a group becomes too tight-knit, members tend to try to maintain group relations at all costs. The result is a phenomenon known as **groupthink**: Critical thinking is sacrificed in order to promote group agreement.[36] Group members begin to think of themselves as incapable of making mistakes. Instead of basing decisions on careful analysis of the facts and the alternative courses of action, they become sloppy and overconfident. They end up making bad decisions or defective products. Because of

this tendency, experts recommend that groups be cautious about letting loyalty to the group become too important.

To promote effective group relations, it is healthy to develop communication patterns that reflect complementary roles, clear-cut norms, and a moderate degree of cohesiveness. Think about the groups you've worked with in the past. What were the roles, norms, and forms of cohesion of the most successful ones?

In addition to good relations between supervisors and subordinates and among work groups, it is also important to become adept at managing organization-wide communication channels. We will explore these channels next. In the following section we look at how orga-

Uniform dress is one way to build identification among members of small groups or organizations. What are some other verbal or nonverbal ways that we shape group cohesion and identity?

nizational cultures develop and at some of the ways workers can adapt to the role demands of complex organizations.

INTERPERSONAL COMMUNICATION IN THE ORGANIZATION

In order to communicate effectively in an organization, you need to develop communication skills that will aid you in dealing with larger groups of people. Your perceptual abilities will also be in demand, for you will need to figure out which messages and which sources are important. Thus, you need to be aware of the organizational culture and the socialization processes related to it, as well as communication networks such as the grapevine and how they function. In addition, you need to master a short list of specific communication skills.

Organizational Culture

Just as individual selves are shaped by national and regional cultures (Chapter 8), and dyads develop relational cultures (Chapter 5), so does each organization form its own unique culture. An **organizational culture** can be defined formally as a system of shared meanings and beliefs expressed through symbolic forms such as rituals, stories, and myths which function to hold a group of people together.[37] More colloquially, organizational members might define it as "the way we do things around here." It is the culture of an organization that gives meaning to messages and events, making them understandable to insiders, but possibly confusing to those unfamiliar with the culture. We know how cultures differ at the societal level. Box 12.2 reveals some of the differences in communication styles between Japanese and American employees. But culture is often more invisible at the

BOX 12.2

When East Meets West: Hidden Differences in Corporate Communication Styles

Not so long ago, an American company sent one of it's best young managers to Japan to take over the Tokyo office. His first decision concerned a new advertising campaign, which he found completely unacceptable. When the New York office urged him to accept the plan anyway, he felt angry and frustrated. These feelings only deepened over time. Meetings seemed disorganized, and department heads were vague about their plans. His plans to reorganize the office and put his own mark on the company met with passive resistance. Six months later, after his top Japanese manager resigned, the young man was recalled.

What happened? In *Hidden Differences: Doing Business with the Japanese,* Edward T. and Mildred Reed Hall explain that cultural misunderstandings lay at the root of the problem. Sending a young man to head the Tokyo office was the first mistake, as Japanese businessmen respect age and experience. The fact that the young man himself failed to do research on Japanese language, culture, and business practices was another error. Finally, sending an ambitious person with a desire to put his own ideas into practice was the third mistake. The Japanese find a competitive, aggressive attitude uncongenial and distressing. The Halls feel that, "despite popular beliefs to the contrary, the single greatest barrier to business success is the one erected by culture."

One difference between Japan and the United States is that Japan, like many countries in East Asia, Africa, and South America, is a collectivist culture, while the United States is an individual-ist country. When collectivists and individualists interact without understanding the hidden differences that characterize their corporate styles, misunderstandings result. According to Harry C. Triandis, Richard Brislin, and C. Harry Hui, individualism-collectivism is a major cultural difference that affects work values, personal styles of interaction, and even concepts of morality. They believe that anyone who wants to work effectively in international business should be trained in how to diagnose and adapt to differences along the individualism-collectivism continuum.

What is the difference between collectivist and individualist cultures? Briefly, collectivists have a "we" orientation. Loyalty to the group is more important than individual achievement, and the smallest "unit of survival" is the collective, whether it be extended family, clan, or organization. In contrast, individualist cultures have an "I" orientation. Here the smallest unit of survival is the individual.

The behaviors of collectivists can seem surprising or distasteful to individualists, and collectivists may find individualist attitudes and action equally inexplicable. What should Americans, as individualists, do when working in a collectivist culture? Triandis and his colleagues offer a number of guidelines, a few of which are listed below.

First, individualists should understand that collectivists let themselves be guided by group norms rather than individual goals. This means that when collectivists change group memberships, their opinions, attitudes, and even their personalities may change. Individualists need to be aware of this factor and not be taken aback.

In addition, collectivists are likely to stress harmony and cooperation more than individualists. Competitive or confrontational situations cause discomfort and embarrassment. If criticism of a coworker becomes necessary, the individualist must be sure the interaction takes place in private and should offer as much positive feedback as possible to allow the other to save face.

Because harmony is so important, individualists should not be put off by unusual shows of modesty from collectivists. It is not uncommon

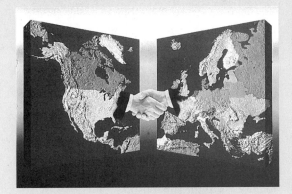

for a collectivist to begin a presentation by saying something like, "Please forgive this unworthy effort." Individualists who give presentations should begin in a more modest way than they are generally used to. Attempts to build credibility by stressing expertness will seem like boasting and will create a negative impression.

Although collectivists are not competitive or boastful, they do recognize and respect status differences. Unlike individualists, they feel more comfortable in vertical than in horizontal relationships. They therefore feel uncomfortable interacting until they know what position in society their partner occupies. Individualists should not hesitate to let collectivists know their age, rank, place of birth, and even income. This information allows collectivists to decide how to proceed. Individualists should also seek out this kind of information and give special respect to collectivists' status and age.

Individual decision making is not as highly valued by collectivists as it is by individualists. Individualists should expect negotiations to take time as collectivists seek out group consensus. Negotiations also take time because collectivists feel the need to establish personal relationships with their individualist partners. In some cases, individualists may feel their privacy is being violated. In an attempt to establish long-term relationships, collectivists may spend a great deal of time visiting their individualist partners, or they

may ask personal questions that individualists feel are intrusive. Although establishing a personal relationship takes time, once the relationship has been defined, collectivists will expect a great deal more loyalty and commitment than an individualist is normally likely to give to a business partner.

Finally, the actual mechanics of doing business may differ dramatically. Collectivists rely less on written contracts than do individualists and may not understand the necessity for signed documents. They may also engage in some acts which are considered illicit in individualist countries. Whereas an individualist might consider paying a government official to expedite paper work to be a bribe, collectivists may see it as a natural part of doing business. Nepotism and other personal connections are much more acceptable in collectivist cultures than in individualist cultures.

Of course, not all collectivist countries are the same, and individualists doing international business must recognize the particular patterns in the country to which they are assigned. Nevertheless understanding the general nature of collectivism can be an important first step in successful intercultural interaction. If you should find yourself working in a collectivist culture some day, you will have to find a way to maintain your own value system while respecting that of others. This is by no means an easy task, but it is absolutely essential in adapting to the hidden differences you are sure to encounter.

SOURCE: Harry C. Triandis, Richard Brislin, and C. Harry Hui, "Cross-cultural Training Across the Individualism-Collectivism Divide," *International Journal of Intercultural Relations* 12 (1988), 269–289.

ADDITIONAL READING

Hall, Edward T., and Mildred T. Hall. *Hidden Differences: Doing Business with the Japanese.* Garden City, N.Y: Anchor Press/Doubleday, 1987.

organizational level. We tend to think of American organizations as sharing essentially the same beliefs about what it takes to be successful. It is only when we transfer from one organization to another that we begin to find different beliefs about the importance of hierarchy and authority, different expectations about working overtime and weekends, tendencies to stifle or thrive on the creative ideas of employees, and so on.

Most scholars recognize organizational cultures to be communicative creations. Differences such as those cited above are not inherent in certain industries or types of organizational tasks. Rather they emerge from the hundreds of conversations and nonverbal displays that members exchange every day. Karl Weick, a noted organizational theorist, likes to compare organizations to spider webs. Each day employees collectively spin the various webs of power, reward, and organizing structures as members interact with one another. At night, when employees go home, the webs fall apart. The next day they are spun again, probably in much the same fashion as the day before, but also exhibiting a few subtle changes so that the structure continues to evolve.[38] Recognition of the influence of organizational culture as a context for shaping meaning is a crucial factor in building one's competence as an organizational communicator.

Communication and Socialization

When a new employee joins an organization, two socializing processes are set in motion: The organization tries to indoctrinate the new recruit, and the new recruit tries to "learn the ropes" and "make her mark" on the organization.

From the organization's perspective the new employee must be taught the values and rituals of the organization's culture. In other words, socialization processes teach one how to be a good employee. Written materials, canned presentations, and informal insights about the beliefs, values, and behaviors expected are the focus of

socialization efforts. While some of this socializing is through formal training and company publications, most of it comes from coworkers and supervisors. But the process is not an automatic one. As Daniel Feldman reports, a certain degree of trust and friendliness has to develop before the "regulars" will share vital information with a new recruit: "Until incumbent employees felt they could trust recruits, they withheld information about supervisors' preferences and personalities, making the recruits less competent in the eyes of the supervisors."[39]

Typically, new recruits are fresh from college or an intensive training period and are eager to show what they have learned. It is infinitely wiser, however, to remain a student for a while — learning from coworkers, conforming to standards you may not really like, and earning trust. This kind of compliant behavior will open the doors to inside information that, according to Fredric Jablin, "helps the new employee decode and interpret the scripts and schemas that prevail in the organization."[40] Then, once you're accepted as one of the group, you can begin making your mark.

Communication Networks

Having learned the ropes in your immediate work unit, it's time to venture out into the larger organization and tap into the flow of information that regulates movement up, down, in, and around the corporation. There are actually many different kinds of communication networks in large organizations, most of them formed informally by people with a need for information that isn't available through regular, formal channels. Some networks, like the grapevine, have been named and are recognized by almost everyone. Others are almost invisible, and even the members of such networks may not realize they exist. An informal network exists whenever members who do not formally report to one another exchange information on a somewhat regular basis. They may talk about almost any informational topic. An "innovation" network, for instance, might include people who share an interest in technology or ideas even though they are located in a variety of units and talk only when they happen to run into one another. Often they find out about new product lines and other techniques months before they are reported in company newsletters and internal memos. A network can be considered an informal group, even though all of its members rarely meet at the same place and time. Since most members communicate regularly with at least some of their network partners, important messages usually get to all of the members in a relatively short time.

The **grapevine** is perhaps the most interesting and certainly the most researched of the networks. People are curious about the action behind the scenes and often talk about what they know or have heard in the hallways, beside the water cooler, or over coffee. Many people rely on the information gleaned from the grapevine to increase their own understanding of the organization, predict future changes, and consolidate their own power by being in the know. People who fail to tune in to the grapevine are often likely to be the subject of rumors. Research verifies that most people have a negative image of the grapevine but would rather have possibly misleading information than no information at all.[41] The most interesting findings, however, are those that dispute popular opinion about the grapevine. Contrary to what most people think, the grapevine is amazingly accurate. One study estimates that nearly 80 percent of the information acquired through the grapevine is basically accurate.[42] Several studies have found that information passed via the grapevine was distorted less than most messages passed through formal channels.[43] Astute managers know the value of the grapevine and frequently use it to spread information that their people need to know but that is too sensitive to be commented on publicly.

In organizations, information is power, and the lack of it can weaken your position in the company. We recommend that you view the grapevine as a viable channel of communication, though always taking what you hear with a grain of salt. Try to cultivate other informal networks as well; you never know when such contacts will pay off. In addition, you'll be the kind of informed employee who can be a true asset to the organization.

To be a well-rounded communicator, you must manage public, impersonal relationships just as well as you do intimate ones. In this chapter we have described the major criteria that shape public encounters. These criteria can serve as general guidelines when other, more specific information is not available. It should also be helpful to consider what we've talked about in this chapter in terms of the model of communicative competence that we have stressed throughout the text.

Professional Relationships and Communicative Competence

Competence in professional and public relationships requires different sensitivities than those called for in family and personal relationship contexts. Public interactions utilize civil discourse that relies on ritualized knowledge instead of personal knowledge about others. To demonstrate competence in this context means balancing a friendly but aloof demeanor so that we can enjoy each other's company without prying or burdening the other with issues in our personal life. In family and intimate relationships we are expected to do just the opposite.

PROFESSIONAL RELATIONSHIPS AND INTERPRETIVE COMPETENCE

Many people who are excellent at deciphering others once they get to know them seem hopelessly inept at initial encounters with strangers.

Organizational communication does not have to take place in stuffy old offices. Imagine trying to keep this bunch in tune.

Such people probably have well-developed cognitive schemas relevant to showing empathy, managing conflict, and reading personal motivations, but need to have extensive personal knowledge of the other before they can put their social skills to work. Ours is a culture that values the personal and tends to devalue impersonal relationships as if they were somehow inferior and unsatisfying. Perhaps that is why we refer to such interactions as small talk. We don't expect big dividends, so we spend little time elaborating or practicing social scripts that go beyond the first two or three minutes of interaction and yet remain at an impersonal level. We seem to have lost what earlier generations referred to as "the art of conversation." However, we do have very efficient scripts for moving interaction in a personal direction. One study of conversational expectations indicated that Americans are predisposed to reveal quite intimate details about themselves within the first 30 minutes to an hour of conversation.[44] Thus, it appears that we have plenty of room for improvement in our interpretive competence at this level but few models to follow.

PROFESSIONAL RELATIONSHIPS AND ROLE COMPETENCE

Another consequence of the infusion of the personal into the public realm is a confusion of roles. Where earlier eras provided clear-cut social roles and codes of etiquette to manage cultural transitions, our age has made informality its badge of honor. But this often blurs role distinctions, as when financial institutions advertise themselves as "your friend" in the community. As Judith Martin (otherwise known as "Miss Manners") has pointed out, if your banker is your friend, you would certainly be understanding and forgiving if a bank officer forgot to process your new home loan until after interest rates had gone up a half-percentage point. The officer meant well. How could you be angry at a friend who was just trying to do his or her job? Role competence is hampered when we don't know the rules for enacting the role. Sometimes the rules are clear to anyone with experience in a given role. The simple remedy in such cases is to learn the role by observing those who are good at it. But in times of profound social change, public roles are often challenged.

One such role undergoing dramatic change today is the role of professional caregivers in the field of human services. Since the rise of the welfare state, social services agents have been trained as professionals whose role was defined as problem solvers for the poor and disabled. The complementary role cast for the client of social services was a "victim," — too weak and powerless to help him or herself. Critics of the welfare state have charged that these role assumptions created a vicious cycle of learned helplessness. Today, many social service agencies are moving toward a model where clients are seen as untapped sources with a capacity to solve their own problems when empowered and given a shared role in making decisions about what resources they really need.[45] Obviously, what counts as role competence for both caregiver and client have changed significantly. Role competent behavior will continue to change as our culture struggles to define our public roles in relation to one another.

Changes in work roles have also challenged our communication competence. Gone are the days when an employee could be successful by not making waves and being loyal to the company. The new rules stress taking risks, being willing to make mistakes, asking for more responsibility, working faster, and shooting for total quality.[46] Being role competent is not getting any easier.

PROFESSIONAL RELATIONSHIPS AND SELF COMPETENCE

While role competence makes sense in work or public settings, concern for self competence may seem oddly out of place. In fact, our discussion of interpretive and role competence implies that there is already too much self-focus and any more would only threaten the public realm further. And yet, there is an important relationship between the self and our public or professional roles. Self-identity is drawn from many sources. When we narrow our definition of self to include only private pursuits, we give up a part of ourselves. Earlier cultures seem to have recognized the importance of a full and fulfilling public life of theatrical play, civic celebration, political involvement, and conversational enjoyment. Sociologist Ray Oldenburg has argued that the best cultures have always had what he calls "third places" (beyond the family and workplace) where neighbors could congregate and experience a public life. Neighborhood cafés, pubs, beauty parlors, and a host of assorted places qualify for third places if we but use them. An important aspect of self-expression awaits us there.

PROFESSIONAL RELATIONSHIPS AND GOAL COMPETENCE

How can we improve goal competence at work and elsewhere in the public realm? Midway through the decade of the 90s, we seem to be charting a course that moves precariously between a work life that must be fulfilling, a pleasure-filled private life, and a subtle but nagging need to re-engage ourselves in the public life of our communities. The problem is one of balance. How do we avoid the tendency for work to become all-consuming? How do we make the time for our families and close friends that we so desire? And what energy will be left to invest in the public realm if we are to save our cities, reinvent democracy, and leave our children a healthy planet? Balancing these concerns in our lives requires skilful communication. We must provide a convincing rationale to the boss that time off from work to spend with family or in the community is not only well-deserved, but will ultimately refresh us and make us more productive at work. In order to fulfill our responsibilities to community and family, we need to demonstrate the value of the entire family giving up its weekend to help a local recycling effort. These are issues that require goal competence. Without careful consideration of our own and other's goals, we will likely bounce back and forth, attempting much but accomplishing little.

PROFESSIONAL RELATIONSHIPS AND MESSAGE COMPETENCE

Translating our professional and public goals into effective verbal and nonverbal messages is the final challenge. Knowledge of how interpersonal communication works is valuable in any organization, but that knowledge must be converted to specific skills to do any good. Over the course of your college education, you will want to develop your public speaking, writing, and interviewing skills. These will enable you to present yourself as an organized and skilled communicator both at work and in public roles. You will also have need to call on many of the interpersonal skills that we have described in this text: listening actively, overcoming stereotypes, managing conversations, taking the perspective of others, and occasionally expressing your feelings or showing empathy. One of the most useful skills in the public realm is the ability to hear diverse points of view and find meaningful ways to integrate or sort them out. In the skill building section of this chapter, we show how to develop the art of negotiation and conflict management.

Skill Building: Creative Conflict Management and Negotiation

Conflicts and differences of opinion are normal parts of all communication contexts, professional or private. On the job or in the home, you can expect to encounter many situations in which your interests conflict with those of others. As a competent communicator you need to know how to use talk to resolve these conflicts of interest; that is, you need to know how to negotiate.

Negotiation is a process whereby two or more parties whose interests are initially opposed use communication to reach a joint decision. When the foreign ministers of two superpowers sign a peace treaty, when business executives enter into an international joint venture, or when city officials and union leaders end a strike, negotiation has taken place. Similarly, when students and teachers agree on an extra credit assignment, when parents and children decide on a fair allowance, or when two friends choose an evening's entertainment, they too have taken part in negotiation. In all these cases, people use talk to get what they want from one another. When their communication works, everyone involved benefits and the relationship is strengthened. When it fails, frustration, anger, and exhaustion are likely results. Thus, the ability to negotiate effectively is an important interpersonal skill.

In this section we'll give you some hints on how to improve your negotiating skills. We'll begin by introducing you to five different styles of conflict, discussing the situations in which each is appropriate, and asking you to think about your own style. We'll then look at some ways people can turn conflict situations into opportunities for creative problem solving. Finally, we'll end with some general rules for cooperative negotiation. While we'll only be able

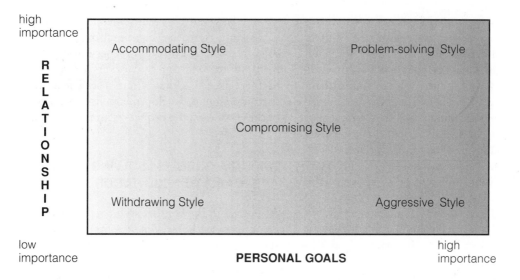

FIGURE 12.1
Conflict styles

to skim the surface of this complex subject, we hope you'll think about your negotiation behavior as you read this section.

CHOOSING YOUR CONFLICT STYLE

Without realizing it, you have probably already developed a negotiation style. Most people have. Some people are overwhelmed by conflict and either walk away from it or give in to keep the peace. Some see conflict as a contest and will do anything to win. Some seek to compromise, while others view conflict as an opportunity for creative problem solving. We can define the five basic conflict styles in terms of their ability to meet two kind of goals: personal and relational. Figure 12.1 shows the relationship between these two goals and conflict style. Let's begin with the lower right-hand quadrant. Here we place people whose primary concern is with achieving personal goals, even at the expense of a relationship. For these people conflicts are competitive games; they may even enjoy fights — as

long as they win. We call their style the **aggressive style.** David Johnson compares each conflict style to a different animal.[47] He describes those who use the aggressive style as sharks.

Moving clockwise, we come to the lower left-hand corner. Individuals who fit here try to avoid conflict. For them nothing is worth the hassle of a fight. When faced with disagreement, they use the **withdrawing style,** backing away from conflict both physically and psychologically. Johnson calls them turtles.

In the upper left-hand quadrant is the **accommodating style,** in which concern for the relationship is high while the need to achieve personal goals is low. People who fit this quadrant try to smooth over all disagreements. If you are the one who gives in just to keep the peace, you fill the role of accommodator. Johnson would describe you as a teddy bear.

In the middle of Figure 12.1 are those who have a moderate concern for personal and relational goals. These individuals often try to cut a deal by using a **compromising style.** Johnson compares them to foxes.

Finally, in the top right-hand quadrant we have individuals who are committed both to personal and relational goals. They seek solutions through which everyone will benefit. Raymond and Mark Ross describe their **problem-solving style** this way: "It is an enlightened style based on the assumptions that conflicts are natural in the human experience; conflicts are amenable to rational, cooperative problem solving; and a sensitive openness is the necessary first step."[48] Johnson likens people who use this style to owls.

Which style is the best? It all depends. While the problem-solving style is the most idealistic choice, it takes skill and effort and may not be right for all situations. There are times when each style should be used. For example, when a goal is more important than a relationship, an aggressive (or at least assertive) style may be called for. When buying a used car, it is not particularly important to forge a close relationship with the salesperson, but it is important to get a good buy. Here the shark will do better than the teddy bear. In some cases neither maintaining the relationship nor getting your way is very important. This is when it makes sense to withdraw. If a very large person wearing leather and chains wants to park a motorcycle in the spot you've been eyeing, why not park somewhere else? Unless you have something to prove, avoidance may be the better part of valor.

When the relationship is important, a more accommodating style is called for. If you and a close neighbor are pooling your money to buy a wedding gift for a friend but you disagree on what to buy, you may decide it is better to give in. If you really don't care a lot about the gift but do care about your neighbor, accommodating may be best.

If your emotional involvement and your needs are equal and moderate, then try to compromise. Perhaps you are involved in business negotiations. You want to maintain a reasonably good business relationship, but you also want to do well for yourself. Negotiating the best overall compromise is the strategy called for here.

Finally, when a lot is at stake, it's a good idea to take time to work things out using a problem-solving strategy. For example, serious disagreements with long-time coworkers or romantic partners need this kind of response. The point is that you should develop the ability to enact all of these styles in the proper circumstances.

TAKING A PROBLEM-SOLVING APPROACH TO NEGOTIATION

Although all the conflict styles we've discussed are appropriate in some circumstances, one stands out as particularly important: the problem-solving or integrative approach. Because this style takes the most interpersonal skill and sensitivity, it warrants further analysis in terms of (1) how it differs from negotiation and (2) what specific strategies are available.

The Difference between Compromise and Problem Solving

Initially, it's easy to confuse compromise with problem solving, but the two are not identical. Perhaps an example will help illuminate the differences. A husband and wife disagree about where to go for vacation. He wants to go to the mountains, while she wants to go to the seashore. A compromise solution might be to split their two-week vacation into equal parts: one week in the mountains and one week at the shore. While this is certainly better than nothing, it is not the ideal solution, for, at least half of the time, one party has to give in to the other. A problem-solving solution looks for a novel alternative that results in at least some benefits to both parties. If, after discussing the reasons for their initial preferences, the couple finds out that what the husband wants from a mountain vacation is the opportunity to hunt, fish, and hike and what the wife likes about the shore is the swimming, sunning, and social interaction, then they are in a position to look for a problem-solving solution. They may find an alternative that meets both their needs: a resort in a warm part of the country, one that has a sandy beach and plenty of activities, but one in an area where hunting and fishing are plentiful.[49]

Problem-Solving Strategies

While the advice to look for a creative solution that will increase the rewards and decrease the costs to both parties is obviously good advice, it's not always obvious how we are to find such solutions. Students of negotiation have identified several ways to reach integrative solutions. In the first two we will look at, one actor gets the other to agree by reducing the other's costs or increasing the other's rewards. In the second two, both parties change their initial positions.

The first strategy is called **cost-cutting**. Usually, when one party objects to a solution, it is because that solution leads to costs. If a way can be found to minimize or eliminate the costs of the objecting party, then agreement can be reached. Geoff may object to going to Serena's home for the holidays because the drive is long and tiring. Serena can cut his costs by promising to drive, by suggesting that they stop at a nice resort on the way, or by arranging to fly.

Of course, not all the costs of an agreement are that concrete — sometimes they are psychological. Once people have taken a position, they often refuse to give in as a matter of pride. One way of cost-cutting is to help the other person save face. We've already discussed the importance of maintaining one's own face and line. The competent communicator is also willing to help others maintain theirs. Suppose that, without thinking, Dr. Foster assigns a test the day after the big homecoming dance. His students would like him to change the date. So far as they can see, there are no costs involved in his making such a simple change. Foster, however, sees the matter differently. He agrees that it would be possible to rearrange his lesson plan without too much trouble. Two things, however, are at

stake: his principles and his status. Foster objects to changing his course simply to accommodate the social needs of his students. He feels that such a change would signal that dances are more important than classes, and more significantly, he feels that if he gives in, he will lose face. The student negotiators must acknowledge these concerns. They should be careful to show him respect and to let him know that they understand the importance of class work. They should frame their discussion as problem solving rather than confrontation, and they should be careful not to challenge his authority. By stressing his reputation for being flexible as well as fair and firm, by trying to minimize the size of the change they are asking, and by offering to take the test earlier rather than later, they may have a better chance to convince him. How would you cut the professor's costs if you were the students involved? What would you agree to if you were the professor?

A second way of reaching a mutually beneficial agreement is **compensation,** or finding a way to pay back the party who is accommodating. An interesting example of compensation occurred during the 1961 Cuban Missile Crisis. In 1961, the Russians began placing nuclear missiles in Cuba. In return for agreeing to remove them, the Russians secretly convinced the United States to withdraw its missiles from Turkey. Compensation allowed the Russians to feel that their decision did not represent unilateral accommodation but instead involved mutual benefits. Interestingly, the U.S. withdrawal was delayed for four months, to help U.S. leaders avoid domestic criticism and save face.[50]

On a more mundane level, if your mother agrees to lend you her car, you could compensate by offering to pick up the cleaning on your way home or, at the very least, by returning it with a full tank of gas. We generally expect some compensation when we do favors for others. Insensitivity to this simple principle can wreck relationships, making one party feel that he or she is being taken advantage of or taken for granted. Often, a simple "thank you" is all that another party wants by way of compensation, illustrating how important simple verbal responses are in maintaining relationships.

A third method of creative negotiation is called **logrolling.** Here both sides make concessions on issues that are important to the other but relatively unimportant to them. That is, the first party concedes on positions A and B while the second concedes on C and D. Assume, for example, that members of a union are asking for a 20 percent increase in the overtime pay rate (a position that is very important to them) as well as 20 minutes more of rest breaks (a position of secondary importance). Assume also that management strongly opposes the rest breaks but is not as concerned with the overtime issue. In this case the union might be willing to drop its request for breaks if management gives up its position on overtime. As Dean Pruitt tells us, "This will typically be better for both parties than a compromise on the two issues (e.g., a 10 percent increase in overtime rate and 10 more minutes of rest time)."[51]

Let's look at another example of logrolling. Geena and Ellen are looking for an apartment. Geena's primary concern is that the place be close to work; secondarily, she would like to live in a modern high-rise. Ellen, on the other hand, can't stand modern apartments; she wants an older place with a fireplace and a large kitchen. Location is of less concern although she would prefer a house in the country. Perhaps both can get their major needs met if they look for a converted duplex in town. Although Geena doesn't get to live in a high-rise and Ellen doesn't get to live in the country, both may be relatively satisfied.

The final strategy we'll look at is **bridging.** Bridging involves finding a new option that satisfies both parties, without either having to concede. Let's look at a classic example. Two people are working in the library. One feels the library is stuffy and so decides to open the window. The other is made uncomfortable by the draft and insists the window be closed. No compromise (for example, opening the window halfway) seems possible. The librarian who comes to investigate the disturbance thinks for a minute and then opens a window in the next room, bringing in fresh air without the draft. Another example of this kind of bridging was illustrated in an old episode of *The Brady Bunch.* The Bradys had accumulated a large number of green stamps, coupons that could be traded in for valuable merchandise. Conflict arose because the boys wanted a rowboat while the girls wanted a sewing machine. If you've seen the episode (many of our students have), you'll know how they bridged their disagreement: They bought a televison, an alternative that was better than either of the original options.

Another way of bridging is called **expanding the pie.** If a conflict arises over sharing resources, one way to solve the problem is to increase the resource. Assume a couple is quarreling over who will get sole possession of a second bedroom. One party, a composer, wants it as a music room. The other, an architect, wants it as a design area. Sharing the room, a compromise solution, won't do, as there isn't enough space for both to spread out and the activities of one would disturb the other. One solution is to build on an addition to the house, thereby expanding the available space so both can have what they want.

RULES FOR COOPERATIVE PROBLEM SOLVING

Negotiating creatively takes imagination and sensitivity. Here we offer some things to think about the next time you find yourself in a conflict situation.

1. *Diagnose your personal and relational goals.* As we have seen, there are times to walk away from a conflict, times to give in, times to take a hard line, and times to compromise. When you encounter a conflict of interest, begin by honestly evaluating your personal and relational goals. If both are high, then a cooperative problem-solving strategy is called for.

2. *Make an effort to understand the other's interests and emotions.* Don't forget the human element. The parties involved in negotiation are flesh-and-blood people who are often frustrated, fearful, or angry and who have their own unique thoughts and perceptions. In Chapter 3 we discussed attribution biases. We saw that it is much easier for people to understand their own motivations than those of others. While seeing things from the other's point of view is not easy, it is worth a try. Often the other's demands are not as arbitrary and unreasonable as you might think.

One block to understanding the other is distinguishing *their* intentions from *your* fears. Roger Fisher and William Ury illustrate how easy it is for us to let our own fears and expectations color our interpretations. They recount the following story: "They met in a bar, where he offered her a ride home. He took her down unfamiliar streets. He said it was a short cut. He got her home so fast she caught the 10 o'clock news." Most people find the ending surprising because they make an assumption based on their own fears and prejudices.[52] Our suspicions are often made even worse during negotiation. The cost is an unwillingness to look for creative solutions.

If you can put aside your prejudices and sense the other's position, you may be better able to reach a settlement. If a father understands that a child's opposition to an early bedtime is prompted by a desire for autonomy rather than a desire to stay up late, he may be able to find another way to let the child feel grown up and important. It's also a good idea to ask yourself how your behavior looks to the other. One party's shyness may seem to the other to be coldness or disdain. If the first person realizes this, he or she can violate the other's perceptions by being more outgoing. Finally, understanding a partner's perceptions also allows you to help the partner save face. Remem-

ber that people may be trapped into a proposal long after they've ceased to believe it. You need to find a way to help them back out gracefully.

3. *Realize that emotions may run high during negotiation and accept them as legitimate.* In public negotiations parties may feel the need to vent anger, either to show a constituency they are not being soft or simply to release tension. While one's first response might be to walk out or shout an angry partner down, a better response is to let the other talk. The same is true of personal disagreements. Once your roommate has expressed anger, he or she may be better able to talk rationally. Fisher and Ury cite a useful rule developed during an industrial negotiation: Members agreed that only one person could get angry at a time. That made it easier for the party being criticized to listen to the other and say, "That's OK. It's his [or her] turn now."[53]

4. *Focus on interests not positions.* Let's return to the example we gave of opening the library window. Each disputant had an initial position: "The window should be opened" versus "The window must be closed." A **position** is the initial solution to the conflict that each proposes. **Interests**, on the other hand, are the underlying needs or concerns of each party. In this example the interests are "to get fresh air" and "to avoid a draft." The disputants couldn't find a solution because they were focusing on positions. The librarian realized what interests were at stake and found a solution that fulfilled both interests.

It is essential to search for the interests behind the position. Assume the parents in a given community are concerned about a dangerous building site.[54] They are afraid that their children will get hurt playing there, so they demand that the construction company fence off the area immediately. The company doesn't understand the reasons behind the demands but rather sees it as unnecessary harrassment. The company is likely to respond defensively if the parents' committee begins discussion by saying, "We demand that you put up a fence within the next 48 hours or we'll bring suit." A better way is to start with common ground: "We believe that we have a problem that needs to be solved. We're concerned about safety, as we know you are. It would be a terrible thing for both of us if an accident occurred. What can we do to make sure that one doesn't occur?" In addition, the parents should demonstrate that they recognize the company's interests as well: "We understand that it's in your interests to get your job done at minimum cost while preserving your reputation for safety and responsibility. Are we correct? Do you have any other important interests?" By responding to interests rather than positions, both parties are more likely to be able to solve the problem.

5. *Consider turning to third parties for help in negotiation.* Many conflicts can be solved if the people involved sincerely want to solve them and if they have the necessary sensitivities and interpersonal skills. But not all can. It is no crime to turn to others for help in the face of conflict. The literature on negotiation distinguishes three types of third-party intervention. Pruitt tells us that "in **mediation,** the third party works with the disputants, helping them reach agreement. In **fact-finding,** the third party listens to arguments from both sides and produces a set of nonbinding substantive recommendations. **Arbitration** is like fact-finding except that the recommendations are binding."[55] Conflicts between management and unions often make use of the latter two types of intervention. Mediation is used for a wide range of personal and community disagreements.

When negotiations reach a deadlock, third parties can help. For professional disputes people often turn to a professional mediator. For personal problems people generally turn to a friend. In both cases the individual chosen must have certain qualities: the ability to establish rapport with both parties, good interpersonal and persuasive communication skills, perceived impartiality, assertiveness, a strong power base,

and a reputation for trustworthiness.[56] Most importantly, the mediator must be skilled at empathic listening. If you believe you have these skills and want to develop them, you might consider taking a course in group problem solving, conflict management, negotiation, or mediation. Each of these areas will build on your interpersonal skills and make you better able to take problem-solving approaches to personal and professional problems.

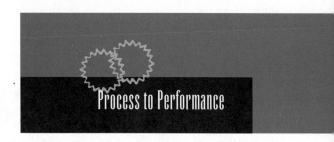

Process to Performance

REVIEW TERMS

The following is a list of major concepts introduced in this chapter. The page where the concept is first mentioned is listed in parentheses.

deference (355)
avoidance rituals (355)
presentational rituals (355)
demeanor (355)
playacting (356)
natural role differences (359)
dysfunctional role difference (359)
upward distortion (360)
warmth (360)
genuineness (360)
accurate empathy (360)
personality traits (366)
leadership (366)
dyadic linkage theory (366)
cohesion (367)
groupthink (368)
organizational culture (369)

grapevine   (373)
negotiation   (376)
aggressive style   (377)
withdrawing style   (377)
accommodating style   (377)
compromising style   (377)
problem-solving style   (378)
cost-cutting   (379)
compensation   (379)
logrolling   (380)
bridging   (380)
expanding the pie   (380)
position   (381)
interest   (381)
mediation   (382)
fact-finding   (382)
arbitration   (382)

SUGGESTED READINGS

Lappé, Frances Moore, and Paul Martin DuBois. *The Quickening of America: Rebuilding Our Nation, Remaking Our Lives.* San Francisco: Jossey-Bass, 1994. Two of America's leading activists for community involvement and social change demonstrate how to master the arts of public conversation and active citizenship. This is a workbook that really helps you think about the range of possible roles in public life and how to have your voice heard in the neighborhood as well as across the nation.

Zunz, Olivier. *Making America Corporate: 1870–1920.* Chicago: University of Chicago Press, 1990. Reconstructing the lives of middle-level managers from the personnel files of five major corporations of the time, Olivier Zunz has shown how their social relationships with one another and the workers they directed formed the corporate bureaucracies that still dominate much of the American workplace. A fascinating look at how many of the communication patterns

of supervisor and subordinate were originally shaped.

Deal, Terrance, and Alan Kennedy. *Corporate Cultures: The Rites and Rituals of Corporate Life.* Reading, Mass.: Addison-Wesley, 1982. An almost anthropological guide to "reading" behavior in the organization. This very enjoyable book shows you all the things to look and listen for when you enter the corporate world: the importance of rituals and stories, the major role players in the communication network, and the heroes who embody the company's real goals and values.

Goffman, Erving. *Interaction Ritual: Essays on Face-to-Face Behavior.* Garden City, N.Y.: Anchor Books, 1967. An in-depth look at the social mechanisms of public life. Essays on face-work, deference and demeanor, embarrassment, and much more. A fascinating look at how we conduct everyday life.

Martin, Judith. *Miss Manners' Guide to Excruciatingly Correct Behavior.* New York: Warner Books, 1988. A very humorous, but nonetheless excruciatingly correct, discussion of "proper" public communication. This book and Miss Manners' newspaper columns have gone a long way to restoring the perception that it's OK to be mannerly.

TOPICS FOR DISCUSSION

1. Discuss the four criteria suggested at the beginning of this chapter for managing public interactions. Are these the only or even the best criteria? What criteria would you add or delete from the list? Do your classmates agree? Discuss any differences of opinion.

2. Review the definition of playacting on page 356. Identify as many ways as you can that strangers playact in public. Do you think that playacting is healthy, damaging, or simply a waste of time? Ask several classmates to react to the claim that "most people today don't know how to interact with strangers, so they just ignore them."

3. Why do you think that upward distortion happens in organizations? Under what circumstances do you think a subordinate should keep quiet, disguise the bad news a bit, or be open and up-front about it?

4. What advice would you give doctors about conducting the medical interview with a patient? Keep in mind these three essentials: efficient use of time, accurate information processing, and patient satisfaction.

5. How important are status differences in the work and social world? When should status barriers be maintained, broken down, or built up? Why?

6. Research indicates that the grapevine is the least trusted but most utilized communication network in most organizations. What do you think should be done, if anything, to change the influence of the grapevine on campus or at work?

OBSERVATION GUIDE

1. Visit a public square, park, or business area where impersonal transactions are likely to take place. Record examples of avoidance rituals and presentational rituals. Note what happens when one person oversteps the boundaries, such as being too polite or too personal. Also, try to label any other rituals or behaviors that you think make impersonal interactions more or less effective.

2. Observe a wide range of customer-clerk interactions. On the sales floor, record the communication patterns on the sale of big-ticket items such as furniture or automobiles as well as small purchases like shoes, groceries, or health foods. In addition, hang around the customer service desk, where you can overhear people returning merchandise. Take notes following each observation, writing down message patterns. Then rate the results of the transaction as (1)

very effective, (2) OK, (3) somewhat problematic, or (4) not effective at all. Summarize what you have observed, noting which patterns of communication are most or least effective. Then compare your observations with the suggestions on page 362.

3. Every college campus is an organization. From your perspective as a student, try to identify as many different informal communication networks as you can. Who are the key members of the grapevine? Who are the most influential decision makers? Who is tapped into the off-campus network? Which faculty seem to be most "connected" on your campus? What influence do these networks have on the goings-on at your campus? You can conduct similar observations at work.

EXERCISES

1. Your instructor will assign everyone a role in a fictitious manufacturing organization. (Instructors, see directions for "Hi-Fli, Inc." in the *Instructor's Guide* to Farace, Monge, and Russell's *Communicating and Organizing,* available from Addison-Wesley.) For two or three class periods, the class will role-play an actual organization going about its everyday work routines. Students should observe their own communication with supervisors, coworkers, messengers, top management, and so on, and write down observations during assigned "coffee breaks." After the exercise is completed, discuss the communication patterns observed: status differences, upward distortion, leadership styles, and so on.

2. Rent a videocassette or film version of one or more movies that include work settings and scenes as a major part of the storyline. Films such as *9 to 5, Network,* and *Games Mother Never Taught You* are good examples. Choose several interesting segments to show in class. Small groups of students may be assigned to analyze different segments. The analysis should reflect research and theory presented in this chapter. For instance, a group could analyze the nature of supervisor-subordinate communication as portrayed in the film clip. Another group might choose to discuss the decision-making style and roles being played in a business meeting, and so on. Each group should organize its analysis for a 15-minute presentation to the class.

3. Each student should think of the best and worst supervisor-subordinate relationship he or she has been involved in. These relationships may have taken place at work, in a volunteer agency, or in a classroom work group — anywhere a clear leader was established. As a class, compile two lists. The first one should include the characteristics of the most and least effective supervisor known. The second list should include characteristics of the most and least effective relationships observed. Be careful to distinguish characteristics attributed to the supervisor from those attributed to the relationships. Once you have completed the two lists, discuss which is the most instructive. Is it better to think in terms of personal traits or relational attributions? Why?

4. Divide the class into groups of three and assign one person each to play the role of therapist, help seeker, and observer. Then role-play the following informal therapeutic relationships. In each situation the "therapist" should try to enact the three essential traits recommended by Carl Rogers: warmth, genuineness, and accurate empathy. The "observer" should record the verbal or nonverbal messages that communicate (or fail to communicate) the three characteristics.

Situation 1:

THERAPIST: Bartender

HELP SEEKER: Regular patron at bar, an independent accountant

SITUATION: Patron reveals a problem relating to a potential client in the basket-weaving mail-order business. He wants the account but cannot find a single topic of conversation on which to conduct small talk. He asks the bartender for advice.

Situation 2:

THERAPIST: Best friend

HELP SEEKER: East Coast young urban professional (yuppie)

SITUATION: Yuppie tells friend about a job offer on the West Coast. She really wants the job but can't seem to convince her boyfriend that there will be opportunities for him. He likes his current job and friends, but she thinks the move will do them good — if he gives it half a chance. She asks her best friend for advice.

Situation 3:

THERAPIST: Attorney

HELP SEEKER: A recent widow, 45 years of age, one child

SITUATION: The young widow consults her attorney. She is trying to put her life back together but cannot decide whether to sell the house and move into an apartment or keep the house and rent out rooms. She is on the verge of tears as she thinks about the changes ahead of her.

When finished role playing, the observer should report what he or she saw, and all three students should discuss how to improve informal therapeutic interactions. When, for instance, is a problem beyond informal help? How can you tell someone he or she needs to seek professional help?

Harriet Powers, who made this quilt, was born a slave in 1837 near Athens, Georgia. Her choice of biblical and astronomical subjects and the proportions of the figures are Western. The appliqued design and the animal figures, however, show an African influence. With other African Americans, Powers reworked and expanded African cultural elements to create a unique black culture.

(Harriet Powers, *Pictorial Quilt*, pieced and appliqued cotton embroidered with yarns, ca. 1895–1898)

13

Cultural and Historical Influences:
Communication Competence in Context

Throughout this text we have emphasized the part that context plays in communication competence. In examining family, intimate, and professional communication, we have already seen how important context can be. Here we expand that discussion by looking at more general contextual influences on communication. In this chapter we consider how culture and history affect the forms and functions of interpersonal communication.

We will begin by looking at some of the ways culture impacts on interpersonal interaction. In the first half of this chapter we will define culture and examine some of the ways cultures differ from one another. We will then look at problems that can occur when people from different cultures confront one another, and we will offer suggestions for improving cross-cultural communication.

In the second half of the chapter we will look at the impact of historical change on inter-

personal communication. Our goal will be to demonstrate that interpersonal communication is not only affected by geographic or spatial factors, but by temporal factors as well. Cultures grow and change, and the competent communicator recognizes and adapts to this process.

Cultural Influences

Culture is that set of values and beliefs, norms and customs, rules and codes, that socially define groups of people, binding them to one another and giving them a sense of commonality. Because we are humans, we ask questions about the world and our place in it. And because we are social beings, we turn to others for answers. In a sense culture is the collective answer to the fundamental questions that puzzle all of us: Who are we? What is our place in the world? How are we to live our lives? Although each of us develops our own responses to these questions, we also carry with us the answers our cultures have given us. And these cultural understandings play a large part in determining how we perceive the world, how we think about ourselves and our relationship to others, how we set and achieve goals, how we define the self, and how we exchange messages.

Although there may have been a time when Americans could sit back complacently and ignore everything that was "foreign," that time is gone. In today's shrinking world it is impossible to avoid cultural contact. More and more of us are crossing cultural boundaries each year, and even those of us who stay "safely" at home find our cultural worlds changing. As a result of technological and social changes, the worlds we are born into are likely to be quite different from those we later work and live in. To get along today, we must be able to adapt to cultural change. One way to begin is to become aware of how our own culture affects us.

AMERICAN CULTURAL PATTERNS

Like everyone else, we Americans are the products of cultural values and understandings. Although you may not share all the beliefs we will discuss, you have undoubtedly been exposed to dominant cultural patterns throughout your life: in schools, in religious organizations, and in the media. Whether you have accepted them without question or rebelled against them, they're still part of your cultural baggage — baggage you'll carry with you when you cross international boundaries. In discussing dominant cultural patterns in America, we'll draw on the work of Larry Samovar and his colleagues; we'll look at American (1) worldviews, (2) activity and time orientations, (3) human nature orientations, (4) perceptions of the self,

(5) social organization, and (6) communication styles.[1]

Worldview

Samovar and his colleagues define **worldview** as "a culture's orientation toward such things as God, man [and woman], nature, the universe, and the other philosophical issues that are concerned with the concept of being."[2] Although members of a culture may find it difficult to articulate their worldview, it is "so deeply imbedded in our psyches that we take it completely for granted and assume automatically that everyone else views the world as we do."[3] In analyzing the American worldview, Samovar discusses the way we separate the individual from nature, the importance we put on science and technology, and our materialism.

While some cultures emphasize unity with nature, Americans tend to separate the natural and the civilized worlds, believing that humans are distinctly different from (and more highly developed than) other living organisms. As a nation we see nature as something to be mastered, as an inexhaustible resource to be exploited for the benefit of humanity — and ourselves. While this view has contributed to our material wealth, it has also led to vast environmental problems we are only now beginning to recognize. Americans also place a high value on science and technology as ways of exploiting and mastering nature. Objectivity and control are two of the basic scientific values that spill over into our worldview and into our communication practices. "Americans tend to value objectivity, empirical evidence, rationality, and concreteness in their communication, and they often experience considerable difficulty in understanding persons who do not reflect these values."[4] Finally, Samovar feels that Americans believe in the goals of material well-being and physical comfort. One measure of an individual's success is the amount of material goods he or she manages to amass. Because Americans expect a high degree of cleanliness and comfort, they often look down on members of "underdeveloped" countries who have not achieved a comparable standard of living.

Activity and Time Orientation

Given the beliefs we've looked at so far, it's not surprising that Americans are active and hard working; value speed, efficiency and practicality; and are oriented toward progress and change. In general, Americans are characterized by **effort optimism,** a belief that if you work hard enough, you can achieve any goal. Of course, the converse of this belief is that if you fail, it is somehow your own fault. All of these values translate into a concern with clear, direct, and rapid channels of communication. Americans expect to be able to communicate instantly and effectively. When they encounter countries in which the telephones don't work and the mail service is unreliable, their response is likely to be anguish or frustration.

Americans' relationship to time is also deeply ingrained. To most of us, "Time is money," and speed is valued over sloth. Failure to show up on time or to meet a deadline is a serious matter. Time is something to be segmented into uniform chunks, and the time we spend in a given activity is regulated not by the nature of the act itself, but by the clock. We tend to make our activities fit our schedules rather than fitting our schedules to our activities.

Human Nature and the Individual Self

One of the questions cultures try to answer is, What is human nature? According to Samovar, Americans believe that although humans are capable of evil deeds, they are essentially perfectable. Whether an individual person becomes mean or noble is partially a function of the op-

portunities he or she is given. Therefore, it should be possible to improve human behavior by providing people with a good education and a healthy environment. Americans also believe that people are basically rational and can be trusted to make their own decisions. This premise, Samovar says, "underlies the democratic ideal, trial by a jury of one's peers, and free enterprise."[5]

As we saw earlier, America is an individualistic culture. The importance of individual identity and self-motivation is shown in the popularity of the "success story" and the respect Americans accord self-made persons. Samovar sums up the importance of the individual self: "The value of individualism in American culture represents a complex cluster of more specific desirable states or conditions such as self-reliance, autonomy of choice, privacy, freedom of expression, respect for other persons, equality, and democratic processes."[6]

Social Organization

Not only do cultures answer fundamental questions about the nature of the self, they provide guidelines for appropriate social relationships. According to Samovar the two most important characteristics of American social organization are **equality** and **future-oriented conformity.** Because of our emphasis on individual autonomy and human dignity, American culture tends to be egalitarian. As communicators we try to establish an atmosphere of equality. The breezy, informal style of the American can be problematic in countries with more hierarchical structures, where it may undermine basic authority structures.

As Samovar points out, one of the requirements of social life in any culture is conformity to basic social rules. The question is not whether a given culture encourages conformity, but what kind it encourages. Americans tend to conform not to traditional but to future-oriented norms.

It is generally far more important for Americans to "keep up with the Joneses" by being "up-to-date" than by conforming to traditions. Thus, Americans keep up with trends and are intrigued by progress and change.

Cultural Patterns and Communication Style

Americans also have unique ideas about how to communicate, ideas that may not be shared by people of other cultures. Let's start with the notion of credibility. If you have taken a public speaking class, you know that the good speaker emphasizes expertise and trustworthiness at the beginning of a speech. In certain Native American cultures, however, it is considered rude to display one's own credentials; the speaker instead opens by apologizing for his or her lack of knowledge, telling audience members that they alone can judge the worth of the speech.

In the interpersonal realm we believe that healthy relationships are built through self-disclosure and that it is important to share personal details with those close to us. In some cultures the sharing of intimate details is distasteful, while in others, speakers are even more blunt than we are. Our ways of handling conflict are also culture-bound. We believe that it is best to confront problems and discuss conflicts directly, but we must be careful in some Asian countries, where criticism causes shame and embarrassment. Successful cross-cultural communication often means reexamining basic beliefs about what represents good and bad communication.

ETHNIC, REGIONAL, AND CLASS DIFFERENCES

As you read the description of American cultural patterns given above, you may have found sections that you personally disagreed with. The beliefs and behaviors described above apply to most of us, most of the time, but they do not

sum us up completely. Nationality is not the only influence on our lives. Our ethnic, regional, and class memberships are also important aspects of our cultural identity. In this section, we look at some of the ways the subcultures Americans belong to shape our lives.

Shifting Cultural Identities

None of us belongs to a single culture. Rather we belong to a number of hierarchically embedded cultures and subcultures, each contributing in its own way to our understanding of the world. Some of the groups to which we belong are very large and diffuse, while others are much smaller and more specific. Some are very important sources of influence and identity, while others affect us only slightly. Some complement each other, and some conflict. Yet each contributes to cultural identity.

Our cultural identities shift back and forth. Sometimes we are influenced by national identity, sometimes by regional or class loyalties. In some situations ethnic and gender identifications shape our attitudes and behaviors, while in others, religious identity comes to the fore. If we are successful, we choose, from among the many voices telling us who to be and what to do, that advice that best fits our own sense of self.

Black and White Communication Patterns

Ethnic identities are one of our main sources of cultural identity; they are also a major source of misunderstanding, for members of different ethnic groups may develop differences in communicator style. One of the best documented of these differences is the difference between black and white communication patterns.

In *Black and White Styles in Conflict*, Thomas Kochman describes some of the common differences he encountered when, as a white, he interacted with blacks. Noticing that he did not always understand his colleagues' and students' points of view and they often misunderstood his, he wondered whether these communication problems might be due to cultural differences. He therefore began looking for patterns that repeated themselves regardless of the individuals involved. He became interested in reconstructing "the cultural factors that shaped the patterns and attitudes that Blacks and Whites brought with them to the communication situation."[7]

At the outset, we should clarify what groups Kochman is talking about when he uses the terms black and white. Kochman describes the groups he observed: Specifically, white is intended to represent the cultural patterns and perspectives of the dominant social group, a group that is also called white middle-class, Anglo, or Anglo-American. Black represents the ethnic patterns and perspectives of black "community" people, called elsewhere ghetto blacks, inner-city blacks, or African-Americans.[8]

Kochman admits that it is hard to separate the effects of social class from ethnic identity. He notes that what he calls the "black culture" will exist most completely among lower-income blacks, while the white patterns he describes are most true for middle- to upper-income-level whites. He contends, however, that the patterns he describes are ethnic as well as economic, even though in our society class and ethnic identity are often confounded.

Before we look at the results of Kochman's research, let's look at two cases that illustrate what happens when blacks and whites fail to realize they are following conflicting communicative rules. The first took place in 1914 when black civil rights activist Monroe Trotter met with President Woodrow Wilson to discuss segregation in the federal government. Wilson explained that segregation would help avoid friction between blacks and whites. Trotter objected strongly, pointing out that black and white clerks has worked together for 50 years without problems. Wilson was incensed by Trotter's argumentative manner and demanded a less offensive spokesman. When Trotter asked what had offended Wilson, the president answered, "Your tone with its background of passion." Trotter responded, "But I have no passion in me, Mr. President, you are entirely mistaken; you misinterpret my earnestness for passion."[9]

Now let's move to a more recent scene on a university campus. Community representatives were meeting with black and white faculty to discuss a proposed graduate program in urban education. The discussion soon became heated. One of the white female members criticized the meeting, likening its atmosphere to a "Baptist revival meeting." In response, a black male faculty member pointed to her and said, "Professor _____ , you need to know something. You can't make me over into your own image. Do you understand that? You can't make me over into your image." When he saw her fright, he softened his voice and said, "You don't need to worry; I'm still talking. When I *stop* talking, then you might need to worry."[10] Afterwards, the whites objected to the emotional tone of the meeting, and the professor who made the revival meeting comment believed she had been personally threatened. The blacks, on the other hand, believed their emotional expressions were perfectly appropriate given their strong feelings about the issues. As for the faculty member who was accused of making threats, he was completely astonished, commenting, "All I did was *talk* to her. Now how can that be threatening?"

If we look at the two scenarios, it's obvious that the disagreement is not so much over content, but over communication style. Kochman believes that blacks and whites hold different views of argument and discussion: "The black mode — that of black community people — is high-keyed: animated, interpersonal, and confrontational. The white mode — that of the middle class — is relatively low-keyed: dispassionate, impersonal, and non-challenging."[11] For black speakers, to show affect (even negative affect) during argument is to show sincerity and seriousness. Holding back emotions indicates distrust. To most white speakers, however,

392 PART 4: RELATIONAL CONTEXTS

anger indicates irrationality; reason and emotion are incompatible. The result? Black speakers may see white speakers as insincere, while white speakers may consider black speakers as out of control.

This effect is increased by differences in turn-taking. Kochman tells us that white speakers generally wait for a pause or a direct invitation to take their turn at talk, then address all of the points that have been made up to that time. The black rule, on the other hand, is to come in as assertively as one can after a single point has been made but then to restrict comments to this one point. Because of these differences both groups will see each other as "hogging the floor." Blacks will be perceived as jumping in too soon, while whites, who wait their turn, will seem reticent. However, once whites get to speak, they will go on for longer than is normal for black speakers.

The style differences one finds in interpersonal communication are also found in public talk. In general, black rhetorical style is intense, dynamic, and animated and often involves verbal interaction between audience members and speaker. Jack Daniel and Geneva Smitherman describe the **call and response pattern** basic to expressive behavior in the traditional black church as well as in secular situations. "Briefly defined, this African-derived process is the verbal and nonverbal interaction between speaker and listener in which each of the speaker's statements (or "calls") is punctuated by expressions ("responses") from the listener. As a fundamental aspect of the Black communications system, call-response spans the sacred-secular continuum in Black Culture."[12]

This highly interactional style is often used by black speakers and audiences who feel that overt responses are necessary to let the speaker know how he or she is "getting over." When blacks interact with whites, who give feedback in more subdued ways, they may assume that the whites are not listening and may "repeatedly punctuate . . . 'calls' with questions such as 'Are you listening to me?' 'Did you hear me?' etc."[13]

To the white speaker these questions seem annoying and unnecessary, for by standing quietly and maintaining eye contact, the white speaker is showing attention. Conversely, when the white speaker takes over and his or her black partners begin adding comments like "Tell it," "I hear you," or "Go 'head, run it down" or even worse, when black listeners actually turn and walk away in response to a particularly choice comment, the white speaker is likely to become completely confused. These indications of black interest and involvement will be interpreted as intrusive and interruptive by most whites.

Yet another source of misunderstanding lies in eye behavior. Molefi Asante and Alice Davis tell us that blacks tend to avoid eye contact with superiors as a show of respect, but whites tend to expect eye contact during listening. A white employer who cannot get a black employee to look him or her in the eye may conclude the worker has something to conceal, while the white listener staring the black employer in the eye may be perceived as disrespectful or, worse, as trying to put something over on the boss.[14]

These are only a few of the best-documented differences between black and white communication styles. There is, in fact, a large literature on the pragmatics of black and white language. Box 13.1 discusses another highly expressive, highly interactive use of language often associated with black male speakers, "playing the dozens." If you have never played the dozens (and you don't necessarily have to be black or male to have done so), you may find the practice a bit unusual. If you have, you may consider it a normal way of interacting with others. In either case it fulfills important functions within the communities in which it is played.

It is important to reiterate that the differences we have looked at are general, group-based differences — they won't apply to every black or white that you know. Still, they should indicate how easy it is for people whose communication styles differ to misunderstand one another. This is, in fact, what happened in the two examples we gave above. In both, the black speakers used a high-involvement style (assertive, emotionally expressive, and expansive) that disconcerted white listeners. Communication broke down because of conflicts in communication style.

Regional and Class Differences

Ethnic differences are not the only sources of communication misunderstandings. Social class and regional indentity also give rise to communication differences. Carley Dodd, for example, lists some of the differences in interpersonal style one is likely to find between the West and East coasts of America. His list includes perceived abruptness; speed of delivery; amount of verbal buffering (that is, introductory phrases in a sentence); amount of eye contact, touch, space, and verbal pausing; manner of leaving a conversation; amount of warmth and openness; amount of animation; amount of dominance; and amount of contentiousness.[15]

Class also determines communicative activity, as we saw in our discussion of Bernstein's elaborated and restricted codes in Chapter 4. There can be great differences between those who have lived in affluence and those who have grown up in poverty. Dodd describes some of the attitudes one is likely to find in poverty-level subcultures. Members of the poverty culture are much more likely to be fatalistic than are the affluent. Many poor people feel that the future is beyond their control, that success is impossible, and failure almost inevitable. Reared in environments in which achievement is difficult, their aspirations are often very limited. This leads to a here and now attitude in which desires are satisfied as rapidly as possible rather than deferred to a future date. Members of poverty cultures are often traditional and conservative, resisting innovations and sticking to tried-and-true ways of doing things. Because of these differences, communication between the rich and poor is often

frustrating for both parties. Table 13.1 (page 396) summarizes some poverty-culture values. The fact that these values differ from those of the middle class means that when middle-class people intervene in poverty neighborhoods, fundamental misunderstandings may occur.

COMMUNICATING ACROSS CULTURE

Whenever we interact with others who have been taught a different set of understandings about the world, we are engaging in **cross-cultural communication.** As we have seen, this kind of communication is not always easy. Although sensitive and intelligent people can often find communicative common ground, even the most well-meaning people experience problems in communication if cultural differences are large. In this section, we'll look at some of the reasons problems occur and we'll discuss some ways these problems can be avoided.

Cross-cultural communication is difficult because we are unaccustomed to dealing with differences. As we have seen throughout this text, people seek out similar others and avoid those who are different. In conversational openings, for example, we try to find something in common to talk about. ("Oh, you're from New Jersey, do you know so-and-so?"). Similarity is such a strong basis for attraction we may actually dislike dissimilar others. As social comparison theory points out, if we find ourselves interacting with someone who is too different, we exert subtle pressures on that person to conform.

One of the reasons we avoid those who are different is that cross-cultural communication usually takes extra effort. Rather than relying on old routines, we have to take the trouble to define new scripts and negotiate new understandings. While this may be a disadvantage in terms of time and energy, it can also be rewarding. Cross-cultural communication forces us to see the world in fresh ways and allows us to make new connections.

If You Can't Stand the Shame, Don't Play the Game: Playing the Dozens as a Conflict-Reducing Ritual

"Sounding" or "playing the dozens" is a game of verbal insults played in black urban communities. Before a group of onlookers, opponents direct rapid-fire insults, often obscene, toward one another's relatives, commenting on their age, beauty, wealth, and the like. "Your mother so skinny she ice-skate on a razor blade" and "Your mother wear high-heeled sneakers to church" are examples of some of the milder sounds. (For more obscene examples, consult the sources below.) One of the goals of the game is to think of new and creative insults that top those of the previous player. At their best, sounds can be clever and even poetic. Players must be quick-witted and highly verbal.

There have been many explanations for this ritual. Some have seen it as displaced aggression resulting from social and economic pressures, while others have viewed it as a working through of Oedipal impulses. Still others argue that, whatever other functions it performs, it teaches safe ways of resolving conflict in daily interaction.

Thurmon Garner believes that people learn important lessons about conflict by playing this game. They learn to confront conflict by talking rather than fighting, to keep cool in tense situations, and to keep their wits about them.

As we have seen, one way to deal with conflict is to repress or minimize it. Another way, illustrated here, is to dramatize it by bringing it out in the open. Hostilities are revealed and expressed, but in an indirect and ritualized form, giving the community a nonviolent forum for conflict.

Participants also benefit personally, learning inventiveness, assertiveness, and poise. They can gain a personal sense of power, since successful players are highly regarded in the community. They also learn not to lose their temper and to "hang in" when the going gets tough. Participants learn to remain composed, calmly taking whatever failures fall their way. Finally, because

BARRIERS TO INTERCULTURAL UNDERSTANDING

Given the kinds of differences we have described, it is no wonder that communication sometimes fails. In this section, we'll look at three barriers to intercultural understanding. We'll begin with prejudice, then briefly discuss two additional problems: ethnocentrism and assumed similarity.

Prejudice

Communicating interculturally means communicating with people who are different, and peo-ple who are different often make us feel uncomfortable. We can do two things in response to this discomfort: (1) we can think about the parts of the new culture we find strange, try to see why people in the culture act as they do, and relish the opportunity to communicate in new ways; or (2) we can reject, devalue, and avoid contact with anyone from the new culture. As we all know, the latter course is too frequently chosen, resulting in prejudice, discrimination, and intergroup conflict.

Prejudice is a negative social attitude held by members of one group toward members of another group, an attitude that biases perceptions and often leads to discrimination. To better un-

contestants must play off one another, following the flow of the game, they learn to coordinate their thoughts and actions. Thus, competition and cooperation are mixed together in a ritual that benefits both the individual and the community.

SOURCE: Thurmon Garner, "Playing the Dozens: Folklore as Strategies for Living," *Quarterly Journal of Speech* 69 (1983): 47–57.

ADDITIONAL SOURCES

Abrahams, Roger D. *Deep Down in the Jungle.* Chicago: Aldine, 1970, pp. 35–54.
Dollard, John. "The Dozens: Dialect of Insults." *American Imago* 1 (1939): 3–25.
Labov, William. "Rules for Ritual Insults." In *Studies in Social Interaction.* David Sudnow, ed. New York: Free Press, 1972.

derstand this definition, let's break it down into separate parts, following the analysis given by Tuen van Dijk.[16]

First of all, *prejudices are attitudes.* An **attitude** is a generalized evaluation of a stimulus object. To see how attitudes work in general, let's take a fairly neutral stimulus object, the horse. People respond to horses in various ways. Some people are crazy about them, some people are scared to death of them, and others simply don't care. Suppose as a young child Bob spent his summers on a farm, where he was allowed to feed the horses. His friends were all crazy about riding and talked about the horses they would one day own. Bob also read books about horses, and for a while *Black Beauty* was his favorite book. Over time he took these experiences and messages and used them to construct a general schema of what a horse was like: strong, swift, and beautiful. He stored this schema in memory, accessing it whenever the topic of horses came up, and using it to color later perceptions. When, on a vacation, he was given a mean-tempered, ill-kempt, sway-backed horse to ride, he measured the poor beast against his original schema, saw that the horse was atypical, and felt sorry that it had been so neglected and mistreated. Compare Bob's experience with Cathy's. Cathy was always told to stay away from horses because they were dangerous and

TABLE 13.1 Perceptions of poverty culture in the U.S.	
Concept	**Poverty culture's view**
Success	generally unattainable, limited only to people with a lot of luck
Failure	inevitable, no hope to overcome inherent failure
Emotions	emotions are made to be expressed, publicly or privately
Future	difficult to envision, so live for now
Money	to be used before it gets away, not saved for the future
Police	unfriendly, out to get us, and should be avoided
Education	useful for poor people with upward aspirations, an obstacle for individuals with low aspirations.
Fate	dominates some people, since various seen and unseen forces control our destiny

Reprinted from Carley H. Dodd, *Dynamics of Intercultural Communication,* 2nd ed. (Dubuque, Iowa: Brown, 1987), p. 80.

wild. She had no personal experience with the animal, but picked up a fear of horses from her mother. Her schema was negative, and when she saw the pitiful sway-backed nag we just described, she said to herself, "See, I was right. Horses are large, dumb, nasty beasts." The generalized conception, or attitude, each developed acted as a guide to perception and action.

Second, prejudices are a special kind of attitude. *Prejudices are attitudes based on group rather than individual opinions.* Some attitudes are merely matters of personal taste. You, for example, may not like people who are tall. If this attitude is not shared by other members of your culture and not used to limit the freedom of those who are tall, it is not a prejudice, although it is a foolish and biased opinion. Other attitudes are developed through communication with **in-group members** (people who share a common group identity) and used to describe **out-group members** (people who come from a different social group). These attitudes, if they are negative, are prejudices.

In all cases of ethnic prejudice, there is a strong emphasis on group identity, on "them" versus "us." "They" are to be feared or mistrusted primarily because they are not like "us." Ethnic prejudices are, in fact, created and reproduced through intergroup communication. Ironically, many people who are strongly prejudiced have never had personal experiences with the targets of their prejudice. Their negative attitudes come from secondary experience, from the talk or texts that make up their cultures.

Third, *prejudice is, by definition, a negative attitude.* Through prejudice we devalue members of other groups for not being the same as us. In a study of the attitudes of the Dutch toward foreign workers (primarily Surinamese, Moroccans, and Turks), van Dijk found three areas of negative evaluation. Out-group members were devalued for being different, for competing for scarce resources, and for threatening the Dutch way of life. First, van Dijk's subjects complained that the foreign workers were lazy, noisy, clannish, dirty, and sexually promiscuous, character-

Members of out-groups often look strange to members of in-groups. The mid-nineteenth-century Japanese artist who drew this portrait of Commodore Perry and his officers seems confused. The officers' eyes are oriental, but their noses are prototypically Western and greatly exaggerated. In this artist's ethnocentric view, all Westerners looked alike!

istics often used to describe out-group members regardless of nationality. Second they accused the foreign workers of taking away their neighborhoods, jobs, and houses, even though, as van Dijk points out, the jobs and houses they took were generally unacceptable to Dutch workers. Again, this complaint is a common one: that out-group members are favored over in-group members, even when by objective measure this perception is untrue. Finally, van Dijk's subjects saw the out-group as threatening to their territory, cultural identity, safety, well-being, and material interests.[17] With such fear, it is no wonder that intergroup conflicts so easily erupt into violence.

Fourth, *prejudices are based on biased cognitive models.* When prejudiced people think about out-group members, they are not trying to represent the world accurately. Rather, their purpose is to draw a line between in-group and out-group members, a line that divides those who are "superior" from those who are "inferior." To do this, prejudiced people often distort reality. Van Dijk explains:

When in-group members interpret "ethnic encounters," their goal in doing so is not primarily to establish a truthful and reliable representation of "what is really going on." Rather, just as in the interpretation of other encounters, people construct a model that is subjectively plausible . . . is coherent with previous models of ethnic encounters, and is a partial instantiation of general knowledge and attitude schemata.[18]

Several cognitive biases maintain prejudice: negative interpretations, discounting, attribution errors, exaggeration, and polarization. By **negative interpretations** we mean interpreting everything that minority members do as negative. If, for example, we see an out-group member sitting in the yard and soaking up the sun, we may interpret this activity as shiftlessness, while an in-group member doing the same thing may be seen as enjoying a well-deserved rest. If out-group members hang out together, they are clannish; if in-group members do so, they are being sociable. Whenever people see what "they" do as bad and what "we" do as good, they are using negative interpretations.

Discounting is a cognitive bias often linked to prejudice. Discounting means dismissing information that doesn't fit preconceived schemata. If, for example, you believe that out-group members are incapable of success and you encounter a very successful individual, you may discount this information by telling yourself that he or she is merely the "exception that proves the rule." Or you may convince yourself that the success was only due to luck or favoritism. In this way your schema never has to be changed, and you can continue to hold your prejudice in the face of contrary evidence.

People also tend to make the **fundamental attribution error** of interpreting another's negative behaviors as due to their disposition rather than due to their situation. This error is particularly strong in prejudiced people. If a prejudiced person finds that an out-group member is unemployed, he or she will believe the reason lies in the out-group member's inherent lack of ability and motivation rather than in an external circumstance like job discrimination. Of course, if the prejudiced person should lose a job, the attribution will be reversed. This time the unemployment will be blamed on external circumstances, for example, that all the jobs are being stolen by out-group members.

Finally, the biases of exaggeration and polarization are often used to support prejudices. Because of fear and anger, individuals may engage in **exaggeration** when they describe the negative character of out-group actions. An out-group member disagreeing with an acquaintance will be perceived as engaging in a violent argument. A mother who scolds her child in public may be seen as abusing the child. Individuals are not the only ones guilty of exaggeration; media reports about out-group members also show this bias. Thus, van Dijk reports that in the Netherlands newspapers frequently use a "flood" metaphor to describe immigration —

for example, a "tide" of Tamil refugees "flood" into the country. These word choices are particularly unfortunate in the Netherlands, given its tradition of battling against the sea for survival.[19]

Polarization is the tendency to magnify differences between in-groups and out-groups. Polarization is also used to categorize people as more different than they are. Thus, an immigrant who has become a citizen and who, for all intents and purposes, is very similar to in-group members will still be excluded and seen as one of "them."

A final characteristic of prejudices is that *prejudices are often used to support discriminatory behavior;* that is, they legitimate the treating of out-group members as inferior. Prejudices make it acceptable to deny out-group members the same rights and privileges given to in-group members. Thus, prejudices are often used to support the power and dominance of in-group members.

Communicating Prejudice

These biased perceptions are kept alive through everyday communication, both mediated and interpersonal. The mass media reproduce prejudices in several ways. First, news items are often written in ways that encourage alarm or anger. Often the most sensational and violent aspects of interethnic interactions are stressed, presumably because this practice sells papers and raises ratings. But whereas minority group members often take center stage in violent happenings, their roles are generally "nonspeaking." That is, they are seldom given the opportunity to explain their perception of events. In addition, the number of minority journalists, especially in high positions, is small. Thus, ethnic events are often described from the majority points of view. Finally, "topics that are relevant for the ordinary daily life of ethnic groups, such as work, housing, health, education, political life, and culture, as well as discrimination in these areas, are hardly discussed in the press, unless they lead to 'problems' for society as a whole or when they are spectacular."[20]

Individuals also spread prejudice through stories, anecdotes, and jokes, through persuasive argument, and through everyday conversations. Because most prejudiced people know that prejudice is considered bad, they try to hide it or to disguise it by using disclaimers ("Some of my best friends are . . . ," "I'm not prejudiced, but . . . ," or "Some of them are perfectly nice, however . . ."). These language forms give the illusion of fairness. Unfortunately, statements such as these are usually followed by negative stereotypes. Because these patterns cloak prejudice and racism, they are generally resented by out-group members.

In a classic 1970 study, Jack Daniel asked black respondents to report statements that white speakers had made to them that indicated insincerity.[21] In analyzing his results, Daniel put the responses into four categories. The first was made up of white attempts to show affinity for black people and included comments like "One of my best friends is a Negro," "You are as good as I am," "My maid is a Negro," and "My son goes to school with a Negro." The second category contained attempts to show an understanding of the black person's experiences through comments like "I am a member of a minority group," "I know exactly how you feel," "I used to live in the Hill District (a black district in Pittsburgh)," and "Once I didn't have what you have." The third category included stereotypic and derogatory comments like "you people," "little colored child," and "show me the latest dance." Finally, the last category consisted of comments that indicated the majority speaker did not understand the problems of minority members: "Negroes should be more grateful," "You have a chip on your shoulder," "If you just wait a little longer . . . ," and "What exactly does the Negro want?"

Do these comments appear prejudiced to you? Have you heard comments like them? If you are a minority group member, you probably have (although the language and content may be updated), and chances are you've found them offensive. If you're a majority group member you may not have realized how inappropriate some of these comments are.

Ethnocentrism

Another barrier to effective intercultural communication, and one that is closely tied to prejudice, is **ethnocentrism,** the belief that our culture is better than any other. While our way of life may be best for us, that does not mean it is best for others, or that our cultural patterns are widely shared. Samovar and his colleagues ask us to consider the possibility that every culture has something to offer and that our culture may not always be the best.

> *The Jew covers his head to pray, the Protestant does not — is one more correct than the other? In Saudia Arabia women cover their faces, in America they cover very little — is one more correct than the other? The Occidental speaks to God, the Oriental has God speak to him — is one more correct than the other? The American Indian values and accepts nature, the average American seeks to alter nature — is one more correct than the other? A listing of these questions is never-ending. We must remember, however, that it is not the questions that are important, but rather the dogmatic way in which we answer them.*[22]

Currently, many colleges are trying to combat ethnocentrism by exposing individuals to multicultural studies. Traditional curricula are being revamped to include the contributions of writers and thinkers from a variety of cultural backgrounds. Because allegiance to one's own cultures is so strong, this attempt has been controversial. Box 13.2 asks you to consider the debate surrounding multiculturalism and invites you to form your own opinion.

Assumed Similarity

There is a final barrier to cross-cultural understanding that may surprise you. This barrier consists of **assumed similarity**; it occurs whenever we ignore differences and assume that everyone is exactly the same. At first glance, this hardly seems like a problem; it seems instead to support the goals of open-mindedness and equality. The problem comes, however, when we ignore true differences and assume everyone is just the same as us. Many of the cross-cultural misunderstandings we have discussed so far have occurred precisely because the participants did not consider that their partners might be seeing the world differently and acting in accordance with those different perceptions. Competent communicators recognize the powerful effects of culture on every aspect of their lives. When interacting with people from another culture they are sensitive to differences in perspective.

Communicative Competence and Culture

It should be clear by now that culture is a powerful force that affects every aspect of our lives. In this section we will look at the relationship between culture and interpretive schema, social roles, goal achievement, notions of the self, and message choices. We will see how sensitivity to cultural norms and values can increase our competence as communicators, and how ignoring

the effects of culture can lead to unsuccessful and unrewarding interactions.

CULTURE AND INTERPRETIVE COMPETENCE

William Brooks gives an excellent example of how cultural sets affect perception. He tells the story of a professor at London University who showed his African students a film about improving health conditions in African villages. After the film he asked the class what they had seen. One student answered, "A chicken!" and the others all agreed. The professor was surprised, for to his knowledge there was no chicken in the movie. He carefully went through the entire film, frame-by-frame, and sure enough he found in the bottom corner of two or three frames, a chicken taking flight. Although the chicken's cameo performance lasted only part of a second, the students saw it quite clearly; what they did not see was the important information (important least to the professor) on eradicating mosquitoes. Several theories were offered for the students' response: the African students' sharp eye for hunting, the religious significance of the chicken, and even the fact that novice film viewers tend to focus on details within a frame rather than on the whole frame. Regardless of the reason, the students' culture clearly had taught them to see the world differently than the professor's culture had.[23]

The example of the chicken points out that people from different cultures see the content of scenes differently. Someone brought up on a farm in Nebraska and someone from inner-city Chicago, if transported to each other's environments, will not see them in the same way. Each will miss a lot of what the other considers to be important. Yet each will probably notice things that are so commonplace to the other that they've become invisible.

Not only does culture determine what we see, it determines how we see. There is evidence that general patterns of information processing also differ culturally. Carley Dodd tells us that general thought patterns, including the kind of logic we use and the ways we sequence events, may also be the products of culture. Members of some cultures, for example, think in terms of linear, sequential, time-ordered patterns, while members of other cultures think in terms of pictures or configurations.[24]

CULTURE AND ROLE COMPETENCE

All cultures categorize people by role. A good example of role-related behavior is the way we react to age. In many cultures the elderly are treated with great respect. The Ashanti of Ghana, for example, address all elderly men by a term that translates as "my grandfather," and they regard older people as repositories of wisdom.[25] In China old age is also respected, and the Chinese have difficulty understanding why Americans separate the generations, paying to send our children to day-care centers and our grandparents to old-age homes. In comparison to the Ashanti and the Chinese, we place less value on old age. In our culture the elderly are often seen (even by themselves) as useless and nonproductive.

The values placed on being men or women are also culture-specific, and everyday customs reflect these values. In parts of India women do not eat at the table with men; they are served separately after the men have finished eating.[26] In Vietnam women must eat smaller portions of food than men, regardless of their hunger.[27] And, of course, in some cultures women wear veils and are completely isolated from the world of men. Not only do gender values differ, but so too do our ways of being masculine and feminine. Although many Americans are brought up to believe that men are naturally more aggressive, more logical, and less emotional than women, in some cultures this pattern is reversed. Edward Hall tells us that in Iran, it is the

In traditional societies, power and prestige are differently distributed. The place of women in such societies is likely to differ sharply from that of men.

men who read poetry, express their emotions freely, and act on intuition rather than logic; women, on the other hand, are considered to be coldly practical.[28]

CULTURE AND GOAL COMPETENCE

Not only does culture specify appropriate role behaviors, it also affects individual goals and aspirations. Carley Dodd discusses the fact that some cultures emphasize task goals, while others emphasize social goals. Members of task cultures believe that self-worth can be measured by how

BOX **13.2**

Recognizing Cultures: The Politics of Multicultural Talk

Novelist Saul Bellow is supposed to have said, "When the Zulus produce a Tolstoy we will read him." Whether or not Bellow actually made the statement, it does capture the sentiment of many who have passed judgment on the raging debate about "multiculturalism." The issues range from the debate at Stanford University regarding which authors should be standard reading fare for freshmen to Rush Limbaugh's declaration that "multiculturespeak" can be summarized as "*Indians are good. White Europeans are bad. Blacks are good. Asians, we're not too sure about* (77)." But what are the issues surrounding multiculturalism and how do they apply to interpersonal communication?

Political scientist Amy Guttman describes the two extremes in the debate as "essentialists" and "deconstructionists." The first camp seems to believe that allowing any new or minority voices to be heard is paramount to forsaking the values of Western civilization. They fear that our society will be balkanized or broken into a thousand different subcultures, because the core values of American society will have been diluted to a point where no "glue" will be left to adhere us together. Deconstructionists, on the other hand, can't understand why the white European canon is so sacred, especially since they see it as perpetuating racism, sexism, and ethnocentrism. But then they take the argument to another

extreme, insisting that there are *no* shared intellectual standards able to provide reasonable answers to the fundamental questions of life, liberty, and happiness. In the end, the values that count are simply the values of those in power. Naturally, this provokes fear in the essentialists, who make another clarion call for minority groups to adopt "our" traditional values or take the next boat back to wherever they supposedly came from. Polarization reigns.

Philosopher Charles Taylor believes this debate turns on a supposed link between recognition and cultural identity. If our personal and social identities are partly shaped by how others recognize us, then a society that does not recognize the heritage of a particular group or mirrors back a demeaning image of that heritage can cause great harm. Interpersonal and intercultural communication are essential in this process because identity is defined in dialogue with others. In earlier times, recognition of one's identity was built into the very fabric of small societies, since it was based on social categories that everyone took for granted. Today, one's personal (and even cultural) identity "doesn't enjoy this recognition a priori. [One] has to win it through exchange, and the attempt can fail" (34–35)."

Taylor sees modern democratic principles as promising equal dignity to all citizens. In theory, this grants each citizen universal access to the same rights and privileges, with society blind to his or her race, gender, creed, or subculture. But alongside this "politics of universalism," Taylor sees the historical emergence of unique personal selves as giving rise to a "politics of difference." In terms of our personal identity and cultural heritage, we do not want to be treated the same, but to be recognized as having "differences" worth preserving. In the multicultural debate, no one has taken the position that it is necessary to give up our individual rights, value preferences or

this presumption does not mean that we accept all cultures as equally valid or as contributing to the human story in equal measure. Taylor calls it an act of breathtaking condescension to grant a favorable judgment to any culture without first attempting to understand what it values and what it might contribute to our own culturally limited view of things. We should expect to find in another culture aspects that we will come to admire as well as those that we will continue to detest. And we should also be open to the real possibility that our own values will be transformed in such a way that we will see things differently, that our own standards will have been enlarged. We might, for instance, discover that the Zulus contribution to humanity will not be another Tolstoy, but a new form of artistic or intellectual or moral excellence that was previously unfamiliar to us.

The debate on multiculturalism will continue to be hashed out on radio talk shows and in our college classrooms. But as long as it remains polarized, we all lose. One measure of our collective intercultural communication competence may be how successful we are at changing the terms of the debate.

differences in personality in order to cohere as a society. Why is it that preserving cultural differences should be any more threatening to the common good? Taylor agrees that we need to preserve diversity and engage ourselves in each other's cultural heritages, but cautions us in terms of how we do it.

In Taylor's view, every culture that has withstood the test of time probably has something important to add to the conversation of human societies. We owe each culture the presumption that it has something valid to contribute, and we owe it to ourselves to make the effort to understand other cultures on their own terms. To offer

SOURCE: Charles Taylor. *Multiculturalism and "The Politics of Recognition"* (Princeton, N.J.: Princeton University Press, 1992); Rush Limbaugh. *See, I Told You So.* (New York: Pocket Star Books, 1993.); Amy Guttman. "Introduction," in C. Taylor, *Multiculturalism and "The Politics of Recognition."*

ADDITIONAL READINGS

Berlin, Isaiah. *The Crooked Timber of Humanity: Chapters in the History of Ideas.* New York: Vintage Books, 1992.

Tarnas, Richard. *The Passion of the Western Mind: Understanding the Ideas That Have Shaped Our World View.* New York: Ballantine, 1991.

much one has accomplished. Dodd tells us that in such cultures, themes such as "no pain, no gain," "get ahead," and "make it to the top" are "the surface structures of a deeper, underlying cognitive dimension of how people are viewed in comparison with tasks. Americans, for instance, are considered highly task oriented."[29] In a more people-oriented culture, task achievement is less important. People develop a more personal style of conversation. In traditional societies, power and prestige are differentially distributed. The place of women in such societies is likely to differ sharply from that of men.

Cultures also tell us whether we should even try to set goals. Certain cultures, marked by fatalism, believe that individuals can do nothing to control their future. Members of these cultures meet their fate with acceptance, endurance, and passivity, assuming that it is wrong to attempt to change what is God's will. Larry Samovar illustrates the difference between fatalism and a sense of accomplishment. "If you ask a Hindu why he got only ten bags of corn from his land while nearby farmers got much more he would say it was the wish of God. An American farmer's answer to the same questions would be, 'Hell, I didn't work hard enough.'"[30] Obviously, members of fatalistic cultures communicate differently from those of more active cultures. They may consider our communication efforts to be aggressive, persistent, and even arrogant.

CULTURE AND SELF COMPENTENCE

As we saw in Box 12.2, cultures also differ in the value they place on the self. **Collectivist cultures** emphasize what Stella Ting-Toomey calls a "we" identity, valuing shared interests, harmony, and collective judgments. **Individualist cultures,** on the other hand, place a premium on an "I" identity, valuing personal identity, competition, and individual decision making.[31] North American and European countries (like the United States, Canada, and Great Britain)

are individualist, while many South American and Asian countries (like Venezuela, Peru, Taiwan, and Thailand) stress collectivism. The individualist countries value freedom, creativity, and economic incentive, but at the same time may inadvertently encourage materialism, alienation, and ecological arrogance. As for communication style, collectivists try to avoid conflict and, when this is impossible, use indirect styles of conflict resolution, while individualists are more confrontational and direct. Collectivists also try to discourage individual accomplishment. In distributing rewards they are more likely to use an **equality norm** (where each member receives the same reward regardless of input) than an **equity norm** (where distribution is based on individual merit); in individualist countries the opposite is true. Because harmony is so important, collectivist cultures value obedience, emphasize smooth intergroup relations, and stress politeness. Family and interpersonal obligations are also important. As Ting-Toomey says, "To be attracted to a member of a collectivistic culture means to take on additional responsibilities and obligations toward the member's social networks."[32]

CULTURE AND MESSAGE COMPETENCE

One of the most obvious signs of cultural difference is language difference. Dodd tells us that there are over three thousand language communities on earth, many of which have yet to be recorded in writing. One of the best points of access to a culture is its language, for language is the primary tool by which a culture transmits its values and beliefs. Yet learning a new language is difficult, because languages differ in what they make expressible. As we saw in our discussion of the Sapir-Whorf hypothesis in Chapter 4, different language communities organize the world in different ways.

While differences in verbal behavior between cultures are obvious, nonverbal differences are

Cultural boundaries shrink every day. These children, photographed in rural southern China, are fascinated by Americans and can already speak a few words of English. While their Western-style clothes make them look like American youngsters, their world views will be uniquely Chinese.

equally important but less obvious. When we cross international borders, we are usually aware of the difficulties of translating our language; we are less aware of the difficulties of translating nonverbal meanings. As we saw in Chapter 3, one area of nonverbal difference is in the meaning and use of space. As Hall tells us:

> Space is organized differently in each culture. The associations and feelings that are released in a member of one culture almost invariably mean something else in the next. When we say that some foreigners are "pushy," all this means is that their handling of space releases this association in our minds.[33]

Hall explains that in Latin American countries people feel comfortable talking at much closer distances than North Americans are used to.

The distance that makes a Latin American feel comfortable may signal either sexuality or hostility to a northerner. Thus, a North American will move away from a Latin American during conversation. "As a consequence, they think we are distant or cold, withdrawn and unfriendly. We, on the other hand, are constantly accusing them of breathing down our necks, crowding us, and spraying our faces."[34] Americans who work closely with Latin Americans have been known to erect physical barricades of desks and chairs to give themselves room, a tactic that so disturbs Latin Americans that they may even climb over the obstacles in order to find a comfortable speaking distance.

Body language and eye contact also differ from culture to culture. In Indonesia, for example, people talk while sitting on the floor, but it is very important for them not to point the soles of their feet toward their conversational partner, for that would indicate the other was beneath them.[35] And even so seemingly natural a behavior as eye contact can carry many messages. E. C. Condon outlines the meanings that are attached to a widening of the eyes in several cultures. For instance, in the dominant American culture widened eyes signify surprise or wonder. If Chinese widen their eyes, however, they may be expressing anger or resentment. For the French the identical movement means "I don't believe you," while for Hispanics, it may signal a lack of understanding.[36]

The examples in this section have shown that culture affects all aspects of communicative behavior. To be an effective communicator, an individual must be sensitive to cultural norms and values. He or she must also be aware that cultural understandings change over time. In the remainder of this chapter, we look at the temporal dimension of communicative contexts.

Historical Influences

As our discussion of cultural influences has shown, communication changes as we travel around the globe. What counts as good communication in San Diego may not be effective in San Juan, and what is acceptable in Berlin may be taboo in Beijing. The same kind of changes occur as we move through time. Communication practices that were acceptable to your parents' generation seem old fashioned now, just as today's communication patterns will seem obsolete to the next generation. No culture can afford to remain static; if a culture is to survive, it must evolve. Understanding a culture therefore involves more than understanding what separates it from other cultures. It also involves understanding how that culture develops over time.

In this section we'll examine temporal changes in the interpersonal communication patterns of Americans — changes that we think will surprise you. We'll discover that the ways our ancestors interacted with friends and neighbors, thought about their families, raised their children, communicated their love to one another, and felt about themselves have changed dramatically over the years. And we'll see that these changes in the private sphere are closely related to social and economic changes in the public sphere.

We'll begin by looking at social conditions in America in three historical periods: the colonial period, the early industrial period, and the modern period. There will, of course, be gaps in our survey, and we will limit ourselves to understanding the lives of middle-class citizens. Nevertheless, this brief overview should give you a general sense of the ways in which personal relationships have evolved over time.

THE COLONIAL PERIOD (1600–1780)

Let's begin with the **colonial period,** a period that extends from about 1600 to about 1780. During this period the early colonists set out to establish themselves in what was to them the New World. Of course, there were regional variations in the ways they went about this task. The Puritans who settled in New England, for example, lived in small, tight-knit villages, closely supervised by religious leaders. Colonists in the Middle colonies were more religiously and economically diverse and experienced greater class disparity. And Southern communities, where much of the population was made up of single males between the ages of 20 and 29, was characterized by a less stable culture involving "conspicuous consumption, profiteering, and hospitality."[37] Despite these differences, however, there were commonalties. The colonial period was characterized by strong social consensus and interdependence, by an acceptance of inequality and rank, and by patriarchal power.

The Colonial Household

The basic interpersonal unit in colonial times was the household, not the nuclear family. Households were large, consisting of husband and wife, children from their marriage and (because of high death and remarriage rates) from previous marriages as well, indentured servants, apprentices, and unmarried relatives. No special favoritism was shown to blood relatives, all household members lived and worked together, and there was no separation between work and family life. The colonial home was a site of production. There food was grown, cloth was woven, furniture was made, schooling was undertaken, and religious instruction was offered.

For most colonists (except the very few who lived on large Southern plantations) personal space was limited. A large family might share a two- or three-room dwelling and might all sleep together in the same room or even many in the same bed. The modern concept of privacy was simply unknown. Community leaders could interfere in the lives of the colonists whenever they liked, removing a child from, or assigning an unmarried adult to, a household. No household was exempt from community scrutiny. Court records, for example, frequently cited testimony of neighbors who just happened to be peering through a window at the time a crime was committed. In one case a couple testified that they heard snoring in the next room. To satisfy their curiosity they stood on a hogshead of tobacco and peered over the wall. Upon catching a glimpse of a couple in bed together, one of the observers pried loose a board to get a better view.[38] Under such close supervision, it is not surprising that individualism and nonconformity were rare.

Rank and Patriarchy

Colonial political life was hierarchical, with older males making all important community decisions. In the words of historian Stephanie Coontz, "the glue that bound individuals to households and households to community was patriarchy."[39] Under **patriarchy** older males ruled all aspects of life. So accepted was male authority that household heads who failed to control their wives, servants, or children could be punished. Inequality and male superiority were seen as a natural part of God's plan. In such a society, knowing how to communicate one's own rank and how to show deference to those of higher rank must have been an important communication competence.

Codes of Conduct

One of the most surprising aspects of colonial life was the relative earthiness of the people. Behaviors we would consider rude or crude today were quite common, although advice manuals of the time did their best to encourage a more civilized code of conduct. A popular advice manual of the time offered the following advice:

Foul not the table cloth.

Put not thy hand in the presence of others to any part of thy body not ordinarily discovered.

Spit not in the room but in the corner, or rather go out and do it abroad.[40]

Accounts of foreign travelers confirm the fact that uncouth behaviors occurred frequently. A Frenchman who visited Virginia in the 1780s marveled at the fact that the people he observed blew their noses either with their fingers or with a single silk handkerchief that also doubled as a necktie and a napkin.[41] It was clear that our colonial ancestors did not have a strong sense of cleanliness or of human boundaries. Nor did the majority view personal violence and cruelty as wrong. Brawling was a major and accepted part of male culture. The problem became so bad, in fact, that legislatures in Virginia, North Carolina, and South Carolina made it illegal to "cut out the Tongue or pull out the eyes," or to bite or cut off the nose "[of] the King's Liege people."[42] Only gradually did more "civilized" sets of manners develop.

Sex, Love, and Marriage

Given such impulsivity, it is not surprising that sex was openly enjoyed and discussed. Sex during colonial times was not a matter for false prudery; it was talked about with great directness, and marriage manuals advised couples to engage "with equal vigor" in the conjugal act.[43] Nevertheless, the proper setting for sex was considered marriage, and sexual practices that did not lead to legitimate procreation were severely punished. Adultery, defined as sex between a man and a married woman, was one such practice, although its prohibition seems to have been as much a matter of protecting (men's) property rights as it was a way of enforcing morality.

Today we believe that love is a necessary prerequisite to marriage. This was not the case in colonial times. Love was a duty, something one learned to feel after marriage. Romantic love, as we know it today, did not develop until the 19th century. Colonial couples based their choice of partners on compatibility rather than on romance and were anxious to pick a mate their parents approved of. According to a popular advice manual of the time: "Children are so much the goods, the possessions of their Parents, that they cannot without a kind of theft, give away themselves without the allowance of those that have the right in them."[44]

Concepts of Identity

In colonial times, identity was clearly fixed by rank and gender. Men and women were considered to be different from one another by nature. Men were controlled, rational, and moral. Women, on the other hand, having inherited Eve's sinful nature, were passionate and tempestuous. Because of these essential differences, men were to guide and teach their wives; and wives were to submit to such teaching. In the words of John Winthrop, governor of the Massachusetts Bay Colony, writing in 1645, "A true wife accounts her subjection [as] her honor and freedom, and would not think her condition safe and free, but in subjection to her husband's authority."[45] This was not an era in which gender roles were questioned or individuality accepted.

Although colonial conformity pressures may seem stifling to us, they did not seem that way to the colonists. Independent decision making had little value, and families made no attempt to teach children social attitudes that might conflict with community standards. It simply never occurred to parents to foster individuality in their children. And the idea that people should look inside themselves to find what makes them unique and should share that uniqueness with others was not to occur for another hundred years or so. Rather than worrying about an individual self, the colonists worried about being accepted by their communities and their God.

THE EARLY INDUSTRIAL PERIOD (1830–1880)

The simple agrarian life of the colonial period did not last long. By the early 19th century, America was experiencing rapid urbanization and industrialization. Young men and women in increasing numbers were leaving the safety of small rural communities and seeking their fortunes in towns and cities. The new conditions they faced led to a great deal of uncertainty.

Social Change and Anxiety

Historian Karen Haltunnen has identified some of the fears that preoccupied Americans during this period.[46] First, 19th-century Americans feared political instability. Now that political leaders were elected rather than appointed by the crown, there was concern about the influence of corrupt politicians. Fear of mob rule was real and immediate. Second, 19th-century Americans feared economic change. The emergence of industrial capitalism ushered in a new era of competition and greed. People worried about the instability of a money economy. Third, 19th-century Americans feared the new social freedoms that surrounded them. No longer under the watchful eye of their elders, suddenly responsible for their own conduct, young men and women found their new freedoms frightening.

S. W. Nissenbaum sums up the situation in which urban migrants found themselves:

> They were on their own, then, in mind and body . . . what loomed before them was not just a bleak future, but an unknowable future — and a far wider range of options than their parents had ever known, and for which nobody was equipped to prepare them. . . . Neighbors were unfamiliar; the new communities were often demographically skewed; the seasonal cycle of seed-time and harvest no longer serve to regulate the rhythm of their lives; even their bodies, which had served to confirm their identity through the physical labor imposed by farm work, were useless and "alien" to the kind of activities demanded of them in colleges or cities.[47]

Social historians argue that it was in response to insecurity brought on by new social conditions that 19th-century Americans developed new ways of relating to one another and to themselves.

The 19th-Century Home

In one sense, 19th-century Americans were right to be concerned about the impact of a changing economy on their lives. The emergence of industrial capitalism had far-reaching effects, not the least of which was that work and home became separated. For the first time in American history, men left home to work, leaving women and children behind. This changed the way 19th-century Americans felt about the home. Americans began to think of their lives as occurring in two different spheres, one ruled over by men and the other belonging to women. The public sphere, where men worked and governed, was characterized by competition and greed. The private sphere, the world of the home, was characterized by sentiment and sympathy. No longer a site of production, the home now became a refuge from the harsh realities of capitalist competition, a "haven in a heartless world." Descriptions of the home dating from this period reveal an almost religious fervor.

> We go forth into the world . . . and the heart is sensible to a desolation of feeling; we behold every principle of justice and honor disregarded, and good sacrificed to the advancement of personal interest; and we turn from such scenes with a painful sensation, almost believing that virtue has deserted the abodes of men; again, we look to the sanctuary of home; there . . . disinterested love is ready to sacrifice everything at the altar of affection.[48]

Not only did the home serve a spiritual function, it also took on a political function. During the Revolution, the patriots had exerted pressure on the British by boycotting foreign products. After the Revolution, the sense that there was a link between patriotism and the home became even stronger. It was in the home that citizens of the new republic were to be educated. The problem of political instability that so worried people of the time could only be solved if young people were educated to be responsible and patriotic. That education took place within the home under the guidance of what came to be called the **republican mother.**

During this period, the physical home was redesigned to reflect changing social conditions, as well as improved standards of living and new notions of propriety. Beds, which in the colonial period, were in open view in the main room of the home, were now placed in separate rooms. Houses became larger and their spaces more specialized. Historian John Kasson says, "by the latter part of the nineteenth century, middle-class houses and apartments were characteristically divided into major zones of society, privacy, and service . . . " Guests were entertained in the parlor and dining room; household members sought privacy in bedrooms and bathrooms; and servants worked in kitchen, pantry, and laundry room.[49]

Rudeness and Civility

Americans responded to the dramatic changes that were occurring around them by developing new codes of conduct. These codes were closely tied to the new public and private spheres. In public, as we saw in Box. 3.1, behavior was characterized by rigid politeness and self-effacement. Gone was the impulsivity of the colonial times. Now anything that remotely touched on personal feeling or on passionate desire was placed off-limits. The public face of 19th-century America was rigid and prudish in the extreme.

In private, another code of conduct developed. People who guarded against any show of emotion in public were free to express their feelings in private, although this emotional expression was expected to be positive and uplifting and was extremely sentimental. One of the reasons communication took this form was that it was considered (as we have already seen in Chapter 8) to be a reflection of the speaker's **character.** Character consisted of a constellation of positive qualites including thrift, hardwork, duty, self-sacrifice, good deeds, integrity, and a spotless reputation, as well as sentimentality, gentility, and kind-heartedness.[50] Character was extremely fragile; it could be destroyed by any hint of crudeness. Therefore, it was something to be constantly worried about and improved upon. Within the private sphere almost any occasion could give rise to character-building. Even a normal dinner could be an opportunity for family members to demonstrate "punctuality, order, neatness, temperance, self-denial, kindness, generosity, and hospitality."[51]

Sex Roles and Personal Identity

As in the colonial period, sex roles were highly differentiated. Men and women were still considered to be different from one another, but the nature of their differences had shifted. Women, who had previously been considered morally inferior to men, now became the moral superiors. No longer could men set the standard for women, for men were now considered to be ruled by base passions. Women were desexualized and described with almost cloying sweetness, as the following passage from a novelist of the time shows:

> But stop. Turn back. We have neglected the heart of the house, the mother's room! The old temple had no such holy of holies. The mother's room! Here came she as a bride. Here only God's angels and her own husband have heard what words the inmost heart of love can coin.[52]

Love, Desire, and Romance

The direct expression of sexual feeling that characterized colonial communication was muted and transformed in the 19th century. Direct talk about sex became taboo, although the resulting secrecy and censorship may actually have enhanced rather than dampened sexual desire.[53] When couples expressed their passion, they expressed it in terms of an idealized and romantic love rather than in terms of physical desire. As we saw in Box 11.2, couples used a lushly romantic and highly emotional style to convey affection.

Although love purified and elevated passion, it was not an excuse for premarital intimacy. Sex was to take place only within the bonds of marriage. An advice manual of the day told men to wait until marriage before engaging in physical intimacy: "You can wait, you are a man; be master of yourself."[54] There was no corresponding need to warn women, for their natural purity protected them from temptation.

THE MODERN PERIOD (1900–1960)

By the turn of the century, social conditions in America were once again changing. The anxieties of early capitalism had waned, and Americans were embracing the very values they had once feared. Americans had finally adjusted to urban life and industrial development. Many of our current beliefs and attitudes toward interpersonal communication were begining to emerge.

Mass Consumption and the American Dream

The early 20th century was a period of unprecedented industrial growth. To Americans of the time, bigger was better. Many towns and cities doubled in size, large corporations began to control the economy, and average citizens began to orient themselves to national news and advertising rather than to local issues.[55] As the economy moved from scarcity to abundance, America became a consumer society. In earlier times, independent families were expected to be self-sufficient, producing all that they needed for themselves. As industries grew, people became dependent "on goods made by unknown hands," on the output of mass production.[56] As Americans wandered through the glamorous new department stores and gazed at piles of brand-name goods, they dreamed of someday displaying these riches in their own homes. For more and more people consumption was a means of reaching happiness. Now every American had an equal right "to desire the same goods and to enter the same world of comfort and luxury."[57]

It was no accident that advertising came into its own at this time. The new mass economy required a high level of consumer demand, the more wasteful and indiscriminate the better. Advertising had to do more than announce the availability of a product, it had to create a demand. In 1919 the associate editor of *Advertising and Selling* made this quite clear: "I want advertising copy to arouse me, to create in me a desire to possess the thing that's advertised, even though I don't need it."[58] Under such pressure, Americans became increasingly materialistic. As Stephanie Cott points out, "the activity of parents became directed less at ensuring that their children should *be* more than themselves than that they should *have* more than themselves."[59]

Home and Family Values

Given this change in attitudes, it is not surprising that the home was no longer seen as a refuge or a temple. It was seen, instead, as a place for further commodification and consumption. The home was a place to display the store-bought goods a family could afford, especially the technological marvels made possible by electricity. The status of a home could be measured by whether it contained an electric range or washing machine; the personality of its owners could be measured by the style and taste of the home's furnishings.

At the same time that the home was becoming filled with consumer goods, it was being emptied of most of its social functions. The moral authority of the home was diminishing, as public schools took over education and government agencies took over the task of providing social welfare. The only social function left was an emotional one. Experts agreed that the

Communication is transformed not only by political and economic change, but by technology as well. New technologies produce new ways of experiencing and relating.

(Stuart Davis, sketch for mural, *The History of Communication,* 1939)

primary social purpose of the home was to "foster emotional health in an industrial society."[60] Social maladjustment was no longer blamed on poverty or genetics, but on a failure of the home. Mothers, in particular, were blamed if children did not turn out to be model citizens for it was their responsibility to provide a stable and nurturing psychological setting within the home.

Personality and Self Expression

By the early 20th century, the codes of conduct that had characterized the 19th century had almost completely dissolved. Middle-class Americans no longer looked to their "betters" for models of genteel behavior. Instead, in the early part of the century, "imitations of working-class and black culture became the rage: middle-class people listened to ragtime, did the cakewalk, copied the tough dancing pioneered by urban working youth, embraced professiontal sports, and started going to amusement parks and nicleodeons."[61] The stiffness and informality of the 19th century was replaced by a new freedom, openness, and vitality.

Friendliness was also a key component of the new communication style. Twentieth-century Americans labored to make themselves liked in ways their ancestors had not. One reason lay in the world of work. The modern workplace had become more and more anonymous. To get ahead in the ranks of white-collar workers, it was necessary to get along with others, to make a good impression on the boss, to stand out in a crowd. This took more than character; it took personality.

The careful, self-controlled man or woman of the 19th century was becoming obsolete in the new consumer culture. Success was no longer measured by diligence and self-control but by one's ability to take risks and to make a personal impression. The quality that best allowed one to make such an impression was **personality.** Personality allowed one to be outgoing and expressive; people who had it were fascinating, stunning, attractive, magnetic, glowing, masterful, creative, dominant, and forceful.[62] The individual with personality knew how to draw attention to him or herself. The individual with personality could win friends and influence people.

Sex and Self-Discovery

Psychologist Howard Gadlin has identified two major features of interpersonal relationships in the early 20th century: the reemergence of repressed sexuality, and an increased acceptance of personal fulfillment as a goal of relationships.[63] As the modern period advanced, sex became freer and more open. During the 19th century, for a man to glimpse a young woman's ankle was considered shocking and improper. By the 1920s flappers were wearing skirts that revealed their knees. In fact, between the years 1913 and 1928 the amount of cloth needed to make a woman's dress diminished from a little over 19 to a mere 7 yards.[64] Gradually, people were revealing both their bodies and their minds to one another.

As we saw in Box 11.1, a new form of courtship, the date, developed in the 20th century. As young people escaped the watchful eyes of chaperones, they were free to experiment with new forms of intimacy. Although virginity was still highly prized until late in the century, "necking" and "petting" became more common. In heterosexual couples, it was considered the woman's task to set sexual limits. It was also considered the woman's fault if control broke down and unsanctioned sexual acts occurred. According to the sexual ideology of the time, there were two types of women, "good girls" who successfully fought off their beaus' advances and "bad girls," who somehow gave off subtle cues that they were "cheap" and thus "got what they asked for." A 1945 dating manual addressed to women warned: "Remember that the average man will go as far as you let him go. A man is only as bad as the woman he is with."[65] The fallacies in this system are clear to us today, but they were not at the time. Prior to the 1960s, few seemed to have found the double standard objectionable. Nor were many particularly offended that men were often portrayed as "potential wolves verging on rapists."[66] As in every other period we have looked at, these sexual stereotypes were considered to be "natural."

Marriage was still an important goal for most couples. As in previous eras it provided financial security and legitimized reproduction. But intimate relationships did more than that in the 20th century: they offered self-fulfillment. Couples believed that interpersonal relationships were a path to self-discovery. Increasingly they turned to one another for the satisfaction of all their emotional needs, expecting togetherness to solve all of their problems. When togetherness did not result in new insights into the self, and when partners were unable to provide each other with complete need satisfaction, disappointment was often bitter, with divorce an inevitable result. As current statistics attest, it has become harder and harder over time for couples to stay together, perhaps because expectations are so high.

Communicative Competence and Historical Change

Our discussion of changing social conditions in America shows that, just as culture affects communicative competence, so too does history. In different periods, people process information differently, take on different roles, set different goals, define themselves differently, and construct messages in substantially different ways. Below, we summarize some of the ways historical change affects each aspect of communicative competence.

HISTORY AND INTERPRETIVE COMPETENCE

Having interpretive competence means being sensitive to context; it means understanding, at any given time, what social information to attend to and what to ignore. In order to make appropriate message choices, individuals must be able to read complex social cues. Over time, the nature of these cues changes; factors that are closely tied to effective communication in one era may be completely unimportant in another.

In the colonial period, for example, rank and social standing determined message choices. Americans of the time had to be able to gauge the exact amount of social distance between themselves and those with whom they communicated. In the 20th century, where displays of deference are not as important as they once were, it isn't necessary to pay as much close attention to these details. Similarly, in the 19th century, social occasions were highly formal and etiquette was exacting. Communicators of that time period had to pay careful attention to social cues that we in the 20th century would hardly notice, and they had to follow exactly social scripts. This does not mean that today we no longer need interpretive competence; rather it suggests that we need to be sensitive to other kinds of social information. In some respects, our task today may be harder than that of our ancestors, for rather than looking at outward indications of others' rank or character, we have to look inward, picking up on subtle differences that tell us who others are as individuals. Clearly, interpretive competence is connected to historical change.

HISTORY AND ROLE COMPETENCE

Over time roles also change. The clearest example of this kind of change lies in gender roles. As we have seen, concepts of men's and women's essential nature have changed dramatically in the last 400 years. And, of course, they are still evolving today.

In any era, knowing how to fit comfortably into appropriate roles without losing one's identity is an important social skill. In a transitional period when role definitions are changing, this kind of role competence is especially important. Women who were born before

World War II, for example, the grandmothers of today's college students, experienced such a role transition. Brought up to believe that their self-worth lay in finding a good husband and in keeping house for him and their children, few considered embarking on a long-term professional career. The woman who chose a career after college ran the risk of being labeled unwomanly or a bad mother or even emasculating. On the other hand, the woman who followed proper role expectations and settled into a domestic role was, by the time she reached middle age, dismissed as "just a housewife." It took exceptional flexibility for a woman of that generaton to find her way through the contradictions of being female.

Men today may be in a somewhat similar position. Male roles seem to be in transition. Older, more "macho" images of man as undisputed head of household, principal wage earner, and protector of wife and child are now being questioned. Like women of earlier generations, men today need to use role competence to adapt to new social expectations without losing their identities. Of course, gender roles are not the only roles that change over time. None of our social roles are static; our attitudes toward family roles, age roles, and professional roles also evolve.

HISTORY AND GOAL COMPETENCE

Like interpretive and role competence, goal competence is also affected by historical change. Both the kinds of goals we set for ourselves and the ways we go about achieving them change over time. As we have seen, definitions of personal fulfillment have evolved over the years. Goals such as ambition and competition are good examples. In preindustrial America, where social mobility was severely limited, these goals were not particularly important to the average person. After industrialization, however, they became more common.

Once new goals become popular, individuals must develop the competence to achieve those goals. In the early 20th century, for example, two new ways of impressing others developed: **pluck** and **charm.** Being plucky meant presenting oneself to others as spirited, resolute, and willing to take risks to get what one wanted. People with pluck were not afraid to blow their own horns to advertise their good qualities. People with charm got their way by being physically attractive and cheerful and by exhibiting brash good humour. Today these persuasive qualities are still admired, so it may seem odd to us that in the 19th century they were not highly valued. Indeed, these qualities were deeply distrusted and associated with the tricks of confidence men [67] In the 19th century had an individual tried to use pluck or charm to achieve a goal, he or she would probably have failed. Today, quite the reverse is true. How we reach our goals changes historically.

HISTORY AND SELF COMPETENCE

If there is one enduring theme in American social history, it is that Americans have become more and more individualistic with the passage of time. Discovering and understanding the self was not of particular concern to our colonial ancestors because they derived their identity through social rank and community membership rather than individual achievement. Individualism became more important in the 19th century, as people began to search for the romantic self, the self that transcended social roles. When personality became a valued attribute in the early 20th century, individuality became even more central to our way of life. Americans turned inward to consider what qualities made them unique and out of the ordinary. Developing a personal style that expressed that self became an essential interpersonal competence.

As the self became increasingly important to Americans, talking about the self became more

and more acceptable. In earlier times, discussing one's most private thoughts and feelings was actually considered unacceptable and rude. Today we see it as a basic prerequisite for any healthy relationship. In fact, self-revelation is becoming an important source of entertainment as talk show hosts from Ricki Lake to Oprah have found out. Americans today love talking and hearing about intimate details of their own and others' lives. Knowing when and how to do so is an important social skill in the late 20th century. Self competence, like the other kinds of competence we have reviewed, is historically determined.

HISTORY AND MESSAGE COMPETENCE

As interpretive, role, goal, and self competence change, so too do the message choices we make. Over time, language itself takes on different forms and functions. Throughout this chapter we have included excerpts from 19th-century novels and letters, excerpts that have probably seemed unusually sentimental and florid to you. Most of us simply do not express ourselves in these ways today. The words and sentences we use nowadays are quite different in tone from those used in previous eras.

Nonverbal behaviors have also changed. We dress and move in a much feer and more open way today than ever before. We express emotions differently too. If, today, we were to use the kinds of nonverbal behaviors popular in either the colonial period or the 19th century, we would seem completely incompetent.

Finally our relational messages have undergone change as well. As the kinds of bonds we seek to forge with others have evolved, so too have our ways of sending relational messages. Although emotional bonding would appear to be a spontaneous and natural kind of communication, it, too, like every other form of competence, is deeply affected by context.

Skill Building: Increasing Sensitivity to Context

In order to communicate effectively, you need to be aware of both historical and cultural contexts. Because it is difficult to predict the future, it is impossible to give specific guidelines for adapting to historical change. At this point all we can say is that the definition of successful communication is constantly changing as new technologies emerge and social conditions change. The more flexible and the more adaptable you can be, the better will be your communication.

It is somewhat easier to discuss cross-cultural skills. So in this section, we'll focus on adapting to cultural differences. We'll begin with some suggestions about how to increase competence in international situations and then offer some suggestions for handling subcultural contact.

ADAPTING TO INTERNATIONAL DIFFERENCES

Many people find it hard to picture themselves in international contexts. Yet statistics show us that more and more people are crossing international borders every year. Here are some guidelines to help you adapt to this kind of communication situation and develop a "third culture" perspective.

1. *Prepare yourself ahead of time. Preparedness is an important aspect of successful adaptation.* While still in this country, read some books, take a course, or try to meet people from your host country. Ask them what you can expect. This knowledge will give you a sense of confidence and will impress host nationals with the effort you've made to understand their culture.

2. *When you travel abroad, expect differences in material culture.* In many countries housing, transportation, sanitation, food, and medical facilities may not meet the standards you are used to. Don't dismiss the importance of these differences, but don't let them overwhelm you either. Know that from time to time the lack of luxury and privacy will be frustrating. Don't take your frustration out on host nationals. Instead of complaining, see how they cope. Above all, practice patience.

3. *Realize that it is naturally stressful to be cut off from familiar customs and landmarks.* When you feel the stress of culture shock, take a break and relax. This may mean periods in which you withdraw a bit until you regain the equilibrium needed to explore your new environment. Give yourself occasional rest periods.

4. *Make friends with host nationals and ask them to introduce you to their culture.* Interpersonal contacts are an important source of information. Host nationals will usually be delighted to show you the ropes, and they can take you places you'd never have the courage to explore on your own. Your trip will be much more rewarding if you have made new friends.

5. *Realize that you will make mistakes.* From time to time you will violate norms of your new culture, and host nationals will undoubtedly violate some of your norms. Laugh off these mistakes and learn from them. If reactions to your behavior suddenly seem strained, ask someone what went wrong and discuss what you should have done instead. Similarly, if a new acquaintance violates one of your customs, explain the violation in a nonjudgmental and nonthreatening way. Like other forms of communication, cross-cultural misunderstandings are best repaired by metacommunication.

6. *Develop an attitude of nonjudgmental curiosity* While it is natural to see differences as "wrong," it is generally nonproductive. When you encounter a new custom, suspend your judgment and try to find out why the custom exists and how it functions within the culture.

Instead of being a critic, be an observer. And remember the old proverb, "To understand all is to forgive all."

INCREASING SUBCULTURAL UNDERSTANDING

Sometimes it seems that the misunderstandings we encounter in our own country are more difficult to correct than those between nations. Members of different subcultures can seem very foreign and very threatening to us. Yet there are some things we can do to increase our ability to understand subcultural communication differences.

1. *Open yourself up to new contacts.* As we have seen, prejudiced persons seldom have any direct contact with the targets of their prejudice. Stop for a minute and think about your own circle of friends. How many people do you know who come from a different racial, ethnic, or religious background than yours? If your answer is few or none, you are avoiding potentially rewarding experiences. The first step in increasing subcultural understanding is to make contact.

2. *Learn about the history and experiences of different subcultures.* Most people know a lot about the history, problems, and customs of their own or of majority groups and very little about those of other people. This tendency is very limiting. If you are fortunate enough to know people from other subcultures, take the time to ask them about their cultural heritage. If not, read or take courses. Most college campuses offer courses on the history, literature, and art of major subcultures. They also often have workshops on social problems of oppressed groups. Take advantage of these programs while you have the opportunity.

3. *Test your stereotypes.* All of us have prejudices of some kind. The person who proudly announces to the world, "I'm not at all prejudiced," probably is. The trick is to be aware of your prejudices. When you feel yourself being judgmental about out-group members, ask yourself why you feel this way and what effect it is having on you. Admit to yourself that you might be wrong, and try to see things more objectively.

4. *Develop empathy.* Don't assume that everyone in the world thinks and feels as you do. Observe other people and listen to what they are saying. Try mentally putting yourself in their place. Also be aware that careless comments can be potentially hurtful. Before you say something that might be offensive, ask yourself, "How would I feel if someone said that to me?"

5. *Work on becoming more self-confident.* If you feel insecure about yourself, you may use others as scapegoats, taking out your insecurities on them. The better you feel about yourself, the more likely you are to be able to feel good about other people and to be willing to learn from them.

REVIEW TERMS

The following is a list of major concepts introduced in this chapter. The page where the concept is first mentioned is listed in parentheses.

culture (387)
worldview (388)
effort optimism (389)
equality (389)
future-oriented conformity (389)

call and response pattern   (392)
cross-cultural communication   (393)
prejudice   (394)
attitude   (395)
in-group member   (396)
out-group member   (396)
negative interpretations   (397)
discounting   (398)
fundamental attribution error   (398)
exaggeration   (398)
polarization   (398)
ethnocentrism   (399)
assumed similarity   (400)
collectivist culture   (404)
individualist culture   (404)
equality norm   (404)
equity norm   (404)
colonial period   (406)
patriarchy   (407)
early industrial period   (408)
republican mother   (409)
character   (410)
modern period   (411)
personality   (412)
pluck   (415)
charm   (415)

SUGGESTED READINGS

Carbaugh, Donald, ed. *Cultural Communication and Intercultural Contact.* Hillsdale, N.J.: Lawrence Erlbaum, 1990. This anthology looks at a variety of cultures. The articles are interesting and important instances of cross-cultural study.

Coontz, Stephanie. *The Social Origins of Private Life: A History of American Families 1600–1900.* London: Verso, 1988, pp. 74–78. Coontz describes social conditions in America prior to the 20th century. She begins by discussing Native American notions of the family prior to the arrival of the colonists.

She then examines changing patterns of family life among the colonists. Her section on slave families provides a brief introduction to a fascinating topic.

Samovar, Larry A. and Richard E. Porter. *Intercultural Communication: A Reader*, 6th ed. Belmont, Calif.: Wadsworth, 1991. An excellent collection of readings about a great many different cultures. A good source for an overview of the field.

Samovar, Larry A. and Richard E. Porter. *Communication Between Cultures.* Belmont, Calif.: Wadsworth, 1991. An intelligent discussion of basic issues in intercultural communication.

Seidman, Steven. *Romantic Longings: Love in America, 1830–1980.* New York: Routledge, 1991. This book offers an engaging study of the meaning of love and sex during the 19th and 20th centuries and helps us understand the origins of current attitudes and values.

TOPICS FOR DISCUSSION

1. As a class, list all of the cultural groups that have affected you. Share with one another the effects membership in these groups has had on you. Why are some more important than others?

2. Is there a country or culture you have always been interested in? Why? What about it seems appealing to you? On the other hand, are there countries or cultures that you characterize negatively? Why? What are your characterizations, and how fair are they?

3. Discuss Samovar's description of the dominant American cultural pattern. Do you agree with it or disagree? If you disagree, decide as a class how you would describe American culture. Now consider how communication patterns are related to cultural values.

4. Have you ever traveled abroad? If so, did you experience trouble in adapting? If you did, how did you resolve your feelings? If you did not, what do you think prevented it?

5. What prejudices do you hold? Where do they come from, and how do you deal with them?

6. What do you think can be done to increase subcultural understanding? Why do you think people from different subcultures have difficulty with one another?

7. Some people have suggested that in America males and females are brought up in two different cultures. Do you believe gender is a culture? Explain.

8. Have you ever been offended by sexist or racist comments? What kinds of comments bother you? Discuss them and explain your concerns.

9. For you personally what would be the advantages and disadvantages of living in each of the other eras we discussed in this chapter?

10. How would you characterize the era in which we live today? What social or technological factors are changing the ways we form relationships and communicate with one another?

11. Imagine how the American home might change in the next ten years and how those changes might affect the families who reside in them.

12. Which of the customs we follow today do you think will look strange to the next generation?

OBSERVATION GUIDE

1. Interview someone from a different culture. Explore differences in worldview, time and activity orientations, attitudes toward human nature and the individual self, and social organization. Analyze how these differences might affect communication. Ask your informant what difficulties he or she has encountered in your country.

2. If you are a fan of science fiction or utopian literature, take a favorite book and analyze the worldview of the major characters. How does the fictional culture described in the novel differ from your own? How would your communication have to change for you to fit in that world?

EXERCISES

1. Often organizations on campus run programs to familiarize students with the problems of minority groups. Invite members of these groups to come to your class and conduct a workshop. If there are no such organizations on your campus, make it a class project to design programs that will increase understanding between majority and minority members.

2. Invite businesspersons or government employees who have worked abroad to attend class and discuss their experiences with you. If your campus has professors who act as consultants in intercultural matters, have them attend too.

References

CHAPTER 1

1. Carl Sagan, ed., *Communication with Extraterrestrial Intelligence (CETI)* (Cambridge, Mass.: MIT Press, 1973), p. 344. This book is a transcript of a conference held in 1971 at Byurakan Astrophysical Observatory, Yerevan, USSR. While it is technically difficult, the chapters "Message Contents" and "The Consequences of Contact" are easy to follow and very illuminating.

2. See, for example, Cyril Ponnamperuma and A. G. W. Cameron, *Interstellar Communication*: Scientific Perspectives (Boston: Houghton Mifflin, 1974). For a more popular discussion, see Carl Sagan, *The Cosmic Connection: An Extraterrestrial Perspective* (Garden City, N.Y.: Anchor Press, Doubleday, 1973).

3. Sagan, *Cosmic Connection*, p. 42.

4. For an excellent history of the study of communication, see Nancy Harper, *Human Communication Theory: The History of a Paradigm* (Rochelle Park, N.J.: Hayden, 1979).

5. Frank E. X. Dance and Carl E. Larson, *Speech Communication: Concepts and Behavior* (New York: Holt, Rinehart & Winston, 1972).

6. S. S. Stevens, "A Definition of Communication," *The Journal of the Acoustical Society of America* 22 (1950): 689–90. Quoted in Frank E. X. Dance and Carl E. Larson, *The Functions of Human Communication* (New York: Holt, Rinehart & Winston, 1976), p. 25.

7. Dean Barnlund, *Interpersonal Communication: Survey and Studies* (Boston: Houghton Mifflin, 1968), p. 6. Quoted in Dance and Larson, *Functions,* p. 25.

8. John T. Masterson, Steven A. Beebe, and Norman H. Watson, *Speech Communication: Theory and Practice* (New York: Holt, Rinehart & Winston, 1983), p. 5.

9. Bernard Berelson and Gary A. Steiner, *Human Behavior: An Inventory of Scientific Findings* (New York: Harcourt Brace Jovanovich, 1964), p. 527. Quoted in Dance and Larson, *Functions*, p. 24.

10. Sarah Trenholm, *Human Communication Theory* (Englewood Cliffs, N.J.: Prentice-Hall, 1986), pp. 4–5.

11. Aldous Huxley, "Words and Their Meanings," in *The Importance of Language,* ed. Max Black (Englewood Cliffs, N.J.: Prentice-Hall, 1962), pp. 4–5.

12. Joost A. M. Meerloo, "Contributions of Psychiatry to the Study of Human Communication," in *Human Communication Theory: Original Essays,* ed. Frank E. X. Dance (New York: Holt, Rinehart & Winston, 1967), p. 132.

13. Ibid.

14. Clifford Geertz, "Deep Play: Notes on the Balinese Cockfight," in *Myth, Symbol and Culture,* ed. Clifford Geertz (New York: Norton, 1971), p. 7.

15. John C. Condon, "When People Talk with People," in *Messages: A Reader in Human Communication,* 3rd ed., ed. Sanford B. Weinberg (New York: Random House, 1980), p. 58.

16. Erving Goffman, "On Face-Work," in *Interaction Ritual,* ed. Erving Goffman (Garden City, N.Y.: Anchor Books, 1967).

17. Ibid., p. 10.

18. Donald J. Cegala, "Interaction Involvement: A Cognitive Dimension of Communicative Competence," *Communication Education* 30 (1981): 109–21; Brian H. Spitzberg and Michael L. Hecht, "A Component Model of Relational Competence," *Human Communication Research* 10 (1984): 575–99; John M.

Weimann, "Explication and Test of a Model of Communicative Competence," *Human Communication Research* 3 (1977): 195–213; David R. Brandt, "On Linking Social Performance with Social Competence: Some Relations Between Communicative Style and Attribution of Interpersonal Attractiveness and Effectiveness," *Human Communication Research* 5 (1979): 233–37.

19. Dell H. Hymes, "On Communicative Competence," in *Sociolinguistics,* ed. J. B. Pride and Janet Holmes (Harmondsworth, England: Penguin, 1972), pp. 269–93; Ruth Ann Clark and Jesse G. Delia, "Topoi and Rhetorical Competence," *The Quarterly Journal of Speech* 65 (1979): 187–206.

20. Stephen W. Littlejohn and David M. Jabush, "Communication Competence: Model and Application," *Journal of Applied Communication Research* 10 (1982): 29–37; Brian H. Spitzberg, "Communication Competence as Knowledge, Skill, and Impression," *Communication Education* 32 (1983): 323–29.

21. Clark and Delia, "Topoi."

22. James C. McCroskey, "Communication Competence and Performance: A Research and Pedagogical Perspective," *Communication Education* 31 (1982): 1–7.

CHAPTER 2

1. The situational approach is fairly standard in our field and can be found in most introductory communication texts. An especially well developed discussion can be found in David L. Swanson and Jesse G. Delia, "The Nature of Human Communication," in *Modules in Speech Communication* (Chicago: Science Research Associates, 1976).

2. For a discussion of the form of "inner speech," see Lev Semenovich Vygotsky, *Thought and Language,* ed. and trans. Eugenia Hanfmann and Gertrude Vakar (Cambridge, Mass.: MIT Press, 1962). An interesting source for a discussion of the elliptical and condensed quality of intrapersonal communication is Sigmund Freud, *The Interpretation of Dreams,* ed. and trans. James Strachey (New York: Avon Books, 1965).

3. William W. Wilmot, *Dyadic Communication,* 2nd ed. (Reading, Mass.: Addison-Wesley, 1979), p. 19.

4. For an interesting discussion of organizational culture, see Ernest G. Bormann, "Symbolic Convergence: Organizational Communication and Culture," in *Communication and Organizations: An Interpretive Approach,* ed. Linda L. Putnam and Michael E. Pacanowsky (Beverly Hills, Calif.: Sage, 1983).

5. Robert Cathcart and Gary Gumpert, "Mediated Interpersonal Communication: Toward a New Typology," *Quarterly Journal of Speech* 69 (1983): 267–77, 268.

6. Sarah Trenholm, *Human Communication Theory* (Englewood Cliffs, N.J.: Prentice-Hall, 1986), pp. 17–18.

7. Gerald R. Miller, "The Current Status of Theory and Research in Interpersonal Communication," *Human Communication Research* 4 (1978): 164–78.

8. Arthur P. Bochner, "The Functions of Human Communication in Interpersonal Bonding," in *Handbook of Rhetorical and Communication Theory,* ed. Carroll C. Arnold and John Waite Bowers (Boston: Allyn and Bacon, 1984), p. 550.

9. Gerald R. Miller and Mark Steinberg, *Between People: A New Analysis of Interpersonal Communication* (Chicago: Science Research Associates, 1975). See also Chapters 1 and 4 in Cassandra L. Book and others, *Human Communication: Principles, Contexts, and Skills* (New York: St. Martin's Press, 1980).

10. Shelley Duvall and Robert A. Wicklund, *A Theory of Objective Self-Awareness* (New York: Academic Press, 1972).

11. Wilmot, *Dyadic Communication,* pp. 9–10.

12. For an overview of general systems theory as related to communication, see the following: B. Aubrey Fisher, "A View from System Theory," in *Human Communication Theory: Comparative Essays,* ed. Frank E. X. Dance (New York: Harper & Row, 1982); B. Aubrey Fisher, *Perspectives on Human Communication* (New York: Macmillan, 1978), especially the chapter on the pragmatic perspective; George A. Borden, *Human Communication Systems* (Boston, American Press, 1985).

13. In his book on small groups, B. Aubrey Fisher presents an excellent discussion of feedback: *Small Group Decision Making: Communication and the Group Process,* 2nd ed. (New York: McGraw-Hill, 1980).

14. For two additional discussions of interpersonal trajectories, see Jesse G. Delia, "Some Tentative Thoughts Concerning the Study of Interpersonal Relationships and Their Development," *Western Journal of Speech Communication* 44 (1980): 93–96; Steve Duck, "Social and Personal Relationships," in *Handbook of Interpersonal Communication,* ed. Mark L.

Knapp and Gerald R. Miller (Beverly Hills, Calif.: Sage, 1985).

15. Bochner, "Interpersonal Bonding," p. 547.

16. William K. Rawlins, "Openness as Problematic in Ongoing Friendships: Two Conversational Dilemmas," *Communication Monographs* 50 (1983): 1–13, and "Negotiating Close Friendship: The Dialectic of Conjunctive Freedoms," *Human Communication Research* 9 (1983): 255–66.

17. The tendency of our culture to desire intimacy in all relationships has been discussed by a number of historians and social critics. See, for example, Howard Gadlin, "Private Lives and Public Order: A Critical View of the History of Intimate Relations in the United States," in *Close Relationships: Perspectives on the Meaning of Intimacy,* ed. George Levinger and Harold L. Raush (Amherst: University of Massachusetts Press, 1977), pp. 33–72; Christopher Lasch, *The Culture of Narcissism* (New York: Norton, 1978); Robert N. Bellah and others, *Habits of the Heart: Individualism and Commitment in American Life* (Berkeley and Los Angeles: University of California Press, 1985); Judith Martin, *Common Courtesy* (New York: Atheneum, 1985).

18. Judee K. Burgoon, "Privacy and Communication," in *Communication Yearbook* 6, ed. Michael Burgoon (Beverly Hills, Calif.: Sage, 1982), p. 225.

19. Ibid., p. 225.

20. Our discussion of relational competence is loosely adapted from the work of Linda Harris. In explaining her model, however, we have omitted its theoretical grounding in CMM theory. For a fuller understanding of her model, see Linda Harris, "Communication Competence: An Argument for a Systemic View," unpublished paper, Department of Communication Studies, University of Massachusetts, 1979.

CHAPTER 3

1. John Fowles, *Daniel Martin* (Boston: Little, Brown, 1977).

2. Judee Burgoon and Thomas Saine, *The Unspoken Dialogue: An Introduction to Nonverbal Communication* (Boston: Houghton Mifflin, 1978), pp. 6–10.

3. Ross Buck, *The Communication of Emotion* (New York: Guilford Press, 1984).

4. George Herbert Mead, *Mind, Self, and Society* (Chicago: University of Chicago Press, 1934).

5. Desmond Morris, *Manwatching: A Field Guide to Human Behavior* (New York: Abrams, 1977), pp. 86–91.

6. Paul Ekman and Wallace Friesen, *Unmasking the Face: A Guide to Recognizing Emotions from Facial Expressions* (Englewood Cliffs, N.J.: Prentice-Hall, 1975).

7. Albert Mehrabian, *Nonverbal Communication* (Chicago: Aldine-Atherton, 1972), p. 2.

8. Daphne E. Bugental, Jacques W. Kaswan, Leonore R. Love, and Michael N. Fox, "Child Versus Adult Perception of Evaluative Messages in Verbal, Vocal, and Visual Channels," *Developmental Psychology* 2 (1970): 367–75.

9. Jeffrey G. Shapiro, "Responsivity to Facial and Linguistic Cues," *Journal of Communication* 18 (1968): 11–17. See also Leon Vande Creek and John T. Watkins, "Responses to Incongruent Verbal and Nonverbal Emotional Cues," *Journal of Communication* 22 (1972): 311–16.

10. Miles Patterson, *Nonverbal Behavior: A Functional Perspective* (New York: Springer-Verlag, 1983), p. 9.

11. Ashley Montagu and Floyd Matson, *The Human Connection* (New York: McGraw-Hill, 1979), p. 17.

12. Abraham Maslow and Norbert L. Mintz, "Effects of Esthetic Surroundings I: Initial Effects of Three Esthetic Conditions upon Perceiving 'Energy' and 'Well-Being' in Faces," *Journal of Psychology* 41 (1956): 247–54.

13. See, for example, Mark L. Knapp, *Nonverbal Communication in Human Interaction* (New York: Holt, Rinehart & Winston, 1978), pp. 83–113; Lawrence Rosenfeld and Jean Civikly, *With Words Unspoken: The Nonverbal Experience* (New York: Holt, Rinehart & Winston, 1976), pp. 161–85.

14. Steven Kaplan, Rachel Kaplan, and John S. Wendt, "Rated Preference and Complexity for Natural and Urban Visual Material," *Perception and Psychophysics* 12 (1972): 334–56.

15. Albert Mehrabian and James Russell, *An Approach to Environmental Psychology* (Cambridge, Mass.: MIT Press, 1974).

16. Rosenfeld and Civikly, p. 147.

17. Stanford Lyman and Marvin Scott, "Territoriality: A Neglected Social Dimension," *Social Problems* 15 (1967): 235–49.

18. Edward T. Hall, *The Silent Language* (New York: Doubleday, 1959).

19. Edward T. Hall, *The Hidden Dimension* (Garden City, N.Y.: Doubleday, 1969), pp. 133–34.

20. Edward T. Hall, *Beyond Culture* (Garden City, N.Y.: Anchor Press, 1970).

21. For a summary of this research, see Burgoon and Saine, *The Unspoken Dialogue*, pp. 93–94.

22. James G. Martin, "Racial Ethnocentrism and Judgments of Beauty," *Journal of Social Psychology* 63 (1964): 59–63; A. H. Illife, "A Study of Preferences in Feminine Beauty," *British Journal of Psychology* 51 (1960): 267–73.

23. Elaine Walster, Vera Aronson, Darcy Abrahams, and Leon Rottman, "Importance of Physical Attractiveness in Dating Behavior," *Journal of Personality and Social Psychology* 4 (1966): 508–16.

24. James E. Maddux and Ronald W. Rogers, "Effects of Source Expertness, Physical Attractiveness, and Supporting Arguments on Persuasion: A Case of Brains over Beauty," *Journal of Personality and Social Psychology* 39 (1980): 235–44.

25. Morris, *Manwatching*, p. 282.

26. See, for example, L. Aiken, "Relationships of Dress to Selected Measures of Personality in Undergraduate Women," *Journal of Social Psychology* 59 (1963): 119–28; Lawrence Rosenfeld and Timothy G. Plax, "Clothing as Communication," *Journal of Communication* 27 (1977): 24–31; Mary B. Harris and Hortensia Baudin, "The Language of Altruism: The Effects of Language, Dress, and Ethnic Group," *Journal of Social Psychology* 91 (1973): 37–41.

27. Thomas F. Hoult, "Experimental Measurement of Clothing as a Factor in Some Social Ratings of Selected American Men," *American Sociological Review* 19 (1954): 324–28.

28. Adam Kendon, "Some Functions of Gaze-Direction in Social Interaction," *Acta Psychologica* 26 (1967): 22–63.

29. Ekman and Friesen, *Unmasking the Face,* p. 40 and p. 52.

30. For a brief review, see D. R. Rutter, *Looking and Seeing: The Role of Visual Communication in Social Interaction* (Chichester, England: Wiley, 1984), pp. 49–54.

31. P. C. Ellsworth, "The Meaningful Look," *Semiotica* 24 (1978): 15–20; Miles Patterson, "An Arousal Model of Interpersonal Intimacy," *Psychological Review* 83 (1976): 235–45.

32. Irenaus Eibl-Eibesfeldt, "Similarities and Differences Between Cultures in Expressive Movements," in *Nonverbal Communication,* ed. Robert Hinde (Cambridge: Cambridge University Press, 1972), pp. 297–312.

33. Michael Argyle, Mansur Lalljee, and Mark Cook, "The Effects of Visibility on Interaction in a Dyad," *Human Relations* 21 (1968): 3–17.

34. Clara Mayo and Marianne LaFrance, "Gaze Direction in Interracial Dyadic Communication," paper presented at the annual meeting of the Eastern Psychological Association, Washington, D.C., 1973. Cited in Clara Mayo and Nancy Henley, eds., *Gender and Nonverbal Behavior* (New York: Springer-Verlag, 1981).

35. Rutter, *Looking and Seeing.*

36. Ibid.

37. Ekman and Friesen, *Unmasking the Face.*

38. For a review of these studies, see Judith Hall, *Nonverbal Sex Differences: Communication Accuracy and Expressive Style (*Baltimore: Johns Hopkins University Press, 1984), pp. 59–84.

39. Paul Ekman and Wallace Friesen, "The Repertoire of Nonverbal Behavior: Categories, Origins, Usage, and Coding," *Semiotica* 1 (1969): 49–98.

40. Morris, *Manwatching*, pp. 50–51.

41. G. L. Trager, "Paralanguage: A First Approximation," *Studies in Linguistics* 13 (1958): 1–12.

42. David W. Addington, "The Relationship of Selected Vocal Characteristics to Personality Perception," *Speech Monographs* 35 (1968): 492–503.

43. James McCroskey, Carl E. Larson, and Mark Knapp, *An Introduction to Interpersonal Communication* (Englewood Cliffs, N.J.: Prentice-Hall, 1971), p. 117.

44. Susan Milmoe, Robert Rosenthal, Howard T. Blane, Morris E. Chafetz, and Irving Wolf, "The Doctor's Voice: Postdictor of Successful Referral of Alcoholic Patients," *Journal of Abnormal Psychology* 72 (1967): 78–84.

45. Ashley Montagu, *Touching: The Human Significance of the Skin* (New York: Columbia University Press, 1971).

46. Brenda Major, "Gender Patterns in Touching Behavior," in *Gender and Nonverbal Behavior,* pp. 15–37.

47. Richard Heslin, "Steps Toward a Taxonomy of Touching," paper presented at the annual meeting of the Midwestern Psychological Association, Chicago, 1974.

48. Major, "Gender Patterns," p. 33.

49. Nancy Henley, "Status and Sex: Some Touching Observations," *Bulletin of the Psychonomic Society* 2 (1973): 91–93.

50. Equilibrium theory was first introduced by Argyle and Dean and has been modified considerably by Miles Patterson. Patterson has renamed the modified theory a "sequential functional model." We have chosen to retain the term equilibrium theory for heuristic purposes. See Michael Argyle and Janet Dean, "Eye Contact, Distance and Affiliation," *Sociometry* 28 (1965): 289–304; Patterson, *Nonverbal Behavior*, pp. 13–34.

51. James Averill, "A Constructivist View of Emotion," in *Emotion: Theory, Research, and Experience,* Vol. 1, ed. R. Plutchik and H. Kellerman (New York: Academic Press, 1980), pp. 305–39.

52. Richard Buttny, "The Discourse of Affect Display in Social Accountability Practices," paper presented at the International Communication Association annual convention, Chicago, 1991.

53. Example cited in ibid., pp. 20–21, and slightly modified for use here.

54. Ronald Adler, *Confidence in Communication: A Guide to Assertive and Social Skills* (New York: Holt, Rinehart & Winston, 1977), p. 178.

55. Janet Beavin Bavelas, Alex Black, Nicole Chovil, and Jennifer Mullett, *Equivocal Communication* (Newbury Park, Calif.: Sage, 1990).

56. Jane Austen, *Sense and Sensibility,* 2nd ed. (Oxford: Oxford University Press, 1982, 1811).

57. Lawrence M. Brammer, *The Helping Relationship: Process and Skills* (Englewood Cliffs, N.J.: Prentice-Hall, 1973), pp. 90–93.

CHAPTER 4

1. Helen Keller, *The Story of My Life* (Garden City, N.Y.: Doubleday, 1905), p. 36.

2. Daniel J. Boorstin, *The Discoverers* (New York; Vintage Books, 1983), Book One: Time.

3. For a nice summary of the differences between verbal and nonverbal codes, see Judee K. Burgoon and Thomas Saine, *The Unspoken Dialogue: An Introduction to Nonverbal Communication* (Boston: Houghton Mifflin, 1978), pp. 18–20.

4. For an attempt at a structuralist breakdown of nonverbal behavior, see Ray L. Birdwhistell, *Introduction to Kinesics* (Louisville: University of Kentucky Press, 1952), and *Kinesics and Context* (Philadelphia: University of Pennsylvania Press, 1970); and for a critique of this attempt, see Allen T. Ditmann, "Review of Kinesics in Context," *Psychiatry* 34 (1971): 334–42.

5. Umberto Eco, *A Theory of Semiotics* (Bloomington: University of Indiana Press, 1976), p. 7.

6. Our list is a composite made up of functions suggested by the following authors: Joost A. M. Meerloo, "Contributions of Psychiatry to the Study of Communication," in *Human Communication Theory: Original Essays,* ed. Frank E. X. Dance (New York: Holt, Rinehart & Winston, 1967), pp. 130–59; Roman Jakobson, "Closing Statement: Linguistics and Poetics," in *Style in Language,* ed. Thomas Sebeok (Cambridge, Mass.: MIT Press, 1960), pp. 350–77; and Dell Hymes, "The Ethnography of Speaking," in *Readings in the Sociology of Language,* ed. Joshua Fishman (The Hague: Mouton, 1968), pp. 99–138.

7. Sigmund Freud, *Introductory Lectures on Psychoanalysis,* trans. and ed. James Strachey (New York: Norton, 1966), pp. 25–79.

8. For a full discussion of the relationship between language and uncertainty see Charles R. Berger and James J. Bradac, *Language and Social Knowledge: Uncertainty Reduction in Interpersonal Relations* (London: Edward Arnold, 1982).

9. Michael Stubbs, *Discourse Analysis: The Sociolinguistic Analysis of Natural Language* (Chicago: University of Chicago Press, 1983), pp. 48–49.

10. If you are not familiar with language structure, you may find Frederick Williams, *Language and Speech: Introductory Perspectives* (Englewood Cliffs, N.J.: Prentice-Hall, 1972), a useful introduction to the subject.

11. *Webster's Third New International Dictionary* (Springfield, Mass.: Merriam-Webster, 1981).

12. Dan I. Slobin, *Psycholinguistics* (Glenview, Ill.: Scott Foresman, 1971), p. 96.

13. John R. Searle, *Speech Acts: An Essay in the Philosophy of Language* (Cambridge: Cambridge University Press, 1969).

14. CMM theory is one of the most popular of recent communication theories; there are many articles on the subject. We suggest you try W. Barnett Pearce, Vernon E. Cronen, and Forrest Conklin, "On What to Look at When Analyzing Communication: A Hierarchical Model of Actors' Meanings," *Communication* 4 (1979): 195–220, and Vernon E. Cronen and W. Barnett Pearce, "Logical Force in Interpersonal Communication: A New Concept of the 'Necessity' in Social Behaviors," *Communication* 6

(1981): 5–67. For an overview and bibliography, see Vernon E. Cronen, W. Barnett Pearce, and Linda M. Harris, "The Coordinated Management of Meaning: A Theory of Communication," in *Human Communication Theory: Comparative Essays,* ed. Frank E. X. Dance (New York: Harper & Row, 1982), pp. 61–89.

15. Edward Sapir, *Selected Writings of Edward Sapir in Language, Culture and Personality* (Berkeley and Los Angeles: University of California Press, 1958), and Benjamin Lee Whorf, *Language, Thought and Reality* (Cambridge, Mass.: MIT Press, 1966).

16. Sapir, *Selected Writings,* p. 162.

17. Henry Allan Gleason, Jr., *An Introduction to Descriptive Linguistics,* rev. ed. (New York: Holt, Rinehart & Winston, 1961), p. 4.

18. Slobin, *Psycholinguistics,* p. 125.

19. Whorf, Language, *Thought and Reality,* p. 240.

20. Ibid., p. 243.

21. Julia T. Wood, *Gendered Lives: Communication, Gender, and Culture* (Belmont, Calif.: Wadsworth, 1994), p. 130; Julia T. Wood, "Defining and Studying Sexual Harassment as Situated Experience," in Gary Kreps, ed., *Communication and Sexual Harrassment in the Workplace* (Cresskill, N.J.: Hampton Press, 1993).

22. Basil Bernstein, ed., *Class, Codes and Control,* Vol. 2 (London: Routledge and Kegan Paul, 1973).

23. The sample dialogue is taken from Raymond S. Ross and Mark G. Ross, *Relating and Interacting* (Englewood Cliffs, N.J.: Prentice-Hall, 1982), p. 93.

24. Two useful reviews of these studies can be found in Chapters 2 and 3 of Barbara Westbrook Eakins and R. Gene Eakins, *Sex Differences in Human Communication* (Boston: Houghton Mifflin, 1978), and Chapter 6 in Judy Cornelia Pearson, *Gender and Communication* (Dubuque, Iowa: Brown, 1985).

25. Robin Lakoff, *Language and Woman's Place* (New York: Harper & Row, 1975).

26. Eakins and Eakins, *Sex Differences,* p. 48.

27. Ibid, p. 49.

28. Cheris Kramarae, *Women and Men Speaking: Framework for Analysis* (Rowley, Mass.: Newbury House, 1981), pp. 1–63. For a general discussion of feminist theories of language see Stephen W. Littlejohn, *Theories of Human Communication,* 4th ed. (Belmont, Calif.: Wadsworth, 1992), pp. 238–245.

29. Carol Gilligan, *In a Different Voice* (Cambridge, Mass.: Harvard University Press, 1982).

30. Littlejohn, *Theories of Human Communication,* p. 241; see also Dale Spender, *Man Made Language* (London: Routledge & Kegan Paul, 1980), pp. 76–105.

31. Eakins and Eakins, *Sex Differences in Communication,* p. 121.

32. Ibid., p. 120.

33. Ibid., p. 141.

34. Robin Lakoff, "Language and Women's Place," *Language in Society* 2 (1973).

35. See Alan Garner, *Conversationally Speaking: Testing New Ways to Increase Your Personal and Social Effectiveness* (New York: McGraw Hill, 1981) and Sharon A. Ratliffe and David D. Hudson, *Skill-Building for Interpersonal Competence* (New York: Holt, Rinehart & Winston, 1988).

36. Mark L. Knapp and others, "The Rhetoric of Goodbye: Verbal and Nonverbal Correlates of Human Leave-Taking," *Speech Monographs* 40 (August 1973): 182–98.

CHAPTER 5

1. Paul Watzlawick, Janet Beavin Bavelas, and Don D. Jackson, *Pragmatics of Human Communication* (New York: Norton, 1967), p. 52.

2. Ibid., p. 51. See also Jurgen Ruesch and Gregory Bateson, *Communication: The Social Matrix of Psychiatry* (New York: Norton, 1951), pp. 179–81.

3. Watzlawick et al., *Pragmatics,* p. 52.

4. Stephen W. King and Kenneth K. Sereno, "Conversational Appropriateness as a Conversational Imperative," *Quarterly Journal of Speech* 70 (1984): 264–73.

5. Julia T. Wood, "Communication and Relational Culture: Bases for the Study of Human Relationships," *Communication Quarterly* 30 (1982): 75–83. See also Mary Anne Fitzpatrick and Patricia B. Best, "Dyadic Adjustment in Relational Types: Consensus, Cohesion, Affectional Expression and Satisfaction in Enduring Relationships," *Communication Monographs* 46 (1979): 167–78, and Gerald M. Phillips and Nancy J. Metzger, *Intimate Communication* (Boston: Allyn and Bacon, 1976).

6. Robert C. Carson, *Interaction Concepts of Personality* (Chicago: Aldine, 1969); see in particular Chapter 6, "Contractual Arrangements in Interpersonal Relations."

7. Ibid., p. 184.

8. See, for example, Gregory Bateson, "Culture Contact and Schismogenesis," *Man* 35 (1935): 178–83; William C. Schutz, *The Interpersonal Underworld* (Palo Alto, Calif.: Science and Behavior Books, 1966); Timothy Leary, *Interpersonal Diagnosis of Personality* (New York: Ronald Press, 1957). For a summary of early relational work, see Malcolm R. Parks, "Relational Communication: Theory and Research," *Human Communication Research* 3 (1977): 372–81.

9. Judee K. Burgoon and Jerold L. Hale, "The Fundamental Topoi of Relational Communication," *Communication Monographs* 51 (1984): 193–214.

10. Frank E. Millar and L. Edna Rogers, "A Relational Approach to Interpersonal Communication," in *Explorations in Interpersonal Communication*, ed. Gerald R. Miller (Beverly Hills, Calif.: Sage, 1976).

11. B. Aubrey Fisher, *Small Group Decision Making*, 2nd ed. (New York: McGraw-Hill, 1980), p. 327.

12. Burgoon and Hale, "The Fundamental Topoi," p. 198.

13. Ibid.

14. For a general overview of some classic research on similarity and attraction, see Ellen Berscheid and Elaine Walster, *Interpersonal Attraction* (Reading, Mass.: Addison-Wesley, 1969). For a discussion of similarity as a device in developing relationships, see Steve Duck, "Interpersonal Communication in Developing Acquaintance," in *Explorations in Interpersonal Communication*. For experimental evidence of the effects of attitude similarity on attraction, see the work of Michael Sunnafrank; for example, "Attitude Similarity and Interpersonal Attraction in Communication Processes: In Pursuit of an Ephemeral Influence," *Communication Monographs* 50 (1983): 273–84.

15. Evelyn Sieburg, "Dysfunctional Communication and Interpersonal Responsiveness in Small Groups," unpublished dissertation, University of Denver, 1969. For a good summary of Sieburg's theory, see Frank E. X. Dance and Carl E. Larson, *Speech Communication: Concepts and Behavior* (New York: Holt, Rinehart & Winston, 1972), pp. 140–43.

16. Watzlawick et al., *Pragmatics*. See Chapter 6 for a discussion of the "logic" of paradox.

17. Gregory Bateson, Don D. Jackson, Jay Haley, and John H. Weakland, "Toward a Theory of Schizophrenia," *Behavioral Science* 1 (1956): 251–64; Jay Haley, *Strategies of Psychotherapy* (New York: Grune & Stratton, 1963).

18. Lynda Rummel, Sarah Trenholm, Charles Goetzinger, and Charles Petrie, "Disconfirming (Double Bind) Effects of Incongruent Multichannel Messages," in *Interpersonal Communication: A Rhetorical Perspective,* ed. Ben Morse and Lyn Phelps (Minneapolis: Burgess, 1980).

19. The Palo Alto group includes Gregory Bateson, John H. Weakland, Paul Watzlawick, Janet Beavin Bavelas, Don D. Jackson, and Jay Haley. To understand this approach, see the section on the pragmatic perspective in B. Aubrey Fisher, *Perspectives on Human Communication* (New York: Macmillan, 1978).

20. For an overview and model of interact sequences, see B. Aubrey Fisher and Leonard C. Hawes, "An Interact System Model: Generating a Grounded Theory of Small Groups," *Quarterly Journal of Speech* 57 (1971): 444–53.

21. See Watzlawick et al., *Pragmatics,* pp. 54–59 for the original example.

22. William W. Wilmot, *Dyadic Communication* (Reading, Mass.: Addison-Wesley, 1979).

23. Ibid., p. 127.

24. Vernon E. Cronen, W. Barnett Pearce, and Lonna M. Snavely, "A Theory of Rule-Structure and Types of Episodes and a Study of Perceived Enmeshment in Undesired Repetitive Patterns ('URPs')," in *Communication Yearbook* 3, ed. Dan Nimmo (New Brunswick, N.J.: Transaction Books, 1979).

25. Wilmot, *Dyadic Communication,* p. 128.

26. Gerald R. Miller and Mark Steinberg, *Between People: A New Analysis of Interpersonal Communication* (Chicago: Science Research Associates, 1975), pp. 167–73.

27. Ross Buck, "Recent Approaches to the Study of Nonverbal Receiving Ability," in *Nonverbal Communication: The Social Interaction Sphere,* ed. John Wiemann and Randall Harrison (Beverly Hills, Calif.: Sage, 1983), pp. 209–42.

28. Ross Buck, "Emotional Communication in Personal Relationships: A Developmental-Interactionist View," in *Close Relationships,* ed. Clyde Hendrick (Newbury Park, Calif.: Sage, 1989), p. 159.

29. B. Aubrey Fischer, *Small Group Decision Making,* 2nd ed. (New York: McGraw-Hill, 1980), pp. 327–29.

CHAPTER 6

1. S. T. Fiske and S. E. Taylor, *Social Cognition* (Reading, Mass.: Addison-Wesley, 1984).

2. E. Tory Higgins and Jacquelynne Parsons, "Social Cognition and the Social Life of the Child: Stages as Subcultures," in *Social Cognition and Social Development,* ed. E. Tory Higgins, Diane Ruble, and Willard W. Hartup (Cambridge: Cambridge University Press, 1983), pp. 15–62.

3. Ellen J. Langer, "Rethinking the Role of Thought in Social Interaction," in *New Directions in Attribution Research* 2, ed. J. H. Harvey, W. Ickes, and R. F. Kidd (New York: Wiley, 1978), pp. 35–58.

4. Ellen J. Langer, *Mindfulness* (Reading, Mass.: Addison-Wesley, 1989), p. 97.

5. Charles Berger and William Douglas, "Thought and Talk: 'Excuse Me, but Have I Been Talking to Myself?'" in *Human Communication Theory,* ed. Frank Dance (New York: Harper & Row, 1982), pp. 42–60.

6. James Applegate and Jesse Delia, "Person-Centered Speech, Psychological Development and the Contexts of Language Usage," in *The Social and Psychological Contexts of Language,* ed. R. St. Clair and H. Giles (Hillsdale, N.J.: Lawrence Erlbaum, 1980); Brant R. Burleson, "Comforting Communication," in *Communication by Children and Adults: Social Cognitive and Strategic Processes,* ed. Howard Sypher and James Applegate (Beverly Hills, Calif.: Sage, 1984), pp. 63–104.

7. James Atlas, "Beyond Demographics: How Madison Avenue Knows Who You Are and What You Want," *The Atlantic Monthly* (October 1984): 49–58.

8. See R. Hastie, "Schematic Principles in Human Memory," in *Social Cognition: The Ontario Symposium* 1, ed. E. T. Higgins, C. P. Herman and M. P. Zanna (Hillsdale, N.J.: Lawrence Erlbaum, 1981). See also S. E. Taylor and J. Crocker, "Schematic Basis of Information Processing," in *Social Cognition: The Ontario Symposium* 1.

9. F. I. M. Craik, "Human Memory," *Annual Review of Psychology* 30 (1979): 63–102.

10. Sally Planalp, "Relational Schemata: A Test of Alternative Forms of Relational Knowledge as Guides to Communication," *Human Communication Research* 12 (1985): 3–29.

11. Nancy Cantor and Walter Mischel, "Prototypes in Person Perception," in *Advances in Experimental Social Psychology* 12, ed. Leonard Berkowitz (New York: Academic Press, 1979).

12. George Kelly, *The Psychology of Personal Constructs* (New York: Norton, 1955).

13. C. McCauley, C. L. Stitt, and M. Segal, "Stereotyping: From Prejudice to Prediction," *Psychological Bulletin* 87 (1980): 195–208.

14. Robert Abelson, "Script Processing in Attitude Formation and Decision-Making," in *Cognition and Social Behavior,* ed. J. S. Carroll and J. N. Payne (Hillsdale, N.J.: Lawrence Erlbaum, 1976).

15. Albert Hastorf, David Schneider, and Judith Polefka, *Person Perception* (Reading, Mass.: Addison-Wesley, 1970).

16. W. W. Grings, "The Verbal Summator Technique and Abnormal Mental States," *Journal of Abnormal and Social Psychology* 37 (1942): 529–45.

17. Stanley Deetz and Sheryl Stevenson, *Managing Interpersonal Communication* (New York: Harper & Row, 1986), p. 58.

18. Joseph Forgas, "Affective and Emotional Influences on Episode Representations," in *Social Cognition: Perspectives on Everyday Understanding,* ed. Joseph Forgas (London: Academic Press, 1981), pp. 165–80.

19. Michael Brenner, "Actors' Powers," in *The Analysis of Action: Recent Theoretical and Empirical Advances,* ed. M. von Cranach and Rom Harre (Cambridge: Cambridge University Press, 1982), pp. 213–30.

20. Steven Duck, "Interpersonal Communication in Developing Acquaintances," in *Explorations in Interpersonal Communication,* ed. Gerald R. Miller (Beverly Hills, Calif.: Sage, 1976), pp. 127–47.

21. Seymour Rosenberg and Andrea Sedlak, "Structural Representations of Implicit Personality Theory," in *Advances in Experimental Social Psychology* 6, ed. Leonard Berkowitz (New York: Academic Press, 1972).

22. Harold H. Kelley, "The Warm-Cold Variable in First Impressions of Persons," *Journal of Personality* 18 (1950): 431–39.

23. Leonard Zunin, *Contact: The First Four Minutes* (Los Angeles: Nash, 1972).

24. Randy Wood, "Deceptive Schemata: Initial Impressions of Others." In *Interpersonal Communication: Evolving Interpersonal Relationships,* ed. Pamela Kalbfleisch (Hillsdale, N.J.: Lawrence Erlbaum, 1993), pp. 69–86.

25. Walter Crockett, "Cognitive Complexity and Impression Formation," in *Progress in Experimental Personality Research* 2, ed. B. A. Maher (New York: Academic Press, 1965). See also Jesse Delia, "Constructivism and the Study of Human Communication," *Quarterly Journal of Speech* 63 (1977): 68–83.

26. Jesse Delia, Ruth Ann Clark, and David Switzer, "Cognitive Complexity and Impression Formation in Informal Social Interaction," *Speech Monographs* 41 (1974): 299–308. See also Claudia Hale and Jesse Delia, "Cognitive Complexity and Social Perspective-Taking," *Communication Monographs* 43 (1976): 195–203.

27. Crockett, "Cognitive Complexity."

28. Mark L. Snyder, "The Self-Monitoring of Expressive Behavior," *Journal of Personality and Social Psychology* 30 (1974): 526–37.

29. Mark L. Snyder, "Self-Monitoring Processes," in *Advances in Experimental Social Psychology* 12, ed. Leonard Berkowitz (New York: Academic Press, 1979), pp. 86–131.

30. Planalp, "Relational Schemata."

31. Robert Carson, *Interaction Concepts of Personality* (Chicago: Aldine, 1969).

32. Edward E. Jones and Keith E. Davis, "From Acts to Dispositions: The Attribution Process in Person Perception," in *Advances in Experimental Social Psychology* 2, ed. Leonard Berkowitz (New York: Academic Press, 1965).

33. Harold H. Kelley, "Attribution Theory in Social Psychology," in *Nebraska Symposium on Motivation* 15, ed. D. Levine (Lincoln: University of Nebraska Press, 1967).

34. Ibid.

35. For a review, see Lee Ross, "The Intuitive Psychologist and His Shortcomings: Distortions in the Attribution Process," in *Advances in Experimental Social Psychology* 10, ed. Leonard Berkowitz (New York: Academic Press, 1977).

36. E. E. Jones and D. McGillis, "Correspondent Inferences and the Attribution Cube: A Comparative Reappraisal," in *New Directions in Attribution Research* 1, ed. J. H. Harvey, W. J. Ickes, and R. F. Kidd (Hillsdale, N.J.: Lawrence Erlbaum, 1976).

37. J. Jaspars and M. Hewstone, "Cross-Cultural Interaction, Social Attribution, and Intergroup Relations," in *Cultures in Contact,* ed. S. Bochner (Elmsford, N.Y.: Pergamon Press, 1982); B. Park and M. Rothbart, "Perceptions of Outgroup Homogeneity and Levels of Social Categorization: Memory for the Subordinate Attributes of In-Group and Out-Group Members," *Journal of Personality and Social Psychology* 42 (1982): 1051–68.

38. J. Miller, "Culture and the Development of Everyday Social Explanations," *Journal of Personality and Social Psychology* 46 (1984): 961–78.

39. Ralph G. Nichols, *Are You Listening?* (New York: McGraw-Hill, 1957), pp. 1–17.

40. Charles Robert Petrie, Jr., "What Is Listening?" in *Listening: Readings,* ed. Sam Duker (New York: Scarecrow Press, 1966), p. 329.

41. See, for example, Andrew D. Wolvin and Carolyn Gwynn Coakley, *Listening* (Dubuque, Iowa: Brown, 1985), and Florence I. Wolff, Nadine C. Marsnik, William S. Tracey, and Ralph G. Nichols, *Perceptive Listening* (New York: Holt, Rinehart & Winston, 1983).

42. See Voncile Smith, "Listening," in *A Handbook of Communication Skills,* ed. Owen Hargie (New York: New York University Press, 1986), pp. 250–51.

CHAPTER 7

1. Peter L. Berger, *Invitation to Sociology: A Humanistic Perspective* (Garden City, N.Y.: Anchor Books, 1963), p. 66.

2. Ibid., p. 78.

3. Ruth Benedict, *Patterns of Culture* (New York: Penguin Books, 1946), p. 2.

4. Theodore M. Newcomb, Ralph H. Turner, and Philip E. Converse, *Social Psychology: The Study of Human Interaction* (New York: Holt, Rinehart & Winston, 1965), p. 326.

5. George J. McCall and J. L. Simmons, *Identities and Interactions* (New York: Free Press, 1966), p. 67.

6. Charles Horton Cooley, "The Social Self: On the Meanings of I," in *The Self in Social Interactions, Vol. I: Classic and Contemporary Perspectives,* ed. Chad Gordon and Kenneth J. Gergen (New York: Wiley, 1968), pp. 87–91.

7. Leon Festinger, "A Theory of Social Comparison Processes," *Human Relations* 2 (1954): 117–40.

8. Daryl J. Bem, "Self-Perception Theory," in *Advances in Experimental Social Psychology* 6, ed. Leonard Berkowitz (New York: Academic Press, 1972).

9. Our review of gender differences is taken from Laurie P. Arliss, *Gender Communication* (Englewood Cliffs, N.J.: Prentice-Hall, 1990). See in particular pp. 63, 67.

10. Ibid., p. 46.

11. Robin Lakoff, *Language and Woman's Place* (New York: Harper & Row, 1975).

12. Barbara Westbrook Eakins and R. Gene Eakins, *Sex Differences in Human Communication* (Boston: Houghton Mifflin, 1978), pp. 48–49.

13. Ibid.

14. Arliss, *Gender Communication,* p. 50.

15. McCall and Simmons, *Identities and Interactions,* p. 67.

16. Erving Goffman, "On Face-Work," in *Interaction Ritual* (Garden City, N.Y.: Anchor Books, 1967).

17. Ibid., p. 226.

18. Erving Goffman, *The Presentation of Self in Everyday Life* (Garden City, N.Y.: Doubleday, 1959), p. 24.

19. Sarah Trenholm, *Human Communication Theory* (Englewood Cliffs, N.J.: Prentice-Hall, 1986), p. 105.

20. Erving Goffman, "Role Distance," in *Encounters: Two Studies in the Sociology of Interaction* (New York: Bobbs-Merrill, 1961), p. 108.

21. Goffman, *Presentation of Self,* pp. 212–28.

22. Morris Rosenberg, "Psychological Selectivity in Self-Esteem Formation," in *Attitude, Ego Involvement, and Change,* ed. Carolyn W. Sherif and Muzafer Sherif (New York: Wiley, 1967), pp. 26–50. Quoted in William Wilmot, *Dyadic Communication* (Reading, Mass.: Addison-Wesley, 1979).

23. W. Barnett Pearce, "The Coordinated Management of Meaning: A Rules-Based Theory of Interpersonal Communication," in *Explorations in Interpersonal Communication,* ed. Gerald R. Miller (Beverly Hills, Calif.: Sage, 1976), pp. 17–35.

24. William F. Lewis, "Telling America's Story: Narrative Form and the Reagan Presidency," *Quarterly Journal of Speech* 73 (1987), 280–302, p. 282.

25. Vivian Paley, *Bad Guys Don't Have Birthdays* (Chicago: University of Chicago Press, 1991)

26. Jerome Bruner, "Life as Narrative," *Social Research* 54 (Spring 1987), 11–32., p. 15.

27. Lewis, "Telling America's Story," p. 282.

28. Ellen J. Langer, "Minding Matters: The Consequences of Mindlessness-Mindfulness," *Advances in Experimental Social Psychology* (1989): 137–73.

29. Milton Rokeach, *The Open and Closed Mind* (New York: Basic Books, 1960), p. 57.

30. Langer, "Minding Matters," p. 140.

31. Ibid., p. 167.

CHAPTER 8

1. John McCrone, *The Ape That Spoke: Language and the Evolution of the Human Mind* (New York: Morrow, 1991).

2. *The New Shorter Oxford English Dictionary,* Vol. 1. (Oxford: Clarendon Press, 1993), p. 483.

3. Philip Rieff, *The Triumph of the Therapeutic: Uses of Faith after Freud.* New York: 1966, p. 2, quoted in Warren I. Susman, *Culture as History: The Transformation of American Society in the Twentieth Century* (New York: Pantheon Books, 1984), pp. 271–285; Charles Taylor, *Sources of the Self: The Making of the Modern Identity* (Cambridge: Harvard University Press, 1989).

4. Susman, *Culture as History,* p. 273.

5. Ibid., p. 273.

6. Ibid., p. 277.

7. Henry Laurent, *Personality: How To Build It* (New York: 1915), p. iv, quoted in ibid, p. 277.

8. See, for example, John Kihlstrom and Nancy Cantor, "Mental Representations of the Self," in *Advances in Experimental Social Psychology* 17, ed. Leonard Berkowitz (Orlando, Fla.: Academic Press, 1984), pp. 1–47.

9. John P. Hewitt, *Self and Society: A Symbolic Interactionist Social Psychology,* 3rd ed. (Boston: Allyn and Bacon, 1984), pp. 89–91.

10. Mark Snyder and William Ickes, "Personality and Social Behavior," in *The Handbook of Social Psychology,* Vol. 2, 3rd ed., ed. Gardner Lindzey and Elliot Aronson (New York: Random House, 1985), pp. 883–947.

11. Charles Horton Cooley, "Looking-Glass Self," in *Symbolic Interaction: A Reader in Social Psychology,* 3rd ed., ed. Jerome G. Manis and Bernard N. Meltzer (Boston: Allyn and Bacon, 1978), p. 169.

12. A. G. Greenwald. "The Totalitarian Ego: Fabrication and Revision of Personal History," *American Psychologist* 35 (1980): 603–618.

13. William J. McGuire and C. V. McGuire, "The Spontaneous Self-Concept As Affected by Personal Distinctiveness," in *Self-Concept: Advances in Theory and Research,* ed. M. D. Lynch, A. A. Norem-Hebeisen and K. Gergen (New York: Ballinger, 1981).

14. William J. McGuire and A. Padawer-Singer, "Trait Salience in the Spontaneous Self-Concept," *Journal of Personality and Social Psychology* 33 (1976): 743–54.

15. S. Coopersmith, *Antecedents of Self-Esteem* (San Francisco: Freeman, 1967).

16. L. Jacobs, E. Berscheid, and E. Walster, "Self-Esteem and Attraction," *Journal of Personality and Social Psychology* 17 (1971): 84–91; Albert Mehrabian, "The Development and Validation of Measures of Affiliative Tendency and Sensitivity to Rejection," *Educational and Psychological Measurement* 30 (1970): 417–28.

17. Michael Lewis and Jeanne Brooks-Gunn, *Social Cognition and the Acquisition of Self* (New York: Plenum Press, 1979), pp. 222–40.

18. Jerome Kagan, *The Nature of the Child* (New York: Basic Books, 1984), pp. 136–42.

19. Andrew J. Lock, "The Role of Relationships in Development: An Introduction to a Series of Occasional Articles," *Journal of Social and Personal Relationships* 3 (1986): 89–99.

20. L. S. Vygotsky, *Mind in Society* (Cambridge, Mass.: Harvard University Press, 1978), p. 57.

21. Vittorio Guidano, *Complexity of the Self: A Developmental Approach to Psychopathology and Therapy* (New York: Guilford Press, 1987).

22. Ibid., p. 32. See also J. Bowlby, *Attachment and Loss,* Vol. 1: Attachment, 2nd ed. (London: Hogarth Press, 1983); C. M. Parkes and J. Stevenson-Hinde, eds., *The Place of Attachment in Human Behavior* (London: Tavistock, 1982).

23. William W. Wilmot, *Dyadic Communication: A Transactional Perspective* (Reading, Mass.: Addison-Wesley, 1975), pp. 44–45.

24. Anthony G. Greenwald, "The Totalitarian Ego: Fabrication and Revision of Personal History," *American Psychologist* 35 (1980): 603–18.

25. Daryl J. Bem, "Self-Perception Theory," in *Advances in Experimental Social Psychology* 6, ed. Leonard Berkowitz (New York: Academic Press, 1972).

26. Hazel Markus, "Self-Schemata and Processing Information About the Self," *Journal of Personality and Social Psychology* 35 (1977): 63–78.

27. Hazel Markus, M. Crane, S. Bernstein, and M. Siladi, "Self-Schemas and Gender," *Journal of Personality and Social Psychology* 42 (1982): 38–50.

28. Eric Berne, *Games People Play* (New York: Grove Press, 1964).

29. W. Barnett Pearce and Vernon E. Cronen, *Communication, Action and Meaning* (New York: Praeger, 1980), p. 136.

30. Steven Berglas and Edward E. Jones, "Drug Choice as an Externalization Strategy in Response to Noncontingent Success," *Journal of Personality and Social Psychology* 36 (1978): 405–17. See also E. E. Jones and S. Berglas, "Control of Attributions About the Self Through Self-Handicapping Strategies: The Appeal of Alcohol and the Role of Underachievement," *Personality and Social Psychology Bulletin* 4 (1978): 200–206.

31. D. C. McClelland, R. Koestner, and J. Weinberger. "How Do Self-Attributed and Implicit Motives Differ?" *Psychological Review* 96 (1989): 690–702.

32. Robert Norton, *Communicator Style: Theory, Applications, and Measures* (Beverly Hills, Calif.: Sage, 1983), p. 58.

33. Donald Darnell and Wayne Brockriede, *Persons Communicating* (Englewood Cliffs, N.J.: Prentice-Hall, 1976), p. 176.

34. Ibid., p. 178.

35. Roderick Hart and Don Burks, "Rhetorical Sensitivity and Social Interaction," *Speech Monographs* 39 (1972): 75–91.

36. Roderick Hart, Robert Carlson, and William Eadie, "Attitudes Toward Communication and the Assessment of Rhetorical Sensitivity," *Communication Monographs* 47 (1980): 1–22.

37. James C. McCroskey, "Oral Communication Apprehension: A Summary of Recent Theory and Research," *Human Communication Research* 4 (1977): 78–96.

38. Ibid.

39. Michael J. Beatty and Ralph R. Behnke, "An Assimilation Theory Perspective of Communication Apprehension," *Human Communication Research* 6 (1980): 319–25.

40. J. Bowlby, *Attachment and Loss: Separation, Anxiety, and Anger* (New York: Basic Books, 1973); C. Hazan and P. R. Shaver, "Love and Work: An Attachment-Theoretical Perspective," *Journal of Personality and Social Psychology* 52(1990): 511–24; Eric P. Simon and Leslie Baxter, "Attachment Style Differences in Relationship Maintenance Strategies," *Western Journal of Communication* 57 (1990): 416–30.

41. See J. Feeney and P. Noller, "Attachment Style as a Predictor of Adult Romantic Relationships," *Journal of Personality and Social Psychology* 58 (1990): 281–91; J. Feeney and P. Noller, "Attachment Style and Verbal Descriptions of Romantic Partners," *Journal of Social and Personal Relationships* 8 (1990):

187–215; Hazan and Shaver, "Love and Work"; N. Collins and S. Read, "Adult Attachment, Working Models, and Relationship Quality in Dating Couples," *Journal of Personality and Social Psychology* 58 (1990): 644–63; M. Levy and K. Davis, "Lovestyles and Attachment Styles Compared: Their Relations to Each Other and to Various Relationship Characteristics," *Journal of Social and Personal Relationships* 5 (1988): 439–71; J. Simpson, "Influence of Attachment Styles on Romantic Relationships," *Journal of Personality and Social Psychology,* 59 (1990): 971–80.

42. K. Bartholomew and L. Horowitz, "Attachment Styles among Young Adults: A Test of a Four Category Model," *Journal of Personality and Social Psychology* 61 (1991): 226–44; R. Kobak and C. Hazen, "Attachment in Marriage: Effects of Security and Accuracy of Working Models," *Journal of Personality and Social Psychology* 60 (1991): 861–69; R. Kobak and A. Sceery, "The Transition to College: Working Models of Attachment, Affect Regulation, and Perceptions of Self and Others," *Child Development* 88 (1988): 135–46; M. Mikulincer and O. Nachshon, "Attachment Styles and Patterns of Self-Disclosure," *Journal of Personality and Social Psycholog,* 61 (1991): 321–31; M. Senchak and K. Leonard, "Attachment Styles and Marital Adjustment Among Newlywed Couples," *Journal of Social and Personal Relationships* 9 (1992): 51–64; J. Simpson, W. Rholes, and J. Nelligan, "Support Seeking and Support Giving Within Couples in an Anxiety-Provoking Situation: The Role of Attachment Styles," *Journal of Personality and Social Psychology* 62 (1992): 434–46.

43. D. P. McAdams. "Human Motives and Personal Relationships," in *Communication, Intimacy, and Close Relationships,* ed. V. Derlega (New York: Academic Press, 1984) p. 45.

44. D. P. McAdams, S. Healy, and S. Krause. "Social Motives and Patterns of Friendship," *Journal of Personality and Social Psychology* 47 (1984): 828–38; D. P. McAdams, R. J. Jackson, and C. A. Kirshnit, "Looking, Laughing and Smiling in Dyads as a Function of Intimacy Motivation and Reciprocity," *Journal of Personality* 52 (1984): 261–73.

45. Judy-Anne Craig, Richard Koestner, and David Zuroff, "Implicit and Self-Attributed Intimacy Motivation," *Journal of Social and Personal Relationships* 11 (1994): 491–508.

46. Mark Knapp and Gerald Miller, eds., *Handbook of Interpersonal Communication* (Beverly Hills, Calif.: Sage, 1985), p. 72.

47. Barbara Montgomery, "Behavioral Characteristics Predicting Self and Peer Perceptions of Open Communication," *Communication Quarterly* 32 (1984): 233–40.

CHAPTER 9

1. Saul V. Levine, "Radical Departures," *Psychology Today* 18 (8) (August 1984): 20–27.

2. Eileen Barker, *The Making of a Moonie* (London: Basil Blackwell, 1984). See also Rodney Stark and William Sims Bainbridge, *The Future of Religion: Secularization, Revival and Cult Formation* (Berkeley and Los Angeles: University of California Press, 1985).

3. Ruth Ann Clark and Jesse G. Delia, "Topoi and Rhetorical Competence," *The Quarterly Journal of Speech* 65 (1979): 187–206, 196.

4. For a thorough overview of all the learning theories, see Frederick H. Kanfer and Jeanne S. Phillips, *Learning Foundations of Behavior Therapy* (New York: Wiley, 1970).

5. The original source is I. P. Pavlov, *Conditioned Reflexes* (London: Oxford University Press, 1927).

6. See, for example, B. F. Skinner, *Science and Human Behavior* (New York: Macmillan, 1953).

7. Albert Bandura, *Social Learning Theory* (Englewood Cliffs, N.J.: Prentice-Hall, 1977).

8. Mary John Smith, *Persuasion and Human Action: A Review and Critique of Social Influence Theories* (Belmont, Calif.: Wadsworth, 1982), p. 202.

9. George Caspar Homans, *Social Behavior: Its Elementary Forms* (New York: Harcourt Brace Jovanovich, 1959); John W. Thibaut and Harold H. Kelley, *The Social Psychology of Groups* (New York: Wiley, 1959).

10. Good discussions of relational currencies are provided in Kenneth L. Villard and Leland J. Whipple, *Beginnings in Relational Communication* (New York; Wiley, 1976), and Kathleen M. Galvin and Bernard J. Brommel, *Family Communication: Cohesion and Change* (Glenview, Ill.: Scott, Foresman, 1982).

11. For an overview of consistency theories, see Smith, *Persuasion and Human Action,* or Richard E. Petty and John T. Cacioppo, *Attitudes and Persuasion: Classic and Contemporary Approaches* (Dubuque, Iowa: Brown, 1981).

12. Fritz Heider, *The Psychology of Interpersonal Relations* (New York: Wiley, 1958).

13. Charles E. Osgood and Percy H. Tannenbaum, "The Principle of Congruity in the Prediction of Attitude Change," *Psychological Review* 62 (1955): 42–55; Percy H. Tannenbaum, "The Congruity Principle Revisited: Studies in the Reduction, Induction, and Generalization of Persuasion," in *Advances in Experimental Social Psychology* 3, ed. Leonard Berkowitz (New York: Academic Press, 1967).

14. Leon Festinger, *A Theory of Cognitive Dissonance* (Stanford, Calif.: Stanford University Press, 1957); Jack W. Brehm and Arthur R. Cohen, eds., *Explorations in Cognitive Dissonance* (New York: Wiley, 1962); Robert A. Wicklund and Jack W. Brehm, *Perspectives on Cognitive Dissonance* (Hillsdale, N.J.: Lawrence Erlbaum, 1976).

15. Charles R. Berger and James J. Bradac, *Language and Social Knowledge: Uncertainty in Interpersonal Relations* (London: Edward Arnold, 1982); Charles R. Berger and Richard J. Calabrese, "Some Explorations in Initial Interaction and Beyond: Toward a Developmental Theory of Interpersonal Communication," *Human Communication Research* 1 (1975): 99–112.

16. Milton Rokeach, *Beliefs, Attitudes, and Values* (San Francisco: Jossey-Bass, 1968), *The Nature of Human Values* (New York: Free Press, 1973), and "Value Theory and Communication Research: Review and Commentary," in *Communication Yearbook* 3, ed. Dan Nimmo (New Brunswick, N.J.: Transaction Books, 1979).

17. Daniel Katz, "The Functional Approach to the Study of Attitudes," *Public Opinion Quarterly* 24 (1960): 163–204.

18. Aristotle, *Rhetoric*, trans. W. Rhys Roberts, and *Poetics*, trans. Ingram Bywater (New York: Modern Library, 1954), pp. 24–25. For more modern formulations of the notion of credibility, see Carl I. Hovland and W. A. Weiss, "The Influence of Source Credibility on Communicative Effectiveness," *Public Opinion Quarterly* 15 (1951): 635–50, and David K. Berlo, James B. Lemert, and Robert J. Mertz, "Dimensions for Evaluating the Acceptability of Message Sources," *Public Opinion Quarterly* 33 (1969): 563–76. For critiques of the credibility construct, see Gary Cronkhite and Jo Liska, "A Critique of Factor Analytic Approaches to the Study of Credibility," *Communication Monographs* 43 (June 1976): 91–107, and Gerald R. Miller and Michael Burgoon, "Persuasion Research: Review and Commentary," *Communication Yearbook* 2, ed. Brent D. Ruben (New Brunswick, N.J.: Transaction Books, 1978), pp. 29–47.

19. John R. French and Bertram Raven, "The Bases of Social Power," in *Studies in Social Power* (Ann Arbor: University of Michigan Press, 1959).

20. Edward E. Jones and Thane S. Pittman, "Toward a General Theory of Strategic Self-Presentation," in *Psychological Perspectives on the Self,* ed. Harry Suls (Hillsdale, N.J.: Lawrence Erlbaum, 1980).

21. Karen Tracy and others, "The Discourse of Requests: Assessment of a Compliance-Gaining Approach," *Human Communication Research* 10 (1984): 513–38.

22. Gerald R. Miller and others, "Compliance-Gaining Message Strategies: A Typology and Some Findings Concerning Effects of Situational Differences," *Communication Monographs* 44 (1977): 37–51; Michael E. Roloff and Edwin F. Barnicott, "The Situational Use of Pro- and Anti-Social Compliance-Gaining Strategies by High and Low Machiavellians," in *Communication Yearbook* 2, ed. Brent D. Ruben (New Brunswick, N.J.: Transaction Books, 1978), pp. 193–205.

23. Gerald Marwell and David R. Schmitt, "Dimensions of Compliance-Gaining Behavior: An Empirical Analysis," *Sociometry* 30 (1967): 350–64.

24. William J. Schenck-Hamlin, Richard L. Wiseman, and G. N. Georgacarakos, "A Model of Properties of Compliance-Gaining Strategies," *Communication Quarterly* 30 (1982): 92–100.

25. Michael J. Cody and Margaret L. McLaughlin, "Perceptions of Compliance-Gaining Situations: A Dimensional Analysis," *Communication Monographs* 47 (1980): 132–48; Michael J. Cody, M. L. Woelfel, and W. J. Jordan, "Dimensions of Compliance-Gaining Situations, *Human Communication Research* 9 (1983): 99–113.

26. Tracy and others, "The Discourse of Requests," pp. 520–22.

27. Ibid., pp. 533–34.

28. Harold H. Dawley, Jr., and W. W. Wenrich, *Achieving Assertive Behavior* (Monterey, Calif.: Brooks/Cole, 1976), p. 15.

29. Ibid., p. 97.

CHAPTER 10

1. John Cheever, "Goodbye, My Brother," in *The Stories of John Cheever* (New York: Knopf, 1978), p. 3. Reprinted with permission.

2. See, for example, Salvador Minuchin, *Families and Family Therapy* (Cambridge, Mass.: Harvard University Press, 1974), pp. 50–51.

3. Virginia Satir, *Peoplemaking* (Palo Alto, Calif.: Science and Behavior Books, 1972).

4. Kathleen M. Galvin and Bernard J. Brommel, *Family Communication: Cohesion and Change* (Glenview, Ill.: Scott, Foresman, 1982), p. 4.

5. Ronald E. Cromwell and David Olson, eds., *Power in Families* (New York: Halstead Press, 1975), p. 5.

6. Basil Bernstein, *Class, Codes, and Control* (London: Routledge and Kegan Paul, 1971).

7. Ralph Turner, *Family Interaction* (New York: Wiley, 1970), pp. 97–116.

8. Minuchin, *Families,* p. 53.

9. David Kantor and William Lehr, *Inside the Family* (San Francisco: Jossey-Bass, 1976).

10. Minuchin, *Families,* pp. 54–56.

11. Christopher Lasch, *Haven in a Heartless World* (New York: Basic Books, 1977).

12. David Olson and Hamilton McCubbin, *Families: What Makes Them Work* (Beverly Hills, Calif.: Sage, 1983), pp. 30–34.

13. D. R. Entwistle and S. G. Doering, *The First Birth* (Baltimore: Johns Hopkins University Press, 1980); B. C. Miller and D. L. Sollie, "Normal Stress During the Transition to Parenthood," *Family Relations* 29 (1980): 459–65.

14. J. H. Meyerowitz and H. Feldman, "Transition to Parenthood," *Psychiatric Research Reports* 20 (1966): 459–65.

15. Hilary Lips and Anne Morrison, "Changes in the Sense of Family Among Couples Having Their First Child," *Journal of Social and Personal Relationships* 3 (1986): 393–400.

16. S. A. Anderson, C. S. Russell, and W. R. Schumm, "Perceived Marital Quality and Family Life Cycle Categories: A Further Analysis," *Journal of Marriage and the Family* 45 (1983): 127–39; B. C. Rollins and K. L. Cannon, "Marital Satisfaction over the Family Life Cycle: A Re-evaluation," *Journal of Marriage and the Family* 36 (1974): 271–82.

17. S. A. Anderson, "Changes in Parental Adjustment and Communication During the Leaving-Home Transition," *Journal of Social and Personal Relationships* 7 (1990): 47–68.

18. Ibid.

19. Anne-Marie Ambert, "Relationship Between Ex-Spouses: Individual and Dyadic Perspectives," *Journal of Social and Personal Relationships* 5 (1988): 327–46.

20. F. F. Furstenberg, "The New Extended Family: The Experience of Parents and Children After Remarriage," in *Remarriage and Step-parenting,* ed. K. Pasley and M. Ihinger-Tallman (New York: Guilford Press, 1987), p. 342.

21. Ambert, "Relationship Between Ex-Spouses."

22. Galvin and Brommel, *Family Communication,* p. 234.

23. Steven Mintz and Susan Kellogg, *Domestic Revolutions: A Social History of American Family Life* (New York: The Free Press, 1988).

24. Jane Howard, *Families* (New York: Simon and Schuster, 1978). Cited in Galvin and Brommel, *Family Communication,* pp. 299–300.

25. See John M. Gottman, *Marital Interaction: Experimental Investigations* (New York: Academic Press, 1979).

26. Mary Anne Fitzpatrick, "A Typological Approach to Marital Interaction: Recent Theory and Research," in *Advances in Experimental Social Psychology* 18, ed. Leonard Berkowitz (New York: Academic Press, 1984), pp. 1–47. See also Mary Anne Fitzpatrick and Diane M. Badzinski, "All in the Family: Interpersonal Communication in Kin Relationships," in *Handbook of Interpersonal Communication,* ed. Mark Knapp and Gerald R. Miller (Beverly Hills, Calif.: Sage, 1985), pp. 687–736.

27. Fitzpatrick and Badzinski, "All in the Family," p. 700.

28. B. Rollins and R. Galligan, "The Developing Child and Marital Satisfaction of Parents," in *Child Influences on Marital and Family Interaction: A Lifespan Perspective,* ed. Richard Lerner and Graham Spanier (New York: Academic Press, 1978), pp. 71–106.

29. Alice Rossi, "Transition to Parenthood," *Journal of Marriage and the Family* 30 (1968): 26–39.

30. Linda K. Acitelli, "When Spouses Talk to Each Other About Their Relationship," *Journal of Social and Personal Relationships* 5 (1988): 185–200.

31. Michael Ross and Diane Holmberg, "Are Wives' Memories for Events in Relationships More Vivid Than Their Husbands' Memories?" *Journal of Social and Personal Relationships* 9 (1992), 585–604.

32. Paul H. Zietlow and Alan L. Sillars, "Life-stage Differences in Communication During Marital Conflicts," *Journal of Social and Personal Relationships* 5 (1988): 223–46.

33. Ibid.

34. See, for example, B. Rollins and D. Thomas, "Parental Support, Power, and Control Techniques in the Socialization of Children," in *Contemporary Theories About the Family,* Vol. 1, ed. Wesley R. Burr and others (New York: Free Press, 1979), pp. 317–64. See also S. Steinmetz, "Disciplinary Techniques and Their Relationship to Aggressiveness, Dependency, and Conscience," in *Contemporary Theories About the Family,* Vol. 2, pp. 405–38.

35. Desmond Morris, *Intimate Behavior* (New York: Bantam Books, 1971), pp. 252–54.

36. Gene Brody and David Shaffer. "Contributions of Parents and Peers to Children's Moral Socialization," *Developmental Revie,* 2 (1992): 31–75.

37. R. R. Sears, E. E. Maccoby, and H. Levin, *Patterns of Childrearing.* (Evanston, Ill.: Row, Peterson, 1957).

38. Brody and Shaffer, 1982, p. 39.

39. M. L. Hoffman, "Identification and Conscience Development," *Child Development* 4 (1971): 400–406.

40. E. M. Hetherington, M. Cox and R. Cox, "The Aftermath of Divorce," in *Mother-Child, Father-Child Relations,* eds. J. H. Stevens and M. M. Mathews (Washington, D.C.: NAEYC, 1978); T. S. Parish. "The Relationship Between Factors Associated with Father Loss and Individuals' Level of Moral Judgement," *Adolescence* 15 (1980): 535–541.

41. James Applegate, Brant Burleson, Julie Burke, Jesse Delia, and Susan Kline. "Reflection-Enhancing Parental Communication," in *Parental Belief Systems: The Psychological Consequences for Children,* ed. Irving Sigel (Hillsdale, N.J.: Lawrence Erlbaum, 1985), pp. 107–142.

42. Roger Jon Desmond, Jerome L. Singer, Dorothy G. Singer, Rachel Calam, and Karen Colimore, "Family Mediation Patterns and Television Viewing: Young Children's Use and Grasp of the Medium," *Human Communication Research* 11 (1985): 461–80.

43. Ibid.

44. William Rawlins and Melissa Holl, "Adolescents' Interaction with Parents and Friends: Dialectics of Temporal Perspective and Evaluation," *Journal of Social and Personal Relationships* 5 (1988): 27–46.

45. Anderson, "Changes in Parental Adjustment."

46. Mark Fine and Lawrence Kurdek, "Parenting Cognitions in Stepfamilies: Differences Between parents and Stepparents and Relations to Parenting Satisfaction," *Journal of Social and Personal Relationships* 11 (1994): 95–112.

47. For a brief review of this research, see Fitzpatrick and Badzinski, "All in The Family." pp. 713–17.

48. A. Goetting, "The Developmental Tasks of Siblingship over the Life Cycle," *Journal of Marriage and the Family* 48 (1986): 703–14.

49. Victor Cicirelli and Jon Nussbaum, "Relationships with Siblings in Later Life," in *Life-Span Communication: Normative Processes,* ed. J. Nussbaum (Hillsdale, N.J.: Lawrence Erlbaum, 1989), pp. 283–99.

50. D. T. Gold, "Sibling Relationships in Retrospect: A Study of Reminiscence in Old Age," doctoral dissertation, Northwestern University, Evanston, Illinois, 1986. (Cited in Cicirelli and Nussbaum, "Relationships with Siblings.")

51. Michael Nichols, *The Power of the Family: Mastering the Hidden Dance of Family Relationships* (New York: Fireside Books, 1988).

52. James Patterson and Peter Kim, *The Day America Told the Truth* (New York: Prentice Hall, 1991).

53. Virginia Satir, *Peoplemaking* (Palo Alto, Calif.: Science and Behavior Books, 1972).

54. J. Bowlby, *The Making and Breaking of Affectional Bonds* (London: Tavistock, 1979); J. A. Simpson. "The Influence of Attachment Styles on Romantic Relationships," *Journal of Personality and Social Psychology* 59 (1990): 971–80.

55. Brant R. Burleson, "Age, Social-Cognitive Development, and the Use of Comforting Strategies," *Communication Monographs* 51 (1984): 140–53.

56. D. R. Lehman, J. H. Ellard, and C. B. Wortman, "Social Support for the Bereaved: Recipients' and Providers' Perspectives on What Is Helpful," *Journal of Consulting and Clinical Psychology* 54 (1986): 438–46.

57. James L. Applegate, "Adaptive Communication in Educational Contexts: A Study of Teachers' Communicative Strategies," *Communication Education* 29 (1980): 158–70.

58. Brant R. Burleson and Wendy Samter, "Consistencies in Theoretical and Naive Evaluations of Comforting Messages," *Communication Monographs* 52 (1985): 103–23.

CHAPTER 11

1. The authors would like to thank Vernon Cronen for providing this example. We have paraphrased the account; any inaccuracies are our own.

2. Howard Gadlin, "Private Lives and Public Order: A Critical View of the History of Intimate Relations in the United States," in *Close Relationships: Perspectives on the Meaning of Intimacy,* ed. George Levinger and Harold Raush (Amherst, Mass.: University of Massachusetts Press, 1977), pp. 33–72.

3. Richard Sennett, *The Fall of Public Man: On the Social Psychology of Capitalism* (New York: Vintage Books, 1976), p. 102.

4. Timothy Stephen, "Communication in the Shifting Context of Intimacy: Marriage, Meaning, and Modernity," *Communication Theory* 4 (1994): 191–218.

5. Ellen Berscheid, Mark Snyder, Allen Omoto, "Issues in Studying Close Relationships: Conceptualizing and Measuring Closeness," in *Close Relationships,* ed. Clyde Hendrick (Newbury Park, Calif.: Sage, 1989), pp. 63–91.

6. Ibid.

7. See William K. Rawlins, "Friendship as a Communicative Achievement: A Theory and an Interpretive Analysis of Verbal Reports," Ph.D. dissertation, Temple University, 1981. See also Kaspar D. Naegele, "Friendship and Acquaintances: An Exploration of Some Social Distinctions," *Harvard Educational Review* 28 (1958): 232–52.

8. Virginia Kidd, "Happily Ever After and Other Relationship Styles: Advice on Interpersonal Relations in Popular Magazines, 1951–1973," *Quarterly Journal of Speech* 61 (1975): 31–39.

9. Diane Prusank, Robert Duran, and Dena DeLillo. "Interpersonal Relationships in Women's Magazines: Dating and Relating in the 1970s and 1980s," *Journal of Social and Personal Relationships* 10 (1993): 307–320.

10. For models of relationship development that portray participants as making rational choices and being highly aware of the process, see Irwin Altman and Dallas Taylor, *Social Penetration: The Development of Interpersonal Relationships* (New York: Holt, Rinehart & Winston, 1973); Charles Berger and Richard Calabrese, "Some Explorations in Initial Interaction and Beyond: Toward a Developmental Theory of Interpersonal Communication," *Human Communication Research* 1 (1975): 99–112. For arguments that people are less conscious of these processes, see Charles Berger, "Self-Consciousness and the Adequacy of Theory and Research into Relationship Development," *Western Journal of Speech Communication* 44 (1980): 93–96; Jesse Delia, "Some Tentative Thoughts Concerning the Study of Interpersonal Relationships and Their Development," Western *Journal of Speech Communication* 44 (1980): 97–103.

11. Harriet Braiker and Harold Kelley, "Conflicts in the Development of Close Relationships," in *Social Exchange in Developing Relationships,* ed. Robert Burgess and Ted Huston (New York: Academic Press, 1979), pp. 136–68.

12. Mark L. Knapp, *Interpersonal Communication and Human Relationships* (Boston: Allyn and Bacon, 1984), p. 192.

13. Warren Shibles and Charles Zastrow, "Romantic Love vs. Rational Love," in *The Personal Problem Solver* (Englewood Cliffs, N.J.: Prentice-Hall), p. 21.

14. See Stanley Schacter and Jerome Singer, "Cognitive, Social, and Physiological Determinants of Emotional State," *Psychological Review* 69 (1962): 379–99; Miles Patterson, "An Arousal Model of Interpersonal Intimacy," *Psychological Review* 83 (1976): 235–45.

15. Gregory L. White, Sanford Fishbein, and Jeffrey Rutstein, "Passionate Love and the Misattribution of Arousal," *Journal of Personality and Social Psychology* 41 (1981): 56–62.

16. Richard Sennett, *The Fall of Public Man* (New York: Random House, 1978).

17. Steven Duck, "Interpersonal Communication in Developing Acquaintance," in *Explorations in Interpersonal Communication,* ed. Gerald R. Miller (Beverly Hills, Calif.: Sage, 1973), pp. 127–48.

18. Elaine Walster, Vera Aronson, Darcy Abrahams, and Leon Rottman, "Importance of Physical Attractiveness in Dating Behavior," *Journal of Personality and Social Psychology* 4 (1966): 508–16.

19. For a summary of this research, see William Griffitt, "Attitude Similarity and Attraction," in *Foundations of Interpersonal Attraction,* ed. Ted L. Huston (New York: Academic Press, 1974), pp. 285–308.

20. Brant Burleson and Wayne Denton, "A New Look at Similarity and Attraction in Marriage: Similarities in Social-Cognitive and Communication Skills as Predictors of Attraction and Satisfaction," *Communication Monographs* 59 (1992): 268–287.

21. Brant Burleson, Wendy Samter, and A. E. Lucchetti, "Similarity in Communication Values as a Predictor of Friendship Choices: Studies of Friends and Best Friends," *Southern Communication Jour-*

nal 57 (1992): 260–276; Brant Burleson, Adrianne Kunkel, and Jennifer Birch. "Thoughts about Talk in Romantic Relationships: Similarity Makes for Attraction (and Happiness, Too)," *Communication Quarterly* 42 (1994): 259–273.

22. Charles Backman and Paul Secord, "The Effect of Perceived Liking on Interpersonal Attraction," *Human Relations* 12 (1959): 379–84. See also Fritz Heider, *The Psychology of Interpersonal Relations* (New York: Wiley, 1958).

23. Benjamin J. Broome, "The Attraction Paradigm Revisited: Responses to Dissimilar Others," *Human Communication Research* 10 (1983): 137–52.

24. See David R. Mettee and Elliot Aronson, "Affective Reactions to Appraisal from Others," in Huston, *Foundations of Interpersonal Attraction,* pp. 235–83.

25. William C. Schutz, *FIRO: A Three-Dimensional Theory of Interpersonal Behavior* (New York: Holt, Rinehart & Winston, 1958).

26. Kenneth Villard and Leland Whipple, *Beginnings in Relational Communication* (New York: Wiley, 1976); U. G. Foa, "Interpersonal and Economic Resources," *Science* 171 (1971): 345–51.

27. John Berg and Richard Archer, "The Disclosure-Liking Relationship: Effects of Self-Perception, Order of Disclosure, and Topical Similarity," *Human Communication Research* 10 (1983): 269–82.

28. Rawlins, "Friendship as a Communicative Achievement."

29. Margaret E. Gruhn, "German-American Language Patterns as Indicators of Cultural Communication Boundaries: A Cross-Cultural Analysis," paper presented at the Speech Communication convention, Denver, Colorado, November 1985.

30. Michael Monsour, Sam Betty, and Nancy Kurzweil. "Levels of Perspectives and the Perception of Intimacy in Cross-Sex Friendships: A Balance Theory Explanation of Shared Perceptual Reality," *Journal of Social and Personal Relationships* 10 (1993): 529–50.

31. Paul H. Wright, "Self-referent Motivation and the Intrinsic Quality of Friendship," *Journal of Social and Personal Relationships* 1 (1984): 115–30.

32. Robert B. Hays, "The Day-to-Day Functioning of Close Versus Casual Friendships," *Journal of Social and Personal Relationships* 6 (1989): 21–38.

33. Suzanna Rose and Felicisima Serafica, "Keeping and Ending Casual, Close and Best Friendships," *Journal of Social and Personal Relationships* 3 (1986): 275–88.

34. Ibid, p. 280.

35. Knapp, *Interpersonal Communication,* pp. 29–58.

36. Paul Mongeau, Jerold Hale, Kristen Johnson, and Jacqueline Hillis, "Who's Wooing Whom? An Investigation of Female Initiated Dating," in *Interpersonal Communication: Evolving Interpersonal Relationships,* ed. Pamela Kalbfleisch (Hillsdale, N.J.: Lawrence Erlbaum, 1993) pp. 51–68.

37. Liana Koeppel, Yvette Montagne-Miller, Dan O'Hair, and Michael Cody. "Friendly? Flirting? Wrong?" in *Interpersonal Communication: Evolving Interpersonal Relationships,* ed. Pamela Kalbfleisch (Hillsdale, N.J.: Lawrence Erlbaum, 1993), pp. 13–32.

38. Robert A. Bell and John A. Daly, "The Affinity-Seeking Function of Communication," *Communication Monographs* 51 (1984): 91–115.

39. Leslie A. Baxter and William Wilmot, "'Secret Tests': Social Strategies for Acquiring Information About the State of the Relationship," *Human Communication Research* 11 (1984): 171–202.

40. James H. Tolhuizen, "Communication Strategies for Intensifying Dating Relationships: Identification, Use and Structure," *Journal of Social and Personal Relationships* 6 (1989): 413–34.

41. Malcolm R. Parks and Mara B. Adelman, "Communication Networks and the Development of Romantic Relationships: An Expansion of Uncertainty Reduction Theory," *Human Communication Research* 10 (1983): 55–80.

42. Leslie A. Baxter, "Symbols of Relationship Identity in Relationship Cultures," *Journal of Social and Personal Relationships* 4 (1987): 261–80.

43. Robert Fulghum, *It Was on Fire When I Lay Down on It* (New York: Random House, 1989).

44. William Rawlins, "Openness as Problematic in Ongoing Friendship: Two Conversational Dilemmas," Communication Monographs 50 (1983): 1–13; Leslie A. Baxter, "Dialectical Contradictions in Developing Relationships," *Journal of Social and Personal Relationships* 7 (1990): 69–88.

45. Baxter, "Dialectical Contradictions."

46. Alan L. Sillars and Michael D. Scott, "Interpersonal Perception Between Intimates: An Integrative Review," *Human Communication Research* 10 (1983): 153–76.

47. Ibid.

48. Steven Duck, *Relating to Others* (Chicago: The Dorsey Press, 1988), pp. 102–21.

49. Sally Planalp and James Honeycutt, "Events That Increase Uncertainty in Personal Relationships," *Human Communication Research* 11 (1985): 593–604.

50. John W. Lannamann, "Interpersonal Communication Research as Ideological Practice," *Communication Theory* 1 (1991): 179–203; Sarah Trenholm and Arthur Jensen, "The Ideology of Intimacy: Public Selves/Private Selves," paper presented at the Eastern Communication Association's annual conference, Atlantic City, May, 1986.

51. Elizabeth House, "Sex Role Orientation and Marital Satisfaction in Dual- and One-Provider Couples," *Sex Roles* 14 (1986): 245–59; Linda Nyquist, Karla Slivken, Janet Spence, and Robert Helmreich, "Household Responsibilities in Middle-Class Couples: The Contributions of Demographic and Personality Variables," *Sex Roles* 12 (1985): 15–34.

52. Morton Deutsch, "Conflicts: Productive and Destructive," in *Conflict Resolution Through Communication*, ed. Fred E. Jandt (New York: Harper & Row, 1973), pp. 155–97, 156.

53. Joyce Hocker Frost and William W. Wilmot, *Interpersonal Conflict* (Dubuque, Iowa: Brown, 1978), pp. 17–19.

54. Raymond S. Ross and Mark G. Ross, *Relating and Interacting* (Englewood Cliffs, N.J.: Prentice-Hall, 1982), p. 124.

55. George R. Bach and Peter Wyden, *The Intimate Enemy: How to Fight Fair in Love and Marriage* (New York: Avon Books, 1970).

56. David W. Johnson, *Reaching Out: Interpersonal Effectiveness and Self-Actualization*, 3rd ed. (Englewood Cliffs, N.J.: Prentice-Hall, 1986), pp. 81–83.

57. Frost and Wilmot, *Interpersonal Conflict*, pp. 136–38. See also Roger Fisher, "Fractionating Conflict," in *Conflict Resolution: Contributions of the Behavioral Sciences*, ed. Clagett G. Smith (Notre Dame, Ind.: University of Notre Dame Press, 1971).

58. Frost and Wilmot, *Interpersonal Conflict*, p. 138.

CHAPTER 12

1. Ken Auletta, "Power, Greed and Glory on Wall Street: The Fall of Lehman Brothers," *New York Times Magazine* (17 Feb. 1985): 29–43.

2. Leon Battista Alberti, *Ten Books on Architecture*, ed. and trans. by J. Leoni (New York: Transatlantic Arts, 1966), p. 175.

3. Lawrence Rosenfeld, "Central Park and the Celebration of Civic Virtue," in *American Rhetoric: Context and Criticism*, ed. Thomas W. Benson (Carbondale, Ill.: Southern Illinois University Press, 1989), pp. 221–66.

4. Warren Leland, "Turning Reality Round Together: Guides to Conversation in Eighteenth-Century England," *Eighteenth Century Life* 8 (1983): 65–87.

5. Henry Fielding, "An Essay on Conversation," in *Miscellanies*, Volume One, ed. Henry Knight Miller (Middletown, Conn.: Wesleyan University Press, 1972), p. 120.

6. Rom Harre, *Social Being: A Theory for Social Psychology* (Totowa, N.J.: Littlefield, Adams, 1979), pp. 22–26.

7. For example, see Richard Sennett, *The Fall of Public Man* (New York: Random House, 1974). See also Christopher Lasch, *The Culture of Narcissism: American Life in an Age of Diminishing Expectations* (New York: Norton, 1979).

8. Erving Goffman, *Interaction Ritual: Essays on Face-to-Face Behavior* (Garden City, N.Y.: Anchor Books, 1967), pp. 47–95.

9. Ibid., p. 76.

10. Ibid., p. 79.

11. Sennett, *The Fall of Public Man*.

12. John Naisbitt, *Megatrends* (New York: Warner Books, 1982).

13. E. Foster and others, *A Market Study for the College of Business Administration*, University of Minnesota, Twin Cities (Minneapolis: College of Business Administration, University of Minnesota, November 1978).

14. Daniel Katz and Robert L. Kahn, *The Social Psychology of Organizations* (New York: Wiley, 1966), pp. 239–45.

15. Gerald A. Goldhaber, *Organizational Communication* (Dubuque, Iowa: Brown, 1983), p. 226.

16. Fredric M. Jablin, "Superior-Subordinate Communication: The State of the Art," *Psychological Bulletin* 86 (1979): 1208.

17. William C. Redding, *Communication Within the Organization: An Interpretative Review of Theory and Research* (New York: Industrial Communication Council, 1972), p. 443.

18. Fredric M. Jablin, "An Exploratory Study of Subordinates' Perceptions of Supervisory Politics," *Communication Quarterly* 29 (1981): 269–75.

19. For a review, see P. D. Krivonos, "Distortion of Subordinate-to-Superior Communication," paper presented at the annual meeting of the International Communication Association, Portland, Oregon, 1976. See also Norman Maier, L. Richard Hoffman, and William Read, "Superior-Subordinate Communication: The Relative Effectiveness of Managers Who Held Their Subordinates' Positions," *Personal Psychology* 26 (1963): 1–11.

20. Cal Downs and Charles Conrad, "Effective Subordinancy," *Journal of Business Communication* 19 (1982): 27–37.

21. Charles B. Truax and Robert R. Carkhuff, *Toward Effective Counseling and Psychotherapy* (Chicago: Aldine, 1967).

22. Loyd Pettegrew and Richard Thomas, "Communicator Style Differences in Formal vs. Informal Therapeutic Relationships," in *Communication Yearbook 2,* ed. Brent D. Ruben (New Brunswick, N.J.: Transaction Books, 1978), pp. 521–37.

23. Ibid., p. 534.

24. Ibid.

25. Daniel Costello, "Health Communication Theory and Research: An Overview," in *Communication Yearbook 1,* ed. Brent D. Ruben (New Brunswick, N.J.: Transaction Books, 1977), pp. 557–67.

26. See, for example, Paul Arntson, David Droge, and Harry E. Fassl, "Pediatrician-Patient Communication: Final Report," in *Communication Yearbook 2,* pp. 505–22; B. Freeman, V. Negrete, V. Davis, and M. Korsch, "Gaps in Doctor-Patient Communication: Doctor-Patient Interaction Analysis," *Pediatrician Research* 5 (1971): 298–311.

27. See "Professionals," *Buyer's Market 2* (3), ed. Luke W. Cole (March 1986): 3.

28. Arntson and others, "Pediatrician-Patient Communication," p. 521.

29. James Dillard, "Close Relationships at Work: Perceptions of the Motives and Performance of Relational Participants." *Journal of Social and Personal Relationships* 4 (1987): 179–93.

30. Ibid.

31. Patrice Buzzanell, "Managing Workplace Romance," paper presented at the annual convention of the Speech Communication Association, Chicago, November, 1990.

32. G. R. Spruell, "Daytime Drama: Love in the Office," *Training and Development Journal* 39 (1985): 21–23; Dennis Mumby and Linda Putnam. "Bounded Rationality as an Organizational Construct: A Feminist Critique," paper presented at the annual conference of the Academy of Management, San Francisco, 1990.

33. For a review of trait research, see R. D. Mann, "A Review of the Relationship Between Personality and Performance in Small Groups," *Psychological Bulletin* 56 (1959): 241–70. For a more current review of personality influences, see Mark Snyder and William Ickes, "Personality and Social Beahvior," in *The Handbook of Social Psychology,* Vol. 2, 3rd ed., ed. Gardner Lindzey and Elliot Aronosn (New York: Random House, 1985), pp. 883–947.

34. Max DePree, *Leadership Jazz* (New York: Doubleday, 1992), pp. 220–25.

35. Charles O'Reilly and David Caldwell, "Informational Influence as a Determinant of Task Characteristics and Job Satisfaction," *Journal of Applied Psychology* 64 (1979): 157–65.

36. Irving Janis, *Victims of Groupthink: A Psychological Study of Foreign Policy Decisions and Fiascos* (Boston: Houghton Mifflin, 1972).

37. Charles Conrad, *Strategic Organizational Communication: An Integrated Perspective* (Fort Worth: Holt, Rhinehart and Winston, 1990), p. 6.

38. Karl Weick, *The Social Psychology of Organizing* (Reading, Mass.: Addison-Wesley, 1979).

39. Daniel C. Feldman, "The Multiple Socialization of Organization Members," *Academy of Management Review* 6 (1981): 309–18.

40. Fredric M. Jablin, "Task/Work Relationships: A Lifespan Perspective," in *Handbook of Interpersonal Communication,* ed. Mark Knapp and Gerald R. Miller (Beverly Hills, Calif.: Sage, 1985), p. 633.

41. Julie Foehrenbach and Karen Rosenberg, "How Are We Doing?" *Journal of Communication Management* 12 (1982): 3–11.

42. Keith Davis, *Human Behavior at Work* (New York: McGraw-Hill, 1972), p. 280.

43. William Davis and J. Regis O'Connor, "Serial Transmission of Information: A Study of the Grapevine," *Journal of Applied Communication Research* 5 (1977): 61–72; Evan E. Rudolph, "Informal Human Communication Systems in a Large Organization," *Journal of Applied Communication Research* 1 (1973): 7–23; Eugene Walton, "How Effective Is the Grapevine?" *Personnel Journal* 38 (1961): 45–49.

44. Charles Berger. "Perceptions of Information Sequencing in Relationship Development," *Human Communication Research* 3 (1976): 29–46.

45. Frances Moore Lappé and Paul Martin DuBois, *The Quickening of America: Rebuilding Our Nation, Remaking Our Lives* (San Francisco: Jossey-Bass, 1994), pp. 137–163.

46. Price Pritchett, *Culture Shift: The Employee Handbook for Changing Corporate Culture* (Dallas: Pritchett & Associates, 1993).

47. For a discussion of relational and personal goals in a management context, see Robert R. Blake and Jane S. Mouton, *The Managerial Grid* (Houston: Gulf, 1964), and Jay Hall, *Conflict Management Survey* (Woodlands, Tex.: Teleometrics International, 1969). See also Raymond S. Ross and Mark G. Ross, Relating and Interacting (Englewood Cliffs, N.J.: Prentice-Hall, 1982), and David W. Johnson, *Reaching Out: Interpersonal Effectiveness and Self-Actualization*, 3rd ed. (Englewood Cliffs, N.J.: Prentice-Hall, 1986), pp. 207–10.

48. Ross and Ross, *Relating and Interacting*, p. 145.

49. Our discussion of negotiation strategies is based on two basic sources: Dean G. Pruitt, *Negotiation Behavior* (New York: Academic Press, 1981), and Roger Fisher and William Ury, *Getting to YES: Negotiating Agreement Without Giving In* (Boston: Houghton Mifflin, 1986).

50. Pruitt, *Negotiation Behavior,* pp. 149, 152.

51. Ibid., p. 153.

52. Fisher and Ury, *Getting to YES,* p. 24.

53. Ibid., p. 32.

54. See ibid., pp. 51–56, for a development of this example.

55. Pruitt, *Negotiation Behavior, p. 201.*

56. Ibid., pp. 215–17.

CHAPTER 13

1. Larry A. Samovar, Richard E. Porter, and Nemi C. Jain, *Understanding Intercultural Communication* (Belmont, Calif.: Wadsworth, 1981); see especially Chapter 3, "Understanding Ourselves: American Cultural Patterns."

2. Ibid., p. 46.

3. Ibid., pp. 46–47.

4. Ibid., p. 68.

5. Ibid., p. 74.

6. Ibid., p. 76.

7. Thomas Kochman, *Black and White Styles in Conflict* (Chicago: University of Chicago Press, 1981), p. 4.

8. Ibid., pp. 13–14.

9. Thomas Kochman, *Black and White Styles,* pp. 16–17. Kochman's source for this story is "Mr. Trotter and Mr. Wilson," *Crisis* (January 1915): 119–27.

10. Ibid., p. 44.

11. Ibid., p. 18.

12. Jack L. Daniel and Geneva Smitherman, "How I Got Over: Communication Dynamics in the Black Community," *Quarterly Journal of Speech* 62 (February 1976): 26–39, 27.

13. Ibid., p. 38.

14. Molefi Kete Asante and Alice Davis, "Encounters in the Interracial Workplace," in *Handbook of International and Intercultural Communication,* p. 387.

15. Carley H. Dodd, *Dynamics of Intercultural Communication,* 2nd. ed. (Dubuque, Iowa: Brown, 1987), p. 71.

16. Tuen A. van Dijk, *Communicating Racism: Ethnic Prejudice in Thought and Talk* (Newbury Park, Calif.: Sage, 1987).

17. Ibid., p. 220.

18. Ibid., pp. 235–36.

19. Ibid., p. 372.

20. Ibid., pp. 44–45.

21. Jack L. Daniel, "The Facilitation of White-Black Communication," *The Journal of Communication* 20 (June 1970): 134–41.

22. Samovar and others, *Understanding Intercultural Communication,* p. 195.

23. William D. Brooks, *Speech Communication* (Dubuque, Iowa: Brown, 1974), p. 24. The original source for this anecdote is John Wilson, "Film Literacy in Africa," *Canadian Communications* 7 (4) (Summer 1961): 7–14.

24. Dodd, *Dynamics of Intercultural Communication,* p. 49.

25. Ibid., p. 44.

26. Samovar and others, *Understanding Intercultural Communication,* p. 119.

27. Dodd, *Dynamics of Intercultural Communication,* p. 45.

28. Edward T. Hall, *The Silent Language* (Garden City, N.Y.: Doubleday, 1959), p. 67.

29. Dodd, *Dynamics of Intercultural Communication,* p. 92.

30. Samovar and others, *Understanding Intercultural Communication,* p. 94. The quote is from K. S. Sitaram and Roy T. Cogdell, *Foundations of Intercultural Communication* (Columbus, Ohio: Merrill, 1976), p. 51.

31. Stella Ting-Toomey, "Identity and Interpersonal Bonding," in *Handbook of International and Intercultural Communication,* p. 352.

32. Ibid., p. 364.

33. Hall, *The Silent Language,* p. 191.

34. Ibid., p. 209.

35. Dodd, *Dynamics of Intercultural Communication,* p. 174.

36. E. C. Condon, "Cross-Cultural Interferences Affecting Teacher-Pupil Communication in American Schools," *International and Intercultural Communication Annual* 3 (1976): 108–20.

37. Stephanie Coontz, *The Social Origins of Private Life: A History of American Families 1600–1900* (London: Verso, 1988), pp. 74–78.

38. John D'Emilio and Estelle B. Freedman, *Intimate Matters: A History of Sexuality in America* (New York: Harper & Row, 1988), p. 29

39. Coontz, *Social Origins,* p. 79

40. Eleazar Moody, *The School of Good Manners* (Portland, Me.: Thomas B. Wait, 1786), pp. 7, 8, 10; quoted in John F. Kasson, *Rudeness and Civility: Manners in Nineteenth-Century Urban America* (New York: Hill & Wang), p. 13.

41. Kasson, *Rudeness and Civility,* p. 14.

42. Ibid., pp. 15–16.

43. Coontz, *Social Origins,* p. 89.

44. D'Emilio, *Intimate Matters,* p. 21.

45. Coontz, *Social Origins,* p. 96

46. Haltunnen, Karen, *Confidence Men and Painted Women: A Study of Middle-Class Culture in America, 1830–1870* (New Haven: Yale University Press, 1982).

47. S. W. Nissenbaum, "From Pleasure to Intimacy: The Glorification of Sexual Love in Early Victorian America, 1830–1860." mss. University of Mass., Amherst, 1966, p. 27; quoted in Howard Gadlin, "Private Lives and Public Order," in *Close Relationships: Perspectives on the Meaning of Intimacy,* eds. George Levinger and Harold L. Raush (Amherst, Mass.: University of Massachusetts Press, 1977), p. 43

48. Kirk Jeffrey, "The Family as Utopian Retreat from the City," *Soundings* 55 (1972), p. 28; quoted in Stephanie Coontz, *The Way We Never Were: American Families and the Nostalgia Trap* (New York: Basic Books, 1992), p. 54.

49. Kasson, *Rudeness and Civility,* p. 170.

50. Warren I. Susman, *Culture as History: The Transformation of American Society in the Twentieth Century* (New York: Pantheon Books, 1984), pp. 273–74.

51. Glenna Matthews, *"Just a Housewife:" The Rise and Fall of Domesticity in America* (New York: Oxford University Press, 1987), p. 25.

52. Ibid., p. 20.

53. Karen Lystra, *Searching the Heart* (New York: Oxford University Press), 1989), p. 88.

54. Ibid., p. 116.

55. Coontz, *Social Origins of Family Life,* p. 335.

56. William Leach, *Land of Desire: Merchants, Power, and the Rise of a New American Culture* (New York: Vintage, 1993), p. 7; quote taken from Wesley Clair Mitchell, *Business Cycles* (Berkeley, Calif.: 1913), p. 12.

57. Leach, *Land of Desire,* p. 6.

58. Matthews, *"Just a Housewife,"* p. 180.

59. Coontz, *Social Origins of Family Life,* p. 351.

60. Matthews, *"Just a Housewife,"* p. 182

61. Coontz, *Social Origins of Private Lives,* p. 337.

62. Sussman, *Culture as History,* p. 277.

63. Gadlin, "Private Lives and Public Order," p. 57.

64. Ibid., p. 62

65. Beth Bailey, *From Front Porch to Back Seat: Courtship in Twentieth-Century America* (Baltimore: Johns Hopkins, 1989), p. 90.

66. Ibid., p. 93.

67. Haltunnen, *Confidence Men and Painted Women.*

Author Index

A

Abelson, Robert, 428
Abrahams, Darcy, 424, 436
Abrahams, Roger D., 395
Acitelli, Linda K., 298, 434
Addington, David W., 74, 424
Adelman, Mara B., 333, 437
Adler, Ronald, 425
Agar, Michael, 111
Aiken, L., 424
Alberti, Leon Battista, 352, 438
Allen, Terre, 338, 339
Altman, Irwin, 436
Ambert, Anne-Marie, 434
Anderson, S. A., 434
Anderson, Stephen, 285, 301
Applegate, James, 305, 428, 435
Archer, Richard, 437
Argyle, Michael, 77, 424
Aristotle, 433
Arliss, Laurie P., 193, 195, 429
Arnold, Carroll C., 422
Arntson, Paul, 439
Aronson, Elliot, 430, 437, 439
Aronson, Vera, 424, 436
Asante, Molefi Kete, 393, 440
Atlas, James, 428
Auletta, Ken, 351, 438
Austen, Jane, 81, 425
Averill, James, 78, 425

B

Bach, George R., 345, 438
Backman, Charles, 437
Badzinski, Diane M., 434
Bailey, Beth L., 331, 441
Bainbridge, William Sims, 243, 432
Baldridge, Letitia, 43
Bandura, Albert, 432
Barker, Eileen, 242–243, 432
Barnicott, Edwin F., 433

Barnlund, Dean, 421
Bartholomew, Kim, 232, 432
Basso, Keith H., 100–101
Bateson, Gregory, 134–135, 138, 426, 427
Baudin, Hortensia, 424
Bavelas, Janet Beavin, 81, 118, 119, 135, 138, 425, 426
Baxter, Leslie A., 331, 333, 431, 437
Beatty, Michael J., 431
Beebe, Steven A., 421
Behnke, Ralph R., 431
Bell, Robert A., 329, 332, 437
Bellah, Robert N., 423
Bem, Daryl J., 190–191, 224, 429, 431
Benedict, Ruth, 186, 206, 429
Benson, Thomas W., 438
Berelson, Bernard, 421
Berg, John, 437
Berger, Charles R., 149, 425, 428, 433, 436, 439
Berger, Peter L., 429
Berglas, Steven, 226, 431
Berkowitz, Leonard, 428, 429, 430, 433, 434
Berlin, Isiah, 403
Berlo, David K., 433
Berne, Eric, 225, 238, 431
Bernstein, Basil, 102, 276, 426, 434
Bernstein, S., 431
Berscheid, Ellen, 314, 427, 431, 436
Best, Patricia B., 426
Betty, Sam, 437
Birch, Jennifer, 437
Birdwhistell, Ray L., 425
Black, Alex, 138, 421, 425
Blake, Robert R., 440
Blane, Howard T., 424
Bochner, Arthur P., 39, 422
Bochner, S., 429
Book, Cassandra L., 422

Boorstin, Daniel J., 425
Borden, George A., 46, 422
Bormann, Ernest G., 422
Bowers, John Waite, 422
Bowlby, J., 431, 435
Bradac, James J., 424, 433
Braiker, Harriet, 319, 436
Brammer, Lawrence, 82, 425
Brandt, David R., 422
Brehm, Jack W., 433
Brenner, Michael, 161, 428
Brislin, Richard, 370–371
Brockriede, Wayne, 230, 431
Brody, Gene, 300, 435
Brommel, Bernard J., 275, 289, 307, 432, 434
Brooks, William D., 440
Brooks-Gunn, Jeanne, 219, 220, 431
Broome, Benjamin J., 323, 437
Bruner, Jerome, 201, 430
Buck, Ross, 56, 69, 78, 79, 136, 423, 427
Bugental, Daphne E., 423
Burgess, Robert, 436
Burgoon, Judee K., 121,123, 124, 423, 425, 427
Burgoon, Michael, 423, 433
Burke, Julie, 435
Burks, Don, 231, 431
Burleson, Brant R. 305, 322, 428, 435, 436, 437
Burr, Wesley R., 435
Bushman, Richard L., 75
Buttny, Richard, 79, 425
Buzzanell, Patrice, 363, 439
Bywater, Ingram, 433

C

Cacioppo, John T., 432
Cahn, Dudley, 237
Calabrese, Richard J., 433, 436

Subject Index

A

abdicrat, 323
abstraction, construct, 165
accenting function, of nonverbals, 59
accommodating conflict style, 377–378
accommodation, in decision making, 277
accommodation, to social change, 284
accurate empathy, and therapeutic communication, 360
activity, as American value, 389
adaptability, family, 290
adaptors, 73
adolescence, 301
adornment, 65
adultery, in colonial times, 408
advertising, 411
affect displays, 72
affection need, 324
affection-hostility messages, 122, 124
affinity-seeking strategies, 329, 332
African-American communication patterns, 390–393
age, cross-cultural views of, 401
aggressive conflict style, 377–378
aggressiveness (vs. assertiveness), 266
agoraphobia, 66
agreement about content, 128
aligning action, 236
all-channel network, 278
altercasting, 44, 201
ambiguity, and the self, 216
American cultural patterns, 388–390
American dream, 411
analogic codes, 88–90
animal communication, 8–9, 54
animated style, 230
antirole, self as, 314–315
Apache language rituals, 100–101
apologies, 364–365
appreciative listening, 177

architecture, 286–287
arousal, in equilibrium theory, 78
arousal cues, in environment, 61
assertiveness, 265–267
assimilation effects, 338
associational learning, 246
assumed similarity, 400
attachment styles, 232
attentive communicator style, 230
attitudes, and prejudice, 395
attraction:
    and filtering theory, 321
    and interpersonal magnets, 321–324
attribution bias, 398
attribution theory:
    biases in, 172–173
    correspondent inferences and, 169–170
    and covariation, 171–172
    defined, 169
autobiography, and identity, 202
autocratic personality, 323
autonomy-togetherness dialectic, 336
avoidance rituals, 355
avoiding stage, 340

B

back region, 200
backchanneling, 68
balance theory, 249
batons, 72
beautiful room/ugly room study, 61
beauty, 64
behavioral constraints, 34
beneffectance, 224
bereavement, 305
black/white communication patterns, 390–393
blanked expressor, 71
body movement, 72–73
body territory, 63

body types, 64
bonding stage, 334
boundaries, 280
boundary-spanning role, 362
boy culture, 198
braille, 88–89
brainstorming, 205
bridging, 380
built environment, 286–287
business communication. *See* professional communication

C

call and response pattern, 393
caregiving, in family, 282
central traits, 164
centralized network, 277
chain network, 278
change:
    in family life cycle, 284–285
    and family stress, 288–289
    ways to cope with, 290–291
character, 212, 410
Charleston Place, Fla., 287
childhood, in 18th century, 292–293
chronemics, 60
cinematography, and perception, 156–157
circumscribing stage, 340
civility, 320, 355, 410
clarifying responses, 128
class differences, 393
classical conditioning, 246
client-counselor interactions, 360–361
closed episodes, 161, 217
closed family, 280–281
closed-ended questions, 110
closed-mindedness, 203–204
closings, conversational 111
CMM theory, 95–98
coercive power, 257

Illustration Credits

Page 2, The Bettmann Archive (16th-century woodcut)

Page 5, Japanese, Shukongo-jin, *Thunderbolt Deity,* wood with traces of polychromy, Kamakura period (1185–1333), ht.: 92.7 cm, Kate S. Buckingham Fund, 1958.120, photograph © 1994, The Art Institute of Chicago. All Rights Reserved

Page 9, Jim Harter, ed., *Animals: 1419 Copyright-Free Illustrations of Mammals, Birds, Fish, Insects, Etc.* New York: Dover, 1979

Page 10, National Gallery of Art, Washington, D.C., Collection of Mr. and Mrs. Paul Mellon (*Breton Girls Dancing, Pont Aven* by Paul Gauguin)

Page 14, The Saint Louis Museum, Museum Purchase (*The Knitting Lesson* by Jean François Millet)

Page 19, Jim Harter, ed., *Animals: 1419 Copyright-Free Illustrations of Mammals, Birds, Fish, Insects, Etc.* New York: Dover, 1979

Page 25, Dale Kennington, Caffe Florian. Private collection/Superstock

Page 27, © The Phillips Collection, Washington, D.C. (*The Luncheon of the Boating Party* by Pierre Auguste Renoir)

Page 29, The Thomas Gilcrease Institute of American History and Art, Tulsa, Oklahoma, 0137.1962, (*Pueblo Green Corn Dance* by Fred Kabotie)

Page 30, © Alex Webb/Magnum Photos, Inc.

Page 35, Egon Schiele, *Seated Woman with Bent Knee,* 1917. The Narodni Gallery of Prague/Bridgeman Art Library

Page 37, The Saint Louis Art Museum, Gift of Mrs. Stratford Lee Morton (*Friendship Quilt,* Baltimore, 1848)

Page 52, Albert Bloch, Ragtime. Christie's of London/Superstock

Page 55, © 1991, The Detroit Institute of Arts, City of Detroit Purchase (*The Wedding Dance,* c. 1566 by Pieter Brueghel the elder, Flemish, 1525/30–1569, oil on panel, 47 X 62 inches, accession no. 30.374)

Page 57, Carol Bellanger Grafton, ed., *Humorous Victorian Spot Illustrations.* New York: Dover, 1985

Page 59, The Metropolitan Museum of Art, Rogers Fund, 1948 (*Memy-Sabu and His Wife,* c. 2420 B.C., Egyptian)

Page 62, center and top left, Jim Harter, ed., *Women: A Pictorial Archive from Nineteenth-Century Sources.* New York: Dover, 1982

Page 62, top center, top right, bottom center, and bottom right, Jim Harter, ed., *Men: A Pictorial Archive from Nineteenth-Century Sources.* New York: Dover, 1980

Page 67, Blanche Cirker, ed., *1800 Woodcuts by Thomas Bewick and His School.* New York: Dover, 1962

Page 70, Photos from P. Ekman and W. F. Friesen, *Pictures of Facial Affect.* Palo Alto, California: Consulting Psychologists Press, 1976. Copyright Paul Ekman

Page 71, Jim Harter, ed., *Men: A Pictorial Archive from Nineteenth-Century American Sources.* New York: Dover, 1980

Page 75, Clarence P. Hornug, ed., *Handbook of Early Advertising Art.* New York: Dover, 1956

Page 86, E. K. F. Von Gekhardt (1830–1925), *The Students.* Superstock

Page 88, Jim Harter, ed., *Animals: 1419 Copyright-Free Illustrations of Mammals, Birds, Fish, Insects, Etc.* New York: Dover, 1979

Page 89, top, The Museum of Modern Art/Film Stills Archives

Page 89, bottom, Hellen Keller, *The Story of My Life.* New York: Doubleday, 1954

Page 90, Tomb Relief of the King's Scribe, Amenhotep and His Wife Renut. Painted limestone, W. 123.1 cm. Egypt, Deir Durunka, Dynasty XIX, 1307–1196. © The Cleveland Museum of Art, 1995, Leonard C. Hanna Jr., Fund, 63.100

Page 94, Bowles and Carver, *Catchpenny Prints: 163 Popular Engravings from the Eighteenth Century.* New York: Dover, 1970

Page 101, Dick Sutphen, ed., *The Pen & Ink and Cross Hatch Styles of the Early Illustrators.* © 1976, Art Direction Book Company, New York

Page 106, The Metropolitan Museum of Art, Gift of Robert E. Tod, 1929 (29.36) (detail of a court robe, late 19th century, Chinese)

Page 116, The Vigeland Sculpture Park, Oslo, Norway (*Father, Mother, and Child* by Gustav Vigeland)

Page 119, A Young Woman Buying a Pink from a Young Man. Black chalk heightened with white chalk, ca. 1720, 42.9 × 54.9 cm. Giovanni Battista Piazetta, Italian, 1692–1754. © The Cleveland Museum of Art, 1995, Purchase from the J. H. Wade Fund, 38.387

Page 123, Jim Harter, ed., *Women: A Pictorial Archive from Nineteenth-Century Sources.* New York: Dover, 1982

Page 131, © Estate of Grant Wood/V.A.G.A., New York/Cincinnati Art Museum, The Edwin and Virginia Irwin Memorial (1959.46) (*Daughters of the Revolution* by Grant Wood)

Page 135, The Metropolitan Museum of Art, The Michael C. Rockefeller Memorial Collection, Gift of Nelson A. Rockefeller, 1968 and Purchase, Nelson A. Rockefeller Gift, 1967 (1978.412.1516) (Mixed media sculpture, 19th–20th century, Papua, New Guinea)

Page 144, M. C. Escher, *Still Life with Reflecting Sphere,* 1934 lithograph, The Escher Estate

Page 148, Bowles and Carver, *Catchpenny Prints: 163 Popular Engravings from the Eighteenth Century.* New York: Dover, 1970

Page 151, Collection of Whitney Museum of American Art. Purchase, with funds from the Richard and Dorothy Rodgers Fund (*'61 Pontaic,* 1968–69 by Robert Bechtle, oil on canvas, 59¾ × 84½ in., 70.16) © 1995 Whitney Museum of Modern Art

Page 156, Photo from an Italian film featuring Constance Dowling. Photo courtesy of Leland Moss

Page 157, Photo from the film, *Duel in the Sun*

Page 159, Nikolaus Braun (1900–1950), *Street Scene in Berlin.* Berlinische Galerie/Superstock

Page 162, The Metropolitan Museum of Art, Bequest of Stephen C. Clark, 1960 (61.101.1). *The Card Players* by Paul Cezanne

Page 167, The Metropolitan Museum of Art, Gift of Howard Mansfield, 1936. From the Japanese illustrated book *Manja,* Vol. VIII by Katsushiko Hokusai

Page 170, © Leonard Freed/Magnum Photos, Inc.

Page 175, Dick Sutphen, ed. *The Pen & Ink and Cross Hatch Styles of the Early Illustrators.* © 1976, Art Directions Book Company, New York

Page 184, Jean Pezous (1815–1885), *Portrait of Charles Deburau.* Musée de la Ville de Paris, Musée Carnavalet/Giraudon — Bridgeman Art Library

Page 187, Albright-Knox Art Gallery, Buffalo, New York. Room of Contemporary Art Fund, 1941 (*Family at Supper* by Pablo Picasso)

Page 191, Jim Harter, ed., *Music: A Pictorial Archive of Woodcuts and Engravings.* New York: Dover, 1980

Page 192, Collection, The Museum of Modern Art, New York, Gift of Mrs. Simon Guggenheim (*Girl Before a Mirror* by Pablo Picasso, 1932. Oil on canvas,

64″ × 51¼″). © 1995 Artists Rights Society (ARS), New York/SPADEM, Paris

Page 194, The Metropolitan Museum of Art, The Michael C. Rockefeller Memorial Collection, Gift of Nelson A. Rockefeller, 1972 (1978.412.323) (Belt Mask, Nigeria, Court of Benin)

Page 195, Rose Art Museum, Brandeis University, Gevirtz-Mnuchin Purchase Fund (*Forget it! Forget Me!* by Roy Lichtenstein)

Page 200, Millard Sheets, *Tenement Flats,* c. 1934. National Museum of American Art, Smithsonian Institution, Transfer from the U.S. Department of the Interior, National Park Service

Page 202, Edward Kienholz, *The Beanery,* 1927. Dwan Gallery/Superstock

Page 210, top left, Giraudon/Art Resource, N.Y. (*Portrait de l'artiste.* 1888 by Vincent van Gogh). Private Collection, Zurich, Switzerland

Page 210, top right, Vincent van Gogh, Dutch, 1853–1890, *Self-Portrait,* oil on artist's board mounted on cradled panel, 1886/87, 41 × 32.5 cm, Joseph Winterbotham Collection, 1954.326, photograph © 1994, The Art Institute of Chicago. All Rights Reserved

Page 210, bottom left, The Metropolitan Museum of Art, Bequest of Miss Adelaide Milton de Groot (1876–1967), 1967 (67.1870.70a) *Self-Portrait with a Straw Hat* by Vincent van Gogh)

Page 210, bottom right, Giraudon/Art Resource, N.Y. (*Self-Portrait* by Vincent van Gogh, 1889. Musée d'Orsay, Paris, France)

Page 214, Pablo Picasso, Spanish, 1881–1973, *The Red Armchair,* oil and enamel on panel, 1931, 130.8 × 99 cm, Gift of Mr. and Mrs. Daniel Saidenberg, 1957.72, photograph © 1994, The Art Institute of Chicago. All Rights Reserved

Page 220, Bowles and Carter, *Catchpenny Prints: 163 Popular Engravings form the Eighteenth Century.* New York: Dover, 1979

Page 223, The Metropolitan Museum of Art, Robert Lehman Collection, 1975 (*Self-Portrait at Age Twenty-Two* by Albrecht Dürer)

Page 227, Jim Harter, ed., *Men: A Pictorial Archive from Nineteenth-Century Sources.* New York: Dover, 1980

Page 228, Charles Mills Gayley, *The Classic Myths in English Literature and Art.* New York: Blaisdell, 1939

Page 233, Edward Hopper, *Compartment C, Car 293,* 1938. Courtesy of IBM Corporation

Page 240, National Gallery of Art, Washington, D. C., Samuel H. Kress Collection (central panel of triptych, *The Fall of Man,* workshop of Albrecht Altdorfer)

Page 254, Jim Harter, ed., *Women: A Pictorial Archive from Nineteenth-Century Sources.* New York: Dover, 1982

Page 258, The Saint Louis Art Museum, Museum Purchase (*The Country School* by Winslow Homer)

Page 259, Layton Art collection, Milwaukee Art Museum (*The Sawdust Trail* by George Bellows)